'This collection of analytic essays on tc
of governance to concepts central to constitutionalism provides a fine
introduction to the state of the field.'

Mark Tushnet, William Nelson Cromwell
Professor of Law, Harvard Law School

'We have entered the golden age of comparative constitutionalism. The
digital revolution has made foreign legal sources more easily accessible,
modern advances in transportation have made the world smaller, and
scholarly collaborations across borders have pushed the boundaries of
our knowledge. And yet many fundamental questions in comparative
constitutionalism remain contested or even unanswered: how to compare,
what to compare, and more importantly why to compare? Masterman
and Schütze have assembled an all-star team of leading authorities in the
study of constitutionalism to guide both experienced scholars and new
students through the most important inquiries in the field. The future
of public law is comparative, and this outstanding volume will be an
invaluable resource for understanding the stakes and challenges that
await.'

Richard Albert, William Stamps Farish
Professor of Law, The University of Texas at Austin

'This *Cambridge Companion to Comparative Constitutional Law* stands
out for its in-depth pursuit of well-selected themes. It offers the scholar
and student an authoritative account of the theoretical foundations and
historical foundations of global constitutionalism, as well as its core
principles, institutions and dynamics.'

Adrienne Stone, Redmond Barry Distinguished Professor,
Melbourne Law School, The University of Melbourne

'In times of flourishing comparative constitutional law studies, this
Cambridge Companion addresses the main issues in the field, with a view
to orient scholarly approaches towards systematic comparative work. In an
ever more connected world, such stimulating enterprise will enhance the
comprehension of the challenges at stake, as well as the communication
among different methodologies and theories.'

Cesare Pinelli, Professor at the Faculty of Law,
University 'La Sapienza'

'This *Companion* assembles a remarkable cast of leading scholars on comparative constitutional law. The chapters adopt a panoramic view in interrogating the field from its theoretical and historical foundations through to its present-day significance. This *Companion* is an important and valuable contribution on a subject of ever-growing significance.'

George Williams, Dean and Anthony Mason Professor,
University of New South Wales

'Combining magnitude and accuracy, here is a new instrument, original in its design, as complete as possible, which will allow any reader to satisfy his curiosity by measuring the importance and interest of this new scientific field. Here is a book that makes it possible to understand better, at the time of globalization, the stakes of a comparative confrontation between the main modes of constitutional arrangement in the world.'

Vlad Constantinesco, Emeritus Professor,
University of Strasbourg

The Cambridge Companion to
Comparative Constitutional Law

What is the purpose of comparative constitutional law? Comparing constitutions allows us to consider the similarities and differences in forms of government, and the normative philosophies behind constitutional choices. Constitutional comparisons offer hermeneutic help: they enable us to see 'our' own constitution with different eyes and to locate its structural and normative choices by reference to alternatives evident in other constitutional orders.

This Cambridge Companion presents readers with a succinct yet wide-ranging introduction to a modern comparative constitutional law course. Its twenty-two chapters are arranged into five thematic parts: starting with an exploration of the theoretical foundations (Part I) and some important historical experiences (Part II), it moves on to a discussion of the core constitutional principles (Part III) and state institutions (Part IV); finally it analyses forms of transnational constitutionalism (Part V) that have emerged in our 'global' times.

Roger Masterman is Professor of Constitutional Law at Durham Law School. His research interests are in constitutional law and reform, rights instruments, and in the interplay between national and international constitutional laws. He is a member of the Executive Committee of the UK Constitutional Law Association, and of the editorial committee of *Public Law*.

Robert Schütze is a Professor of European Law and Co-Director of the Global Policy Institute at Durham University as well as Visiting Professor at LUISS Guido Carli University (Rome). He is a constitutional scholar with a particular expertise in the law of the European Union and comparative federalism and co-directs the Oxford Comparative Constitutionalism Series.

Cambridge Companions to Law

Cambridge Companions to Law offers thought-provoking introductions to different legal disciplines, invaluable to both the student and the scholar. Edited by world-leading academics, each offers a collection of essays which both map out the subject and allow the reader to delve deeper. Critical and enlightening, the Companions library represents legal scholarship at its best.

The Cambridge Companion to

Comparative Constitutional Law

Edited by

Roger Masterman
Durham University

Robert Schütze
Durham University

CAMBRIDGE
UNIVERSITY PRESS

CAMBRIDGE
UNIVERSITY PRESS

University Printing House, Cambridge CB2 8BS, United Kingdom

One Liberty Plaza, 20th Floor, New York, NY 10006, USA

477 Williamstown Road, Port Melbourne, VIC 3207, Australia

314–321, 3rd Floor, Plot 3, Splendor Forum, Jasola District Centre, New Delhi – 110025, India

79 Anson Road, #06-04/06, Singapore 079906

Cambridge University Press is part of the University of Cambridge.

It furthers the University's mission by disseminating knowledge in the pursuit of education, learning, and research at the highest international levels of excellence.

www.cambridge.org
Information on this title: www.cambridge.org/9781107167810
DOI: 10.1017/9781316716731

© Cambridge University Press 2019

First published 2019

Printed in the United Kingdom by TJ International Ltd, Padstow Cornwall

A catalogue record for this publication is available from the British Library.

Library of Congress Cataloging-in-Publication Data
Names: Masterman, Roger, editor. | Schütze, Robert, editor.
Title: The Cambridge companion to comparative constitutional law /
edited by Roger Masterman, Robert Schütze.
Description: Cambridge, United Kingdom; New York, NY:
Cambridge University Press, 2019. | Series: Cambridge companions to law
Identifiers: LCCN 2019019723 | ISBN 9781107167810 (hardback) |
ISBN 9781316618172 (paperback)
Subjects: LCSH: Constitutional law – Comparative studies. | BISAC: LAW / Comparative.
Classification: LCC K3165.C34425 2019 | DDC 342–dc23
LC record available at https://lccn.loc.gov/2019019723

ISBN 978-1-107-16781-0 Hardback
ISBN 978-1-316-61817-2 Paperback

Contents

Contents

Notes on Contributors

Denis Baranger is Professor of Public Law at the Université Panthéon-Assas, Director of the Institut Michel Villey and Co-director of the Law School (*école de droit*). He has received several prizes and distinctions (François Furet Prize, 2001; grand prix de l'académie des sciences morales et politiques, 2018). He has been elected to the Institut Universitaire de France (junior member, active 2008–2013, now honorary). He was a member of the French National Assembly's committee on constitutional reform (2014–2015).

Raffaele Bifulco is Full Professor of Constitutional Law at LUISS Guido Carli University in Rome. His main research interests focus on: federalism, Italian regionalism, state liability and deliberative democracy. He has also been engaged in EU law and more specifically he has written on the Charter of Fundamental Rights of the European Union. He is national leader of the Horizon 2020 project 'Reconciling Europe with its Citizens through Democracy and Rule of Law' (RECONNECT).

Paul Craig is Professor of English Law at St John's College Oxford, FBA QC (Hon). His research covers constitutional law, administrative law, EU law and comparative public law. He is the UK alternative member of the Venice Commission on Law and Democracy.

Philipp Dann is Professor of Public and Comparative Law at Humboldt University of Berlin. He has published widely on comparative constitutional and EU law, on the law of international organizations and 'law and development'. He is the editor-in-chief of the comparative law journal *World Comparative Law/Verfassung und Recht in Übersee* that focuses on issues of public law in the Global South.

Mark Elliott is Professor of Public Law at the University of Cambridge and a Fellow of St Catharine's College, Cambridge. From 2015 to 2019 he served as a Legal Adviser to the House of Lords Select Committee on the Constitution.

Conor Gearty is Professor of Human Rights Law at the London School of Economics and Political Science, and a barrister at Matrix Chambers. He is the author of numerous books on human rights, civil liberties and terrorism, most recently *On Fantasy Island: Britain, Strasbourg and Human Rights* (Oxford University Press, 2016). With Costas Douzinas he has edited the *Cambridge Companion to Human Rights Law* (Cambridge University Press, 2012). He has been Director of the LSE's Centre for the Study of Human Rights and (more recently) its Institute of Public Affairs.

Claudia Geiringer holds the Chair in Public Law at Victoria University of Wellington, New Zealand, and is a Co-director of the NZ Centre for Public Law. Her scholarship focuses on the New Zealand Bill of Rights Act in its domestic and comparative context. She has worked for both the New Zealand and Victorian governments, advising on their respective statutory human rights charters, and has appeared in human rights litigation before the New Zealand and Victorian courts.

Gábor Halmai is Professor and Chair of Comparative Constitutional Law, and Director of Graduate Studies at the European University Institute in Florence. His primary research interests are comparative constitutional law, and international human rights. He has published several books and articles, as well as edited volumes on these topics in English, German and Hungarian. His most recent book *Perspectives on Global Constitutionalism* (Eleven International Publishing, 2014) deals with the use of foreign and international law by domestic courts.

Ran Hirschl (PhD Yale University, 1999) is Professor of Political Science and Law at the University of Toronto, and holder of the Alexander von Humboldt Professorship in Comparative Constitutionalism at the University of Göttingen. He is the author of several award-winning books and over one hundred articles on comparative constitutional law and its intersection with closely related fields. In 2014, he was made Fellow of the Royal Society of Canada – the highest academic accolade in that country.

Vicki C. Jackson is the Thurgood Marshall Professor of Constitutional Law at Harvard Law School, and teaches and writes on US constitutional law, federal courts and comparative constitutional law. Her recent work includes *Proportionality: New Frontiers, New Challenges* (Cambridge University Press, 2017) (co-editor Mark Tushnet); *Comparative Constitutional Law* (Foundation Press, 3rd ed., 2014) (with Mark Tushnet); *Constitutional Engagement in a Transnational Era* (Oxford University Press, 2010).

Jan Klabbers teaches international law at the University of Helsinki, concentrating on international organizations, treaties and matters of global ethics. He is the author of several books on international law, international organizations law, and EU law; co-author of *The Constitutionalization of International Law* (Oxford University Press, 2009), and co-editor of *The Challenge of Inter-Legality* (Cambridge University Press, 2019). He has held visiting positions at various institutions of higher learning, including NYU School of Law, the Graduate Institute of International and Development Studies, the Erasmus Law School Rotterdam, and the Sorbonne.

Nicola Lupo is Full Professor of Public Law and Director of the Center for Parliamentary Studies at LUISS Guido Carli University in Rome. He holds a Jean Monnet chair in 'Understanding European Representative Democracy' and directs a Masters program in 'Parliament and Public Policies'. He was also counsellor at the Italian Chamber of Deputies. His publications concern sources of law, parliamentary rules of procedure, legislative drafting, budgetary procedures, regional councils, parliaments in the EU and the European Parliament.

Roger Masterman is Professor of Constitutional Law at Durham Law School. His research interests are in constitutional law and reform, rights instruments, and in the interplay between national and international constitutional laws. He is a member of the Executive Committee of the UK Constitutional Law Association, and of the editorial committee of *Public Law*.

Christoph Möllers is Professor of Public Law and Jurisprudence at Humboldt University of Berlin and a Permanent Fellow at the Berlin Institute for Advanced Study. His most recent book publications include *The Three Branches* (Oxford University Press, 2011), *Die Möglichkeit der Normen* (Suhrkamp, 2015) and – as co-author – *The Court without Borders* (Oxford University Press, 2019).

Thomas Poole is a Law Professor at the London School of Economics and Political Science. His research focuses on public law, constitutional theory, and the history of law and empire. His most recent book is *Reason of State: Law, Prerogative and Empire* (Cambridge University Press, 2015).

Anashri Pillay is an Associate Professor in Law at Durham University where she teaches Comparative Constitutional Law, International Human Rights and Public International Law. Before joining Durham Law School in 2013, she held posts at the University of Leeds and the University of Cape Town. Anashri's research focuses on the role of judges in giving effect to economic and social rights in South Africa, India and the UK. She has also written on judicial appointments systems in India and South Africa.

Susan Rose-Ackerman is the Henry R. Luce Professor of Law, Emeritus, at Yale Law School. She has published widely on comparative administrative law, the political economy of corruption and regulatory policy. Her most recent books are *Due Process of Lawmaking: The United States, South Africa, Germany and the European Union* (Cambridge University Press, 2015) (with Stephanie Egidy and James Fowkes) and *Corruption and Government: Causes, Consequences and Reform* (2nd ed., Cambridge University Press, 2016) (with Bonnie Palifka).

András Sajó is University Professor at the Central European University, Budapest. He served as Vice-President of the European Court of Human Rights until 2017. He holds a PhD (Hungarian Academy of Sciences) and was recurrent Visiting Professor at various American law schools. He has published extensively on comparative constitutional law, law and emotions and sociology of law. His latest book is *The Constitution of Freedom* (with Renata Uitz, Oxford University Press, 2017).

Cheryl Saunders is Laureate Professor Emeritus at Melbourne Law School. She writes in the field of comparative constitutional law from a global perspective. She is the founding Director of the Centre for Comparative Constitutional Studies, a President Emeritus of the International Association of Constitutional Law, a senior technical advisor to the Constitution Building Program of International IDEA and a joint convenor of the Constitution Transformation Network.

Robert Schütze is a Professor of European Law and Co-Director of the Global Policy Institute at Durham University as well as Visiting Professor at LUISS Guido Carli University (Rome). He is a constitutional scholar with a particular expertise in the law of the European Union and comparative federalism. He is a co-editor of the Oxford Series in 'Comparative Constitutionalism' (with Richard Albert) as well as the Hart Series on 'Parliamentary Democracy in Europe' (with Nicola Lupo).

Kaarlo Tuori is Professor Emeritus of Jurisprudence at Helsinki University. He has published extensively in the fields of legal theory and national and transnational public law. His legal theoretical works include *Critical Legal Positivism* (Ashgate, 2002) and *Ratio and Voluntas* (Ashgate, 2011). In European constitutional law his main works are *The Eurozone Crisis – A Constitutional Analysis* (together with Klaus Tuori, Cambridge University Press, 2014) and *European Constitutionalism* (Cambridge University Press, 2015). Tuori is a long-time member and former vice-president of the Venice Commission.

Cal Viney is an Australian lawyer focused on public law and policy. He has served as an adviser to the Premier of Victoria, Australia, and the Prime Minister's Department, Australia, where he has advised on constitutional reform, international public and private law, and public and administrative law. He holds an LLM (Public Law) from the London School of Economics and Political Science, where he studied as a Chevening Scholar, and an LLB/BA from Deakin University.

Qianfan Zhang joined the law faculty of Peking University in 2003, where he is the Director of the Center for the People's Congress and Parliamentary Studies. He has published widely in the areas of Chinese and comparative constitutional law, moral and political philosophy, including *The Constitution of China: A Contextual Analysis* (Hart Publishing, 2012) and *Human Dignity in Classical Chinese Philosophy: Confucianism, Mohism, and Daoism* (Palgrave Macmillan, 2016). He has been the vice president of the Chinese Constitutional Law Association since 2004.

Acknowledgements

This *Cambridge Companion to Comparative Constitutional Law* was conceived some years ago when the editors jointly designed a course on comparative constitutional law. The present book, written by over twenty academics, is now – unsurprisingly – much richer than we initially imagined, and we are extremely grateful to the distinct and brilliant voices within this volume. Our fellow contributors have been exemplary collaborators whose patience (and courage) to work with us has been outstanding. We are equally indebted to Cambridge University Press, and especially to Valerie Appleby, who commissioned this work; as well as Marianne Nield, who helped us bring it to fruition. Finally, we wish to offer our profound thanks to María José Pérez-Crespo and Nick Kilford for their invaluable assistance in the preparation of this manuscript.

Acknowledgements

The Cambridge Companion to Shakespeare ...
...

...

Table of Cases (Selection)

Australia

Al-Kateb v. *Godwin* [2004] HCA 37, 493
Australian Capital Television Pty Ltd v. *Commonwealth* (1992) 177 CLR 106, 86
In Re Judiciary and Navigation Acts (1921) 29 CLR 257, 418
Lange v. *ABC* (1997) 189 CLR 520, 481
McCloy v. *New South Wales* [2015] HCA 34, 494
Momcilovic v. *The Queen* [2011] HCA 34, 494

Canada

British Columbia (Attorney General) v. *Christie* 2007 SCC 21 [2007];
    1 SCR 873, 277
British Columbia v. *Imperial Tobacco Canada Ltd.* 2005 SCC 49; [2005]
    2 SCR 473, 277
Canada (AG) v. *PHS Community Services Society* [2011] 3 SCR 134, 283
Quebec v. *Montreal* 2000 SCC 27; [2000] 1 SCR 665, 573
R v. *Drybones* [1970] SCR 282, 558
Reference re s 94(2) of Motor Vehicle Act (British Columbia) [1985]
    2 SCR 486, 281, 283
Reference re Secession of Quebec [1998] 2 SCR 217, 476
Roncarelli v. *Duplessis* [1959] SCR 121, 275, 276
Winnipeg School Division No 1 v. *Craton* [1985] 2 SCR 150, 573

European Convention on Human Rights

Al-Dulimi and Montana Management Inc. v. *Switzerland,* Application
    No 5809/08 (21 June 2016), 266, 276
Baka v. *Hungary,* Application No. 20261/12 (23 June 2016), 284
Běleš and Others v. *the Czech Republic,* Appl. No. 47273/99 (12 November
    2002), 276
Blokhin v. *Russia,* Application No. 47152/06 (23 March 2016), 271
Čudak v. *Lithuania,* Application No. 15869/02 (23 March 2010), 278

European Union Cases

France

Germany

India

New Zealand

South Africa

United Kingdom

United States

Abbreviations

BverfGE	Entscheidungen des Bundesverfassungsgerichts
CA	Constituent Assembly
CC	*Conseil Constitutionnel* (France)
CCP	Chinese Communist Party
DHR	Directorate of Human Rights
ECHR	European Convention on Human Rights
ECJ	European Court of Justice
ECtHR	European Court of Human Rights
EU	European Union
GC	German Constitution
GFC	Global Financial Crisis
HRA	Human Rights Act
IFI	Independent Fiscal Institution
IMF	International Monetary Fund
LPG	Local People's Government
NPC	National People's Congress
OBR	Office for Budget Responsibility
PIL	Public Interest Litigation
RoL	Rule of Law
SPC	Supreme People's Court
TFEU	Treaty on the Functioning of the European Union
TEU	Treaty on European Union
UN	United Nations
WTO	World Trade Organization

Introduction

The Editors

What is the purpose of comparative constitutional law? What is 'comparative' and what is 'constitutional' about it; and to what extent should the former be relevant to the latter?

The objects of constitutional law are constitutions. But what are 'constitutions'? From a purely *descriptive* point of view, constitutions simply reflect the institutions and powers of government; and comparative constitutional law here becomes an exercise in 'comparative government'.[1] From a normative perspective, on the other hand, constitutions 'order' societies according to particular political philosophies; they thus do not merely describe political societies but *prescribe* their actions.

Both the prescriptive and descriptive view come into sharp relief in the sphere of *comparative* constitutional law. For comparing constitutions requires us to consider differences (and similarities) in forms of government as well as the normative philosophies behind constitutional choices. This comparison will often lead us to take a step back from the primary objects of comparison – the constitutions themselves – so as to examine the social phenomena and normative concepts that form the elementary 'constituents' of our political imagination. The process and product of comparison are thus of equal importance. For only the two of them, joined together, will allow us to illuminate previously unseen elements of individual constitutions from the vantage point of a new – outside – perspective.[2] Legal comparisons here offer hermeneutic help: they allow us to see 'our' own constitution with different eyes and to locate its structural and normative choices by reference to alternative choices made in other constitutional orders. For example: anyone wishing to explain the French 'presidential' system may wish to contrast it to the United Kingdom's 'parliamentary' system; and which better way to contrast

---

[1] S.E. Finer, *Comparative Government* (The Penguin Press, 1970).
[2] M. Siems, *Comparative Law* (Cambridge University Press, 2014), 2–5.

American 'federalism' than to see it against the backdrop of the French 'unitary' state?[3]

Apart from this hermeneutic function, comparative constitutional law may also serve a 'constructive' function. This constructive or creative function often comes to the fore in times of political crisis or social transformation. For whereas a mature constitutional order tends to 'reflect the principles of the social order that it seeks to regulate',[4] this relationship is often inverted for new ones, as new constitutions are often designed to create new social orders.[5] What is the best way to proceed here? While a search for the 'ideal' constitution may often turn out to be quixotic,[6] a borrowing or refinement of 'real' constitutional principles from other States (or historical epochs) might sometimes be the best solution to accommodate for revolutionary changes or reformist adaptations. True, revolutionary changes tend to be relatively rare, yet constitutional reforms are surprisingly common in today's world. For the need for regular constitutional change has dramatically accelerated in recent decades during which the forces of globalization have 'integrated' many states into the world economy. And though the 'autobiographical' and 'idiosyncratic' characteristics of national constitutions remain worthy of note,[7] their special characteristics have

[3] For this comparative constitutional approach, see only A. de Tocqueville, *Democracy in America* (edited: P. Bradley, Vintage, 1954).

[4] W.G. Friedmann, *The Changing Structure of International Law* (Stevens, 1964), 3. The classical statement of this idea comes from none other than Montesquieu. In his *The Spirit of the Laws* (edited by: A.M. Cohler et al., Cambridge University Press, 1989), we thus read (ibid., 8): 'Laws should be so appropriate to the people for whom they are made that it is very unlikely that the laws of one nation can suit another. (...) They should be related to the physical aspect of the country; to the climate... to the properties of the terrain... to the way of life of the peoples... they should relate to the degree of liberty that the constitution can sustain, to the religion of the inhabitants, their inclinations, their wealth, their number, their commerce, their mores and their manners; finally, the laws are related to one another, to their origin, to the purpose of the legislator, and to the order of things on which they are established.'

[5] The classic example here may be the 1791 French Constitution, whose main purpose is to abolish the 'old' social order; see Preamble: 'The National Assembly, wishing to establish the French Constitution upon the principles that it has just recognized and declared, abolishes irrevocably the institutions that have injured liberty and the equality of rights.'

[6] In the words of Francis Bacon: 'As for the philosophers, they make imaginary laws for imaginary commonwealths; and their discourses are as the stars, which give little light, because they are so high.'

[7] S.E. Finer, V. Bogdanor and B. Rudden, *Comparing Constitutions* (Oxford University Press, 1995), 7.

partly been 'flattened' through a process of social symbiosis and legal adaptation.[8]

This process of constitutional symbiosis is not confined to States alone. Today, the very idea of what a 'constitution' is has migrated from the national to the supranational or international sphere. Of course, the days of the nation state are surely not yet counted, and yet the state-centred definition of what a 'constitution' is – a definition that became prevalent in the eighteenth and nineteenth century – has come to be challenged in the twentieth and twenty-first century by such legal phenomena as the European Union and the United Nations. But can we really speak of the European Treaties or the UN Charter as 'constitutions'; and, if so, to what extent have they taken ideas from the constitutional traditions of their Member States? The European Court of Justice certainly thinks so;[9] and even within the context of international law, 'constitutionalizing' forces have famously been identified.[10]

What, then, is the purpose of this (text)book? The idea behind this *Cambridge Companion* is to present the interested reader with the core elements of a – modern – comparative constitutional law course. While no match, in terms of size, to the 1,500-page American hornbooks,[11] we nonetheless hope that our collection offers a wide-ranging yet concise introduction to the subject; and we have thereby particularly tried to refer to more modern constitutional phenomena, such as the rise of independent fiscal institutions and various forms of 'multi-constitutionalism'.

---

[8] For this excellent point, see O. Kahn-Freud, 'On Uses and Misuses of Comparative Law' (1974) 37 *Modern Law Review* 1 at 9: 'Would Montesquieu have written about cultural diversities the way he did, had he been able to anticipate that everywhere people read the same kind of newspaper every morning, look at the same kind of television pictures every night, and worship the same kind of film stars and football teams everywhere? Industrialisation, urbanisation, and the development of communications have greatly reduced the environmental obstacles to legal transplantation – and nothing has contributed more to this than the greater ease with which people move from place to place.'

[9] Cf. Opinion 1/91 (*European Economic Area*), [1991] ECR I-6079, [21]: '[T]he [EU] Treaty, albeit concluded in the form of an international agreement, none the less constitutes the constitutional charter of a [Union] based on the rule of law.'

[10] J. Klabbers, A. Peters and G. Ulfstein, *The Constitutionalization of International Law* (Oxford University Press, 2009).

[11] See only N. Dorsen, M. Rosenfeld, A. Sajó and S. Baer, *Comparative Constitutionalism: Cases and Materials* (West Publishing, 2016); as well as V. Jackson and M. Tushnet, *Comparative Constitutional Law* (Foundation Press, 2014). The former book comprises over 1,700 pages; the latter book is over 1,900 pages long!

Pedagogically, we have arranged our twenty-two chapters into several thematic parts: beginning with an exploration of the theoretical foundations (Part I) on which comparative constitutionalism builds and having revisited some important historical experiences (Part II), the core constitutional principles (Part III) and state institutions (Part IV) will be analysed before we finally investigate forms of transnational constitutionalism (Part V) that have emerged in our 'global' times.

Part I thereby aims to clarify the contours of comparative constitutional law by better defining the two core elements of the discipline, namely what is 'comparative' and what is 'constitutional' within comparative constitutional law.

Part II presents a (highly selective) number of State constitutions and their historical evolution. Complementing the generalist aspects of Part I, it is meant to offer concrete illustrations of five – diverse – constitutional orders; and we have primarily selected them as specific manifestations of particular constitutional structures or philosophies. The UK Constitution here embodies not only the quintessential 'unwritten' and 'descriptive' constitution, but it also establishes one of the oldest 'monarchical' states of the world. The French and the American Constitutions, by contrast, represent the prototypes of the modern 'normative' constitution, which are both based on the 'republican' distinction between 'constituting' and 'constituted' power. These three constitutional orders also offer an excellent contrast between pure 'parliamentarism' (the United Kingdom) and pure 'presidentialism' (the United States) with the French constitutional system lying in between the two extremes. The British and French constitutional orders are furthermore excellent expressions of unitary constitutional orders, whereas the American and Indian Constitutions are excellent examples of federal constitutional systems. The Indian Constitution is also a potent and powerful illustration of a vibrant Asian and post-colonial legal order, whereas the Chinese Constitution may today be characterized as 'the' paradigm case for a modern socialist constitution.

Part III analyses key structural principles of contemporary constitutionalism. The five 'ruling' ideas for us here are: (representative) democracy, the separation of powers, the rule of law, the protection of human rights and federalism. Each of these core ideas of modern constitutionalism emerged independently; yet there are also positive and negative correlations between them. For example, the democratic principle arguably stands in clear tension with the separation of powers principle;[12] and it equally collides with the idea of fundamental rights removed from the democratic will represented by the majority. The rule of law, on the other hand, accords very well with both the separation of powers principle as well as the idea of fundamental human rights. The constitutional principle that undoubtedly stands mostly on its own is here federalism. For whereas the other constitutional concepts are 'unitary' concepts that determine who holds power among a number of (horizontal) institutions, federalism concerns the vertical division of powers between two levels of government. And this duplication of the constitutional levels within a 'compound' republic raises very interesting questions with regard to, for example, democracy but also the protection of fundamental rights.[13]

Part IV explores five governmental institutions that are the key players within most liberal democratic states. The democratic principle within modern constitutions indeed insists – first and foremost – on the existence of a 'parliament' as the representative of the 'people'. The idea that the legislative function belongs to parliament has become so engrained in our constitutional imagination that older forms of 'royal' legislation have nearly disappeared.[14] Following the separation of powers principle, the legislature ought to exist in isolation of the executive; and with the rise of the 'administrative State' in the nineteenth century,[15] many modern constitutions here further distinguish between 'governmental' and 'administrative' functions. To the list of 'parliaments', 'governments', 'administrations', 'courts' must of course be added as the institution charged with the judicial function; but we have also decided to add a fifth – emergent – branch: independent fiscal institutions (IFIs). Though IFIs have a longstanding presence in some constitutional systems, their rise to prominence in the wake of the global financial crisis suggests that

---

[12] In the provocative words of C.H. McIlwain, *Constitutionalism: Ancient and Modern* (Liberty Fund, 2008), 132: 'Political balances have no institutional background whatever except in the imaginations of closet philosophers like Montesquieu. When in modern times representative assemblies took over the rights and duties of earlier kings, they assumed a power and a responsibility that had always been concentrated and undivided.'

[13] On this point, see Chapter 2, dealing specifically with the question of a separate 'federal' constitutionalism.

[14] On the powers of the British 'crown' and its 'royal' prerogatives, see M. Sunkin and S. Payne, *The Nature of the Crown: A Legal and Political Analysis* (Oxford University Press, 1999).

[15] On this point, see Chapter 15 as well as G. Lawson, 'The Rise and Rise of the Administrative State' (1993–94) 107 *Harvard Law Review* 123.

they are coming to be seen as performing an essential extra-governmental (and extra-legislative) function in the regulation and monitoring of public finances.

Part V finally takes account of the fact that most state constitutions no longer live in splendid isolation (even if some pretend they do).[16] Our contemporary world is a global world; and today, many nation-states are deeply embedded in a wider network of transnational legal structures. Can we thus speak of transnational constitutionalism; and if so, what are its horizontal and vertical dimensions? Transnational constitutionalism may be found in a number of places, and the rise of international organizations – like the United Nations and the World Trade Organization – here only represent the most general and universal phenomena. Regional transnational structures can be found in the context of the European Union and the 'Commonwealth of Nations'. The European Union represents the most developed form of supranational constitutionalism – a constitutionalism that has extensively 'borrowed' from the constitutional traditions of federations, like the United States and Germany.[17] But more often, constitutional 'transplants' take place horizontally between state legal orders; and the various informal and formal instances of constitutional borrowing and transplants will be discussed in our last chapter.

We are acutely aware that this *Cambridge Companion* has left some very important topics untreated. African and Latin American constitutionalism would have deserved some special treatment;[18] and the re-emergence of theocratic constitutions might have equally deserved a special chapter.[19] The post-communist constitutions within Central and Eastern Europe would have offered a fascinating case study in both

[16] See T. Cottier and M. Hertig, 'The Prospects of 21st Century Constitutionalism' (2003) 7 *Max Planck Yearbook of United Nations Law* 261.
[17] See for example R. Schütze, *European Constitutional Law* (Cambridge University Press, 2015), Chapter 2. For the failed attempt of a 'reverse' borrowing, see *Printz* v. *United States*, 521 US 898 (1997), where Justice Scalia held (ibid., 921): 'Justice Breyers's dissent would have us consider the benefits that other countries, and the European Union, believe they have derived from federal systems that are different from ours. We think such comparative analysis inappropriate to the task of interpreting a constitution, though it was of course quite relevant to the task of writing one.'
[18] For an excellent treatment of the latter, see R. Gargarella. *Latin American Constitutionalism, 1810–2010: The Engine Room of the Constitution* (Oxford University Press, 2013).
[19] For a modern example of a theocratic constitution, see only A. Schirazi, *The Constitution of Iran* (Tauris, 1998).

constitutional design and transitional regimes,[20] while the rise of authoritarian regimes in the world – whether it be Turkey or North Korea – could have provided a contrasting tonic to liberal triumphalism.[21] And yet: each introduction to a subject must make some 'hard choices'; and the choices we have made will of course be revaluated in a future second edition.[22] Last but not least: in order to help students with the various jurisdictions and materials within this *Cambridge Companion*, we would like to draw attention to the existence of a companion website. The latter can be found under www.masterman-schutze.eu, and here students will not only find links to all the relevant cases and readings mentioned in each of the chapters but can also use a range of extra materials designed to complement this book.

---

[20] See for example W. Sadurski, *Rights Before Courts: A Study of Constitutional Courts in Post-Communist States in Central and Eastern Europe* (Springer, 2008).

[21] For an overview here, see T. Ginsburg and A. Simpser (eds.), *Constitutions in Authoritarian Regimes* (Cambridge University Press, 2014).

[22] For any suggestions in this respect, please feel free to contact us via email; or, more traditionally, by post.

Part I

Theoretical Foundations

Comparative Methodologies   1

Ran Hirschl

Introduction

From its beginnings as a relatively obscure and exotic subject studied by a devoted few, comparative constitutionalism has developed into one of the more vibrant and exciting subjects in contemporary legal scholarship, and has become a cornerstone of constitutional jurisprudence and constitution-making in an increasing number of countries worldwide. This tremendous renaissance in comparative constitutional inquiry reflects a confluence of factors. Chief among them are extensive democratization and constitutionalization trends worldwide; the internalization of the legal profession and of legal education; and the rise of communication and information technologies that facilitate considerably the diffusion of constitutional concepts, and foster cross-national jurisprudential dialogue. The result has been an ever-expanding interest among scholars, judges, practitioners and policymakers in the transnational migration of constitutional ideas, and in the comparative study of constitutions and constitutionalism more generally.

And yet, despite this tremendous renaissance, and in stark contrast to other areas of research that define themselves as comparative (including comparative constitutional law's neighbouring fields – comparative law and comparative politics – both of which sport extensive and sophisticated methodological debates), the methodological, research

design, case selection and data analysis aspects of comparative constitutional inquiry – how should we study constitutionalism as a distinct phenomenon with multiple forms and manifestations across time
and place – remain largely undertheorized and until recently, seldom
discussed.[1]

In the following pages, I outline a few elements that are vital to
understanding the array of comparative methodologies deployed in the
study of constitutions and constitutionalism across time and place. Such
understanding, I suggest, is essential for sustaining the current revival of
comparative constitutionalism as a distinct and valuable area of scholarship. The discussion proceeds in three main steps. I begin with two basic
distinctions concerning the meaning of the 'comparative' in comparative
constitutional inquiry: (i) the various epistemological branches of constitutional law scholarship and the comparative angle in them; and (ii)
the various professions and stakeholders engaged in comparative constitutional inquiry and their different aims and practices. In the second
part, I identify and discuss the main methodologies and research designs
commonly deployed in comparative study of constitutions and constitutionalism across time and place.

These various approaches to comparative inquiry may be distinguished
from one another based on their aimed level of abstraction and generalization, and include the generation of encyclopaedic knowledge,
classifications or taxonomies; self-reflection through analogy and contrast; concept formation through multiple description; idiographic studies
that aim to produce in-depth understanding of given constitutional setting;

---

[1] For an initial attempt to deal with these questions, see R. Hirschl, *Comparative Matters: The
Renaissance of Comparative Constitutional Law* (Oxford University Press, 2014); as
well as J. Husa, 'Comparison', in D.S. Law and M. Langford (eds.), *Research Methods
in Constitutional Law: A Handbook* (Edward Elgar Publishing, 2018); S. Gardbaum,
'How Do and Should We Compare Constitutional Law', in Samantha Besson et al. (eds.),
Comparing Comparative Law (Schulthess, 2017), 109–126; T. Ginsburg, 'How to Study
Constitution-Making: Hirschl, Elster, and the Seventh Inning Problem' (2016) 96 *Boston
University Law Review* 1347–1358; R. Hirschl, 'From Comparative Constitutional Law to
Comparative Constitutional Studies' (2013) 11 *International Journal of Constitutional Law*
1–12; V.C. Jackson, 'Comparative Constitutional Law: Methodologies', in Michel Rosenfeld
and András Sajó (eds.), *The Oxford Handbook of Comparative Constitutional Law* (Oxford
University Press, 2012), 54–74; V.C. Jackson, 'Methodological Challenges in Comparative
Constitutional Law' (2010) 28 *Penn State International Law Review* 319–326; R. Hirschl,
'The Question of Case Selection in Comparative Constitutional Law' (2005) 53 *American
Journal of Comparative Law* 125–155; M. Tushnet, 'The Possibilities of Comparative
Constitutional Law' (1999) 108 *Yale Law Journal* 1225–1309.

and nomothetic studies that draw on controlled comparisons to formulate and test hypotheses with some general applicability to the comparative constitutional universe. In the third part, I address some of the structural and disciplinary difficulties embedded in the comparative constitutional inquiry and point to the rise of cross-disciplinary, multi-method and collaborative research as providing a set of plausible solutions to some of these challenges.

The upshot of the chapter is threefold: (i) there is no magic bullet or one-size-fit-all research design 'formula' for a field as rich and diverse as comparative constitutional studies; therefore, methodological pluralism is an asset and a necessity; (ii) the sensibility and rationality of comparisons boil down to the concrete perimeters of any given comparison, the scope and nature of the substantive claim they purport to advance, and whether the case-selection criteria and research methodologies deployed are properly tailored to suit the theoretical or empirical question a given comparative study is set to address; and (iii) ultimately it is the *comparative* element that separates comparative constitutional law from its older, more established, supposedly self-contained and undoubtedly less cosmopolitan sibling – constitutional law. Hence, an understanding of the 'comparative' in comparative constitutional law – its various rationales, methods, limitations and possibilities, alongside the contours and contents of the audacious comparativist's toolkit – is essential for the field's renaissance to persist.

1 What is Comparative Constitutional Law? Two Basic Distinctions

Before exploring the various methodologies and research designs deployed in comparative constitutional law, two basic distinctions should be made. First is the distinction between constitutional law, constitutional theory, constitutional studies, and the comparative aspect in each of these branches of scholarship. The better part of academic writing about the constitutional domain – often referred to as *constitutional law* – focuses on constitutional texts or on constitutional jurisprudence, often construed as the study of judicial interpretation of constitutional provisions and constitutional principles. The epistemological focus of this branch of scholarship is often on the internal logic, hierarchy and interpretive coherence of constitutional law as an autonomous legal system. Critical assessment of constitutional rulings and judicial reasoning, furtherance or departure from relevant precedents and established approaches, innovative structures or doctrines and their intra-constitutional effects, and debates about how a given court should have decided a given case or set of cases are, generally speaking, the prevalent scholarly genres here.

In recent years, this type of constitutional law scholarship increasingly engages with closely related legal fields such as international law or administrative law, and occasionally also with immigration law or criminal law, to the extent that the norms and practices established in these areas of public law are or ought to be in close dialogue with constitutional principles. Legal periodicals in North America and Europe, and to an increasing extent in leading Asian and Latin American centres of high learning too, present countless examples of this type of constitutional scholarship. As it focuses on intra-constitutional analysis, much of this type of scholarship is read exclusively by stakeholders within the legal profession: legal academics, judges, law students and lawyers.

So-called *constitutional theory* is another important branch of constitutional scholarship. It often departs from analysis of the constitutional text and its judicial interpretation to explore foundational principles and normative considerations that ought to guide the constitutional domain and its various stakeholders. It engages in a search for ethically sound and morally appealing approaches to common problems in constitutional law such as the legitimacy of judicial review, or the desired scope and nature of abstract notions such as 'equality' or 'human dignity'. Most contributors to this area of scholarship have formal training or at least solid background in political philosophy or legal theory; the main mode of scholarship is philosophical or normative argumentation akin to scholarly modes deployed in closely related fields such a philosophy, political theory or the history of ideas. Academic writings within this genre of constitutional scholarship are frequently read beyond the lawyerly circles, most notably by philosophers and political theorists interested in the normative foundations of the constitutional order, what should be its moral priorities, and the justifiable interpretation of its constitutive texts.

A rapidly expanding body of literature – elsewhere I referred to it as *constitutional studies* – complements the legal and normative approaches to the study of constitutions, by deploying more social-scientific approaches and methods to the study of constitutions and constitutional development more broadly. Generally speaking, this emerging branch of scholarship sees the constitutional domain as an integral part of the broader political context, whether institutional, ideological, societal or material, within which the constitutional domain evolves and operates. Consequently, the constitutional domain is perceived as extending beyond constitutional texts, constitutional principles or constitutional jurisprudence, to encompass historical trends, political interests, economic incentives, strategic choices and power struggles that affect and are shaped by constitutional institutions. Certain threads within this body of scholarship, most notably the study of constitutional design, combine social-scientific empirical research with an explicit normative outlook (peace, stability, democracy). Many contributors to this type of constitutional scholarship have acquired formal training or possess some background in disciplines such as history, sociology, political science or economics. Consequently, social science research methods such as statistical analysis of large data sets, surveys, archival work, in-depth interviews, computerized content analysis, and occasionally multi-method studies are deployed in an attempt to understand the constitutional domain in its broader context.

The advent of *comparative* constitutional inquiry adds another epistemological layer to the study of constitutionalism. It is increasingly evident in all three branches of constitutional inquiry: constitutional law (e.g. reference to comparative constitutional jurisprudence or comparative accounts of proportionality and other approaches to constitutional interpretation); constitutional theory (e.g. comparative normative analysis of concepts such as 'human dignity', 'equality' or 'freedom of expression'); and constitutional studies (comparative studies of the origins and consequences of constitutional institutions or comparative analyses of the constitutional sphere's interaction with the social and political environment within which it operates). Colloquially, the word 'comparative' is often used in the sense of 'relative to' (e.g. 'he returned to the comparative comfort of his home') or to refer to words that imply comparison (e.g. 'better', 'faster', etc.). The scientific use of 'comparative' is defined in the *Oxford English Dictionary* as 'involving the systematic observation of the similarities or dissimilarities between two or more branches of science or subjects of study'. These definitions seem intuitive enough – yet, the meaning of the *comparative* in comparative constitutional law has proven quite difficult to pin down. Situated between constitutional law and comparative law, and, more generally, between law and political science – constitutional law regulates political life and as such is arguably the most overtly political branch of all legal fields – comparative constitutional law has become a bit of a catch-all label to what in effect are quite different types of studies. In its most basic definition, it refers to the study of constitutional systems or their various components across time and place, with an aim of generating some kind of analytical yield by the act of comparison. The nature of that analytical yield itself may be descriptive, taxonomical, hermeneutic, conceptual, normative, explanatory or any combination of these and other types of scholarly inquiry.

The most basic understanding that virtually all contributors to comparative constitutional inquiry share is that elements and manifestations of constitutionalism across time and place share many common features and are therefore comparable. As such, comparative constitutional inquiry rejects the 'culturalist-relativist' view within comparative law according to which each legal system is an idiosyncratic, non-comparable by-product of its own shared history, culture and aspirations. It also objects to the constitutional sovereigntist view that denounces comparative constitutional inquiry, in particular in its comparative constitutional jurisprudence guise, as it is undermining domestic constitutional traditions and institutions viewed as inherently more authentic than any external constitutional orders or preferences. However, even if one brushes aside the extreme contextualist position, it is undeniable that due to its epistemological nature, the comparative study of constitutions has taken a distinctly more cosmopolitan direction than that taken by its more established relative – the study of constitutional law in a given country (the United States is of course a prime example) that has long been dominated by jurists and legal academics who are based in that country and who master its own laws.

A second key distinction is who is conducting the comparative constitutional inquiry, in what capacity and for what purpose? Unlike other comparative disciplines (e.g. comparative literature or comparative psychology) that are confined, by and large, to the academic world, comparative constitutional inquiry is pursued within and beyond the ivory tower itself. What makes the understanding of the 'comparative' in comparative constitutional law so essential is the various vocational, jurisprudential, academic and scientific stakeholders involved in practising the art of comparison.

Undoubtedly, the constitutional lawyer, the judge, the law professor qua professor, the constitutional drafter, the normative legal theorist and the social scientist engage in comparison with different ends in mind. A lawyer, for instance, may be forgiven for selectively using comparative evidence in an attempt to enhance her client's case. This is, after all, her professional and ethical prerogative. A judge who wishes to make a good public policy decision may look carefully at other jurisdictions that have been contemplating the same issues. Her goal is to write an informed, well-reasoned judgment. A comparative quest for what appears to be the 'best' or 'most suitable' constitutional solution to a given problem, seems appropriate and relevant. It often involves comparisons by distinction, analogy and contrast. Similarly, constitutional drafters who are seeking an effective solution for a troubled polity, would be advised to comparatively explore relevant alternatives that have been tried in other, similarly situated, settings.

A law professor trying to illustrate to her students the variance across countries with regard to, say, the law of reproductive freedoms would be well advised to survey the state of affairs with respect to the right to have an abortion in a few pertinent polities. Such type of comparison contributes to what may be termed 'concept formation through multiple description'. It may take the form of a systematic taxonomical account of all forms and manifestations of a given constitutional phenomenon (e.g. 'federalism', 'equality', 'judicial activism' or 'freedom of religion'), or a more selective account of the main displays of that phenomenon, so as to effectively accomplish the pedagogical goal. Aptly, this approach serves as the organizing principle of most leading textbooks in comparative constitutional law.[2] Likewise, a social scientist who wishes to illustrate to her students the significance of certain constitutional phenomena (e.g. 'parliamentarism', 'presidentialism', 'bi-' or 'uni-cameralism') rightly draws on descriptive accounts involving analogy and contrast to illustrate the point. The constitutional drafter or consultant involved in a given constitution-making exercise is interested in concrete constitutional mechanisms deployed in other, similarly situated, constitutional settings. Meanwhile, the legal philosopher or constitutional theorist is interested in formulating moral justifications or principles for best

---

[2] See, e.g., V.C. Jackson and M. Tushnet, *Comparative Constitutional Law* (3rd edition; Foundation Press, 2014).

practices at the *ought* (rather than the *is*) level, and may thus be forgiven for supporting her insights with a small number of favourable yet possibly unrepresentative cases. However, an attempt to explain or establish causality warrants a more methodologically astute approach. One cannot move freely from engaging with a specific purpose for comparative work (e.g. descriptive, taxonomical, normative, causal, etc.) to engaging with another without adjusting one's case-selection principles and applicable methodologies correspondingly. Accordingly, the researcher whose aim is to understand the causes and consequences of a given constitutional dynamics must consider seriously principles of controlled comparisons, inference-oriented research design, case selection and data analysis.

2 Comparative Methodologies and Research Designs

Within constitutional scholarship that is widely accepted as comparative, the term 'comparative' is often used indiscriminately to describe what, in fact, are several different types of scholarship: (i) freestanding, single-country studies – often quite detailed and 'ethnographic' in nature – that are characterized as comparative by virtue of dealing with a country other than the author's own (as any observer is immersed in their own (constitutional) culture, studying another constitutional system involves at least an implicit comparison with one's own); (ii) genealogies and taxonomic labelling of types or categories of constitutional systems, old or new; (iii) multi-author studies (often in the form of symposium journal issues or edited collections) of constitutional law in selected polities within a given region or continent; (iv) surveys of foreign constitutional law aimed at finding the 'best', most effective or most suitable set of constitutional rules or constitutional principles across cultures; (v) references to the constitutional mechanisms or high court rulings of other countries aimed at engendering self-reflection through analogy and contrast; (vi) concept formation through multiple descriptions of the same constitutional phenomena (e.g. equality, expression, reproductive freedoms) across countries; (vii) normative or philosophical contemplation of abstract concepts such as 'constitutional supremacy', 'constitutional identity', 'transnational/supranational/global constitutional order', etc., often accompanied by casual reference to constitutional jurisprudence in one or more jurisdictions; (viii) careful 'small-N' analysis of a handful of case studies aimed at advancing causal arguments that may be applicable beyond the studied cases; and (ix) 'large-N' studies that draw upon multivariate statistical analyses of a large number of observations, measurements, data sets, etc. in order to determine correlations among pertinent variables or the spread over time and space of certain constitutional structures and practices. More often than not, these last two research modes purport to draw upon controlled comparison and inference-oriented case-selection principles in order to assess change, explain dynamics, and make inferences about cause and effect. As such, these modes of inquiry are often deployed by scholars who study constitutional development over time and across space, or by scholars who are interested in the efficacy of certain constitutional mechanisms across various settings.

Taken as a whole, these various comparative research designs may be distinguished from one another based on their *aimed level of abstraction and generalization* (e.g. generation of encyclopaedic or taxonomical knowledge; self-reflection through analogy and contrast; concept formation through multiple description; idiographic/hermeneutic study; nomothetic study). Clear response to this question provides the scholar with a direction with respect to methodology, case selection and research design. In the following pages, I consider the basic logic of these comparative research designs and illustrate their successful deployment in comparative constitutional scholarship.

Arguably the most fundamental type of comparative constitutional inquiry is ontological in nature, engaging in mapping and classifying elements of worldwide constitutional universe in a systematic way that provides basic vocabulary and categorizations, surveys pertinent developments, and allows researchers, jurists and policy makers to gain knowledge of constitutional systems and to engage in simple comparisons in an ever-changing constitutional environment worldwide. As in any scientific domain, the creation of ontologies, taxonomies, conceptual maps and semantic webs, let alone the provision of accurate information delivered in a sophisticated, well thought out fashion, are an essential building bloc of theory-building. It is hard to overstate the significance of such studies, not least as linguistic barriers and access to up-to-date information remain two of the main practical obstacles in the comparative study of constitutions and constitutional institutions across time and place.

Three recent illustrations of this mode of scholarship, which all utilize in a sophisticated way advancements in information technology to provide an invaluable service to the comparative constitutional community worldwide, are the *Constitute* dataset and website (provides a searchable dataset of all written national constitutions from the late eighteenth century onwards; allows for synchronic and diachronic comparisons by hundreds of pre-defined terms and categories); the *ICONnect* ongoing 'year in review' project (provides approximately fifty single-country annual surveys on major constitutional developments and debates in each of the surveyed countries; each report is written by a team of local experts and addresses *de facto*, so-called 'small-c' constitutionalism, in addition to formal, *de jure* developments); and the *ConstitutionNet* project (provides 'real-time' commentary on constitutional developments worldwide, with a focus on global south settings that are often absent from standard academic discourse).

It is material to note that, unlike in comparative law, classification of a given constitutional system within the 'legal traditions' or 'family trees for legal systems' matrix coined by Rene David and further developed by Zweigert, Kötz and others, is not common in comparative constitutional inquiry. This may be because the rise of transnational and international rights regimes and the emergence of so-called 'global constitutionalism' – a supposedly Esperanto-like language of constitutional law and jurisprudence – are increasingly defying classical legal families (e.g. common law, civil law) distinctions. Although 'legal tradition' still accounts for considerable differences in modes of constitutional adjudication, reasoning and foreign citation sources, legal families cannot explain why constitutional jurisprudence in countries as different as Germany, Spain, Canada, Korea, Colombia and South Africa looks progressively similar.

An increasingly common mode of comparative constitutional inquiry, engages with cross-jurisdictional constitutional 'pollination' pertaining to several different objects of migration: constitutional structure (i.e., the very architecture of a given constitutional system and its organs); constitutional interpretation techniques and modes of analysis (e.g., originalism, purposive interpretation, proportionality); and comparative jurisprudence, namely selective judicial reference to constitutional concepts and constitutional court rulings, precedents and legal analysis. In the latter scenario, foreign constitutional jurisprudence may be referenced as a 'persuasive authority', as an interpretive aid (so that the ruling does not appear arbitrary), as a testament to a given rule's functionality in other jurisdictions, as a benchmark against which to compare a given constitutional system's take on the issue at stake, or more strategically as a legitimacy-enhancing means.

As is well known, in its landmark 1995 *Makwanyane* ruling – determining the unconstitutionality of the death penalty – the newly established South African Constitutional Court examined in detail pertinent jurisprudence from Botswana, Canada, Germany, Hong Kong, Hungary, India, Jamaica, Tanzania, the United States, Zimbabwe, the European Court of Human Rights and the United Nations Committee on Human Rights. In total, it refers to no less than 220 foreign case citations from eleven national and three supranational courts.[3] Observers often point out that Article 39 of the South African Constitution explicitly permits courts to look to foreign jurisprudence and in fact mandates that they consult international law when dealing with rights cases. It is hardly surprising that Justice Dikgang Moseneke, Deputy Chief Justice of South Africa, stated in 2010 that: '[I]t is no exaggeration to observe that our decisions read like works of comparative constitutional law and where appropriate we have not avoided relying on foreign judicial dicta or academic legal writings in support of the reasoning we resort to or conclusions we reach.'[4] Even the US Supreme Court – often considered (though perhaps incorrectly) the last bastion of principled resistance to foreign citations among the world's leading national high courts – has hesitantly joined the comparative reference trend.[5] Whereas on substantive grounds such comparative reference may be convincingly justifiable, on pure methodological grounds, it is sometimes pursued in an a-systematic, result-driven fashion that inadvertently lends credence to the 'cherry-picking' critique targeted at it.

In its more advisory, policy-oriented guise, the 'quest for best practice' mode of comparative constitutional inquiry takes the form of academic or think-tank reports on possible constitutional solutions to transitional

[3] See C. Rautenbach and L. du Plessis, 'In the Name of Comparative Constitutional Jurisprudence: The Consideration of German Precedents by South African Constitutional Court Judges' (2013) 14 *German Law Journal* 1539–1577.

[4] D. Moseneke, 'The Role of Comparative and Public International Law in Domestic Legal Systems: A South African Perspective', *Advocate* (December 2010).

[5] See, e.g., S. Breyer, *The Court and the World: American Law and the New Global Realities* (Knopf, 2015).

post-conflict or post-authoritarian settings or to polities torn along ethnic, religious and linguistic lines. The common principle that guides such reports is identifying the best or most suitable set of constitutional solution to a given polity by looking at a variety of comparable or potentially applicable arrangements in similarly situated polities. The emphasis is on result-driven comparative engagement in search for 'success stories'; a given set of constitutional arrangements that has proven effective in addressing a certain set of problems in polity X, may be implemented in similarly situated polities Y or Z. Since such reports are often written with an explicit policy goals mindset (e.g. quest for political stability, institution-building, democratization, power-sharing, peace-keeping), they do not aspire to draw on random sampling or on comprehensive surveys of all available settings or solutions, but focus instead on what has been proven workable or effective in comparable settings.

When we turn our gaze to more conventional academic modes of comparative constitutional scholarship, a continuum may be drawn between idiographic and nomothetic modes of inquiry. At one end stand idiographic studies that draw on thorough, nuanced analysis of a single constitutional system. This type of study may yield illuminating 'ethnography-like' accounts of constitutional transformation in given polities.[6] Ideally, it may also spawn general insights or lessons for other, similarly situated constitutional settings, although the stated purpose of such studies is often more modest than that, and is confined to understanding the unique traits of the constitutional domain in a single setting. Recent examples of well-executed 'constitutional ethnographies' are Michaela Hailbronner's *Tradition and Transformation* (a meticulous account of the rise of German constitutionalism in the post-World War II era);[7] Benjamin Sconthal's examination of Buddhism-infused constitutionalism in Sri Lanka;[8] Donald Horowitz's *Constitutional Change and Democracy in Indonesia*;[9] Brian Ray's *Engaging with Social Rights* (a detailed study of social rights jurisprudence and implementation in post-apartheid

---

[6] K.L. Scheppele, 'Constitutional Ethnography: An Introduction' (2004) 38 *Law & Society Review* 389–406.

[7] M. Hailbronner, *Tradition and Transformations: The Rise of German Constitutionalism* (Oxford University Press, 2015).

[8] B. Schonthal, *Buddhism, Politics and the Limits of Law: The Pyrrhic Constitutionalism of Sri Lanka* (Cambridge University Press, 2016).

[9] D. Horowitz, *Constitutional Change and Democracy in Indonesia* (Cambridge University Press, 2013).

South Africa);[10] or the various single-country volumes published under the auspices of the Constitutional Systems of the World book series (e.g. Cheryl Saunders's *The Constitution of Australia: A Contextual Analysis*, Shigenori Matsui's *The Constitution of Japan: A Contextual Analysis*, Andrew Harding's *The Constitution of Malaysia: A Contextual Analysis*, as well as other books published in the same series on the constitutions of Canada, France, Germany, the United Kingdom, Ireland, Brazil, Poland, China, Indonesia, Pakistan, Thailand, Vietnam and Israel).[11] In recent years, entire research handbooks have been devoted to constitutional law in a given polity (e.g. *The Oxford Handbook of the Canadian Constitution* or *The Oxford Handbook of the Indian Constitution*).[12] Each of these studies carefully canvasses a single constitutional system, explains its form and operation, and provides a critical evaluation of its foundations, evolution and contemporary challenges. Unique elements in each setting are defined as such by reference to comparative anchors.

Critical reflection by an external observer on a given polity's constitutional law and institutions is a subcategory in this genre of comparative constitutional studies. The study of constitutional system X by a researcher steeped in constitutional background Y, it may be argued, meets the basic requirement of comparative analysis – the existence of at least two targets of observation or points of view – because the observer at least implicitly perceives and describes system X in contrast with system Y. Montesquieu's *Persian Letters* or de Tocqueville's *Democracy in America* are prime examples of this type of implicit comparison. Within constitutional studies, Alexei Trochev's detailed account of the Russian Constitutional Court's 'difficult childhood' years, and of its jurisdictional 'wars' with other courts and the political sphere, makes a most valuable contribution to the understanding of how newly established courts in post-transition settings begin to gain traction and authority.[13] Likewise,

---

[10] B. Ray, *Engaging with Social Rights: Procedure, Participation, and Democracy in South Africa's Second Wave* (Cambridge University Press, 2016).

[11] C. Saunders, *The Constitution of Australia: A Contextual Analysis* (Hart Publishing, 2010); S. Matsui, *The Constitution of Japan: A Contextual Analysis* (Hart Publishing, 2010); A. Harding, *The Constitution of Malaysia: A Contextual Analysis* (Hart Publishing, 2012).

[12] P. Oliver, P. Macklem and N. Des Rosiers (eds.), *The Oxford Handbook of the Canadian Constitution* (Oxford University Press, 2017); S. Choudhry, M. Khosla and P.B. Mehta (eds.), *The Oxford Handbook of the Indian Constitution* (Oxford University Press, 2016).

[13] A. Trochev, *Judging Russia: The Role of the Constitutional Court in Russian Politics 1990–2006* (Cambridge University Press, 2008).

Lisa Hilbink's meticulous exploration of the culture of formalism and pas-
sivity in Chilean courts is a prime illustration of how a carefully crafted
constitutional ethnography of a single country can be pursued in a way
that contributes to general theory-building.[14]

However, even without such a general contribution or other concrete
payoffs, 'one can unapologetically study a foreign legal system simply
for its own sake.'[15] As Tom Ginsburg argues (in the context of studying
Japanese law):

Even if one starts with a more instrumentalist premise, we cannot conceivably
know whether any particular legal rule or institution will be of broader theoretical
or practical interest until we know what it is we are looking at. And this requires
a certain degree of local knowledge, of willingness to understand legal systems on
their own terms. There is therefore virtue in having a group of scholars studying
foreign legal systems for their own sake, independent of the need to resolve any
particular theoretical or practical question.[16]

At the same time, qualitative studies in comparative constitutionalism
are expected to subscribe to the established norms of qualitative work in
other human sciences. Within the academic domain, they should not be
conflated with fabulous storytelling about constitutional loci overseas or
with over-extrapolation from a very small yet frequently invoked set of
examples (e.g. the effect of the *Brown v. Board of Education* ruling, or
the constitutionalization of social and economic rights in South Africa).
Advocacy of qualitative approaches in comparative constitutional studies
must not be confused with methodological sloppiness or a retreat from
gold-standard practices such as field or archival work, linguistic profi-
ciency, and close acquaintance with the history, culture, law and politics
of the studied polity.

A different level of abstraction is at the basis of comparative inquiry
meant to *generate concepts and analytical frameworks for thinking critically about constitutional norms and practices.* This mode of comparative
constitutional scholarship involves a quest for a detailed understanding
of how people living in different cultural, social and political contexts
deal with constitutional dilemmas that are assumed to be common to

[14] L. Hilbink, *Judges beyond Politics in Democracy and Dictatorship: Lessons from Chile*
(Cambridge University Press, 2007).
[15] T. Ginsburg, 'Studying Japanese Law Because It's There' (2010) 58 *American Journal of
Comparative Law* 15–25, 15.
[16] *Id.*, 16.

most modern political systems. Its focus is not on a single jurisdiction, but on a single practice (or a set of closely related practices) as carried out in or encountered by different jurisdictions. More often than not, this type of comparative scholarship takes a universalist tone, emphasizing the broad similarity of constitutional challenges and functions across many relatively open, rule-of-law polities. By studying various manifestations of and solutions to roughly analogous constitutional challenges, our understanding of key concepts in constitutional law, such as separation of powers, statutory interpretation or equality rights, becomes more sophisticated and analytically sharp. The intellectual end often sought from this exercise is novel concept formation or the introduction of new thinking tools through multiple description.

Works dealing with innovative mechanisms designed to mitigate the tension between constitutionalism and democracy – mechanisms such as the Canadian Charter of Rights and Freedoms' 'limitation' and 'override' clauses, the New Zealand Bill of Rights Act's 'preferential' model of judicial review, and the UK Human Rights Act's 'declaration of incompatibility' – provide a good substantive illustration of the 'concept formation through multiple description' approach. Drawing on a comparative examination of such mechanisms, comparativists such as Stephen Gardbaum and Mark Tushnet have introduced the concept of the 'Commonwealth model of judicial review' or 'weak-form judicial review'. In doing so, they have enriched and brought new life to the debate about the questionable democratic credentials of constitutionalism in the United States.[17] Similar research design logic underlies other important comparative constitutional works of the concept formation genre, for example Yaniv Roznai's *Unconstitutional Constitutional Amendments*;[18] Gary Jacobsohn's masterful formation of the concept of constitutional identity;[19] and Vicki Jackson's introduction of modes of engagement with foreign constitutional jurisprudence in a transnational era.[20] This mode of inquiry is also prevalent in edited collections devoted to the analysis of a given

[17] See, e.g., S. Gardbaum, *The New Commonwealth Model of Constitutionalism: Theory and Practice* (Cambridge University Press, 2013); M. Tushnet, *Weak Court, Strong Rights* (Princeton University Press, 2009).

[18] Y. Roznai, *Unconstitutional Constitutional Amendments: The Limits of Amendment Powers* (Oxford University Press, 2017).

[19] G.J. Jacobsohn, *Constitutional Identity* (Harvard University Press, 2010).

[20] V.C. Jackson, *Constitutional Engagement in a Transnational Era* (Oxford University Press, 2010).

constitutional phenomenon across countries; here, a thematic introduction sets up the stage for a series of country chapters.[21] Hence, concept formation through multiple description. In recent years, an advanced version of this genre of edited collections combines various theoretical and theme-based essays with a selection of individual polity chapters by country experts, to provide a comprehensive, in-depth theoretical and empirical account of important constitutional phenomena (e.g. democratic backsliding, illiberal constitutionalism).[22]

Another type of comparative constitutional studies differs from concept formation in that it aims to engage in *theory testing and explanation through causal inference*. At the most abstract level, this type of scholarship is concerned with how two or more things or processes are related, why a certain phenomenon is happening, and why it is happening the way it is. Causation, however loosely or rigorously perceived, is a key element, perhaps even the main marker of identity of this scholarly enterprise. Controlled comparison and methodologically astute case selection and research design are critical to accomplishing these goals. There must also be a clear distinction between conditionality (a given phenomenon cannot occur without condition X, but that condition is not the *cause* of the phenomenon) and causality, as well as between direct factors and intervening factors, and between necessary and sufficient conditions.

Systematic examination of a small number of carefully selected cases (small-N), and statistical analysis of large data sets (large-N) are the two main research designs deployed in this inference-oriented mode of comparative constitutional studies. In his classic *A System of Logic*, John Stuart Mill spoke of a 'method of difference' and a 'method of agreement' in selecting comparative cases.[23] Using this method of inferential reasoning, comparative political scientists have for generations developed and applied various case selection ideal-types in the small-N mode of theory.[24] These ideal-types include: (i) the 'most similar cases' principle

---

[21] See, e.g., A.H.Y. Chen (ed.), *Constitutionalism in Asia in the Early Twenty-First Century* (Cambridge University Press, 2014); T. Groppi and M.-C. Ponthoreau (eds.), *The Use of Foreign Precedents by Constitutional Judges* (Hart Publishing, 2013).

[22] See M. Graber, S. Levinson and M. Tushnet (eds.), *Constitutional Democracy in Crisis?* (Oxford University Press, 2018).

[23] J.S. Mill, *A System of Logic, Ratiocinative and Inductive* (Longmans, Green, & Co., 1906).

[24] A sophisticated body of literature in political science deals with inference-oriented case-selection principles in single-case study or small-N research designs. See, e.g., J. Gerring, *Case Study Research: Principles and Practices* (Cambridge University Press, 2007);

(comparison of cases that, as much as possible, are identical but for the factors of causal interest); (ii) the 'most different cases' principle (comparison of cases that are different but for the factors of causal interest); (iii) the 'prototypical cases' principle (the studied cases feature as many key characteristics as possible that are found in a large number of cases); (iv) the 'most difficult case' principle (if a theory passes a 'most difficult' test case, our confidence with its predictions increases; conversely, if a claim or hypothesis does not hold true in a 'most likely' or a 'most favourable' case, its plausibility is severely undermined); and (v) the 'outlier cases' principle (studying case or cases that are not adequately explained by extant theories; because the studied phenomenon occurs frequently or in a significant fashion absent of the known causes or existing explanations, there ought to be another explanation).[25]

Two additional points are worth bearing in mind in this context. First, longitudinal comparisons of the same constitutional setting over a long stretch of time may be as instructive as cross-national comparisons. This may also serve as a more general cautionary note that contemporary discussions in comparative constitutional law often proceed as if there is no past, only present and future.[26] The reality is that the migration of constitutional ideas and critical encounters with the constitutive laws of others have been taking place long before the last few decades. Methodologically astute researchers should bear this in mind, and draw on longitudinal comparisons when applicable. Second, while mastery of context and language when studying a given constitutional setting remain essential, examining common patterns across different settings becomes easier as certain variants of constitutionalism become exceedingly common worldwide. Applying common sense is essential: clearly, an old water well and the concept of infidelity are hardly comparable. But a duck and a stork are. In other words, comparability requires unity

---

C. Ragin, *Redesigning Social Inquiry: Fuzzy Sets and Beyond* (University of Chicago Press, 2008); C. Ragin, *Fuzzy-Set Social Science* (University of Chicago Press, 2000).

[25] For a detailed elaboration and illustrations of the basic logic of each of these case selection principles and their deployment in contemporary comparative constitutional studies, see R. Hirschl, 'The Question of Case Selection in Comparative Constitutional Law' (2005) 53 *American Journal of Comparative Law* 125–156, and R. Hirschl, *Comparative Matters: The Renaissance of Comparative Constitutional Law* (Oxford University Press, 2014), 224–281.

[26] R. Hirschl, 'Remembrance of Things Past' (2015) 13 *International Journal of Constitutional Law* 1–8.

and plurality.[27] Plurality is essential, as there is not much sense in comparing things that are perfectly identical; little would be gained by such a comparison. Likewise, there is hardly any utility in comparing things that share little or nothing in common. Either way, a plausible proposition in this regard is that there are areas of constitutional jurisprudence – most notably the interpretation of rights – where cross-jurisdictional reference is more likely to occur than in other areas, such as the more aspirational or organic (e.g. federalism, separation of powers and amending procedures) features of the constitution, where national idiosyncrasies and contingencies are more prevalent.[28]

As mentioned earlier, the 'most similar cases' principle is the most commonly drawn upon research design and case selection principle in inference-oriented small-N studies. Tom Ginsburg's *Judicial Review in New Democracies* – a carefully constructed comparative study of the catalysts behind the emergence of independent constitutional review regime during the early stages of democratic liberalization in post-authoritarian polities – is an example of an effective application of the 'most similar cases' methodology to the study of comparative constitutionalism.[29] Ginsburg's argument – judicial review is a solution to and a function of the problem of uncertainty in constitutional design – is carried out through an exploration of the formation of constitutional courts, and the corresponding judicialization of politics, in three new Asian democracies: Taiwan, Mongolia and Korea. The three countries share a roughly similar cultural context. Each underwent a transition to democracy in the late 1980s and early 1990s, and in each the newly established constitutional court has struggled to maintain and enhance its stature within a political environment that lacks an established tradition of judicial independence and constitutional supremacy. Despite these commonalities, however, there has been significant variance in judicial independence among the three countries.

Another commonly invoked research design principle in 'small-N' comparative constitutional law is the 'prototypical cases' logic. A couple

---

[27] C. Valcke, 'Comparative Law as Comparative Jurisprudence – The Comparability of Legal Systems' (2004) 52 *American Journal of Comparative Law* 713–740, 720–721.

[28] See generally V.C. Jackson, 'Comparative Constitutional Federalism and Transnational Judicial Discourse' (2004) 2 *International Journal of Constitutional Law* 91–138.

[29] T. Ginsburg, *Judicial Review in New Democracies: Constitutional Courts in Asian Cases* (Cambridge University Press, 2003).

of books that draw on such a design to question the supposed uniformity of proportionality analysis in comparative constitutional jurisprudence provide textbook illustrations. In their book *Proportionality and Constitutional Culture*, Moshe Cohen-Eliya and Iddo Porat present a detailed comparison of the origins and practice of proportionality analysis in Germany and balancing analysis in the United States to advance the argument that the scope and nature of proportionality/balancing analysis in a given polity may be affected by the concrete origins of the practice as well as the legal, political and philosophical culture in that polity.[30] Whereas in Prussia, to pick one aspect of this comparative analysis, 'proportionality stepped into the vacuum created by the absence of constitutional protection for rights, and introduced into administrative law an element of rights-protection through the notion of the rule of law', in the United States balancing emerged as a rights-limiting mechanism that, in lieu of a limitations clause in the Bill of Rights, facilitated a pragmatic, rights-restricting jurisprudential approach in cases involving conflicting interests. The particular historical context, Cohen-Eliya and Porat show, 'shaped the conception of these doctrines: proportionality as pro-rights and balancing as pragmatic and limiting rights.' They go on to illustrate that political culture accounts for the centrality and the intrinsic value accorded proportionality in German constitutional law as an effective means for shaping and optimizing German society's values, as opposed to the relative marginalization of balancing in American constitutional law and its conceptualization as a pragmatic exception to the construction of rights as categorical limitations on state power. In short, the conceptualization of proportionality analysis may vary from one polity to another; the differences may be culturally based.[31]

A different variant of this mode of inquiry in comparative constitutionalism is evident in edited volumes featuring collections of single-country accounts of constitutional law in a selection of polities within a given

---

[30] M. Cohen-Eliya and I. Porat, *Proportionality and Constitutional Culture* (Cambridge University Press, 2013). For a similar research design, theme and case studies, see J. Bomhoff, *Balancing Constitutional Rights: The Origins and Meanings of Postwar Legal Discourse* (Cambridge University Press, 2014).

[31] An earlier illuminating example of inference-oriented small-N 'prototypical cases' research design in comparative constitutional reasoning is Mitchel Lasser's comparative account of constitutional reasoning styles. See, Mitchel de S.-O.-l'E. Lasser, *Judicial Deliberations: A Comparative Analysis of Judicial Transparency and Legitimacy* (Oxford University Press, 2004).

region or continent (e.g. South East Asia, Latin America, post-communist Europe, etc.).[32] The underlying research design logic of this sort of comparative work is that, taken as a whole, the comparison of various constitutional elements in polities that share pertinent historical, legal, political and cultural background factors implicitly follows a 'most similar cases' logic, thereby facilitating the identification of pan-regional or pan-continental patterns of convergence or divergence on any given constitutional axis. A number of such collections that focus on the European scene follow instead a 'most different cases' logic, deployed to help assess the effects of the emerging pan European constitutional regime on constitutional law within a number of very different polities that are all subject to that regime (e.g. the twenty-eight-member European Union or the forty-seven-member Council of Europe and its European Convention of Human Rights).[33] In so doing, these collections aim to assess the effects of a similar, across-the-board exogenous 'treatment' on different constitutional cultures and traditions.

At the nomothetic end of the generalization spectrum in comparative constitutional inquiry stand large-N studies that aim to generate widely transferable insights (nomothetic knowledge) through analyses of large sets of observations, and ideally even the entire studied population. In simplistic terms, the idea here is to study the entire constitutional forest, not individual constitutional trees. Such an approach might provide a response to heuristics and case-selection biases, as well as to the limited generalizability associated with single-case and small-N research. With many phenomena, the sheer number of cases makes a complete analysis infeasible. However, when it comes to studying the world's constitutions, the full number of cases is still only in the hundreds. For many purposes this is a manageable number, and as long as quantitative studies limit themselves to what they can plausibly extract and deduce from constitutional texts (and possibly other cross-national indicators), they should be a most welcome addition to comparative constitutional studies. Large-N analyses are particularly useful as a means to consider broader trends in

---

[32] E.g. M. Tushnet and M. Khosla (eds.), *Unstable Constitutionalism: Law and Politics in South Asia* (Cambridge University Press, 2016); R. Dixon and T. Ginsburg (eds.), *Comparative Constitutional Law in Latin America* (Edward Elgar, 2017); A. Fruhstorfer and M. Hein (eds.), *Constitutional Politics in Central and Eastern Europe* (Springer, 2017).

[33] See, e.g., A. Jakab and D. Kochenov (eds.), *The Enforcement of EU Law and Values: Ensuring Member States' Compliance* (Oxford University Press, 2017).

constitutionalism – to focus on the general picture, not on specific details or individual observations. If properly executed, such analyses may likewise elude the clichés, heuristics and biases that emerge from decades of over-studying a handful of cases and instead become able to actually test some of the canonical insights of constitutional theory or shed new light on causal links within the constitutional universe.

This mode of inquiry becomes exceedingly relevant in the relentless global convergence towards constitutionalism and as increasingly comprehensive databases and advanced information technology make a rich body of pertinent information readily available to researchers and scholars worldwide. It is now possible – perhaps for the first time – to engage in serious, methodological, interdisciplinary dialogue between ideas and evidence, theory and data, normative claims, and empirical analysis. In so doing, large-N studies of comparative constitutional phenomena may help alleviate the legitimate concerns over 'cherry-picking' raised by opponents of a-systematic reference to foreign legal sources and may likewise mitigate the overreliance on a small number of 'usual suspect' constitutional settings (at the expense of over 150 others) by treating all constitutions as equally worthy of observation or status as data points.[34]

The number of large-N constitutional studies published to date remains modest, but it has been growing exponentially in recent years. It has been drawn upon to assess the global decline of American constitutional legacy;[35] to determine why countries adopt constitutional review;[36] to trace and explain patterns of judicial decision-making in

---

[34] This may be the right place to say that the common focus in much of the literature on the constitutional 'North' betrays not only certain epistemological and methodological choices but also a normative preference for some concrete set of values that the 'Northern' setting seems to uphold. The near-exclusive focus on a dozen liberal democracies in comparative constitutional law reflects the field's deeply liberal bent. But moving away from its normative facet to the positivist, real-life one, the relevance of the Global South critique becomes more qualified. Whether the selective Northern (or 'Western') emphasis in comparative constitutional law limits the applicability or value of canonical scholarship in the field hinges on the specific question being posed. A given constitutional setting may belong to the Global South in one context or comparative dimension, but not in another.

[35] D. Law and M. Versteeg, 'The Declining Influence of the United States Constitution' (2012) 87 *NYU Law Review* 762–858.

[36] T. Ginsburg and M. Versteeg, 'Why Do Countries Adopt Constitutional Review?' (2014) 30 *Journal of Law, Economics and Organization* 587–622.

constitutional adjudication,[37] or patterns of constitutional court reference to foreign law;[38] to examine the global spread of economic and social rights;[39] to measure the effects of such rights;[40] and to study the efficacy of constitutional mechanisms such as formal amendment rules or term limits.[41]

A notable example of how large-N studies may contribute to comparative constitutional studies is *The Endurance of National Constitutions* by Zachary Elkins, Tom Ginsburg and James Melton.[42] At the core of this pioneering book is an ostensibly simple question: 'Why do the lifespans of national constitutions vary? Why is it that some live much longer than others?' To answer this, the authors build a data set of constitutions of the world from 1789 to 2005 – a mere 216 years of modern constitutionalism. The data reveal some stunning results (e.g. while constitutions are written to last, they vary considerably in terms of their endurance; only half of all constitutions last more than nine years, with an overall average of less than twenty years). It also shows that while extra-constitutional factors do affect a constitution's endurance, design choices matter more. All things considered, enduring constitutions tend to be specific, to emerge by virtue of a relatively open drafting stage that engenders 'buy-in' by diverse constituencies, and to be adaptable as a result of amending formulae and provisions for incorporating modern practices. These three design choices 'result from the constitution-making process itself, but are also features of ongoing practice. All three mutually reinforce each other

---

[37] See, e.g., G. Helmke, *Courts Under Constraints: Judges, Generals, and Presidents in Argentina* (Cambridge University Press, 2005); S. Dothan, *Reputation and Judicial Tactics* (Cambridge University Press, 2014); J. Segal and H. Spaeth, *The Supreme Court and the Attitudinal Model Revisited* (Cambridge University Press, 2002).

[38] E. Mak, 'Reference to Foreign Law in the Supreme Courts of Britain and the Netherlands: Explaining the Development of Judicial Practices' (2012) 8 *Utrecht Law Review* 20–34; E. Mak, *Judicial Decision-Making in a Globalised World: A Comparative Analysis of the Changing Practices of Western Highest Courts* (Hart Publishing, 2013).

[39] C. Jung, R. Hirschl and E. Rosevear, 'Economic and Social Rights in National Constitutions' (2015) 62 *American Journal of Comparative Law* 1043–1094.

[40] A. Chilton and M. Versteeg, 'Rights Without Resources: The Impact of Constitutional Social Rights on Social Spending' (2017) 60 *Journal of Law and Economics* 713–748.

[41] T. Ginsburg and J. Melton, 'Does the Constitutional Amendment Rule Matter at All?' (2015) 13 *International Journal of Constitutional Law* 686–713.

[42] Z. Elkins et al., *The Endurance of National Constitutions* (Cambridge University Press, 2009).

to produce a vigorous constitutional politics in which groups have a stake in the survival of the constitution.'[43]

As with any other research design and case selection approach, a comparative constitutional scholar needs to tread with caution when considering the suitability of a large-N study for her planned study. The apparent weaknesses of large-N studies have been addressed repeatedly, most notably (though not exclusively) by proponents of contextual, purportedly deeper research.[44] Perhaps most significant for the study of constitutionalism is that large statistical data sets tend to overlook context or take it too lightly, ignore the crucial 'law on the ground' or 'soft law' aspects. Subsequently, it is quite common to take issue with large-N studies' marked difficulty capturing the vital nuance and the multilayered – social, cultural and political – context in which constitutional development occurs. Concepts such as 'constitutional identity' or 'constitutional culture' are not easily amenable to inquiry that is insensitive to details, stripped of nuance and context, and reliant on oversimplified coding schemes.

Extant data sets of constitutional texts do not tell us much, if anything, about constitutional interpretation by courts or on-the-ground implementation and impact (in fairness, those studied do not aim to address that type of issue). More generally, large-N studies often focus on observable or quantifiable phenomena but lack the tools to deal with non-observable, non-quantifiable ones. Consequently, they tend to focus on questions and phenomena that lend themselves a priori to quantitative analysis of concrete observations. This, in turn, may lead to what Ian Shapiro succinctly describes as 'a flight from reality in the human sciences'.[45] As well, it is sometimes argued that large-N studies pour tremendous effort into sophisticated data-analysis techniques, possibly at the expense of net theoretical yield or substantive ingenuity.

There is more than a kernel of truth in all these concerns. Yet, analyses of large data sets are still a valuable addition to theory-building

---

[43] *Id.*, 89.

[44] For a critique of economics' reliance on numbers to capture the complex nature of law in various contexts, see P. Legrand, 'Econocentrism' (2009) 59 *University of Toronto Law Journal* 215–222. Legrand begins his critique with an epigraph quote from Nietzsche: 'the reduction of all qualities to quantities is nonsense.' For further discussion see H. Spamann, 'Empirical Comparative Law' (2015) 11 *Annual Review of Law & Social Science* 131–153.

[45] I. Shapiro, *The Flight from Reality in the Human Sciences* (Princeton University Press, 2005).

and testing in comparative constitutional studies. To be clear, the claim here is not that explanation, causality or numerical comparative inquiry should serve as the field's golden standard or intellectual Holy Grail. However, as Mila Versteeg, one of the leading young voices in what may be termed 'empirical constitutional studies' suggests that 'the field of comparative constitutional law is filled with causal claims, including, inter alia, the following notions: constitutions constrain government; judicial review protects human rights; socio-economic rights are unenforceable; and constitutional law is converging upon a global paradigm. These claims, which often take the form of unarticulated assumptions, are essentially empirical claims that have largely gone untested.'[46] Along similar lines, Frederick Schauer, one of America's most prominent constitutional thinkers, suggests that the intuitions and hunches of law professors concerning the impact of constitutional law ought to be subject to empirical testing. He asks: '[D]oes constitutional law make a difference to official behavior? Do the texts of constitutions influence official action? Do the emanations of courts affect the actions of officials? Affirmative answers to these questions are commonly assumed, but perhaps the time is ripe to examine such assumptions more critically in comparative context.'[47] When taken with a healthy dose of scepticism and awareness to their acknowledged limitations, empirical studies on the effects of constitutional texts, traditions, designs and rulings can only contribute, not harm the state of knowledge on these matters.

3 Cross-Disciplinary, Multi-Method and Collaborative Research

Around the world, in numerous countries and in several transnational entities, constitutional law plays a key role in regulating politics and in delineating the scope of rights protections. Because the complex symbioses of today's world admit neither constitutionalism-free political

---

[46] A. Meuwese and M. Versteeg, 'Quantitative Methods for Comparative Constitutional Law', in M. Adams and J. Bomhoff (eds.), *Practice and Theory in Comparative Law* (Cambridge University Press, 2012), 233.

[47] F. Schauer, 'Comparative Constitutional Compliance: Notes Towards a Research Agenda', in M. Adams and J. Bomhoff (eds.), *Practice and Theory in Comparative Law* (Cambridge University Press, 2012), 213.

systems nor apolitical constitutional law, it is increasingly common for comparative constitutional inquiry to embrace an interdisciplinary approach. Consequently, the array of research methods deployed in comparative constitutional inquiry has expanded beyond traditional legal analysis of legislation, jurisprudence and reasoning, to the deployment of social science methods such as interview fieldwork and participatory observations, archival work, surveys, assembling and statistical analysis of large data sets, game theory and formal modelling, computerized content analysis or the study of constitutional diffusion and convergence through network science.

This does not detract from the power of doctrinal analysis per se. The more prevalent constitutional terminology and constitutional jurisprudence become in addressing core ethical, political and public policy dilemmas, the more relevant mastery of doctrinal constitutional analysis turn out to be. Comparative constitutional law professors hold a clear and undisputed professional advantage in their ability to identify, dissect and scrutinize the work of courts and to critically assess the persuasive power of a given judge's opinion. Understanding jurisprudence on its own terms or explicating modes of judicial reasoning and interpretation has traditionally been the domain of law professors. As long as comparative constitutional analysis is focused on these facets, no one is better positioned to pursue it than law professors well-versed in doctrinal legal analysis.

However, theorizing about the constitutional domain of a broader world requires closer engagement with and openness towards disciplines that study the broader context with which constitutions and constitutional institutions constantly and organically interact. It requires some familiarity with the history of modern constitutional thought (the field's ever-expanding terminology includes phrases such as 'liberal constitutionalism', 'authoritarian constitutionalism', 'global constitutionalism' or 'theocratic constitutionalism'); awareness to the study of judicial behaviour (an overwhelming body of evidence suggests that extrajudicial factors play a role in constitutional court decision-making); an understanding of the origins of constitutional change and stalemate (a variety of theories point to the significant role of ideational and strategic factors in both); the promise and pitfalls of various constitutional designs (the relevance of the social, political and cultural context in settings where such designs are deployed is obvious); and the study of the actual capacity of constitutional jurisprudence to induce real change on-the-ground,

independently of or in association with other factors (the social sciences
are essential for studying the actual effects of constitutions beyond the
courtroom). Contributions to these types of comparative constitutional
scholarship require a researcher to adjust her research design and methodological approach to better fit the study's thematic goal or aim. The
question then is not *why* engage in interdisciplinary comparative constitutional inquiry – few open-minded legal scholars or intellectually honest
political scientists would disagree that in an ideal world that would be
a preferable approach – but rather *how* should such an interdisciplinary,
multi-method inquiry be effectively pursued.

The interdisciplinary turn in comparative constitutional inquiry
encounters some obvious resistance from both sides of the disciplinary
divide. Such resistance has much to do, I suspect, with various training,
vocational and sociology of knowledge factors, most notably political
scientists and sociologists' inclination to conceptualize the constitutional
domain as mere reflection of broader societal, political or cultural forces
and undercurrents, as well as the vocational and licensing aspects of legal
education and the legal profession's collective interest in maintaining
the autonomous and a political image of constitutional law. It remains
to be seen whether the multi-faceted nature of constitutionalism worldwide continues to promote interdisciplinary inquiry in comparative constitutionalism or whether professional interests in maintaining doctrinal
boundaries prevail.

Under any scenario, comparative constitutional inquiry requires a fair
degree of knowledge about and expertise in the studied jurisdictions
and their political context in addition to their legal and constitutional
traditions. This is no easy task, even if it has been facilitated somewhat
by dramatic advancements in information technology and the improved
availability of pertinent comparative materials. It likewise necessitates
rich linguistic skills and jurisdiction-specific acquaintance with so-
called 'small-c' constitutionalism – the de facto, on-the-ground practice,
meaning and power of constitutional law, constitutional ideals and constitutional norms in a given polity, in addition to acquaintance with that
polity's 'large-C' constitutionalism, namely the formal, de jure or textual
elements of the constitutional domain. Taken as a whole, these and other
related difficulties embedded in the comparative study of constitutionalism
across time and place call for greater emphasis, already underway in some
respects, on jointly authored work and greater openness to collaborative

group projects that address similar constitutional phenomena.[48] It likewise suggests that multi-method research projects – studies that combine various legal and social science research designs, or blend qualitative and quantitative research methods may be gaining momentum in the years to come.[49] Such multi-method research is underpinned by the principle of triangulation, which means that researchers should ensure they are not over-reliant on a single research method, and should instead follow more than one measurement procedure when investigating a research problem. In this way, multi-method research enhances confidence in findings.

Among its many advantages, collaborative, multi-method research projects may help alleviate one of the lingering challenges in comparative constitutional law – the field's long-standing reliance on a small number of overanalysed, 'usual suspect' constitutional settings or court rulings that do not necessarily represent the entire constitutional universe while the constitutional experiences of entire regions, mostly in the Global South – from sub-Saharan Africa to Central America and to Central and South East Asia – remain understudied and generally overlooked. Whereas no student of comparative constitutionalism may consider herself a master of the field without exposure to the constitutional legacy of the United States, the innovative features of the Canadian constitution or the extensive jurisprudence of the European Court of Human Rights, she must likewise question the validity of purportedly universal insights that are based on a handful of frequently studied and not always representative settings or cases.

Conclusion

The renaissance of comparative constitutionalism has been characterized by blissful methodological pluralism. Indeed, no concept of constitutionalism's scope and nature can be exhaustively and comparatively assessed using a single research design, approach or method. Thus, there is no, and there cannot be, a single, unified 'official' method in the comparative study of constitutional law, constitutional institutions and

---

[48] See R. Dixon, 'Towards a Realistic Comparative Constitutional Studies' (2016) 64 *American Journal of Comparative Law* 193–199.

[49] See, generally, L.B. Nielsen, 'The Need for Multi-Method Approaches in Empirical Legal Research', in P. Cane and H. Kritzer (eds.), *The Oxford Handbook of Empirical Legal Research* (Oxford University Press, 2010), 951–975.

constitutional practice. That said, collective understanding of what may be considered methodologically sound scholarship is the hallmark of every thriving discipline or research enterprise. Appreciation of and attention to the nature of various comparative methodologies and their compatibility with the various meanings, types, aims and purposes of comparative constitutional inquiry are vital for the continuation of the field's current renaissance. When executed poorly (fortunately, a diminishing act), comparative constitutional inquiry may amount to little more than result-oriented cherry-picking of favourable cases, which is precisely the kind of practice that opponents of reference to foreign law (most notably the late Antonin Scalia of the US Supreme Court) base their objections on. Precisely because the concern with the a-systematic 'cherry-picking' of 'friendly' examples may not be easily dismissed, those who wish to engage in systematic comparative work ought to pay closer attention to research methods, and the philosophy of comparative inquiry more broadly. The response to the cherry-picking concern is not to abandon comparative constitutional work; rather, it is to engage in comparative work while being mindful of key historical foundations, ontological distinctions, epistemological directions, and methodological considerations that define *comparative* constitutional inquiry as a distinct area of scholarship and practice.

Further Reading

S. Gardbaum, 'How Do and Should We Compare Constitutional Law', in Samantha Besson et al. (eds.), *Comparing Comparative Law* (Schulthess, 2017), 109–126.

R. Hirschl, 'The Question of Case Selection in Comparative Constitutional Law' 2005 53 *American Journal of Comparative Law* 125–155.

'From Comparative Constitutional Law to Comparative Constitutional Studies' 2013 11 *International Journal of Constitutional Law* 1–12.

Comparative Matters: The Renaissance of Comparative Constitutional Law (Oxford University Press, 2014).

V.C. Jackson, 'Methodological Challenges in Comparative Constitutional Law' 2010 28 *Penn State International Law Review* 319–326.

'Comparative Constitutional Law: Methodologies', in Michel Rosenfeld and András Sajó (eds.), *The Oxford Handbook of Comparative Constitutional Law* (Oxford University Press, 2012), 54–74.

A. Meuwese and M. Versteeg, 'Quantitative Methods for Comparative Constitutional Law', in Maurice Adams and Jacco Bomhoff (eds.), *Practice and Theory in Comparative Law* (Cambridge University Press, 2012), 230–256.

M. Reimann, 'Comparative Law and Neighboring Disciplines', in Mauro Bussani and Ugo Mattei (eds.), *The Cambridge Companion to Comparative Law* (Cambridge University Press, 2012), 13–34.

K.L. Scheppele, 'Constitutional Ethnography: An Introduction' 2004 38 *Law & Society Review* 389–406.

M. Tushnet, 'The Possibilities of Comparative Constitutional Law' 1999 108 *Yale Law Journal* 1225–1309.

2 Constitutionalism(s)

Robert Schütze

Introduction

Constitutionalism is the set of ideas that defines what a constitution is or ought to be. For some, there exists an essential core meaning of the term;[1]

---

[1] C.H. McIlwain, *Constitutionalism: Ancient and Modern* (Liberty Fund, 2008).

while for others, the concepts of 'constitution' and 'constitutionalism' have fundamentally changed over time.[2]

Various conceptions of constitutionalism have indeed developed in legal history. According to a descriptive constitutionalism, a constitution is the factual description of the institutions and powers of government.[3] By contrast, a normative constitutionalism insists that constitutions do not merely *describe* the existing governmental structures, but rather *prescribe* their composition and powers. From a formal point of view, constitutional laws are thus those norms that, as the highest laws within a society, stand above the government.[4] This formal definition has, in the last two hundred years, competed with a *material* understanding of what a constitution ought to be. This material constitutionalism links the legal concept of the constitution with a particular *political* philosophy that is meant to *legitimize* the constitution. According to a 'democratic' constitutionalism, a genuine constitution thus only exists where it is based on the idea of a 'government of the people, by the people, for the people'.[5] A 'liberal' constitutionalism, on the other hand, believes that a constitution is only a 'true' constitution if it sets limits to the powers of government, and the two traditional constitutional limits here are the separation of powers and fundamental rights.[6]

The various 'constitutionalisms', and their relations to each other, can be seen in Figure 2.1; and the aim of this chapter is to briefly introduce each of them (Sections 2–4). The main purpose behind this chapter is thus to sensitize the reader to the fact that the many *constitutional* phenomena discussed in this book are not only geographically variant but that the very idea of what counts as *constitution* is historically constructed and

---

[2] Cf. 'Verfassung', in: O. Brunner, W. Conze and R. Koselleck, *Geschichtliche Grundbegriffe –* Volume 6 (Klett-Cotta, 2004), 831–899.

[3] This descriptive sense of 'constitution' can be found in Aristotle, *Politics* (trans: E. Baker, Oxford University Press, 1998), Book III, §§ 6 and 7.

[4] This normative sense of 'constitution' can be found in T. Paine, 'Rights of Man' in *Political Writings* (Cambridge University Press, 1997), 89: 'A Constitution is a thing antecedent to a government, and a government is only the creature of a constitution.'

[5] This democratic sense of 'constitution' can be found in A. Lincoln, 'Gettysburg Address, 1863', in H.S. Commager and M. Cantor (eds.), *Documents of American History*, vol. I (Prentice Hall, 1988), 429.

[6] This liberal sense of 'constitution' can be found in the 1789 Declaration of the Rights of Man and of the Citizen, whose Article 16 states: 'Toute Société dans laquelle la garantie des Droits n'est pas assurée, ni la séparation des Pouvoirs déterminée, n'a point de Constitution.'

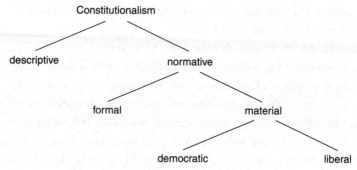

Figure 2.1 Main Variants of Constitutionalism

will often be influenced by a pre-commitment to a particular *constitutional* theory. The most prevailing element of any constitutional theory in the past three hundred years has thereby been the link between the idea of a constitution and that of the modern (unitary) state. Yet as Section 4 hopes to show, the state-centred idea of a constitution cannot explain federal unions, such as the (early) United States or today's European Union, in which there are two levels of government making a constitutional claim over the same people(s).

1 Descriptive Constitutionalism: Forms of Government

a Constitutional Forms I: The Legacy of Classic Antiquity

The discovery that there exist different types of 'governments' and 'constitutions' was made in antiquity. The most enduring constitutional classification here comes from Aristotle, whose description of the various forms of government continues to shape our modern understanding of the forms of State.[7] For Aristotle, political communities are best classified by using a quantitative and a qualitative criterion. Quantitatively, he first identified three main types depending on the number of people ruling (one, minority, majority); and this basic division is completed by a qualitative criterion that asks whether public power is exercised for the benefit

---

[7] H. Kelsen, *Allgemeine Staatslehre* (Springer, 1925), 320 (my translation): 'All modern theories of state forms continue to be decisively shaped by antiquity, and here particularly by the Aristotelian theory.'

Table 2.1 Aristotelian Forms of Government

	For the Benefit of All	For its own Benefit
Power Exercised by One	Monarchy	Tyranny
Power Exercised by a Minority	Aristocracy	Oligarchy
Power Exercised by the Majority	Polity	Democracy

of all people or only for the benefit of the number of people holding power. The resulting six constitutional forms can be seen in Table 2.1.

These 'pure' forms have been passed on to us (almost) unchanged.[8] From the very beginning, however, they were complemented by the idea of the 'mixed' constitution. The latter is a combination of elements taken from the pure forms; and for Aristotle, as for other classic scholars, it was heralded as the most stable constitutional arrangement because of its 'balance' between competing structures.[9] In an early instance of constitutional borrowing,[10] it is the Greek idea of the mixed constitution that becomes one of the core principles of the Constitution of Rome. Famously analysed by Polybius,[11] the governmental institutions of ancient Rome are thus seen to reflect three distinct constitutional principles: the 'monarchical' principle is expressed through the Consuls, the 'aristocratic' principle finds its manifestation in the Senate, and the 'democratic' principle comes to life in the public assemblies. The mixed nature of the Roman Constitution therefore inevitably pushed a new word to the foreground: the idea of a 'republic' (*res publica*) or 'commonwealth'.[12] This new notion henceforth neutrally referred to the 'political community' without the Aristotelian connotations in the older concept of 'polity'.

---

[8] The principal difference today, however, is that the negative connotations of democracy have disappeared; and we now identify 'polity' with 'democracy' and the negative aspects of democracy with 'populism'.

[9] On this point, see A. Lintott, 'Aristotle and the Mixed Constitution', in R. Brock and S. Hodkinson (eds.), *Alternatives to Athens: Varieties of Political Organization and Community in Ancient Greece* (Oxford University Press, 2003), 152.

[10] See Chapter 22 in this volume.

[11] See only: A. Lintott, *The Constitution of the Roman Republic* (Oxford University Press, 1999), Chapter III.

[12] Cicero, *On the Commonwealth and on the Laws* (editor: J. Zetzel, Cambridge University Press, 1999). This new concept comes to generically stand for a 'political community' and is consequently broader than the modern conception of a 'republic' that is opposed to a 'monarchy'.

Leaping over the 'dark' Middle Ages,[13] many of these classic concepts experienced a renaissance in the sixteenth and seventeenth century. Bodin's 'Six Books on the Commonwealth' drew once more on the Aristotelian tradition when they distinguished between three commonwealths: 'If sovereignty lies in a single prince, we will call it monarchy; if all of the people have a share, we will say that the state is democratic (*populaire*); if it is only the lesser part of the people, we will hold that the state is aristocratic.'[14] Yet determined to position the idea of a single and indivisible sovereignty at the centre of each commonwealth, the possibility of a mixed constitution is now vehemently rejected;[15] and, according to Bodin, any 'scientific' analysis of constitutions must equally eschew a qualitative classification into 'good' and 'bad' constitutions.[16]

Instead, a new distinction is introduced – a distinction that has survived to the present day: the distinction between 'forms of state' and 'forms of government'.[17] The former comes to refer to who is seen as the 'sovereign' or 'head' of State, while the latter refers to the manner or institution through which sovereignty is exercised. A State can henceforth easily be classified as a 'monarchy' (because sovereignty is seen to lie in one person), yet also have an 'aristocratic' or 'democratic' government because the monarch exercises his or her power 'through' a council or 'through' a parliament. Elaborated in the eighteenth century, and especially through the work of Montesquieu (and Kant), this 'trick' brings the idea of the mixed constitution partly back via the principle of the separation of powers; while it equally accommodates the rise of parliaments in societies that formally adhere to the monarchic principle of hereditary and dynastic power.[18]

[13] See only: O. von Gierke, *Political Theories of the Middle Ages* (Cambridge University Press, 1900); as well as: W. Ullmann, *Principles of Government and Politics in the Middle Ages* (Methuen, 1961).

[14] Bodin, *On Sovereignty* (editor: J. Franklin, Cambridge University Press, 1992), 89. He continues: 'But it is clear that to have true definitions and resolutions in any subject matter, one must fix not on accidents, which are innumerable, but on essential differences of form. Otherwise one could fall into an infinite labyrinth which does not admit of scientific knowledge.'

[15] Ibid., 92: '[T]o combine monarchy with democracy and with aristocracy is impossible and contradictory, and cannot even be imagined. For sovereignty is indivisible, as we have shown, how could it be shared by a prince, the nobles, and the people at the same time?'

[16] Ibid., 89.

[17] Bodin distinguishes three forms of government: despotic, royal and tyrannical; and all three forms can be found in all three types of state.

[18] See only Article 85 (1) Belgian Constitution: 'The constitutional powers of the King are hereditary through the direct, natural and legitimate descent.'

Be that as it may, the rise of parliaments and their identification with (representative) democracy causes the perhaps greatest semantic revolution to the classic constitutional vocabulary. For after the American and French revolutions, a new – modern – understanding of 'republicanism' comes to re-define almost all categories of classic constitutionalism; and it is to this semantic revolution that we must now turn.

b Constitutional Forms II: Modern Classifications

aa The Rise of Democracy and Representative Government

With the American and French Revolutions, old words were given a new meaning, and it is this modern meaning that is still with us today.[19] This modern understanding of what constitutions are or ought to be finds its clearest expression in *The Federalist*.[20] Deeply influenced by the classic tradition, James Madison here famously coined the modern vocabulary of representative democracy by deliberately contrasting a 'pure Democracy' with a 'Republic' within 'which the scheme of representation takes place'.[21] Claiming that the past had hitherto not clearly produced the republican form, the latter is now defined as follows:

What then are the distinctive characters of the republican form? (...) If we resort for a criterion, to the different principles on which different forms of government are established, we may define a republic to be, or at least may bestow that name on, a government which derives all its powers directly or indirectly from the great body of the people; and is administered by persons holding their offices during pleasure, for a limited period, or during good behavior. (...) The House of Representatives, like that of one branch at least of all the State Legislatures, is elected immediately by the great body of the people. The Senate, like the present Congress, and the Senate of Maryland, derives its appointment indirectly from the people. The President is indirectly derived from the choice of the people, according to the example in most of the States. Even the judges, with all other

---

[19] On the importance of the eighteenth century as a 'Sattelzeit', see R. Koselleck, Einleitung, in: O. Brunner et al. (eds.), *Geschichtliche Grundbegriffe* (n. 2) – Volume 1, XV; and with regard to France in particular, see F. Schrader, *Zur Politischen Semantik der Revolution: Frankreich* (1750–1850) (VS Verlag, 2010).

[20] A. Hamilton, J. Madison and J. Jay, *The Federalist* (editor: T. Ball, Cambridge University Press, 2003).

[21] Ibid., 43–44.

officers of the Union, will, as in the several States, be the choice, though a remote choice, of the people themselves.[22]

The 'republican' constitution is here intrinsically linked with the idea of (democratic) representation; and for the American revolutionaries, such a 'republic' is a better form of government than a 'democracy' because of its ability to control 'factions' or political parties.[23] The idea of *indirect* democracy in which office holders are regularly elected by the people applies with particular force to the American Parliament: the House of Representatives. Indeed, our modern idea of 'democracy' has today come to mean 'parliamentarism', that is a constitutional arrangement whereby decisions are not taken by the people themselves but by their representatives. (And using the classic constitutional vocabulary, this is of course a form of 'aristocracy' in which a 'minority' is elected to take decisions on behalf of the majority.) When the republican notion of representation applies to the head of state, we arrive at another constitutional concept: presidentialism in which an elected 'monarch' reigns in the name of the people for a limited period of time.

Thanks to the overwhelming rise of the idea of representative democracy in the twentieth century (see Section 3), almost all modern states today adhere to this new vocabulary. Thus: depending on whether the dominant representative institution is composed of one person, few persons or many persons; and subject to whether we think of it in positive or negative terms, six modern forms of government can be distinguished (Table 2.2).[24] Presidentialism here refers to a governmental system dominated by an (elected) executive officer – like in the United States, while its negative manifestation may be captured by the modern idea of dictatorship.[25] Parliamentarism, by contrast, refers to a system in which

---

[22] Ibid., 182–183.

[23] Ibid., 45: 'Extend the sphere, and you take in a greater variety of parties and interests; you make it less probable that a majority of the whole will have a common motive to invade the rights of other citizens; or if such a common motive exists, it will be more difficult for all who feel it to discover their own strength, and to act in unison with each other.'

[24] These six 'democratic' forms of government may of course be mixed – as is the case in most modern democracies. France is thus often described as a semi-presidential system that combines presidentialism with parliamentarianism. For a discussion of this point, see Chapters 4 and 14.

[25] C. Schmitt, *Die Diktatur* (Duncker & Humblot, 2006).

Table 2.2 Modern Forms of Government: Republican Categories

	Positive Expression	Negative Expression
Power Exercised by One	Presidentialism	Dictatorship
Power Exercised by a Minority	Parliamentarism	Party State
Power Exercised by the Majority	(Direct) Democracy	Populism

an (elected) assembly of citizens deliberates on the future of the polity; whereas a 'party state' refers to a situation in which a small group of career politicians takes most decisions behind closed doors.[26] Forms of direct democracy are also known in some modern States (but even they contain elements of 'representation').[27] The negative expression of such direct democracy is the uninformed power of the masses that is labelled as 'populism'. It is a form of government, where not the public 'interest' but public *opinion* – often manipulated by powerful private interests – governs society.

bb The Rise of Liberal Values and Private Property

This republican classification has sometimes come to compete with a categorization based on liberal values. A liberal classification here arranges constitutions alongside a spectrum that spans from governments that protect a maximum sphere of private right to a government that establishes a total 'public' sphere. The two extremes are probably best manifested in the laissez-faire libertarian state of nineteenth century-Britain on the one hand, and the totalitarian Fascist state of the twentieth century on the other.[28] In between lies the authoritarian state in which governmental

---

[26] C. Schmitt, *Die geistesgeschichtliche Lage des heutigen Parlamentarismus* (Duncker & Humblot, 2010), 62 (my translation): 'The great political and economic decisions that determine the fate of the people are no longer (if they have ever been) the result of a balancing of arguments and counter-arguments in a public parliamentary debate... Smaller and smaller party committees decide today, behind closed doors, what the representatives of big industry have previously agreed upon[.]'

[27] For example: the people voting in a referendum are seen as representatives of the (historic) nation.

[28] On the 'totalitarian' state, see the classic study by H. Arendt, *The Origins of Totalitarianism* (Harcourt, 1973).

Table 2.3 Modern Forms of Government: Liberal Categories

	Private Rights Generally	Private Property Rights
High Protection	Libertarian Regimes	Capitalist Regimes
Low Protection	Authoritarian Regimes	Socialist Regimes
No Protection	Totalitarian Regimes	Communist Regimes

institutions repress some individual liberties for the (supposed) public good of the nation at large.[29]

A special and interesting version of this liberal categorization emerges when the focus is set on one of the most central fundamental rights within modern liberal societies: the right to property. The most liberal regime here is a capitalist regime that allows for all forms of private property, whereas in communist societies, all private property is theoretically replaced by public property.[30] Socialist regimes occupy a middle ground in that they typically restrict the private right to property by excluding private ownership in the means of agricultural or industrial production.[31] For an overview of the possible forms of government according to a liberal standard see Table 2.3.

2 Formal Constitutionalism: The Constitution as Supreme Law

Formal constitutionalism defines a 'constitution' as the set of those norms that stand at the apex of the legal hierarchy. Constitutional norms are the highest norms and as such enjoy absolute – legal – supremacy over all other norms. This implies two things. First, constitutional law must be 'law' and as such it must be enforceable.

[29] On the modern form of the authoritarian constitution, see M. Tushnet, 'Authoritarian Constitutionalism' (2015) 100 *Cornell Law Review* 391.
[30] The question of property arguably constitutes the 'essential core' of all communist constitutions; yet there is of course a bundle of ideas that have equally been identified with communist constitutional theory. See only: W.B. Simons (ed.), *The Constitutions of the Communist World* (Sijthoff, 1980), XIII.
[31] See only: ex-Article 11 USSR Constitution: 'The state owns the basic means of production in industry, construction, and agriculture; means of transport and communication; the banks; the property of state-run trade organisations and public utilities, and other state-run undertakings; most urban housing; and other property necessary for state purposes.'

Enforcement could here theoretically mean physical resistance by the people,[32] yet we no longer identify these 'extra-legal' enforcement mechanisms as legal enforcements. Legal enforcement requires judicial enforcement, and such judicial enforcement may be done either centrally (through a special constitutional court), or decentrally via the ordinary courts.[33] But more importantly still: as the highest law within a legal order, constitutional review must, secondly, mean that all governmental acts – including legislative acts – should be reviewable as against the constitution. For if the government (in the wide sense of the term) can arbitrarily change the law, it is not subject to it; and instead of the 'law' it is the 'parliament' that is supreme. From this – normative and formal – point of view, neither the British nor the Chinese Constitutions are 'real' constitutions.[34]

a American Origins and Constitutional Review

The first modern constitution that complies with the formal idea of a judicially enforceable law that stands above all acts adopted by the government is the 1787 US Constitution. The latter was expressly conceived as 'the supreme Law of the Land; and the Judges in every State shall be bound thereby';[35] and it was quickly argued that the reason for imposing constitutional limits – even on the legislative branch – derived from republican principles:

There is no position which depends on clearer principles, than that every act of a delegated authority, contrary to the tenor of the commission under which it is exercised, is void. No legislative act therefore contrary to the constitution can be valid. To deny this would be to affirm that the deputy is greater than his principal; that the servant is above his master; that the representative of the people are superior to the people themselves ... A constitution is in fact, and must be, regarded by the judges as a fundamental law.[36]

---

[32] For this excellent point, see J.-E. Lane, *Constitutions and Political Theory* (Manchester University Press, 1996), 27–29.
[33] On this point, see Chapters 10 and 11.
[34] On the nature of the British and Chinese Constitutions, see Chapters 3 and 7.
[35] 1787 US Constitution, Article VI (2).
[36] A. Hamilton, J. Madison and J. Jay, *The Federalist* (n. 20), 379. On the historical background to this, see E.S. Corwin, 'The "Higher Law" Background of American Constitutional Law' (1928) 42 *Harvard Law Review* 149.

The American constitutional order here confirmed a distinction between a higher 'fundamental' law and 'ordinary' legislation; and it derived this distinction from the contrast between the people acting directly as constituent power (in French: *pouvoir constituant*) and the people acting indirectly through their government as the constituted power (in French: *pouvoir constitué*).[37] The higher status given to the Constitution is thus rooted in and legitimized by its more direct link with the will of the people.

For the American Founders, the best way to protect the people's original will against the government was thereby seen to be 'through the medium of the courts of justice'.[38] For the judiciary was regarded, in line with Montesquieu, as not having an independent will of its own; a court will only '*declare* the sense of the law'.[39] This position was confirmed in 1803. In *Marbury* v. *Madison*, the US Supreme Court famously held that 'all those who have framed written Constitutions contemplate them as forming the fundamental and paramount law of the nation, and consequently the theory of every such government must be that an act of the Legislature repugnant to the Constitution is void'.[40] And in the eyes of the Court, constitutional review was indeed no exercise of public power, because '[i]t is emphatically the province and duty of the Judicial Department to say what the law is'.[41]

b Towards a General and Purely Legal Understanding

But let us take a step back. The American Founding Fathers had derived the distinction between a higher fundamental law and ordinary legislation from *republican* principles; yet from a purely formal perspective, the democratic origin of a norm with constitutional status is irrelevant. All that ought to count for a norm to be seen as constitutional is that it enjoys the *status* as the highest law of the land. Norms that are given that constitutional status can be produced in a variety of ways. They may be established by 'the people' (as in the American case) but they could

[37] For the French ideas here, see only: E. Sieyès, *Political Writings* (editor: M. Sonenscher, Hackett, 2003).
[38] A. Hamilton, J. Madison and J. Jay, *The Federalist* (n. 20), 379.
[39] Ibid., 381.
[40] *Marbury* v. *Madison*, 5 US 137 (1803), 177.
[41] Ibid. For an extensive analysis of the case, see W.W. Van Alstyne, 'A Critical Guide to *Marbury* v. *Madison*' (1969) 18 *Duke Law Journal* 1.

equally be seen as given by 'God'.[42] They can be granted by a monarch;[43] or they may result from custom. For from a purely formal or legal point of view all that counts is that constitutional law stands on top of a hierarchical legal order. It is the last 'law'; and this ironically means that its legal validity cannot be derived from other legal norms:

> If we ask why the constitution is valid, perhaps we come upon an older constitution. Ultimately we reach some constitution that is the first historically and that was laid down by an individual usurper or by some kind of assembly. The validity of this first constitution is the last presupposition, the final postulate, upon which the validity of all the norms of our legal order depends ... The basic norm is not created in a legal procedure by a law-creating organ. It is not – as a positive legal norm is – valid because it is created in a certain way by a legal act, but it is valid because without this presupposition no human act could be interpreted as a legal, especially as a norm-creating act.[44]

The central point behind a purely formal understanding of a constitution is consequently this: a constitution 'is' the highest law but why it 'ought' to be the highest law is beyond legal analysis. The 'why' question concerns the *material* legitimacy of a constitution; and that question is simply not a legal question because constitutions are never legally adopted but *socially* postulated.[45] According to this view, every new constitution is always the result of a revolutionary break with the past; and it therefore cannot draw its legitimacy from the previously existing – legal – status quo. The normative validity of any constitution thus lies in its facticity – that is the fact that people *consider* it to be the highest law; and the reason why people consider it as such may significantly vary. The American revolutionaries, for example, regarded popular sovereignty as the core of their constitutionalism, whereas nineteenth-century European constitutionalism considered the crucial element of why a constitution

---

[42] This was the case in the Middle Ages. See C.H. McIlwain, *Constitutionalism: Ancient and Modern* (n. 1), Chapter IV.

[43] For an illustration of a monarchic constitutionalism, see the 1820 Vienna Final Act. According to its Article 57, 'the entire authority of the state must, according to the basic concepts provided thereby, remain united within the head of state, and the sovereign can therefore only in the exercise of particular rights be constitutionally bound to the participation of the estates'. On the 'monarchic' principle within nineteenth-century German constitutionalism, E.R. Huber, *Deutsche Verfassungsgeschichte seit 1789 – Volume I* (Kohlhammer, 1960) 653 *et seq.*

[44] H. Kelsen, *General Theory of the State* (Transaction Publishers, 2005) 115–116.

[45] Ibid., 118.

should be called a constitution its liberal content. We shall explore both material constitutional philosophies in Section 3.

c Formal Constitutionalism and the Amendment Power

The very essence of formal constitutionalism is the distinction between a (higher) fundamental law adopted by a *constituent* power and a (lower) ordinary law adopted by the *constituted* powers. Would this distinction imply that only the original constituent power could amend the constitution? Many constitutional orders have not completely adhered to this logic. On the contrary, they often allow their constituted powers to formally or informally amend constitutional law. For example, Article 79 of the German Basic Law allows the legislature to amend the Constitution by a statute; and these 'constitutional' statutes enjoy the same legal rank as the constitution.

The adoption of constitutional statutes adopted by the ordinary legislature has come to significantly blur the distinction between constituent and constituted power. For even if the legislature is forced to act by means of a qualified voting procedure, the originally 'extra-legal' power to change the constitution is here delegated to an organ of the State. To nevertheless protect some core areas reserved for the constituent power, an increasing number of constitutional orders has therefore identified *unamendable* parts within their constitutions.[46] These essential constitutional choices cannot be 'delegated' to the government acting through constitutional statutes. Article 79(3) of the German Basic Law, to use this example again, consequently outlaws all amendments that affect its core identity, such as the division of the German Federal Republic into *Länder* and the democratic and social character of the German State. These matters are seen to be eternal; yet they are of course only eternal in the sense of being removed from amendment under the *existing* constitutional order. For instead of binding the sovereign,[47] they *reserve* this power to the original constituent power.

---

[46] For a wonderful analysis of this phenomenon, see Y. Roznai, 'Unconstitutional Constitutional Amendments – The Migration and Success of a Constitutional Idea' (2013) 61 *American Journal of Comparative Law* 657.

[47] For the opposite view see T. Ginsburg, 'Constitutionalism: East Asian Antecedents' (2012) 88 *Chicago-Kent Law Review* 11 at 17 (emphasis in original): 'Constitutionalist norms are those of *a legal character that constrain the sovereign itself, not merely the agents of the sovereign.*'

Express 'eternity clauses' will often be found in constitutions whose amendment procedures offer a significant level of flexibility. But even in the absence of such provisions, any formal constitution will always recognize *implicit* limits governing its amenability.[48] For an amendment to something must, by definition, remain a non-essential change that needs to respect the 'identity' of the thing to be amended.[49] The amendment power within a constitution should consequently never allow for 'fundamental' changes to a State's fundamental law. A State ought thus not be able to legally transform itself from a republic to a monarchy;[50] nor should a federal union be allowed to legally transform itself into a unitary state. The idea of implicit limits to the amendment power has been accepted by several constitutional courts; and a good illustration is here offered by the Indian constitutional order and its 'basic structure' doctrine:

[I]f by constitutional amendment, Parliament were granted unlimited power of amendment, it would cease to be an authority under the Constitution, but would become supreme over it, because it would have power to alter the entire Constitution including its basic structure and even to put an end to it by totally changing its identity. It will therefore be seen that the limited amending power of Parliament is itself an essential feature of the Constitution, a part of its basic structure, for if the limited power of amendment were enlarged into an unlimited power, the entire character of the Constitution would be changed.[51]

This brings us to discuss one final point: formal constitutionalism may, paradoxically, allow for informal constitutional amendments. The reason for this lies in the fact that a formal constitution must not necessarily mean a 'written' constitution. A formal constitution can be composed of written as well as customary norms that have come to enjoy 'formal' constitutional status. The meaning of the constitution may thus be 'amended' by a judicial interpretation that is seen to have constitutional status. For example: when the US Supreme Court holds two very different interpretations of the Commerce Clause before and after the New Deal, an *informal*

---

[48] For the classic treatment here, see C. Schmitt, *Verfassungslehre* (Duncker & Humblot, 2010), 101–112.

[49] See for example § 112 of the Norwegian Constitution: 'Such amendment must never, however, contradict the principles embodied in this Constitution, but solely relate to modifications of particular provisions which do not alter the spirit of the Constitution[.]'

[50] For the express provision here, see Article 89 of the 1958 French Constitution: 'The Republican form of government is not subject to revision.'

[51] *Minerva Mills Ltd. and Others* v. *Union of India and Others*, AIR 1980 SC 1789 at 1824.

constitutional amendment has taken place.[52] A formal constitution can thus still be a 'living constitution'.[53] Yet to remain within the parameters of formal constitutionalism, all constitutional amendments – whether written or unwritten – must be distinct from the ordinary legislative procedure; for else the key characteristic of the formal idea of a constitution as a fundamental law is lost.

3 Material Constitutionalism: 'Democratic' and 'Liberal' Constitutions

The formal idea of a constitution as the highest law within a political community competes with the idea that only certain kinds of constitutions are 'real' constitutions.[54] The material understanding of what a constitution ought to do (to be styled as such) emerged in the long nineteenth century and has since become the dominant understanding. It links the idea of the constitution with two 'material' ideas: (representative) democracy and limited government. A democratic constitutionalism thus insists on a 'government of the people, by the people, for the people', while a liberal constitutionalism claims that only those constitutions that guarantee a separation of powers and (human) rights will be 'real' constitutions. Constitutions that lack any of these elements are 'façade' constitutions.

a Democratic Constitutionalism: Popular Sovereignty and Representative Government

Constitutionalism seen through the democratic lens insists that all power must, directly or indirectly, be exercised by the people; and where this is not the case, we cannot speak of a constitution in the first place.

On a foundational level, democratic constitutionalism therefore demands that it must be the people that create a constitution: 'The constitution of

---

[52] B. Ackerman, *We the People – Volume 2: Transformations* (Harvard University Press, 1998), especially Chapter 11: 'The Missing Amendments'.

[53] See especially: B. Ackerman, 'The Holmes Lectures: The Living Constitution' (2007) 120 *Harvard Law Review* 1737 at 1742: 'It is judicial revolution, not formal amendment, that serves as one of the great pathways for fundamental change marked out by the living Constitution.'

[54] For the idea of 'façade' constitutions, see G. Sartori, 'Constitutionalism: A Preliminary Discussion' (1962) 56 *American Political Science Review* 853; and for a more recent look, see D.S. Law and M. Versteeg, 'Sham Constitutions' (2013) 101 *California Law Review* 863.

a country is not the act of its government, but of the people constituting a government.'[55] Popular sovereignty can thereby express itself either directly or indirectly. A strict version would require that the people directly adopt their constitution through a referendum;[56] yet a softer version of democratic constitutionalism allows this task to be delegated to an elected 'constitutional' assembly that can adopt the constitution on behalf of the people.[57] This foundational dimension is however only one element of democratic constitutionalism. For an undemocratically created constitution might still set up democratic institutions, while a popular referendum might create an undemocratic regime.[58]

A governmental system is traditionally regarded as democratic when it is composed 'of' the people. The modern 'translation' of this democratic ideal is, as we saw in Section 1(b), representative democracy. Within a representative government, democracy means that the legislature, the executive and even the judiciary, should be *elected* by the people. Yet hardly any State constitution has created completely democratized governmental structures: not only is the judicial branch often unelected, non-democratic elements may also be found in the legislative branch.[59] The democratic credentials of a constitutional regime will therefore typically depend on the powers possessed by the legislature. But what about the executive? Here, two models of democratic government have developed: the parliamentary model and the presidential model. In the parliamentary model, the (governing) executive – the prime minister and the cabinet – will be elected and controlled by parliament; whereas a presidential system will typically invest the – independent – executive with its own direct democratic legitimacy.[60]

Finally, what about the idea of a government *for the people*? This third element of democratic constitutionalism emphasizes that elected officials must exercise public power not only in the name of the people but also

---

[55] See T. Paine, *Rights of Man* (n. 4), 89.
[56] For example, the (current) French Constitution for the Fifth Republic was adopted by a referendum.
[57] For an illustration of this indirect democratic source, see the 1919 (Weimar) Constitution of Germany. The 1949 German Constitution was also originally adopted by the state parliaments.
[58] The 1852 Constitution of the Second French Empire was ratified by a plebiscite; and yet it established an undemocratic government.
[59] In the United Kingdom, the second chamber (the House of Lords) is not elected.
[60] On these points, see Chapters 13 and 14 in this volume.

for their benefit. This qualitative criterion behind republican constitutionalism has however lost most of its meaning today. It can perhaps still be
found in moments when a Head of State or a constitutional court vetoes a
legislative act that – while formally democratic – is nevertheless not seen
to reflect the 'public good'; or where a parliament refuses to adhere to a
referendum result because it would significantly hurt future generations
and the prosperity of the political community as such. These forms of
'guardianship' on behalf of the people are often seen with suspicion; and
yet, they are theoretically and historically an integral part of democratic
constitutionalism.

b Liberal Constitutionalism: Limiting the Powers of Government

aa Limited Government I: The Separation of Powers Principle

The central tenet of liberal constitutionalism is to establish limits to 'the
[i]nconveniences of [a]bsolute power'.[61] It aims to protect freedom by
establishing a 'government of laws, and not of men'.[62] For governmental
power, even democratic governmental power is dangerous when used
arbitrarily.[63]

One of the oldest constitutional devices of limiting absolute power is
to split it, therefore 'balance[ing] the [p]ower of [g]overnment, by placing several parts of it in different hands'.[64] However, the central question
behind the separation of powers doctrine has always been this: which governmental *parts* should be placed into which governmental *hands*? Liberal
constitutionalism has here built on a tripartite division that was originally
developed by a French aristocrat: Baron Charles de Montesquieu. When
he published *The Spirit of Laws* in 1748, three powers were famously
identified:

---

[61] J. Locke, *Two Treatises of Government* (Cambridge University Press, 2005), II § 107 = 338.
[62] J. Harrington, as quoted in W.B. Gwyn, *The Meaning of the Separation of Powers*
(Martinus Nijhoff, 1965) 13.
[63] In the famous words of J. Madison in 'Federalist No 51' (n. 20), 252: 'If men were angels,
no government would be necessary. If angels were to govern men, neither external nor
internal controls on government would be necessary. In framing a government which is
to be administered by men over men, the great difficulty lies in this: you must first enable
the government to control the governed; and in the next place oblige it to control itself.
A dependence on the people is, no doubt, the primary control on the government; but
experience has taught mankind the necessity of auxiliary precautions.'
[64] J. Locke, *Two Treatises of Government* (n. 61), II § 107 = 338.

In each state there are three sorts of powers: legislative power, executive power over the things depending on the rights of nations, and executive power over the things depending on civil right. By the first, the prince or the magistrate makes laws for a time or for always and corrects or abrogates those that have been made. By the second, he makes peace or war, sends or receives embassies, establishes security, and prevents invasions. By the third, he punishes crimes or judges disputes between individuals. The last will be called the power of judging, and the former simply the executive power of the state.[65]

And having acknowledged three governmental 'powers' or functions, Montesquieu then moved on to advocate their distribution between different institutions:

When legislative power is united with executive power in a single person or in a single body of the magistracy, there is no liberty, because one can fear that the same monarch or senate that makes tyrannical laws will execute them tyrannically. Nor is there liberty if the power of judging is not separate from legislative power and from executive power. If it were joined to legislative power, the power over the life and liberty of the citizens would be arbitrary, for the judge would be the legislator. If it were joined to executive power, the judge could have the force of an oppressor.[66]

But did distribution here mean that each separate power would need to be given to a separate institution? Liberal constitutionalism has given two distinct answers to this question. According to the *functional separation* version, each governmental institution must not be given more than one governmental power.[67] The separation between the making of laws and their (administrative or judicial) execution is here designed to create a 'rule of law' in which the men who made the law would also be subject to it. This idea was subsequently expanded to define the – liberal – constitutional prohibition on the legislature not to pass 'individual laws', that is, laws that are tailored for a single individual or a limited group of individuals.[68] At the same time, the executive is – theoretically – not

[65] C. de Montesquieu, *The Spirit of the Laws* (edited by A. Cohler et al., Cambridge University Press, 1989), 156.
[66] Ibid., 157.
[67] The theory of a functional separation of powers finds (almost) no matching constitutional practice.
[68] For the US Constitution, see Art I, Section 9: 'No Bill of Attainder or ex post facto Law shall be passed.'

allowed to exercise any law-making power, as this is an exclusive power of the legislature.

According to the *institutional cooperation* version, on the other hand, each governmental function should be distributed over more than one institution: 'In order to form a moderate government, one must combine powers regulate them, temper them, make them act; one must give one power a ballast, so to speak, to put it in a position to resist another[.]'[69] The exercise of the legislative function should thus ideally involve more than one institution: '[The] legislative body is composed of two parts, the one will be chained to the other by their reciprocal faculty of vetoing. The two will be bound by the executive power, which will itself be bound by the legislative power.'[70] The idea behind this second version is to create a system of checks and balances; and from that second point of view, the modern English 'parliamentary system' violates the separation of powers doctrine, since it is based on a 'fusion' – not a separation – of the legislative and executive branch.[71]

bb Limited Government II: Fundamental Rights

The idea of fundamental rights is an achievement of liberal constitutionalism. It is based on the discovery of the 'individual' – a discovery that ultimately led to the protection of an inviolable private sphere.[72] This idea was minted into constitutional form during the American Revolutionary War. The 1776 Virginia Declaration of Rights stated: 'That all men are by nature equally free and independent and have certain inherent rights, of which, when they enter into a state of society, they cannot, by any compact, deprive or divest their posterity'.[73] This idea of inalienable rights was to eventually inspire the adoption of the US 'Bill of Rights'; and it was subsequently expressed in the 1789 (French) Declaration of the

---

[69] C. de Montesquieu, *The Spirit of the Laws* (n. 65), 63.

[70] Ibid., 164.

[71] In the words of W. Bagehot, *The English Constitution* (Oxford University Press, 2001) 11: 'The efficient secret of the English Constitution may be described as the close union, the nearly complete fusion, of the executive and legislative powers. According to the traditional theory, as it exists in all the books, the goodness of our constitution consists in the entire separation of the legislative and executive authorities, but in truth its merit consists in their singular approximation. The connecting link is *the cabinet*. By that new word we mean a committee of the legislative body selected to be the executive body.'

[72] E. Wolgast, *Geschichte der Menschen- und Bürgerrechte* (Kohlhammer, 2009), 33.

[73] 1776 Virginia Declaration of Rights, Art. 1.

Rights of Man and of the Citizen.[74] The declaration famously insisted on 'natural' rights that even bound the constitution-makers;[75] and it soon became the symbol and stimulus for the liberal constitutionalism of the nineteenth century.

In the twentieth century, the protection of fundamental rights has become a central task of most constitutions.[76] Unlike the separation of powers doctrine that operates as a *political* safeguard of liberalism, the protection of human rights is typically conceived of as a *judicial* safeguard of liberalism that is identical with constitutional review of governmental action.[77] A thin liberal constitutionalism here restricts judicial review to actions of the executive.[78] A thick liberal constitutionalism, on the other hand, insists that even parliamentary legislation must be judicially reviewed in light of possible violations of fundamental rights.[79]

But which types of human rights are seen as essential human rights? The eighteenth and nineteenth century (almost) exclusively thought of 'liberal' rights, such as freedom of property. (For Locke, the very purpose of why people would create a government was 'the preservation of their property'.[80]) Within the twentieth century, these liberal or 'negative' rights were complemented by a set of 'positive' or welfare rights. Political communities came to be seen as solidarity communities in which the State must guarantee all individuals a decent human life. The welfare state or 'social state' must actively assist the poor through a redistribution of private wealth.[81] In capitalist societies, this is generally done via taxation. In socialist societies, on the other hand, the process of wealth generation

---

[74] For an analysis and historical interpretation of the declaration, see Wolgast, *Geschichte der Menschen- und Bürgerrechte* (n. 72), Chapter 2.

[75] These rights were not 'founded' but simply 'declared' – hence the title: 'Declaration' – by the constitutional assembly.

[76] On human rights as constitutional rights, see A. Sajó, *Limiting Government* (Central European University Press, 1999), Chapter 8.

[77] See M. Cappelletti, *Judicial Review in the Contemporary World* (Bobbs-Merrill, 1971).

[78] Traditionally, this is the case for the United Kingdom. On this, see Chapters 3 and 11 in this volume.

[79] The classic example here is the United States. On this, see Chapter 5 in this volume.

[80] J. Locke, *Two Treatises of Government* (n. 61), II §124 = 351. Contrast this 'English' view with the 'French' view as offered by Montesquieu (n. 65), 455: 'A few alms given to the naked man in the streets does not fulfil the obligations of the state, which owes all the citizens an assured sustenance, nourishment, suitable clothing, and a kind of life which is not contrary to health.'

[81] For the German idea of the 'social state', see Article 20 Basic Law. See also Article 1 of the French Constitution as well as Article 1 of the Spanish Constitution.

is itself controlled; as the means of production were here held to be 'state property' or 'people property'.[82]

The balance between liberal rights and social rights has always been one of the most pressing questions for liberal constitutionalism. The danger of overemphasizing liberal rights lies in creating a libertarian society in which formal equality masquerades over a society of dramatic material inequalities,[83] and in which democracy will no longer work for everyone because re-distributive questions have been removed from the democratic process.[84] The danger of overemphasizing equality lies in ignoring differences of private ability and enterprise, with a totalitarian public sphere repressing all individual differences. Most modern liberal democracies have therefore tried to stir a middle path between individualism and communitarianism. With regard to organizing their economies, many nation states thus combine a private market economy with public elements to create a 'mixed' economic constitution.[85]

4 Excursion: Federal Constitutionalism as a Distinct Standard

The notions of 'constitution' and 'constitutionalism' have, in the past three hundred years, been mainly identified with the (unitary) state. The classic definition here holds: 'The fundamental [law] that determines the manner in which the public authority is to be exercised, is what forms the *constitution of the State*. In this is seen the form in which the nation acts in quality of a body politic[.]'[86]

This view correlates the concept of the constitution with that of the State;[87] and this state-centred definition has meant that other phenomena,

---

[82] See n. 31.

[83] This is perhaps best expressed in the *bonmot* by Anatole France according to which 'the majestic equality of the laws prohibits the rich and the poor alike to sleep under the bridges, beg in the streets and to steel bread'.

[84] For the idea that a degree of 'social' equality is necessary for democracy to work, see A. de Tocqueville, *Democracy in America, Volume I*, (trans. H. Reeve, P. Bradley (ed.)) (Vintage 1954), Volume 1 – Chapters 3 and 4.

[85] For the masterful Italian study here, see S. Cassese, *La Nouva Constituzione Economica* (Laterza, 2012).

[86] E. de Vattel, *The Law of Nations* (trans. J. Chitty) (Johnson & Co., 1883), Book I, §27.

[87] For this outdated conceptual 'nationalism', see the work of D. Grimm, 'Does Europe Need a Constitution?' (1995) 1 *European Law Journal* 282.

such as Unions of States, have traditionally not easily fitted into the constitutional categories discussed above. But when the United States (in the plural when founded) adopted their 'constitution', they did not conceive of the Union as a nation state; and since each of the States within the Union had its 'constitution',[88] there now existed two parallel constitutional orders for each American citizen, each of whom was represented in two parallel parliaments and each of whom was potentially protected by two parallel bills of rights. In what sense, then, does a federal order therefore require its own – federal – constitutionalism?

Let us explore this question in this final section.

a Formal Perspective: Two Competing Constitutional Claims

We saw above that formal constitutionalism defines a constitution as the highest law within a legal order; and it should therefore follow that there can only be one supreme – constitutional – law within a political community. This 'unitary' theory has however never lived up to the constitutional practice of federal orders, where both the Union *and* its Member States are seen to have *constitutional* claims. In addition to federal constitutional law there has always existed state constitutional law;[89] and the co-existence of two constitutional levels here derives from the co-existence of two political bodies in a compound structure.

But more importantly still: unlike unitary States, where the supremacy issue is settled, federal unions are often characterized by a situation in which the locus of sovereignty remains suspended. When 'fundamental' questions here arise – say, the abolition of slavery in nineteenth-century America – significant constitutional conflicts may emerge that cannot be solved by legal means and that will often be decided by the force of fact or the facticity of force.[90]

This fundamental insight into the constitutional plurality of Unions of States has today become marginalized in some of the older federal unions,

---

[88] For the perhaps most famous one here, see the 1776 Virginia Constitution.

[89] For the German federal order, see for example the discussion on the constitutional law of Saxony by C. Degenhart, *Staats- und Verwaltungsrecht Freistaat Sachsen* (Müller, 2013).

[90] On the existence of constitutional conflicts in the United States before and after the Civil War, see R. Schütze, 'Federalism as Constitutional Pluralism: Letter from America', in M. Avbelj and J. Komárek (eds.), *Constitutional Pluralism in the European Union and Beyond* (Hart Publishing, 2012), 185.

such as the United States and Germany. However, the pluralist constitutionalism within federal orders has been 're-discovered' in the context of the European Union. Here, two supremacy claims – one from the Union and one from its Member States – still openly compete. In *Costa* v. *ENEL*,[91] the European Court of Justice thus insisted on the supremacy of all EU law over all Member State law; yet this EU perspective is – unsurprisingly – not shared by the Member States. For while accepting that the EU constitutes a 'new legal order' distinct from classic international law, many Member States continue to insist that the validity of European law must ultimately be measured against their national constitutions. This dual perspective on the supremacy question within Europe has been taken up by an academic movement called 'constitutional pluralism',[92] but the better view has always been to simply see it as a manifestation of constitutional federalism or federal constitutionalism.

b Material Perspective: Dual Democracy and Dual Fundamental Rights

Who embodies the 'constituent power' within a federal union? Believing that the 1787 US Constitution had 'split the atom of sovereignty',[93] early American constitutionalism conceived of the constituent power as a plurality of peoples. The 1787 Constitution had thus been ratified 'by the people, *not as individuals composing one entire nation*, but as composing the distinct and independent States to which they respectively belong'. 'Each State, in ratifying the Constitution, [was] considered as a sovereign body, independent of all others, and only to be bound by its own voluntary act.'[94] The famous phrase 'We, the People' in the US Constitution must

---

[91] Case 6/64 *Costa* v. *ENEL* [1964] ECR 585.

[92] The movement gained momentum in the aftermath of the *Maastricht* judgement by the German Federal Constitutional Court. See J. Baquero-Cruz, 'The Legacy of the Maastricht-Urteil and the Pluralist Movement' (2008) 14 *European Law Journal* 389.

[93] *US Term Limits, Inc* v. *Thornton*, 514 US 779 (1995), 838 (Justice Kennedy).

[94] J. Madison in A. Hamilton et al., *The Federalist* (n. 20), 184–185. To bring the point home, Madison continues (ibid., 185): 'Were the people regarded in this transaction as forming one nation, the will of the majority of the whole people of the United States would bind the minority, in the same manner as the majority in each State must bind the minority; and the will of the majority must be determined either by a comparison of the individual votes, or by considering the will of the majority of the States as evidence of the will of a majority of the people of the United States. Neither of these rules have been adopted.'

therefore be read with two qualifications in mind. First, it did not refer to a popular referendum; and, secondly, it also did not refer to the 'American people' but instead the peoples of the several states.[95]

The best theoretical generalization of a 'federal' constituent power has come from the pen of Carl Schmitt.[96] Accordingly, the normative foundation of every Union of States is a 'federal treaty'. This 'federal treaty' is an international treaty of a constitutional nature.[97] 'Its conclusion is an act of the *pouvoir constituant*. Its content establishes the federal constitution and forms, at the same time, a part of the constitution of every Member State.'[98] Each Union of States is here seen as a creature of international and national law.[99] Unlike unitary constitutionalism, the constitution-making power therefore lies not in the unitary body of 'the' people, because the idea of a *single* sovereign subject is replaced with that of a pluralist constituent power. From the perspective of democratic constitutionalism, the constituent power behind a Union of States will always be the state *peoples* instead of a single 'demos'.

This duplication of the democratic base can also be found vis-à-vis the constituent powers. For unlike unitary States, where parliamentary democracy demands that all legislative power should be placed in one parliament, in a Union of States, there will always be *two* democratic constituencies: each State will have its own 'demos', while the Union will also have a 'demos' that is constructed out of the various State populations. Each of these democratic constituencies offers an independent source of democratic legitimacy; and a federal constitutionalism must take account of this dual democracy. Thus: the division of legislative powers within a federal Union means that depending on the area, either the federal

---

[95] The original 1787 draft preamble indeed read: 'We, the people of the States of New Hampshire, Massachusetts, Rhode-Island and Providence Plantations, Connecticut, New-York, New-Jersey, Pennsylvania, Delaware, Maryland, Virginia, North-Carolina, South-Carolina, and Georgia, do ordain, declare and establish the following Constitution for the government of ourselves and our posterity.' However, due to the uncertainty about which of the thirteen States would succeed in the ratification (according to Art. VII of the Constitution-to-be, only nine states were required for the document to enter into force), the enumeration of the individual States was dropped by the 'Committee of Style' (M. Farrand, *The Framing of the Constitution of the United States* (Yale University Press, 1913), 190–191).

[96] C. Schmitt, *Verfassungslehre* (n. 48), esp. Part IV.

[97] Ibid., 367 and 368 (all my translations).

[98] Ibid.

[99] Ibid., 379.

parliament or the state parliaments will be competent; and even with regard to the composition of the federal legislator we often find it made up of two chambers. In this bicameralism, every union law is dually legitimized by reference to two democratic sources: the consent of the Union 'people' and the consent of the State peoples.

The same duplication can be found in relation to other material elements within modern constitutionalism. For example, we saw above that a liberal constitutionalism demands that for there to be a constitution, there needs to be a separation of powers and the protection of fundamental rights. And each of these elements will typically be found both within the federal as well as the state constitutions. With regard to fundamental rights in the United States (or the European Union) for example, we will thus encounter two levels of fundamental rights protection. Federal rights will apply against the federal government, while state fundamental rights apply against a State government.[100] Table 2.4 summarizes the differences between the unitary and the federal standard across our three variants of constitutionalism.

Conclusion

This chapter has explored the question what a constitution is or ought to be. Various conceptions of such 'constitutionalism(s)' have emerged in legal history; and the predominant way of thinking about constitutions today is offered by 'liberal democratic' constitutional thought. The latter identifies a constitution by means of three elements. First, a constitution is formally seen as the highest law that applies within a State (or Union). According to the democratic element, this higher law must – secondly – be adopted by the people(s). Finally, the liberal element insists that all public power must be limited and principled.

Historically, the third element is thereby often seen as the most important one: 'in all its successive phases, constitutionalism has one essential quality: it is a legal limitation on government.'[101] Yet this liberal

---

[100] In the past, many federal orders have nevertheless insisted that federal fundamental rights might, in certain situations, be 'incorporated' into the state constitutional orders. For a comparative overview of the US and EU approaches here, see R. Schütze, 'European Fundamental Rights and the Member States: From "Selective" to "Total" Incorporation?' (2011–2012) 14 *Cambridge Yearbook of European Legal Studies* 337.

[101] C.H. McIlwain, *Constitutionalism: Ancient and Modern* (n. 1), 21.

Table 2.4 Unitary and Federal Constitutionalism: An Overview

	Unitary Standard	Federal Standard
Formal Constitutionalism	There is *one* constitution in *one* polity, where the supremacy issue has *one* solution.	There are *two* constitutional levels in a *compound* polity, where the supremacy issue has *no* solution.
Democratic Constitutionalism Foundational Origin Parliamentary Structure	The constitution is founded by *one* people ('We, the People'). The legislator is (ideally) composed of *one* Parliament and represents *one* people.	The constitution is founded on the basis of a *treaty* between multiple *peoples* ('We, the Peoples'). The legislator is composed of *two* chambers, whereby the first represents the federal *people* and the second the state *peoples*.
Liberal Constitutionalism Separation of Powers Human Rights	There is one horizontal separation of powers. There is (typically) *one* Bill of Rights.	There is a horizontal *and* a vertical separation of powers. There is (typically) a federal and a State Bill of Rights.

identification of constitutionalism with 'limited government' is deeply reductionist. It reduces the task of a constitution to a negative or guaranteeing function and thereby discards its positive and 'constructivist' purpose.[102] Constitutions may indeed not only abolish ancient institutions or social orders;[103] they can positively create new ones. This creative dimension has led some scholars to identify constitutions with the very process of political integration;[104] and the classic eighteenth-century example of

---

[102] This positive function has also been called 'revolutionary constitutionalism'. See S. Gardbaum, 'Revolutionary Constitutionalism' (2017) 15 *International Journal of Constitutional Law* 173.

[103] For this positive aspect, see especially the 1791 French Constitution: 'The National Assembly, wishing to establish the French Constitution upon the principles it has just recognized and declared, abolishes irrevocably the institutions which were injurious to liberty and equality of rights.'

[104] R. Smend, *Staatsrechtliche Abhandlungen und andere Aufsätze* (Duncker & Humblot, 1994), especially: 'Verfassung und Verfassungsrecht' (1928).

creating and integrating a 'new order' has been the United States. With the failure of the socialist constitutions in the twentieth century, the best contemporary illustration of such a constructivist constitution may well be the EU Constitution. For this 'new legal order' represents the most dynamic transnational constitutional order in the world today.[105]

Further Reading

R. Albert, *Constitutional Amendments: Making, Breaking, and Changing Constitutions* (Oxford University Press, 2019).

G. Casper, Constitutionalism (1987) *University of Chicago Law* Occasional Papers No. 22.

T. Cottier and M. Hertig, 'The Prospects of 21st Century Constitutionalism' (2003) 7 *Max Planck Yearbook of United Nations Law* 261–328.

S. Gordon, *Controlling the State: Constitutionalism from Ancient Athens to Today* (Harvard University Press, 1999).

J.-E. Lane, *Constitutionalism and Political Theory* (Manchester University Press, 1996).

M. Loughlin, *The Idea of Public Law* (Oxford University Press, 2003).

C.H. McIlwain, *Constitutionalism: Ancient and Modern* (Liberty Fund, 2008).

J.E.K. Murkens, 'The Quest for Constitutionalism in UK Public Law Discourse' (2009) 29 *Oxford Journal of Legal Studies* 427–455.

G. Sartori, 'Constitutionalism: A Preliminary Discussion' (1962) 56 *American Political Science Review* 853–864.

R. Schütze, 'Constitutionalism and the European Union', in C. Barnard and S. Peers (eds.), *European Union Law* (Oxford University Press, 2017), 71–96.

[105] R. Schütze, *European Constitutional Law* (Cambridge University Press, 2015).

Part II

Historical Experiences

The United Kingdom Constitution 3

Mark Elliott

Introduction

'In law context is everything.' So said Lord Steyn in the case of *R (Daly)* v. *Secretary of State for the Home Department.*[1] In doing so, he was perhaps making a statement of the blindingly obvious, but that does not undermine either the veracity or the broad pertinence of the observation. Indeed, it is an insight onto which the comparative lawyer in particular, and perhaps the comparative constitutional lawyer even more especially, must fasten. One of the great virtues of comparative study is its capacity to illuminate one's comprehension of a given legal phenomenon or system through an appreciation of how and why things are done differently elsewhere. Understanding why such differences arise can illuminate one's 'home' jurisdiction in fresh ways, subtly, or even radically, changing one's perspective, and opening up new avenues of inquiry. This can be particularly instructive when the jurisdictions under consideration are, in general, relatively similar – for in such circumstances, individual points

[1] [2001] UKHL 26; [2001] 2 AC 532, [28].

of contrast are not readily dismissible as functions of macro-divergence. It is for this reason that comparative scholarship that examines different members of a jurisdictional family, such as the common law systems that form the focus of this book, can be so fruitful.

Against that background, and with Lord Steyn's aphorism firmly in mind, the purpose of this chapter is to examine the constitution of the United Kingdom in a way that identifies elements of it that form essential components of the context to which the comparativist must be appropriately sensitive. In doing so, two types of constitutional phenomena are considered. The first comprises classical aspects of the UK constitution which, taken in combination, produce a tableau that conforms to the expectations that those with a passing knowledge of the system might be likely to entertain. But therein lies the trap for the incautious comparativist, for a second set of phenomena – which challenge traditional understandings and complicate the comparativist enterprise as it pertains to the UK constitution – must also be considered if our understanding of the context is to be satisfactory. It is only when these two sets of phenomena are taken together that a suitably binocular view of the UK constitution comes into focus. The picture that emerges is of a constitution which, its deep historical roots notwithstanding, is in a state of considerable flux – a state of affairs that poses a challenge for anyone seeking to make sense of the UK constitution today, and perhaps particularly for the comparativist who seeks to identify the essence of the 'British approach' when it comes to matters constitutional. Understanding the UK constitution, as we will see, thus depends upon an appreciation of the sometimes subtle, and occasionally bewildering, interaction of the old and the new.

1 Sovereignty and the 'Unwritten' Constitution

If the UK is known – in constitutional terms – for anything, it is perhaps known for 'not having' a constitution. That is certainly a perception held by many people who live in the UK. It is also strongly arguable that it is a misconception. But it is one that does at least have a discernible root in the UK's lack of a 'written' constitution. It is, then, here that we begin to see what it is about the UK's constitutional arrangements that make them genuinely distinctive: namely, that there exists no text that gathers together fundamental constitutional rules, singling them out for special treatment. If, then, one wishes to identify the British constitution, one must look for something other than a 'capital-C Constitution'.[2] And it is in the legal vacuum created by the lack of such a constitutional text that the principle of parliamentary sovereignty,[3] according to which there are no legal restraints upon the legislature's power, exists – the absence of a (power-limiting) written constitution and the existence of the principle of parliamentary sovereignty being, at least to some extent, two sides of a single coin.

Taken in combination, the absence of a written constitution and the acknowledgment of legislative supremacy conspire to produce a picture that can, to the outsider, seem disorientating at best, bizarre at worst. Indeed, it might be thought to take us full circle back to the notion – perhaps now revealed as a truth, rather than a misconception – that the UK 'has no constitution'. However, the persuasiveness of that view must turn upon our prior sense of what it means to have (and, therefore, to lack) a constitution. And our answer to that question may, in turn, depend upon the baggage that we bring along with us – baggage that may, for the comparativist, be informed in part by preconceptions formed by reference to a 'home' jurisdiction. Those steeped in the notion of the constitution as a foundational text may be inclined to adopt a somewhat formal perspective, casting doubt on whether any state can lay claim to a constitution properly so-called in the absence of such a text. Similarly, for those whose legal compass is set by reference to constitutions that allocate and demarcate state authority, the notion that an organ of the state may possess legally unlimited power might seem inconsistent with the very idea of a constitution.

It follows that if the UK has a constitution, it is a constitution that differs markedly from, and challenges standard preconceptions about, constitutions generally. Herein, then, lies one of the merits in comparative engagement with the British system: it is liberal-democratic in nature, it has much in common, in institutional and legal-doctrinal

---

[2] On the notion of 'capital-C' constitutions, see generally A. King, *The British Constitution* (Oxford University Press, 2010), Chapter 1. On constitutionalism generally, see Chapter 2.

[3] The idea of parliamentary sovereignty is considered later in this chapter. For very helpful discussions of this concept, see J. Goldsworthy, *The Sovereignty of Parliament: History and Philosophy* (Clarendon Press, 2001) and A. Young, *Parliamentary Sovereignty and the Human Rights Act* (Hart Publishing, 2009).

terms, with many other common law jurisdictions, and yet its constitutional arrangements, at least *prima facie*, are very different from those of most other such systems.[4] So different, in fact, that the interested outsider might, as we have seen, be led to wonder whether the UK really has a constitution, or at least a 'proper' constitution, at all. Yet the comparativist willing to take a second look – and, perhaps, to lay her own constitutional baggage to one side – might perceive things somewhat differently. She might do so on the ground that the UK system demonstrates that a constitution can meaningfully exist even if it does not impose the sort of hard restraints upon power that are a *sine qua non* of many constitutional regimes. She might also do so on the ground that closer study of the UK system shows that state authority can be conditioned in a variety of ways, and that an absence of hard legal restraints is not to be confused with a lack of meaningful constitutional controls. And she might do so on the further ground that focussing on the presence or absence of a foundational text is revealed, by the British experience, to be an unduly formalistic approach, the more important question being whether a constitution, properly so-called, can be discerned from an array of relevant, albeit diverse, legal and political resources.

Such considerations implicate features of the modern British constitution to which we will turn below – namely, its traditionally political character and its contemporary juridification. But before we examine those matters, it is worth pausing to ask *why* the British constitution exhibits characteristics that, from the comparativist's perspective, might seem so eccentric. The answer lies in both the substance and the nature of the constitutional history of the UK and of its constituent parts. Detailed consideration of that history lies far beyond the scope of this chapter, but two points are worth highlighting. The first is that the origins of the principle of parliamentary sovereignty – the existence of which, as we have seen, precludes a constitution in the classically power-constraining sense – lie in *realpolitik* as distinct from law. The principle emerged in the late seventeenth century as a part of a constitutional settlement that limited monarchical power by scotching, once and for all, assertions that such power could be used to override Parliament, and by instead treating ultimate legislative authority as being vested in

---

[4] The difference with New Zealand is, of course, less stark.

the monarch-in-Parliament. Hence the need, to this day, for royal assent to bills before they can become law.

So far, so unremarkable; it is inevitable that, from time to time, polities encounter events that involve the drawing of a line in the constitutional sand, and events in late seventeenth-century England can fairly be regarded in such terms. But (and here is our second point) such events – such 'constitutional moments' – generally entail transcribing a newly established political settlement into legal form through the adoption or revision of a legal-constitutional text. And such constitutional texts usually end up allocating and determining the powers of the various organs of the state. In contrast, England in the late seventeenth century, and the UK subsequently, did not pursue such a trajectory. Thus, for instance, the political consensus that ultimate law-making authority lies with the monarch-in-Parliament remains that – a consensus that exists in political terms, but which has never been clothed in legal-constitutional garb. There is, then, no legal-constitutional text that *accords* legislative authority to the monarch-in-Parliament, meaning that the source of such authority is, in the final analysis, extra-legal, or political, in nature.[5]

This resistance to line-in-the-sand, constitutional-moment-embracing legal-constitutional reform is central to any understanding of how the British constitution works. Indeed, it is precisely this that accounts for the absence of any constitution at all if that concept is viewed in terms of the systematization and codification of rules that are functionally constitutional, or in terms of the legal-constitutional allocation and delimitation of the powers of the state. It is not, of course, that the UK has uniquely failed to encounter the sort of constitutional issues that would tend elsewhere to precipitate fundamental, constitution-making reform. Indeed, there have been many such phenomena in the UK's long history, the formation of the UK through the union of England and Wales with Scotland and then Ireland being paramount examples. But even events such as those did not trigger the adoption of any overarching constitutional text. Nor did the radical realignment of the territorial constitution effected by the creation of new devolved legislatures and governments in the late 1990s. And nor (yet) have such significant constitutional events as joining and, now, leaving the European Union. Through all of these

---

[5] For the classic account of this point, see H.W.R. Wade, 'The Basis of Legal Sovereignty' (1955) 13 *Cambridge Law Journal* 172.

changes, the UK has resorted to nothing more than regular legislation, the enactment of which is itself rooted ultimately in a legislative capacity which derives from nothing more than *realpolitik*.

2 A Political Constitution

If, to the comparativist, this all looks very odd, then the (or at least a) key to understanding matters is to recognize that it is all of a piece with a very British way of doing things. Thus we find that there is resistance to big-bang reform in favour of incrementalism; a preference for historical continuity over fresh starts; a tendency to make do and mend rather than engaging in fundamental systemic redesign; and a deeply pragmatic mindset that prioritizes 'what works' over conceptual tidiness. It is against the background of such predilections that we encounter the notion of the British constitution as a 'political constitution'.[6] We have already met what is, perhaps, the cardinal aspect of this phenomenon, in the form of the paradox that the unbounded legal power that Parliament is (generally) acknowledged to possess is attributable to a political consensus rather than to any form of legal-constitutional conferral. But there are at least two other critical (and related) manifestations of the 'political' nature of the British constitution that ought to be noted here.

The first concerns the role played by constitutional conventions.[7] In a number of respects, the legal aspects of the British constitution are archaic, in the sense that they do not reflect the reality of modern political practice and fail to align with contemporary constitutional values. An example – which we noted in passing above – concerns the legislative role of the monarch. As we have seen, a Bill becomes an Act of Parliament only with the monarch's assent – a fact that is traceable to the political consensus that emerged in late seventeenth-century England concerning the relative powers of the monarch and the legislature. This is obviously archaic in the sense that it appears to assign to an unelected head of

[6] A key point of reference on the notion of political constitutionalism is J.A.G. Griffith's seminal article 'The Political Constitution' (1979) 42 *Modern Law Review* 1. For helpful discussion, see also G. Gee and G. Webber, 'What is a Political Constitution?' (2010) 30 *Oxford Journal of Legal Studies* 237.
[7] See generally D. Feldman, 'Constitutional Conventions', in M. Qvortrup (ed.), *The British Constitution: Continuity, Change and the Influence of Europe – A Festschrift for Vernon Bogdanor* (Hart Publishing, 2013).

state a power to veto legislation enacted by the (partially)[8] democratically elected Parliament. But the reality of political practice is very different, it being more than three centuries since a monarch disregarded ministers' advice to grant royal assent to a Bill.

Over that period, a constitutional convention that assent is given as a matter of course developed and hardened into something that is so ingrained within the British constitutional order that it is every bit as compelling as a law. This does not mean that convention and law should be casually conflated, or that courts will enforce conventions as if they were laws.[9] Nevertheless, conventions such as that which governs the granting of royal assent to Bills play a fundamental part in the operation of the constitution, in effect serving to politically neutralize discretion that the law appears to accord, so as to ensure that, in practice, archaic legal authority cannot be wielded in a way that subverts contemporary constitutional morality. This, then, is a significant respect in which the British constitution is 'political', the legal authority of constitutional actors being controlled in important part not by law or courts, but by the entrenchment of fundamental values in institutional practices that are 'enforced' by political rather than judicial means.[10]

A second important sense in which the constitution is 'political' relates back to the idea of parliamentary sovereignty. As we have seen, thanks to that feature of the UK constitution, the legislature is legally free to enact whatever laws it wishes:[11] it has 'the right to make or unmake any law whatever', and 'no person or body is recognised by the law ... as having a right to override or set aside the legislation of Parliament'.[12] To those from other jurisdictions familiar with the existence of hard legal limits upon legislative authority that serve to counterbalance law-making power and mitigate the risk of its abuse, this may well be an arresting proposition,

[8] 'Partially' because the upper chamber, the House of Lords, is not elected, albeit that its powers are inferior to the elected House of Commons.
[9] *R. (Miller)* v. *Secretary of State for Exiting the European Union* [2017] UKSC 5; [2018] AC 61.
[10] Conventions can, however, exert indirect legal influence. For a good example, see *Evans* v. *Information Commissioner* [2012] UKUT 313 (AAC).
[11] We are concerned here with the UK, or Westminster, Parliament. The position is different as far as the devolved legislatures are concerned; their powers are conferred and limited by UK legislation.
[12] A.V. Dicey, *Introduction to the Study of the Law of the Constitution* [1885] (Macmillan, 1959), 10th ed., 39.

given that it legally sanctions the enactment of any, including heinous, laws. That such laws remain unenacted in the UK is thanks ultimately to the constraining effect of politics, not law.

The two matters mentioned above – that is, the role of conventions and the rocks of parliamentary sovereignty upon which other constitutional values, including those enshrined in conventions, ultimately founder – coalesce in relation to the arrangements for multi-layered governance in the UK. Since the late 1990s, legislative and administrative power has been devolved to newly created assemblies and governments in Scotland, Wales and Northern Ireland.[13] The UK Parliament has not relinquished its authority to any of those institutions and, as a matter of law, remains capable of overriding them or otherwise legislating on matters devolved to them. That legal position is glossed by the 'Sewel convention', which holds that the UK Parliament will not normally legislate on such matters without the consent of the relevant assembly. The convention, however, is legally unenforceable, meaning that a fundamental aspect of the British constitutional order concerning the balance of power between national and territorial tiers of government – a matter that in many other constitutional systems would be a matter of law to be determined by courts – remains an ultimately political matter. The UK Parliament and Government must be trusted to respect the convention: and, if they do not, the devolved assemblies' and administrations' recourse, if any, lies on the political, not the legal, plane. In this way, for all that devolution in the UK might look, at first glance, a lot like federalism, it is significantly different from that model, thanks to deep-seated elements of the constitutional order onto which the new model of territorial governance has been grafted. In this way, the old and the new interact so as to produce institutional structures that may, to the comparativist, have a ring of familiarity, but which are at the same time distinctive.

3 Taking Stock

What has been said so far seeks to set out, necessarily by way of an outline sketch, a traditional picture of the British constitution. It depicts a constitution dominated by the notion of parliamentary sovereignty – a

---

[13] Devolution in Northern Ireland has, however, been suspended on several occasions.

notion that itself derives from a historical-political consensus that is relevantly unclothed by law, and which appears to bequeath and coexist with a constitutional order that is similarly political in nature, thanks both to a British tendency to secure constitutional modernity other than via fundamental, systemic reform, and to the fact that legislative authority is neither conferred nor cabined by law, meaning that political vigilance and restraint are the only viable antidotes to the potential abuse of such authority.

If 'context is everything', then understanding these basic truths about the British system is imperative – for, in spite of what follows in the remainder of this chapter, they remain basic truths in the sense that they continue to supply important aspects of the conceptual underpinning of the contemporary constitution. However, to stop here would be to supply a highly incomplete and misleading impression, for these traditional aspects of the UK constitution are today heavily influenced by a set of interlocking contemporary developments to which the comparativist seeking to make sense of the British system – and to understand how it differs from, and is similar to, her own – must be suitably sensitive. Prominent among those developments are the Europeanization and juridification of the British constitution, along with the already-mentioned dispersal of constitutional authority across the UK's constituent territories. The combined effect of these developments is to render the UK system, at least in some respects, rather less exceptionalist that it has traditionally tended to be, albeit that European influences arguably move the British system further away from other common law jurisdictions in certain respects. As we will see, the picture that emerges for the comparative constitutional lawyer trying to make sense of all of this is a complex but also a rich one.

4 Europeanization

The extent to which the UK remains fully a member of the family of common law jurisdictions, including those with which this book is concerned, is called into some doubt by the extent to which its legal and constitutional system has been Europeanized. Such Europeanization has resulted in the implantation of concepts, such as the doctrine of proportionality, and conceptual structures, such as the notion of the supremacy of European Union ('EU') law, that are either not entirely familiar or wholly alien to most other common law systems. This process of Europeanization has, of course, occurred as a result of the UK's membership of the EU as well as its being a party to the European Convention on Human Rights ('ECHR') to which domestic effect is given by the Human Rights Act 1998 ('HRA').

It is far beyond the scope of this chapter to chart the many legal changes that these European associations have wrought. Nor will any attempt be made to speculate in specific terms about the likely nature or implications of the process of *de-Europeanization* that is now in train, as a consequence of the UK's decision to leave the EU. However, it is instructive to reflect in broader terms upon the general, structural implications that the UK's European associations have (had) – implications that, for reasons that will be suggested, are liable to be of enduring relevance, exit from the EU notwithstanding, and even if, as is far from inconceivable, the UK withdraws from the ECHR in the future. Those general, or structural, implications arise from the way in which EU membership and involvement with the ECHR, as given domestic effect by the HRA, have challenged traditional perceptions about the extent of legislative authority and about the role of law and of courts in cabining such authority. Consistently with the 'British approach' described earlier in this chapter, this challenge has been oblique rather than direct. But it has nonetheless significantly impacted upon traditional understandings, even if there has not been radical and explicit departure from them.

What, then, is the nature of the challenge? It relates to that most fundamental of constitutional matters – namely, the location and extent of legal authority. We have already seen that, in the UK, at least on a traditional understanding of the system, ultimate authority is vested in Parliament, making notions about the (legal) constraint of lawmaking power that are elsewhere familiar quite alien in the British context. However, the UK's European associations have – albeit, perhaps, without mounting a head-on challenge to it – at least called into question that constitutional worldview. They have done so by forcing novel (at least in British terms) forms of interaction between international legal orders that know nothing of parliamentary sovereignty and a domestic constitutional framework to which that notion is foundational and central.

5 The European Union

The point arises most obviously and directly in relation to the UK's membership of the EU, to whose legal order the notion of the supremacy of EU law is as axiomatic as the doctrine of parliamentary sovereignty is to the UK's. It is unnecessary for present purposes to explore the full breadth of the constitutional scholarship – and head-scratching – that has been stimulated by what looks like the meeting of an irresistible force and an immovable object.[14] What is, however, pertinent is the fact that such reflection has been necessitated – and that it has led to the refining of, if not departure from, the sort of 'traditional' vision of the constitution set out earlier in this chapter. That much is plain from what can fairly be regarded as the leading judicial attempt to rationalize domestic constitutional accommodation of the EU supremacy principle – an attempt that consists of the judgment of Laws J in *Thoburn*[15] and the joint judgment of Lord Neuberger and Lord Mance in the *HS2* case.[16]

One of the defining aspects of the doctrine of parliamentary sovereignty has generally been taken to be what might be called the equality of primary legislation. On that view, all such legislation – whatever its subject matter and however important, constitutionally or otherwise, it might be – is taken to exist on a constitutionally level playing field. Every Act of Parliament thus has the same legal status as every other, with conflicts between provisions in different pieces of primary legislation falling to be resolved by reference to a simple temporal criterion – the principle being, under the doctrine of implied repeal, that the more recent Act prevails in the event of interpretively irreconcilable incompatibility. Thus, as Dicey

[14] Useful contributions to this debate include P. Craig, 'Sovereignty of the United Kingdom Parliament after *Factortame*' (1991) 11 *Yearbook of European Law* 221; H.W.R. Wade, 'Sovereignty – Revolution or Evolution?' (1996) 112 *Law Quarterly Review* 568; Young, n. 3, ch. 2.

[15] *Thoburn* v. *Sunderland City Council* [2002] EWHC 195 (Admin); [2003] QB 151.

[16] *R. (HS2 Action Alliance Ltd.)* v. *Secretary of State for Transport* [2014] UKSC 3; [2014] 1 WLR 324. The idea of constitutional legislation was also embraced by the Supreme Court in *H* v. *Lord Advocate* [2012] UKSC 24; [2013] 1 AC 413, while in *Miller*, the majority in the Supreme Court recognized that the ECA is a statute that has a 'constitutional character'. The extent to which the 'constitutional' status of the ECA played a part in the reasoning in *Miller* is debateable, but the majority appears to understand the notion of constitutional statutes in terms that are consistent with those set out in *Thoburn* and *HS2*: see *Miller*, n. 9, [67].

famously put it, 'neither the Act of Union with Scotland nor the Dentists Act 1878 has more claim than the other to be considered a supreme law'.[17]

But this traditional understanding has been placed under pressure by EU membership in two ways. First, difficult questions have arisen about whether – and, if so, how – it is possible, given the principle of equality of primary legislation, for the European Communities Act 1972 (ECA) to ascribe primacy to EU law so as to privilege it over other, including post-1972, domestic primary legislation. Second, questions have arisen about the *extent* to which EU law enjoys primacy – in particular, about whether its primacy over domestic law is so unyielding as to enable it to override even fundamental constitutional principles and legislation that institutionalizes them. In confronting those difficult questions, the courts have begun to articulate a vision of the British constitution that is, in important respects, at odds with the orthodox version of it sketched at the beginning of this chapter. In particular, the courts have articulated and begun to develop a notion of 'constitutional legislation' that is impervious to implied repeal, and which is thus capable of taking priority over other, including subsequent, legislation that is inconsistent with it. Moreover, the judgment of Lords Neuberger and Mance in *HS2* indicates that the category of constitutional legislation may itself be hierarchically gradated. In that way, it was suggested, the ECA – albeit a constitutional statute – may neglect to confer upon EU law a legal status that enables it to override constitutionally fundamental principles enshrined in the Bill of Rights 1688, on account of the latter being, in effect, not merely constitutional but super-constitutional in nature.

It is the UK's membership of the EU that has served as the anvil upon which these jurisprudential innovations have been beaten out. But their significance will outlast such membership, and their implications are relevant not only to the UK *qua* EU Member State. The need to confront the difficult legal issues occasioned by EU membership will thus cause the UK to leave the EU with a constitution that is, in significant respects, different from – or, perhaps more accurately, is *understood* differently from – that which obtained when it joined. All of which raises something of a paradox. The incorporation of EU law and integration within the EU legal order are generally taken to have eroded some of what the UK shares in common with other common law systems. Yet at the same time,

---

[17] Dicey, n. 12, 145.

the UK's exposure to these European influences has actually yielded – or has at least yielded the articulation of – a constitution that is (very modestly) hierarchically ordered in a way that renders it somewhat less exceptionalist in nature, and which, to that extent, enhances that which it has in common with most other constitutional systems.

6 The Human Rights Act

The other respect in which the UK constitutional order has been exposed to significant European influence is via the UK being a party to the European Convention on Human Rights and through the domestic effect accorded to the ECHR by the Human Rights Act 1998. The legal issues here are quite different from those that arise in respect of the EU, and the challenge to conventional constitutional wisdom is more subtle. But it is nevertheless important and, as we shall see, relates to, and perhaps feeds into, other such challenges.

Traditionally, the UK has eschewed the notion of individual rights that are ring-fenced against State interference. For instance, writing in 1985, Browne-Wilkinson LJ, in a case that was concerned with freedom of expression, said that in the UK the 'freedom of the person' – and so freedom of speech – 'depends on the fact that no one has the right lawfully to arrest the individual save in defined circumstances'. It followed that to the extent that the UK could be said to acknowledge 'fundamental freedoms', they subsisted not as 'positive rights' but as an 'immunity from interference by others'.[18] Ultimately, this approach to rights – or freedoms – is an inescapable corollary of the principle of parliamentary sovereignty. After all, if the legislature's authority is unconstrained by the terms of any constitution, it must follow that the individual lacks any legal trump card that can be played in the event of a legislative incursion into what is – or, prior to the incursion, was – one of the individual's fundamental freedoms. Moreover, this constitutional truth has a cascade effect that shapes the position of the individual vis-à-vis the State in its non-legislative guises: if, for instance, the legislature is legally capable of doing whatever it wishes, including in relation to the limitation of basic freedoms, it follows that it can also authorize others, such as the administrative branch and other public bodies, to interfere with such freedoms,

[18] *Wheeler* v. *Leicester City Council* [1985] AC 1054, 1065.

thereby denying the individual any opportunity to challenge not only legislation but other official action on fundamental rights grounds.

Against this background, the ECHR and, in particular, the HRA have operated as a significantly disruptive force, not by challenging this orthodoxy brazenly – for that is not the British way – but subtly. The ECHR has never sat entirely comfortably with the notion of parliamentary sovereignty, in that the former prevents the exploitation of the latter in way that undermines fundamental rights if the UK wishes to avoid breaching its international obligations. But any direct challenge to parliamentary sovereignty is avoided, given that the UK's is a dualist system, and that any infraction of international law occurs on an international plane that regulates the UK's actions as State, without prejudice to the institutional capacity of the UK Parliament to do as it wishes as a matter of national constitutional law. On this view, the constraining force of treaty obligations such as those contained in the ECHR and the domestic legal capacity of the UK Parliament are ships that pass in the night – or trains running on parallel tracks. The possibility of collision does not arise.

The HRA, however, changes things somewhat. It assigns relevance in domestic law to Convention rights in several ways, including by requiring public authorities to act in accordance with such rights (unless required to do otherwise by primary legislation),[19] instructing courts to construe domestic legislation compatibly with those rights so far as is possible,[20] and authorizing courts to quash nearly all forms of legislative provisions that cannot be interpretively reconciled with Convention rights. The HRA does not, however, go as far as to permit courts to quash Acts of Parliament, allowing them only to declare that such legislation is incompatible with Convention rights when the two cannot be interpretively reconciled with one another.[21] The latter point may appear to imply that the system is a relatively weak one that is readily subject to legislative override. But the reality is different, precisely because the HRA is not merely a domestic statute, but is rather a means of ascribing domestic relevance to legal norms that are binding on an international plane on which the notion of parliamentary sovereignty is no answer to a charge

[19] Human Rights Act 1998, s. 6.
[20] Human Rights Act 1998, s. 3.
[21] Human Rights Act 1998, s. 4.

that treaty obligations have been breached. The upshot is that the legislative discretion formally accorded by the HRA to ignore declarations of incompatibility largely evaporates, given that it is widely understood that any attempt to leverage such discretion will subsequently very likely result in an adverse judgment in the European Court of Human Rights, thus triggering the liability of the UK as a State in international law.

An analogy can be drawn with the way in which constitutional conventions operate so as to neutralize, or at least heavily circumscribe, apparent legal capacities. The obvious difference, of course, is that conventions operate as political restraints whereas the ECHR, via the HRA, operates as a legal restraint, albeit one that bites on the international rather than the domestic plane. But that difference obscures a broader truth: namely, that the HRA leverages the same form of indirect, subtle cabining of legal authority in the service of fundamental values, thus affording such values a degree of constitutional security that confounds their (domestic) legal fragility. In this way, a mere declaration of incompatibility is invested with far greater potency than may, at first glance, be assumed. By the same token, Parliament's capacity to reverse bold judicial interpretations rendered under the HRA so as to bend Acts of Parliament to the requirements of Convention rights is far slighter than it might seem.

The UK's willingness – for the time being – to open up its legal system to a European human rights regime that is binding in international law terms thus significantly influences the nature of its own constitutional order. In particular, it shaves some of the hard edges off the principle of parliamentary sovereignty and supplies a domestic human rights system that has at least some things in common with models of human rights protection that are rooted in foundational constitutional texts. These things are accomplished, however, without any explicit denial of the *status quo* as set out in the first part of this chapter. As a result, they exploit what may seem to be – at least to an outside observer, steeped in a different kind of constitutional traditional – the paradoxical possibility of something being simultaneously legal and unconstitutional. Just as conventions – or, more specifically, the values that they institutionalize – serve as benchmarks by which to measure the constitutionality, as distinct from the legality, of what relevant constitutional actors do, so Convention rights, as mediated by the HRA, operate in effect as a means of calibrating the extent of Parliament's respect for fundamental constitutional values – in the form of basic rights – without ultimately delimiting its legal authority to disregard them. This gives rise to what might be considered a gap between the legal and the political constitutions: that is, a gap between things that can lawfully be done and things that can be done with constitutional propriety; the legal 'is' and the constitutional 'ought'.

The British constitution has long leveraged this distinction, using the latter as an indirect restraint upon, as opposed to a direct challenge to, the former. But recent developments – and the UK's European interfaces in particular – have served to emphasize, and place greater weight upon, this *modus operandi*. Such thinking is evident in relation to the accommodation of the supremacy of EU law, which, as we have seen, was rationalized in terms not of Parliament's incapacity to override it, but by reference to the constitutional status of the ECA which made it immune to implied (but not express) repeal. Similarly, the HRA disincentivizes legislation that would place the UK in breach of its international obligations by rendering those obligations domestically front and centre, without going so far as to treat them as absolute constraints upon Parliament as a domestic institution.

In this way, whatever superficial impression might be conveyed by the axiomatic place that parliamentary sovereignty occupies within British constitutional tradition, and by the associated fact that a power-conferring and restraining text is anathema to that tradition, the reality is more complex. Appearances, then, can be deceptive, and the comparativist seeking to understand the contemporary nature of the UK constitution must thus immerse herself not only in its classical architectural features but in the ways in which understandings of those aspects of the constitution have shifted in the light of the connections that have been forged between European legal systems and the British system. Indeed, the capacity of the British system to adapt in this almost chameleonic way, without the need for obvious and fundamental constitutional reform, is itself a defining characteristic of that system: it speaks volumes about its radical malleability. And while it is something that can be a trap for the comparativist who is insufficiently attentive to contemporary context, it is also an important aspect of the UK constitution that itself repays study, including in comparative perspective. Indeed, it serves to underscore the paradoxical question of whether the capacity of the British constitution to adapt casts doubt upon any claim that the UK has a 'proper' constitution to begin with.

7 Common Law Constitutionalism

Unlike the matters considered above, the common law *per se* is hardly a modern element of the UK system. However, the position is rather different in relation to what is often referred to as 'common law constitutionalism'. What this term means is something of a moveable feast, but it is generally understood to refer to the greater judicial willingness evident in recent years to treat the common law as a source – and, to some extent, as a guarantor – of fundamental constitutional values and rights. Even this phenomenon (as distinct from the moniker) is not entirely new. After all, courts have long been willing, via their powers of judicial review, to evaluate the validity of executive action by reference to constitutional values that, at least on one view, find expression as common law principles of good administration.[22] And it is now more than half a century since the Appellate Committee of the House of Lords, in the *Anisminic* case,[23] demonstrated its preparedness to insist upon the courts' capacity to do such things even in the face of legislation that appeared to rule out the possibility of judicial review, thus upholding what is, in modern parlance, the constitutional right of access to court.

Nevertheless, the prominence that is today accorded to the common law as a repository of constitutional values and rights and as a mechanism for protecting them undoubtedly marks a departure with the past. The seeds of the modern outlook in this regard were evident as long ago as the 1990s, as courts in the UK began to develop, increasingly explicitly, the notion of common law constitutional rights.[24] In doing so, they were – consciously or otherwise, deliberately or otherwise – in sync with developments elsewhere in the common law world, where the notion of fundamental rights was gaining a new prominence. In some instances, this was thanks to legislative intervention, the enactment of the New Zealand Bill of Rights Act 1990 being one example. Elsewhere, however, judges, like their counterparts in the UK, were themselves innovating – including in Australia, where the High Court began to find implied rights

---

[22] It is unnecessary, for present purposes, to examine the debate about whether principles of judicial review are best thought of as functions of statutory construction or as common law principles. On that debate, see C. Forsyth (ed.), *Judicial Review and the Constitution* (Hart Publishing, 2000).

[23] *Anisminic Ltd* v. *Foreign Compensation Commission* [1969] 2 AC 147.

[24] See, e.g., *R* v. *Lord Chancellor, ex parte Witham* [1998] QB 575.

in the text of the Constitution.[25] It is beyond the scope of this chapter to speculate about cause and effect in this regard, but it is at least noteworthy that British and Australian judges simultaneously found themselves exploring the boundaries of rights protection in constitutional systems that, although different in important respects, were united by the absence of any bill of rights. In this context, and particularly given the comparative focus of this volume, it is worth bearing in mind the capacity of the common law to serve as a means by which ideas may be transplanted from jurisdiction to jurisdiction[26] – a capacity that exists in the public law sphere, as in other spheres, albeit that it is necessarily curtailed by differences of constitutional architecture.

Somewhat ironically, however, the enactment of the HRA in the UK served both to emphasize UK public law's distinctiveness from its common law cousins – by rendering the European Convention on Human Rights the principal point of orientation in rights-related matters – and to disrupt the trajectory upon which the common law had by then tentatively begun. Thus it was that, in 2006, Lord Rodger appeared to consign the notion of common law rights to the status of historical curiosity, observing that while they might have had their use prior to the enactment of the HRA, the 'heroic efforts' of judges who had developed the idea of common law rights were no longer necessary.[27] The upshot, according to one commentator, was that 'the coffin lid on [common law] constitutional rights was well and truly screwed down'.[28]

However, reports of the death of common law constitutional rights in fact turned out to have been greatly exaggerated. Indeed, they find themselves today in nothing less than rude health – and, far from being eclipsed by the HRA, they have arguably been invigorated by it. None of this is to suggest that the HRA remains anything other than enormously significant, or that its repeal could be met with equanimity by those who favour strong judicial protection of individual rights. Nevertheless, a

---

[25] See, e.g., *Australian Capital Television Pty Ltd* v. *Commonwealth* (1992) 177 CLR 106.

[26] See, e.g., C. Harlow, 'Export, Import. The Ebb and Flow of English Public law' (2000) *Public Law* 240; R. French, 'The Globalisation of Public Law: A Quilting of Legalities', in M. Elliott, J.N.E. Varuhas and S. Wilson Stark (eds.), *The Unity of Public Law? Doctrinal, Theoretical and Comparative Perspectives* (Hart Publishing, 2018).

[27] *Watkins* v. *Secretary of State for the Home Department* [2006] UKHL 17; [2006] 2 AC 395, [64].

[28] B. Dickson, *Human Rights and the United Kingdom Supreme Court* (Oxford University Press, 2013), 28.

series of bellwether judgments delivered in recent years by the Supreme Court has served to re-emphasize the common law as a site of rights protection, as well as to underline the capacity of the common law to evolve. Thus, among other things, it has been said that domestic law, including the common law, remains the 'natural starting point' in this context, the availability of Convention rights under the HRA notwithstanding;[29] that a discernible tendency to 'overlook' the common law in human rights cases is a 'baleful and unnecessary one';[30] that human rights 'continue to be protected by our domestic law, interpreted and developed in accordance with the [HRA] when appropriate';[31] and that the common law's development 'did not come to an end on the passing of the Human Rights Act 1998'.[32]

Taking these points in combination, the clear message is that the common law's capacity to protect fundamental rights not only survives the enactment of the HRA, but may have been augmented by it given the capacity of the common law to develop, including in the light of the HRA itself. Admittedly, the common law does not at present explicitly recognize the whole gamut of rights available under the HRA. But the absence of current recognition should not necessarily be taken to signal the common law's incapacity in the future to embrace a wider range of rights. Such considerations will become particularly important if – as is far from inconceivable, at least in the medium term – the HRA is repealed and the ECHR withdrawn from, thereby necessitating greater recourse to the common law in this field.

It might be retorted that common law *recognition* of constitutional rights is all very well, but that it is clear, from what has already been said in this chapter, that that cannot ultimately get us very far in the face of the principle of parliamentary sovereignty. As observed above, the HRA is a greater match for that principle than might at first be supposed, given that it places in the domestic spotlight obligations that are internationally binding. In contrast, it might be thought, the common law is no such match, its hierarchical inferiority to Acts of Parliament being a necessary

---

[29] *Kennedy* v. *Charity Commission* [2014] UKSC 20; [2015] AC 455, [46], *per* Lord Mance.
[30] *Kennedy* (n. 29), [133], *per* Lord Toulson.
[31] *R. (Osborn)* v. *Parole Board* [2013] UKSC 61; [2014] AC 1115, [57], *per* Lord Reed.
[32] *R (Guardian News and Media Ltd)* v. *City of Westminster Magistrates' Court* [2012] EWCA Civ 420; [2013] QB 618, [88], *per* Toulson LJ. Lord Toulson, as he had by then become, made similar remarks in the Supreme Court in *Kennedy* (n. 24), [133].

function of parliamentary sovereignty. But the position is not quite so straightforward. For one thing, the courts have increasingly demonstrated a willingness to uphold common law constitutional rights, along with other fundamental constitutional values, even in face of apparently contrary legislation by engaging in interpretation at least as bold as that which has been evident in HRA cases.[33] Some judges, however, have gone still further by suggesting that there may be circumstances in which a court could legitimately strike down or decline to enforce legislation on the ground of its offensiveness to constitutional fundamentals, which would go *beyond* what can be done under the HRA. Such suggestions were prominently made in extra-curial interventions as long ago as the mid-1990s.[34] More recently, however, such apparently heterodox sentiments have issued from the bench as well, albeit only by way of *obiter dicta*.[35]

In this way, the prominence of the notion of common law constitutionalism proves to be a further trap for the unwary comparativist, and further underlines the need not only to be aware of the UK constitution's traditional features, but also to be sensitive to a contemporary context in which those features are being viewed in a new perspective and, in some instances, openly questioned, including at the highest judicial level. Not only does this represent a challenge of sorts to the axiom of parliamentary sovereignty: it also calls into question the extent to which the UK constitution can continue to be considered a 'political' one, given the propensity of the courts to infer from the common law constitutional order increasingly penetrating legal constraints upon the authority of public bodies up to, and perhaps including, Parliament. It is true, of course, that there has been no seismic constitutional case amounting to a naked judicial power grab and entailing an outright refusal to acknowledge the validity of primary legislation. But a change in tone, at least in some judicial quarters, is certainly evident.

The net effect is somewhat paradoxical. For while the comparativist who has a passing familiarity with the orthodox tenets of British constitutional law might be caught out by the recent direction of travel, the common law constitutionalist perspective arguably moves the UK

---

[33] See, e.g., *R. (Evans)* v. *Attorney General* [2015] UKSC 21; [2015] AC 1787; *R. (Unison)* v. *Lord Chancellor* [2017] UKSC 51; [2017] 3 WLR 409.

[34] See, e.g., Lord Woolf, '*Droit Public* – English Style', [1995] *Public Law* 57; Sir J. Laws, 'Law and Democracy' [1995] *Public Law* 72.

[35] See, e.g., *R. (Jackson)* v. *Attorney General* [2005] UKHL 56; [2006] 1 AC 262.

constitution onto territory that is more familiar to the outsider, thus rendering the British system at least a little less exceptionalist in nature. Indeed, a possible logical endpoint for the common law constitution-alist enterprise – or, depending upon one's perspective, its *reductio ad absurdum* – is the fashioning of a power-constraining constitutional order that leaves the UK system shorn of its most distinctive characteristics, save that the 'constitution' would remain formally uncodified. Arrival at such a destination is unlikely, given that the path leading to it is strewn with danger – not least for the judiciary.[36] But the very fact that the journey has been embarked upon has significant implications for how the UK constitution ought today to be situated when it is examined in com-parative perspective.

Conclusion

The British constitution is, in many senses, a very old one. A strong pref-erence for continuity over rupture has resulted in a system whose roots lie deep in history, undisturbed by reform so radical as to entail any formal or definitive break with the past. At the same time, however, the UK con-stitution has been renewed in recent years and decades, not least as a result of the developments traced in the course of this chapter. In most constitutional orders, change is managed at a micro-level through con-stitutional amendment and through judicial interpretation and reinter-pretation of the constitutional text, and at a macro-level by big bang reform such as the adoption of a constitutional text or the replacement of an existing text with a new one. Something that sets the UK apart is that none of these change-management strategies have any purchase in the context of its constitutional system. The notions of constitutional amendment and (re)interpretation are beside the point, there being, in the first place, no relevant text capable of alteration or (re)construction. Meanwhile, as we have seen, drastic change such as the adoption of a new – or, in the case of the UK, just *a* – constitutional text has been resisted because of a conservative political-cultural tradition that prizes stability over radical reform.

---

[36] See D. Oliver, 'Parliament and the Courts: A Pragmatic (or Principled) Defence of the Sovereignty of Parliament', in A. Horne and G. Drewry (eds.), *Parliament and the Law* (Hart Publishing, 2018).

The upshot is that the British constitution today is a curious admixture of the old and the new, which enables – or, at least, may enable – a system that is in some senses archaic or that otherwise sits in tension with contemporary constitutional and political mores to operate in functional terms in a way that is sensitive to those matters. It is for this reason that the outsider who wishes to understand the UK constitution and perhaps to compare it with her own must exercise great caution. The basic, architectural aspects of many constitutional systems remain relatively stable unless and until explicit, hard-to-overlook reform occurs. In contrast, the famously flexible British constitution finds itself in a state of constant evolution – and today arguably finds itself in a state of rather more significant flux. The dispersal of governmental power via devolution, the exposure of the British constitutional system to European influences, and the development of thinking about the role of the common law as a source of constitutional principle each serve to bring the old and the new into relationship – and sometimes tension – with one another.

Standing back and viewing these developments cumulatively, the question arises whether the 'British way', which insists upon weaving the contemporary into an ancient and delicate constitutional tapestry, will continue to be sustainable. There is no definitive answer to that question. But it is fair to say that to suppose that the UK's constitutional fabric is infinitely malleable would imply foolish complacency. At the very least, it must be acknowledged that the constitutional fabric is presently being pulled in a number of different directions and its strength tested, not least by the senses of constitutional plurality that have developed as a result of devolution and the sharp relief into which such differences have been thrown by the decision to withdraw from the EU.

The UK system has tended to rely – to what might seem to many outsiders to an astonishing and imprudent degree – on trust. In the absence of the sort of constitution that lays down hard, justiciable parameters upon legislative authority, the public must inevitably place considerable faith in political actors and institutions to operate not only within the letter of the law, but also within the spirit of the constitution. It is ironic, to say the least, that the UK has been so instrumental – first as a colonial power, and then through the transitional role it has played in many parts of the world in the context of decolonization – in the adoption of written constitutional instruments, while eschewing that model at home. In the light of the circumstances discussed in this chapter, the question arises whether the UK's brand of constitutional exceptionalism is capable of being maintained in the longer term. It would be naïve baldly to assert that it is not. After all, the present system has endured, in perpetually evolving iterations, for centuries. But it would be equally naïve to dismiss out of hand the possibility that the UK's current constitutional model is capable of enduring come what may.

The fissiparous effects of devolution, the implications of Europeanization and the as-yet-unknown consequences of de-Europeanization, and what might be thought of as flirtation at common law with elements of hard-legal, albeit still-uncodified, constitutionalism conspire to produce a moment of uncertainty for the UK system – and one that, just might, form the impetus for a 'constitutional moment' productive of more funda-mental re-evaluation and change. If that does come to pass, then, in time, the UK might become a less disorientating system for the comparativist. But if the direction of travel sketched here is one that is pursued, then British constitutional lawyers will themselves have to become more intrepid comparativists. After all, the path towards 'capital-C' constitu-tionalism is a well-trodden one, even if the UK, were it to set out down that route, would arrive somewhat late at the party.

Further Reading

V. Bogdanor, *The New British Constitution* (Hart Publishing, 2009).

B. Dickson, *Human Rights and the United Kingdom Supreme Court* (Oxford University Press, 2013).

D. Feldman, 'None, One or Several: Perspectives on the UK's Constitution(s)' (2005) 64 *Cambridge Law Journal* 329.

House of Lords Select Committee on the Constitution, *The Union and devolution* (HL Paper 149, 2015–16), available at: https://publications.parliament.uk/pa/ld201516/ldselect/ldconst/149/149.pdf

Sir J. Laws, *The Common Law Constitution* (Cambridge University Press, 2014).

A. Tomkins, *Our Republican Constitution* (Hart Publishing, 2005).

A. Young, *Parliamentary Sovereignty and the Human Rights Act* (Hart Publishing, 2009).

4 French Constitutional Law

Denis Baranger

....

Introduction

This chapter aims at providing readers with an introduction to French constitutional law and, more generally, to France's constitutional tradition. France's constitutional culture is dominated by a paradox: it is a revolutionary culture with frequent constitutional changes and amendments, but also some remarkably stable key characteristics. Amongst these is the establishment of a republican culture in a country governed for centuries by monarchs. This may explain France's very special position with regard, in particular, to systems of government. While France chose parliamentarism during the nineteenth century, the 1958 Constitution – an embodiment of the ideas of General de Gaulle – is characterized by an insistence on presidential powers that many observers compare with a presidential monarchy. This is just one, albeit maybe the most conspicuous, of France's constitutional paradoxes.

Although most countries in the world now have a constitution, the core notions, institutions, and underlying ideas of constitutional law – also called 'constitutionalism' – have been elaborated in certain specific historical contexts, mostly in Britain, continental Europe and the United States in the course of the seventeenth and eighteenth century. In this regard, France plays a particular role in the history of constitutional law. It has drawn most of its founding ideas and institutions from England and the United States. In many regards, thus, the contribution of the French constitutional tradition can appear as a limited one; one could even say that France has an impressive record of failures and drawbacks in many dimensions of its constitutional experience, such as its long-lasting incapacity to build up a form of government adjusted to its own needs. Yet the French approach to constitutional law is also marked by a focus on republican principles understood in a radical way. The keyword to this approach to constitutionalism – often derided by non-French observers as unrealistic or even utopian – is collective political autonomy. As far as constitutional law is concerned, the meaning of the French revolution can be summed up in one proposition: that law must be the result of political activity on the part of the citizenry at large, and that this political activity ought to be the ultimate source of law-making. This is as universal a proposition as it gets in the field of constitutional law and as a matter of fact, despite all the shortcomings of the French constitutional experience, this is a lesson that was more clearly understood in revolutionary France than in eighteenth-century Britain or during the American revolution.

Since 1789, France has been governed under several monarchies (1791, 1814, 1830) and two empires (1804–1814 and 1815, 1852–1870). It has known ultra-democratic (1793) as well as fairly reactionary (1795, 1814, 1830, 1851) governments, not to mention the infamous Vichy regime (1940–1944). Instability and diversity seem to be the key features of French constitutional history. Yet there seems to be an underlying principle of continuity that – beyond several experiments going in other directions – unites the revolutionary era (1789–1799) and the republican parliamentary regimes established since 1875: France has approached

constitutionalism from the point of view of the consolidation of republicanism (collective self-government of citizens) and individual human
rights, autonomy and dignity. There has been no small amount of interest
in the mechanics of government, but the abundant imagination of French
constitution-drafters has not given birth to an effective and sustainable model of government. After a long chain of dismal experiments,
France has reluctantly adhered to parliamentary government, while never
renouncing its revolutionary principles: national sovereignty, law as the
expression of the general will, and so on.

There is no guarantee that the Westminster approach to separation of
powers on one side, and the French concern for national sovereignty on
the other can merge harmoniously. As early as 1778, Turgot – a French
philosopher and civil servant – had blamed the constitutions of the newly
independent north American states for 'establishing different bodies'
(separating powers) while what mattered most in his view was to 'bring
all the authorities into one, that of the nation'.[1] This paramount concern
for unity is key to French constitutional history. Legitimacy comes first;
other liberal concerns – such as the separation of powers – only come
second. Political liberty is first and foremost guaranteed by granting
power to the 'nation', thus giving political freedom to the collective body
of citizens. The 1789 Declaration of the Rights of Man and Citizen is as
much a catalogue of classical liberal individual rights as it is the palla-
dium of national sovereignty (Article 3); it insists on the separation of
powers (Article 16) as well as on the principle that every parliamentary
statute (in French: *loi*) expresses the general will (Article 6). The presence
of all these values in the 1789 Declaration, as well as the absence of other
ones – such as religious transcendence – is evidence of a republican constitutional philosophy in which man asserts himself as the bearer of rights
while at the same time he claims to be a citizen whose participation in
public life can only be fulfilled in a certain type of institutionalized political community: a 'constitution' based on the 'separation of powers', a
'guarantee of rights' and an autonomous polity in which the sovereign is
the supreme legislator.

In the French tradition of public law, *loi* being the expression of the
general will, any *loi*, however banal in its content, is 'higher law'. During
the Third Republic (1875–1940), the French lawyer Raymond Carré de

---

[1] A.-R. Turgot, *Œuvres* – Volume II (Reprint of the 1844 edition; Zeller, 1966), 807.

Malberg (1861–1935) expressed some dismay at the fact that the authority of the written constitution was not sufficiently guaranteed: the constitution, he thought, was not effectively entrenched since it could be amended by the same assemblies which were entrusted with ordinary legislative power.[2] The entrenched constitution was not as much a 'higher law' as in, say, the United States. Be that as it may, what really mattered in fact was that, symmetrically, 'ordinary' statutes were treated with greater reverence. As far as France was concerned, parliamentary law-making was in fact 'higher law-making'. Especially, there was no provision in the constitution for a mechanism of constitutional review of statutes. In American constitutional law, national sovereignty and legislative supremacy are not intertwined. 'We the people' have enacted the 1787 Constitution and the Constitution alone. Congress is only a representative body in a 'constitution of limited powers'. Conversely, in the French tradition prior to 1958, statutes were granted a special dignity while written constitutions only enjoyed a somewhat diminished level of prestige. This is why it took so long for France to embrace judicial review and to follow the model set by *Marbury* v. *Madison* in the United States in 1803.

As a whole, however, the fact that France began its modern constitutional history by adopting a declaration of rights – as a preamble to enacting a constitution – shows that it had engaged into a process of promoting political autonomy in the sense of the capacity to 'form, revise and rationally pursue its conception of what gives value to its collective life'. The 1789 Declaration also provided the nation with 'a public conception of justice' on which to act.[3] That the Declaration has been constantly in the background, and, since 1971, a part of the body of positive rules applied by the courts, is an illustration of this continuity of purpose.

1 The Republican Framework: The State and Political Autonomy

a Constituent Power

If France has played an important role in the building of modern constitutionalism, it is first and foremost because it is the country whose

---

[2] Article 8 of the Constitutional Act of 25 February 1875.
[3] J. Rawls, 'Kantian Constructivism in Moral Theory: The Dewey Lectures 1980' (1980) 77 *Journal of Philosophy* 515.

main concern was that of establishing an institutionalized political community from an act of deliberate choice with as little concern as possible for history or tradition. Frenchmen – and especially the polemicist and constitution-drafter Abbé Sieyès – have claimed as their own the invention of the idea of constituent power, though it was more probably an American invention. Even worse: while the Americans have invented specialized constituent conventions, French drafters have, more often than not, been unable to clearly distinguish between higher law-making (drafting constitutions) and the use of ordinary legislative powers: most of France's constituent assemblies indeed were at the same time legislative bodies.

The reason for this lies in the principle of national sovereignty and the theory according to which the will of the nation is only legitimately expressed through representative assemblies. While the monarchy came to an end in 1792 and was definitively rejected in 1884, the monarchical idea of sovereignty was maintained and transposed to the nation. At the same time, the nation as an abstraction, was fully and exclusively represented by an elected assembly. This assembly – in the revolutionary era and later in the Third and Fourth Republics (1875–1958) – was entrusted with the plenary authority of the popular sovereign. It enacted the constitution, sometimes in one piece, sometimes in a piecemeal fashion, but it also legislated. Moreover, and not infrequently, assemblies were also entrusted with the executive power (1793) or, at least, they held – as during the Third Republic – great sway over the executive through their standing committees. This phenomenon became known as 'absolute representation' in the words of Carré de Malberg. The paradox here is that nowhere does constitutional law insist more on the existence of the people as a legal as well as a political sovereign than in France while nowhere has the nation's power been more systematically confiscated by representatives, be they assemblies or more recently the head of State.

b The State: Monarchical Leftovers in a Republican Constitution?

The other major contribution of France to the building of a frame of political life and political activity for citizens is the idea of a State. While France has fared poorly in the field of engineering political regimes, it has done very well in building a state and a system of public law.

While many constitutions have been tried and abandoned, the State has developed on a pattern of continuity, as Tocqueville was one of the first to identify. In France, ever since the *Ancien Régime* (prior to 1789), there has been a deeply embedded culture of the State, first eulogized by the French sixteenth- and seventeenth-century jurists (for example, Bodin, Loyseau and Coquille) who were also proponents of the idea of sovereignty. Its cogs and wheels have been, without recourse to a fully-fledged underlying theory, elaborated by unsung generations of chancery officers and official lawyers of all denominations. As Tocqueville clearly observed, the development of the State was not disrupted by the French Revolution. After the Napoleonic reforms, there developed a court-based *droit administratif* from which emerged the roots of French public law. The *Conseil d'Etat* is as much an institution of French constitutional law as any other, despite its role as a judge of the legality of administrative action. Finally, following the path of the German *Staatslehre*, French lawyers of the Third Republic developed a 'General Theory of the State' based on the French constitutional experience. Despite this theoretical effort, the state is rarely seen in the rulings of the French courts and in constitutional texts. Yet, its importance should not be underestimated. The state plays a major role in public law, and also in political and social life, promoting political autonomy by embodying collective authority. At the same time, this strong and efficient administrative state may also play a less positive role, insofar as it acts *on behalf of citizens* without being sufficiently accountable *to citizens* – and even to their elected representatives – and without enough regard for their opinions and their rights.

In French law, the state is a corporate body the existence of which is acknowledged by positive law. 'State' is not only – as in the United Kingdom – a term of art reserved to political scientists or to be used by lawyers mostly in the specific context of the law of the European Union; neither is it, as in the United States, a word the use of which is made more difficult by federalism, as this requires that there be two levels of public authorities.

As opposed to the United Kingdom – in which this role is played in part by the legal concept of 'Crown' – French public law knows of a corporate 'state', which plays a very prominent role in the functioning of public law. A good example of this, at the crossroads of constitutional and administrative law, is to be found in the French approach to state liability in torts. In France, civil servants are state employees. The default position is that if they cause a tort to a third party, it is the State, not the agent, which appears in court and is held liable. There is an exception to this principle if the agent's fault is such (ie. so serious) that it cannot be related to the activity of the public authority and is therefore 'detachable' from it. This is the exact reverse of the common law mechanism of vicarious liability. And this is a very clear result of the existence of a 'State'. The state always stands in the background of French public law. The case law of France's administrative courts has, ever since the Third Republic, granted the executive unwritten regulatory powers to maintain the 'continuity' of the state's activity. This has been replicated in the French Constitution of 1958: the President is the 'guardian of the continuous functioning of public powers as well as of the continuity of the state' (Article 5).

c Law as the Expression of the General Will

Constitutional law is the law of self-government. A constitution in the modern sense is an instrument of self-government. It is a legal *instrumentum* which aims at establishing self-government in the sense of individual and collective autonomy. French constitutionalism reads as a constant experiment of a nation aiming at governing itself with the utmost level of autonomy. As early as the Declaration of the Rights of Man and Citizen (August 1789) France has embraced a fairly radical approach to individual autonomy, insisting on individual liberties and rejecting the idea that bills of rights should include a reference to God (as demanded by the clergy in 1789) or to human duties (as in the protestant tradition). The individual self (man and citizen) was put to the forefront as much as the collective self (the nation). The latter was held to be sovereign and the first consequence seems to have been drawn in Article 6 of the 1789 Declaration: '*la loi*' (not 'the law' but statutes) voted by the national assembly expresses the 'general will'. The legal consequences of that principle were as important as their political and philosophical import. For a long time, legislation was the main source of the French legal system. Despite the fact that France has had a written constitution since 1791, statutes enjoyed a status of paramountcy and centrality until the late establishment (1958) of a constitutional court. 'Legicentrism' was the word forged to express the fact that parliamentary statutes could not be questioned before a court and/or judicially quashed. This immunity from review reflected a deep faith in the ability of statutory law to further the republican agenda of promoting human rights and of building society according to principles of equality and collective agency. This approach has only partly given way to the primacy of the constitution since 1958 and the establishment of a constitutional court, the '*Conseil Constitutionnel*' (CC). In 1985, in a celebrated ruling, the CC held that the purpose of constitutional review was 'to make sure that parliamentary bills, which only express the general will insofar as they are in pursuance with the constitution' can be amended in order to be constitutional.[4]

2 The Problem of Government: Presidentialism vs. Parliamentarism ... or both at the Same Time?

a A Longstanding Difficulty

In French constitutional culture the 'people' are held to be sovereign as a matter of 'principle', while the 'exercise' of sovereignty is devolved to individual voters and representatives. This distinction was expressed in Article 3 of the Declaration of 1789 and more recently in Article 3 of the 1958 Constitution. Ever since the Revolution, the idea of self-government encapsulated two potentially contradictory ideas: that of a 'collective self' (Rousseau), which is the bearer of political supremacy, and that of an effective activity of governance (or 'exercise' of sovereignty). The French constitutional tradition has always fared better in pursuing the agenda of defining, expanding and extolling the virtues of that collective self (be it the 'people' or the 'nation' finally merging into the formula of Article 3 of the 1958 Constitution: 'national sovereignty belongs to the people') than when it undertook to elaborate a form of government.

France has experimented with many political regimes during its history. It was only reluctantly that it eventually embraced parliamentary government. The Westminster model, based on a sharing of power between representative assemblies and an accountable executive, thus came into tension, when transposed to France, with the idea of national sovereignty that by definition is one and indivisible. The revolutionary attempts to make Parliament hold the entirety of power were obvious failures, as was the 1795 attempt to divide it almost

---

[4] Décision No. 85–197 DC of 23 August 1985.

entirely. The British solution was more or less replicated during the monarchical restoration of 1814 and in 1830: an executive, initially politically dependent on the monarch, became accountable to parliament in large part because of the rise of modern party politics and of a majority/opposition pattern. Yet France is not wholeheartedly attached to the idea of parliamentary government, which it has had recourse to while being at the same time obsessed with the idea that the actual power – or at least a decisive weight – should be granted either to the representative body itself (1793, 1875, the first constitutional draft of April 1946, the 1946 constitution) or to a head of state elected by universal suffrage (1848 and since 1962).

b The 1958 Regime: An Imperfect Synthesis between Republicanism and the Monarchical Tradition?

Throughout its history, France has had fifteen constitutions – a figure that does not include some more temporary arrangements – as well as a great many constitutional crises. However, the underlying revolutionary principles and the necessity to adhere to a model of parliamentary government have been left unshaken. Along with universal suffrage and the concern for equality before the law, they form the component parts of the republican tradition. The Third (1875–1940) and the Fourth (1946–1958) Republics were here the clearest examples of a 'dualist' model of parliamentary government as well as the best instances of its shortcomings; and, in the case of the Fourth Republic, of what has been unjustly held as a complete failure. The 1946 regime was faced with an ultimate blow to its authority by the crisis of Algerian independence. To overcome it, General De Gaulle – the founding father of the Fifth Republic – proposed a new constitutional blueprint in which he merged his own personal and historical legitimacy with that of the administrative state. Since 1946 ('Bayeux' discourse), he had asserted the principles of representative government and universal suffrage but also of collective ministerial accountability to Parliament. These principles were retained in the 1958 Constitution (Articles 20 and 49).

But the key to the new regime was the *Président de la République* to whom, in the very words of De Gaulle, 'the entirety of the authority of the state is devolved'. Article 5C makes the President the head of the executive but also the guardian of the state's continuity and the integrity of the constitution. While the President enjoys the classical powers of a parliamentary head of state (dissolution, appointing of cabinet ministers, countersigning orders in council, promulgating acts of parliament, etc.), his – written as well as unwritten – executive powers extend far beyond those of the previous regimes' presidents. In the normal functioning of the state, a set of constitutional conventions have expanded the president's powers beyond the black letter of the constitution. For instance, he/she can force the prime minister to resign even though the latter enjoys (as in April 1972), the full confidence of the lower house. In extraordinary times, the President enjoys, thanks to Article 16, wide emergency powers which amount to a temporary fusion of powers. In 1961, for instance – the only time at which a President has triggered this emergency procedure – General de Gaulle amended legislation by way of executive regulations. This vast array of powers and the even wider area delineated by the 'presidentialist' interpretation of the Constitution explain to a large part why the President is, since 1962, elected directly by the 'people' and not by the assemblies alone (1875–1958) or by a larger electoral college mostly composed of parliamentarians and local officers (1958–1962). Or at least this explains why the presidential election matters so much in French politics: the head of state is elected in other countries (such as in Portugal, Finland and Austria) but nowhere, maybe, does the president hold so much sway over the regime as in France. The move from a seven-year term to a five-year term enacted by a constitutional amendment in 2000 has not changed this state of affairs, but it has somewhat destabilized the presidency and maybe the entire regime. Presidents have been tempted to become 'hyperactive' (i.e. to act as their own prime minister and be enmeshed in the intricacies of day-to-day governmental business) but in fact they have been reduced to a condition of relative weakness and inefficiency. This is all the more worrying as the *Président de la République* is not politically accountable, be it to Parliament or the people (except through re-election). This feature, frequently singled out at as one of the main drawbacks of the Fifth Republic, has only marginally been corrected by the introduction in 2007 of a so-called impeachment procedure *à la française* which allows for a destitution by a 'high court' should the President act in a manner incompatible with the requirements of his office (Article 68).

For better or for worse, the President is the first (and main) pillar of the Constitution. The other pillar is a fully-fledged, if somewhat subdued, system of parliamentary government. The Prime Minister and all other ministers ought to resign if they lose the confidence of the National Assembly (and it alone, because the second chamber, the Senate, has no role here) under one of the procedures spelled out in Article 49C. Another mechanism – heavily discussed in the recent period, notably by the left – is that by which the prime minister can force the National Assembly either to accept without a vote, and without amendments, a bill, or to be forced to express its loss of confidence and thereby possibly incur a dissolution (Article 49(3)). This being said, parliamentary government works in France as everywhere else: Article 20 clearly spells out the working relationship between the ministerial cabinet ('gouvernement') and the majority in the national assembly. The cabinet 'determines and conducts the policy of the nation'. Not only can the Prime Minister (and upon statutory authorization, ministers generally) enact executive regulations in reserved areas (Article 37C) or implement legislation (Article 34C), but; more importantly, the Constitution grants ministers important powers in the course of the legislative procedure. They can introduce bills, reject amendments not adopted in standing committees, and eventually give the last say to the National Assembly in case of a deadlock with the Senate, the second chamber representing local authorities. Symmetrically, according to Article 24C 'parliament passes legislation, it controls the activity of the *gouvernement* and it evaluates the implementation of public policies'. Votes of no confidence are as rare in France as in other parliamentary regimes (the only one since 1958 took place in 1962). Indeed, as anywhere else, parliamentary government is first and foremost based on a working relationship between the executive and the ruling parliamentary majority. Yet in France this relationship is overshadowed by presidential primacy: the majority in parliament is, under normal circumstances, held to be 'the president's majority' and the Constitutional Council has sanctioned that this justified holding general elections after the presidential election, rather than before.[5] When this is not the case, the President belongs to a party and the parliamentary majority to another. This is called '*cohabitation*' (as in 1986–1988, 1993–1995 and 1997–2002): a French variety of divided government which is generally considered temporary and pathological.

[5] Décision No. 2001–444 DC of 9 May 2001.

c France and Europe

France has adhered to many multilateral treaties like other countries around the world. This has had an obvious impact on its Constitution and legal system. The French approach to international law is well expressed in the Constitution: treaties, once incorporated into French law by way of a statutory instrument are superior to French statutes. Yet this supremacy does not amount to full monism as the constitution itself is held to be superior to international law. The normative ranking of international treaties (and indeed other sources of international law) is defined by the constitution itself.[6]

Nevertheless, the rise of international law has had a deep effect on the French legal system. The case of the European Union is perhaps the most illustrative example of the kind of situation that this generates in constitutional terms. In general, this situation is better approached in terms of an interaction between a national constitution and a very integrated transnational legal system of a higher order than in terms of a 'global constitutional law' or, in the case of the EU, of a 'European Constitution'.

France joined the EEC in 1957 and was one of the proponents of its transformation into a 'European Union' in 1992 (Maastricht Treaty) with greater legislative powers given to the institutions of the EU. This section will leave aside the functioning of the EU institutions as such and rather focus on the nature of the EU as an integrated legal order enjoying, since the landmark ECJ cases *Costa* v. *Enel* and *Van Gend en Loos*, primacy and direct effect over national norms. Primacy and direct effect were, not without some reluctance, accepted by French national courts during the 1970s. The adhesion to the EU has received constitutional sanction by way of a constitutional amendment incorporating into the 1958 Constitution a chapter on the 'European Union'. Article 88(1), the inaugural section of that chapter, states that 'the French Republic takes part to the European Union, which is composed of states which have freely chosen to exercise in common some of the competences in pursuance of the treaty on the European Union'.

The implementation of EU law does not generate massive practical problems, but this masks a lingering constitutional issue of great magnitude: the compatibility between EU membership and the implementation of EU law and the principle of national sovereignty, expressed in

---

[6] *Conseil d'Etat*, 'Sarran' Décision of 30 October 1998.

Article 3 of the Constitution. The compatibility between those two clauses has been asserted by the Constitutional Court in several 1992 rulings collectively known as the 'Maastricht' rulings.[7] Especially, in keeping with the French constitutional culture of formalism and a rejection of 'supraconstitutionality', the Court here insisted that the constituent power was allowed to derogate from the wider, and otherwise still applicable, principle of national sovereignty by enacting Article 88(1)C.

Despite the fact that the Court could do little else, this apparent neutrality illustrates the shortcomings of the current French practice when it comes to amending constitutions. This practice consists of complementing a general principle with a derogation of a more limited scope. As a result, the normative conflict is solved (there is no contradiction between national sovereignty and adhesion to the European Union) but the fundamental problem remains. France and its Constitution retain their supremacy while the EU institutions claim supremacy for the law of their own making. This has several consequences. First, it increases the power of the judiciary, as the main interpreter of the Constitution and of EU law; and it increases the need for a 'dialogue' between national and European courts in order to avoid clashes. Second, this widens the gap between national democratic systems and the European institutions. At no point did the rise of the European Union as an integrated 'legal community' generate a 'direct relation between community norms and the peoples of Europe'.[8] Actual democracy takes place at the national level, something that has been evidenced in France by the rejection of the so-called Treaty establishing a Constitution for Europe in 2005, as well as by the heated debate on Europe that dominated a large part of the French presidential electoral debate in 2017.

3 The Law and the Constitution

a France and the Rule of Law

French public law has developed a rather specific approach to the rule of law, so specific in fact that the expression does not translate well into

---

[7] Ruling N°92–308 DC of 9 April 1992; Ruling n°92–312 DC of 2 September 1992; and Ruling n°92–313 DC of 23 September 1992.

[8] For this view, see M.P. Maduro, 'The Importance of being called a Constitution: Constitutional Authority and the Authority of Constitutionalism' (2005) 3 *International Journal of Constitutional Law* 332.

French and that its closest equivalent (*Etat de droit*) was only transposed belatedly into French legal parlance. In English-speaking countries, the rule of law is often associated with a concern for legality as well as for certain core human rights (as in England with a concern for individual liberty). France is sometimes called the 'homeland' of human rights, notably because of its revolutionary declarations, but as a matter of fact it is not in France that the modern machinery of protecting and promoting human rights was developed with the utmost energy. The history of civil liberties in the nineteenth century and early twentieth century in France is a wayward one. Written constitutions and the 1804 Civil Code emphasized certain specific liberties – such as private property. The French public law courts acknowledged the existence of unwritten general principles of law such as procedural defence rights for civil servants or equality before the law; and certain important statutes did indeed promote particular freedoms (such as the freedom of association in 1901). Yet, civil liberty was also hampered by the expansion of police powers and the Third Republic has sometimes been depicted as having also worked 'against liberties'.[9]

It is, however, another dimension of the rule of law – legality – that has risen at the same time. While France has had written (entrenched) constitutions since 1791, it did not adopt constitutional review until 1958. It was only in the middle of the twentieth century that France developed a constitutional court, and only since the 1970s that this court has effectively gone to the path of protecting human rights, and only since 2008 that it has allowed direct access to the court by individual litigants. In the meantime, the concern for legality has been as strong in France as in other Western countries, but it was associated there with a concern for the state and the strength of public action. *Loi* was central to the functioning of civil society, as evidenced by the role of the (legislative) civil code of 1804 and the rise of the French administrative state. A specific body of administrative courts, topped by the *Conseil d'Etat*, developed a body of rules and unwritten principles aiming – with success – at harnessing administrative discretion and ensuring that administrative authorities acted in keeping with 'legality'. This concern for a strong administrative state was not incompatible with judicial review of administrative action; and, as a matter of fact, the two concepts went hand in hand.

---

[9] J.-P. Machelon, *La République contre les libertés?* (Presses de la FNSP, 1976).

Judicial review was thereby, from 1790 onwards, taken out of the hands of ordinary courts and endowed to ministers and a special hierarchy of administrative courts. Only in the 1889 *Cadot* case was it acknowledged that this top administrative court – the *Conseil d'Etat* – also had ordinary jurisdiction to hear applications for judicial review. Previously, ordinary jurisdiction belonged, in the absence of special statutory provisions, to the minister. Yet, along with judicial review there was a growing degree of protection for legal subjects, as for instance in the field of state liability for torts. This is the core reason why Dicey was misguided when he understood French *droit administratif* as another word for arbitrary public power.

b Constitutional Justice and the Changing Meaning of the 'Constitution'

aa The Framework of Constitutional Justice in France

From its creation in 1958 up until 2008, the Constitutional Council (*Conseil Constitutionnel*) had stood apart from most other comparable constitutional courts in the West in that it only reviewed acts of parliament *before* they came into force. This model of *a priori* abstract review was (and still is) embodied in two main constitutional provisions. First, under Article 61(2) C, which states:[10]

Acts of Parliament may be referred to the C.C., before their promulgation, by the President of the Republic, the Prime Minister, the President of the National Assembly, the President of the Senate, sixty Members of the National Assembly or sixty Senators.[11]

Second, Article 54C creates another procedural vehicle for constitutional review. It has a separate purpose, namely to allow for a check on the compatibility between treaties and the Constitution before those treaties are ratified. Finally and importantly, since the constitutional reform of 2008, a new mechanism permits individuals to challenge

[10] Article 61(1)C creates a procedure of mandatory review for organic laws, referendary bills, and the standing orders of the Houses of Parliament.

[11] All the translations of the 1958 Constitution (quoted as 'Article xx C' used in this chapter) are from the *Légifrance* website: www.conseil-constitutionnel.fr/conseil-constitutionnel/francais/la-constitution/la-constitution-du-4-octobre-1958/la-constitution-du-4-octobre-1958.5071.html.

statutes already in force that infringe their constitutional rights. This new procedure for a preliminary reference,[12] known as *Question prioritaire de constitutionnalité*, has not, however, induced the court to significantly alter the way in which its cases are drafted. The court's 'style' – concise in the extreme – has remained essentially the same.

bb The Theory of the Constitution

The CC's rulings are remarkably laconic. The Council can hardly be said to give reasons, yet its decisions are not unprincipled. The decisions point to reasons, by using certain standards such as (in our case) 'the spirit of the constitution', or the 'direct expression of national sovereignty'. One can imagine that those who decided these cases had very precise and articulated arguments in their support. Yet the decisions merely stand as a kind of syllabus briefly (if at all) spelling out these reasons. They are relegated to the background as if they were better left unarticulated. In a Western legal culture dominated by the values of transparency and rationality, which imply (amongst other things) the *giving* of reasons, the level of rationality of the CC's case law does not go beyond a certain limit. Though this is ultimately bound to have a negative impact on its legitimacy, this is how French courts often decide cases; and the question is therefore not so much of approving or disapproving this phenomenon as to inquiring into its meaning. In Germany, India or the United States, opinions are given by individual judges and often reflect a lengthy and quasi-doctrinal pursuit of the meaning of the law. In France those standards are expressed in unanimous rulings that are expressive of the will of the State rather than of the opinion of a constitutional judge. Because of the way the decisions are drafted, what comes to the forefront is authority rather than what, in the words of classical common law thinking, was called the 'artificial reason' of the law.

Yet these rulings rely on a coherent set of doctrinal justifications which have been developed over time in legal literature. Leading amongst its supporters are academic authors who were very close to the court itself, either because they were former members of its judicial panel (Georges Vedel, Robert Badinter) or its *Secrétaire Généraux* (Bruno Genevois,

---

[12] Translation suggested by G. Neuman, 'Anti-Ashwander: Constitutional Litigation as a First Resort in France' (2010) 43 *New York University Journal of International Law and Politics* 15 at 17.

Jean-Eric Schoettl). This supporting doctrinal literature tends to come to
the defence of the rulings by using broadly similar arguments. The views
of Georges Vedel and Bruno Genevois will be referred to mostly here
since they express admirably what may be called a 'sceptical' theory of
the constitution. The following paragraphs will only attempt to sketch
out the broad lines of this theory, which approaches the constitution
in purely formal terms and which is very reluctant to admit that there
can be actual limits (other than procedural) to the amending power. The
sceptical doctrine also rejects 'supraconstitutionality' as well as most
legal distinctions between the initial enactment of the constitution and
its amendments.

   This doctrinal literature has adhered for quite a long time to a very distinctive understanding of the Constitution. It has not lost its impetus with
the rise of the normative account of the Constitution that has followed the
development of the case law of the CC. Rather, the sceptical account and
the normative understanding of the Constitution have coexisted rather
harmoniously, although some disagreements could appear along the way.
According to the sceptical interpretation, the concept of a constitution is
purely formal: there is no 'material' (in the sense of substantive) content
that would be inherent to the constitution. George Vedel has summed up
that 'formal' definition of the constitution (as opposed to a political or
material meaning) by saying that 'the constitution is such a norm as can
only be altered according to certain procedures'.[13]

   In keeping with this doctrinal approach, the case law of the CC is
underpinned by a theory of constitutional sources which has three main
characteristics: (1) It is *formalist* to the extreme: it discards all the possible resources of constitutional law that do not possess a proper pedigree
in positive law. (2) It is *textualist*: all the constitutional 'norms' applicable in positive constitutional law must derive from a written instrument. Therefore, as a matter of principle, 'unwritten law' is normally not
a source of law. (3) In French doctrinal literature, the general approach
to principles, rules, fundamental rights, etc. is a *normative* one. All the
component parts of a judicial decision are 'norms' belonging to different
normative categories.

   This formalist and textualist approach is encapsulated in the doctrine of
the '*bloc de constitutionalité*'. This orthodox account of the French source

---

[13] Id. 112.

system aims at describing the 'norms' which the *Conseil Constitutionnel* uses as 'references' for its constitutional review of parliamentary statutes and treaties. Up until 1971, the view prevailed that the Preamble to the 1958 Constitution was not a part of positive law and could therefore not be used to quash statutory enactments. A famous decision of 16 July 1971 – preceded by a few other cases – created a sea change in this regard with just a few words: 'according to the Constitution and especially its Preamble' ('*vu la constitution, et notamment son préambule*'). As a matter of fact, the Preamble itself refers to several types of norms: 'The French people solemnly proclaim their attachment to the Rights of Man and the principles of national sovereignty as defined by the Declaration of 1789, confirmed and complemented by the Preamble to the Constitution of 1946, and to the rights and duties as defined in the Charter for the Environment of 2004'.

The mere reference to the 1958 Preamble as part of positive law thus meant that, by extension, the seventeen articles of the 1789 Declaration; the fourteen principles explicitly enumerated in the 1946 Preamble; the unwritten principles referred to in the same preamble as 'fundamental principles recognized by the republican laws'; and finally since 2005, the 'Charter for the Environment were now part of positive law'.

This entailed a sea change in the definition of the very concept of constitution. For the word does no longer refer to the 1958 text but also to the many other 'norms' contained in these several texts. The 1971 landmark case indeed decided that freedom of association was one of the 'fundamental principles recognized by the republican laws' based especially on the important 1901 law on associations. In 1973, the CC logically extended its recognition to the 1789 Declaration. Since then, it has developed a particular methodology in using the Preamble which can be summed up in the following fashion: (1) Only the texts referred to in the Preamble are used as norms of reference. As a matter of principle, international treaties and the standing orders of parliamentary assemblies have thus been excluded. However, while the CC declines to consider conformity with international treaties as a condition of the constitutionality of statutes, ordinary courts (*Conseil d'Etat* and *Cour de cassation*) do exercise a control over the compatibility of ordinary statutes with international 'conventions' (hence the term of art: '*contrôle de conventionnalité*'). Yet a statute held to be '*inconventionnel*' will not be quashed; rather it will be set aside in the litigation where the incompatibility is declared. (2) All the component parts of the texts belonging to the 'block' have constitutional force. The CC has steadily declined to engage in a process of 'cherry picking' some clauses and setting aside others. (3) All the 'norms' contained in those texts have the same normative value. There is no hierarchy of constitutional norms. For instance, the principle of equality before the law does not take precedence over other principles of supposedly lesser importance.

These doctrines appear to be very clear. Yet for several reasons they are not as clear-cut as they might be: (1) The CC has softened the exclusion of treaties from the 'block' of constitutional norms of reference. Ever since the 1990s, constitutional review has indeed taken into account international norms when they are 'expressly referred to' by the Constitution. This is notably the case for the EU Treaties as the Constitution has been amended (Articles 88(1) to 88(4)) to allow for France's membership of the European Union. Ordinary as well as 'organic' legislation has to be in keeping with those treaties. (2) Similarly, the constitutional 'block' has been expanded to make room for other legal instruments of lesser normative rank. Certain important 'organic' statutes – especially the one creating the procedure for appropriation acts and taxation acts – are also held to be norms of reference for constitutional review. In even rarer cases, this can also be the case of some clauses in the standing orders of the two assemblies and, even more rarely, of ordinary statutes.

However, the main loophole in the theory of the 'block' of constitutional norms of reference does not come from these various exceptions but from the fact that the Court very freely creates new norms out of the blue when needs be. The mode of adjudication in French courts, including the CC, is 'hyperformalist': judicial reasons are based on the deductive mode and there is apparently no room for policy arguments or policy analysis. Yet on closer inspection, the CC has made abundant use of such policy arguments. Elements of judicial reasoning that operate like policy arguments are squeezed into pre-existing normative categories – some drawn from the Constitution or its (enforceable) Preamble, such as the 'fundamental principles recognized by the laws of the republic'; others created by the Court itself or by doctrinal writing – such as the 'objectives of constitutional value' or other *sui generis* categories such as 'principles of constitutional value' (for instance, the 'constitutional principle of the protection of public health'[14] which was also called, in the same decision,

---

[14] Decision n° 90–283 DC of 8 January 1991: 'Loi relative à la lutte contre le tabagisme et l'alcoolisme'.

an 'imperative'). In other cases, the Court has used a broad categorization, such as 'goal of general interest' or 'protection of general interests'. This was the terminology used in 1985 to define some broad objectives of environmental policy, such as a duty to respect the 'natural character of spaces', the 'quality of landscapes', or the 'ecological equilibrium'.[15] But beyond these broad normative categories, what should one call the 'necessity to defend public health', or to 'protect natural spaces', or to ensure a certain degree of pluralism in the medias, if not policy arguments? More often than not, these policy arguments indeed appear without any reference to a normative category. This has been the case of the 'goal of political or social appeasement' which has justified a statute of amnesty in 1988.[16] More recently, the CC has mentioned 'the legal complexity of the law regarding the enforcement of punishments'. This complexity, the Court said, was an obstacle to the participation of ordinary citizens in certain judicial panels.[17]

Conclusion

This chapter has emphasized the continuing tension between certain key features of French constitutional culture. This tension generates insoluble political contradictions that are still visible to this day. In particular, a continuing thirst for autonomy and human rights is matched by an equal propensity of the nation to opt for strong executives and swift governmental intervention in times of upheaval. Yet the tension has also been productive. It may explain the framework of state and administrative law that underpins France's social and political life and is a factor that needs to be assessed by anyone wishing to understand French constitutional law. It is in this context that France has faced the challenges of constitutional modernity. After a long era in which – through a great deal of crises and upheavals – French constitutional law has adhered to the classical principles of '*légicentrisme*' and republicanism, France has more recently taken on-board most of the 'modern' mechanisms and practices of constitutionalism practiced throughout the world: constitutional review made

[15] Decision n° 85–189 DC of 17 July 1985: 'Loi relative à la définition et à la mise en oeuvre de principes d'aménagement'.
[16] Decision n° 88–244 DC of 20 juillet 1988: 'Loi portant amnistie'.
[17] Decision n° 2011–635 DC of 4 August 2011: 'Loi sur la participation des citoyens au fonctionnement de la justice pénale et le jugement des mineurs'.

available (to some extent) to individual litigants; frequent 'technical' constitutional amendments adjusting the fundamental law to the needs of the day and especially to a growing number of multilateral international treaties; and more generally, an embrace of global law (EU, ECHR and transnational regulatory regimes). The rise of constitutional review, and the growing body of case law that has accompanied it, has been met with enthusiasm. Constitutional law has been held by some to have been truly revived and to be for the first time able to be taken seriously as *'vrai droit'*. This optimism, however, may be open to doubt. The glorious rise of constitutional review seems to come at the expense of what represents, as this chapter has tried to suggest, the peculiarity of the French constitutional tradition, namely: self-government and a concern for the political participation of citizens.

Further Reading

D. Baranger, *Droit constitutionnel* (Presses Universitaires de France, 2016).

R. Carré de Malberg, *Contribution à la théorie générale de l'État* (Dalloz, 1919–1922).

S. Cassese, *La construction du droit administratif: France et Royaume-Uni* (Montchrestien, 2000).

M. Gauchet, *La révolution des droits de l'homme*, (Gallimard, 1989).

M. Gauchet, *La révolution des pouvoirs: la souveraineté, le peuple et la représentation*, (Gallimard, 1995).

R. Halévi and F. Furet, *La monarchie républicaine: la Constitution de 1791* (Fayard, 1996).

M. Troper and F. Hamon, *Droit constitutionnel* (LGDJ-Lextenso, 2014).

US Constitutional Law and History   5

Vicki C. Jackson

Introduction

Although the US Constitution is quite short, it is also quite old. The structures it called forth – including the presidency, the bicameral Congress, the Supreme Court – survive, even as their relationships have evolved. Its brief provisions have also spawned a complex body of jurisprudence on many issues that has shifted over more than two centuries; there are now more than 560 volumes of the official 'US Reports', that is, of cases decided by the US Supreme Court.[1]

In the first four decades after the Constitution came into effect, the Supreme Court, dominated by Chief Justice John Marshall, issued foundational opinions on issues of judicial review, the scope of federal power, and the supremacy of federal over state law. In the decades leading up to the Civil War of 1861–1865, the Court struggled increasingly with a bitter sectional divide, reflected nowhere more starkly than in its infamous decision, *Dred Scott* v. *Sandford*,[2] treating African Americans as permanently incapable of being citizens, a decision overruled by the post-Civil

---

[1] *Opinions: Bound Volumes*, Supreme Court of the US, www.supremecourt.gov/opinions/boundvolumes.aspx (last visited 1 November 2018) (noting 569 official volumes).
[2] 60 US 393 (1857).

War amendments. Following the Civil War and an all-too brief period of 'Reconstruction' when federal troops and officials sought to secure the rights of the newly freed former slaves in the South, from the 1870s until well into the twentieth century the Court and the country were faced with challenges arising out of the changing industrial conditions. Increased efforts by state and federal legislatures to respond to changing economic conditions clashed with commitments to a private sphere of liberty protecting the rights of freedom to contract. Not until the 'New Deal' of the 1930s did the caselaw take a decisive turn that, for most of the next eighty years, allowed the federal and state legislatures substantial latitude over economic regulation.

In the mid-twentieth century the Court began to invigorate an individual rights jurisprudence, in criminal procedure rights, religious and speech freedoms. The decision in *Brown* v. *Board of Education*,[3] reflecting the organized efforts of the movement for African American equality, initiated the 'Civil Rights' era in the Court and the nation: rights against racial segregation and racial discrimination were elaborated, as well as rights of privacy, gender equality, reproductive freedom, among others, especially by the Court led by Chief Justice Earl Warren Court and, in its early years, the Court led by Chief Justice Warren Burger. In the 1990s, under Chief Justice Rehnquist and in the twenty-first century continuing under Chief Justice Roberts, a new set of issues emerged, in a jurisprudence that includes revived judicial interest in enforcing federalism-based limitations on national power. As some areas of rights for traditionally disadvantaged groups have expanded (e.g., rights to same-sex marriage), other jurisprudence has become increasingly concerned with protecting rights to use economic power (e.g., corporate speech) or money (e.g., in campaign contributions).[4]

As this all-too brief introduction indicates, the range of topics developed in US constitutional caselaw is vast. Some important aspects of the US Constitution, moreover, are rarely if ever litigated but foundational to the structures of the national and state governments. This brief chapter, then, cannot be comprehensive. It will address selected topics, in an effort to

---

[3] 347 US 483 (1954).
[4] Cf. P.S. Karlan, 'Foreword: Democracy and Disdain' (2012) 126 *Harv. L. Rev.* 1, 29–32 (describing *Citizens' United* as prioritizing the Court's conception of liberty as against the legislature's conception of equality).

provide some sense of the scope and history of important parts of this constitutional tradition.

What topics to address depends, in part, on whether one takes the perspective of an insider or outsider to the constitutional system. From an insider perspective, the theme of change in US constitutional law is at least as important as continuity. From an outsider perspective, some particularities of how US constitutional law deviates from that of many otherwise comparable constitutional democracies are worthy of comment. To illustrate these and other perspectives, this chapter will take up the Constitution as a written text; debates over its interpretation and the role of the courts; federalism, the supremacy of federal law and the scope of state and federal regulatory powers; selected rights, with a focus on the Fourteenth Amendment's due process and equal protection clauses (considering the 'incorporation' of criminal procedure rights, racial and gender discrimination, and 'substantive' aspects of liberty protected by the due process clause); and US exceptionalism (discussing the death penalty, speech and guns). Only limited aspects of each of these topics can be discussed. Missing entirely are such other large topics such as the amending process; the constitutionally mandated decennial census; federal and state control of elections; the independent constitutional powers of the President; separation of powers among the branches of the federal government, including war powers, or limitations on the appointment power; the constitutional basis for and constraints on administrative regulation; the range of procedural due process, contract and property rights; treaties and international law; inter-state relations and agreements; and justiciability limitations on the judicial power. It is hoped that what is covered will provide a useful introduction.

1 The Constitution as Written Instrument

The original text of the US Constitution came into force in the late 1780s, having been drafted in 1787 and then ratified by a sufficient number of states.[5] Although often referred to as a story of continuity (the 'world's oldest continuous constitution'), its still-brief text reflects periods of avulsive change, as well as the increasing difficulty of formal amendment.

---

[5] For a superb account of the conditions in which the Constitution was drafted, see J.N. Rakove, *Original Meanings: Politics and Ideas in the Making of the Constitution* (Knopf, 1996).

The original Constitution was built on two major compromises over representation in the national government: one that built in over-representation, in the Senate, of smaller population states (by giving each state two Senators) and the other that built in over-representation in the House of the white slaveholding South (through the 'three-fifths' rule). Although amending rules were liberalized from the unanimity require-ment under the predecessor instrument, amendment was designedly difficult, requiring two-thirds of both houses of Congress to agree on a proposed amendment which had then to be ratified in three-fourths of the states.[6] A special rule provides that 'no State, without its Consent, shall be deprived of its equal Suffrage in the Senate', that is, essentially requiring unanimity to depart from each state having equal votes in the Senate. Twelve amendments were sent to the states by the First Congress, of which ten were timely ratified and became what is called the 'bill of rights' of the Constitution.[7] The Eleventh Amendment was added shortly thereafter to overcome a Supreme Court decision permitting suit against a state by a private person on a contract, and the Twelfth Amendment was enacted in response to a constitutional defect, revealed by the 1800 election, in not specifying separate votes for the offices of president and vice president.

There followed more than half a century of stasis in the constitutional text. But the Civil War, occasioned by the attempted secession of several southern states (in order, among other things, to preserve slavery), was a tectonic event. US deaths (per capita and in absolute numbers) exceeded those in World War I and World War II. The War ended with a Northern victory, military occupation of the southern states and a requirement that, in order to regain representation in Congress, the southern states ratify the Fourteenth Amendment. The three-fifths rule was abandoned with the abolition of slavery in the Thirteenth Amendment. The Fourteenth Amendment not only overruled *Dred Scott*, by declaring all persons born in the United States to be citizens thereof, it also provided for important rights against the State governments. The Fifteenth Amendment, enacted in 1870, prohibited discrimination in voting based on race, colour or prior condition of servitude. But even in this deadly period of constitutional

[6] US Const. art. V (also providing – as an alternative, thus far unused route – that on request of two-thirds of the state legislatures, Congress should convene a convention to propose amendments, which would then need to be ratified in three-fourths of the states).
[7] The Twenty-seventh Amendment, discussed below, was one of the twelve originally sent for ratification in 1789 but was not declared part of the Constitution until 1992.

crisis, there was no change in the structure of the Senate. And the extent of the change that should be attributed to the three Civil War amendments, especially the Fourteenth, is debated; by the 1890s, the Fourteenth Amendment, which initially had been understood as constraining the states on behalf of equal citizenship for the newly freed slaves, had been transformed into an instrument for businesses to attack state regulation of novel forms of competition or industrial power.

The Progressive Era was another period of major changes in constitutional text, including the Sixteenth Amendment (1913) authorizing a federal income tax, the Seventeenth Amendment (1913) requiring the direct election of Senators, and the Nineteenth Amendment (1920) prohibiting sex discrimination in voting. The federal income tax may be regarded as essential to the expansion of federal power in the twentieth century and the direct election of the Senators, though largely ratifying a shift that the state legislatures had already moved to, further solidified the national character of the government but without resolving the problem of population disproportion in the representation in the Senate.

Between 1919 and 1971, Prohibition was enacted and repealed, the lame duck period of Congress shortened and provisions for succession in the event of the President's death made, a two-term limit on presidents imposed, voting in presidential elections extended to the District of Columbia, the poll tax barrier to voting in federal elections prohibited, further provisions enacted concerning the death or disability of the President, and the voting age lowered to eighteen. An Equal Rights Amendment for women was introduced and almost gained ratification in the 1970s, but fell short by three states. There has been no sustained effort to engage in serious constitutional amendment since the ERA. A twenty-seventh amendment, prohibiting congressional pay rises from taking effect without an intervening election, was seemingly added to the Constitution in 1992, through a process of state ratifications stretching over two centuries; the constitutionality of this process has not been adjudicated by the Court. With this possible (and sui generis) exception, there has been no change in the Constitution's text since 1971.

It had been the hope of James Madison, a principal architect of the Constitution of 1789, that the Constitution would gain a degree of affection from the people, towards which end it was designedly difficult to amend. Over the more than two centuries since it came into force the Constitution succeeded in becoming a national symbol. Despite critique by many it has become a kind of sacralised instrument.[8] This too may change, but in recent decades efforts to amend the Constitution have been defeated, in part by appeals to its sacralised nature. In this respect it differs from many other constitutions in the world, which were designed to be (or in practice have been) more easily amended.

2 Interpretation and the Role of the Courts

The US Constitution has been developed in significant ways through processes of judicial interpretation, a phenomenon that has prompted lively and extensive debate over approaches to interpretation and about the relationship between judicial interpretation of the Constitution and its interpretation in other branches of government. Unlike some more contemporary constitutions, the US Constitution does not address judicial review of legislation in so many words but it does extend the judicial power to 'all Cases, in Law and Equity, arising under this Constitution', words that, together with other features of the Constitution, have long been held to authorize judicial review. Nonetheless, the absence of more explicit language has sometimes fed concerns about what Alexander Bickel called the 'counter-majoritarian' character of judicial review.

Responses to those concerns often focus on claims about how the courts should go about their interpretive task. 'Originalists' and some other constitutional positivists seek to anchor the federal courts' role as one of implementing prior decisions taken by 'the people,' as against departures from those decisions by elected officials.[9] Others, like John Hart Ely, argue that courts should play a special role in protecting minorities disadvantaged by irrational prejudice from defects in the political process.[10] Still others argue for the importance of judicial review in protecting a range of constitutional values from majoritarian abuse.[11]

---

[8] See S. Levinson, *Constitutional Faith* (Princeton University Press, 1988).

[9] On originalism, see, e.g., A. Scalia, 'Originalism: The Lesser Evil (1989) 57 *U. Cinn. L. Rev.* 849. For a more dynamic but also arguably 'positivist' account, anchoring changed interpretations of the Constitution to decisions made by 'the people', the positive source of authority, in special constitutional moments, see B. Ackerman, *We the People: Volume I, Foundations* (Harvard University Press, 1991); B. Ackerman, *We the People: Volume II, Transformations* (Harvard University Press, 1998).

[10] See J.H. Ely, *Democracy and Distrust: A Theory of Judicial Review* (Harvard University Press, 1980).

[11] See, e.g., R. Dworkin, *The Moral Reading of the Constitution*, N.Y. Rev. Books 46 (21 March 1996) (arguing for a moral reading of broad constitutional guarantees); J.

Methods of constitutional interpretation in the US Supreme Court have been described as 'eclectic',[12] or 'multi-valenced',[13] drawing on textual interpretation; original understandings; precedent and history; purposive or structural analyses; moral reasoning, 'ethos' or community values; and consequentialist understandings. Many of these sources are similar to those used in other constitutional systems.

There are at least two distinctive features of the judicial practice of constitutional interpretation in the United States. First, 'originalism' – what the enacting generation understood constitutional texts to mean – plays a significant role at least in interpretive debates,[14] and occasionally in decisions.[15] The Court is by no means always originalist; a dramatic illustration was in its 1954 decision, *Bolling* v. *Sharpe*,[16] treating the Fifth Amendment, ratified in 1791 when slavery was still protected by the Constitution, as including the same 'equal protection' component as the Fourteenth Amendment, enacted after the Civil War. Second, the US's 'clause-bound' interpretation,[17] has not accommodated 'proportionality analysis' as a general method for analysing the constitutionality of rights limitations, though there are distinct balancing tests in US constitutional law that resemble aspects of proportionality review.[18]

E. Fleming, *Securing Constitutional Democracy* (2006) (arguing that protection of basic liberties subsumed by the idea of autonomy is necessary to democracy); see also, e.g., V.A. Blasi, 'The Pathological Perspective and the First Amendment' (1985) 85 *Colum. L. Rev.* 449 (arguing that in interpreting free speech protections courts should be concerned with possible government pathologies of hostility to speech). Cf. R.E. Barnett, *Restoring the Lost Constitution: The Presumption of Liberty* (Princeton University Press, 2003) (linking certain natural rights to originalist, contractarian claims).

[12] M. Tushnet, 'The United States: Eclecticism in Service of Pragmatism', in J. Goldsworthy (ed.), *Interpreting Constitutions: A Comparative Study* (Oxford University Press, 2006).

[13] See V.C. Jackson, 'Multi-Valenced Constitutional Interpretation and Constitutional Comparisons: An Essay in Honor of Mark Tushnet' (2006) 26 *Quinnipiac L. Rev.* 599.

[14] See, e.g., A. Scalia, 'Originalism: The Lesser Evil' (1989) 57 *U. Cinn. L. Rev.* 849.

[15] *District of Columbia* v. *Heller* 554 US 570 (2008).

[16] 347 US 497 (1954) (extending *Brown*'s ban on state-segregated public schools to Washington, DC, the capital, under federal control).

[17] For critiques of 'clause-bound' approaches that do not consider the entire text, or the structure and relationships established thereby, see, e.g., C.L. Black, *Structure and Relationship in Constitutional Law* (1969); J.H. Ely, *Democracy and Distrust* (1980), 11–41; B. Ackerman, 'Robert Bork's Grand Inquisition' (1990) 99 *Yale L.J.* 1419, 1425–1427; A.R. Amar, 'Intratexualism' (1999) 112 *Harv. L. Rev.* 747, 800–801.

[18] On proportionality, see V.C. Jackson, 'Constitutional Law in an Age of Proportionality' (2015) 124 *Yale L. J.* 3094; J. Greene, 'Foreword, Rights as Trumps?' (2018) 132 *Harv. L. Rev.* 28.

The relationship of judicial interpretation to the constitutional role of other branches has been the subject of at least two major sets of debates over many generations: first, over the role of judicial deference to the positions of other branches and second, over the binding force of final judicial judgments.

On deference, the Court in *Lochner* v. *New York*,[19] controversially, overturned the constitutionality of a New York law limiting bakery workers to no more than ten hours of a work a day, on the ground that it was an unjustified interference in the freedom of contracting. For the next three decades the Court sought to define a line between permissible and impermissible economic regulation, in case law that in some respects paralleled developments in federalism on the scope of national power. In the mid-1930s a crisis arose, with the Supreme Court striking down federal legislation that the President and Congress supported. After the 1936 election, the Supreme Court adopted a different approach, reverting generally to deference to legislatures in reviewing economic legislation.[20] *Carolene Products'* 'footnote 4' was particularly influential in framing the Court's view of its role vis-à-vis other branches over the next several decades. It indicated that: 1) there was less room for deference, or any 'presumption of constitutionality when legislation appears on its face to be within a specific prohibition of the Constitution, such as those of the first ten amendments;' 2) 'more exacting judicial scrutiny' may be called for in reviewing 'legislation which restricts those political processes which can ordinarily be expected to bring about repeal of undesirable legislation', such as restrictions on voting, dissemination of information, political organizations or peaceable assemblies; and 3) 'prejudice against discrete and insular minorities may be a special condition, which tends seriously to curtail the operation of those political processes ordinarily to be relied upon to protect minorities', and might justify heightened judicial scrutiny of 'statutes directed at particular religious, ... or national, ... or racial minorities'.[21] The Warren Court's decisions on reapportionment, religious freedom, racial segregation and criminal procedure rights are sometimes explained within this 'Footnote 4' framework, see Ely (1980), as are its decisions allowing broad scope for federal and state regulation

---

[19] 198 US 45 (1905).
[20] See *West Coast Hotel Co.* v. *Parrish* 300 US 379 (1937) and *United States* v. *Carolene Products Co.* 304 US 144 (1938).
[21] Id. at 152–153, n. 4.

of economic matters. However, by the late twentieth and early twenty-first centuries, the Court was asserting itself in ways that seemed to some scholars to depart from this framework, for example by enhancing protection of 'commercial' speech in regulatory contexts, or by providing heightened scrutiny to laws claimed to disadvantage majority races as well as minorities.

On the bindingness of Supreme Court decisions, debate has moved between polls of 'departmentalism', holding that each of the three branches of the federal government have equal authority to determine what the law is on matters within their jurisdiction, and a 'judicial supremacist' view that the Supreme Court's determinations of issues of federal law are binding on all other constitutional actors. The roots of the latter view can be found as far back as *Marbury* v. *Madison*,[22] in a passage asserting that '[i]t is emphatically the province and duty of the judicial department to say what the law is.' Responding to defiance of lower court desegregation orders following *Brown* v. *Board of Education*, the Court spoke more strongly in *Cooper* v. *Aaron*,[23] asserting that 'the interpretation of the Fourteenth Amendment enunciated by this Court in the *Brown* case is the supreme law of the land', binding on all of the states, even those states not parties to the original *Brown* judgment. An example of the 'departmentalist' position is found in President Andrew Jackson's 1832 veto of a bill to modify and continue the national bank, the constitutionality of which had been upheld by the Supreme Court in *McCulloch* v. *Maryland*.[24] President Jackson's Veto Message stated that even '[i]f the opinion of the Supreme Court covered the whole ground of this act, it ought not to control the coordinate authorities of this Government. The Congress, the Executive, and the Court must each for itself be guided by its own opinion of the Constitution. Each public officer who takes an oath to support the Constitution swears that he will support it as he understands it, and not as it is understood by others.'[25] President Lincoln's First Inaugural Address acknowledged that Supreme Court 'decisions must be binding in any case upon the parties to a suit as to the object of that suit', but argued that although 'entitled to very high

---

[22] 5 US 137, 177 (1803).

[23] 358 US 1, 18 (1958).

[24] 17 US 316 (1819).

[25] President Jackson's Veto Message Regarding the Bank of the United States; 10 July 1832, http://avalon.law.yale.edu/19th_century/ajveto01.asp.

respect and consideration in all parallel cases by all other departments of the Government', they could not 'irrevocably' control 'the policy of the Government upon vital questions affecting the whole people' without threatening self-government.[26] Many 'departmentalists' would agree with Lincoln's distinction between the binding force of a judicial decision to the particular parties and the binding force of the decision on the general issue. The Supreme Court has continued to assert its authority to make final interpretive decisions, see *City of Boerne* v. *Flores*,[27] and its judgments are typically respected by other actors.

3 Regulatory Powers

Supremacy of federal law. The Supremacy Clause of Article VI of the Constitution has been understood since the Founding era to stand for two important propositions: first, that all statutes, state and federal, must conform to the Constitution and second, that all valid federal laws – the Constitution, and also federal statutes and treaties – are supreme over conflicting state laws. The narrative here is one of continuity, from *Marbury* and *McCulloch* through the recent unanimous 2016 decision in *James* v. *City of Boise, Idaho*,[28] which treated the Court's prior interpretation of a civil rights attorney's fee statute as binding on the state courts.

   Scope of Congress's Power to Regulate Commerce: One of the principal additional powers given to the Congress by the Constitution, beyond those held under the prior Articles of Confederation, was the power to 'regulate Commerce with foreign Nations, and among the several States'. There has been both continuity and discontinuity in conceptualization of this power, and much change in application. In early nineteenth-century caselaw the power was described in relatively broad terms.[29] By the late nineteenth and early twentieth century, the Court had developed a variety of tests designed to constrain federal regulation,[30] while also at

---

[26] First Inaugural Address of Abraham Lincoln, 4 March 1861, http://avalon.law.yale.edu/19th_century/lincoln1.asp.

[27] See *City of Boerne* v. *Flores*, 521 US 507, 536 (1997).

[28] 136 S. Ct. 6875 (2016).

[29] See *Gibbons* v. *Ogden* 22 US 1, 195 (1824) (indicating that only commerce which is 'completely internal' to a state, 'which do[es] not affect other States,' is beyond Congress's reach).

[30] See, e.g., *US* v. *E.C. Knight*, 156 US 1 (1895); *Hammer* v. *Dagenhart*, 247 US 251 (1918) (holding that the federal Commerce Power cannot be exercised if the goal is to affect production, which is exclusively for the states to regulate); *Carter* v. *Carter Coal*, 298 US 238 (1936) (to similar effect).

times constraining state regulation under the due process clause (as in *Lochner*). In the late 1930s, the Court moved towards a more 'realistic', effects-oriented test, one that eschewed categorical limits on the scope of the commerce power based on the nature of the activity,[31] arguably returning to the broader framing of cases like *Gibbons*. This approach controlled until 1995, when the Court began reinvigorating limits on Congress's power in a categorical way, denying it authority to regulate 'non-economic' activity that affects commerce only through an aggregation of effects, see *United States* v. *Lopez*;[32] *United States* v. *Morrison*,[33] or the power to require persons to engage in commercial transactions, *NFIB* v. *Sebelius*.[34] As this brief discussion suggests, during the last 150 years the Court has veered between resistance and deference towards new forms of regulation.

'Dormant' Commerce Clause: The grant of power to the federal government to regulate certain forms of commerce was early on viewed as creating a sphere of exclusive federal power, in which states were not free to regulate at all. The dividing line under such a view assumed great importance. By the mid-nineteenth century, however, the Court was developing a more nuanced view, one that treated only some aspects of federal power as necessarily exclusive and larger aspects as presumptively concurrent.[35] Well into the later part of the nineteenth century, however, there was uncertainty whether the Constitution's allocation of exclusive competence was unchangeable by Congress, leaving somewhat unclear Congress' authority to authorize state regulation of areas otherwise deemed within exclusive federal competence. However, by the mid-twentieth century the Court came to regard Congress as having the power to authorize such state regulation, treating the Commerce Clause's effect on state legislative competence as creating a default rule, administered by the Court, subject to change by Congress. Thus, for example, although the Court held that states could not exclude waste product from other states, *Philadelphia* v. *New Jersey*,[36]

---

[31] See, e.g., *NLRB* v. *Jones & Laughlin Steel Corp.*, 301 US 1 (1937); *Wickard* v. *Filburn*, 317 US 111 (1942). The Court likewise relaxed prior due process based constraints on economic regulation by states. See, e.g., *West Coast Hotel Co.* v. *Parrish*, 300 US 379 (1937).

[32] 514 US 549 (1995).

[33] 529 US 598 (2000).

[34] 567 US 519 (2012).

[35] See, e.g., *Cooley* v. *Bd of Wardens*, 53 US 299 (1851).

[36] 437 US 617 (1978).

it upheld federal legislation providing special permission under certain conditions for states to do precisely that, see *New York* v. *United States*.[37]

Federalism and 'States Rights': Although the Constitution's proponents argued that enumerating powers of the national government would preserve areas for exclusive regulation by the states, many contemporary scholars doubt its effectiveness in so doing. In the early twentieth century Louis Brandeis extolled states as laboratories of democratic experimentation,[38] but to the extent that federal law has grown (with its potential preemptive force on state law under the Supremacy Clause), the possibility of conflict between federal and state law has also grown. In the last twenty-five years the Court has developed doctrine on what has been called the 'etiquette of federalism',[39] under which certain methods of promoting state compliance with federal law are found to be prohibited by unwritten structural elements of the federal system. Thus, beginning in *New York* v. *United States*,[40] the Court developed an 'anti-commandeering' doctrine prohibiting federal statutes from *requiring* state legislatures or executive officials to carry out federal statutory directives. The Court reasoned that Congress may authorize direct federal regulation of private persons but may not coerce states to implement the regulation for the federal government, although federal grants to the states may be conditioned on states voluntarily agreeing to certain requirements (including enactment of legislation).[41] Moreover, the scope of states' immunity from suit under otherwise valid federal law has expanded.[42]

From Laboratories of Democracy to Code for Racism and Beyond? The valence of 'states' rights' in US federalism has shifted dramatically – for example, from Brandeis's progressive 'laboratories of experimentation', to organized resistance to desegregation and racial equality, and recently, to a more complex picture in which some states have positioned themselves

---

[37] 505 US 144 (1992).

[38] *New State Ice Co.* v. *Liebmann*, 285 US 262, 311 (1932) (Brandeis, J., dissenting).

[39] See M.D. Adler and S.F. Kreimer, 'The New Etiquette of Federalism' (1998) *Sup. Ct. Rev.* 71, 72.

[40] 505 US 144 (1992); see also *Printz* v. *United States*, 521 US 898 (1997). For a recent decision, arguably expanding the doctrine, see *Murphy* v. *National Collegiate Athletic Ass'n*, 138 S. Ct. 1461 (2018).

[41] See, e.g. *New York* v. *United States*, 505 US 144 (1992); see also *NFIB* v. *Sebelius*, 567 US 519 (2012) (finding that a new condition for state receipt of federal Medicaid funds was coercive, not voluntary).

[42] See, e.g., *Seminole Tribe of Florida* v. *Florida*, 517 US 44 (1996).

in opposition to the party in power in the White House, including in the bringing of litigation.[43]

4 Rights

US constitutional law has a very large body of caselaw dealing with rights, including rights under the First Amendment (dealing with speech, association, the press and religion), the Fourth Amendment (protection from unreasonable searches and seizures), and the Fifth and Fourteenth Amendments (embodying principles of equal treatment by governments and due process of law). The Constitution also provides that takings of property must be for a public purpose and accompanied by just compensation, and prohibits laws impairing the obligation of contracts. In addition, the Constitution protects a number of other specific procedural rights primarily in the criminal process, including rights to counsel and to confront (and cross-examine) witnesses, rights against compelled self-incrimination and double jeopardy, and prohibitions on ex post facto or bill of attainder laws. Additional rights exist, but the main point is that the jurisprudence is so vast it eludes summary here.

Accordingly, the discussion below will focus on only a small number of issue areas, which have been the focus of considerable caselaw or recent controversy and which illustrate some of the distinctive features and concerns, including federalism, of US constitutional rights jurisprudence. As noted earlier, US constitutional rights have been developed in a somewhat siloed, or 'clause-bound', manner, making accurate general statements across all rights areas more difficult.

Criminal Procedure: Increasing attention to criminal procedure rights began in the early part of the twentieth century, with the Court occasionally applying the due process clause to condemn trials infected by fear of mob violence;[44] the use of coercion to obtain confessions;[45] and trials of indigents without counsel.[46] In some of these cases, concern for racially

---

[43] See, e.g., J. Bulman-Pozen, 'Partisan Federalism' (2014) 127 *Harv. L. Rev.* 1077.

[44] *Moore* v. *Dempsey*, 261 US 86 (1923).

[45] See, e.g., *Brown* v. *Mississippi*, 297 US 278 (1936); *Chambers* v. *Florida*, 309 US 227 (1940); see also *Rogers* v. *Richmond*, 365 US 534 (1961) ('convictions following the admission into evidence of confessions which are involuntary, i.e., the product of coercion, either physical or psychological, cannot stand').

[46] *Powell* v. *Alabama*, 287 US 45 (1932); see also *Gideon* v. *Wainright*, 372 US 335 (1963).

unjust systems of criminal prosecution may have influenced the development of criminal procedure rights. Constitutional criminal procedure law's development is related to both the 'incorporation' debate and the opening and closure of constitutional law to affirmative obligations to the poor.

Gideon v. *Wainright* (1963) illustrates both. In a pre-Civil War decision,[47] the Court had held that the Bill of Rights' procedural protections applied only to the federal and not to the state governments. Over time, the Fourteenth Amendment has had a transformative effect on the application of constitutional rights to the states. In *Gideon*, the Court held that the Due Process Clause of the Fourteenth Amendment, applicable to the states, necessarily incorporates the Sixth Amendment right to the assistance of counsel.[48] (Although the Court had previously held that in federal criminal prosecutions counsel must be provided for indigent defendants on their request,[49] it had denied that this rule applied in *state* criminal cases.[50]) In *Gideon*, the Court reasoned that the Sixth Amendment right to counsel in criminal cases was of such fundamental importance to a fair trial in the US adversary system that it should be applied (or 'incorporated' as) to the states by the Due Process Clause of the Fourteenth Amendment, overruling contrary authority.[51]

Although the right of compensation for takings of property was incorporated early,[52] in the first part of the twentieth century the Court had rejected arguments that various criminal procedure rights were incorporated against the states by the Due Process Clause.[53] For decades the Court applied the Fourteenth Amendment's due process clause based on the 'totality of the facts', determined case-by-case in review of state criminal convictions.[54] Gradually, however, the Court began to 'selectively incorporate' specific protections into the Fourteenth Amendment's

---

[47] *Barron* v. *Baltimore*, 32 US 243, 250 (1833).

[48] *Gideon* v. *Wainright*, 372 US 335 (1963).

[49] *Johnson* v. *Zerbst*, 304 US 458 (1938).

[50] *Betts* v. *Brady*, 316 US 455, 473 (1942).

[51] *Gideon*, 372 US at 345 (overruling *Betts*).

[52] See *Chicago, B. & Q. R. Co.* v. *Chicago,* 166 US 226 (1897) (treating such compensation as an essential element of due process).

[53] See, e.g., *Twining* v. *New Jersey*, 211 US 78 (1908) (denying that federal constitutional protection from compelled self-incrimination applies as against the states).

[54] See, e.g., *Betts* v. *Brady*, 316 US 455, 462 (1942) ('Asserted denial [of due process to criminal defendant] is to be tested by an appraisal of the totality of facts in a given case;' denying defendant's constitutional challenge to the failure to appoint counsel to represent him at trial); *Powell* v. *Alabama*, 287 US 45, 71 (1932) (reversing conviction and death sentence of black defendant, holding that 'in a capital case, where the defendant

due process clause, including virtually all of the criminal procedure protections. In addition to *Gideon*, see, for example, *Mapp* v. *Ohio*,[55] which overruled an earlier decision and applied the Fourth Amendment exclusionary rule to state court criminal trials, or *Duncan* v. *Louisiana*,[56] which held that jury trial rights extended to a category of state court criminal trials.

Second, *Gideon* held that where an indigent defendant in a felony case requests an attorney but cannot afford one, the trial court must appoint counsel.[57] The Court's opinion emphasized that without an attorney, a poor person cannot have as fair a trial as one wealthy enough to hire an attorney. The 'noble ideal' that 'every defendant stands equal before the law', the Court wrote, 'cannot be realized if the poor man charged with crime has to face his accusers without a lawyer to assist him'.[58]

Poverty: In *Gideon* and other mid-twentieth-century cases,[59] the Court seemed open to creating a jurisprudence requiring affirmative measures to assure fair process to the poor. In *Harper* v. *Va. State Bd of Elections*,[60] the Court found unconstitutional a poll tax on voting in state elections, reasoning that '[w]ealth, like race, creed, or color, is not germane to one's ability to participate intelligently in the electoral process', and stating that '[l]ines drawn on the basis of wealth or property, like those of race … are traditionally disfavored'. These cases led some to believe that the Court would more generally engage in heightened review of laws claimed to disadvantage people based on their poverty. However, by the early 1970s the Court made clear it was not willing to treat adverse effects on the poor as generally triggering heightened review.[61]

Racial equality: Brown v. *Board of Education*.[62] Slavery had some degree of protection in the original Constitution. The 'fugitive slave'

is unable to employ counsel, and is incapable adequately of making his own defense because of ignorance, feeble-mindedness, illiteracy, or the like, it is the duty of the court, whether requested or not, to assign counsel for him as a necessary requisite of due process of law').

[55] 367 US 643 (1961) (overruling *Wolf.* v. *Colorado*, 338 US 25 (1949)).

[56] 391 US 145 (1968) (holding that right to a jury trial extended to state criminal trials for serious offences, including those carrying a punishment of up to two years in prison).

[57] *Gideon* v. *Wainright*, 372 US 335, 344 (1963).

[58] Id.

[59] See, e.g., *Griffin* v. *Illinois* 351 US 12 (1956) (requiring that if a transcript is needed to take an appeal as of right the state must enable indigents to obtain such transcripts).

[60] 383 US 663, 668 (1966).

[61] See *Dandridge* v. *Williams*, 397 US 471 (1970); *San Antonio Indep. Sch. School Dist.* v. *Rodriguez,* 411 US 1 (1973).

[62] 347 US 483 (1954).

clause required the return of runaway slaves. The 'three-fifths' clause counted 'Persons' who are not 'free' as three-fifths of a person for purposes of apportioning seats in the House of Representatives, thereby increasing the power of white slave-owners in those states maintaining slavery. The Court's early caselaw on racial equality condemned state laws that prohibited black persons from serving on juries,[63] but, in *Plessy* v. *Ferguson*,[64] the Court upheld state laws requiring the separation of the 'white and colored races' on public conveyances.[65] The *Plessy* decision opened the doors to a massive hierarchical system of racial segregation – separate water fountains, separate seating, separate schools.

After successful challenges to particular graduate programmes that separated white and black students (including by paying the tuition of black students at out-of-state schools) on the grounds that under the circumstances such separation did not treat blacks and whites equally,[66] the Supreme Court accepted a head-on challenge to racial segregation and ruled it unconstitutional, in the context of public education, in *Brown* v. *Bd of Education*. Historical evidence of the specific intended meaning of the Fourteenth Amendment was 'inconclusive', the Court found, and it 'cannot turn the clock back to 1868, when the Fourteenth Amendment was adopted, or even to 1896 when *Plessy* v. *Ferguson* was written.'[67] By 1954, it emphasized, education was the most important function of state and local government, and the 'segregation of children in public schools solely on the basis of race, even though the physical facilities and other "tangible" factors may be equal, deprive[s] the children of the minority group of equal educational opportunities.'[68] Although *Brown* rested in part on the importance of public education, it was rapidly extended to ban segregation in public transportation and other public facilities. But not until 1967, in *Loving* v. *Virginia*,[69] did the Court hold that state laws prohibiting interracial marriage violated the Equal Protection Clause; the Court's delay is widely attributed to the massive resistance in several southern states to allowing implementation of the *Brown* ruling.

---

[63] *Strauder* v. *West Virginia*, 100 US 303 (1879).

[64] 163 US 537 (1896).

[65] Id. at 540.

[66] See *Missouri ex rel Gaines* v. *Canada*, 305 US 377 (1938); *Sweatt* v. *Painter*, 339 US 629 (1950).

[67] *Brown*, 347 US at 489, 492.

[68] Id. at 493–495.

[69] 388 US 1, 7–12 (1967).

Segregation laws such as those at issue in *Brown* and *Loving* made explicit reference to race. But with respect to laws that do not use an explicitly racial criteria, the Court has held that the Equal Protection Clause treats as presumptively invalid *only* those government actions intended to discriminate by race. In some cases, the Court has readily inferred a racially invidious intent.[70] In most contemporary cases, however, outright reference to racial motives is less common. And unlike in some legal systems that consider both 'effects' and 'purpose' in constitutionally evaluating laws claimed to discriminate, the US Court will not infer a racially discriminatory motive (and hence, the need for strict scrutiny) even from a significant disproportionate effect in the use of a purportedly neutral criteria: 'neutral' criteria that have a disparate adverse effect on a racial minority, or on women, are not, as such, treated as 'suspect' for purposes of the standard of review under the Equal Protection clause.[71] Even showing that government decision-makers were *aware* of the adverse effect on racial minorities or one sex but continued use of the criteria does not necessarily lead to heightened scrutiny.[72] Unless a discriminatory purpose is shown, facially neutral laws challenged for their disparate effects will be upheld as long as there is any rational basis for use of the criteria. These holdings have been subject to vigorous critique, but the jurisprudence has remained unchanged.

However, any use of an explicitly racial criterion will trigger 'strict' scrutiny; the use does not have to be invidious or malign in character, nor need it target a racial minority. In a series of challenges to affirmative action plans, the Court has held that strict scrutiny must be applied

---

[70] See, e.g., *Hunter* v. *Underwood*, 471 US 222 (1985) (invalidating state constitutional provision dating to 1901 disenfranchising those convicted of offenses such as vagrancy, in light of evidence that the intent of the law was to exclude blacks from voting); *Yick Wo* v. *Hopkins*, 118 US 356 (1886) (finding that municipal ordinance was unconstitutionally applied to deny only persons of Chinese descent permission to run laundries in wooden buildings while allowing the operation in wooden buildings of laundries operated by those of other races). Cf. *Smith* v. *Allwright*, 321 US 649 (1944) (concluding that Texas laws permitting state political parties to organize themselves, determine their own membership, and hold primaries, violated the Fifteenth Amendment's ban on race discrimination in voting when the Texas Democratic party excluded African Americans from voting).

[71] A different approach is followed under some federal civil rights statutes, including Title VII. See *Griggs* v. *Duke Power Co.*, 401 US 424 (1971).

[72] See *Washington* v. *Davis*, 426 US 229 (1976) (rejecting challenge to civil service exam that disproportionately disadvantaged black applicants for the police in Washington D.C.); *Personnel Adm'r of Mass* v. *Feeney*, 442 US 256 (1979).

regardless of whether the purpose of the racial consideration is to injure or assist previously disadvantaged groups.[73] It is thus easier to justify and sustain a facially neutral programme with disproportionate adverse impacts on racial minorities than it is to justify and sustain a programme that explicitly takes race into account in an effort to promote more diverse state schools.[74]

Equal Protection, Substantive Due Process and Standards of Review: The Court's decision in *Brown* did not refer to or articulate a 'standard of review', although in *Korematsu* v. *United States*,[75] an infamous World War II era case upholding the federal government's internment of citizens having Japanese ancestry, the Court had said that 'all legal restrictions which curtail the civil rights of a single racial group are immediately suspect'. By the early 1970s, the Court had made clear that racial classifications that injured minority group members were presumptively unconstitutional, and could be sustained only by meeting the rigorous requirements of 'strict scrutiny'. By 1976, in *Craig* v. *Boren*,[76] the Court settled on a standard of 'intermediate scrutiny' for sex classifications, having recently rejected a gender preference among persons of equal relation in designating executors for intestate decedents as unconstitutional,[77] and a law that assumed that service members' wives, but not husbands, were dependents for purposes of certain benefits.[78] Intermediate scrutiny requires an important (though not necessarily compelling) purpose and the use of means that are 'substantially related' to achieving that purpose (rather than being 'narrowly tailored' to do so). Both 'strict scrutiny' for racial classifications and 'intermediate scrutiny' for sex classifications

---

[73] See, e.g., *Adarand Constructors, Inc.* v. *Pena*, 515 US 200 (1996) (challenge by unsuccessful nonminority bidders on government contracts that their equal opportunity to work for the government was impaired by measures designed to favour minority-owned businesses); *Gratz* v. *Michigan*, 539 US 244 (2003) (challenge by unsuccessful white student-applicants arguing that affirmative action programs for racial minority students had denied them equal opportunities for admission at public universities); cf. *Regents, University of California* v. *Bakke*, 438 US 265 (1978) (in challenge by white student of a set aside of seats for minority applicants, Justices split on standard of review but struck down the programme).

[74] See, e.g., R. Siegel, 'Foreword: Equality Divided' (2013) 127 *Harv. L. Rev.* 1 (discussing 'restricting minority-protective equal protection review' and 'expanding majority-protective equal protection review').

[75] 323 US 214, 216 (1944).

[76] 429 US 190 (1976).

[77] *Reed* v. *Reed*, 404 US 71 (1971).

[78] *Frontiero* v. *Richardson*, 411 US 677 (1973).

stand in marked contrast to the 'rational basis' form of review adopted for most areas of regulation in *Carolene Products*, discussed above. However, the standards of strict scrutiny can be met, as they were in *Grutter* v. *Bollinger*[79] and *Fisher* v. *Univ. of Texas at Austin*,[80] in both of which the Court upheld affirmative action plans that took explicit account, albeit in limited ways, of race.

An example of 'rational basis' review is found in *N.Y.C. Transit Auth.* v. *Beazer*,[81] which held that banning all methadone users from employment in the city transportation system was rationally related to safety objectives and thus constitutional, even though the rule was broader than necessary in light of evidence that, after one year, methadone users had safety records equivalent to other drivers. Likewise, in *Armour* v. *City of Indianapolis*,[82] the Court upheld, as rational, a municipal decision to completely forgive outstanding taxes on sewer line hookups paid on an instalment basis but providing no credit to taxpayers who had paid in full at the outset for the same service. On rare occasion the Court has applied 'rational basis with bite', for example, in *Plyler* v. *Doe*,[83] holding that a rational person would require a stronger reason to impose hardship on innocent children and thus striking down a Texas law forbidding undocumented non-citizen children from receiving a free public education. More typically, rational basis review has been highly deferential.

In deciding what 'liberties' are subject to high levels of protection, the influence of the '*Lochner*' decision should be noted. *Lochner* treated as substantively protected from regulation the freedom of contracting, a nontextual right read into the liberty protected by the Due Process Clause. Although *Lochner* became an 'anti-canonical' cases for most jurists, its existence has not precluded recognition of other atextual rights as fundamental substantive aspects of the liberty protected by the Fifth and Fourteenth Amendments. These include, inter alia, rights of parents to control the upbringing of their children,[84] rights to live with extended family members,[85] rights of pregnant women to terminate their pregnancies,[86]

---

[79] 539 US 306 (2003).

[80] 136 S Ct 2198 (2016).

[81] 440 US 568 (1979).

[82] 566 US 673 (2012).

[83] 457 US 202 (1982).

[84] *Pierce* v. *Society of Sisters*, 268 US 510 (1925).

[85] *Moore* v. *City of East Cleveland*, 431 US 494 (1977).

[86] *Roe* v. *Wade*, 410 US 113 (1973).

rights to marry,[87] and rights of sexual intimacy.[88] Claimed intrusions on other liberties, relating to business activities, for example, are generally subject to review under a more relaxed 'rational basis' standard (whether they are challenged under the equal protection clause or as a matter of substantive due process).

By the end of the Warren Court, doctrine indicated that if a law or government action used a 'suspect' classification, such as race, or if a classification trenched upon a 'fundamental right', like the right to vote, it would need to be justified by a compelling government interest and be narrowly tailored, or the least restrictive alternative, towards achieving that goal. However, in recent years the clarity and significance of this approach has diminished, with the Court retreating from strict scrutiny in voting rights cases,[89] and abortion rights cases.[90] Moreover, while the Court continues to apply strict scrutiny to evaluate overt racial classifications, and intermediate scrutiny to evaluate overt sex discriminations, no new 'suspect' classifications as such have been recognized in recent years. In constitutional cases challenging sexual orientation discrimination between 1996 and 2003, the Court seemed deliberately to avoid the standard-of-review issue while at the same time shifting ground to extend the protections of equal protection and due process; most recently, it held that states could not deny to same-sex couples the 'fundamental' right to marry.[91]

Ten years after rejecting a constitutional challenge to a criminal sodomy law in *Bowers* v. *Hardwick*,[92] the Court, in *Romer* v. *Evan*,[93] held unconstitutional a state constitutional amendment that prohibited the enactment or application of any anti-discrimination legislation to protect persons from discrimination based on their sexual orientation. Such a law was explainable only on the basis of dislike of homosexuals, the Court said. Although a legislative classification that 'neither burdens a fundamental right nor targets a suspect class, ... [will be upheld] so long

[87] See *Loving* v. *Virginia*, 388 US 1, 12 (1967); *Obergefell* v. *Hodges*, 135 S Ct 2584 (2015).
[88] See *Lawrence* v. *Texas*, 539 US 558 (2003).
[89] See e.g., *Burdick* v. *Takashi*, 504 US 428 (1992) (rejecting a challenge to restrictions on write-in voting).
[90] See, e.g., *Planned Parenthood of SE Pennsylvania* v. *Casey*, 505 US 833 (1992) (permitting certain state regulation of abortion decisions before viability as long no 'undue' burden is imposed on the pregnant woman's decision to terminate the pregnancy).
[91] *Obergefell* v. *Hodges*, 135 S Ct 2584 (2015).
[92] 478 US 186 (1986).
[93] 517 US 620 (1996).

as it bears a rational relation to some legitimate end,' the Colorado law, the Court reasoned, 'fails, indeed defies, even this conventional inquiry,' because it 'impos[es] a broad and undifferentiated disability on a single named group,' whose 'sheer breadth is so discontinuous with the reasons offered for it that the amendment seems inexplicable by anything but animus toward the class it affects.'[94] Animus towards a group, the Court held, does not pass rational basis review: 'It is not within our constitutional tradition to enact laws of this sort. Central both to the idea of the rule of law and to our own Constitution's guarantee of equal protection is the principle that government and each of its parts remain open on impartial terms to all who seek its assistance.'[95] Because the law failed rational basis review, there was no need to resolve whether sexual orientation was a suspect classification.

In *Lawrence* v. *Texas*,[96] the Court overruled *Bowers*, concluding that states could not impose criminal sanctions on private, consensual, sexual activity between persons of the same sex. The majority found this to be an unconstitutional intrusion on the liberty protected by the Due Process Clause, linking the issue to questions of marriage and procreation that the Court had previously found protected, treating *Bowers* as having misunderstood and demeaned the liberty claim presented there. As the dissenters point out, however, the majority did not assert a fundamental right to engage in certain forms of sexual conduct, thereby eliding the fundamental rights/ordinary liberty line suggested by earlier cases.[97] Justice O'Connor wrote separately, arguing that the Texas law was unconstitutional on equal protection grounds, insofar as it treated the same sexual acts performed by two persons of the same sex differently than if performed by two persons of the opposite sex.[98] She applied 'rational basis review', while suggesting that when classifications inhibit personal relationships, rational basis review is more likely to lead to invalidation.[99] And she avoided deciding '[w]hether a sodomy law that is neutral both in effect and application ... would violate the substantive component of the Due Process Clause', expressing confidence 'that so long as the Equal

---

[94] Id. at 631–632.
[95] Id. at 633.
[96] 539 US 558 (2003).
[97] Id. at 586 (Scalia, J., dissenting).
[98] Id. at 578 (O'Connor, J., concurring in the judgment).
[99] Id. at 580.

Protection Clause requires a sodomy law to apply equally to the private consensual conduct of homosexuals and heterosexuals alike, such a law would not long stand in our democratic society.'[100]

The overlap between equal protection and substantive liberty claims is suggested by this passage in the majority opinion in *Lawrence*: 'Equality of treatment and the due process right to demand respect for conduct protected by the substantive guarantees of liberty are linked in important respects ... When homosexual conduct is made criminal by the laws of the State, that declaration in and of itself is an invitation to subject homosexual persons to discrimination both in the public and in the private spheres.'[101] The majority overruled *Bowers*, whose 'continuance as precedent demeans the lives of homosexual persons'.[102]

Twelve years later, *Obergefell* v. *Hodges* concluded that the right to marry is a 'fundamental' one that same-sex couples cannot be denied.[103] Refusing to limit the substantive protections of the Due Process Clause to specific versions of rights recognized by tradition,[104] the Court rejected arguments that same-sex marriage would depreciate opposite-sex marriage as resting on a 'counterintuitive' set of ideas about the 'personal, romantic and practical considerations' that motivate couples to marry.[105] Again noting the 'interlocking' nature of the guarantees of equal protection and substantive liberty, but without explicit discussion of the standard of review, the Court found the state's limits on the right to marry violated both the liberty protected by the due process clause and the guarantee of equal protection of the law.[106]

Abortion and same-sex intimacy cases both raised questions about the Court's role in protecting newly-framed rights asserted under capaciously worded constitutional texts, generating considerable debate over criteria for determining what claimed liberties are 'fundamental'. In both lines of cases, dissenters accused majorities of making *Lochner*-esque errors.

[100] Id. at 584–585.
[101] Id. at 575 (Kennedy, J., for the Court).
[102] Id.
[103] 135 S.Ct. 2584, 2604 (2015).
[104] Id. at 2782 (noting but rejecting in this context caselaw indicating that 'liberty under the Due Process Clause must be defined in a most circumscribed manner, with central reference to specific historical practices'); see K. Yoshino, 'A New Birth of Freedom? *Obergefell* v. *Hodges*' (2015) 129 *Harv. L. Rev.* 147.
[105] 135 S.Ct. at 2607.
[106] Id. at 2604.

Scholars as well as judges have vigorously debated these questions, which are enduring ones, across generations and subject areas.

5 US Exceptionalism?

A much mooted topic is the degree to which US constitutional law is 'exceptional'. The US Constitution, to be sure, does not include provisions for positive social rights. Moreover, the Supreme Court's present conception of the right not be deprived of life, liberty or property without due process of law does not generally impose justiciable obligations on governments to prevent violent harm.[107] In these respects US constitutional law differs from that of some other constitutional democracies and bears the imprint of its eighteenth-century Founding era rather than of more recent periods of constitutional change in the world. I touch on three other topics here: the death penalty; freedom of expression; and the right to bear arms.

US constitutional law permits imposing the death penalty for a limited group of crimes committed by adults; the death penalty cannot, for example, be imposed for the rape of a child that did not result in and was not intended to result in death.[108] Litigation over the constitutionality of the death penalty under the Eighth Amendment's ban on 'cruel and unusual punishments' has frequently invoked the law of other countries. In *Roper* v. *Simmons*,[109] the Court held that the death penalty could not constitutionally be applied to a person who was a juvenile (that is, below the age of 18) at the time of the murder for which he was convicted. The Court referred to foreign and international law, described the United States as 'now stand[ing] alone in a world that has turned its face against the juvenile death penalty' and acknowledged the relevance of 'the overwhelming weight of international opinion against the juvenile death penalty'.[110] Most of the Court's opinion, however, was devoted to analysis of the trend in the states, the maturity and moral culpability of a juvenile, and its own independent evaluation of the 'proportionality' of the death penalty for particular crimes or classes of offenders. Interestingly, the majority

---

[107] See, e.g., *Deshaney* v. *Winnebgao Cty. Soc'l Serv. Dept*, 489 US 189 (1989); *Town of Castle Rock* v. *Gonzalez*, 545 US 748 (2005).

[108] *Kennedy* v. *Louisiana*, 554 US 407 (2008).

[109] 543 US 551 (2005).

[110] Id. at 577–578.

rejected Justice O'Connor's argument for a case-by-case analysis of the death penalty's proportionality for juveniles, adopting a bright-line rule.[111] The death penalty may be imposed on adults found to have committed murder, provided the state specifies criteria for the decisionmaker to use to limit the death penalty only to the most heinous of those crimes and also affords sufficient discretion for the decisionmaker to make an individualized decision taking into account the particular defendant's circumstances.[112] Notwithstanding these procedural requirements for its use, the death penalty has been subject to widespread criticism as inequitable and arbitrary, in part because of the uneven and frequently poor quality of counsel for indigent capital defendants.[113]

On freedom of expression, the US caselaw embodies some distinctions that are echoed in free speech jurisprudence elsewhere. For example, it has emphasized the importance of protecting freedom of political expression, as in *New York Times* v. *Sullivan*,[114] although in recent years it has focused considerable attention on protecting commercial speech, see, e.g., *Cent. Hudson Gas & Elec. Corp.* v. *Pub. Serv. Comm'n of New York*;[115] *44 Liquormart* v. *Rhode Island*,[116] and campaign contributions (based on the link between money and political speech), see *Citizens United* v. *Fed. Election Comm'n*.[117] It has allowed more latitude for 'time, place, and manner' limitations (e.g., no noisy amplifiers late at night in residential neighbourhoods) than for prohibitions of speech based on content. Although the Court sometimes articulates a close to absolute rule against 'content based regulation', there are permissible forms of 'content' regulation of speech; for example, compelled disclosures in connection with securities offerings, prohibitions on fraud, prohibitions on pornography or on obscene material marketed to children.

---

[111] For her dissenting opinion, see id. at 587 (O'Connor, J., dissenting).

[112] See *Gregg* v. *Georgia*, 428 US 153 (1976); *Lockett* v. *Ohio*, 438 US 586 (1978).

[113] See, e.g., C.S. Steiker and J.M. Steiker, 'Sober Second Thoughts: Reflections on Two Decades of Constitutional Regulation of Capital Punishment' (1995) 109 *Harv. L. Rev.* 355, 398–399.

[114] 376 US 254 (1964) (holding that common law liability for defamation could not constitutionally be imposed on a newspaper that published an advertisement critiquing official conduct in the absence of a showing of a knowing or deliberately indifferent a falsehood).

[115] 447 US 557, 561 (1980).

[116] 517 US 44 (1996); see also *Sorrell* v. *IMS Health Inc.*, 564 US 552 (2011).

[117] 558 US 310 (2010).

But it is also true that the United States at times treats free speech rights as close to absolute, although intrusions on speech may in theory be justified under 'strict scrutiny'. The Court has a very strong presumption against the constitutionality of governmentally-imposed 'prior restraints' on speech, thus holding, in the *Pentagon Papers Case*,[118] that a lower court had erred in enjoining publication of leaked, classified documents about the Vietnam war, leaving open the possibility of a later criminal prosecution of the newspaper for the publication.[119]

Another area in which the seeming absolutism of the US jurisprudence has been remarked upon is its approach to regulation of hate speech. *In R.A.V. v. St. Paul*,[120] the Court held unconstitutional a statute prohibiting the placing of objects, including a burning cross or swastika, on property knowing that it would arouse anger, alarm or resentment based on race, colour, creed, religion or gender. The majority assumed that the statute was limited only to 'fighting words', that is, words 'which by their very utterance inflict injury or tend to incite an immediate breach of peace', which ordinarily can be prohibited.[121] However, the Court invalidated the statute because it made content- and viewpoint-based distinctions, which could be avoided by a more broadly drawn ban; the content-based distinction was between fighting words on the specified subjects of race etc., and other fighting words; the viewpoint distinction was between pro- and anti-tolerance speech.[122] The Court's vigilance in protecting hateful speech is a noteworthy feature of other recent cases as well,[123] as is the high standard it has imposed to uphold laws limiting campaign contributions and its narrow conception of what constitutes corruption.[124] As noted earlier, the United States has not adopted proportionality review as a general approach to evaluating the permissibility of rights-infringing actions.

[118] *New York Times Co.* v. *United States*, 403 US 713 (1971).
[119] See id. at 730 (Stewart, J., concurring); id. at 733 (White, J., concurring).
[120] 505 US 377 (1992).
[121] *See id.* at 380 (quoting *Chaplinsky* v. *New Hampshire,* 315 US 568, 572 (1942)).
[122] The prohibition of more speech is an unusual application of strict scrutiny's narrow tailoring requirement. See also id. at 401 (White, J., concurring in the judgment).
[123] See, e.g., *Snyder* v. *Phelps*, 562 US 443 (2011) (invalidating as an unconstitutional intrusion on free speech an award of damages against a religious group that picketed a soldier's funeral, hailing the death as a sign of divine punishment for US tolerance of homosexuality).
[124] See *Citizens United* v. *Fed. Election Comm'n.*, 558 US 310 (2010).

US jurisprudence on defamation in matters of public concern also reflects an especially speech-protective approach: government officials and public figures may not recover for defamation unless they can show that the defendants acted with knowledge of the falsity of what they were reporting or in reckless disregard of the truth; mere negligence in reporting cannot give rise to liability. The reasons behind this rule include concerns that erroneous statements are inevitable in vigorous public debate and that political speech can easily be chilled by threat of tort liability, as well as a 'profound national commitment to the principle that debate on public issues should be uninhibited, robust, and wide-open'.[125] Some have argued that such hardiness comes more easily to members of an empowered majority than to members of minority groups that have suffered persecution.

On the right to bear arms, the quite unusual constitutional text of the Second Amendment states: 'A well regulated Militia, being necessary to the security of a free State, the right of the people to keep and bear Arms, shall not be infringed.' In *United States* v. *Miller*,[126] a constitutional challenge to a federal law banning a particular kind of rifle was rejected, the Court concluding that the rifle bore no relation to having a militia and thus there was no Second Amendment right at issue. But almost seventy years later, in *District of Columbia* v. *Heller*,[127] the Court, rejecting the link to the militia emphasized in *Miller*, concluded that the original meaning of the Second Amendment had to be determined based only on its 'operative clause' (beginning 'the right of the people'), without regard to the prefatory clause's statement of purpose. Justice Scalia has written that the purpose of written constitutions is to 'obstruct modernity', but this decision made some wonder if the Constitution could have been intended to weaponize modernity. Nonetheless, the opinion made clear that some regulation of firearms would be upheld, for example, 'prohibitions on carrying concealed weapons ... possession of firearms by felons and the mentally ill, ... carrying of firearms in sensitive places such as schools and government buildings, or laws imposing conditions and qualifications on the commercial sale of arms.'[128]

---

[125] *New York Times* v. *Sullivan*, 376 US 254, 270 (1964). For critique of US law on defamatory speech against public figures, see, e.g., *Hill* v. *Church of Scientology of Toronto*, [1995] 2 S.C.R. 1130, paras. 127–138 (Can.).

[126] 307 US 174 (1939).

[127] 554 US 570 (2008).

[128] Id. at 626–627. For the Scalia quote above, see A. Scalia, 'Modernity and the Constitution', in E. Smith (ed.), *Constitutional Justice Under Old Constitutions* (Kluwer Law International, 1995).

Conclusion: Constitutional Crises and towards the Future

The US Constitution has survived challenging political times. In 1800 the national election was very contested; it was ultimately decided after many votes in the Congress and ended with the Federalist Party losing power. Power was transferred, peacefully, based on the election results, though with some significant challenges to the authority of the courts. The Civil War was an enormous crisis, culminating in immense violence and loss of life and threatening dissolution of the Union. It was resolved by military force and included multiple forms of constitutional crises, including the near removal from office of President Andrew Johnson (who had been Lincoln's vice-president and assumed office upon Lincoln's assassination). In 1876, there was another deeply contested election, which Congress opted to have resolved by a specially created commission (in contrast to Congress itself resolving contests over electoral votes, as apparently contemplated by the Constitution). The ultimate decision gave the election to the Republican candidate but this was followed by the removal of federal troops from the South, with ensuing losses in gains that freed slaves had made in moving towards full citizenship.

In the twentieth century, many thought that President Franklin Roosevelt's proposal to expand the Supreme Court amounted to a serious threat to judicial independence; the issue was fiercely contested. Shortly thereafter the Supreme Court's jurisprudence shifted to a more generous understanding of government power to regulate the economy, thereby averting pressures for significant change in the structure of the Court. In the 1950s, several of the Southern States engaged in a campaign of 'massive resistance' to compliance with the *Brown* v. *Board of Education* decision; federal troops had to be called out to enforce orders.[129] In 1974, President Richard Nixon resigned in disgrace, following a unanimous Supreme Court opinion holding that he was required to comply with a subpoena for the production of certain tapes, sought in connection with indictments alleging criminal acts by White House aides and persons involved in the committee to re-elect the President.[130] And in 2000, a dispute over electoral and popular votes in the State of Florida was resolved,

---

[129] See *Cooper* v. *Aaron*, 358 US 1 (1958), discussed above.
[130] See *United States* v. *Nixon*, 418 US 683 (1974).

not in the Congress, but by the Supreme Court, in *Bush* v. *Gore;*[131] the loser accepted the Court's decision and Bush became President.

Many in the United States today are concerned about threats to the rule of law. Even strong institutional structures may bend or break under the weight of major constitutional actors who lack appreciation for democratic, constitutional values. Yet the multiplicity of constitutional and political actors provides reason for hope that US constitutional democracy will weather the current period.

Further Reading

A. Bickel, *The Least Dangerous Branch* (Bobbs-Merrill, 1962).

C.L. Black, Jr., *Structure and Relationship in Constitutional Law* (Ox Bow Press, 1985 reprint) (originally Lousiana State University Press, 1969).

W.J. Brennan, Jr., 'State Constitutions and the Protection of Individual Rights' (1977) 90 *Harv. L. Rev.* 489.

P. Brest, 'The Misconceived Quest for the Original Understanding' (1980) 60 *B.U. L. Rev.* 204.

J.H. Ely, *Democracy and Distrust* (Harvard University Press, 1980).

C.R. Lawrence, 'The Id, the Ego, and Equal Protection: Reckoning with Unconscious Racism' (1987) 39 *Stanford Law Review* 317.

A. Scalia et al., *A Matter of Interpretation* (Princeton University Press, 1997).

R. Siegel, 'Reasoning from the Body: A Historical Perspective on Abortion Regulation and Questions of Equal Protection' (1992) 44 *Stan. L. Rev.* 261.

K. Sullivan, 'The Justices of Rules and Standards' (1992) 106 *Harv. L. Rev.* 22.

C. Sunstein, 'Foreword: Leaving Things Undecided' (1996) 110 *Harv. L. Rev.* 4.

J.B. Thayer, 'The Origin and Scope of the American Doctrine of Constitutional Law' (1893) 7 *Harv. L. Rev.* 129.

H. Wechsler, 'The Political Safeguards of Federalism: The Role of the States in the Composition and Selection of the National Government' (1954) 54 *Colum. L. Rev.* 543.

[131] 531 US 98 (2000).

The Constitution of the Republic of India   6

Anashri Pillay

Introduction

The Constitution of India, adopted in 1949 and still in force today, was one of the earliest post-colonial Constitutions. Where the constitutional systems of most other newly independent states of the 1960s and 1970s have been marked by revolution, constitutional repeal and suspension, the Indian Constitution is remarkable for its durability. In fact, there are only a handful of states, with or without a colonial history, whose Constitutions have proved more resilient. The Indian Constitution is also the longest Constitution in the world, with the original draft consisting of 395 articles, eight schedules and a huge amount of administrative detail. There have also been 101 Amendments to the Constitution.

As the length of the document indicates, the Constitution is ambitious – in addition to setting up political institutions and delineating fundamental rights, its provisions are aimed at social reform. The transformative nature of the Constitution is perhaps best illustrated by its recognition of positive discrimination and various economic and social rights as directive principles of state policy. That the Constitution was innovative for its time and broadly successful in setting out a blueprint for the democratic government of a highly populous, heterogeneous state is beyond question. For these reasons, the Indian Constitution occupies an important space in studies of comparative constitutional law.

At the same time, studies of constitutionalism in India are critical of the fact that India's successes – a reasonably well-functioning democracy of over sixty years' standing, broad respect for the rule of law, a vibrant judicial system and rapid economic growth – have not served to transform the lives of the country's most vulnerable people. Poverty remains a huge challenge for India, with recent data showing that, even on conservative estimates, about 30 per cent of the population lives below the poverty line. Furthermore, the lack of accountability of India's large public sector has also arisen as a major concern – infrastructure in areas such as power supply is notoriously poor, and corruption is rife. This chapter examines key features of the Indian Constitution – from its drafting history to current challenges.

1 History and Background

The years leading up to India's independence from Britain were marked by violent repression of the independence movement by colonial authorities. When Britain finally agreed to grant independence to a Republic of India in 1947, it was due to a range of factors including an increasingly well-organized independence movement, the pressures that World War II had placed on the colonial power and the coming into power of the Labour Party, which had always favoured self-rule. India's formal independence was preceded by gradual devolution of power by the British government through constitutional legislation. By 1947, India had spent two years as a dominion in the British Empire. During this period, India was governed under the Government of India Act of 1935.

But the recognition of India as a fully independent state demanded agreement between the Indian National Congress, which had emerged as the party likely to lead a new Indian government, the leaders of the 'princely states' within India – which had never been under British rule but had entered into alliances with the colonial power – and the Muslim League. Conflict with the Muslim League proved intractable. As Muslims comprised only 20 per cent of the population, dominance of the Hindu population in a new government was inevitable and the Muslim separatist movement had been steadily gaining ground. The Muslim League itself gained popularity when it made the demand for a new independent state of Pakistan – to be created by partition of India – its rallying cry. In what has been heavily criticized as an ill thought-out and ill-timed move, the British government acceded to this demand. The partition of India resulted in large-scale communal violence and turmoil. It also left a large number of Muslims in the new Indian state. India is home to approximately 11 per cent of the world's Muslim population. Thus, partition also resulted in India having one of the world's largest minority populations.

It was against this background that the Constitutional Assembly, indirectly elected through provincial assemblies in 1946, completed its work of drafting a new Constitution for India.

2 Constitutional Drafting Process

The formation of a Constituent Assembly (CA) was put forward as a key demand of the Indian National Congress in the mid-1930s. By the time the partition of India had been effected, the CA had 299 members. The CA was made up of a wide range of people from different political, socio-economic, religious and professional backgrounds, including prominent political leaders, jurists, trade unionists and economists. To some extent, the scope of the CA's work had been set by the Cabinet Mission Plan of 1946. This plan had emerged from the visit of three British cabinet ministers to India in February 1946. Their aim was to facilitate the move to independence through negotiations with various stakeholders. They were unable to secure agreement amongst the major players (particularly Congress and the Muslim League) and ultimately devised a set of proposals of their own, which became known as the Cabinet Mission Plan.

The plan was not greatly detailed, nor did it bind the CA in any formal sense. However, its directives, including that a Constitution should deal with 'Foreign Affairs, Defense, and Communications; and should have the powers necessary to raise the finances required for the above subjects', and that 'all subjects other than the Union subjects and all residuary powers should vest in the Provinces' assumed importance because of the differences of opinion within India.[1] When a unified India was deemed no longer to be possible and partition became a reality, the CA ostensibly had more freedom to decide on how power would be devolved between the centre and the states. In fact, some form of federalism remained inescapable because of the need to secure the agreement of the rulers of the princely states to accede to an independent Indian Republic.

Somewhat controversially, the 1935 Government of India Act also proved highly influential during the constitutional drafting process. There was little enthusiasm for the Act when it came into effect. Intended to allow for a certain amount in self-rule in India, it was critiqued as being too radical in Britain and as not going far enough in India. However, when it came to drafting a Constitution for an independent India, the 1935 legislation provided a framework. Whilst the drafters wanted the Constitution to reflect a new India, they were also not opposed to constitutional borrowing, even from the former colonial power. Many of the provisions of the Constitution were taken directly from the 1935 Act. This textual similarity may be seen 'merely as a template for further constitutional development'. However, it has contributed to an ongoing debate about Indian constitutional identity.[2]

After the provincial elections of 1945–1946 and India's formal independence from Britain in 1947, the CA was largely a Congress Party body. During this time, the CA functioned both as a constitutional drafting body and as the legislative body for the interim Government of India. It was only in 1951–1952 that India held its first general election based on universal suffrage. On one level, the constitutional drafting process was a Congress Party affair. However, as the leader of the independence movement, with a broad ideological base, one of the party's policies was to ensure the representation of a wide range of viewpoints on the CA. And, in fact, the group was made up of people from different political, socio-economic, religious and professional backgrounds, including

[1] P.K. Tripathi, 'Perspectives on the American Constitutional Influence on the Constitution of India' (1988) 98 *Contemporary Asian Studies Series Reprint* 56, 63.

[2] B. Seetharamanan and Y. Kumar, 'The Quest for Constitutional Identity in India' (2013) 6 *Indian Journal of Constitutional Law* 191.

prominent political leaders, jurists, trade unionists and economists. Apart from ensuring that a certain number of individuals (approximately twelve) with expertise in constitutional law and public administration became members of the CA and recommending that the provincial legislatures pay attention to minority and gender representation, the Congress Party left the provincial legislatures to decide on their representatives to the CA. The emphasis on a united nation also influenced the leaders of the drafting process to reach decisions by consensus, rather than voting – the objective was to adopt a Constitution with broad-based support. The draft Constitution was widely circulated from February to October 1948 to allow for public comment.[3]

The British constitutional system was not the only one to have influenced the Indian drafters. The model of judicial review in the Constitution was based on the American Constitution and the Indian Constitution's approach to federalism also drew inspiration from the United States. For the directive principles of state policy, the drafters drew upon the Irish Constitution. The drafters were clear about the fact that they were happy to draw upon the experiences of various jurisdictions but that, ultimately, the Indian Constitution would not be modelled on any one Constitution – it would have to be responsive to the needs of the new democracy. The Constitution came into effect on 26 January 1950 with widespread support. When the first democratic elections were held in 1951–1952, the Congress Party won by a landslide and retained power until 1977. The party's policies are on the centre-left of Indian politics. Congress is a secular party that champions social-liberalism. In its early years, the party followed socialist economic policies. However, since the early 1990s, it has favoured economic liberalization. The Congress Party remains one of two main political parties in India. The other, the Bharatiya Janata Party (BJP), is currently the majority party in government. Its policies are socially conservative. Whilst the BJP has traditionally upheld Hindu nationalist interests, when in government it has followed a neo-liberal agenda and shifted focus away from more controversial policies such as the adoption of a uniform civil code (discussed further below).

---

[3] Tripathi, n. 1, 72.

3 Key Features

a Indian Federalism

The Indian Constitution is formally thought of as being federal in nature. The twenty-three states all have their own governments. However, the idea of a strong centre took hold in the very early drafting days and led to several provisions which suggest that the Constitution is not fully federal. Thus, states in India do not have separate constitutions. Furthermore, in terms of Article 356, the President may dissolve a state government 'in case of failure of constitutional machinery' and rule that state from the centre. This provision has been used on numerous occasions. Article 249 gives Parliament the power to legislate on a matter in the exclusive State List if it is in the national interest to do so and the upper house has passed a resolution allowing for this by at least a two-thirds' majority. This provision, as well as that allowing for the Union to take over legislative and executive control of states during a declared state of emergency (Article 353) have been employed on rare occasions. But, on balance, the need for the Constitution to reflect a united nation was prioritized in the immediate aftermath of colonial domination.

b Parliamentary Democracy

Despite Gandhi's influence on the independence movement, his proposal that the political system be based on the indigenous model of the villages as primary units of social organization, was ultimately rejected. A level of administrative devolution to village panchayats (assemblies) was incorporated into the Constitution. But a village-based system was not seen as an alternative to parliamentary democracy by the Congress Party leadership. Liberal democracy and its institutions had become both familiar and widely respected in India. Perhaps most importantly, the incumbent leaders of an independent India saw liberal democracy based on a centralized Constitution as the only feasible way of responding to the key issues of socio-economic reform and stability. At the time, food scarcity was a huge problem in parts of the country and communal violence had escalated dramatically. Thus, a centralized Constitution based on the British model of parliamentary democracy ultimately won the day. An elected President is the nominal head of state but exercises little power. The head of government is the Prime Minister. The President appoints the executive – the Union Council of Ministers or Cabinet – on the advice of the Prime Minister. Like the British system, there are two houses of parliament – the Lok Sabha, which has 545 members, is the main legislative body. In practice, it is the party with a majority in the Lok Sabha which elects its leader as Prime Minister. The Rajya Sabha or Council of States, consisting of 233 members indirectly elected by the legislative assemblies of the states and 12 appointed by the President, was essentially designed to be a federal chamber. In most matters, the balance of power rests very much with the Lok Sabha. This is especially so with respect to the power to make legislation. In terms of Article 107, bills may be introduced by either house. They cannot be referred to the President for assent unless both houses agree. Critically, however, disagreements between the two houses are solved in a joint sitting in which the Lok Sabha wields a significant numerical advantage.

Critics of the parliamentary system point to the fact that coalition politics have resulted in successive governments being unable to take decisive action, their resources focused instead on maintaining an, often tenuous, hold on power. From 1989 until 2014, India was governed by a series of coalition governments. In 2014, the Bharatiya Janata Party became the first party to secure a majority in twenty-five years. As the Supreme Court of India has found the current system of government to be part of the basic structure of the Constitution, a doctrine discussed further below, a move to a presidential system is not feasible. But proposals for such a move continue to be made. Similarly, the first-past-the-post electoral system has also been heavily critiqued on the basis that, whilst easy to administer, it does not accurately reflect the will of the people with candidates being elected to parliament despite their political parties having attained a comparatively low proportion of the national vote.

c Fundamental Rights

The Indian Constitution's inclusion of justiciable fundamental rights is a significant departure from the British model. Article 13 of Part III imposes an obligation on the state to refrain from enacting laws which are inconsistent with fundamental rights. Any such laws will be void. Under Article 32, the courts have wide remedial powers for the enforcement of these rights. The fundamental rights chapter contains a typical list of civil and political rights: freedom, equality, freedom of religion. The inclusion of the cultural and educational rights of minorities and the right against exploitation speak more obviously to the Indian experience. Under Article 16, which protects 'equality of opportunity in matters of public employment', caste is specified as a prohibited basis for discrimination. Also, Article 17 of the fundamental rights chapter abolishes untouchability.

The sections dealing with equality have given rise to a vast jurisprudence on affirmative action. India's system of reservations speaks to the constitutional goal of moving from a caste-based, hierarchical societal structure to an egalitarian one. In line with this objective, a certain number of jobs in the public sector, places at publicly funded universities or colleges and positions in many elected assemblies are reserved for disadvantaged groups. A key concern has been to identify the beneficiaries of these reservations. Much of the debate in recent decades stems from the category of 'other backward classes' or OBCs. Article 16(4) of the Constitution allows for reservations of appointments or positions for 'any backward class of citizens which, in the opinion of the State, is not adequately represented in the services under the State'. Article 16(4A) deals with reservations for Scheduled Castes and Scheduled Tribes in a general way; the Constitution also contains several other, more specific provisions (covering reservations in relation to public office and education, for instance). By virtue of Articles 341 and 366 of the Constitution, the Scheduled Castes and Schedules Tribes have been identified in Presidential Orders. The Constitution contains no definition of 'backward classes'. As Choudhry points out, the practice has been to treat OBCs as a residual category that is, backward classes that are neither scheduled castes nor scheduled tribes.[4] Whilst the impact of the reservations policy on India's worst-off has been challenged, reservations for the Scheduled Castes and Tribes have been relatively uncontroversial in principle. This is due to a combination of factors – a clear understanding of who these groups are, that they constitute a minority of the population and that reservations with respect to the Scheduled Castes and Tribes is incontrovertibly linked to a history of discrimination and deprivation.[5] The same cannot be said of OBC reservations.

[4] S. Choudhry, 'How to do Constitutional Law and Politics in South Asia', in M. Tushnet and M. Khosla (eds.), *Unstable Constitutionalism* (Cambridge University Press, 2015) 18, 30.
[5] Ibid., 31.

The key issues with OBCs lie with their definition and the expansion of OBC reservations. The 1955 report of the First Backward Classes commission relied largely on caste in defining backward classes. By this understanding, the commission concluded that 32 per cent of the population were OBCs. It recommended 'the reservation of 25 to 40 percent of open positions in the public sector'.[6] The Congress Party's rejection of the report led to increased and widespread OBC political mobilization. When the Janata Party, which provided a platform for OBC voters, came to power in 1977, government set up a second Commission – known as the Mandal Commission. Where the First Commission 'relied on caste as a proxy for social and economic backwardness ... the Second Commission diagnosed caste as the principal cause of social and economic backwardness'.[7] Importantly, the Mandal Commission found that 52 per cent of the population fell into the OBC category. By the time the Commission had completed its work, the Congress Party was again in power. It was only in 1989 that the Janata Dal Party implemented the recommendations through an executive order. The now-defunct Janata Dal Party was formed through the merger of a number of political parties, including factions from the original Janata party which had led the movement against the State of Emergency. The party's ideology did not differ markedly from that of the Congress Party. Janata Dal won the 1989 election on a platform opposed to the high levels of inflation and corruption in government. The party consisted of three major political wings: one espousing the earlier Indian socialist policies, another consisting of dissident leaders of the Congress Party and the third coming from the 'middle peasantry and the so-called "backward castes" of Uttar Pradesh and Bihar'.[8] The 1989 executive order was challenged before the Supreme Court in *Indra Sawhney* v. *Union of India*.[9] A five-judge bench referred the matter to be heard by nine Supreme Court justices. By majority decision, the Court held that reservations for OBCs were constitutionally permissible.

The court approved the use of caste as a means of determining who are OBCs. The judges recognized the connection between caste, occupation and poverty but were careful to note that reference to caste was not the only acceptable method of determining OBC status. The court upheld

---

[6] Ibid.

[7] Ibid., 32–33.

[8] L. Pickett, 'The Rise and Fall of the Janata Dal' (1993) 33 *Asian Survey* 1151.

[9] 1992 Supp (3) SCC 217.

the 27 per cent quota for backward classes, which had emerged from the Mandal Commission and held that, in general, reservations could not exceed 50 per cent. Furthermore, they could only be applied at the entry level (they did not apply to promotions). Finally, Justice Reddy sounded a warning note in his judgment when he referred to the concern that reserved posts were being occupied by members of a 'creamy layer' of the backward classes. He held that these socially advanced sections of the OBC category should be excluded from the reservations. A majority (though made up of different judges) also agreed with this aspect of the judgment. The creamy layer exclusion did not apply to the Scheduled Tribes and Scheduled Castes. This part of the judgment is controversial as there are different levels of socio-economic disadvantage within the Scheduled Tribes and Castes as well. However, most criticism of the *Indra Sawhney* decision centred on the relationship between caste and class. Commentators have argued that the judgment encourages a caste-focused, and therefore overly simplistic, approach to reservations. Socio-economic inequality is often the result of factors other than caste.

The creamy layer exclusion was the focus of another key Supreme Court decision in 2006 – *Ashoka Thakur* v. *Union of India*.[10] This time, the issue was the government's approach to affirmative action in education. The 93rd Amendment to the Constitution allowed for special measures to be taken for the advancement of India's 'socially or educationally backward classes of citizens or for the Scheduled Castes or the Scheduled Tribes in so far as such special provisions relate to their admission to the educational institutions'. By this time, OBC reservations had attracted a wide measure of Parliamentary approval, reflecting the political mobilization of OBCs and their increased electoral clout.[11] The court unanimously upheld the OBC reservations but held that the 27 per cent quota for OBCs should not include the 'creamy layer'. The Court left government a wide measure of discretion with respect to determining who fell within the 'creamy layer' exclusion but the reasoning on the 'creamy layer' exclusion is both detailed and significant. Chief Justice Balakrishnan noted that:

When socially and educationally backward classes are determined by giving importance to caste, it shall not be forgotten that a segment of that caste is economically advanced and they do not require the protection of reservation ... As

---

[10] *Ashoka Thakur* v. *Union of India* (2008) 6 SCC 1.
[11] Choudhry, n. 4 at 37.

noticed earlier, determination of backward class cannot be exclusively based on caste. Poverty, social backwardness, economic backwardness, all are criteria for determination of backwardness. It has been noticed in Indra Sawhney's case that among the backward class, a section of the backward class is a member of the affluent section of society. They do not deserve any sort of reservation for further progress in life. They are socially and educationally advanced enough to compete for the general seats along with other candidates.[12]

To some extent, these concerns about the appropriate beneficiaries of reservations policies had been raised in *Indra Sawhney* as well. However, the Supreme Court in *Ashoka Thakur* gave more carefully reasoned and unanimous support for the idea that reservations should not apply to those most privileged amongst OBCs.

As an approach to affirmative action India's longstanding reservations policy is unusual – both because it is applied to a majority of the population and because it consists of a highly detailed quota system. The system continues to meet with criticism. The policy has been steadily expanded over the years. Despite the ruling that reservations cannot generally exceed 50 per cent of governmental posts, reservations in states with large OBC populations are as much as 80 per cent.[13] Whilst the number of people from 'backward classes' in public posts has increased, it is not clear that the broader aims of the policy are being met. A relatively small proportion of the population are employed in government jobs. There is a concern that other forms of discrimination and disadvantage (in the private sector and outside the employment context) are being neglected. Combined with this is the worry that political elites within 'backward classes' benefit most from the policy. Many argue that the policy is marginal to the objectives of tackling structural inequalities and moving away from a caste-based society.

The term 'secular' was added to the Preamble of the Constitution through the passing of the 42nd Amendment in 1976. This inclusion did not mark a change in the state's relationship with religion, however. The commitment to secularism was agreed upon by the CA and expressed in the protection of 'freedom of conscience and free profession, practice and propagation of religion' in Article 25. In addition, the Constitution protects the freedom to manage religious affairs (Article 26) and prohibits

[12] *Asoka Thakur*, n. 10, paras. 144 and 147.
[13] 'Affirmative action: Indian Reservations', 29 June 2013, www.economist.com/blogs/banyan/2013/06/affirmative-action (accessed 6 March 2018).

the payment of taxes for the promotion of any religion (Article 27). Article 28(1) states that 'no religious instruction shall be provided in any educational institution wholly maintained out of State funds'. Article 28(2) qualifies this general prohibition as follows: 'Nothing in clause (1) shall apply to an educational institution which is administered by the State but has been established under any endowment or trust which requires that religious instruction shall be imparted in such institution.' Even before the 42nd Amendment was passed, the Indian Supreme Court had found secularism to be one of the 'basic features' of the Constitution in the *Kesavananda case*[14] (discussed below).

But the eventual agreement over the place of religion in the Constitution of a newly independent Indian state was hard-won. The question of whether the word 'secular' should be included in the Preamble took up a great deal of the CA's time. Debate over this issue was heated. The CA faced the problem of drafting clauses dealing with religion in the context of a deeply religious society and against the background of widespread communal violence. As Jacobsohn and Shankar have noted, 'from the very beginning of constitutional governance in independent India, official indifference to what transpired within the religious domain was never a plausible option'.[15] The social structure of the state was inextricably tied to religious belief. As a result, the government would not have been able to pursue any policy of socio-economic transformation without some intervention into religious matters. For India's first Prime Minister, Nehru, the commitment to a secular state was bound up with the commitment to socialism. Communalism – which he understood as being the dominance of one religious group – was antithetical to social and political equality. Thus, the Indian model does not envisage a strict separation between religion and state. Instead it is based on religious accommodation or tolerance and on the equal treatment of religious groups. The complexity of ensuring religious accommodation whilst also protecting women's rights, employment rights and socio-economic equality, for example, has given rise to a significant amount of deliberation and litigation.

[14] *Kesavananda Bharati Sripadagalvaru and Ors* v. *State of Kerala and another* AIR (1973) SC 1461.

[15] G.J. Jacobsohn and S. Shankar, 'Constitutional Borrowing in South Asia: India, Sri Lanka and Secular Constitutional Identity', in S. Khilani, V. Raghavan and A. Thiruvengadam (eds.), *Comparative Constitutionalism in South Asia* (Oxford University Press, 2013) 189.

The question of a Uniform Civil Code is a source of perennial debate in India. Article 44 of the Constitution provides that 'the State shall endeavour to secure for the citizens a uniform civil code throughout the territory of India'. Even though the Article is a directive principle of state policy rather than a justiciable right, the fact that such a Code has not come into being is an indication of how fraught an issue this is in Indian law and politics. As India has a series of other common codes – dealing with criminal law, criminal procedure and civil procedure – and universally applicable laws in various other areas of law, it is in the field of personal law that the absence of a common code is felt. Family-related matters such as marriage, adoption and inheritance are dealt with by the religious laws of various communities. Calls for a uniform code have come from a number of groups – but it is perhaps in the area of gender justice that the lobby has been most vocal.

Over the years, government has been responsive to the concern that personal laws may discriminate against women. An early example is the Dissolution of Muslim Marriages Act, 1939, which allowed women to sue for divorce on certain, limited grounds. The Indian Divorce (Amendment) Act of 2001 removed gender-based discrimination from Christian divorce laws. Hindu laws of succession were amended in 2005 to give daughters and sons equal inheritance rights (Hindu Succession Act, 2005). A number of judicial decisions have also effected reform in this area. Thus, in *Mohammed Ahmad Khan* v. *Shah Bano*,[16] the Supreme Court upheld the petitioner's claim for maintenance for herself and her children despite the fact that Muslim Personal Law only provided for such maintenance for a period of approximately three months. The case was hugely controversial. The Rajiv Gandhi-led government responded by passing an amendment to the Criminal Procedure Code that appeared to nullify the Court's decision. The Muslim Women (Protection of Rights on Divorce) Act of 1986, through which the amendment was brought into effect, was later challenged before the Supreme Court. The Court managed to uphold the Act and the rights of Muslim women to regular maintenance by interpreting the reference in the new section 3(1)(a) to 'a reasonable and fair provision and maintenance'. According to Justice Babu, rather than overturning the ruling in *Shah Bano*, this provision made it

---

[16] AIR 1985 SC 945.

clear that the amendment affirmed the payment of maintenance beyond the three-month period.[17]

The practice by which Muslim men may divorce their wives by simply pronouncing a 'triple talaq' has also come under fire over the years. Recently, a five-judge bench of the Supreme Court ruled against the practice and prohibited it for a six-month period whilst government drafts new legislation.[18] However, the two dissenting judgments and differences in reasoning amongst the judges generally highlight the fact that a potential move towards a Uniform Civil Code remains highly divisive. Whilst many would see the move as a triumph for gender equality, others fear that it would go against the pluralistic nature of Indian society. There is also an argument that continued steady reform of the laws would be preferable to the blunt instrument of a common code. Perhaps most worryingly, commentators fear that the UCC-lobby is being used as a political tool against a Muslim minority by the Hindi majority and that a focus on personal laws has resulted in the neglect of issues such as gender-based violence. During the constitutional drafting debates, secularism was seen as the only feasible way to accommodate a wide range of religious values whilst furthering social reconstruction. But it meant that many complex issues were simply postponed to a later date. Secularism has become an important part of India's constitutional identity, but its meaning and impact continue to be debated politically and in the courts.

d Directive Principles of State Policy

The term 'socialism' also did not appear in the Constitution. It was introduced into the Preamble by the controversial 42nd Amendment, discussed later in this chapter. But socialist principles were there from the beginning. Austin notes that the fundamental rights and directive principles chapters represent the 'core of the commitment to a social revolution'.[19] However, there was disagreement as to how the transformative aims of the incoming leaders would be best captured in the Constitution. Members of the CA were concerned that the protection of rights should not hinder the government's capacity to effect widespread social reform.

[17] *Danial Latifi* v. *Union of India* (2001) 7 SCC 740.
[18] *Sharaya Bano* v. *Union of India and others* Writ Petition No. 118 of 2016 (22 August 2017).
[19] G. Austin, *The Indian Constitution: Cornerstone of a Nation* (Oxford University Press, 1999), 50.

India's new political leaders had fought in the struggle for independence, whereas the judges were colonial appointees drawn from the elite in Indian society. One of the concerns of the members of the CA was that an unelected judicial body could use the fundamental rights provisions to protect established economic interests thereby thwarting attempts at reform. The leaders of the independence movement did not see the need to separate economic and social rights from civil and political rights; in the end this is what the CA did.

Drawing from the Irish Constitution, members of the CA decided to set out the social and economic duties on the state such as securing the right to an 'adequate means of livelihood' for all citizens (Article 39(a)); securing the right to work, education and certain forms of social security' (Article 41); and raising the levels of nutrition and public health (Article 47) as directive principles of state policy in Part 4 of the Constitution, separate from the fundamental rights detailed in Part 3. Article 37 of the Constitution, dealing with the application of the directive principles states:

The provisions contained in this Part shall not be enforceable by any court, but the principles therein laid down are nevertheless fundamental in the governance of the country and it shall be the duty of the State to apply these principles in making laws.

Thus, the directive principles were not intended to be enforceable by courts. Instead, the drafters of the Constitution saw them as guiding principles for the central and state governments in the development of their policies. This is clear from Article 37 itself, as well as the terms such as 'the State shall regard', 'the State shall endeavour to secure', 'the State shall, within the limits of its economic capacity and development, make effective provision for securing', and 'the State shall, in particular, direct its policy towards securing' used in the subsequent Articles of the chapter on directive principles.

Chairperson of the constitution drafting committee, B.R. Ambedkar, noted that the intention of the CA was that the directive principles be made the 'basis of all executive and legislative action'. In presenting the Fourth Constitutional Amendment Bill before Parliament in 1954, India's first Prime Minister and one of the most important figures in the drafting process, Jawaharlal Nehru, reiterated the significance of the principles:

We stress greatly and argue in Courts of Law about the Fundamental Rights. Rightly so, but there is such a thing also as the Directive Principles of Constitution...

Those are, as the Constitution says, the fundamentals in the governance of the Country... if... there is an inherent contradiction in the Constitution between the Fundamental Rights and the Directive Principles of State Policy... it is up to this Parliament to remove the contradiction and make the Fundamental Rights sub-serve the Directive Principles of the State Policy.

The approach to individual liberty was also controversial as preventive detention is constitutionally permissible. There was a strong public reaction against this, but the CA ultimately decided that due process protection would limit the state's ability to act in the interests of peace and security. Both the directive principles and the maintenance of the possibility of preventive detention also speak to the attitude of the CA to judicial review: the general view was that judicial review should be closely contained. Fault-lines in the Constitution were highlighted by key events over the next few decades, leading to the state of emergency declared in 1975. These are discussed later in the chapter.

e Judicial Selection and Appointment

Articles 124(2) and 217(1) of the Indian Constitution provide for judges to be appointed through a consultative process. With respect to Supreme Court judges, the President of India is required to consult with the Chief Justice of India and, with respect to High Court appointments, with the Governor and Chief Justice of the respective High Court. The issue of what the duty to consult entails has given rise to some controversial jurisprudence. When the matter first came before the Supreme Court in 1981,[20] the Court interpreted the constitutional sections to mean that the judicial consultees did not have to concur in the President's selection of judges. Judges did not have primacy in the judicial appointments process. However, this all changed when the Supreme Court handed down its Advisory Opinion of 1993.[21] In the later case, the Court found that the Constitution envisaged a move away from political control over judicial appointments. It emphasized that the aim of the consultative process was to reach consensus on judicial nominees. However, the Court was clear that, in the case of any disagreement, the view of the Chief Justice would prevail.

---

[20] *S.P. Gupta* v. *President of India* AIR 1982 SC 149.
[21] *Supreme Court Advocates-on-Record Association* v. *Union of India* (1993) 4 SCC 441.

In the *Third Judges* case in 1998,[22] the court set out the system that currently still applies in India – collegiums consisting of the Chief Justice and two or four senior judges recommend names to the President. Effectively, the President is then bound by those recommendations. All three decisions were handed down in the context of heightened fears over threats to judicial independence (discussed further below). At the same time, judicial dominance over the appointments process has met with sustained criticism. In 2014, the Bharatiya Janata Party-led government was able to pass legislation aimed at moving the country towards a commission-based system of judicial appointments. However, the Supreme Court held that the Constitution (Ninety-Ninth Amendment) Act, 2014 (ninety-ninth Amendment) and the National Judicial Appointments Commission Act of 2014 would impinge on judicial independence and were, thus, unconstitutional.[23]

4 Land Redistribution, Basic Structure and the State of Emergency

The basic structure doctrine is one of the more unusual features of the Indian constitutional system. It arose from a protracted battle between the legislature and the judiciary over land reform. As was predicted during the CA's debates, the fundamental rights were used as a tool to question the legislature's authority to effect social reform. In the years following the enactment of the Constitution, several states passed legislation intended to stimulate agricultural reform. Amongst other things, the legislative reforms abolished the 'zamindari system' in terms of which the zamindars (wealthy landowners) could collect taxes from small landowners. The reforms also allowed for government to pay different rates of compensation for land acquisition. But landowners resisted the legislative enactments, relying on their rights to property and equality before the courts. In response, Parliament passed the Constitution (First Amendment) Act, 1951. In a statement of 'objects and reasons' introducing the Act, the legislators noted:

---

[22] *Special Reference No. 1 of 1998* (1998) 7 SCC 729.
[23] *Supreme Court Advocates-on-Record Association and others* v. *Union of India and others*, WP (Cl) 13/2015 (Supreme Court, 16 October 2015).

The validity of agrarian reform measures passed by the State Legislatures in the last three years has, in spite of the provisions of clauses (4) and (6) of article 31, formed the subject-matter of dilatory litigation, as a result of which the implementation of these important measures, affecting large numbers of people, has been held up. The main objects of this Bill are, accordingly to amend article 19 for the purposes indicated above and to insert provisions fully securing the constitutional validity of zamindari abolition laws in general and certain specified State Acts in particular... It is laid down in article 46 as a directive principle of State policy that the State should promote with special care the educational and economic interests of the weaker sections of the people and protect them from social injustice. In order that any special provision that the State may make for the educational, economic or social advancement of any backward class of citizens may not be challenged on the ground of being discriminatory, it is proposed that article 15(3) should be suitably amplified.[24]

The zamindars were not always successful before the courts. An attempt in 1952 to invalidate the First Amendment on the basis that constitutional amendments could not be used to infringe fundamental rights was rejected by the Supreme Court.[25] Crucially, however, a few years later the Supreme Court found that government had to pay a 'just equivalent' of the value of any private property acquired for a public purpose and that the determination of what was a just equivalent was justiciable.[26] Parliament then passed the Constitution (Fourth Amendment) Act in terms of which the entire process through which private property was acquired by the state was immune from judicial review. The amended Article 31A (I) stated that the acquisition of an 'estate' could not be deemed to be void on the basis that it violated the right to equality, free expression or property. But, in the case of *Karimbil Kunhikoman* v. *State of Kerala*,[27] the Supreme Court was able to strike down the Kerala Agrarian Reforms Act by defining the term 'estate' narrowly. Again, Parliament responded with a constitutional amendment – the Constitution (Seventeenth Amendment) Act, 1964.

Matters reached a turning point in the 1967 *Golaknath* case.[28] The petitioners challenged two state-enacted pieces of land reform legislation,

---

[24] The Constitution (First Amendment) Act, 1951.
[25] In *Shankari Prasad Singh* v. *Union of India and State of Bihar (and other cases)* 1952 SCR 89.
[26] In *State of West Bengal* v. *Mrs Bela Banerjee and others* 1954 SCR.
[27] 1961 AIR 723.
[28] 1967 SCR (2) 762.

thereby questioning the validity of the First, Fourth and Seventeenth Amendments. A majority of the judges found that Parliament could not amend the Constitution in a manner which took away or abridged a fundamental right. By virtue of this decision, a huge number of Acts would have been rendered invalid. However, the Court opted for prospective overruling, leaving in place legislation aimed at land reform that had been passed consistently with earlier Supreme Court judgments. The decision was contentious – it raised questions both about the relative importance of the directive principles and the limits of the judicial role. Following the general elections of 1971, Parliament passed a number of amendments which were designed to retain wide powers to restrict property rights and amend the Constitution. Predictably, these Acts were also challenged before the Supreme Court in the seminal *Kesavananda* case.[29] *Kesavananda* overruled the decision in *Golaknath* but found that the power to amend the Constitution was limited – it could not be used to impinge on a basic feature or the basic structure of the Constitution. Chief Justice Sikri identified these basic features as:

(1) Supremacy of the Constitution;
(2) Republican and Democratic form of Government;
(3) Secular character of the Constitution;
(4) Separation of powers between the Legislature, the executive and the judiciary;
(5) Federal character of the Constitution.

Other judges have elaborated the content of the basic features to include, for instance, the equality of status and equal opportunity of individuals and the rule of law. The position since *Kesavananda* has been that it is up to the Court to determine whether an amendment conflicts with what is an evolving, judicially constructed basic structure doctrine. Initially, this instance of judicial activism was highly controversial, especially as it arose in the context of the Court upholding established property interests. But the Court has been cautious in its use of the doctrine, finding infringements of it in relatively few cases over the years. Moreover, the doctrine gained a level of approval when the Court used it to find governmental action curbing fundamental rights during the 1975–1977 state of emergency to be constitutionally invalid.

[29] n. 4.

The emergency was a hugely significant event in India's constitutional history. Indira Gandhi, India's third Prime Minister and leader of the Congress Party, had won a narrow victory in the 1967 election. Despite her lack of popularity with certain sections of the Party, in 1971, Mrs Gandhi managed to lead the Congress Party to a more convincing election win. However, her election to Parliament was soon challenged before the Allahabad High Court on the basis that she had committed election fraud. The Court set aside her election and, before the Supreme Court could decide on the merits of her appeal, the executive declared a state of emergency. This was swiftly followed by the passing of a succession of constitutional amendments effectively insulating various government acts – including the election of a Prime Minister, censorship laws and other laws infringing fundamental rights – from judicial review. In *Indira Gandhi* v. *Raj Narain* (known as the *Election case*),[30] the Supreme Court held that the Thirty-Ninth Amendment, which purported to remove the election of the Prime Minister and the Speaker from judicial scrutiny, was invalid on the basis that it violated the basic structure of the Constitution. In a decision criticized for lack of conceptual clarity, the judges variously referred to democracy (including free and fair elections), the rule of law, judicial review and the Supreme Court's Article 32 power to issue remedies as basic features of the Constitution. The case painted the doctrine in a new light. As noted by former Justice of the Supreme Court, O. Chinnappa Reddy:

The year 1973 was indeed a watershed in the constitutional history of India. Until then, it looked as if Parliament was asserting and consolidating its power as a democratic institution committed to the goals of abolition of all semblance of feudalism, introduction of land reforms, and the pursuit of the Directive Principles of State Policy... [w]hile the earlier constitutional amendments up to 1973 were aimed at securing to Parliament the power to legislate without question in regard to the goals just mentioned, the amendments made subsequently appear... to be aimed at securing more and more power to the executive. The road signposts clearly changed from democracy to authoritarianism.[31]

The amendments challenged in the cases above were not the only governmental assaults on judicial powers and independence during the

---

[30] AIR 1975 S.C. 2299.
[31] O. Chinnappa Reddy, *The Court and the Constitution of India* (Oxford University Press, 2008), 65–66.

emergency period. The government resorted to packing the court to try to overturn the basic structure doctrine. When this did not work, they passed the 42nd Amendment. Apart from introducing the terms 'secular' and 'socialist' into the Preamble, features which were retained when the other aspects of the Amendment were later found to be unconstitutional, this Amendment also placed severe limitations on the judiciary. In this context, the Court's decision in the *Election case* amounted to the use of the basic structure doctrine to protect democratic freedoms from an increasing repressive government.

However, this interpretation of the role of the basic structure doctrine was difficult to maintain when the Court handed down its decision in *Additional District Magistrate, Jabalpur* v. *SS Shukla*,[32] the *Habeas Corpus* case, another landmark decision from the emergency period. The case also concerned authoritarian emergency laws – this time, wide powers of detention. Thousands of people, including members of rival political parties and journalists were held under preventive detention laws. In the face of pervasive reports of human rights abuses, which included the use of torture by the police, the Supreme Court held, with a single dissent by Justice Khanna, that the detentions were not amenable to judicial review because the emergency laws prevented access to the courts.

The reasons for this highly criticized decision – repeatedly cited as the lowest point in the Supreme Court's history – have been much debated. The fact that the judiciary felt itself to be under threat at the time certainly seems to have played a role. Both immediately before and during the emergency, there were signs of governmental interference with judicial independence. In the aftermath of *Kesavananda*, with the imminent retirement of Chief Justice Sikri, the government had to appoint a successor to lead the Supreme Court. In the ordinary course, the convention of selecting the most senior judge on the bench would have been followed. However, Indira Gandhi's government chose to appoint Justice A.N. Ray, passing over three more senior judges in the process. This supersession of judges seen to be less friendly to governmental policies was widely condemned – there were protests by former judges, the Law Commission and the Supreme Court Bar Association, for instance. In addition, during the emergency, government transferred sixteen High Court judges who had ruled against preventive detention measures away from their home

---

[32] 1976 SCR 17.

Courts. These judges did not consent to their transfers – in several cases, they were transferred in the face of their express objections.

In 1977 Mrs Gandhi, concerned for her international image and her political future, called for fresh elections. Her Congress Party suffered a crushing defeat to the Janata party, an alliance of various parties opposed to Congress. The Janata party provided a platform for groups with highly divergent ideological and political positions to unite against the State of Emergency. However, once it assumed power, the party's ideological divisions proved an obstacle to any significant economic reforms. Its support began to weaken. By the late 1980s, the party had ceased to exist in its original form. Nevertheless, the party was instrumental in bringing the state of emergency to an end. Emergency politics continued to exert a profound influence on India's constitutional development.

5 Public Interest Litigation and the Directive Principles of State Policy

The public interest (or social action) litigation (PIL) model in India originated with a small group of lawyers and judges. The idea was to make the courts more easily available to ordinary citizens who wished to exercise their rights. At the heart of the movement was the idea that courts would only be able to contribute to social reform if the traditional procedural rules surrounding litigation were relaxed so that claims from people who were vulnerable, often illiterate and with little access to resources could be facilitated. Thus, for example, the Supreme Court accepted a letter written to a judge, complaining of the violation of fundamental rights, as a legitimate means through which an individual could bring a matter before the court.[33] The movement involved a departure from an adversarial approach to litigation and included flexible pleading rules, new methods of fact-finding such as the appointment of socio-legal commissions[34] and expanded remedial powers including supervisory jurisdiction[35] over court orders.[36]

[33] *Sunil Batra* v. *Delhi Administration and others* 1979 SCR (1) 392.

[34] *Bandhua Mukti Morcha* v. *Union of India and others* 1984 SCR (2) 67.

[35] See, for example, *Indian Council for Enviro-Legal Action and others* v. *Union of India and others* 1996 (2) SCR 503.

[36] B. Neuborne, 'The Supreme Court of India' (2003) 1 *International Journal of Constitutional Law* 476.

This more relaxed approach to procedure was married with a generous approach to the interpretation of rights. Article 21 became a focal point of the PIL movement. The Article states that '[n]o person shall be deprived of his life or personal liberty except according to procedure established by law'. For some time, this Article was interpreted very restrictively as a guarantee only that any interference with the right was carried out through the mechanism of law. Provided there was some piece of legislation in place, the court would not enquire further into the soundness of that law and its effects on the individuals concerned. This changed with the case of *Maneka Gandhi* v. *Union of India and Another*.[37] The case concerned the government's power to impound passports without giving the affected individuals a hearing. Justice Bhagwati, in whose opinion all the judges but one concurred, held that the procedure by which the Article 21 right is impinged on 'cannot be arbitrary, unfair or unreasonable'. In addition, the majority gave a generous meaning to the *content* of the right protected in Article 21:

The expression 'personal liberty' in Article 21 is of the widest amplitude and it covers a variety of rights which go to constitute the personal liberty of man and some of them have been raised to the status of distinct fundamental rights and given additional protection under Article 19.[38]

Following this line of reasoning, in the later case of *Francis Mullin*,[39] the Supreme Court held that the right to life included the protection of '[e]very limb or faculty through which life is enjoyed' and by necessary extension 'the faculties of thinking and feeling'. Most importantly, the Court held that this meant protection of human dignity and all that is attached to that: 'namely, the bare necessaries of life such as adequate nutrition, clothing and shelter and facilities for reading, writing and expressing oneself in diverse forms.' Given the interpretation of Article 21 favoured in these cases, with the judges' emphasis on human dignity and the 'bare necessaries of life', it was not long until the directive principles of state policy began to make their way into the jurisprudence. In the following years, the Court found that Article 21 includes a right to adequate medical facilities or health care,[40] and would be violated in cases

---

[37] (1978) 1 SCC 248.
[38] n. 4, 670–671.
[39] *Francis Coralie Mullin* v. *The Administrator, Union Territory of India and others* 1981 SCR.
[40] *Paschim Banga Ket Mazdoor Samity* v. *State of West Bengal* (1996) 4 SCC 37; *Consumer Education and Research Centre* v. *India* (1995) 3 SCC 42.

of deprivation of livelihood.[41] In addition, the Court found that the right to equality protected in Article 14 included a right to primary education.[42] In these cases, the court interpreted justiciable civil and political rights in light of directive principles of state policy. Sometimes, the reference to directive principles only gave rise to procedural protections but, in some cases, civil and political rights were interpreted to include substantive economic and social guarantees. This marked a radical move away from the notion that the directive principles were non-justiciable.

There have been many attempts to explain and to understand the judicial activism displayed by the Supreme Court at this time – a complex range of factors were, and still are, at play. As noted above, the continued impact of the emergency was certainly a relevant feature. The repressive measures government took against the Indian population created a gap in legitimacy which the court attempted to fill by holding the government accountable for its constitutional promises of liberty and socioeconomic reform. Sathe attributes the post-emergency judicial activism to the court's realization that its reputation as a site of social privilege would not protect it against future attacks by a 'powerful political establishment' – in short, the court needed the people of India on its side.[43] Government's policies with respect to the judiciary were treated with a high level of distrust. Again, this could be traced to emergency politics in the form of the supersession and transfer of judges. It was also during this post-emergency period that the Supreme Court secured judicial control over the judicial selection and appointments process by handing down its decisions in the *Second* and *Third Judges* cases discussed above.

6 The Indian Supreme Court and the Nature of Judicial Power

In recent years, a sizeable scholarship has developed on the question of the role of the Indian Supreme Court. The post-emergency narrative of the Court as facilitator of social reform and protector of individual rights against governmental excesses has been difficult to maintain in

---

[41] *Olga Tellis and Others* v. *Bombay Municipal Corporation and Others* 1986 AIR 180.

[42] *Unnikrishnan* v. *State of Andra Pradesh* 1993 (1) SCC 645.

[43] S.P. Sathe, *Judicial activism in India: Transgressing Borders and Enforcing Limits* (Oxford University Press, 2002) 107.

light of later jurisprudence. In the much-criticized *Narmada Bachao Andolan* v. *Union of India* case,[44] for instance, the Court held that the Sardar Sarovar Dam Project could go ahead even though the environmental clearance required by legislation had not been given and in the face of evidence that government's plan to rehabilitate displaced people was woefully inadequate. Tellingly, Justice Kirpal criticized Narmada Bachao Andolan, the non-governmental organization that had brought the case to court seven years after the construction of the dam had begun:

When such projects are undertaken and hundreds of crores of public money is spent, individual or organisations in the garb of PIL cannot be permitted to challenge the policy decision taken after a lapse of time. It is against the national interest and contrary to the established principles of law that decisions to undertake developmental projects are permitted to be challenged after a number of years during which period public money has been spent in the execution of the project.

The Court failed to acknowledge that the delay was due to an ongoing period of engagement between Narmada Bachao Andolan and governmental authorities in which the NGO had been attempting to get government to agree to a comprehensive environmental assessment. The Court found that there was no need for independent experts to evaluate the studies which had been carried out. There was no reason to question the accuracy of the studies or to believe that government would not be able to manage any problems that arose. The Court refused to address concerns about the construction of the dam itself, finding that the only justiciable issue was whether the rehabilitation measures were being properly implemented. The Court accepted without discussion government's assertions that the project would lead to benefits for the displaced population and, on that basis, held that the right to life in Article 21 was not threatened. In a development related to this case, the Court used its contempt powers against the novelist Arundhati Roy, a vocal critic of certain of its judgments in the Sardar Sarovar Dam matter.

In *Calcutta Electricity Supply Corporation (CESC) Ltd. Etc.* v. *Subash Chandra Bose and Ors,*[45] a majority of the judges held that people working for Subash Chandra Bose, which CESC had contracted to carry out work

---

[44] (2000) 10 SCC 664.
[45] 1991 SCR Supl (2) 267.

on public roads, did not fall within the definition of 'employees' in the State Insurance Act of 1978. Under that Act, an employee was someone:

employed by or through an immediate employer on the premises of the factory or establishment or under the supervision of the principal employer or his agent on work which is ordinarily part of the work of the factory or establishment or which is preliminary to the work carried on... or incidental to the purpose of the factory or establishment'.[46]

According to the majority, CESC's final approval or rejection of the work carried out was not 'supervision'. As a result, the workers were not entitled to health and welfare benefits. In his dissenting judgment, Justice Ramaswamy adopted an approach to constitutional interpretation much more consistent with the early PIL cases described above. He referred to the protection of health and workers' rights in the Universal Declaration on Human Rights and the International Covenant on Economic, Social and Cultural Rights. He noted that Article 39(c) of the Constitution provided that state policy should be directed at securing the health and strength of workers. He also took into account the fact that the purpose of the legislation was to extend health benefits. According to Ramaswamy J., the level of supervision needed depended on the nature of the work and the term could encompass the kind of legal control as existed in this case.

Certain Supreme Court judges have expressed wariness about judicial activism in strong terms. An example here is Justice Katju in the *Aravali Golf Club* case.[47] Criticizing the Delhi High Court for straying 'into the executive domain or in matters of policy', he raised a concern that government would respond to high levels of judicial intervention by limiting judicial power. He suggested that judicial activism was appropriate only in exceptional circumstances. In general, the role of judges was merely to enforce pre-existing laws on, amongst other things, 'criteria for free seats in schools, supply of drinking water in schools, number of free beds in hospitals on public land, use and misuse of ambulances... begging in public'. Cases like these suggested a retreat from judicial activism. But they have been accompanied by other, far-reaching decisions aimed at socio-economic reform.

Litigation over the right to food is a well-known example. The case arose in the context of a famine in parts of rural India. Grain stocks were

---

[46] *CESC*, n. 44, 279.
[47] 2007 (12) SCR 1084, 2008(1) SCC 683.

overflowing, and government had already developed a Famine Code and several schemes for the distribution of food. However, these plans were not being implemented. Using its power of continuing mandamus, the Court has handed down a series of interim orders in the case, each designed to enforce aspects of the distribution schemes. The most important of the early orders was that handed down on 28 November 2001,[48] in which the Court recognized the schemes' benefits as legal entitlements. In a 2009 decision, a mere two years after his comments about judicial activism in *Aravali Golf Club*, Justice Katju converted an earlier judicial recommendation that central government appoint a group of distinguished scientists to conduct research on how to solve the country's water shortage crisis, into an order of the court.[49] Thus, the idea that the Court had experienced a post-emergency activist phase, led by particular judges, which simply gave way to judicial caution in later decades is overly simplistic.

In considering what may account for the Court's ambiguous relationship with the transformative objectives of the Constitution, the commentary on the history of PIL in India raises several concerns. It suggests that there is a tendency for judges to treat claims made on behalf of the most vulnerable and poorest members of society less favourably. The reasons for this are undoubtedly complex but the argument, based on empirical evidence, is that PIL is not benefitting the most marginalized groups in the country.[50] Whilst judicial decisions have had a positive impact on particular groups and individuals, they are not useful in addressing the structural causes of poverty. Economic liberalization and a governmental emphasis on national development have impacted significantly on judicial decision-making. There are numerous cases in which these governmental objectives have been prioritized over land reform, housing rights and tribal rights, amongst other things.[51] The academic debate has also centred on the inconsistencies in the Court's approach – that is, rather than identifying a general trend against pro-poor decision-making, this scholarship

---

[48] *Peoples' Union for Civil Liberties* v. *Union of India* (2001) 5 SCALE 303; 7 SCALE 484.

[49] *Balakrishnan and others* v. *Union of India and others* 2009(5) SCC 507.

[50] V. Gauri, 'Public Interest Litigation: Overreaching or Underachieving?', The World Bank Development Research Group Policy Research Working Paper 5109, November 2009, www-wds.worldbank.org/external/default/WDSContentServer/WDSP/IB/2009/11/03/000158349_20091103104346/Rendered/PDF/WPS5109.pdf (accessed 7 March 2018).

[51] B. Rajagopal, 'Pro-human Rights but Anti-poor? A Critical Evaluation of the Indian Supreme Court from a Social Movement Perspective' (2007) 18 *Human Rights Review* 157, 161 and 166.

focuses on the variability of the Court's judgments. To some extent, this variability must be laid at the door of the Court's structure. There are currently thirty justices on the bench. The judges divide into subject-matter benches, usually consisting of somewhere between five and fifteen judges. But relaxed standing rules and a generous approach to the admissibility of cases have meant that decisions are commonly handed down by two-judge Division Benches. These factors have contributed to inconsistency.[52]

Most recent attempts to account for the Court's changeable approach focus on the relationship between the judiciary and other arms of government. In this context, Khosla has developed a 'conditional rights thesis', suggesting that the court's approach is determined by whether the state has taken any action to implement the rights at issue. Where the state has breached an existing undertaking or acted negligently (by failing to maintain a state hospital, for example), the Court will hand down a remedy. If there has been prior state action which allows the Court to conclude that a duty has been reached, it has wide remedial powers encompassing compensation and supervisory jurisdiction, amongst other things.[53] This argument speaks to concerns about the Court's institutional security. Decisions broadly aimed at facilitating social reform and wide-ranging remedies are seen as less interventionist, and therefore less susceptible to governmental resistance, when they emanate from existing governmental commitments.

Describing the Court's role as 'promiscuous' in the sense that it is 'both wide-ranging and largely at the Supreme Court's own whims and pleasures', Mehta has recently argued that the Court's style is driven by conflict management. Reviewing a range of anti-corruption decisions in which the Court has positioned itself as an instrument of accountability, Mehta suggests that the Court's approach is instrumentalist rather than unprincipled. As is fitting in a 'messy political democracy', the Court's understanding of its role diverges from an orthodox understanding of the rule of law which emphasizes certainty and consistency.[54] Similarly, in

---

[52] A. Sengupta 'Inconsistent Decisions', *Frontline* Vol. 30(8), 20 April–3 May 2013, www .frontline.in/cover-story/inconsistent-decisions/article4613887.ece (accessed 8 March 2018).

[53] M. Khosla, 'Making Social Rights Conditional: Lessons from India' (2010) 8(4) *International Journal of Constitutional Law* 739.

[54] P.B. Mehta, 'The Indian Supreme Court and the Art of Democratic Positioning', in Tushnet and Khosla, n. 4, 233.

discussing the 'polyvocality' of the Supreme Court's decisions, Robinson suggests that:

finality and coherence may be overvalued, and that a degree of limited plurality may have undervalued benefits. These may include experimentation, encouraging disputing parties to keep returning to the judicial system for redress, and an ability to allow for more situational justice.[55]

These accounts of how the Supreme Court has positioned itself serve both to explain the variability of the Court's approach and to defend it as necessary in the context of Indian constitutionalism. At the same time, these commentators and others are alive to the dangers of the approach. One of these is a potential backlash from government against judicial intervention. More broadly, the expansion of the Supreme Court's role and power means that judicial accountability and independence are ever more pressing issues. Against this background, the fact that judges continue to be appointed through an opaque process that is formally dominated by the judiciary and, at the same time, susceptible to unwarranted executive influence is problematic.

Conclusion

The Indian Constitution occupies an important space in studies of constitutionalism and comparative constitutional law. It is a Constitution made in the Western liberal mode but adapted, textually and in practice, for the Indian context. In a sense, it is this tension which has informed discussion about Indian constitutionalism ever since the Constitution came into effect. Thus, concerns about what secularism means in India and debate about the impact of the Constitution's transformative agenda loom large in the scholarship. Communal violence, widespread poverty and high levels of corruption are troubling features of India's democracy. At the same time, the fact that the Constitution has endured through the decades, providing a level of stability for a vast, heterogeneous population is impressive.

The Indian Supreme Court has played an unusually significant role in giving content to constitutional values and ensuring a level of

---

[55] N. Robinson, 'Structure Matters: The Impact of Court Structure on the Indian and US Supreme Courts' (2013) 61 *American Journal of Comparative Law* 173, 206.

constitutional stability. In the process, the Court has – often controversially – expanded its powers. It has done so by responding to gaps in legitimacy, acting against repressive governmental measures and situating itself as a public interest institution. The much-discussed variability of the Court's approach highlights concerns about its own democratic legitimacy. Acting as it has done involves a careful balancing exercise – 'providing enough to be a locus of hope but also restraining itself in its actual effects so as not to provoke a backlash'.[56] Whether it can, and should, continue to play such a role depends on a host of complex factors. Thus far, the Court's has secured a level of public legitimacy for itself because it is seen to be acting when representative institutions have failed to do so. In the coming decades, the Court's understanding of its own limits and enhanced judicial accountability mechanisms will be crucial.

Further Reading

G. Austin, *Working a Democratic Constitution: A History of the Indian Constitution* (Oxford University Press, 2003).

G. Austin, *The Indian Constitution: Cornerstone of a Nation* (Oxford University Press, 1999).

S. Choudhry, M. Khosla and P.B. Mehta, *The Oxford Handbook of the Indian Constitution* (Oxford University Press, 2016).

S. Krishnaswamy, *Democracy and Constitutionalism in India: A Study of the Basic Structure Doctrine* (Oxford University Press, 2011).

S.P. Sathe, *Judicial Activism in India: Transgressing Borders and Enforcing Limits* (Oxford University Press, 2002).

H.M. Seervai, *Constitutional Law of India* (Universal Law Publishing Company, 2004).

A.K. Thiruvengandam, *The Constitution of India (Constitutional Systems of the World Series)* (Bloomsbury, 2017).

[56] Mehta, n. 54, 240.

Qianfan Zhang

Introduction: Does China Have a Constitution?

Does China have a constitution? That depends on the way in which the word 'constitution' is understood. It is commonly thought that China did not have a written constitution until 1908, when the last dynasty enacted the Outline of Imperial Constitution (*qinding xianfa dagang*), but this does not mean that traditional China was not governed by basic rules and norms. As I argued previously, the Confucian cultural tradition that dominated China for over 2,000 years was centred on the fundamental moral precepts of humanity (*ren*) and righteousness (*yi*), around which an elaborate body of rules on rites, ceremonies, etiquette, and other aspects of human behaviour was developed.[1] Taken together, they formed a vast normative system of 'propriety' (*li*, sometimes translated as 'rites'),[2] which

[1] Q. Zhang, 'Propriety, Law and Harmony: A Functional Argument for the Rule of Virtue', in J. Tao et al. (eds.), *Governance for Harmony in Asia and Beyond* (Routledge, 2010), 282–314.

[2] See J. Legge, *The Sacred Books of China*, vols. 27 & 28 (Clarendon Press, 1885).

stood for a set of customs, conventions and procedures to be practiced in daily life for the purposes of cultivating moral virtue, directing and containing human passions, and preserving a well-ordered society. Indeed, these rules were collected in a dense *Book of Rites* (*Li Ji*) and enforced by generations of the Confucian gentry, to various degrees of efficacy. To that extent, the traditional China did have a constitution – even a written constitution, if 'constitution' is meant to be a set of fundamental rules that govern society.

On the other hand, modern China has experienced a series of written constitutions. Unfortunately, none except the Nationalist Constitution (of the Republic of China) enacted in 1946 and now enforced in Taiwan has had any binding force of law. The current constitution applicable to mainland China, enacted in 1982, emphatically states in its Preamble that the constitution 'is the fundamental law of the state and has supreme legal authority'. In that sense China clearly has a constitution. In reality, however, the constitution cannot be applied in the courts, and cases abound where the constitutional provisions or principles are violated without effective remedy. If one takes the word 'constitution' seriously, a constitution should consist of binding norms that govern the state, more than mere words printed on paper. On this reading, mainland China does not seem to have a real constitution; at most, it has only a feeble constitution, one without any 'teeth' in the sense that its provisions for protecting individual rights and regulating public powers have failed to control the practical operation of the state. A constitution without constitutionalism is necessarily a weak, if not a downright fake, one.[3]

There are roughly four scenarios under which a constitution exhibits different degrees of binding force. First, a constitution is strongest when both the people it governs and their government are motivated to enforce it – to be more precise, when the people, who are naturally motivated to enforce the constitution that protects their rights, are able to oblige the government to do the same through political and legal mechanisms, often provided in the constitution itself, e.g. periodic elections and judicial review.[4] Good examples are the Constitution of the United States, widely regarded as the first written constitution in the modern world, and the

---

[3] Q. Zhang, 'A Constitution without Constitutionalism? The Paths of Constitutional Developments in China' (2010) 8 *International Journal of Constitutional Law* 950–976.

[4] See e.g. L.D. Kramer, *The People Themselves: Popular Constitutionalism and Judicial Review* (Oxford University Press, 2004), 3–6, 73–91.

constitutions of other developed democracies established thereafter. Since the modern constitution is designed to define and limit the power of the government, a rationally self-interested government actor is motivated to abide by the constitution only if he is obliged to do so – failing to enforce the constitution would cost even more than the inconveniences imposed by the constitution on the free exercise of public power.

Second, a constitution is decisively weakened when the people are not empowered to enforce and defend it, but the government and social elite are somehow interested in enforcing its norms. This was the case with traditional China, an authoritarian regime that enforced a hierarchical order defined in its social constitution (*li*), which favoured the interest of the ruling elite. The ordinary people participated in the practice of *li* and obeyed social norms in an orderly state, but such practice was largely passive because these norms were not created by them and some of the norms worked plainly for the interest of the ruling elites at their expense.[5] An authoritarian constitution, buttressed by the elites without popular support, would decay when the elites became incapable of maintaining the moral norms and social order. In the case of traditional China, it was the irreplaceable status of the Confucian culture in an isolated inland civilization that was able to revitalize once again the decayed social norms (*li*) after the order was reinstalled, producing a cycle of dynasties sharing primarily the same moral constitution. The written constitutions of Saudi Arabia (1993) and the United Arab Emirates (1971) are modern examples of this category, with barely disguised authoritarian inclinations. And China's Constitution after the 2018 amendment seems to be moving towards this direction when it eliminated the term limit of the President of the State and put the leadership of the Communist Party in the very first article of the Constitution, even though the ruling party also promised 'constitutional review' for the first time since 1949.

Third, a constitution is rendered empty words when it is filled with lofty declarations that exalt the nominal 'people' above everything else without, however, empowering any real people to defend it, as in the case of socialist republics, including the former Soviet Union and its East European satellites and contemporary China. In these totalitarian states,

---

[5] It is impossible, for example, for a woman to voluntarily support the foot-binding custom that used to bring misery to generations of Chinese women, unless she has been brainwashed into believing that it is for some reason a 'virtuous' act.

it does not take long for the ruling elites to find constitutional enforcement plainly against their self-interest, even though it *is* in their personal interest to pay lip service to the constitution. In reality, they will use every means available to prevent the people from exercising their constitutional rights to limit the abuse of public powers. In the end, no one is in the position to enforce the constitution and, sure enough, the constitution will become a pure façade, a 'noble lie' – with only the ruling elites as a whole being shrewd enough to know that it is nothing but a lie, under which the state is used as a convenient weapon for plundering its people. Such a situation is, of course, not limited to the totalitarian constitutions; the same tendency is seen in virtually all the authoritarian states dressed in the cloak of 'democratic republic', but it is most accentuated in the totalitarian states, e.g. the Soviet Union and the socialist republics established after WWII,[6] where the omnipotent state power is monopolized by one ruling party, often ultimately by one man, and the constitution is but a piece of propaganda for political beautification.

Last, though not the least, and certainly the most relevant here, the situation in these countries gets somewhat better when the people have realized that constitutional enforcement is after all in their own interest and some of them are courageous enough to endeavour to realize what was supposed to be purely nominal. It will be terribly difficult for them to achieve anything since the whole state machinery works against them. But, who knows? With some luck and perhaps benevolence on the conscientious part of the ruling elites, institutional improvements are occasionally achievable. Such is the situation with China since 1978, when it entered the era of 'reform and opening' (*gaige kaifang*). For example, soon after the twenty-seven-year-old Sun Zhigang was beaten to death by fellow inmates when he was illegally detained by the police in Guangzhou, the State Council abolished its notorious Detention and Repatriation Regulation under the mounting public protest on the internet.[7] Of course, achievements of this sort are purely ad hoc and reversible. In recent years, the government has significantly tightened ideological control and reduced intellectual freedom on public discussion, so much so that

---

[6] The conception of totalitarianism was originally used for the fascist regimes and applied to the communist regimes after the WWII. For a conceptual analysis, see C. Friedrich and Z.K. Brzezinski, *Totalitarian Dictatorship and Autocracy*, 2nd ed. (Praeger, 1967).

[7] See Zhang, 'A Constitution without Constitutionalism', 964–967.

the very term of 'constitutionalism' became one of the 'sensitized words' (*min'gan ci*), forbidden at least in formal publications.[8]

It is under such background that this chapter describes the constitution of China. The chapter first provides a brief constitutional history of China, centring on the cycles of order and chaos, liberty and repression, reform and revolution. Next, it discusses the conservative (orthodox) and liberal (new) principles that coexist in the same constitutional text. This is followed by a description of the state institutions defined in China's constitution. It ends with a summary explanation of why China's constitution remains unenforced and what it will take to make it enforceable.

1 A Brief History

Over two millennia ago, Mengzi once famously said: 'The world (*tianxia*) has long been created, and has been alternating between good governance (*zhi*) and chaos (*luan*).'[9] Since China was violently united by the First Emperor (*Qin Shihuang*) in 221 BC, it had experienced a dozen major dynasties.[10] During a dynasty, China often experienced 'good governance', meaning that the imperial authority was capable of maintaining social order and enforcing social norms (*li*), but usually without moral and intellectual freedom. The end of the dynasty would witness serious disruption of social and moral order, a state of unlimited 'freedom' plagued by wars, civil unrest and significant loss of human lives. The Confucian scholar would lament helplessly the collapse of *li* and the decay of norms imposed on the people and the ruling elites. After the restoration of order, a new dynasty would be established on the basis of the old moral and social order; the collapsed social norms defined in *li* would be reinforced and applied once again in full vigour, thus perpetuating the periodic dynastic cycle.[11]

Since the first Opium War in 1840, the last (Qing) dynasty, established by a small ethnic minority, Manchu, faced a fundamentally different

---

[8] In May 2013, the CCP internal document listed 'seven taboos' (*qi bujiang*), including universal values, press freedom, civil society, civil rights, historical mistakes of the CCP, crony capitalism and judicial independence.

[9] *Mengzi*, 3B: 9.

[10] Twenty-four if one counts minor ones and three pre-Qin dynasties: Xia, Shang and Zhou.

[11] For *li* as a constitutional norm, see C. Hahm, 'Ritual and Constitutionalism: Disputing the Ruler's Legitimacy in a Confucian Polity' (2009) 57 *American Journal of Comparative Law* 135.

challenge: competition of ideas, goods and gun powers from the Western world. By 1894–1895, when China was defeated in fateful battles with the quickly developing Japan, the imperial court decided, after a long lag and with much unwillingness, to embark on an experiment by enacting a modern constitution, culminating in 1908 with the Outline of Imperial Constitution. Throughout the whole period, the rule of the last dynasty was frequently compromised by wars with foreign forces, domestic violence and revolutionary insurrections. On the other hand, the same era afforded intellectual freedom that allowed the Chinese elites to thoroughly reflect on the social and political order on which the future state was to be founded. Before long, both liberalism and Communism were introduced to marginalize the elitist Confucian tradition, which suffered its first major blow in 1905 with the abolition of the official examination system by which the ruling elites had been selected for over a thousand years. The old regime was left alone without its elite defenders.[12]

The dynastic cycle was finally broken in 1911, when China established the very first republic in Asia, way before Japan did so, at the end of WWII (1946), and India, following its independence (1950). As Kongzi once preached, however: 'more haste, less speed.'[13] Broken was the cycle of dynasties, but not the alternation between order and chaos. Unlike India, which inherited the British common law tradition and the spirit of gradualist reform, China has been caught in seemingly endless cycles of oppressive order and violent ruptures. In 1927–1928, following years of feuds with the remnants of the old regime and various warlords, the Nationalists, who initially established the first republic, eventually reunified China by reorganizing the party on the Soviet model. The political order was soon challenged, however, first by the violent purge of the Communists and then by the Japanese invasion. In 1935–1936, when Nehru was travelling 50,000 miles in rural India, delivering speeches to and gathering votes from millions of peasants,[14] the Red Army led by the Chinese Communist Party (CCP) embarked on the Long March to escape military annihilation by the Nationalists. In less than fifteen years, however, the CCP surprised the world by toppling the Nationalist regime after

[12] See J.D. Spencer, *The Search for Modern China* (W.W. Norton, 1990), 230–243.
[13] *Analects*, 13: 17.
[14] N.G. Jayal, *Democracy in India* (Oxford University Press, 2001), 22–23.

three years of bloody civil war following years of the Japanese invasion and established a totalitarian regime that has lasted to this day.

With unchecked party-state powers, the pendulum of Chinese history once again swung to the extreme of order with unbearable oppressiveness, erupted by man-made chaos and persecutions. The first three decades of the Communist regime established in 1949 are known for their major human disasters and political movements on an unprecedented scale. None of the three Communist constitutions (enacted in 1954, 1975 and 1978) were able to save the country from falling into the abyss of extreme form of arbitrary and abusive rule. Mao Zedong permanently shelved the constitution he himself drafted by initiating the Great Leap Forward (1958–1960), which led to the great famine that cost the lives of tens of millions, and the Great Cultural Revolution (1966–1976), which virtually plunged the country into civil war in order to save his personal power from the challenge of his comrade rivals.[15] Before the personal whim of the supreme leader, constitutional norms were nothing more than superfluous decoration for a self-proclaimed socialist republic.

Recovering from the great traumas, China began its reform and opening in 1978. The pendulum seemed to swing towards the side of moderate governance with limited freedom. In the next three decades, China has experienced speedy economic growth and gradual loosening of the state control over society. In 1982 the CCP, under the leadership of Deng Xiaoping, enacted the current constitution, which was amended successively in 1988, 1993, 1999, 2004 and 2018. As the Tiananmen tragedy in 1989 attested, however, China is still learning to live in the state of 'ordered liberty'[16] and to put an end to the seemingly endless vacillation between chaotic freedom and oppressive order. Unfortunately, the liberal trend seems to have been reversed since 2013, when the new regime took over, and the political pendulum is swinging back once again to the Communist past. The backlash is attested by the constitutional amendment in March 2018, which heightened the pitch of political ideology and aggravated the fusion between the party and the state by, among other things, establishing the supervisory commission (*jiancha weiyuanhui*).

---

[15] For a succinct review of Chinese political history, see K. Lieberthal, *Governing China: From Revolution Through Reform*, 2nd ed. (W.W. Norton & Co, 2003).

[16] See J. Cardozo's exposition in *Palko* v. *Connecticut*, 302 US 319 (1937).

2 Principles of the 1982 Constitution

Though a mark of the new order, the 1982 Constitution was in nature by and large a reversion to the pre-Cultural Revolution era under the dominance of the CCP's moderate mainstream. As such, it inherited the basic socialist spirit from the 1954 Constitution and, indeed, even the 1949 Common Programme (a founding document for the People's Republic that laid down the orthodox Marxist principles coupled with Chinese characteristics). In practice, these principles served only as formalities through which the party-state powers were exercised, without playing any substantive role in regulating the exercise of the public powers. All the old principles are still in the constitution, however; they are like zombies in the desert, occasionally resurrected to remind people of the distant past. In spite of them, China has evolved during the last three decades towards a more or less open society characterized by market economy, rule of law, and a large and growing internet community – in other words, a radically different world from the totalitarian state established during the 1950s. The new social reality necessarily gives rise to new norms and principles that are widely accepted today by the Chinese society, some of which are codified in the constitutional amendments. These new principles point to the direction towards which contemporary China has been developing until recent years.

a Orthodox Constitutional Principles

The 1982 Constitution contains 143 articles in four chapters. Paraphrasing the Marxist ideology expressed in the 1949 Common Program, the first chapter on General Principles defines the nature of the state as 'a socialist country of people's democratic dictatorship led by the working class and founded on the worker-peasant alliance', where socialism is the 'fundamental system' of the state, the disruption of which is strictly 'prohibited' (Art. 1). These terms are so outdated that even the official party documents have long ceased to bother paying them lip service.

To highlight the new order under the party leadership, the Preamble explicitly expressed Deng Xiaoping's insistence on the Four Cardinal Principles (*sixiang jiben yuanze*), which included the political leadership of the CCP, the state foundation on the 'people's democratic dictatorship', the economic system of the 'socialist road', and the ideological guidance of Marxism, Leninism and Mao Zedong Thought. Added to this list are the 'Deng Xiaoping theory', the 'important thoughts of three represents' (*sange daibiao*), which demands that the ruling CCP should 'represent the most fundamental interest of the overwhelming majority of the people', the 'concept of scientific development' and 'Xi Jinping's thought on socialism with the Chinese characters in the new era', by the constitutional amendments of 1999, 2004 and 2018, respectively. In practice the most important and perhaps the only relevant principle today is the CCP leadership, which ironically runs counter to the spirit of constitutionalism.

The Preamble did highlight the legal nature of the constitution by defining it as 'the fundamental law of the state with supreme legal effect'. The legal force of the Constitution is reaffirmed by Article 5, which explicitly provides that 'no laws or administrative and local rules or regulations may contravene the Constitution'. In practice, however, the CCP has consistently refused to adopt any form of judicial review as a necessary means for constitutional enforcement. In fact, it has so far declined even to establish a constitutional committee within the legislative branch to oversee the constitutionality of legal norms.

Politically, all state powers belong to the people, who exercise their powers through the National People's Congress (NPC) and local people's congresses (LPC) at various levels of government (Art. 2). The state institutions follow the principle of 'democratic centralism' (*minzhu jizhongzhi*), which means that the NPC and LPC at various levels are made 'responsible to the people' by periodic elections, and that the deputies thus constituted in turn supervise all administrative, judicial and procuratorial departments by electing the leadership of these departments at their levels. As a compound of two opposite orders, one bottom-up and the other top-down, the principle of democratic centralism also implies that a people's congress at a higher level is to be created either by one at a lower level or directly elected by their constituencies (the democratic element), but the government at the higher level is to direct and supervise the ones below (the centrist element). In practice, given the ineffectiveness of elections and electoral checks on power, the centrist inclination has always overwhelmed its democratic counterpart, thus reducing the apparently balanced principle to a lopsided structure in which the top-down supervisions alone exert force. The Constitution makes no effort to delimit the central and local powers, but adopts a vague principle of 'giving full scope to the initiative and enthusiasm of the local authorities under the unified leadership of the central authorities' in attempt to guide their functional divisions (Art. 3).

b New Constitutional Principles

The 1982 Constitution was drafted and promulgated in the initial stage of China's opening and reform, when Chinese society had barely begun to reopen itself to new ideas after decades of revolutionary bigotry, self-enclosure and self-destruction. It inherited from the 1949 Common Program and the 1954 Constitution the political and ideological framework that badly needed adjustments, to say the least, in order to comply with the fast-changing demands arising both from economic developments and from legal and constitutional consciousness that never cease to penetrate into the minds of ordinary people. Fortunately, China's unitary constitution allows timely revisions through a simple procedure, merely requiring an approval of a two-thirds majority of the NPC. As a result, the Constitution was amended in 1988, 1993, 1999, 2004 and 2018. So far, most amendments have been revisions of the economic system defined in the Preamble and the General Principles, but a few amendments did supplement fundamental constitutional principles on the rule of law and human rights that were previously absent in the constitution.[17]

In April 1988, the NPC approved two constitutional amendments, both on the economic system. The first supplemented Article 10.4 by allowing that 'the rights to the use of land be transferred according to law', thus giving limited space to market transactions within the straitjacket of public land ownership – the hallmark of socialism purporting to have under public ownership every major 'means of production' (*shengchan ziliao*). The second supplemented Article 11 of the Constitution by allowing 'the private sector of the economy to exist and develop within the limits prescribed by law'. The private economy, which used to be the target for 'transformation' (*gaizao*), was now 'a complement to the socialist public economy', which is to be 'guided, supervised, and controlled' by the state, but whose lawful rights and interests will also be protected by the same state.

In March 1993, the NPC approved a total of nine amendments. It changed the Preamble to highlight that China was in 'the primary stage

---

[17] See D. Cai, 'The Development of Constitutionalism in the Transition of Chinese Society' (2005) 19 *Columbia Journal of Asian Law* 1.

of socialism', during which the basic task of the state was 'socialist modernisation along the socialist road with Chinese characteristics'. The purpose of this amendment is to defend the ongoing economic reform against the orthodox leftist attacks. In order to reflect the new idea of separating management from ownership, whatever enterprises used to be 'state-run' were all changed to 'state-owned', implying that the state was no longer in charge of daily management of public enterprises. The planned economy provisions in Articles 15, 16 and 17 were deleted and replaced by the notion of 'socialist market economy' and 'macro regulation' to be implemented by the state through economic legislation. The 1993 amendment also deleted, belatedly, the term of 'People's Commune', and changed the definition of collective ownership in rural areas to the primary form of household responsibility system. Last but not least, the term of the LPCs at county level was extended from three to five years (Art. 98); the LPCs at the township level were not extended to the same term until 2004, when the constitutional amendment made the People's Congresses at all levels a uniform five-year term.

In 1999, the NPC approved six amendments. First, it reassured the validity of the previous amendment by making the emphasis that 'China will be in the primary stage of socialism for a long time to come', during which the public economy as the principal component in the socialist economic system was to develop together with 'multiple forms of economies' (Art. 6). The status of the private sector was elevated from 'a complement' in the 1988 Amendment to 'the important constituent component' of the socialist market economy (Art. 11). And the political notion of 'counter-revolutionary activities' punished by the state was changed to a more legalistic jargon of 'unlawful activities that harm state security' (Art. 28), followed by corresponding changes in the Criminal Law. More significantly, the 1999 Amendment inserted in the beginning of Article 5 that China is committed to 'administration of the state according to law' and construction of a 'socialist rule of law state'.

In comparison to the previous amendments, the amendment in 2004 was the most extensive in scope, revising as many as fourteen provisions. It was the product of the new regime headed by Secretary-General Hu Jingtao, who succeeded ex-President Jiang Zemin in 2003, shortly before the outbreak of the SARS epidemic and the landmark Sun Zhigang incident.[18] The latter prompted the ruling party to give constitutional recognition to 'human rights' for the first time since the founding of the People's Republic, a notion that used to be ridiculed for its 'petit bourgeois sentiment', and inserted a broad declaration in Article 33: 'The state respects and protects human rights.' It deviated from the classical Marxist conception of a 'class constitution' since what are now respected and protected are not only rights for workers, peasants or any particular 'good class', but 'human' rights in general, that is, rights of all human beings which, literally understood, include even such 'enemies' as those who used to be named 'counter-revolutionaries'. The 2004 amendment, then, signifies a partial repudiation of the Marxist class-based cosmology underlying all previous constitutions. The class language in the Preamble and General Principles remain intact in the 1982 Constitution, however, which creates tensions between the original text and recent amendments that are products of quite a different spirit. The new cosmology is confirmed in corresponding amendments to the Preamble by expanding the 'patriotic united front' to embrace 'all socialist working people, builders of the socialist cause' and by inserting the 'Three Represents' theory, according to which the CCP is supposed to 'represent the most fundamental interests of the broadest range of the people'.

Consistently with the general ideological shift and carrying the momentum of the previous amendments, the 2004 Amendment further strengthens the equal protection of the private economy. The notion of 'individual and private' sectors is generalized to that of 'non-public' economies, whose 'lawful rights and interests' are protected by the state (Art. 12.2). The new Article 13 goes so far as to declare that the 'lawful private property of citizens is inviolable', almost a paraphrase of Article 12, which dictates that 'socialist public property is holy inviolable'. Not only is the status of private property enhanced to almost parallel with that of public property, but taking of private property for the public interest explicitly gives rise, for the first time, to a requirement to provide 'compensation' (Art. 13).[19] Although mere 'compensation', if literally taken, is

---

[18] See Q. Zhang, *The Constitution of China: A Contextual Analysis* (Hart Publishing, 2012), 75–80.

[19] The 1982 Constitution does provide for the 'public interest' condition for taking, though without requiring 'compensation'. The other major revisions include the authorization of the State President to conduct 'state visits' (Art. 81) and change of vocabulary from 'martial law' to 'state of emergency' (Art. 67.20) in wake of the SARS epidemic in 2003,

meaningless without the 'just' requirement, these revisions reflect significant changes in the constitutional consciousness of China's legislators, officials, scholars and ordinary people since the promulgation of the 1982 Constitution.

An obvious backlash came with the latest amendment in 2018, however, when it inserted in Article 1 that 'the CCP leadership is the most essential character of socialism with the Chinese characters'. Although it made room for constitutional review by changing the Law Committee within the NPC to the 'Constitution and Law Committee' (Article 70), it eliminated the term limit of the President of the State (Article 79) and inserted before the provisions on the judiciary a whole section on the new supervisory commission (Articles 123–127), which essentially incorporates the party's disciplinary committee into the state. It remains to be seen whether these textual changes will withstand the test of time.

Overall, although the 1982 Constitution is a 'socialist constitution', there is hardly anything 'socialist' left in its substance. Not only has the socialist ideology been diluted by the new, more liberal amendments, but the socialist promises in the Constitution have never been delivered. The imprint of a socialist constitution is, for example, visible in its numerous positive rights, such as the right to labour and rest, the right to education, the right to social insurance, and the rights of women and the handicapped, which *are* defined in Articles 42–49 in the 1982 Constitution.[20] But these rights hardly mean anything in reality. And, for a 'socialist' country living with its totalitarian legacy, this is necessarily the case. Not only do positive rights, the implementation of which requires adequate state capacity, fail to have any effect, but such standard constitutional safeguards as freedom of speech and belief are regularly breached, and the electoral scheme is systematically manipulated by the party-state. Indeed, the only provision of which the people feel the daily effect is one of the Cardinal Principles in the Preamble: the CCP leadership. If the one-party monopoly is the last and lasting essence of every social

when the central or local governments were compelled to take compulsory non-military action for protecting the public interest.

[20] These rights are usually coupled with constitutional duties, e.g. duties to work (Art. 42), to receive education (46), to exercise birth control (Art. 49), etc. For a critique of including duties and unscrupulous positive rights in the constitution, see Q. Zhang, 'What a Constitution Should Not Provide For' (2005) 3 *ECUPL Journal* 25.

constitution, then one may be able to say that China's constitution is still 'socialist', but that is all that is socialist it is left with.

3 State Institutions

The 1982 Constitution does provide a formal framework of the governing structure in Chapter 3. As a socialist system, China's constitution adopted a unitary framework from its very founding, with the People's Congresses situated at the apex of the power structure. Beneath the People's Congresses are 'one government and two (judicial) chambers' (*yifu liangyuan*). If the 1982 Constitution establishes a unique unicameral legislature with two chambers and a dual judiciary, it establishes an even more unique 'triplet' administrative structure, with three institutions sharing what are normally categorized as 'administrative' powers: the head of the state, the chief executive, and the military commander. The government and the judiciary are supposed to be elected and supervised by the People's Congresses at their respective levels, while maintaining independence among themselves, though it is common for the government to dominate over the judiciary.

a The Unitary Legislature

To begin with, the 1982 Constitution, resembling the British parliamentary model but rejecting the US model of separation of powers, vests China's primary legislatures, the NPC and LPC at various levels alone with the constituent and thus nominally supreme power. Consistent with the socialist ideology, which usually presupposes the presence of a simple majority will,[21] all People's Congresses are made unicameral legislatures, and any law or local regulation needs only to pass one particular Congress to take effect.

Each People's Congress above the county level is equipped with a Standing Committee, which is sometimes seen as the 'second chamber'; it *is* a 'second chamber' in view of its independent authority to pass laws or

---

[21] Chinese constitutional scholars are well aware of the dilemma raised by the French scholar, Sieyes, a century ago: if the House and the Senate in a bicameral system disagree, which should be seen as representing the 'general will' expressed by the majority of the people? See M. Lianying, 'The Legislature', in Z. Qianfan and X. Zesheng (eds.), *The Study of Constitutional Law*, 2nd ed. (Law Press, 2008), Ch. 7.

local regulations alone. This does not, however, make China's legislature 'bicameral', since both a whole Congress and its Standing Committee are capable of passing legislations of almost equal legal force, and since the work of a Standing Committee is also supposedly subject to review of the entire Congress (Constitution Art. 62); in this sense a Standing Committee is an inferior though independent and alternative legislature. Above all, the Standing Committees were created not for the purpose of an alternative representative scheme (for example, regions rather than population) or legislative check and balances, but rather to facilitate law-making and, indeed, to lead the whole Congress.

It is perhaps somewhat justified to characterize China's representative system as 'quasi-bicameral' since, in addition to the People's Congresses and their Standing Committees, the Political Consultative Committees at various levels also play some legislative role, and convene at the same time with their congressional counterparts every year. The PCC is not, however, a formal institution defined in the Constitution, and its resolutions, however influential on state policy making, lack formal binding force. To be accurate, the NPC and LPC are the sole legislative bodies from which other state institutions are created.

b The Triplet Executive

While modern 'mixed' constitutions incorporate a presidency within a parliamentary framework and result in the 'dual heads' scenario, usually a directly elected president and a cabinet created by and accountable to the parliamentary majority, the powers of China's most powerful central government are divided among three institutions. If the State President serves mostly as an honorary symbol of the state, the State Council holds most substantive powers of administration in its capacity as the Central People's Government (CPG, *zhongyang renmin zhengfu*), and the military power is vested in a separate Central Military Commission, which ordinarily overlaps with its counterpart in the CCP with exactly the same name.[22] Deviating significantly from the 1954 Constitution, where the military power was vested in the State President, this arrangement is often criticized as an instrument for politicizing the military and facilitating the CCP's ultimate

---

[22] For exceptional cases where the two CMCs do not exactly coincide, see Zhang, *Constitution of China*, 152–153.

control over the state.[23] From 1982 until now, the pattern of distribution has been changing in China. The three powers used to be controlled by separate hands, but a stable pattern gradually formed after 1989, after Jiang Zemin replaced Zhao Ziyang as the Secretary-General of the CCP in the aftermath of the June Fourth Incident. Nowadays the Secretary-General is also the head of the state and military commander, and forms a 'troika', as it were, with the NPCSC Chairman and the chief executive (Premier).

The powers of the President, defined in Articles 80 and 81 of the Constitution, are largely limited to authenticate the decisions made by the NPC or its Standing Committee. These include the decisions to 'promulgate statutes', to appoint or remove the Premier, Vice-Premiers, State Councillors, Ministers, the Auditor-General and the Secretary-General of the State Council, to issue orders of special pardons, to declare war or state of emergency, to issue mobilization orders, to appoint or recall plenipotentiary representatives abroad, and to ratify or abrogate treaties and important agreements concluded with foreign nations. The apparent lack of substantial power is in sharp contrast to the real power exercised daily by the President – in the capacity of being the Secretary-General of the CCP rather than the President himself, as the two positions have merged in the same person since late 1989. This contrast prompted the constitutional amendment in 2004, which conferred on the President 'the capacity of conducting activities of national affairs'. Despite this somewhat vague empowerment, the nature of the presidential power remains symbolic.

The military power removed from the president by the 1954 Constitution was taken over by the newly formed CMC (*zhongyang junwei*), the most cryptic institution in the 1982 Constitution, regulated only by two articles. Article 93 of the Constitution defines the CMC as the supreme military organ in charge of leading the national military force. It is led by a Chairman, who is elected by the NPC and is responsible to the NPC and its Standing Committee (Art. 94). Unlike the State Council or local governments, the CMC is not regulated by organic law or other types of statutes. Although the Law on Legislation barely mentions in its 'Supplementary Provisions' that the CMC 'enacts military regulations in accordance with the Constitution and other laws' (Art. 93), it specifies

---

[23] Thus, China's liberals often call for the 'nationalization of armies' (*jundui guojia hua*). See Charter 08 signed by over 300 intellectuals in China and published on 10 December 2008, www.vckbase.com/bbs/viewtopic2.asp?rid=3537795&tsf=96.

no mechanism for ensuring conformity of military regulations with the Constitution and laws.

With the exception of the military and defence power, all other substantive powers of the central government are lodged in the most important administrative organ – the State Council (*guowu yuan*). In fact, the State Council *is* the Central People's Government, 'the executive body of the highest organ of state power' and 'the highest organ of state administration' (Art. 85). The State Council is composed of the Premier and Vice-Premiers, State Councillors, Ministers in charge of ministries or commissions, Auditor-General, and Secretary-General. While the Premier assumes 'overall responsibility for the work of the State Council', the Ministers assume 'overall responsibility' for the specific areas of which they are in charge, and the State Councillors are entrusted by the Premier to take charge of special tasks or specific areas of work and may conduct foreign affairs on behalf of the State Council (Organic Law of the State Council, Art. 6). Important issues are decided after discussions at plenary meetings attended by the whole Council or, more often, at the executive meetings (*changwu huiyi*) attended by the Premier and Vice-Premiers, the State Councillors, and the Secretary-General (Art. 4). All these meetings are chaired by the Premier.

Unlike most democratic countries, in which the audit offices are usually affiliated with the parliament, China's auditing office is established within the administrative branch itself, with the purpose of 'supervis[ing] through auditing the revenue and expenditure of all departments under the State Council and of the local governments at various levels, and the revenue and expenditure of all financial and monetary organizations, enterprises and institutions of the state' (Art. 91). To guarantee its independence and fairness, however, the Constitution does place this office under the immediate direction of the Premier in order that it 'independently exercises its power of supervision through auditing in accordance with the law, subject to no interference by any other administrative organ or any public organisation or individual' (Art. 91).

c The Dualist Judiciary

Unlike most countries where legal prosecution is normally part of the administration, consistently with the pivotal role it had played in imperial China, the procuratorate was made a separate and supposedly independent institution within the judicial branch (Art. 134), and constitutes, along with the courts, a 'dualist' judiciary. While the judges are in charge of trials and appeals, the procurators are primarily responsible for prosecutions and investigations for official corruption. The two judicial branches with separate functions check against each other in some respects, but often act in concert on major policy initiatives. The discussion below focuses on the courts, though the procuratorate has undergone similar – indeed, more dramatic – reform, since parts of its power will be allocated to the new supervision system.[24] Through the 2018 constitutional amendment, a new structure of the supervisory commissions was inserted *before* the judicial structure, essentially incorporating the CCP's disciplinary function into the state. The new institution is supposed to orchestrate the judicial functions in handling duty-related crimes by 'cooperating with judicial organs, procuratorial organs, and law enforcement organs, with mutual checks' (Art. 127).

Recovering from the lawless destruction of the Cultural Revolution and recognizing the importance of law, the 1982 Constitution reaffirms the courts as 'judicial organs of the state' (Art. 128), composed of the Supreme People's Court (SPC), local courts at various levels, military courts and other special courts. Inheriting the revolutionary tradition, however, the courts are not kept independent once created, but subject to the supervision of the People's Congresses at the same levels (Art. 133). Article 131 does provide that 'the people's courts exercise judicial power independently, in accordance with the provisions of the law, and are not subject to interference by any administrative organ, public organisation or individual'. But the significance of this provision has been questioned on at least two grounds. First, it excludes interferences from the government, individuals, organizations and possibly political parties if they are interpreted to be a form of 'public organization', but it is silent about the People's Congresses and the procuratorates for reasons that both are in charge of supervising the courts – the former through the elections of the judges and supervision of the court performance as a whole, and the latter through the protestation procedure used against individual judgments they deem wrong. It was once debated whether the People's Congresses could supervise individual cases (*ge'an jiandu*), and this question has been

[24] Q. Ailing, 'The Emerging "State Supervisory commission"', *Southern Reviews*, 10 February 2017, www.nfcmag.com/article/7055.html.

answered in the negative; deputies may, according to the Constitution and laws, investigate or remove judges who improperly performed their functions, but such power does not authorize them to inquire into cases they find to be wrongfully decided.[25]

Second and more profoundly, Article 131 provides for the 'court independence' rather than independence of individual judges. Literally understood, a court enjoys institutional protection against interferences from other institutions or individuals, but individual judges do not enjoy the same protection in daily judicial practice; in other words, they may be subject to the direction and supervision of the court leaders, and in fact they are. The Organic Law of the People's Courts establishes the so-called 'president responsibility system' (*yuanzhang fuzezhi*), by which the president, assisted by the judicial committee (*shenpan weiyuanhui*), is held responsible for all the judgments made by the court. If the president finds 'definite error in the determination of facts or application of law' in a legally effective judgment of his court, he is obliged to submit the judgment to the judicial committee for disposal (Art. 14). Presided over by the court president and staffed by the vice presidents and senior judges, the judicial committee is a 'court' within the court structure whose major task is to practice 'democratic centralism' by 'summing up judicial experience and discussing important or difficult cases' (Arts. 36–37). In fact, it directly decides cases and replaces different judgments made by presiding judges even though none of the committee members may have heard the case.

To summarize, in the shadow of revolutionary legacy, the Chinese judiciary has been suffering from a 'syndrome' that is an interlocking combination of dysfunctional symptoms: (1) local protectionism that seriously undermines the uniformity of law; (2) overall low professional and moral quality of the judges, making them prone to corruption and unfit for the impartial administration of justice; (3) primacy of bureaucratic management of the courts and political control of the judges, which is at odds with the generally recognized principle of judicial independence and impartiality; and (4) the lack of adequate material provisions (income, funding and working conditions) that are necessary

---

[25] C. Dingjian, 'The Current Status and the Reform of the People's Congress's Individual Case Supervision', in C. Dingjian (ed.), *Supervision and Judicial Fairness: A Study and Case Report* (Beijing: Law Press, 2005), 69.

for the effective functioning of the courts.[26] In 1999, the SPC felt compelled to launch judicial reform, which was meant to eradicate China's judicial syndrome. Since then, China's judicial reform has experienced ebbs and flows, with limited substantive progress towards an independent judiciary. On the whole, judicial reform has fallen far short of its original aim.[27]

After years of standstill, it appears that China's judicial reform has suddenly accelerated. In July 2014, the SPC announced an outline of the Fourth Five-Year Reform Plan of the People's Court (2014–2018). This includes as many as forty-five reform measures in eight major areas, which can be summarized by four aspects: (1) improving the classification system of judicial personnel; (2) establishing judicial accountability by reducing the administrative powers of the court presidents and judicial committees; (3) realizing the occupational protection of judicial personnel; and (4) establishing the vertical administration of courts and procurator of offices below the provincial level.[28] These measures are elaborated in the full-length plan published near the end of February 2015. The SPC's Opinion on 'Comprehensively Deepening the People's Court Reform' contains sixty-five points of judicial reform, focusing on the establishments of a jurisdictional system that is adequately detached from the administrative zones, and a litigation system centred on adjudications, the optimization of functional distribution within the courts and the operational mechanism of judicial power, the construction of an open and transparent judicial system, promotion of professional development of judges, and the independent and impartial exercise of judicial power.

4 Local Governments

In comparison to the central government, China's local governments are placed in a much humbler position in the Constitution, but wield substantial powers delegated by the central government for the purpose of implementing laws and policies. Of course, unchecked local powers can

---

[26] Q. Zhang, 'The People's Court in Transition: The Prospects of the Chinese Judicial Reform' (2003) 12 *Journal of Contemporary China* 69.

[27] Q. Zhang, *Judicial Reform in China: An Overview*, in J. Garrick and Y.C. Bennett (eds.), *China's Socialist Rule of Law Reform under Xi Jinping* (Routledge, 2016), 17–29.

[28] Y. Dingbo, 'Judicial Reform Needs Be Promoted', *Legal Daily*, 18 July 2014.

be no less dangerous to individual liberty than unlimited national powers. The structure of local governments mirrors that of the national government by following the same congressional and 'one government, two chambers' model, with the LPC as the supreme local power electing and supervising the major leaders in the Local People's Government (LPG), court and procuratorate at the same level. Without the military and symbolic (presidential) components, the structure of a LPG is a good deal simpler than that of the national government.

The only complication comes from the fact that government at each level is matched with a party organization, which is in charge of overseeing the government decision-making. In fact, the party is an omnipotent and omnipresent shadow over every branch of public power; the two judicial branches and even the LPC are likewise under the supervision of their own party organizations. The structure of the ruling party is not stipulated in the 1982 Constitution other than the general leadership dictated by Article 1 and the first 'Cardinal Principle' in the Preamble, but it is the decisive factor for allocating powers to each formal institution defined in the Constitution.

The political party system is particularly important to China's central–local relationship since the organizing mechanism and power of parties matter a great deal to the division of central and local powers in practice. The former Soviet Union had contained even a dozen 'republics' together with their 'presidents',[29] a constitutional context that would suggest an extremely loose confederation made of over a hundred ethnic minorities, but the reality was precisely the opposite owing to the orchestrating role of the Soviet Communist Party. It is the same with its Chinese progeny, which has maintained a tight grip on society and governments at all levels since 1949 and produced a highly centralized governance structure in an extremely diverse country through its rigorously organized party machine. A strict hierarchy has been established within the party, which commands rigorous obedience of party members and cadres to

---

[29] This is still the case with the current Russian Constitution enacted in 1993 (see Art. 5). As a result, the Russian federalism underwent ebbs and flows during the Yeltsin era, but resumed unitary character after the powerful Putin took over since 2000. See K. von Beyme, 'Federalism in Russia', in U. Wachendorfer-Schmidt (ed.), *Federalism and Political Performance* (Routledge, 2000), 23–37; M. Filippov and O. Shvetsova, 'Federalism, Democracy, and Democratization', in A. Benz and J. Broschek (eds.), *Federal Dynamics: Continuity, Change, and the Varieties of Federalism* (Oxford University Press, 2013), 170–173.

their superiors so as to ensure the will expressed from the top of the power pyramid, now the Standing Committee of the Politburo, be carried out unimpeded through all levels until it reaches the very bottom. The parallel control the CCP exercises over the state institutions at various levels then enables the mere seven members of the Standing Committee to carry out their supreme political commands over the whole of China, and replaces the essentially bottom-up democratic design expressed in the People's Congress provisions of the 1982 Constitution with a top-down control mechanism in daily political practice.

However, is the Politburo or the new National Supervisory Commission, powerful as they are, capable of overseeing all levels of local party and state officials in every location? The strict top-down scheme may work in a country the size of Monaco, or even France. But China is a giant country with a population of 1.4 billion, a vast territory, with five (more accurately, six) levels of government. According to the national census conducted in 2015, China has, on the provincial level, 23 provinces together with 4 directly governed municipalities (*zhixiashi*) and 5 nationality autonomous regions (*shaoshu minzu zizhiqu*), which are subdivided into 291 large cities (at the prefecture level) and 361 cities (at the county level), over 1,500 counties and autonomous counties, nearly 40,000 towns and townships, and almost 700,000 villages,[30] each exercising some degrees of public power. The civil servants working in the various levels of governments (not including the armies, state-owned enterprise employees and teachers and researchers on the public payroll) are estimated to exceed 7 million, and over 10 million if the party organs are included. A single national government simply cannot keep its eyes over any local government for long and prevent it from abusing its power. Even a sophisticated cascade supervisory mechanism will not do, since the chain of supervision is too long to remain tight, and the force of the central command is dissipated at every joint and dwindle to insignificance before it reaches the lower end. This is why exclusive dependence on such partisan mechanisms as the disciplinary committees will necessarily fail to eradicate corruption. Even if it works to an extent, it might not be surprising at all to find that these committee members themselves turn out to be most corrupt since they hold the unchecked power to check everyone else, which is the very source of corruption.

---

[30] See http://data.stats.gov.cn/adv.htm?m=advquery&cn=C01.

Thus, in order to keep in check the powers of the party-state govern-ance at various levels, it is necessary to empower the people to elect their local officials and the courts to invalidate unlawful government acts so that the abuses of public power can be minimized at the local level. Failure to do so simply brings embarrassments to the rule of law. The Chinese lawmakers, knowing that the local governments cannot be trusted in exercising legislative powers over their own people who do not vote them in, deliberately keep some legislative powers away from them. One prominent example is Article 8 of the Law on Legislation, which reserves the 'restriction of personal freedom', among other important items, as a matter to be legislated exclusively by the NPC or its Standing Committee.[31] Thus, the local legislature is without power to regulate any matter that involves the restriction of personal freedom. Given China's size and diversity, however, the local governments surely feel the need to resort to the restriction of personal freedom as an effective means of law enforcement under some circumstances, and since these needs may well arise from purely local situations, the national legislature will not feel any urge in making such legislation; even if it chooses to act, a national legislature making essentially a local law is neither wise nor efficient. In the end, the local government is compelled to choose between either leaving the matter unresolved or acting without legal authoriza-tion. On the other hand, the local governments *are*, by necessity, left with many powers that, if unchecked, will invariably be abused and corrupted. This is attested by millions of 'petitions' (*shangfang*) gathering in Beijing every year, each appealing to redress some abuse of power at certain level of government somewhere in this vast land.[32] The central govern-ment, unable to investigate the deluge of petitions and full of dread of the mounting social pressure in the capital, simply commands the local officials to haul back all the petitioners in their jurisdictions at the risk of losing their post. A giant country like China is simply ungovernable without democracy and rule of law.

---

[31] The same provision also prohibits the State Council from exercising the same power without the national legislative authorization, and this is the very legal issue involved in the Sun Zhigang case, where the police acted according to the State Council's Detention and Repatriation Regulation, providing for the restriction of personal freedom without authorization required by the Law on Legislations. See Zhang, *Constitution of China*, 78–80.

[32] Z. Xiaojian, 'Political Economy Behind the Land New Deal' (2004) 21 *Finance* 90–93.

Conclusions: The Constitution in a One-Party State

The constitutional power structure delineated above is simple enough. Had the practice of the governments followed the rules laid down in the Constitution, China would have been the world's largest democracy, quite akin to the Westminster model. As was pointed out at the beginning, however, China still lives with its totalitarian past and a socialist constitution which is, in reality, without binding force. The political practice has been following a set of 'latent' rules rather than the constitutional text – if there are any rules at all for the raw political power game. In essence the power structure of the ruling party, the moving force behind the daily flow of things in the real world, completely subverts the power structure defined in the Constitution; anything expressed there will be interpreted as consistently as possible with the dictates of the party, and be ignored to the extent that such interpretation is impossible.

Thus, although the People's Congresses are given supreme status in the Constitution, they have long been dubbed 'rubber stamps' since their ordinary roles are largely reduced to endorsing official acts decided by the ruling CCP, the holder of real supreme power in China, whose 'leadership' is explicitly enshrined in the Preamble to the 1982 Constitution. The deputies, usually appointed by the party rather than genuinely elected by the people, are supposed to exercise their constitutional powers over government officials, but in reality they are made docile to the government by party discipline, and this is no surprise since well over 70 per cent of deputies are party cadres, whose ranks are lower than those who hold key posts in the governments. No wonder that the people's congresses and the deputies disappear almost completely from the national scene. No-one even expects them to step out and express their voices on such important occasions as the Sun Zhigang event, and they are duly absent as expected.

The same cause accounts for the lack of judicial review and constitutional enforcement. This is particularly obvious with respect to the enforcement of constitutional rights. To take an extreme example, the right to assembly and demonstration is stipulated in Article 35 of the Constitution, but since 1949 there has hardly been a single peaceful assembly that has been legally approved by the authority. Dr Xu Zhiyong, who finished serving his four-year sentence in July 2017, was imprisoned for organizing migrant parents to demonstrate for their children's right to examination and for setting up a poster by himself alone, appealing for officials to disclose their assets.[33] More recently, activist Wu Gan, nicknamed the 'butcher' (of corrupt officials) and responsible for organizing artful demonstrations against corrupt judges outside the courthouse, was sentenced to eight years imprisonment for 'subversion of the state power'.[34] Such cases abound where the constitutional rights of ordinary people are abridged by the abusive public power. The court, lacking institutional independence even though such independence is explicitly provided for in the Constitution (Art. 131), cannot provide any remedy to rectify the wrongs since it has abandoned its power and duty of judicial review. In the Qi Yuling case decided in 2001,[35] the SPC did try to establish a form of judicial review. Since then it has become amply clear that China needs to establish some sort of judicial review to confer meaning on the words of its Constitution, yet not only has there never been any positive action along this direction, but the Qi Yuling decision itself was repealed by the SPC after several years, and the whole subject matter of 'constitutional judicialization' (*xianfa sifahua*) has been banned from publication, leaving the constitution judicially unenforced.

The major cause for the lack of constitutional enforcement in China lies in the simple fact that its constitution and state are overshadowed by a ruling party whose boundary of power is hardly defined in the Constitution and the law. The 1982 Constitution does highlight in the Preamble the leading role of the CCP as the first 'cardinal principle' and the party's 'obligation to uphold the dignity of the Constitution and ensure its implementation', but its power is never defined in the Constitution or in any law or regulation of the state. In fact, the CCP and its satellite parties are not registered as legal entities in China, thus leaving no ground for estimating their legal status and capacities. In reality, however, the CCP as the sole ruling party has completely permeated China's social structure by extending its control over every corner of its governance. Governments and organizations at all levels are paired with and led by the party committees at the same levels, which decide the key personnel of the leadership circles; even private law firms are required to establish

---

[33] A. Jacobs and C. Buckley, 'China Sentences Xu Zhiyong, Legal Activist, to 4 Years in Prison', *New York Times*, 26 January 2014.

[34] C. Buckley, '"Vulgar Butcher" Activist in China Is Sentenced To 8 Years for Shaming Officials', *New York Times*, 25 December 2014.

[35] Zhang, 'A Constitution without Constitutionalism', 960–964.

party organizations. Unlike the Nationalist 'tutelage politics' during the late 1920s and 1930s, when there was to be 'no single party outside this (Nationalist) party', there *are* eight satellite 'democratic parties' (*minzhu dangpai*) now recognized as legitimate by the CCP, but they are totally subordinated and supposed to play only supplementary roles under the CCP's leadership. And like its Nationalist predecessor, the CCP also leaves virtually 'no politics outside the party', having taken charge of all major policy initiatives by itself.

Ultimately, the lack of judicial review and constitutional enforcement is a deliberate political choice of the CCP, which is unwilling to be shackled by constitutional limitation of its powers. The ruling party will not change this self-interested choice unless there is a countervailing force sufficiently great that demands the opposite. And this force can come from nowhere other than among the people themselves. If the people take their constitutional rights seriously, then they have to take the constitution as their own and stand up and insist on establishing effective institutional mechanisms for enforcing the constitution. Before that takes place, it is safe to expect that China's constitution will remain 'toothless' despite the overture to constitutional review in the most recent amendment.

To be sure, this phenomenon is *not* limited to China. Constitutional scholars have been talking about 'constitutions without constitutionalism', for example, in many African states,[36] where the situation is very similar to that in China. And the root cause is also nearly identical, i.e. a ruling party that is too powerful to leave any space for meaningful elections, separation of powers and judicial independence. The constitution is foremost an institutional instrument that defines, regulates and limits political power, but if the political power is so strong as to defy every substantive limitation, the constitution is rendered meaningless. The limitation of political power is both a consequence of and precondition to constitutionalism. In China as in Africa, Latin America or other parts of Asia that are in the midst of political transition, this precondition has to be met before the constitutions can be meaningfully discussed and compared. If this condition is unfulfilled, the effect of a constitution is necessarily at the mercy of the major power players. At best it

---

[36] H.W.O. Okoth-Ogendo, 'Constitutions without Constitutionalism: Reflections on an African Political Paradox', in D. Greenberg et al. eds., *Constitutionalism and Democracy: Transitions in the Contemporary World* (Oxford University Press, 1993), 68–78.

is a document that records (rather than produces) social progress and describes the form of the governing power without the potential to regulate its substance.

Further Reading

D. Cai, 'The Development of Constitutionalism in the Transition of Chinese Society' (2005) 19 *Columbia Journal of Asian Law* 1.

H. (Albert) Chen, *An Introduction to Legal System of the People's Republic of China*, 4th ed. (LexisNexis Butterworths, 2011).

Y.N. Cho, *Local People's Congresses in China: Development and Transition* (Cambridge University Press, 2010).

H. He, 'The Dawn of the Due Process Principle in China' (2008) 22 *Columbia Journal of Asian Law* 57.

K. Lieberthal, *Governing China: From Revolution Through Reform*, 2nd ed. (W.W. Norton & Co, 2003).

B.L. Liebman, 'China's Courts: Restricted Reform' (2007) 21 *Columbia Journal of Asian Law* 1.

K.J. O'Brien, *Reform without Liberalization: China's National People's Congress and the Politics of Institutional Change* (Cambridge University Press, 2008).

Q. Zhang, *The Constitution of China: A Contextual Analysis* (Hart Publishing, 2012).

Part III

Constitutional Principles

Democracy 8

Paul Craig

Introduction

This chapter addresses the issue of democracy, in the context of this book on comparative constitutional law. It is readily apparent that the topic could be addressed from very different perspectives. Thus, the entire chapter could be directed towards differences between democratic and non-democratic constitutions. It might, alternatively, consider differences between constitutions within democratic polities, examining whether there are, or should be, constitutional differences that flow from different forms of democracy, or how far such differences result from the elevation of socio-economic norms to constitutional status. The chapter might have a different, more empirical, emphasis, with discussion as to the relative importance of constitutions in different countries. These are all significant issues, and each would occupy the entire chapter. They are not, however, addressed here.

The focus of this chapter is, rather, on the relationship between constitutional review and democracy. This is, in itself, a major task, given the volume of literature devoted to the issue. It, nonetheless, remains an important topic, and the balance of opinion has ebbed and flowed over time. What follows is not, however, a literature review. It is, moreover, not possible within the space available to address all issues pertinent to this debate, nor to examine each issue in the depth that it might warrant. The objective is, however, to provide the reader with a view of some central facets of the debate in this area, including also issues that are relevant to the discourse, but which are commonly ignored or treated interstitially. The structure of the argument is as follows.

The first section considers strong constitutional review, and begins by reiterating the core argument against such review advanced in the literature. This is followed by closer analysis of certain key issues that are central to this debate. They include the relationship between law and disagreement; the relevance of constitutional or legislative choice for such a mode of review; and the relationship between the existence of such powers of review, and the standard and intensity with which they are deployed. The first section ends with examination of strong constitutional review in the EU, which provides an interesting example against which to test a number of the issues raised hitherto.

The second section addresses soft constitutional review, and begins by examining the rationale for this form of review. The ensuing discussion reflects on a number of the prominent issues that have arisen in debate about this form of review. They include the legitimating function of legislative choice for this form of review; the critique that the line between strong and soft constitutional review is largely illusory; the democratic tension that flows from the strong principles of interpretation that are commonly used in this form of review; and the relationship between the existence of such powers of review, and the standard and intensity with which they are deployed.

The final section proffers some brief thoughts concerning the relationship between non-constitutional review and democracy. This book is about comparative constitutional law, but the line between constitutional and non-constitutional review can be a fine one. This is the rationale for the brief discussion as to the relationship between non-constitutional review, representative democracy and participatory democracy.

1 Strong Constitutional Review

a The Core Argument

The general issue as to whether there should be constitutional review of statute has generated a veritable mountain of literature, more especially where the courts have power to invalidate primary legislation. We should, however, be wary of allowing US–UK common law preoccupations to dominate the intellectual arena, when the context is the study of comparative constitutional law. With this cautionary note, we can, nonetheless, begin with the discourse as it unfolds in some common law regimes.

Waldron[1] and Bellamy[2] are the leading modern opponents of rights-based constitutional review of statute.[3] Waldron is a court-sceptic, but not a rights-sceptic. Bellamy's position is more complex. He is certainly a court-sceptic, and is also more sceptical about rights insofar as he believes that citizenship should not be equated with a narrow concept of individuals being rights-holders against the state but comprises a 'continuously reflexive process, with citizens reinterpreting the basis of their collective life in new ways that correspond to their evolving needs and ideals'.[4]

There is, nonetheless, much common ground in the reasons for their court-scepticism. Thus, the central premise to Waldron and Bellamy's argument is the prevalence of disagreement concerning the rights that should be included within any Bill of Rights and their interpretation.

---

[1] J. Waldron, *Law and Disagreement* (Oxford University Press, 1999) and 'The Core of the Case against Judicial Review' (2006) 115 *Yale LJ* 1346.

[2] R. Bellamy, *Political Constitutionalism, A Republican Defence of the Constitutionality of Democracy* (Cambridge University Press, 2007).

[3] See also, M. Tushnet, *Taking the Constitution away from the Courts* (Princeton University Press, 1999); L. Kramer, *The People Themselves: Popular Constitutionalism and Judicial Review* (Oxford University Press, 2004); G. Webber, *The Negotiable Constitution: On the Limitation of Rights* (Oxford University Press, 2009); G. Webber, P. Yowell, R. Ekins, M. Köpcke, B. Miller and F. Urbina, *Legislated Rights: Securing Human Rights through Legislation* (Cambridge University Press, 2018).

[4] R. Bellamy, 'Constitutive Citizenship versus Constitutional Rights: Republican Reflections on the EU Charter and the Human Rights Act', in T. Campbell, K.D. Ewing and A. Tomkins (eds.), *Sceptical Essays on Human Rights* (Oxford University Press, 2001), 15. See also, Bellamy (n. 2) 48–50, 141, Chapter 6.

For both writers such disagreement pervades the very foundational ideas of justice on which society is grounded. They maintain, therefore, that whether viewed in terms of process, or in terms of outcome, it is preferable for such matters to be decided ultimately by the political and not the legal process, more especially because this thereby avoids the anti-majoritarian dimension of judicial review, whereby a judicial decision overturns that of the elected legislature. The detailed arguments for and against this position are complex, and cannot be examined fully here. It is, however, necessary to clarify the focus of this challenge, since there are differences between Waldron and Bellamy.

Waldron's argument concerns judicial review of legislation, not executive or administrative action. It is premised on strong constitutional review as it operates in the United States, whereby courts are empowered to decline to apply a statute for non-conformity with rights embodied in the Constitution, and encompasses constitutional regimes where courts can formally invalidate statute on rights-based grounds.[5] It is also conditioned on four more particular assumptions: democratic institutions are in reasonably good working order; the same being true for judicial institutions; commitment by most members of society and officials to the idea of individual and minority rights; and 'persisting, substantial and good faith disagreement about rights'.[6]

There is a further important premise to Waldron's thesis, which is that the strong constitutional review occurs against the backdrop of legislative recognition of the contestable rights-based issue, the paradigm being clear legislative determination of matters such as abortion, campaign financing and the like. Thus, he acknowledges that in other instances it may not be easy for the legislature to see what issues concerning rights are embedded in a legislative proposal, or when they might arise from its subsequent application. Waldron is willing in such instances to countenance weaker forms of constitutional review.[7] He makes clear that his target is strong judicial review,[8] and thus he does not include in his attack the weaker form of review found in the Human Rights Act 1998, whereby UK courts may not decline to apply a statute for violation of Convention rights, although they can make a declaration of incompatibility that triggers

[5] Waldron, 'The Core of the Case' (n. 1) 1354–1355.
[6] Ibid. 1360.
[7] Ibid. 1370.
[8] Ibid. 1354.

recourse to Parliament and use of the fast track procedure to remedy the deficiency.[9]

Bellamy differs in this respect, being less willing to distinguish between a Bill of Rights contained in a Constitution, and the schema in the Human Rights Act 1998. He acknowledges the difference between the two, but is nonetheless also critical of the latter, since he perceives it as suffering from the same infirmities as the former, in particular the substitution of the court's view for that of the legislature. Thus, Bellamy argues that while it is open to the legislature not to accept the court's view under the HRA, he maintains that 'it is ultimately judicial review by the judges sitting in the relevant court which decides the issue', with the consequence that 'legislators come under pressure to anticipate the court's result rather than to elaborate a view of their own'.[10]

b Constitutional Review, Law and Disagreement

The existence of disagreement is, as seen above, central to the argument against strong constitutional review. There is force in the argument, and it will be considered further below. There is, nonetheless, a danger of reductionism. There is a tendency for public lawyers to reason as if the problem of moral disagreement was, in some way, particular to the constitutional terrain. This does not withstand examination.

If the premise against constitutional review is that courts should not be involved in cases where there are contentious value assumptions or difficult balancing exercises then the premise is unsustainable, since it would destroy adjudication across private as well as public law. The disagreement endemic within plural democratic societies concerning the more particular meaning to be ascribed to abstract concepts such as liberty, equality and security in public law, is matched by analogous disagreement in private law on these and related issues.

This is attested to by the debates about theory in, for example, contract, tort, restitution and crime, where commentators discuss the values that should underpin the subjects. Courts in private law routinely develop doctrine that is reflective of defensible, albeit contestable, normative assumptions and will often balance competing values. Judicial doctrine

---

[9] Ibid. 1355.
[10] Bellamy (n. 2) 47–48.

within criminal law is premised on conceptions of moral responsibility and justifiable excuse. Contract law is shaped by considerations relating to matters such as consent, autonomy, bargain and the like. Tort theorists debate as to whether the law should be informed by corrective or distributive justice, or some admixture of the two, and if so what precisely that mix should be. Similar academic debates and judicial discourse are apparent in areas as diverse as restitution and trusts.

It might be argued by way of response that the disagreement that besets the realm of public law is more 'significant' than that applicable within private law. This argument must, however, be sustained, not merely stated. It is not readily apparent that the disagreement that besets private law, criminal law and international law is less 'significant' than that which pertains within public law. Thus, if the criterion of significance is judged by the number of times that an individual engages with the relevant body of law, then contract and tort are almost certainly more 'significant' than public law. If, by way of contrast, the criterion is the importance of the relevant body of rules for freedom from incarceration, then the legal criteria used to determine criminal guilt and defences are more important. If disagreement within the realm of public law is felt to be more 'significant' than in other legal spheres, then this is for consequentialist reasons. Strong constitutional review leads to the invalidation of legislation, preventing the legislature from attaining its desired end when there may be disagreement concerning the meaning to be accorded to the contested right, whereas in other instances where there may be disagreement, it is open to the legislature to have the last word.

c Constitutional Review, and Constitutional or Legislative Choice

The core argument against strong constitutional review is premised in part on legitimate disagreement as to the meaning of rights. It is also predicated, less obviously, on the assumption that the power of constitutional review has been arrogated by the courts, in circumstances where there is no express warrant for this in the founding constitutional document, and no basis for it in legislative choice. This is the tableau against which debates concerning constitutional review in the United States are conducted, since there is no express provision for such review in the US Constitution, with the consequence that the legitimacy of the reasoning in

Marbury v. *Madison* has been contested ever since the decision was made. I have nothing to add to that debate, which will not be revisited here.

We should not, however, regard the contingent historical circumstance of constitutional review in the United States as the empirical norm, more especially in a book on comparative constitutional law. The reality is that in a great many countries there is express provision for constitutional review in the constitution, or in primary legislation duly enacted by the sovereign legislature.[11]

Those opposed to constitutional review might think that structural or rights-based constitutional pre-commitment policed by courts is bad constitutional design, and that the argument based on pre-commitment[12] is fraught with conceptual and theoretical difficulty.[13] They might consider that expression of such choice through primary legislation is scarcely less bad, and that not every decision made by a democratically elected legislature necessarily enhances democracy, in outcome terms at least. They are perfectly entitled to such views.

There is, nonetheless, a very real tension here, given that disagreement is the driving force behind Waldron and Bellamy's argument, leading to the preference for democratic choice as opposed to judicial decision. This disagreement can perforce affect a plethora of issues concerning constitutional content, including whether constitutional review is desirable. Such disagreement can likewise impact views about the wisdom of any particular piece of legislation. Where there is express provision for constitutional review in the constitution or legislation, it provides the clearest evidence as to how this particular aspect of constitutional design should be resolved within that polity.

It follows that express provision for constitutional review carries with it constitutional legitimacy, unless and until the constitution is amended. It equally follows that the UK legislature's imprimatur to the softer constitutional review embodied in the Human Rights Act 1998 imbues it with democratic legitimacy. The fact that particular commentators believe

---

[11] T. Ginsburg and M. Versteeg, 'Why do Countries Adopt Constitutional Review?' (2013) *Journal of Law, Economics and Organization* 1.

[12] S. Holmes, 'Pre-commitment and the Paradox of Democracy', in J. Elster and R. Slagstad, eds, *Constitutionalism and Democracy* (Cambridge University Press, in collaboration with the Maison des Sciences de l'Homme, 1988), Chapter 7.

[13] Waldron, *Law and Disagreement* (n. 1) Chapter 12; J. Elster, *Ulysses Unbound, Studies in Rationality, Precommitment, and Constraints* (Cambridge University Press, 2000), Chapter 2.

such steps to be unwise in no way undermines this. It attests to the very disagreement that pervades choices about the optimal way of dealing with such issues.

This is more especially so, given that the reasons why the framers of a constitution, or the legislature, chose some form of constitutional review are commonly eclectic. Thus, the constitutional framers might have believed that constitutional pre-commitment policed by the judiciary is optimal as a matter of principle. They might have thought that it was warranted by contingent historical circumstance of that particular country, where political forces had hitherto been imperfectly democratic or worse. They might have disagreed with, for example, Bellamy's argument, concerning the relationship between rights and majority rule. The contrary argument, that there should be some rights-based constraints policed by a court in a constitutional democracy, has been advanced from a liberal perspective by Rawls[14] and Dworkin,[15] and from a republican perspective by Pettit,[16] Sunstein[17] and Michelman.[18]

We should, moreover, be mindful of the fact that constitutions are not necessarily drafted with philosophical acuity, but are the result of the complex interplay of a range of forces that affect the content of the resulting document. There may be many provisions thereof that are philosophically contentious, but that does not serve to deny their constitutional legitimacy until they are amended or repealed, and much the same is true for legislation. There may, as noted above, be a range of political and historical considerations that influence the decision to opt for strong constitutional review in a particular system. There is, in addition, the ongoing philosophical disagreement as to the relationship between rights and majoritarian democracy.

---

[14] J. Rawls, *Political Liberalism* (Columbia University Press, 1996).

[15] R. Dworkin, *Freedom's Law: The Moral Reading of the American Constitution* (Oxford University Press, 1996). See also, C. Eisgruber, *Constitutional Self-Government* (Harvard University Press, 2001); L. Sager, *Justice in Plainclothes: A Theory of American Constitutional Practice* (Yale University Press, 2004).

[16] P. Pettit, *Republicanism, A Theory of Freedom and Government* (Clarendon Press, 1997).

[17] C. Sunstein, 'Interest Groups in American Public Law' (1985) 38 *Stan LR* 29 and 'Beyond the Republican Revival' (1988) 97 *Yale LJ* 1539.

[18] F. Michelman, 'Foreword: Traces of Self-Government' (1986) 100 *Harv LR* 4.

d Constitutional Review, Grounds of Review, Intensity of Review and Democracy

The existence of strong constitutional review, the grounds of review and the intensity of review deployed by the courts when exercising their power, are distinct issues. The first tells us that it is open to the reviewing court to invalidate primary legislation for incompatibility with the constitution, and the bill of rights contained therein. The second issue is directed to the kind of error that must exist before the court does so. This may be specified in the constitution, or in an analogous treaty document. The reality is that choice as to the grounds of review will often reside with the courts. The third, and related issue, concerns the standard of review, or the intensity with which the particular ground of review is applied. Thus, if proportionality is recognized as a ground of constitutional review it is still open to the reviewing court to vary the intensity of its application depending upon the circumstances of the case. The intensity of review can, moreover, vary in fundamental rights' cases, depending on the nature of the right in issue. This is reflective of the normative reality that not all rights are of equal significance; a right not to be tortured is more important than a right to trade. It is reflective also of the fact that not all violations of the same right are of equal importance; a right to freedom of speech during an election is more significant than assertion of such a right in the context of the opening of a shop selling sex products.

We shall return to this issue in more detail when considering softer forms of constitutional review, and the debates about standards of review in the UK. Suffice it to say for the present that variable standards of review, as exemplified by the distinction between strict scrutiny and rationality review that prevails in the United States, serve as a mechanism whereby courts can, even in regimes of strong constitutional review, accord some leeway to the legislature. The same is true in relation to variation in the intensity of review. There are, in addition, other devices commonly used in such systems that soften the impact of judicial power. Thus, the mere fact that the courts have the power to invalidate the legislation does not preclude exercise of other juridical devices designed to forestall this eventuality. These include, inter alia, strong interpretive rules, through which the courts read the contested legislation to be compatible with the constitution. The courts may also have recourse to temporal techniques, so as to accord time to the legislature to modify the legislation to bring it into line with the constitution.[19]

e The European Union and Strong Constitutional Review

A number of the preceding points concerning strong constitutional review are brought into sharp comparative focus through consideration of EU law. It is particularly interesting in this respect, since the EU regime combines express authorization for constitutional review, with judicial creativity as to what the grounds of review should be and how intensively they should be applied.

The constituent treaties provided, from the outset, express authority for constitutional review. Article 19 TEU states that the Court of Justice shall ensure that in the interpretation and application of this Treaty the law is observed. It was, however, what is now Article 263(1) TFEU, which contained more specific powers, stipulating, inter alia, that the EU courts shall review the legality of legislative acts of the EU institutions.[20] This is complemented by Article 267 TFEU, which allows for indirect scrutiny of, inter alia, the validity and interpretation of EU acts, including legislative acts, in the context of a legal action that begins and ends in the national court.

The CJEU developed the grounds of review so as to facilitate constitutional and non-constitutional review. These grounds are specified in Article 263(2) TFEU, and remain unchanged since the inception of the EEC: lack of competence, infringement of an essential procedural requirement, infringement of this Treaty or of any rule of law relating to its application, or misuse of powers, which bear the imprint of French juristic thought.[21]

---

[19] See, e.g., E. Young, 'Protecting Member State Autonomy in the European Union: Some Cautionary Tales from American Federalism' (2002) 77 *NYULRev* 1612.

[20] Article 173 EEC contained the analogous power in the original Rome Treaty. The terminology of 'legislative acts' did not exist prior to the Lisbon Treaty, but this does not alter the force of the point being made in the text. This is because Article 173 EEC provided express authority for the ECJ to review the legality of any legal act, including the primary regulations or directives governing an area, which would, in post-Lisbon terminology, be regarded as a legislative acts.

[21] J. Schwarze, *European Administrative Law* (Office for Official Publications of the European Communities/Sweet & Maxwell, revised edition, 2006), 40.

The phrase infringement of 'any rule of law relating to its application' provided fertile ground for development of legal principles designed to enhance legislative and administrative accountability. The intent might have been to ensure merely that Commission decision-making complied not only with the primary Treaty articles, but also regulations, directives etc. passed pursuant thereto. The framers' intent was, however, broader, envisaging a role for general principles of law in the emerging Community legal order.[22] The phrase thereby captured not only the need for compliance with Community legislation, but also with general principles of law, such as proportionality, legitimate expectations, fundamental rights, the precautionary principle, equality and due process, read into the Treaty by the CJEU.[23]

The legal force of such principles was enhanced by their placing in the EU hierarchy of norms, where they sit below the constituent Treaties and above all else. They can, therefore, be used as interpretive guides in relation to primary Treaty articles, legislative acts, delegated acts and implementing acts. While they cannot be used to invalidate a Treaty article, they can function as a ground of review in relation to all other EU acts, including legislative acts, and for Member State acts that fall within the scope of EU law.

Fundamental rights were initially read into the Treaty as one type of general principle of law. The original Treaties contained no express provisions concerning the protection of human rights, in part by way of reaction to the failure of ambitious attempts to create a European Political Community (EPC) in the mid-1950s,[24] which convinced advocates of closer integration to scale down their plans. The CJEU read rights into the Community legal order, the catalyst being the need to head off a potential revolt from the German courts, which threatened not to apply a Community regulation because it infringed rights protected by the German constitution. The ECJ's response was double-edged:[25] it denied that the validity of a Community measure could be judged against principles of national

---

[22] P. Craig, *UK, EU and Global Administrative Law: Foundations and Challenges* (Cambridge University Press, 2015), Chapter 3.

[23] T. Tridimas, *The General Principles of EU Law* (Oxford University Press, 2nd ed., 2006); P. Craig, *EU Administrative Law* (Oxford University Press, 3rd ed., 2018).

[24] G. de Búrca, 'The Evolution of EU Human Rights Law', in P. Craig and G. de Búrca (eds.), *The Evolution of EU Law* (Oxford University Press, 2nd ed., 2011), Chapter 16.

[25] Case 11/70 *Internationale Handelsgesellschaft v Einfuhr- und Vorratstelle für Getreide und Futtermittel* [1970] ECR 1125.

constitutional law, but held that respect for fundamental rights formed an integral part of the general principles of Community law protected by the ECJ. This signalled the start of the CJEU's fundamental rights' jurisprudence, which developed incrementally on a case by case basis.

The EU institutions felt, however, in the late 1990s, that it would be preferable if fundamental rights could be listed more formally, and this was the catalyst for what became the EU Charter of Rights.[26] It was agreed to by the Member States in 2000, but its precise legal status was not resolved until the Lisbon Treaty. Article 6(1) TEU now specifies that the Charter has the same legal value as the Treaties. It can be used to challenge all EU acts, including legislative acts, and Member State action that falls in the scope of EU law.

It is interesting to reflect on constitutional review and democracy in the EU in the light of the more general concerns about such judicial power adumbrated at the outset of this chapter. It is helpful in this respect to disaggregate discussion of treaty authorization for constitutional review, and judicial creativity concerning general principles of law.

The Rome Treaty provided express authorization for strong constitutional review from the very inception of the Community. There have been numerous Treaty amendments since then, and there has been no suggestion during any such Treaty revision that this key feature of judicial power should be changed. The existence of such constitutional review is, in that sense, constitutionally legitimate. Moreover, the counter-majoritarian objection voiced against rights-based constitutional review, viz., that a court is replacing its judgment over the meaning of contestable rights for that of the democratically elected legislature, did not apply in the EC when the fundamental rights' jurisprudence was developing, given that the legal provisions subject to review had limited democratic credentials. This was because, prior to 1986, the European Parliament had scant role in the legislative process, which was dominated by the Commission and Council, as captured in the aphorism 'the Commission proposes, the Council disposes'.

It remains to be seen whether the Lisbon Treaty makes any difference in this respect. Most legislation challenged before the EU courts is now

---

[26] Charter of Fundamental Rights of the European Union [2007] OJ C303/1; Explanations Relating to the Charter of Fundamental Rights [2007] OJ C303/17. The Charter was reissued with the Lisbon Treaty, [2010] OJ C83/2.

made in accord with the ordinary legislative procedure with input from the Commission, Council and European Parliament. The extension of the ordinary legislative procedure, and the symbolic change in nomenclature from that of co-decision, strengthened the European Parliament's role in the EU political order and further enhanced the democratic legitimacy of EU legislation. The interpretation of Charter rights may well be contestable and there will inevitably be cases where EU courts substitute their view for that of the legislature on the meaning and interpretation of such a right. The counter-majoritarian aspect of constitutional review will, therefore, be more apparent than hitherto. There is, however, little sign of change in this respect thus far. This is, in part at least, because preoccupation with the legitimacy of constitutional review has a higher profile in common law jurisdictions, and does not feature so prominently within academic or judicial discourse in civil law countries. There are, perforce, very real differences in approach across different civil law countries, but a constant theme is, nonetheless, the superiority of the constitution, and the rights contained therein, with the courts policing conformity with these precepts.

Let us then turn to the second issue, recognition of general principles of law. There is a strong argument that recognition of such principles by the CJEU, and the fleshing out of the treaty grounds of review, was defensible in terms of principle. The development of general principles of law served to reassure Member States and national courts that the rapidly growing Community power would be subject to proper legal scrutiny, in accord with principles analogous to those in national legal orders. In developing these concepts, the EU courts drew on doctrine from the Member States, although they did not systematically trawl through each national legal system to find principles that they had in common. The same point can be put in a different manner. It would be difficult to construct an argument that precepts such as due process, legal certainty or proportionality should have no place in a Community legal order that aspired to comply with the rule of law.

There are, nonetheless, concerns in this respect. The category of general principles of law accords the CJEU with very considerable power. This follows from the fact that recognition of such principles resides with the CJEU; from their placing in the hierarchy of norms, with the consequence that they can only be changed through Treaty amendment; and from the fact that infirmity in relation to any general principle of law, not just fundamental rights or the Charter, can lead to annulment of a legislative act.

These concerns should be taken seriously. They are, however, alleviated by the intensity with which general principles of law are applied. To put the same point in a different way, the intensity of review is an essential part of the story of constitutional review, since it directly impacts on the relative frequency, or rarity, with which the courts will invalidate legislative acts. The reality in the EU is that the CJEU has rarely struck down legislative acts for non-compliance with, for example, fundamental rights or proportionality.[27] Thus, the CJEU has, for example, reasoned that the right allegedly violated, such as a right to property or a right to trade, is not absolute, that the limitation on the right did not affect its central core, and that the limit was justified.[28]

There is, moreover, as Grimm has noted, a democratic cost of constitutionalization.[29] His central thesis is that the EU Treaties are over-constitutionalized, with the consequence that they are thereby taken off the agenda of normal politics, notwithstanding the fact that many such issues would be regarded as within the province of ordinary law in Member States: 'in the EU the crucial difference between the rules for political decisions and the decisions themselves is to a large extent levelled.'[30] It is inherent in the nature of constitutions that they function as the framework for political decisions, with the consequence that elections 'do not matter as far as constitutional law extends'.[31] There may be too little constitutionalism, but there may also be too much, with the consequence that the democratic process is fettered.[32] While there are no universally applicable principles for determining the content of a Constitution, the 'function of constitutions is to legitimise and to limit political power, not

---

[27] For recent instances where the CJEU has invalidated legislative acts, Cases 293 and 594/12 *Digital Rights Ireland Ltd* v. *Minister for Communications, Marine and Natural Resources*, EU:C:2014:238; Case C-362/14 *Maximillian Schrems* v. *Data Protection Commissioner*, EU:C:2015:650, [78]; O. Lynskey, 'The Data Retention Directive is incompatible with the rights to privacy and data protection and is invalid in its entirety: Digital Rights Ireland' (2014) 51 *CML Rev* 1789.

[28] Craig (n. 23), Chapter 16.

[29] D. Grimm, 'The Democratic Costs of Constitutionalization: The European Case' (2015) 21 *ELJ* 460.

[30] Ibid. 470.

[31] Ibid. 463.

[32] Ibid. 464.

to replace it', with the consequence that constitutions are a 'framework for politics, not the blueprint for all political decisions'.[33]

2 Soft Constitutional Review

a Soft Constitutional Review, Constitutional Tradition and Democracy

Strong constitutional review, whereby courts can invalidate primary legislation, may be ill-suited to polities where constitutional tradition affords primacy of place to parliamentary sovereignty. This is the rationale for the legislative choice in favour of softer forms of constitutional review in the UK and a number of Commonwealth countries.[34] It is exemplified by the Human Rights Act 1998, the framers of which were not in favour of strong constitutional review, since it was felt to be unsuitable for the UK, with its traditions of parliamentary sovereignty.

The HRA therefore encapsulates a softer form of constitutional review in relation to the scrutiny of legislation. The HRA schema is that before legislation is enacted the relevant minister must attest that the Bill is compatible with rights derived from the European Convention on Human Rights, or that although unable to make such a statement, the government wishes to proceed with the Bill.[35] If legislation is challenged, section 3 HRA provides that 'so far as it is possible to do so, primary legislation and subordinate legislation must be read and given effect in a way which is compatible with the Convention rights'. Where a court is satisfied that primary legislation is incompatible with a Convention right then it can, pursuant to section 4 HRA, make a declaration of that incompatibility.[36] This does not, however, affect the validity of the legislation, but serves to send it back to Parliament, which can then decide whether to amend it so as to bring it into line with the reasoning of the court.

This is not the place for detailed exegesis on the case law and secondary literature in relation to the HRA. The ensuing discussion will, in keeping with the remit of this chapter, focus on issues concerning the interplay

---

[33] Ibid. 465.
[34] S. Gardbaum, *The New Commonwealth Model of Constitutionalism: Theory and Practice* (Cambridge University Press, 2013).
[35] HRA s. 19.
[36] Ibid. ss. 4(1)–(2).

between softer forms of constitutional review and democracy. This form
of constitutional review has been criticized on democratic grounds, notwithstanding that the final word resides with Parliament. It is, therefore,
all the more important to disaggregate and assess these critiques.

b Soft Constitutional Review, Democracy and Legislative Choice

The preceding discussion has already touched on this issue, and it can
therefore be dealt with relatively briefly. The HRA is a statute, not a
Constitution; it does not embody strong constitutional review in the sense
articulated by Waldron; and it was made by a democratically elected
legislature.[37] The natural mode of parliamentary expression is through
legislation, which is the quintessential mode of expression of majority
preference. The HRA, therefore, has democratic legitimacy, unless and
until Parliament in exercise of its sovereign power chooses to decide
differently.

It might be argued, by way of response, that not every decision by a
democratic legislature enhances democracy. There is some force in this
as a general argument, but it is far more difficult to sustain in this context. The UK, through the HRA, made a choice for some rights-based
review, which has been made by a very large number of countries in the
world. The reasons that informed the choice were, as in most analogous
instances elsewhere, eclectic. They included, in the UK context, the desire
to bring rights home, such that they could be adjudicated directly by UK
courts, without the need for recourse to Strasbourg, and the belief that
there should be some rights-based constraints on the legislature, even if
the latter still had the last word.

The fact that some might believe that such constraints are either unwarranted philosophically, or undesirable pragmatically, comes nowhere close
to showing that the legislation fails to enhance democracy. The counter
to the philosophical strand of the critique is that a range of prominent
thinkers across the spectrum of political theory, such as Dworkin, Rawls,
Pettit, Michelman and Sunstein, believe that such constraints are philosophically warranted, and are in that sense an integral part of the very

---

[37] It can, nonetheless, consistent with this argument be acknowledged that the HRA has
a special constitutional status, in the sense that the courts will not conclude that its
provisions have been overridden unless there is some very compelling justification for
such a conclusion.

definition of democracy. The counter to the pragmatic argument is that it seldom ventures beyond the general or abstract. The fact that some judicial decisions concerning rights are open to criticism simply shows that all institutions, including courts and legislatures, are imperfect. It does not show that there is some structural fault in the regime.

This does not, as stated earlier, preclude criticism from those who feel that courts should never have been invested with such power. It does mean that such criticism cannot readily be couched in terms of democratic legitimacy, more especially where it forms part of a broader critique of judicial power, which is predicated on the assumption that courts are going beyond their proper remit. I do not believe that the latter case is sustained,[38] but it is in any event important to guard against the elliptical use of language, in this instance, legitimacy, to mean two quite different things. There is the contention that the judiciary is over-reaching in ordinary judicial review cases by exercising such review in a manner that is too intrusive, and hence trespasses on the role of the legislature/executive. There is also the claim that the judiciary are making judgments of a kind for which they are ill-suited under the HRA, or which should be the preserve of the legislature, even though when doing so they are fulfilling an express constitutional or legislative obligation cast on them. There is the world of difference between a 'legitimacy crisis' cast in terms of courts allegedly trespassing on the legislature's terrain; and such a crisis that connotes the difficulties said to flow from the discharge of a constitutional or legislative mandate expressly accorded to the courts.[39]

c Soft Constitutional Review, Democracy and Legislative Reaction

There is a second line of criticism of soft constitutional review, to the effect that there is scant difference in outcome between strong and soft constitutional review, when considered from the fulcrum point of legislative response to judicial decisions. There are those, such as Waldron, who maintain that the form of constitutional review, whether strong or weak, still matters, since Parliament has the last deliberative word in regimes such as the HRA. There are, however, many who share Bellamy's view that even in regimes such as the HRA the legislature feels constrained to

[38] P. Craig, 'Judicial Power, the Judicial Power Project and the UK' (2017) 36 *University of Queensland Law Journal* 355.
[39] Ibid. 360–362.

modify primary legislation in accord with judicial decisions. Soft constitutional review is, on this latter view, inherently unstable, with the strong likelihood being that it will veer towards judicial dominance, even though Parliament has the final say. There is a considerable literature debating this point.[40]

Arguments concerning legislative capitulation to courts are, however, more complex than is often presented. Academic commentary often equates modification of primary legislation in accord with judicial decisions, with legislative capitulation to judicial interpretation of the contested meaning of a protected right. The picture is more nuanced, in large part because the circumstances in which such cases arise are more varied than is often recognized. Consider the following four possibilities.

The first is where Parliament was unaware of all rights-based issues in a legislative proposal, or which might arise from its subsequent application. This can frequently occur. The legislation may be long and complex, and the possible clashes with rights may not be readily foreseeable. When these become apparent in subsequent litigation Parliament is content with the judicial resolution and makes the required changes. A number of the UK cases are arguably of this nature.[41] This is borne out by a detailed study of legislative reaction to judicial declarations of incompatibility, where King noted that 'most of the cases raised issues that Parliament had not considered in great depth (where there was an absence of legislative focus) and about which it often had no strong feelings'.[42] Secondly, there may be instances where Parliament has expressed some considered view on the rights-based issue, but on further reflection acknowledges that

---

[40] See, Gardbaum (n. 34); S. Gardbaum, 'The New Commonwealth Model of Constitutionalism' (2001) 49 *AJCL* 707; J.L. Hiebert, 'Parliamentary Bills of Rights: An Alternative Model' (2006) 69 *MLR* 7; J.L. Hiebert, 'New Constitutional Ideas: Can New Parliamentary Models Resist Judicial Dominance when Interpreting Rights?' (2004) 82 *Texas LR* 1963; J.L. Hiebert, 'Parliament and Rights', in T. Campbell, J. Goldsworthy and A. Stone (eds.), *Protecting Human Rights* (Oxford University Press, 2003), Chapter 11; M. Tushnet, 'New Forms of Judicial Review and the Persistence of Rights and Democracy-based Worries' (2003) 38 *Wake Forest L Rev* 813; R. Bellamy, 'Political Constitutionalism and the Human Rights Act' (2011) 9 I-*CON* 86; J. King, 'Parliament's Role Following Declarations of Incompatibility under the HRA', in H. Hooper, M. Hunt and P. Yowell (eds.), *Parliaments and Human Rights* (Hart Publishing, 2015), Chapter 8.

[41] See, e.g., *Matthews* v. *Ministry of Defence* [2002] 3 All ER 513; *R (on the application of International Transport Roth GmbH)* v. *Secretary of State for the Home Department* [2003] QB 728; *Re S (children: care plan)* [2002] 2 AC 291; *Ghaidan* v. *Godin-Mendoza* [2004] 2 AC 557.

[42] King (n. 40) 187.

the judicial view is preferable. Thirdly, there may be yet other instances where the minister responsible for the legislation does not wholly agree with the judicial determination, but decides that it is not worth the fight. Fourthly, Parliament feels pressure to accept the judicial decision, lest it be portrayed as insufficiently protective of rights, even where it genuinely believes that its determination of the right was preferable. It therefore makes the changes, even though the HRA allows Parliament to stick to its original view.

It is the last such instance that most troubles commentators about the HRA, although it is unclear whether this is a real problem. Thus, King concluded that there is 'little evidence that the Government and Parliament feel dominated by judges under the HRA'; the evidence 'instead supports a view of collaboration and divided responsibilities, with courts adjudicating cases and setting out findings on narrow issues, while the Government and Parliament work from these conclusions to refashion policy accordingly.'[43]

Insofar as there might be a problem, the response is that courts and Parliament both have responsibility in this respect.[44] The courts should acknowledge that there can be disagreement about the more concrete meaning of rights, with the consequence that the legislative choice should be treated with respect. The dialogue should not be merely one-way, with the courts ignoring considered legislative choices concerning the contested right, but we shall see below that courts recognize this and afford respect to the legislature. Parliament also has a responsibility. This is not just to take the judicial decision seriously, which it does, but also to be willing not to accept it if Parliament truly believes that its original legislative determination was indeed consistent with rights, and preferable to that contained in the court's judgment. Parliament is the repository of sovereign authority, and should exercise it where it feels that this is appropriate.

d Soft Constitutional Review, Democracy and the Limits of Interpretation

The details of soft constitutional review vary in different legal systems, but principles of interpretation tend to be found in most such regimes.

---

[43] Ibid. 187.
[44] A. Young, *Democratic Dialogue and the Constitution* (Oxford University Press, 2017).

They can also play a role in regimes of strong constitutional review, in order to read the contested legislation in accord with the constitution, thereby forestalling the need for invalidation. Interpretive principles nonetheless tend to assume greater prominence in systems where soft constitutional review prevails, since they provide the principal tool available to courts when faced with rights-based challenges.

Such principles will commonly be invested with democratic imprimatur, since there will be express legislative provision directing the courts to engage in the interpretive exercise, as exemplified by section 3 HRA, which directs the courts, so far as possible, to read other legislation to be compatible with Convention rights. There can, nonetheless, be democratic tensions in such a regime, since it demands the drawing of a line between the interpretation and the rewriting of contested legislation. It is accepted that there are limits to what can be achieved even through strong interpretation, and accepted also that it does not invest the courts with the power of the legislature to reshape the contested legislation. There are, however, differences of view, judicially and academically, as to where that line falls.

The issue is thrown into sharp relief by the UK case law concerning the limits of what the courts could achieve through section 3 HRA. The early case law revealed divergent judicial views, with some judges taking the view that almost all cases of legislative inconsistency with Convention rights could be resolved in this manner,[45] while others took a more cautious view as to the bounds of legitimate interpretation.[46] The leading decision is now *Ghaidan*,[47] where the House of Lords sought to tread a line midway between the views expressed in the earlier case law. Their Lordships held that section 3 could be used even in the absence of legislative ambiguity. The statutory wording was not, therefore, conclusive, such that courts could read down and read in provisions to render the legislation compatible with Convention rights. This was, however, tempered by limits: the courts should not adopt a meaning that was inconsistent with the fundamentals of the legislation being reviewed, nor should they use section 3 to adopt an interpretation of legislation for which they

---

[45] *R* v. *A* [2002] 1 AC 45, [44]–[45], L. Steyn.
[46] Ibid. [108], L. Hope; *R* v. *Lambert* [2002] 2 AC 545, [79]–[81]; *Re S (children: care plan)* [2002] 2 AC 291, [40].
[47] *Ghaidan* v. *Godin-Mendoza* [2004] 2 AC 557.

were ill-equipped, such as where the interpretation would bring about far-reaching change of a kind that was best dealt with by Parliament.[48]

There will, doubtless, be those who disagree with this approach, or its application in particular cases, believing that it accords the judiciary too much power to alter legislation in the name of interpretation, and hence trespasses on the realm of the legislature. My view is that the approach in *Ghaidan* is sound, that it coheres with the intent underlying the HRA, and that it has, in general, been applied sensibly by the courts in subsequent cases. Courts have not hesitated to issue a declaration of incompatibility where they concluded that compliance with Convention rights could only be secured through significant revision of the statutory scheme, or where the changes were at odds with fundamentals of the contested legislation.[49]

e Soft Constitutional Review, Democracy and Intensity of Review

The earlier discussion revealed the significance of intensity of review to the way in which strong constitutional review operated. The same is true in relation to soft constitutional review, as attested to by the judicial and academic discourse concerning the extent to which the courts do, and should, afford some respect or deference to the legislature or executive when exercising powers under the HRA.[50] This is not the place for a detailed exegesis on all aspects of this debate.[51] It is, once again, the connection between this debate and democracy that is salient for the present chapter. It can be explicated as follows.

There is no a priori connection between the existence of soft constitutional review and the particular standard or intensity of review adopted by the courts of a particular legal system. Let it be assumed that there

---

[48] See also the concerns voiced by Sir J. Beatson, 'Common Law, Statute and Constitutional Law' (2006) *Stat. L. Rev.* 1, 13–14 concerning the problems flowing from the fact that a statute that has been subject to interpretation via s. 3 HRA may no longer mean the same as appears from the written text.

[49] See, e.g., *A* v. *Secretary of State for the Home Department* [2005] 2 AC 68; *R (Wilkinson)* v. *Inland Revenue Commissioners* [2005] 1 WLR 1718; *R (Clift)* v. *Secretary of State for the Home Department* [2007] 1 AC 484; *AS (Somalia)* v. *Entry Clearance Officer (Addis Ababa)* [2009] UKHL 32; *R (Wright)* v. *Secretary of State for Health* [2009] 1 AC 739; *R(F)* v. *Secretary of State for the Home Department* [2011] 1 AC 331.

[50] See P. Craig, *Administrative Law* (Sweet & Maxwell, 8th ed., 2016), Chapter 20, fn 256 for a list of the relevant literature.

[51] My views can be found in Craig (n. 22), Chapter 2.

is express foundation for such constitutional review in a statute or the constitution. These foundational documents may specify the standard or intensity of review with some exactitude, they may furnish some less specific guidance in this respect. Insofar as they do so, there is then a contingent connection between the existence of such review and the standard or intensity of review to be deployed thereunder. It is contingent in the sense that the framers of the constitution or legislation have chosen to address not only the existence of such review, but also the second order issue concerning the standard or intensity thereof.

It is, however, often the case that the constitution or legislation establishing soft constitutional review says little or nothing about the second order issue. Thus, it is commonly the case, as with the HRA, that the legislation states that if there is a violation of protected rights then certain consequences follow, such as a declaration of incompatibility, while stating nothing more about the standard or intensity of review that should be used to decide whether such a breach has occurred. There is, in such circumstances, no a priori connection between the existence of soft constitutional review, and the criteria to be used to determine whether a violation has occurred.

To the contrary, there is a range of options in this respect, and, as might be expected, those who advocate a particular standard or intensity of review will naturally argue that this best coheres with the text, and purpose, of the legislation that embodies soft constitutional review, and more generally with the judicial and constitutional traditions of that particular polity. The discourse could scarcely be conducted in any other terms. This does not, however, mean that there is an a priori connection between the existence of such review and the intensity with which it is applied. It reveals, rather, contestation in this regard, in which varying positions are supported by a plethora of textual, normative and consequentialist argument, which include, importantly, assumptions about the relationship between such review and the precepts of democracy. It might be contended that the courts should, in the light of the preceding criteria, substitute judgment on all legal issues broadly conceived that arise, and that they should exercise very tight controls over discretionary determinations, according little, if any weight, to the views of the legislature or executive. It might, by way of contrast, be argued that the existence of soft constitutional review is perfectly consistent with greater respect being afforded to the legislature and executive where difficult determinations have to be made concerning the meaning and application of rights in particular contexts.

It is these considerations that have played out in UK debates as to whether to give deference,[52] respect[53] or weight[54] to legislative determinations when adjudicating under the HRA. The types of consideration that courts should take into account when according such respect or weight to the legislature are especially pertinent to this chapter. It is generally accepted that this can be done for epistemic, institutional or constitutional reasons. The primary decision-maker might have greater knowledge of the relevant matter than any reviewing court; it might, independent of epistemic considerations, have a deeper understanding of the contested issue by reason of its institutional place within the fabric of government; or the legislature might express a considered view as to the meaning of a right in legislation in circumstances where it has no particular epistemic or institutional advantage over courts.

There is a considerable measure of agreement among commentators that it is legitimate for epistemic and institutional considerations to be taken into account by courts when applying the precepts of judicial review, either when defining the relevant right, or in the context of proportionality review. Courts also give respect to the primary decision-maker in accord with such epistemic or institutional considerations, although they do not abjure judgment on the matter, which remains in their hands.[55]

There is more disagreement among commentators as to whether deference, respect or weight should be given on constitutional grounds.[56] The paradigm instance is as to whether such weight or respect ought to be given to the legislature, by reason of its democratic pedigree, where there are no independent epistemic or institutional reasons to do so. The rationale for affording weight to the legislative choice resides ultimately

---

[52] *R* v. *DPP, ex p Kebilene* [2000] 2 AC 326.

[53] *R (ProLife Alliance)* v. *BBC* [2004] 1 AC 185, [75]–[76].

[54] *Huang* v. *Secretary of State for the Home Department* [2007] 2 AC 167, [16].

[55] See, e.g., *R (Lord Carlile of Berriew QC)* v. *Secretary of State for the Home Department* [2014] UKSC 60.

[56] See, e.g., A. Kavanagh, *Constitutional Review under the UK Human Rights Act* (Cambridge University Press, 2009); T.R.S. Allan, 'Human Rights and Judicial Review: A Critique of "Due Deference"' [2006] *CLJ* 671; A. Kavanagh, 'Defending Deference in Public Law and Constitutional Theory' (2010) 126 *LQR* 222; T. Hickman, *Public Law after the Human Rights Act* (Hart Publishing, 2010), 160–161; Young (n. 44).

in the fact that there is room for legitimate disagreement as to the meaning and application of constitutional rights.

The courts do not have a monopoly of wisdom in this respect, and judges not infrequently disagree among themselves as to what is demanded by a protected right in particular circumstances. A considered legislative choice is, therefore, deserving of respect as embodying its reflective view as to what the right means in a particular context. It deserves this respect on constitutional grounds as the elected legislature charged with making such choices. To afford such respect is not inconsistent with the HRA, its wording or the principles underlying it. This does not mean that the court should abstain or capitulate, but that it should give respect to the legislative choice when making its own final determination. Thus, as Lord Sumption stated in *Carlile*, 'even in the context of Convention rights, there remain areas which although not immune from scrutiny require a qualified respect for the constitutional functions of decision-makers who are democratically accountable',[57] examples being decisions involving important policy choices, broad questions of economic and social policy, or issues involving the allocation of finite resources. The reality is, moreover, that UK courts have frequently accorded respect or weight on constitutional grounds to legislative determinations under the HRA.

This approach is exemplified by the decision in *Animal Defenders*.[58] In deciding that a blanket ban on political advertising on television was compatible with Convention rights, Lord Bingham held that weight should be accorded to Parliament's judgment for a number of reasons: it was reasonable to expect that democratically elected politicians would be sensitive to measures necessary to safeguard the integrity of our democracy; the ban had been enacted because television was the most potent form of advertising and therefore those with the deepest pockets could sway elections; Parliament had decided, after considering the options, that anything less than a wholesale ban would be ineffective; and legislation had to lay down general rules, and it was for Parliament to decide where the lines should be drawn.

The approach is evident in *Carson*,[59] where the House of Lords adopted the US distinction between strict scrutiny for discrimination on grounds

---

[57] *Carlile* (n. 55) [28].

[58] *R (Animal Defenders International)* v. *Secretary of State for Culture, Media and Sport* [2008] 1 AC 1312. See also, *R (Nicklinson)* v. *Ministry of Justice* [2014] UKSC 38.

[59] *R (Carson)* v. *Secretary of State for Work and Pensions* [2006] 1 AC 173.

of race, gender, sexual orientation and the like, with rationality review being applicable to other forms of differential treatment. The instant case was held to fall into the latter category, with the result being that where differences of treatment were made on grounds such as ability, occupation, wealth or education the courts would demand some rational justification. These differences in treatment were, said Lord Hoffmann, normally dependent on considerations of the public interest, which were 'very much a matter for the democratically elected branches of government'.[60]

The House of Lords reasoned in a similar manner in *Hooper*.[61] The claimants were widowers, who alleged discrimination contrary to Article 14 and 8 ECHR on the ground that if they had been widows they would have been entitled to certain benefits that were denied to them as widowers. The House of Lords acknowledged that the discrimination was based on gender and therefore subject to strict scrutiny. It, nonetheless, upheld the legislative scheme. Lord Hoffmann surveyed the legislative rationale for, and history of, such pensions. He concluded that differential treatment between men and women was justified given that older widows as a class were likely to be needier than older widowers as a class, more especially given that for much of the last century it was unusual for married women to work. It was for Parliament to decide when the special treatment for women with respect to this particular benefit was no longer required.

There is, as stated at the outset of this section, no a priori connection between the existence of soft constitutional review and the more particular standard or intensity of review through which it will be decided whether there has been a violation of a right in a particular case. In the UK, courts have been willing to give respect to legislative choice on epistemic, institutional and constitutional grounds. This is, in my view, consistent with the HRA, fits with broader UK constitutional traditions and is justified in normative terms.

The preceding cases reveal how the constitutional justification for respect operates. The House of Lords might have simply decided the rights-based issue for itself and substituted judgment, without any particular consideration of the imperatives driving the legislative choice. They did not do so.

---

[60] Ibid. [16], [55].
[61] *R (Hooper)* v. *Secretary of State for Work and Pensions* [2005] 1 WLR 1681.

They considered the legislative determination concerning rights against the problem that the legislation sought to resolve, giving due weight to the reasons for that choice. The courts did not abstain from adjudication, or merely accept, without more, the legislative choice as conclusive, but gave it respect when deciding the case.[62] This approach was sound, and its application will perforce depend on the extent to which there is evidence that the legislature has addressed the salient issue. There will, by way of contrast, be rights-based claims made in relation to legislation where the legislature was not aware in advance that a particular legislative provision was problematic, since the issue only became apparent when the legislation became live.

This does not mean that the same judicial approach will, or should, be adopted in other legal systems. To the contrary, the very fact that there is no a priori connection between the existence of review powers, and the standard/intensity of review, means that judicial choices concerning the latter will be affected by constitutional traditions in the particular country, and by assumptions concerning the respective roles of courts and legislatures, which may differ from those set out above. A value of comparative constitutional law is, however, that it enables us to see how analogous issues are dealt with in different jurisdictions. This thereby shakes implicit assumptions that the way that such matters are currently dealt with in a particular system is pre-ordained, or the only option. This value retains force, even if, after considering ways of dealing with analogous issues elsewhere, it is decided to stick to the status quo in that particular country.

3 Non-Constitutional Review

This chapter has considered the relationship between democracy and constitutional review, in the context of a book concerned with comparative constitutional law. The boundary line between constitutional and non-constitutional review can, however, be a fine one. It is fitting, therefore, to

---

[62] For discussion as to whether this can be conceptualized in terms of constitutional dialogue between courts and Parliament, see A. Young, 'Is Dialogue Working under the Human Rights Act 1998?' [2011] *PL* 773; Young (n. 44); T. Hickman, 'Constitutional Dialogue, Constitutional Theories and the Human Rights Act' [2005] *PL* 306; P. Sales and R. Ekins, 'Rights-Consistent Interpretation and the Human Rights Act 1998' (2011) 127 *LQR* 217.

say a few words concerning the relationship between non-constitutional review and democracy.

There are connections between non-constitutional review and representative democracy, and they do not all pull in the same direction. Thus, a standard feature of academic discourse in all systems of administrative law is whether courts are going 'too far', and thereby intruding into spheres that should be properly left to democratically elected politicians, who are accountable to the national parliament. This discourse features particularly prominently in the context of the proper degree of judicial control of discretionary power accorded by legislation to a minister or agency. Viewed from this perspective the relationship between non-constitutional review and representative democracy is cast in terms of tension. This can be acknowledged, but we should not thereby ignore the ways in which such review is supportive of representative democracy. The transmission belt theory of administrative law, whereby courts do no more than effectuate the will of the parent legislature, has numerous shortcomings. It is, however, misguided to believe that it has no kernel of truth. The reality is that key administrative law doctrines, such as error of law, are designed to ensure that the body to whom the parent legislature has delegated power has not strayed beyond the bounds thereof. In that sense, non-constitutional review is supportive of representative democracy, by keeping administrative bodies within the remit granted to them by the democratic legislature. There may well be judicial choices as to the standard of review in relation to, for example, error of law, but this does not alter the point being made here. While there can, therefore, be tensions between non-constitutional review and democracy, the former can also support the latter.

There are also connections between non-constitutional review and participatory democracy, which arise most prominently in the context of whether participatory rights should be afforded to interested parties when the administration fulfils its legislative remit through rulemaking, or some form of secondary legislation. The answer may be provided by a code of administrative procedure, which are very common in European countries. Where the code does not provide the answer, or where there is no such code, the issue will necessarily fall to the courts to decide. The salient issue is whether precepts of due process, which courts in most systems have read as a requirement when a decision is made that affects a particular individual or individuals, should also be required when the administration makes rules. Courts have a creative choice in this regard, and the response in many systems, such as the United States, United Kingdom, the EU and Germany, is to deny the analogy between hearing rights in adjudication and participatory rights in rulemaking.[63] This choice is driven by an admixture of normative and pragmatic considerations that are contestable. Courts in many systems are, however, supportive of participatory democracy where there is some foundation for such participation in a statute, or Treaty provision. In such instances the courts will help to ensure the effectiveness of the participation, through insistence that there is notice of the participatory exercise, that it is given in good time, that relevant information is provided in advance and that the responses are taken seriously, even though they are not determinative of outcome.

Conclusion

Constitutions are pivotal in all legal systems, and constitutional law equally so. This is unsurprising given the importance of the matters addressed therein. Thus, constitutions will commonly have horizontal, structural and vertical dimensions.

The horizontal dimension is manifest in the rules that establish the main organs of government, their powers, and the ways in which they inter-relate. There may be procedural rules in this respect, as exemplified by constitutional provisions stipulating how legislation is to be enacted, and whether special majorities are required. There will be substantive rules that define the powers of the legislature, the executive and the courts. The definition of executive power tends to be most problematic across constitutional systems, because of the very duality in meaning of the term execute, connoting both policy formation and policy execution.

The structural dimension of constitutions is concerned with different levels of government within a polity. Thus, in nation states which are federal, or where there is some measure of devolution, the structural provisions of the constitution will identify the respective powers of the federal and state or regional government. These may be set out with varying degrees of specificity or abstraction. Many constitutions tend towards the latter in this regard, thereby requiring more of courts when

---

[63] On 'courts' as governmental institutions, see Chapter 16.

they are called on to engage in constitutional adjudication as to the level of government that has the power to act.

The vertical dimension deals with rules that regulate the interrelationship between citizen and state, the paradigm situation being the existence of rights-based constraints on government action, through a Bill of Rights enshrined in the Constitution. This is, as is evident from this chapter, the typical ground to which strong or soft constitutional review pertains. Contestation as to the desirability or not of such review has been a hallmark of this body of law ever since its inception. It shows no sign of waning, as attested to by the continuing body of literature devoted to the subject. This chapter has sought to contribute to this discourse by disaggregating some of the central issues, and by including in the debate issues that are too often ignored, or accorded only exiguous treatment, in discussion about the relationship between strong and soft constitutional review and democracy.

Further Reading

R. Bellamy, *Political Constitutionalism, A Republican Defence of the Constitutionality of Democracy* (Cambridge University Press, 2007).

R. Dworkin, *Freedom's Law: The Moral Reading of the American Constitution* (Oxford University Press, 1996).

S. Gardbaum, *The New Commonwealth Model of Constitutionalism: Theory and Practice* (Cambridge University Press, 2013).

D. Grimm, 'The Democratic Costs of Constitutionalization: The European Case' (2015) 21 *ELJ* 460.

H. Hooper, M. Hunt, and P. Yowell (eds.), *Parliaments and Human Rights* (Hart Publishing, 2015).

A. Kavanagh, *Constitutional Review under the UK Human Rights Act* (Cambridge University Press, 2009).

J. Waldron, 'The Core of the Case against Judicial Review' (2006) 115 *Yale LJ* 1346.

A. Young, *Democratic Dialogue and the Constitution* (Oxford University Press, 2017).

9 Separation of Powers

Christoph Möllers

Introduction

'Separation of powers' is a concept that is much used, much criticized, but rarely reflected on in contemporary comparative constitutional law.[1] Before it can be discussed properly, we have to elaborate some basic distinctions. Separation of powers can be used as a shorthand description of the organization of government as a whole. Political scientists and lawyers have widely applied the notion in this way even though there is nothing distinctively normative about it. The concept can also serve as a legal argument in constitutional reasoning. Both uses are not mutually exclusive; even though the first does not refer to a normative concept, it seems to be helpful for constitutional lawyers who want to analyse the organizational structure of governments. The second one might also help non-legal researchers to understand one important element of constitutional reasoning and both uses can be intertwined on different levels. The legal argument strives to guarantee a certain organization of government, and it is applied by institutions, namely by courts, which are part of this organization. In the academic debate, both uses are often combined. Especially in the American realist tradition, legal arguments are connected with institutional analyses.[2] This is fine, but it should be ensured that the argument remains clear about its claims and keeps both levels not necessarily separated, but distinct. As long as there is a methodological difference between 'comparative constitutional law' and 'comparative government', this distinction will play a role.[3]

---

[1] At least when compared to the literature on rights, federalism and constitutional review, but see: D. Kyritsis, *Where Our Protection Lies* (Oxford University Press, 2017); J.S. Martinez, 'Horizontal Structuring', in M. Rosenfeld and A. Sajó (eds.), *The Oxford Handbook of Comparative Constitutional Law* (Oxford University Press, 2012), 547–575; A. Kavanagh, 'The Constitutional Separation of Powers', in D. Dyzenhaus and M. Thorburn (eds.), *Philosophical Foundations of Constitutional Law* (Oxford University Press, 2016), 221–239; C. Saunders, 'Theoretical Underpinnings of Separation of Powers', in G. Jacobsohn and M. Schor (eds.), *Comparative Constitutional Theory* (Edward Elgar, 2018), 66–85; and C. Möllers, *The Three Branches*, (Oxford University Press, 2013).

[2] B. Ackerman, 'New Separation of Powers' (2000) 113 *Harvard Law Review* 633–729.

[3] The question if there is a difference is obviously contested: R. Hirschl, *Comparative Matters* (Oxford University Press, 2014); A. von Bogdandy, 'Comparative Constitutional Law as a Social Science? A Hegelian Reaction to Ran Hirschl's *Comparative Matters*' (2016) 55 *Der Staat* 103–115; C. Möllers and H. Birkenkoetter, 'Towards A New Conceptualism in Comparative Constitutional Law, or Reviving the German Tradition of the Lehrbuch' (2015) 12 *International Journal of Constitutional Law* 603–625.

1 Histories and Historiographies

a A Variety of Histories

Even within the relative short history of democratic constitutionalism after the Atlantic revolutions, there is a wide range of understandings and institutional applications of the idea of separated powers. If one tries to group different models of 'separation of powers' according to the institutional dangers they attempt to prevent, the complexity becomes obvious. For the French revolutionary tradition, the courts are the most dangerous branch, an institution prone to endorse individual privileges against the general democratic will.[4] For the American Framers, the legislature was the problematic branch because the experiences with the early state constitutions were so unsatisfactory. Radicalized assemblies sentenced individual persons and printed money.[5] Therefore, any meaningful separation of powers had to protect the system from those evils.[6] While both the critique of too powerful courts and the fear from legislative usurpation are still relevant motives in constitutional law and theory, they have been overshadowed by the critical attention that the executive branch now widely receives.[7] Starting in the late nineteenth century with the advent of the bureaucratic state, the executive became the most plausible threat to any constitutional system, be it as the machine of a political leader or as a seemingly neutral technocratic bureaucracy. Most recently, constitutional courts have also come into the focus of attention.

These different focuses imply different meanings of the concept itself: to date, constitutional orders that are influenced by the early republican traditions like France or the Netherlands remain hesitant with regard to granting strong judicial review, particularly when it comes to the establishment of constitutional courts, wheras other constitutional orders have introduced different kinds of safeguards against legislative encroachment. The idea of parliamentary sovereignty – originating with pre-modern English constitutionalism, but formally re-defined under

---

[4] M. Gauchet, *La Révolution des Pouvoirs* (Gallimard, 1995).

[5] S.M. Elkins and E.L. McKittrick, *The Age of Federalism* (Oxford University Press, 1993), 10–11.

[6] *The Federalist Papers*, No. 47.

[7] For a comparative overview: J.S. Martinez, 'Inherent Executive Power: A Comparative Perspective' (2005–2006) 115 *Yale Law Journal* 2480–2511.

modern conditions[8] – remains a rather exceptional approach and perhaps the strongest place of resistance against the introduction of constitutional adjudication.[9] Regarding the rise of the executive branch, however, no remedy seems to be at hand though there are solid indicators that independent judicial review may make a difference.

In addition to that variety, the institutional history of separation of powers cannot be fully understood without looking at the other grand organizational principle of the constitutional state: federalism.[10] Many institutional arrangements relevant for the separation of powers are due to a federal system. This is true for different versions of legislative bicameralism, and in many cases it also applies to the introduction of constitutional review.[11] The idea of reviewing state action in a federal order is often the beginning of a complete constitutional review of all kinds of legislation. Another important feature of federalism concerns the level of control that the federal entity can exert over the execution of its own legislative program. Here, the United States on the one hand, and the European Union (EU) (and within the EU countries like Germany) on the other, represent two different ideal types of a clearly separated or integrated executive federalism,[12] which respectively have important effects on the organization of the three branches.

b The Common Historical Narrative

Though the history of separation of powers is full of variations and path dependencies that pose a serious challenge for any claim to a unified concept, the historical narrative that is told in many accounts is more simple and straightforward. It is the story of an idealized past and its inevitable decay. Once, there was a classical and formalist idea of separated powers

---

[8] A.V. Dicey, *Introduction to the Study of the Law of the Constitution* (Liberty Fund, 1982).
[9] S. Gardbaum, *The New Commonwealth Model of Constitutionalism: Theory and Practice* (Cambridge University Press, 2013).
[10] On federalism, see Chapter 12 as well as Chapter 2, Section 4 in this volume.
[11] O. Beaud, 'De Quelques Particularités de la Justice Constitutionelle dans un Système Fédéral', in C. Grewe et al. (eds.), *La Notion de 'Justice Constitutionelle'* (Dalloz, 2005), 49. On constitutional review generally, see Chapter 16 in this volume.
[12] D. Halberstam, 'Comparative Federalism and the Issue of Commandeering', in K. Nicolaidis and R. Howse (eds.), *The Federal Vision: Legitimacy and Levels of Governance in the United States and the European Union* (Oxford University Press, 2001), 213–251.

prevailing in continental Europe, but this idea has now become out-dated through different social and institutional realities: the complex regulatory structures of the welfare state, the privatization of public functions, the rise of constitutional courts, and the internationalization of law.[13] This narrative of decline has been widely spread since at least the 1920s and can be traced back to the late nineteenth century. It belongs to fascist as well as to communist stories about liberal constitutionalism, but also to the technocratic world-view of the New Dealers and to the liberal economic critique of corrupt political processes and cumbersome administrative procedures. Yet, the fact that it is widely endorsed does not mean that it is true.

As we have already seen, a more accurate history would have to develop many distinctions and keep in mind many caveats: distinctions between the theory and its institutional practice, between the normative and the descriptive claims of the concept and between democratic and other constitutional systems. It would also try to avoid a linear historical narrative. One core flaw of the dominant narrative lies in the assumption that there was a classical era of pure separation of powers in continental Europe. But even in countries like Germany and France, with all their differences, neither a strong separation of parliament and government, nor a judiciary that has merely been applying legislative rules were the institutional rule.[14] Comparable problems appear with regard to the assumption of a steady decline of parliamentary power. Though it can be plausibly claimed that executive branches are very powerful today, it is obviously hard to measure such a development, and it is not entirely clear how far this development is at cost to the other branches. In any case, it is important that the distribution of power between organs is no zero-sum game.[15] Adding power to one branch does not necessarily diminish the power of the other branches. Finally, it may not be easy to assess and compare different forms of political power and to attribute it to a particular branch. In particular, the political power of parliaments remains

---

[13] For more recent examples in the literature, see: E. Carolan, *The New Separation of Powers* (Oxford University Press, 2009), 1–17; F. Vibert, *The Rise of the Unelected* (Cambridge University Press, 2007).

[14] This cliché is e.g. presented in A.S. Sweet, *Governing with Judges* (Oxford University Press, 2000), 56, 90 et seq., 127 et seq., 137, 146. For the situation in Germany and France: J. Krynen, *L'emprise contemporaine des juges* (Gallimard, 2011), 104, 191; R. Ogorek, *Richterkönig oder Subsumtionsautomat* (Klostermann, 1991).

[15] G. Tsebelis, *Veto-Players: How Political Institutions Work* (Princeton University Press, 2002).

an under-reflected topic[16] because it is exercised in the rather abstract manner of rule-making and political influence through discourse. If one underestimates the power of formal rules,[17] one will also underestimate parliaments. Under these epistemological conditions, it remains open if the general narrative about the loss of parliamentary power is correct and against which historical backdrop this could be proven. All in all, we are still missing a conceptual underpinning for a thorough comparative history that could escape such clichés.

2 Meanings

a The Value and Uses of Conceptual Distinctions

Separation of powers in a wider sense is not necessarily about 'separation'. The expression is a 'misnomer'.[18] Most accounts distance themselves from the idea that different governmental branches should work separately from each other, and rightly so.[19] The word 'separation' refers to different ideas of the organization of government that have in common that they do not deal with strict separations, but with the distinction between branches, with balancing of their respective powers, with the protection of their institutional autonomy or with the prohibition to usurp unsuited functions. Their positive common denominator and the substantial core of all models of separation of powers is the tripartite distinction between legislative, executive and judicial action. To claim that this distinction is reductionist or does not reflect institutional realities misses the very point of normative conceptual distinctions in two ways. Firstly, the distinction, like any other, is not refuted by its blurred boundaries. It is one of the central functions of the distinction that it allows us to describe transgressions and hybrid phenomena and it is not defeated because it allows for vagueness. Secondly, a normative distinction expresses a claim, not a factual practice. If the norm is ignored, this is a matter of justification and not of description.

---

[16] But see M.A. Cameron, *Strong Constitutions* (Oxford University Press, 2013), 39–42.

[17] For a counter-critique of (typically US-American rule scepticism): F. Schauer, *Playing by the Rules* (Oxford University Press, 1993); A.L. Stinchcombe, *When Formality Works* (University of Chicago Press, 2001).

[18] L.H. Tribe, *American Constitutional Law* (Foundation Press, 2000), 137.

[19] A. Kavanagh, 'The Constitutional Separation of Powers', in D. Dyzenhaus and M. Thorburn (eds.), *Philosophical Foundations of Constitutional Law* (Oxford University Press, 2016), 221–239.

Yet, this will not suffice. On the one hand, it seems rather fruitless to abandon the traditional conceptual field of separated powers in favour of artificial new words.[20] On the other hand, some conceptual work has to be done in order to develop a framework that can be used for comparative constitutional law. In a first step, a more precise picture will be drawn of the possible meanings of separation of powers.[21] This will be done in this section before I can have a look at its wider theoretical underpinnings in the following sections. With regard to its meaning, we will distinguish three perspectives: institutional autonomy; balancing; and the prohibition of functional usurpation.

b Institutional Autonomy

The simplest concept of separated powers demands a certain degree of autonomy of governmental organs from their respective counterparts. Many constitutional systems know this principle, though the way it is framed may differ. It may be understood as giving an organ the power to make some basic decisions about its self-organization, or it may shield this organ from at least some information requests from other organs or from judicial review before a final decision is taken. The basic idea is that any organizational actor must enjoy a certain degree of operational independence to maintain its ability to work, especially to develop an institutional determination (or 'will') of its own. The degree of autonomy depends on its legitimacy within a constitutional order. A directly elected parliament can more plausibly claim autonomy than a subordinate administrative agency.

With regard to one governmental branch, the quest for autonomy is widely accepted: judicial independence as an instrument of autonomous decision-making by courts. Though the implications that are attached to this principle do widely differ in various constitutional orders, and though the principle is coming under increasing pressure in the context of

---

[20] For an elaborate description of the phenomena that does not really explain the model it seems to apply: J.S. Martinez, 'Horizontal Structuring', in M. Rosenfeld and A. Sajó (eds.), *The Oxford Handbook of Comparative Constitutional Law* (Oxford University Press, 2012), 547–575.

[21] One reason for the general confusion lies in the complex and shifting jurisprudence of different courts. For an attempt to make sense of the jurisprudence of the US Supreme Court: A.Z. Huq and J.D. Michaels, 'The Cycles of Separation-of-Powers Jurisprudence' (2016) 126 *Yale Law Journal* 346.

the global authoritarian surge, there still seems to be some consensus on its core. Judges must not *ex ante* be instructed by other branches on how to decide a concrete case beyond the legislative program that is in force, and they must not be *ex post* sanctioned for their decisions.

With regard to the relation between the two other branches, the legislative and the executive, the question of autonomy is very much dependent on the difference between parliamentary, presidential and semi-presidential systems.[22] While much of the debate has been centred around the problem which of these systems is preferable,[23] it seems important to take a step back and take account of the fact that the option for one of these alternatives has implications for many other constitutional questions,[24] though all three of them have their own forms of separation of powers.[25] The fact that in a presidential system parliament and president can claim their own political legitimacy, while in a parliamentary system both branches derive their legitimacy from the same parliamentary election determines the solution of standard problems like delegation, parliamentary control and oversight or the function of hierarchy within the executive.[26] This is especially important for comparative constitutional law, in which standard arguments in favour of parliamentary control or limited delegation fluctuate through different systems, thereby losing much of their argumentative bite. This is all the more the case as the US constitution still serves as a common denominator in the field, though its purely presidential system is rarely utilised outside Latin America and Africa and, therefore, only of relative use for comparative constitutional law. A conscientious treatment of the respective branches' different states of institutional autonomy seems to be a necessary condition for a fruitful comparison of more fine-grained problems.

---

[22] For this term: C. Skach, 'The "Newest" Separation of Powers' (2007) 5 *International Journal of Constitutional Law*, 93–121.

[23] B. Ackerman, 'New Separation of Powers' (2000) 113 *Harvard Law Review* 633–729.

[24] The term 'government' itself seems to better fit with a parliamentary system than with a monocratic presidential executive.

[25] R. Albert, 'Presidential Values in Parliamentary Systems' (2010) 8 *International Journal of Constitutional Law* 207–236.

[26] C. Möllers, *The Three Branches* (Oxford University Press, 2013), 110–126.

c Balance

While the idea of autonomy of an organ provides us with a relatively simple concept, the notion of a 'balance' of governmental powers seems to be less clear and more demanding at the same time. The branches shall not only be 'independent', but also 'harmonious'.[27] The idea that the three branches of government shall work in a well-balanced manner has an attractive ring, but it also seems to be conceptually weak. It is therefore not totally surprising that this notion is especially attractive to courts.[28] If it is true that the success of balancing tests in the constitutional jurisprudence on rights can be explained by the fact that this approach gives a lot of leeway for judicial decision-making,[29] this may also be true for its use in separation of powers doctrine.

The source of the idea of balancing is pre-modern and pre-democratic. It stems from Polybius' idea of mixed constitutionalism that combines democratic, aristocratic and monarchic elements.[30] Clear traces of this thinking become apparent in the design of House, Senate and Presidency in American constitutional law.[31] Today, the idea often serves as a kind of holistic justification for judicial interventions into the organization of government. It is also a reminder of the fact that a sound doctrine of separation of powers can, despite of its wording, give reasons for the co-operation between different state organs.[32] One example for the use of the balancing argument may be mentioned: the reference to 'institutional balance' is the standard formula in the constitutional law of the EU as interpreted by the Court of Justice.[33] Though many of these arguments

---

[27] Art. 2 Constitution of Brazil.

[28] Examples are the CJEU: for a reading of the case law from a contemporary perspective, see: D. Yuratich, 'Article 13(2) TEU: Institutional Balance, Sincere Co-Operation, and Non-Domination During Lawmaking?' (2007) 18(1) *German Law Journal* 99–126; and with regard to Germany: C. Möllers, *The Three Branches* (Oxford University Press, 2013), 45–47.

[29] A.S. Sweet, *Governing with Judges* (Oxford University Press, 2000), but for serious doubts compare now N. Petersen, *Proportionality and Judicial Activism* (Cambridge University Press, 2017).

[30] Polybius, *Histories*, 6.4.6-II. See also Chapter 2 in this volume.

[31] G. Casper, *Separating Powers* (Harvard University Press, 1997).

[32] A. Kavanagh, 'The Constitutional Separation of Powers', in D. Dyzenhaus and M. Thorburn (eds.), *Philosophical Foundations of Constitutional Law* (Oxford University Press, 2016), 221–239.

[33] For an analysis, see K. Lenaerts and A. Verhoeven, 'Institutional Balance as a Guarantee for Democracy in EU Governance', in C. Joerges and R. Dehousse (eds.), *Good Governance in Europe's Integrated Market* (Oxford University Press, 2002), 35–88.

can claim plausibility with regard to their results, their justification is not equally convincing. Balancing remains a methodologically uncertain procedure.[34] This is the more the case in separation of powers law, which, contrary to rights' jurisprudence, has no normative presumption in the direction of individual freedom behind its reasoning.

d Functionalism: Prohibition of Usurpation

The modern theory of separated powers, beginning with Montesquieu,[35] does not concern institutional actors or organs as such, but addresses the necessary or possible relations between such actors and their normative 'functions'.[36] Legislation, execution of laws and adjudication are 'functions' that the states or other public authorities fulfil and that are carried out by respective 'branches'. In this context, the notion of 'function' refers to different types of legally relevant actions. Most constitutions from the US of 1787 to the South African of 1996 are built on the mostly implicit assumption that there is a difference between these three functions, without giving much guidance on how to define them.[37] The fact that constitutions refer to these distinctions is the central reason why it is not possible to give up the notion or to replace it with other concepts.[38] In order to define these functions in an applicable manner,

---

[34] For a recent critique: F.J. Urbina, *A Critique of Proportionality and Balancing* (Cambridge University Press, 2017).

[35] Montesquieu, *The Spirit of Laws*. Complete Works. Volume 1 (T. Evans, 1777) vol. II, Ch. 11.

[36] This seems somehow to be missed by the American debate between functionalists and textualists in separation of powers law, which is more or less one version of the debate between originalists and functionalists, being because of its specificity to American law (and politics) of no further concern here.

[37] For some examples compare only Art. 2 Constitution of Brazil; Art. I, II, III US const.; Art. 20 (3) German Basic Law; Chapter III, Art. 24 (1) Constitution of Indonesia; Art. 70, 92, 101 Constitution of Italy; Sections I, II and III Constitution of Argentina; Art., 4, 5, 6 Constitution of Nigeria. As a counter-statement that, yet, presupposes the distinction between branches and functions: '[...] the Indian Constitution does not expressly vest the different sets of powers in the different organs of the State.' R Dehli Lawa Act 1912 AIR 1951 SC 332 [285].

[38] It is another question if the concept should include more elements, such as political parties: S. Gardbaum, 'Political Parties, Voting Systems, and the Separation of Powers' (2017) 65 *American Journal of Comparative Law* 229–264. But this inclusiveness may be rather helpful with a thick description of one system rather than with a conceptual framework. A concept does not necessarily become more useful by being more inclusive.

help is given by procedural and organizational provisions that constitute the organs to which one of these functions is assigned: we look at the rules constituting parliament and its procedures in order to better understand what legislation means and we look at procedural rules for courts to define what adjudication means. But this inductive method has obvious limits. Not everything a parliament does can be considered legislation, and with regard to the executive branch we do not even have an exemplary form of action.[39] Systematic clarification is needed.

This clarification of functions and their respective relation to the organs that have to carry them out lies at the core of any serious legal argument on separated powers. One might wonder about the value of such constructive questions, but as long as one keeps a minimal trust in the value of conceptual arguments, the problems do not seem to be more intricate than in any other legal field. In addition to that, in most cases the reference to the notion of separation of powers will be very specific, embedding the point to be made in the context of concrete constitutional norms and particular political practices in a given constitutional jurisdiction. Comparative constitutional law should be able to analyse differences and parallels in constitutional reasoning, but it will not provide us with any meta-concept that can be applied as a *passepartout* across different jurisdictions. So far, this aspect of comparative law remains underdeveloped in favour of purely institutional perspectives. Still, there is room for theory and comparison as long as individual constitutions leave room for the clarification of the general concepts. We will have a closer look at this in the following sections.

Parliaments, administrative organizations and courts are three types of state organs that have to carry out the three functions. In an ideal world of functionally ordered powers one could assume a perfect correspondence between one function and one organ: only parliaments legislate and they only legislate, only executives execute and they only execute, only courts adjudicate and they only adjudicate. The riddle of separated powers would be solved by means of a functional interpretation. But there are at least three problems with this.

The first problem is, as we have seen, the definition of the function: Where does legislation begin and where does it end? In many accounts

---

[39] C. Möllers, *The Three Branches* (Oxford University Press, 2013), 96–101.

this question is treated as a somehow unsolvable issue of formalist juris-prudence. But if 'formalism' means to make sense of normative concepts, it seems rather difficult to avoid it, without giving up the legal trade as such. If one tries to make a theoretical effort to develop criteria for the functions, three come to mind.[40] The personal and factual scope of a legal decision: legislative law-making is potentially inclusive, while judicial decisions refer to a highly individualized object, a 'case' between only two parties. The temporal orientation: legislative decisions address the future while judicial decisions concern past events. It is, therefore, no accident that retroactive legislation is treated as a constitutional problem in many jurisdictions. Finally, the degree of legalization of the respective decisions (including the degree of legalization of the other two criteria): while legislative action is ideally only moderately constrained by wide constitutional rules that allow for different politically alter-native decisions, judicial decisions are treated as being determined by law.[41] In this model, the executive will take an intermediate position in all three regards.[42] Despite this effort to better define the functions, in most concrete cases one will try to avoid general definitions in favour of the application of more specific constitutional norms.

The second problem lies in the definition of the organ: which features are the necessary elements in order for a court to be a court? Independence from political pressure or life tenure of the judges? The third, most dif-ficult problem concerns the relation between the two triplets. In many cases, organs co-operate in order to fulfil a function. In parliamentary systems, governments usually initiate legislation while parliaments regu-larly participate in administrative actions. These hybrid procedures may or may not be problematic from the point of view of legitimacy, but they are surely not unconstitutional as long as they follow some explicit constitutional rules.

[40] Ibid, 79–80.

[41] Note that it is of little interest if the assumption of legal determinacy is well founded or not. More relevant is the fact that judicial decisions are treated like this with the important consequence that the courts cannot claim an institutional will of their own beyond the law. Also note that constitutional review has to be analysed in a different manner.

[42] It is, therefore, no accident that the executive is the branch that is hardest to define. Connecting political law-making and relatively determined adjudication of rules mostly by means of a hierarchic organization makes executive action more diverse than the task of the other branches.

Therefore, the constitutional principle that is attached to the idea of a functional distribution of powers is regularly not phrased in positive but in negative terms. Functional separation of powers is no principle that requires – in Alexian terms – an optimal distribution of functions to organs,[43] but instead prohibits what is called a usurpation or encroachment of one function by an unsuited organ.[44] Such an argument will also only work within the more specific framework that the constitution is providing – it cannot be turned against specific constitutional provisions. In a parliamentary system, the addressee of this prohibition will most often be the legislature, which often has the power to distribute particular tasks to specific organs. But it is also possible that other organs encroach upon powers. Courts can encroach upon the legislature by issuing too broad decisions. The administration can encroach upon the legislature by issuing decisions against or without a statutory principle. And the administration can encroach upon courts by intruding into their independence or by sanctioning individuals without due process.[45] Again, in most cases the recourse to separation of powers will be unnecessary because more concrete norms are at hand. The normative direction of an argument from separated powers will regularly be indicated by more specific rules like a *domaine réservé* to a parliamentary statute or a 'cases and controversies' clause for courts. But as a background principle, the notion may give relevant normative orientation.

In general, usurpation can take two forms. Firstly, one of the functions can be skipped in a given procedure. Examples would be a law that infringes immediately upon individual rights without any intermediate executive intervention or an executive action that infringes upon rights but is immunized from judicial review. Secondly, it may encompass the deformation of an organ so it can no longer adequately discharge its functions. An example would be a politically dependent body that has to carry out judicial functions or a body with primary legislative tasks that does not represent dissenting political positions.

---

[43] With regard to rights: R. Alexy, 'Rights, Legal Reasoning and Rational Discourse' (1992) 5(2) *Ratio Juris* 143–152.

[44] For the term usurpation see: *The Federalist Papers*, No. 48.

[45] S. Rose-Ackerman, S. Egidy and J. Fowkes, *Due Process of Lawmaking* (Cambridge University Press, 2015); and see Chapter 15 in this volume.

3 Cognitive and Normative Rationales for Separated Powers

a Descriptive Rationales

Why separation of powers? There is nothing self-evident in dividing an organization of government into different parts or in assigning specific functions to them. Obviously, the notion needs some form of a rationale. As we will see, most justifications for our concept make normative claims. But there are also non-normative approaches.[46] Less demandingly, they make a descriptive use of the notion of separation of powers by pointing to the simple fact that the distinction between legislative, executive and adjudicative acts is a helpful instrument to describe and analyse the actions of public authorities on all governmental levels. It is important to see that this usage does not depend on any endorsement of separation of powers either as a normative principle or as an institutional reality. To the contrary, in many accounts about its 'decline' the distinction itself is employed – for instance when complaining about legislation by administrators or executive action done by courts. The notion remains a conceptual tool to describe institutional practices even if they seem to clearly deviate from any normative ideal. And using just one of its elements – legislative, executive or judicial action – does not make any sense without at least an implicit distinguishing reference to the respective other two and, hence, to the whole triplet.

b Cognitive Rationales

To be distinguished from its descriptive value are possible *cognitive* qualities of institutional differentiation through separated powers. Providing for specialized legislative, executive and adjudicatory bodies may have instrumental advantages. It can be helpful to demarcate the distinction between rather political and more technical issues within the state organization even if this distinction will often be contestable and the political devil may lie in the technical detail. It may also be efficient to allocate rule-making and rule-application to different organizations with different procedures. Such instrumental advantages remain independent from the

---

[46] M.A. Cameron, *Strong Constitutions* (Oxford University Press, 2013).

question of how political or another kind of legitimacy is generated in a constitutional system. The Vatican constitution draws a distinction between three functions, though its system is built on a solidly monocratic organization with spiritual legitimacy.[47] To be clear, such organizational advantages do not lead authoritarian systems to introduce features like parliamentary control of the executive or judicial independence for the sake of efficiency; there is no stabilized harmony between a legitimate and an efficient organization of the state that could cause a general adherence to some meaningful version of our principle. But, vice versa, it seems clear that systems that are built on centralized monocratic authoritarian institutions, which make, execute and adjudicate rules at the same time, may not only be politically questionable but also suffer from organizational deficiencies.

In this context, it would be tempting to look for functional equivalents of the notion of separated powers in authoritarian systems. Decentralization could be one example for that.[48] Another one could lie in the differentiation between (one-)party and state administration and in collegial structures within these.[49] Another example could be informal, but practically relevant demands for consensual decision-making within a ruling party or a royal family. A completely different complement may be seen in aggressive political campaigns against corruption that have to compensate for a lack of independent judicial or autonomous political controls by judges and legislators. The authoritarian claim to ubiquitous political control over the state apparatus as well as society is obviously very demanding in terms of organization. In the moment in which this claim can be realized by means of technology, the future of our idea of separated powers will become even bleaker. A fundamental incentive for political actors to let loose in order to achieve would be gone.

c Normative Rationales

The oldest and still most common rationale of the principle of separated powers lies in the protection from tyranny and despotism. In a more

---

[47] Art. 1 (1) Fundamental Law of Vatican City State.

[48] Q. Zhang, *The Constitution of China* (Hart Publishing, 2012), 149–160; and see also Chapter 7 in this volume.

[49] Again for China, see ibid., 121–147, though such distinctions seem to be more and more under pressure.

modern version this leads to a framework in which constitutionalism is identified with the limitation of political powers through law.[50] While this idea is already dominant in Montesquieu's pre-modern and pre-democratic model,[51] it has survived the Atlantic revolutions, being even a core part of its American version. The Framers' fear of legislative despotism led to a constitutional design that still has a certain preference for political inaction through the inclusion of different constitutional veto players.[52] This rationale is based on an idea of negative individual freedom in which persons can better follow their preferences as long as governmental action does not interfere with them.[53] One of its implications is a factual priority of the social status quo over politically induced change, which is by no means politically neutral.[54] Still, the limitation of state powers seems, in the academic debate and outside of the United States, to be the most accepted justification for the principle. By connecting the justification of separated powers to a legalist idea of constitutionalism[55] this model empowers lawyers and the law. It is therefore no accident how dominant this justification still is within the global legal community.

But a negative or legal constitutionalist rationale is not the only possible normative justification for separated powers that is at hand. As a matter of fact, if one perceives a differentiated model of separated powers as a means to make state action more effective,[56] then it is also a means to empower democratic self-determination. This assumption is backed by the historical fact that the constitutionalization of state action in the nineteenth and twentieth century was accompanied by a considerable growth of its political power. This reference to state power must not be

---

[50] Claims for constitutionalist predecessors in antiquity notwithstanding: A. Riklin, *Machtteilung: Geschichte der Mischverfassung* (Wissenschaftliche Buchgesellschaft, 2005).

[51] Montesquieu, *The Spirit of Laws*. Complete Works. Volume 1 (T. Evans, 1777).

[52] *The Federalist Papers*, No. 59.

[53] For an extreme version: F.A. Hayek, *Law, Legislation, Liberty* (University of Chicago Press, 1983).

[54] C.R. Sunstein, *The Partial Constitution* (Harvard University Press, 1998).

[55] For the distinction between political and legal constitutionalism, see on the one hand R. Bellamy, *Political Constitutionalism* (Cambridge University Press, 2007); and, on the other hand, H. Kelsen, *Allgemeine Staatslehre* (Springer, 1925).

[56] S. Holmes, *Passions and Constraints* (University of Chicago Press, 1995), 164–166; C. Möllers, *Gewaltengliederung* (Mohr Siebeck, 2005); C. Möllers, *The Three Branches* (Oxford University Press, 2013). For the important idea of 'articulated governance', see J. Waldron, 'Separation of Powers in Thought and Practice' (2013) 54 *Boston College Law Review* 433.

confused with a reference to mere efficiency; while the latter only gives a weak instrumentalist justification, there is a stronger case to be made on the basis of political constitutionalism. From this point of view, a system of separated powers is a necessary condition for democratic self-government. On this account, constitutionalism is not a system of legal limitations to the political will, but rather a means to enable political action by empowering and protecting a political process. Behind this justification lies a positive concept of freedom that is achieved through state action, not against it,[57] the idea of a democratic community that empowers its members without threatening its freedom. We have already noticed that the fact that separation of powers is more often interpreted as a limiting concept may be due to the preference of lawyers for this kind of rationale,[58] but it is by no means inherent in a concept that explicitly leaves room for a political legislator.

Taking this one step further, it seems possible to develop a reconstruction of the normative core of separated powers that integrates legal and political constitutionalism, and, respectively, a negative individualistic and a positive democratic concept of freedom.[59] While there is much more to be said about the relationship between legal and political constitutionalism or liberal and republican understandings of democracy, one might argue that the very core of a meaningful justification of separated powers lies in a mechanism that guarantees the institutional articulation of both through means of procedure and organization. If the conceptual core of the principle entails a differentiation of public authorities into three functions, then one may also see political and legal constitutionalism as poles of a system of branches that are represented by the legislature and by the judiciary.[60]

---

[57] Möllers, *The Three Branches* (Oxford University Press, 2013), 86–89.
[58] Cf. e.g. R. Albert, 'Presidential Values in Parliamentary Systems' (2010) 8 *International Journal of Constitutional Law* 211–215 who lists only limiting values of separation of powers, and efficiency; see also C. Saunders 'Theoretical Underpinnings of Separation of Powers', in G. Jacobsohn and M. Schor (eds.), *Comparative Constitutional Theory* (Edward Elgar, 2018), 66–85.
[59] Christoph Möllers, *The Three Branches* (Oxford University Press, 2013), Ch. 2, III.
[60] This leaves open the question what to do with the executive. The short answer is: it provides for public action that is neither addressing the political community as a whole nor individual subjects, but intermediaries.

4 Problems

It is one of the weaknesses of our notion that every problem of constitutional structure can be reformulated in its terms. As we have already seen, this is taken care of by the fact that most legal problems are resolved by more concrete norms. The idea remains a normative background principle whose meaning is also determined by its context in a given constitutional jurisdiction. Still, it may be helpful to have a look at some of the more concrete debates. After a very short look at the difference between parliamentarism and presidentialism, the choice of examples will follow a simple scheme: an exemplary look at one problem that addresses the relationship between the legislator and the executive (delegation), at one problem that addresses the relationship between the executive and the judiciary (judicial review) and at one that addresses the relationship between the judiciary and the legislator (constitutional review).[61]

a Parliamentary and Presidential Systems

Though the distinction between presidential and parliamentary systems belongs to the most debated questions in the context of our notion, it may also be a rather fruitless one.[62] To be sure, there are arguments for or against one of the two,[63] and there is an especially strong case against semi-presidential systems.[64] However, most of these arguments are based on empirical research regarding stability or policy outcomes[65] and are hard to integrate into a constitutional argument given the fact that there is no obvious difference in democratic legitimacy between the two. As mentioned above, many problems of constitutional structure can only be solved within the framework of one of the two systems while overarching answers quickly become too unspecific.

---

[61] For a comparable take: C. Schmitt, *Verfassungslehre* (Duncker & Humblot, 1928), § 15.

[62] For a depiction of its variations, see Chapters 13 and 14.

[63] B. Ackerman, 'New Separation of Powers' (2000) 113 *Harvard Law Review* 633–729.

[64] C. Skach, 'The 'Newest' Separation of Powers' (2007) 5 *International Journal of Constitutional Law* 93–121.

[65] See the influential but much criticized J.J. Linz, 'The Perils of Presidentialism' (1990) 1(1) *Journal of Democracy*, 51–69; and, J.J. Linz, 'The Virtues of Parliamentarism' (1990) 1(4) *Journal of Democracy* 84–91.

b Delegation

One classical problem of separated powers is legislative delegation to the executive branch. From a principled point of view, two observations seem important. First, delegation cannot per se be understood as the abdication of the legislative function to another branch. Because legislative rules must be applied by the executive, delegation is better interpreted as a procedure in which the legislator makes use of the means of the executive.[66] Since in many jurisdictions there is no general rule as to what has to be legislated upon, delegation can also be the indication of a powerful legislator. Reversibility of the legislative act seems to be more relevant than its scope. Second, delegation operates differently in parliamentary and in presidential systems.[67] In parliamentary systems, there is a necessary political trust relation between parliament and government.[68] Therefore, delegation might be a problem from a rights perspective with regard to the vagueness of legislative rules[69] and the protection of legitimate expectations, but this is, against a long-standing tradition that never produced feasible criteria, hardly the case with regard to arguments from constitutional structure.[70] This is different for presidential systems in which president and parliament compete for control over the subordinate executive. Therefore, delegation comes often with specific means of parliamentary oversight that might be problematic as such.[71]

c Judicial Review

Can judicial review of the executive branch, the epitome of the rule of law, become a problem for separated powers? It can, when it is skipped. That is to say that any legislative rule that immunizes executive action from

[66] C.R. Sunstein, 'Nondelegation Canons' (2000) 67 *The University of Chicago Law Review* 315–343.
[67] K. Strøm, 'Parliamentary Democracy and Delegation', in K. Strøm, W.C. Müller, T. Bergman (eds.), *Delegation and Accountability in Parliamentary Democracies* (Oxford University Press, 2004), 55–106.
[68] Most prominently described in W. Bagehot, *The English Constitution* (Cornell University Press, 1966).
[69] E.g. *Sessions* v. *Dimaya*, 584 US (2018) (Kagan, J.) vagueness of a deportation rule; BVerfGE 143, 38 (2016): vagueness of a criminal sanction.
[70] For examples of fruitlessness: C. Saunders, *The Constitution of Australia* (Hart Publishing, 2011), 131–132.
[71] W. Wilson, *Congressional Government* (Houghton Mifflin Co., 1885); *INS* v. *Chadha*, 462 US 919 (1983).

judicial review can be seen as a functionally deficient state of separated powers. On the other hand, judicial review might become problematic when it loses contact with its procedural origin, the individual complaint, or when its course of action requires procedures that assimilate courts with the administration. As we can see in India or the United States, courts can assume functions beyond the decision of cases, they can factually run public administrations such as prisons[72] or decide how their own decisions shall be executed. Such practices have been justified as a progressive development in judicial organization.[73] Still, the more similar courts become in their actions to the administration they are supposed to control, the less able they become to fulfil their own specific function. The procedural sense of judicial review of administration lies in the institutional differences between both. One of the implicit assumptions of all models of separated powers is that the respective organization and procedure of the different branches are only legitimate as long as they are different from the organization and procedure of the other branches.

d Constitutional Review

Constitutional review is often seen as a solution to the problem of separated powers.[74] However, if there had ever been a classical doctrine of separated powers, constitutional review would certainly not have been part of it. To the contrary, a body that operates like a court in deciding cases while articulating general claims about the constitutionality of statutes is highly problematic. The idea that one organ can finally decide all questions of constitutional law, including the meaning of separation of powers, seems very much to go against the concept of separated powers. The debate about these problems is well-known, if not worn out. Still, there are at least three aspects in which the concept of separation of powers could contribute to the further discussion. First, one could try

---

[72] For examples: R. Pal, 'Separation of Powers', in S. Choudhry, M. Khosla and P.B. Mehta (eds.) *The Oxford Handbook of the Indian Constitution* (Oxford University Press, 2016), 264–266.

[73] A. Chayes, 'The Role of the Judge in Public Law Litigation' (1976) 89 *Harvard Law Review* 1281.

[74] S. Gardbaum, 'Separation of Powers and the Growth of Judicial Review in Established Democracies (or Why Has the Model of Legislative Supremacy Mostly Been Withdrawn from Sale?)' (2014) 62 *American Journal of Comparative Law* 613–640.

to embed constitutional review into a model of separated powers.[75] This might help to define more procedural limits to it, limits not only regarding the substantial standard of review, but also the way review courts are accessed and organized. Second, every critique of constitutional review that treats constitutional courts as somewhat illegitimate substitutes for parliaments misses the procedural differences between the two.[76] These differences may not justify constitutional review as such, but they remind us of the fact that the operational mode of deciding cases is not necessarily better located in a parliamentary assembly or committee. Finally, if we accept that separation of powers functions as a background principle that cannot derogate more explicit legal decisions, then the same is true for the critique of constitutional review. It becomes a critique of specific cases in which supreme courts have invented themselves as constitutional courts, like in Israel and the United States. It is much less relevant for the many other jurisdictions in which the constitution-maker has explicitly opted for constitutional review.

5 Challenges

While the problems referred to above can at least be addressed, though not solved, by reference to separation of powers, there may be other developments that might more fundamentally challenge the concept.

a Internationalization

Though one canonical attempt to conceptualize the idea of separated powers explicitly addressed external affairs,[77] it seems clear that the idea of tripartite government is designed for domestic action. The rise of international law-making is therefore the most urging challenge for our notion. It appears on two levels: as a need for the adaptation of domestic structures and as a question of how to organize international law-making. This second question leads us beyond the scope of this

---

[75] D. Kyritsis, *Where Our Protection* Lies (Oxford University Press, 2017); W. Heun, *Funktionell-rechtliche Schranken der Verfassungsgerichtsbarkeit* (Nomos, 1992).

[76] Most prominently J. Waldron 'The Core of the Case against Judicial Review' (2006) 115 *Yale Law Journal* 1346–1406.

[77] J. Locke, *The Treatises of Government* (Cambridge University Press, 1988 (ed.) Laslett), 364–372 (II, Ch. XXII, XXIII).

chapter and into the field of international institutional law.[78] Still, one observation seems to be relevant. The EU, as the most advanced international organization, may not be considered a state, but resembles more and more a differentiated organization in which the three branches and their respective functions can be distinguished.[79] While this has become a standard characteristic of EU law, this development shows the value of our notion even on levels beyond the nation state.[80]

The more pressing problem is whether there are means of adapting domestic separation of powers to the internationalization of law-making. The fact that states are, according to international law, represented by their governments poses problems for both other branches. Parliaments are not sufficiently involved in law-making procedures that are legislative in substance and courts often only get a belated chance to exercise meaningful review. In addition, governments can informally extend the mission of international organizations by intergovernmental consensus without giving notice to the other branches. The task of bringing the other branches back into a legitimate institutional division of labour may then be faced with three remedies: parliaments have to be informed and involved *ex ante*, as is the case in the US Fast Track procedures in Trade Law[81] or more recently in German constitutional law.[82] Courts must get the opportunity for an anticipatory review or an advisory control. More generally and most speculatively, one might wonder how necessary the concept of a unified external representation of states really is. Perhaps the internal political pluralism of liberal states deserves different modes of representation.[83]

---

[78] See Chapters 19 and 20 in this volume.

[79] R. Schütze, *European Constitutional Law*, 2nd ed. (Cambridge University Press, 2015), 150–154.

[80] For one examples of this usage: S. Talmon, 'The Security Council as World Legislature' (2005) 99 *American Journal of International Law* 175–193.

[81] H. Shapiro and L. Brainard, 'Trade Promotion Authority formerly known as Fast Track: Building Common Ground on Trade Demands more than a Name Change' (2003) 35 *George Washington International Law Review* 1.

[82] B. Zwingmann, *Separation of Powers the 'German Way'? The Relationship of the German Federal Government and Parliament in the EU Context* (Ph.D. Cardiff, 2017).

[83] I. Ley, 'Opposition in International Law – Alternativity and Revisibility as Elements of a Legitimacy Concept for Public International Law' (2015) 28 *Leiden Law Journal of International Law* 717–742.

b Modern Regulation

Under this heading, two distinct but strongly connected challenges are discussed: the rise of expertocratic administrative agencies and the privatization of administrative agendas.[84] Both are typical of encounters between the administrative state and capitalism. The rise of expertocratic agencies has been a topic of interest at least since the New Deal and, while there is a problem with administrations that claim to derive their legitimacy from their (alleged) expertise, it is important to see that a constitutional question only appears in cases in which the political decision to unbind the agency is either irreversible or too broad. A comparison may illustrate this: while a Congressional statute determines the mandate and the independence of the US Federal Reserve,[85] in the case of the European Central Bank,[86] both features are entrenched in the European Treaties that can only be amended by unanimous decision of the Member States. Therefore, the constitutional question seems more dramatic in the case of the EU in which the institutional design cannot be reversed by a political decision. Meaningful criteria for the detection of such problems can only be made through such comparisons and, while sweeping allegations of the 'rise of the unelected' are often lacking an empirical fundament, in many cases the political power behind administrative agencies seems to be underrated.[87]

This is different with regard to the privatization of public services. On the one hand, separation of powers itself does not give any criteria to limit privatization. Nevertheless, it is clear that governmental functions that are carried out by formally privatized state agencies, or even by private organizations, may slip out of parliamentary and judicial review. One might argue for a rule where, at least in the case of state ownership, the private form should not make a difference in this regard.[88] But even

---

[84] See Chapters 15 and 17 in this volume.
[85] For a critical assessment: P. Conti-Brown, *The Power and Independence of the Federal Reserve* (Princeton University Press, 2016).
[86] For a maximalist approach to its independence that seems to declare outside of all kinds of reviews and controls: C. Zilioli and M. Selmayr, 'The Constitutional Status of the European Central Bank' (2007) 44 *Common Market Law Review* 355–399.
[87] For the case of the EU: D. Curtin, *Executive Power of the European Union* (Oxford University Press, 2009).
[88] Concerning parliamentary controls in a recent decision of the German Federal Constitutional Court, BVerfGE 147, 50–148 (2017).

this seems to stretch our concept and needs argumentative support from other normative sources.

c Authoritarianism

The oldest challenge to our principle and its historical *raison d'être* is also the most recent one: authoritarianism and despotism. Political claims for hegemony by reference to the people's will have challenged democratic constitutional systems in many countries in all parts of the world. Often, these developments are reconstructed as 'populist' attacks on the rule of law, though one might wonder how far democracy is meant when populism is addressed.[89] This is not convincing. It accepts the democratic claim of authoritarian movements, and it misses the point that core values of democratic self-government can only be preserved under the condition of respect for open legal procedures.[90] Even the most basic majority rule requires respect for every vote to be counted and for a process in which the opportunity to win is equally distributed at the institutional level and protected by independent review.

Yet, it is far from clear if constitutional safeguards like the separation of powers are able to contain a dangerous political development. Could a 'better' constitution have saved the Weimar Republic from slipping into National Socialism? Maybe the Weimar Constitution was the best for the Weimar Republic. At least, we can refute the myth that the Weimar legal order did not care for its own protection.[91] If this case can teach us anything, the lesson could be that it is misleading to look for an ultimate legal bulwark against despotism. We rather have to look for procedures that are able to slow down a process that is meant to overthrow a democratic system.[92] We should be less interested in absolute limits and more in relative institutional resilience. This resilience is a highly contextualized matter in most cases since the constitutional design and its political and social environment in a given jurisdiction are so specific that it is

---

[89] J.-W. Mueller, *What is Populism?* (University of Pennsylvania Press, 2016). For a critique: D. van Reybrouck, *Against Elections: The Case for Democracy* (Bodley Head, 2016).

[90] J. Habermas, *Between Facts and Norms* (MIT Press, 1998).

[91] C. Gusy, *Weimar – Die Wehrlose Republik?* (Mohr Siebeck, 1991).

[92] S. Issacharoff, *Fragile Democracies: Contested Power in the Era of Constitutional Courts* (Cambridge University Press, 2015).

hard to find general rules of engagement. Many solutions will lie in the petty detail rather than in a grand design. The appointment of judges by bureaucrats may be a curse or a blessing, it very much depends on the way bureaucrats function, the kind of legal system we are addressing, and the question of how the bureaucrats are appointed themselves. If there is room for more general and comparative speculations about constitutional resilience, its claims should be modest. The analysis of constitutional trade-offs, of prices to be paid for remedies, is a legitimate topic for comparative constitutional scholarship, but it seems to be less helpful to provide concrete advice for constitutional reform.

The authoritarian risks we observe today stem from the political organs, from the executive and the legislative branches. With regard to the executive, there are different strategies to mitigate these risks, though none of them belongs to any 'classical' doctrine of separated powers and all of them produce other risks. The first one is the diffusion of political power. This diffusion is probably less convincingly organized around independent administrative authorities that try to counter the vicissitudes of politics with non-politics. It is far from clear how such institutions can bear this burden without any further genuine claim to legitimacy. The idea that political power is organized in a non-political institutional environment seems rather prone to fuel the current anti-institutional sentiment.

Two other strategies are more promising: firstly, the diffusion must be created through a multiplication of political procedures. This is the function of federal systems and local self-government – they counter politics with politics. Such a multiplication depends on a constitutional system that avoids too tight couplings between the different layers of government – like in the United States and Switzerland with regard to the states/cantons and in Germany with regard to the local governments. If the national level makes a strong constitutional claim for internal sovereignty, it is easier to reign in these counter-procedures. But the effects of local decentralization are especially under-researched in comparative constitutional law. The price that is being paid for this multiplication lies normatively in the fragmentation of democratic equality and practically in a potential inability of the system to take effective political action. A conservative status quo bias may be the result, but this may be better than an authoritarian coup.

Secondly, the executive should be based on a civil service that is politically responsible without being politicized itself by developing a culture of reflective legality. To bolster members of the public service with a certain institutional and habitual independence is an old instrument to buffer a constitutional system against political volatility. This is again not necessarily living up to any purely democratic ideal and we can observe how the civil service was an important element of anti-religious or anti-rural political parties in countries as different as Thailand and Turkey. No rule of law can transform a civil service into a neutral institution, but, especially in systems with a defined democratic tradition, it may have a stabilizing function without assuming an oligarchic role.

The idea of the pluralization of political power seems also relevant for legislative decisions and its equivalents. Constitutional systems are especially sensitive to monocratic justificatory claims, may they come from unicameral parliaments, the direct election of a head of state or plebiscites. One may argue that this is the only way to make the sovereign speak,[93] but one of the core assumptions of any meaningful doctrine of separation of powers is that the sovereign must have more than one voice in order to have a voice at all. Therefore, bi-cameralism, democratic representation and only carefully embedded use of direct democracy may be means to protect democracy from itself.

One might wish for a constitutional organ that could be entrusted with the protection of the constitution as its 'guardian'.[94] Instead, what we see is a trilemma that can be reconstructed by reference to our three branches.[95] Political organs have the best claim to protect the political order, they are legitimized and powerful, yet they either tend to be the problem or they refuse to intervene for the sake of their own political interests (like the Member States of the EU against other Member States). Executive and administrative organs may claim expertise and neutrality, but they seem unable to bear the justificatory burden that goes along with such a kind of conflict. The European Commission is the most visible example, but the same is true for national agencies that fight corruption and monitor human rights violations. Courts, finally, are often lacking

---

[93] For the history of this argument in political theory: R. Tuck, *The Sleeping Sovereign* (Cambridge University Press, 2016).

[94] C. Schmitt, 'Der Hüter der Verfassung', *Archiv des öffentlichen Rechts* 55 (N.F. 16), No. 2 (1929), 161–237 versus H. Kelsen, 'Wer soll Hüter der Verfassung sein?', *Die Justiz* 6 (1931), 576–628.

[95] C. Möllers and L. Schneider, *Demokratiesicherung in der EU* (Mohr, 2018).

both the ability to enforce a contested order and the legitimacy to counter a politically mobilized attack on the constitution.

Conclusion

'Separation of Powers' can be used as a shorthand description of the organization of government as a whole. Political scientists and lawyers have widely applied the term in this way although there is nothing distinctively normative about it. The concept can also serve as a legal argument in constitutional reasoning. Both uses are not mutually exclusive. Even though the first use of the concept does not refer to a legal notion of separated powers in a normative sense, it seems to be helpful for constitutional lawyers who want to analyse the organizational structure of governments. The second one might also help non-legal researchers to understand one important element of constitutional discourse.

While the first use is widely applied by constitutionalists, the latter one seems rather neglected. We do not know much from a comparative perspective about the different usages of our concept in constitutional reasoning. And, while the first use has been proven to be a useful tool, especially as a conceptual bridge between law and empirical political sciences as well as normative political theory, its use has been relatively one-sided and blurred by a typically legal bias. Therefore, the institutional constraints that the idea of separated powers demands for the political process seem somewhat overrated, while its enabling function for all forms of democratic politics is too often ignored. Only a model that includes both elements may serve as a tool to describe the challenges that modern constitutionalism is facing through phenomena such as internationalization, privatization and the recent surge of authoritarianism, and it may then also give some normative orientation.

Further Reading

B. Ackerman, 'New Separation of Powers' (2000) 113 *Harvard Law Review* 633.
M.A. Cameron, *Strong Constitutions* (Oxford University Press, 2013).
A. Kavanagh, 'The Constitutional Separation of Powers', in D. Dyzenhaus and M. Thorburn (eds.), *Philosophical Foundations of Constitutional Law* (Oxford University Press, 2016).

D. Kyritsis, *Where Our Protection Lies* (Oxford University Press, 2017).

C. Möllers, *The Three Branches* (Oxford University Press, 2013).

H.-M. Ten Napel and W. Voermans (eds.), *The Powers That Be* (Leiden University Press, 2016).

G. Tsebelis, *Veto-Players: How Political Institutions Work* (Princeton University Press, 2002).

J. Waldron, 'Separation of Powers in Thought and Practice' (2013) 54 *Boston College Law Review* 433.

10 The Rule of Law

András Sajó

Introduction

Currently the European Union is in the process of applying certain sanctions in respect of Member States that are allegedly in violation of the rule of law (RoL), a fundamental requirement of membership. Sizeable sums of development aid and international loans directed to developing countries are held back for non-observance of the RoL and loans are conditional on satisfying requirements of the RoL. Countries (and international credit rating agencies) measure legal systems against one or another standard of the RoL. The comparative law hypothesis is that there are certain common patterns in the mix of principles, rules and practices that constitute the RoL and within these clusters of patterns certain commonalities emerge. But there has been little systematic comparative study of the RoL in constitutional law, the problem being that what is considered crucial to the RoL in one country is not necessarily required in another. Yet constitutional and international courts, as well as politicians, regularly rely on the concept in adjudication, international treaties and political action. It is therefore a matter of practical importance to understand through comparison what are the common and diverging features of the RoL. Unfortunately, most of the literature on the RoL deals with its normative concepts and not what courts and other servants and masters of the law do with it (or in its name).

The diverging legal understandings (or uses) of the RoL cannot be separated from theoretical debates and approaches to the RoL, even if these different concepts often serve as inspiration for practical legal work and constitutional theory building, and in international and domestic politico-legal evaluations. The contemporary analysis of the RoL is mostly rooted in political or legal theory and is primarily normative. The comparative analysis is therefore limited by the needs of such theories.[1] In constitutional law, and in law in general, the RoL is considered as a problem of national law and is not approached in a systematically comparative way. One of the problems is that the RoL is narrowly understood as a constitutional concept or principle while the real constitutional relevance can be understood only in view of its presence in the specific areas of law (RoL that emerges in the whole legal system and not only when a constitutional court refers to it).[2] In particular, these discussions of the RoL do not look into the specific uses of RoL considerations and socio-legal and political practices in terms of functional comparison.[3] Some theories of the RoL hint at the importance of the social understanding of the RoL as a rule of law *based* legal system which is expected to reflect fundamental expectations and intuitions of the subjects of law. Indeed, this social aspect of the RoL becomes central in practical work when the RoL is promoted internationally.

---

[1] The social relevance of the RoL varies across societies (see also its 'introduction' or 'imposition' in the process of state building). Americans (or at least American lawyers) today, like Dicey more than a hundred years ago claim that 'respect for the Rule of Law is central to our political and rhetorical traditions, possibly even to our sense of national identity.' R. Fallon, 'The Rule of Law as a Concept in Constitutional Discourse' (1997) 97 *Columbia Law Review* 1, 3. Where there is no such respect the RoL may be seen as intrusion notwithstanding international agreement concerning its prevalence.

[2] In certain areas administrative law takes over many functions of constitutional law; it is also constitutional law in action. For the European Union see e.g. M. Hartmann, 'Administrative Constitutionalism and the Political Union' (2013) 14 *German LJ* 695.

[3] The need for such approach is clear in the sociological approaches to the RoL (see: M. Krygier , 'The Rule of Law: Pasts, Presents, and Two Possible Futures' (2016) 12(1) *Annual Review of Law and Social Science* 199–229).

This chapter will apply a functional comparison. Functional comparison here refers to the comparison of specific sets of practices leading to comparable functions of governance. To use a less 'scientific' jargon: assuming that the RoL provides *legal* protection against arbitrariness coming from power holders (especially government) there are different principles, sets of rules and practices to achieve this primarily constitutional aim which are carried out (justified) in the name of the RoL or, conversely, which are subsumed by scholarly and judicial analysis under the heading of the RoL. The comparative law hypothesis is that there are certain common patterns in the mix of principles, rules and practices and within these clusters of patterns certain commonalities emerge with their own normative power both domestically and internationally. (This explains the current interest and importance of national RoL experiences: they are used both domestically to legitimize, develop and criticize the legal system and internationally to enable external control and development of national legal systems.)

The argument of this chapter is that, notwithstanding the formal constitutional relevance of the RoL and the justification of the RoL in constitutional theory, only a systematic comparison (that we are short of at the moment, and even without a proper methodology) can show the domain of uses of a concept which varies depending on the structure of the constitutional system. For example, the extent to which RoL considerations can be enforced depends on the extent to which constitutional law can penetrate private relations. While international documents push for a worldwide recognition of the RoL as a value this argument, both as an international imposition and a domestic claim, remains contested in light of the existing national and even branch-of-law experiences.

Following a survey of conceptual issues, a brief survey of the historical development of the concept and its application follows, as such historically determined practices create a certain path-dependence for contemporary uses. This is followed by a survey of the constitutionalization of the concept, which serves as an introduction to the central thesis of the chapter, namely that the constitutional text is not decisive in the practical uses and scope of the term in different constitutional contexts. As the last part of the chapter indicates, without knowing what is produced in the name of the constitutionalized and internationally acclaimed concept and its derivatives we run the risk of accepting unconditionally an ideology that may not provide guidance, and is easily hijacked for regime legitimation and abuse.

1 Conceptual Issues

The Rule of Law (fundamental justice or natural justice in common law jurisdictions) and *Rechtsstaat* (the German term is translated in different languages as state of law or state governed by law) are part of the constitutional vocabulary all over the world. 'Rule of Law' and *'Rechtsstaat'* (hereinafter RoL for both expressions, albeit they reflect different historical experiences in different countries) refer to some kind of *legal* protection and security against the arbitrariness of power holders (especially government). The security provided by the RoL (eminently present in commercial law as non-interference) enables social and governmental cooperation and it makes credible public and private promises and expectations. Credibility through the RoL is in the interest of the ruler;[4] from the citizens' perspective it enables the planning of their life – even in otherwise oppressive regimes.

It is costly to operate a system of commands or rules without legitimacy and such legitimacy comes from the respect of the RoL. It is respected not only for its social performance, i.e. the foreseeability provided by rule observance: RoL cannot be fully separate from social expectations and practices of minimal social fairness. As 'natural justice' or 'law of reason', it was historically related to the prevailing common sense. It is for this reason that common law lawyers, like Dicey, claimed that 'respect for the Rule of Law is central to our political and rhetorical traditions, possibly even to our sense of national identity'.[5]

Is the RoL an unqualified good? The philosopher Judith Shklar has claimed that the RoL 'has become meaningless thanks to ideological abuse and general over-use ... No intellectual effort need therefore be wasted on this bit of ruling-class chatter.'[6] It can also be argued that the RoL, with its emphasis on legal formalities, prevents justice from prevailing. It distorts human relations by turning them into juridical relations ('juridification of

---

[4] See S. Holmes 'Lineages of the Rule of Law', in J.M. Maravall-Q. Przeworski (eds.), *Democracy and the Rule of Law* (Cambridge University Press, 2003), 32–33.

[5] Fallon (n. 1), 3.

[6] J.N. Shklar, 'Political Theory and The Rule of Law', in A.C. Hutchinson and P. Monahan (eds.), *The Rule of Law: Ideal or Ideology* (Carswell, 1987).

the life world', what is termed 'judicialization' in case of judicial involve-ment) and contributes to an excessive power of judges to the detriment of democracy ('juristocracy').[7] It is easy to see that the necessary formalities of the RoL can become impediments to what Max Weber would call 'material justice'. Improper pleading precludes a court to notice an injustice and pro-hibitive court fees and other formal obstacles may hamper access to justice in a way that is incompatible with the RoL.[8] In such circumstances a RoL abiding administration of justice becomes an accomplice to injustice by inaction. However, even if only partly realized, if it were a legal utopia, it has all the advantages utopia has for positive action.

'The Rule of Law is a human ideal, and theories of the Rule of Law are inevitably framed to serve political or moral interests.'[9] Given its instru-mental use, there are differences in the actual frames of the ideal. For example, it is argued that in Russia a pre-revolutionary legal positivism determines the meaning of the RoL[10] and in China the RoL is written with Chinese characters. Even in matters of commercial law Confucian com-munitarianism prevails where the words (e. g. good faith) are translations of Western legal concepts.[11] The meaning and legal consequences vary historically and even within a given legal system there are differences in the use among the legal branches.

In legal theory the RoL is often understood as a minimum that makes law into a system, into 'legal': it is a matter of legitimacy. Political theory considers the concept within a model of state governance where law plays a crucial role, while constitutional theory, in a related way, considers the RoL as a restriction of governmental arbitrariness. This constitutional concern was expressed early on by Locke: 'Where-ever law ends, tyr-anny begins.' There is an element of self-limitation present here: as Hans Kelsen has pointed out, the civil servants and judges who administer the

---

[7] G. Teubner (ed.), *Juridification of Social Spheres: A Comparative Analysis in the Areas of Labor, Corporate, Antitrust and Social Welfare Law* (de Gruyter, 1987); R. Hirschl, *Towards Juristocracy: The Origins and Consequences of the New Constitutionalism* (Harvard University Press, 2004).
[8] See *Weissman and Others* v. *Romania,* Application No. 63945/00 (24 May 2006); *Teltronic-CATV* v. *Poland,* Application No. 48140/99 (10 January 2006).
[9] Fallon (n. 1), 7.
[10] E. Lukyanova, 'On the Rule of Law in the Context of Russian Foreign Policy' (2015) 3(2) *Russian Law Journal* 10–36.
[11] L.A. DiMatteo, "Rule of Law" in China: The Interaction of Freedom of Contract and Good Faith with Cultural Norms'. Available at SSRN: https://ssrn.com/abstract=2994344 (accessed 28 June 2017).

law have to believe that the rules of the law have to be followed, and they have to believe so because this is what makes their action legitimate in their own eyes and in the eyes of those who must follow their decisions.

The RoL is one of the most open constitutional law concepts. The differences in legal and political theory are so deep that it is even the essentially contested conceptual nature of the RoL is contested. 'An "essentially contestable concept"... has evaluative as well as descriptive elements, and its correct application cannot be fixed simply by appeal to ordinary usage.'[12] Nevertheless, there are a few oft-quoted concepts and ideas which shape normative expectations about the RoL. The fundamental difference is captured in the division between formal and substantive (material) theories or concepts.[13] 'Substantive concepts accept that the rule of law has ... formal attributes ..., but they wish to take the doctrine further. Certain substantive rights are said to be based on, or derived from, the rule of law. The concept is used as the foundation for these rights, which are then used to distinguish between "good" laws, which comply with such rights, and "bad" laws which do not.'[14] The practical legal consequence can be that administrative decisions, regulations, laws can be reviewed by courts in terms of their 'goodness', serving a choice of 'good life'. Formalist theories find this extension of the RoL unacceptable and insist on structural elements of the law: the mere fact that government action is authorized by law (rule by law) would not be sufficient, although it is the precondition for any form of RoL.

Among the formal perspectives, Dicey's late nineteenth century intuition is still influential. Relying on superficial, second-hand comparisons, he equated the English RoL with the supremacy of the law (i.e. the subordination of officials to the law).[15] The RoL is 'contrasted with every system of government based on the exercise by persons in authority of wide, arbitrary, or discretionary powers of constraint.'[16] The RoL includes the equality of all persons before the law; 'equality, or of the universal

---

[12] See Fallon (n. 1).

[13] P. Craig, 'Formal and Substantive Conceptions of the Rule of Law: An Analytical Framework' (1997) *Public Law* 467; Fallon (n. 1).

[14] See Craig (n. 13).

[15] See however *Malone* v. *Commissioner for the Metropolitan Police (No.2)* [1979] 1 Ch 344. This was held not to meet the prescribed by law requirement by the ECtHR, see below.

[16] A.V. Dicey, *Introduction to the Study of the Law of Constitution*, 8th ed. (Macmillan, 1959), 1.

subjection of all classes to one law administered by the ordinary Courts, has been pushed to its utmost limit. With us every official, from the Prime Minister down to a constable or a collector of taxes, is under the same responsibility for every act done without legal justification as any other citizen.'[17] Law serves all citizens (roughly) equally.

Joseph Raz explains the need for the formal features of law being related to the subjects of law and not to the sovereign: the formal RoL enables individuals to plan their lives.[18] Laws should be prospective, not retrospective; they should be relatively stable; particular laws should be guided by open, general (i.e. impersonal) and clear rules; there should be an independent judiciary; there should be access to the courts; and the discretion which law enforcement agencies possess should not be allowed to undermine the purposes of the relevant legal rules. One could add that all those rules have to be enacted and applied in conformity with pre-existing rules of procedure. 'But there are more reasons for valuing the rule of law. We value the ability to choose styles and forms of life, to fix long-term goals and effectively direct one's life towards them.' From the perspective of legislation, the existence of certain characteristics of the rules provide internal morality to law.[19]

Most constitutional theories emphasize that the administration of the rules shall be subjected to an independent and impartial judiciary. The judicial function requires that trials be fair which implies hearing and equality of arms, although fair written proceedings are also part of the Western legal tradition.

The substantive approach to the RoL adds the procedural fairness component and so recognizes the subject of the law as a rights holder who deserves respect. This is regarded as a substantive value or goal, but the procedural aspects of the RoL (the idea that rules shall provide for fair proceedings where people have the opportunity to express their point of view in front of an impartial decider) is a purely formal requirement, even if it is triggered by the substantive consideration that rights are best protected and obligations are best determined by an impartial trier of facts, preferably a judge. It is argued that the procedurally just treatment

---

[17] A.V. Dicey (n. 16), 114.
[18] J. Raz, 'The Rule of Law and its Virtue' (1977) 93 *Law Quarterly Review* 195, 220.
[19] L.L. Fuller, *The Morality of Law* (Yale University Press, 1969), 33–38.

(hearing, equality of arms) increases the legitimacy of the justice system, although it is quite possible that the source of the legitimacy lies in the perception that the authorities are legitimate.[20] The divine legitimacy of a religious arbiter can survive his apparent arbitrariness.

The internal (formal) requirements are primarily the functional needs of a modern legal system that intends to regulate complex social relations in the most efficient way. This requires uniformity but some circumstances and/or ages permit discretion. Discretion does not mean arbitrariness; at least when the decision-maker has to look at proportionality or to the justice of the outcome.

From the constitutional perspective of the limitation of governmental arbitrariness, the formal requirements of the RoL serve as instruments of such limitation. It is argued, however, that formalities and formalism cannot prevent biased results; after all, in Nazi Germany considerable effort was put into deciding which body was competent to pay the German railways for the deportation of the Jews.[21] Notwithstanding its formalism, law in Nazi Germany did not satisfy the equality and access to impartial administration criteria, and it was characterized by unlawfulness and legal chaos.

In the spirit of the search for substantive justice that resurfaced after World War II,[22] Lord Bingham, in his reformulation of the requirement of impartial administration of the law called for substantive review. He added to the list of the RoL components that the law must afford adequate protection of fundamental human rights.[23] This implies that 'our understanding of concepts such as fairness, reasonableness, and equality is inevitably influenced by our evolving view of the individual who is subject to the law, the legal subject for short, and thus in recent times by the claim that the legal subject has to be regarded primarily as a bearer of human rights.'[24] The Venice Commission adopted a similar position where

---

[20] T.R. Tyler, *Why People Obey the Law? Procedural Justice, Legitimacy, and Compliance* (Yale University Press, 1990); D.S. Nagin and C.W. Telep, 'Procedural Justice and Legal Compliance' (2017) 13 *Annual Review of Law and Social Science* 5–28.

[21] R. Hilberg, 'The Bureaucracy of Annihilation', in F. Furet (ed.) *Unanswered Questions: Nazi Germany and the Genocide of the Jews* (Schocken Books, 1989), 119–133, 123.

[22] See *The Declaration of Delhi* (1959).

[23] T. Bingham, *The Rule of Law* (Penguin, 2010), 66.

[24] D. Dyzenhaus, *The Constitution of Law. Legality in a Time of Emergency* (Cambridge University Press, 2006), 13.

respectful treatment of the individual is combined with procedural elements: 'the notion of the rule of law requires everyone to be treated by all decision-makers with dignity, equality and rationality and in accordance with the law, and to have the opportunity to challenge decisions before independent and impartial courts for their unlawfulness, where they are accorded fair procedures.'[25]

Such human rights-inspired concepts have considerable impact on the more traditional, formal elements of the RoL such as fairness. In specific constitutional circumstances, as in Poland (see below) the principle of the 'state ruled by law' became a nearly all-encompassing concept and it has included principles establishing representative democracy and specific political and legal institutions, in addition to principles of separation of powers and the more common above-mentioned elements. It is often argued that the ECtHR assimilates human rights protection, constitutionalism and the RoL.

The resulting comparative constitutional law question is this: to what extent are the above-described substantive concept(s) reflected in national systems, especially as a function of the RoL, and what are the constitutional consequences of such understanding in terms of separation of powers, legitimacy, effective enforcement of fundamental rights, and so on?

The substantive approach may be problematic for the formal RoL. The advantage of the formal RoL approach is that it does not require the analysis of the underlying political or social injustice. A substantive approach runs the risk of being political but it promises to be more ethical and socially just:

The law has its limits, even human rights law. Tensions arise between the demands of justice for the relatives of victims and the imposition of unrealistic burdens on law enforcement agents governed by the rule of law. The judicial resolution of such disputes, ... requires that a delicate balance be struck ... based on the objective and dispassionate application of clear and foreseeable legal standards.[26]

The introduction of even elementary procedural fairness *contra legem* will 'not promote the rule of law. It is a dead end, as it leaves the State concerned in a legal limbo.'[27] However, the demands of the formal RoL

---

[25] www.venice.coe.int/webforms/documents/CDL-AD(2011)003rev-e.aspx ([16]) (accessed 4 December 2017).

[26] Judge Spano, dissenting in *Talpis* v. *Italy*, Application No. 41237/14 (2 March 2017).

[27] Judge Nussberger, dissenting in *Al-Dulimi and Montana Management Inc.* v. *Switzerland*, Application No. 5809/08 (21 June 2016).

form just one of the virtues of law that may be sacrificed for more important considerations; but sacrifice it will be. How often and on what grounds such sacrifice takes place is a matter of future research. In a case concerning the punishment of communist crimes, the Hungarian Constitutional Court limited permissible departure from the formal RoL to situations where a concurring constitutional principle makes this imperative and proportional; this is the case of the revision of a criminal conviction based on a provision that was later declared unconstitutional. Sheer injustice, or the violation of material justice per se, does not provide a substantive right to a remedy.[28]

2 The RoL/*Rechtsstaat* in Historical Comparison

The comparative study of the RoL often refers to models of historical development. Plato accepted the RoL as second best compared to the rule of wise men, while Aristotle, relying on comparative material claimed that '[i]t is more proper that law should govern than any one of the citizens: upon the same principle, if it is advantageous to place the supreme power in some particular persons, they should be appointed to be only guardians, and the servants of the laws.'[29] Roman law and medieval law, including canon law, contained maxims and rules which are today nuts and bolts of the comprehensive RoL concept (e.g. no-one should be a judge in his own cause). Apparently, these are common sense rules of conflict resolution that apply in different cultures across different times; these expectations are considered just or fair in the sense of natural justice or as corresponding to (natural) reason. In this sense, the common law legitimized the RoL (as it was to be 'found' by judges) to be the rule of reason. (Of course, in view of the differences in conflict resolution, these statements of reason are far from universal.) Among these ancient ideas one can find the supremacy of the law over all office holders which emerged in the Middle Ages as a response to the attempts of the monarch. Stuart absolutism relied on the principle of *princeps legibus soluta est*; Sir Edward Coke (1552–1634), a common law judge, responded with an old medieval maxim of the common law: the King is subordinated to

---

[28] Decision 9/1992 (I. 30.) of the Constitutional Court of Hungary.
[29] Aristotle, *Ethics and Politics* (ed. by A. Uyl, Devoted Publishing, 2017), 161 (3.16).

God and law. Moreover, in *Dr Bonham's case* he seems to have considered the possibility that the laws of Parliament could be void if in violation of 'common right and reason'. Some of the institutions that constitute the RoL today were finally codified in the Bill of Rights 1689 and judges were given security in tenure in 1701.

Likewise, it was the use of sovereign power that, deemed arbitrary, mobilized the American colonies to institutionalize a RoL system by enacting state and federal constitutions during and after the War of Independence. In the United States, many elements of the RoL became constitutional rights and rules (e.g. prohibition of *ex post facto* laws) and it was argued that the Republic is a government of laws, and not of men,[30] and the observance of laws and the constitution was safeguarded judicially, e.g. by judicial review.

The desire to limit governmental arbitrariness was also central in the continental Enlightenment but the focus of interest was on individual rights and legal certainty. Revolutionary France constitutionalized the supremacy of laws (partly because of the supremacy of the law-maker, the people). Fundamental rights could be regulated or limited only by law. However, courts were not trusted with rights protection in the common law sense as pre-revolutionary judges were regarded as the source of arbitrariness. France was frozen in a stage of 'legal state' (*État légal*); laws were beyond constitutional control but the administration increasingly had to act within the frame of the law and was subjected to the control of the *Conseil d'Etat*. Legality, the '*principe de légalité*' was a major concern of the State in the sense of preventing abuse of power by the administration, but administrative discretion was widespread. The factual review of administrative decisions in an administrative court became accepted only around 1960. Judges who traditionally dealt with civil and criminal law cases were bound to mechanically apply the law as required by the prevailing technique of interpretation of the law (*exegése*). However, law was understood to apply to all in the spirit of the equality before the law and there was a strong sense of legality in private legal relations. Currently, however, with the privatization of government services, it is a major concern to what extent the RoL, ordinarily applicable in public administrative law, will be applicable where a private party will carry out the functions previously exercised by the administration.

---

[30] *Marbury* v. *Madison* 5 US (1 Cranch) 137 (1803).

The idea that the state is to be governed by law emerged differently in Germany where modern market society was late to arrive and absolutism prevailed. Following Kant, the concept of a *Rechtsstaat* (a system of legal guarantees including constitutional fundamental rights, against the intrusion of the State) became a political demand;[31] it was the battle cry of the reformist bourgeoisie. In opposition to the illiberal police state, the individual in the *Rechtsstaat* is left free and intervention in his affairs is subject to legal formalities. The State can realize its aims only if legally authorized to act, and only using authorized means. In the era of legal positivism, the control of law from an external ethical perspective became unacceptable and the formal legality of the activities of the public administration became central, abandoning the substantive elements of the *Rechtsstaat*. In this positivist sense Kelsen, who is credited for introducing constitutional review of laws in Austria, intended to limit such control to formal constitutionality. Judicial review, under his influence, objects to the idea of substantive RoL (*Rechtsstaat*). While legal scholarship envisioned the need for the constitutional control of legislation (the ultimate RoL expectation in terms of legality control), the implementation of this idea started to take off only after World War II (see the German Basic Law and the Italian Constitution). At this time a substantive concept of the RoL resurfaced, inspired by human rights concerns. These concerns included a right to welfare or livelihood (in the name of dignity), and in view of the functions of the state which was constitutionally defined as a social state. Combining the state of law with the state's welfare function, constitutional theory and the constitutional law of a number of continental countries speak of social *Rechtsstaat*. Many contemporary German scholars argue that in the German constitutional system the *Rechtsstaat* is not only formal but material too, guaranteed by the supremacy of the Basic Law, which in turn means attachment to the content of the Basic Law.[32]

---

[31] The Italian and Spanish equivalents *stato di diritto, estado de derecho* reflect similar political aspirations. The French version of the Canadian Charter of Rights and Freedoms uses '*la primauté du droit*' for RoL.

[32] H. Konrad, 'Der Rechtsstaat im Verfassungssystem des Grundgesetzes', in M. Tohidipur (ed.), *Der bürgerliche Rechtsstaat* (Suhrkamp, 1978), 290–314, 295. For Switzerland, see U. Hafelin, W. Haller and H. Keller (eds.), *Schweizerisches Bundesstaatsrecht* (Schulthess Verlag, 2012), 53.

As to English law, by the end of the nineteenth century, Professor Dicey (with some exaggeration) confirmed the existence of a common law based RoL in England (and in common law ruled territories under the Imperial Crown). Thirty years later he had to admit that the 'ancient veneration for the rule of law has in England suffered during the last thirty year a marked decline. The truth of this assertion is proved by actual legislation, by the existence among some classes of a certain distrust both of the law and of the judges, and by a marked tendency towards the use of lawless methods for the attainment of social or political ends.'[33]

In fact, with the appearance of the welfare state the RoL was losing ground even in democracies, and not only in common law countries. The RoL was considered an impediment to welfare services which were provided by efficiency driven bureaucracies. Welfare administration in the United Kingdom departed from the RoL and unfettered discretionary power was preferred in the name of innovation and flexibility.[34] Distrust in legal formalism also became prevalent in the United States at the time of the New Deal when the Supreme Court moved away from substantive review of laws. Rule-making under the National Industrial Recovery Act 'dispense[d] with one of the most basic elements of a fair legal system: notice through published laws.' The NRA [the regulatory agency] 'boasted' that it 'would not be bound by "legalisms" or "legalistic requirements" in its law-making'.[35] It is true that in 1946 the Administrative Procedure Act introduced a highly RoL oriented rule-making system with hearings and judicial review that turned rule making into adjudication but 'since it is virtually impossible to make rules this way, Congress rarely requires this procedure and the Supreme Court has avoided interpreting statutes to conclude that it does. Thus, section 553

---

[33] Dicey (n. 16).

[34] See P. Craig, 'The Common Law, Reasons and Administrative Justice' (1994) *Cambridge Law Journal* 282–302; M. Adler and S. Asquith (eds.), *Discretion and Welfare* (Heinemann, 1981); F.A. Hayek, *The Road to Serfdom* (Routledge, 1944) and P. Kegan, and J. Jowell, 'Administrative Law', in V. Bogdanor (ed.), *The British Constitution in the Twentieth Century* (Oxford University Press, 2003), 373–400.

[35] N.S. Zeppos, 'The Legal Profession and the Development of Administrative Law' (1997) 72 *Chicago-Kent Law Review* 1126–1128. For a contemporary wave of anti-RoL (where RoL is under pressure for being part of the administrative state) see G.E. Metzger, Foreword: '1930s Redux: The Administrative State under Siege' (2017) 131 *Harvard Law Review* 1–95.

informal rulemaking is the most formal process by which administrative rules are made.'[36]

The antipathy towards formalities was so great that not even criminal law could resist it. Under the influence of theories of 'social defence', fundamental requirements of the RoL were disregarded in the treatment of criminals (the accused), especially in the context of juvenile delinquency. The paradigm of the crime (with its procedural guarantees) was replaced by social work and therapeutic intervention.[37]

Today, the RoL is more cherished than ever. In terms of substantive concepts of the RoL, the individual is not a welfare recipient but a rights holder and the administration is to honour this with procedural fairness and substantive considerations regarding the individual. Nevertheless, it can be argued that in the post-liberal order of the welfare state, because of the intervention of the state into the economy and other social relations, legal texts have become more open with purposive legal interpretation destroying the formal qualities of the RoL, irrespective of the return to procedural RoL.[38]

3 The Place of the RoL in Contemporary Constitutional Law

Today at least 102 constitutions refer to the RoL (state governed by law, etc.) and another eight to natural justice, mostly in the Preamble or among their General Principles. Due process clauses are also common, with special rules of criminal law and procedure complementing the RoL.

The German Basic Law referred to *Rechtsstaat* as early as 1948 as a duty of the constituent Länder.[39] In the wake of decolonization some former colonies with a common law tradition referred to the RoL in the constitution as a general concept (see e.g. Nigeria, 1960, section 32: '"law"

---

[36] E.L. Rubin, 'Bureaucratic Oppression: Its Causes and Cures' (2012) 90 *Washington University Law Review* 291, 362.

[37] Even in 2016 it was still an issue whether juveniles deserve full procedural rights, see *Blokhin* v. *Russia*, Application No. 47152/06 (23 March 2016). The US Supreme Court held already forty years earlier that due process applies in juvenile justice: *Kent* v. *the United States* 383 US 541 (1966).

[38] See R.M. Unger, *Law in Modern Society* (The Free Press, 1976), 176–181, 192–223.

[39] Article 28(1). The constitutional order in the Länder must conform to the principles of a republican, democratic and social state governed by the rule of law, within the meaning of this Basic Law.

includes an unwritten rule of law'). When the dictatorships gave way on the Iberian continent to the constitutional self-definition of the state, it was considered necessary, at least at the level of the Preamble, to define the State as one governed by law. (For example, the Preamble of the 1976 Portuguese Constitution refers to the Portuguese People's decision 'to ensure the primacy of a democratic state based on the rule of law'.) Further, among the principles of the first democratic Portuguese Constitution it was stated that the state is subordinated to the constitution and democratic legality, while in the version in force today the now worldwide standard formula has been added: 'the Portuguese Republic is a democratic state based on the rule of law.'

There are alternative formulations. According to the Canadian Charter of Rights, Canada 'is founded upon the principles that recognize the supremacy of God and the rule of law'. Sierra Leone turns the RoL into a specific state obligation: 'The State shall ... enforce the rule of law.' Exceptionally, even a legal definition of the content of the RoL is provided, as in Article 5 of the Swiss Constitution on the *Rechtsstaat (Principes de l'activité de l'Etat régi par le droit)*:

1. All activities of the state are based on and limited by law.
2. State activities must be conducted in the public interest and be proportionate to the ends sought.
3. State institutions and private persons shall act in good faith.[40]
4. The Confederation and the Cantons shall respect international law.

Legality, that is, the need for state authorities to have the authorization of the law, is central to this approach.

Older constitutions with unchanged text do not mention expressly the RoL but many of its elements are present in the text (e.g. the supremacy of laws and the constitution, the binding nature of laws on authorities,[41] etc.). Fundamental rules and sub-principles of the RoL in criminal law and procedure are also part of these constitutions. It is generally accepted that, even in the absence of explicit reference, the RoL is a fundamental (even unamendable) principle or value of the constitutional order. In Germany, where Article 20 of the Basic Law refers only to certain aspects of the RoL (subordination of the authorities to law), the scholarly literature

---

[40] Good faith was a traditional value of Swiss law originating in the Code of Obligations.
[41] See e.g. Art. 18 §1 Constitution of Austria.

considers that this fundamental principle exists in a combination of specific rules and sub-principles of the Basic Law. The consequence is that the legal practice does not rely on an abstract *Rechtsstaat* ideal or model, it is argued that no further principles or rules can be deducted from the RoL principle; however, it nonetheless remains crucial in constitutional interpretation.[42]

Behind the general trend of including the RoL as a fundamental constituent element of the constitutional order, there are important differences related to national constitutional development. For example, the right to the natural judge is an express provision in post-totalitarian constitutions, in view of past abuses. No case can be decided by any judge other than that who is entitled to hear that case, according to the criteria previously laid down by the law (see Article 25 of the Italian Constitution). Similar provisions are to be found in the German, Italian, Spanish and Portuguese Constitutions, but in France, during the Vichy regime, court presidents determined which judge would deal with a specific case; and currently a decree sustains that system. However, to state that the RoL is imperfect where such a rule is not observed, for example in view of the administrative involvement of the Listing Officer in the distribution of cases in the UK, would seem odd as the impartiality of that officer is taken for granted.

The comparative constitutional law question is this: does the consolidation of the concept (i.e. when it became a stand-alone constitutional principle or a concept of comparable status) make a practical difference in adjudication or legislation? Even in the absence of a systematic empirical study the answer seems to be affirmative. At least some courts (not necessarily under the guise of interpretation) deduce new standards from a constitutional concept of the RoL.

The specific standards developed in the name of the RoL concern primarily the quality of the law and the procedure applied in the decision-making. Another area where the reference to the ideal makes a difference concerns the external evaluation of a legal system: draft laws and national systems (internationally) are discussed in RoL terms.

Quality of the law. Legal certainty is an uncontested principle of the RoL. Legal certainty, related to the demands of the *Rechtsstaat*, requires

---

[42] For a summary of the literature and practice see Münch and Kunig (eds.), *Grundgesetzkommentar*, 6. Auflage (C.H. Beck, 2012) 1420–1430 (F.E. Schnapp).

not only that norms be unequivocal but also that the operation of legal institutions is predictable.[43] The ECtHR is also of the view that the quality of the law is essential for rights protection: it has to be foreseeable, certain and comprehensible. However, the ECtHR has accepted that changing and new legal practice can qualify as foreseeable source of law. Even complex legal regulation is transparent and foreseeable because of available professional legal advice.

The level of legal precision may depend on the nature of the constitutional value protected. In the United States, the First Amendment requires that speech restrictions be particularly specific to avoid the censorial effect of a broad prohibition. Overbreadth and vagueness are grounds of unconstitutionality.

The complex language of the law can be contrary to legal certainty and clarity in Germany (*Bestimmtheitsgebot, Klarheit*). Recently, security (surveillance) laws were declared partly unconstitutional in Germany for this reason. However, in the application of legal clarity the German CC does not directly refer to the principle of the RoL. Legal certainty (security) and the protection of legitimate expectations (*Rechtssicherheit und Vertrauensschutz*) are discussed in conjunction with fundamental rights. Ensuring the reliability of the legal order is an essential condition for self-determination over one's own life plan and its implementation;[44] reference can be made to the specific needs of a fundamental rights protection. Privacy rights are difficult to protect where the laws are non-transparent,[45] hence the unconstitutionality.

Procedural requirements. The RoL can shape the existing constitutional and other rules. For example, it makes 'fair trial' or Habeas Corpus or non-retroactivity etc. more robust and perhaps less isolated in the legal system. The RoL may be extended to new areas, such as where procedural requirements are introduced in tax law or in proceedings, etc., where the sphere of executive privilege is diminished and proper guarantees are introduced in the promulgation and cessation of emergency etc. Hearing and equality of arms follow from the substantive requirement of the RoL that all people shall be treated with full respect.

---

[43] See for Hungary Decision 24/2016. (XII. 12.) of the Constitutional Court of Hungary.
[44] BVerfGE 60, 253, 267f. The ECtHR is of the same view.
[45] See e.g. the need to protect the fundamental right to privacy in telecommunications BVerfGE 100, 313 [281] (*TelekommunikationsüberwachungG*).

4 The Uncertain Status of RoL Today

As mentioned, the constitutional status of RoL varies. It is described as a principle, a constitutional value, or an interpretative tool. Even the reference to principle can be understood differently in different legal systems: ideal, axiom, postulate,[46] standard, maxim, criterion, even rule. It may contain further principles (fair trial) or specific rules (prohibition of the bill of attainder).[47] Generality of the law is one of the standard requirements of the RoL and it is related to equality. It may dictate specific bright line rules (access to counsel) or can be satisfied by a comprehensive balance, without reliance on specific rules,[48] showing a certain indeterminacy of the concept.

What remains for the comparative research is to consider the practices which emerge in reference to the term. But such comparison runs the risk of being one sided. A comparison or evaluation of a constitutional system or government of a country cannot be limited to the use of the specific term; a comparative analysis needs a normative concept. Whichever concept is chosen as the relevant one is a value judgement that will determine the outcome of the comparison: a country may qualify as a RoL -compliant country by one account but not by another one, and a specific judicial ruling or legal reform will be in conformity with one concept but not under another.

The functions of the RoL are manifold and non-exclusive, i.e. in different situations RoL is used differently. There are, however, a few typical techniques that are used with some regularity:

- *RoL as a tool of interpretation.* 'The Court reiterates that the right to a fair hearing,[49] as guaranteed by Article 6 § 1 of the European Convention, *must be construed in the light of the rule of law,* which requires that ... everyone has the right to have any claim relating to his

---

[46] See the *Roncarelli* formula, Supreme Court of Canada (n. 55 below).
[47] See also Venice Commission at its 90th Plenary Session (Venice, 16–17 March 2012, CDL-AD (2012) 001).
[48] *Ibrahim and Others* v. *The United Kingdom,* Applications Nos. 50541/08, 50571/08, 50573/08 and 40351/09 (13 September 2016) (requirement of overall fairness); contrast with *Salduz* v. *Turkey,* Application No. 36391/02 (27 November 2008) ('rights of the defence will in principle be irretrievably prejudiced when incriminating statements made during police interrogation without access to a lawyer are used for a conviction'); [55].
[49] Fair hearing most often means fair trial.

civil rights and obligations brought before a court or tribunal. In this way, Article 6 § 1 embodies the 'right to a court', of which the right of access, that is, the right to institute proceedings before courts in civil matters, constitutes one aspect only.'[50]

- *RoL as an axiomatic ground for principles or rules.* 'In a *Rechtsstaat* the secrecy of state intervention measures is the exception and it requires special justification.'[51] Likewise, for the Supreme Court of India it is 'unthinkable that in a democracy governed by the rule of law, that the executive, government or any of its officers should possess arbitrary power over the interest of the individual. Every action of the executive Government must be informed with reason and should be free from arbitrariness.'[52] For the Hungarian Constitutional Court 'legal security is a necessary component of the RoL, without which one cannot speak of *Rechtsstaat.*'[53]

- *RoL as a source to generate specific (most likely procedural) rights.* Here RoL generates standards, rules (e.g. access to an attorney from the beginning of detention) or institutional guarantees. This is rather common in matters of fair proceedings: All litigants should have an effective judicial remedy enabling them to assert their civil rights.[54] By simple reference to the RoL the Hungarian Constitutional Court has extended judicial review to all decisions of the public administration affecting fundamental rights, not only to administrative acts.

- *RoL as the ground for a specific decision.* Given that the RoL is fundamentally about the restriction of arbitrariness, RoL was historically used against manifestly biased used of discretionary power to show that political leaders are subject to the ordinary law of the land.[55]

It is of comparative importance that a court may construe a specific standard of the RoL without relying on the RoL, for example in

---

[50] Case of *Al-Dulimi and Montana Management Inc.* v. *Switzerland* (supra n. 27). It is an inherent contradiction of the RoL that whenever it is applied to declare clearly stated rules of jurisdiction contrary to the RoL it creates uncertainty.

[51] 118 BVerfGE 168 at 197, [134] (2007, *Kontostammdaten*).

[52] *Kamana Dayaram, Shetty* v. *The International Airport Authority of India,* [1979] 3 SCR 1014, 1032.

[53] Decision 11/1992 (III. 5) of the Constitutional Court of Hungary (law unconstitutional for allowing proceedings for serious communist crimes notwithstanding the statute of limitations.)

[54] *Běleš and Others* v. *the Czech Republic,* Appl. No. 47273/99 (12 November 2002), [49].

[55] *Roncarelli* v. *Duplessis* [1959] SCR 121.

consideration of the needs of effective rights protection or separation of powers (see the surveillance cases of the German Constitutional Court above).

5 Varying Scope and Varying Intensity of Scrutiny

The practical meaning of the RoL cannot be fully appreciated and compared without considering the intensity of the scrutiny triggered by RoL considerations (and resulting intensity of actual respect). Constitutional law recognizes that RoL can be restricted for the sake of other constitutional principles and values and rights too. Moreover, where there is a finding that the RoL has been violated, other RoL considerations, legal certainty in particular, may limit the effects of the finding. Some statutes expressly leave it to the constitutional court to determine the retroactive applicability of the finding of unconstitutionality and the default rule is that the rule in question is voided *ex nunc*.

Moreover, the RoL seems to have inherent limits. Access to court that is relentlessly carved out by constitutional courts remains limited, something that is acknowledged by those same courts, probably in all countries of the world. The ECtHR has limited the right of access to court to certain subject matters, namely to civil rights and to criminal charges only (where 'civil' remains an open matter and subject to further limitation, see scope). Secondly, there are several permitted limitations to this access, depending on the nature of the right claimed and competing public interest at stake, in particular the needs of the administration of justice. 'The right of access to the courts is not absolute. ... there is room, apart from the bounds delimiting the very content of any right, for limitations permitted by implication.'[56] The Supreme Court of Canada has also narrowed down its reliance on the RoL as a constitutional principle, allowing retroactive civil legislation and lack of representation in tax cases.[57]

---

[56] *Golder* v. *The United Kingdom*, Application No. 4451/70 (21 February 1975), [38].

[57] M. Carter, 'The Rule of Law, Legal Rights in the Charter, and the Supreme Court's New Positivism' (2008) 33 *Queen's Law Journal* 453; *British Columbia* v. *Imperial Tobacco Canada Ltd.* 2005 SCC 49; [2005] 2 SCR 473; *British Columbia (Attorney General)* v. *Christie* 2007 SCC 21 [2007]; 1 SCR 873.

a Level of Scrutiny

Constitutional courts often state that the importance of the interest to be protected by law shall determine the level of scrutiny and procedures concerning the realization or sanctioning of fundamental rights are more intense than when it comes to other matters. Consequently, the RoL will have more or less strict standards depending on the interest affected.

Fundamental rights protection generally triggers all the RoL guarantees including the rule that only laws can limit (or regulate) fundamental rights. In the judicial review of the procedural aspects of the RoL, strict scrutiny, or at least intensive proportionality analysis applies and in the case of personal liberty restrictions, judicial pre-authorization is required (e.g. search and arrest warrants).

Beyond the demands of a RoL scrutiny in matters of fundamental rights and important statutory interests, the RoL may, as an independent consideration, dictate certain standards: if it is recognized as a constitutional principle this opens up specific procedural requirements of a hearing and so on.

b Situations Allowing for the Disregard of the RoL

Notwithstanding the international celebration of the RoL as a 'universal' principle, there remain important legal relations where it does not apply or is of limited impact. This is true of the remnants of the (royal or executive) prerogative, for example in matters of foreign relations and security, although officially this concept does not exist in many constitutional systems. Sovereign immunity, even if under stress, is still alive.[58] Blackstone claimed in the eighteenth century: 'That the king can do no wrong is a necessary and fundamental principle of the English constitution.' While in principle administrative decisions are subject to judicial review in the United Kingdom, the Crown's responsibility in torts was recognized only in 1947 (Crown Proceedings Bill) and the Crown's liability did not apply to the armed forces and remains a delicate matter.[59] In the United States the Federal Tort Claims Act (FCTA) (1946) subjects the government to torts law with exceptions, including the 'discretionary function exception'. When a federal employee has acted 'based upon the

---

[58] See for example *Čudak* v. *Lithuania*, Application No. 15869/02 (23 March 2010).
[59] See *Matthews* v. *Ministry of Defence* [2003] UKHL 4.

exercise or performance or the failure to exercise or perform a discretionary function or duty..., whether or not the discretion involved be abused', sovereign immunity applies.[60] However, unless it is statutorily excluded federal courts have the power to award damages for violation of 'constitutionally protected interests' without special statutory authorization because such interests traditionally (i.e. this being logically part of the RoL) need appropriate damages as remedy.[61]

As to the case law of the ECtHR, fair trial guarantees apply to civil rights only: what comes under *imperium* is not covered under the Convention except where civil servants have already access to court in the domestic system. Further, the RoL may apply only partly to legislation. In many countries where unconstitutional laws may be voided for being contrary to the RoL, the available remedies, in particular damages, remain contested; elsewhere, like in Poland, harm done by an action of an organ of public authority, contrary to law results in an obligation of compensation, including harm by legislative act if the unconstitutionality of the statute has been established.[62] As to the European Union, there is responsibility for damage caused by legislation that is contrary to EU law but this principle is not accepted in all EU Member States when it comes to national legislation. For example, the German law that has provided for state responsibility (*Staatshaftungsgesetz*) for serious rights violations by public power was held unconstitutional but only for its disregard of the competences of the Lander.[63]

In addition to these limitations, '[i]n time of war or other public emergency threatening the life of the nation there can be derogation from the Convention subject to the review of the ECtHR' (Article 15.1, European Convention). Such exceptions, especially concerning judicial review are sometimes written into the constitution on grounds of expedience: Habeas Corpus can be suspended under the US Constitution in cases of 'Rebellion or Invasion' (I.9.[2]). The German Basic Law grants an exception to access to courts in matters of telecommunications (privacy) for the protection of the democratic basic order or security of the country (GG 10 (2)), etc.[64]

---

[60] T. Longoria, 'Bureaucracy that kills: Federal sovereign immunity and the discretionary function exception' (2002) 96 *American Political Science Review* 335–349.

[61] See *Bivens* v. *Six Unknown Named Agents*, 403 US 388 (1971).

[62] The Constitution of the Republic of Poland of 2nd April, 1997. Art. 77 (1).

[63] BverfGE 61, 149 (1982).

[64] BVerfGE 100, 313 – *Telekommunikationsüberwachung*, see above.

Emergencies, like war and other national security considerations remain the test for the seriousness of the RoL commitment. When it comes to security, as in post-9/11 cases, adherence to the RoL becomes a matter of balancing. Scrutiny of such security measures in the United Kingdom remains limited: in control order cases where special advocates are confronting certain witnesses, in deciding whether the hearing infringed the controlee's rights under Article 6 ECHR by nondisclosure of closed materials (not accessible to the judge either) the question is 'whether, taken as a whole, the hearing was fundamentally unfair to the controlee, or he was not accorded a substantial measure of procedural justice or the very essence of his right to a fair hearing was impaired'.[65]

In Canada, the security certificate regime (where denial of the certificate leads to deportation/detention) was found unconstitutional but not on general RoL grounds: 'Neither the inability to appeal the reasonableness of the certificate, nor the automatic detention of foreign nationals and detention of permanent residents on the basis of an executive decision offend the rule of law.'[66] In matters of detention of enemy combatants, the US Supreme Court, while insisting on notice and fair opportunity to rebut charges, has accepted that such cases do not require a judge as a neutral decision-maker.[67] Again, there are important counterexamples which can be explained by the specificities of the given constitutional system. The Court of Justice of the European Union, a supranational court that is less concerned with national security and is independent of national political pressure introduced hearing requirements into the UN Security Council terrorist asset freeze regime.[68] However, this was concluded not on RoL grounds but because the freeze regime departed 'from the scheme of judicial protection of fundamental rights' as 'the persons concerned ... had no real opportunity of asserting their rights'.

RoL requirements may considerably diminish the intensity of the review as a matter of respect of the competence and expert knowledge of other

---

[65] In *Secretary of State for the Home Department* v. *AF* [2008] EWCA Civ 1148. But see *Secretary of State for the Home Department* v. *AF and another* [2009] UKHL 28.

[66] M. Bloodworth, A. Coleman, E. Mendes and A. Rock, 'The Rule of Law in Canada: A Global Template?' (2013) 31 *National Journal of Constitutional Law* 111, 124.

[67] *Hamdi* v. *Rumsfeld*, 542 US 507, 533 (2004).

[68] *Yassin Abdullah Kadi and Al Barakaat International Foundation* v. *Council of the European Union and Commission of the European Communities*, Joined Cases C-402/05 P and C-415/05, [2008] ECR I-6351 ([322], [323]).

branches. Deference can be particularly paralysing when the administration has evaluated a fact or circumstance (by certification, affidavit etc.). The attitude is exemplified by the approach taken by the House of Lords in *Liversidge* v. *Anderson* (a wartime detention case predating *Wednesbury*). Here it was accepted that where the Secretary of State has exclusive discretion, the words reasonable suspicion might well mean that if the Secretary 'acting on what he thinks is reasonable cause (and, of course, acting in good faith) believes the thing in question' and 'if the thing to be believed is something which is essentially one within the knowledge of the Secretary' his decision could not be questioned in a court of law.[69] In peacetime the judicial review in administrative law was limited by the reasonableness test: under *Wednesbury*, an English court will not overturn an administrative decision as long as '[t]he subject-matter with which the condition deals is one relevant for its consideration. They have considered it and come to a decision upon it. It is true to say that, if a decision on a competent matter is so unreasonable that no reasonable authority could ever have come to it, then the courts can interfere.'[70] Reasonable is what is appropriate for good administration – as it is seen by administrators. In the context of administrative rule-making the US Supreme Court held that courts should defer to agency interpretations of such statutes as long as 'the agency's answer is based on a permissible construction of the statute'.[71]

6 Substantive RoL Resulting in Procedural Fairness

A substantive concept of the RoL in constitutional adjudication seems to be present in 'substantive due process' (United States and India), and in 'fairness', 'natural justice' or 'fundamental justice' review of legislation affecting fundamental rights[72] but it seems to be resisted in other common law countries. The Supreme Court of Canada (per Justice Lamer, in the majority) rejected what was considered an American 'either/or' approach

---

[69] *Liversidge* v. *Anderson* [1942] AC 206, 220.
[70] *Associated Provincial Picture Houses Limited* v. *Wednesbury Corporation* [1948] 1 KB 223, 229–230. Arguably, at least for human rights (under the European Convention) a proportionality test applies today: *R (Daly)* v. *Secretary of State for the Home Department* [2001] UKHL 26.
[71] *Chevron USA, Inc.* v. *Natural Resources Defense Council, Inc.*, 467 US 837 (1984), 843.
[72] See Canadian Charter of Rights and Freedoms.

to substantive due process: 'the characterization of the issue in such fashion pre-empts an open-minded approach to determining the meaning of "principles of fundamental justice."'[73] Substantive due process refers to a specific use of a standard constitutional provision which, in the original version of the Fifth Amendment of the US Constitution, prohibits that any person be deprived 'of life, liberty, or property, without due process of law'.

In the Canadian Charter property is replaced by security and due process by principles of fundamental justice. This can trigger a procedural obligation for the state, e.g. today individual 'deprivation' notice is required in welfare cases, as well as a hearing in front of an impartial trier of facts and law. In certain instances, due process was understood as requiring the judicial control of the content of legislation, in particular its compatibility with economic liberties. This approach became politically unacceptable at the time of the Great Depression, the legal objection being that it deprives legislation of its constitutional power to enact proper regulation. The contemporary use refers primarily to the review of the substance of legislation related to constitutionally enumerated rights, laws that affect discrete and insular minorities and to the 'finding' of rights 'implicit in the concept of ordered liberty'.[74] Here the review considers the nature of the impairment, and not only the specific process applied in the rights deprivation and in the remedial proceedings. The disapplication of laws on substantive grounds is criticized (judicially too) for being contrary to the idea of legal certainty, rule bound decision and the separation of powers. The criticism is that judges become legislators. Indeed, one can ask: what kind of rule by rules is where decision-makers can depart from the clear meaning of, or legislative intent behind, the rule?

The answer seems to be that blatant governmental arbitrariness which affects fundamental liberty interests necessitate judicial control, with the judge being called to consider the substantive element of the RoL (in the sense of elementary or natural justice). Canada offers an interesting and non-conclusive example. With reference to human dignity[75] and the RoL, the Supreme Court of Canada ruled that a law imposing imprisonment on a suspended driver where the driver was not required to know about the

---

[73] *Reference re s 94(2) of Motor Vehicle Act (British Columbia)* [1985] 2 SCR 486 (J. Lamer), para 17.

[74] *United States* v. *Carolene Products Company,* 304 US 144 (1938) fn 4.

[75] Cf. with *Olga Tellis* (n. 85), decided in the same year (1985).

suspension (a kind of absolute liability) is contrary to a derivative concern of fundamental justice, namely that the innocent shall not be punished. The law as worded had the potential to yield such results.[76] While the RoL was used quite formalistically in later cases, more recently, in a fundamental justice case, the Supreme Court found that discretion granted to the administration does not allow a grossly disproportionate restriction of fundamental rights of applicants even if the government was applying a legitimate policy through legitimate means.[77] In the United States the use of discretionary powers by the Secretary of Labor to protect health at the workplace was also set aside. The Secretary had no unbridled discretion to adopt standards designed to create absolutely risk-free workplaces, regardless of cost. This was construed as a strict statutory interpretation case: the issue was about the meaning of 'safe'.[78] The four dissenting Justices used a formal RoL argument: 'In cases of statutory construction, this Court's authority is limited. If the statutory language and legislative intent are plain, the judicial inquiry is at an end. Under our jurisprudence, it is presumed that ill-considered or unwise legislation will be corrected through the democratic process; a court is not permitted to distort a statute's meaning in order to make it conform with the Justices' own views of sound social policy.'[79]

The protection of fundamental rights triggers a strict application of the RoL. According to the ECtHR specific requirements regarding the formal quality of the law prevent arbitrary interference into human rights (see clarity above). Moreover, where there are 'no legal rules concerning the scope and manner of exercise of the discretion enjoyed by the public authorities', this does not satisfy the requirement of lawfulness either.[80] In the German doctrine, legal clarity (precision) and clear proceedings serve the protection of fundamental rights, not only the RoL.[81]

The substantive references in the RoL context typically consist of procedural considerations and trigger procedural safeguards. In a leading US welfare rights case, *Goldberg* v. *Kelly*[82] a most 'substantive' justification of

---

[76] *Reference re s 94(2) of Motor Vehicle Act (British Columbia)* [1985] 2 SCR 486 (n. 73.).

[77] *Canada (AG)* v. *PHS Community Services Society* [2011] 3 SCR 134.

[78] *Indus. Union Dept.* v. *Amer. Petroleum Inst.*, 448 US 607 (1980).

[79] *Indus. Union Dept.* v. *Amer. Petroleum Inst.*, 448 US 607 (1980), 688.

[80] *Malone* v. *United Kingdom*, Application No. 8691/79 (2 August 1984), [67], [79].

[81] BVerfGE 134, 242 (*Garzweiler*).

[82] *Goldberg* v. *Kelly*, 397 US 254 (1970) 264–265.

procedural RoL was applied, namely that a hearing is needed as a means of recognizing human dignity. The constitutional consideration of procedural due process triggered an evidentiary hearing and therefore a right to hearing and counsel even in the absence of a substantive constitutional right. As Justice Brennan for the majority has stated: 'important governmental interests are promoted by affording recipients a pre-termination evidentiary hearing. From its founding, the Nation's basic commitment has been to foster the dignity and wellbeing of all persons within its borders. We have come to recognize that forces not within the control of the poor contribute to their poverty.' But it is one thing to use a substantive argument for the RoL (creating a procedural right to *promote* a substantive right) and quite another to use the RoL to *create* substantive rights or substantive justice. The finding and protection of 'new' rights is not based on abstract unwritten principles derived from the RoL, but refer instead to social and legal practices. 'Ordered liberty is found in deeply rooted traditions' (which can be recent practices). Consider also that the judicially created part of French constitutional rights are those which were recognized in the existing, long-held laws of the Republic.

Notwithstanding the confusing use of the terms, human rights and RoL considerations are treated as conceptually separate, but this does not exclude important interaction. 'In order to assess the justification of an impugned measure [interfering with a convention right], ... the fairness of proceedings and the procedural guarantees afforded to the applicant are factors to be taken into account when assessing the proportionality of an interference with the freedom of expression guaranteed by Article 10.'[83] The absence of an effective judicial review or its inadequate quality may support a finding of a substantive violation of Article 10.[84]

The Supreme Court of India (following *Goldberg* v. *Kelly*) held that the forcible eviction and removal of pavement dwellers of their hutments deprived them of their means of livelihood and consequently right to life because the right to life includes the right to livelihood. In the relevant part of the decision there is no reference to the RoL. The RoL is mentioned in the determination of the remedy that is triggered by a right. The starting point is the 'substantial agreement in juristic thought that the great purpose of the rule of law notion is the protection of the

---

[83] *Baka* v. *Hungary*, Application No. 20261/12 (23 June 2016), [161].
[84] *Lombardi Vallauri* v. *Italy*, No. 39128/05 (20 October 2009), [45]-[56].

individual-against arbitrary exercise of power wherever it is found'. The removal procedure (depriving the applicants of livelihood) was held reasonable and fair (these were the specific standards that were derived from RoL – not a very demanding standard in the context of an individual constitutional right). What was found incompatible with *natural justice* was that the specific eviction orders were issued *without hearing*.[85] Moreover, formal RoL will set limits to substantive justice: against the interests of Polish tenants the Polish Constitutional Tribunal held 'that, having regard to the principle of maintaining citizens' confidence in the State and the law made by it and the principle of legal certainty' excessive rent control cannot be upheld.[86]

RoL considerations may generate specific rules and rights in the procedural context but contrary to the claims of substantive RoL theories, they do not generate fundamental rights. However, they may play a role in the generation of specific procedural rights on the basis of already recognized procedural demands (related to fair trial) or constitutional institutions (requirements related to the independence of the judiciary). The right of access to justice works as a consideration of procedural fairness; equality of rights may trigger the duty of the state to provide legal representation in criminal cases[87] (on the basis of the right to counsel); RoL (fair trial) may require that there shall be access to a lawyer from the very beginning of the detention.

7 Rule of Law, Abuse and Correction

The RoL is called a universally accepted value but it has also:

become an unavoidable cliché of international organizations of every kind. International donors now spend billions of dollars on rule of law promotion, notwithstanding a seriously underwhelming record of success. Before, the rule of law was not an item to be considered, still less waste money on; now they're eager to do so. Economists now recommend it as necessary for economic development; democrats as integral to their projects; constitutionalists as another name for

---

[85] *Olga Tellis & Ors* v. *Mumbay Municipal Corporation & Ors* (10 July 1985).
[86] The judgment of 12 January 2000, P 11/98. (2000) 46(003) Official Journal, quoted in *Hutten-Czapska* v. *Poland*, Application No. 35014/97, Judgment of 19 June 2006. However, in Germany material justice has prevailed in upholding tenants' rights against apartment owners. See BVerfGE 68, 361 (1985).
[87] *Johnson* v. *Zerbst*, 304 US 458 (1938). See further *Gideon* v. *Wainwright*, 372 US 335 (1963).

the business they are in; those who rush to repair 'failed', 'post-conflict', 'post-dictatorial', 'transitional' states always carry rule of law promotional devices in their toolkits.[88]

This interest can be explained by the positive contribution of the institutional design of the rule of law to capitalist economic development, as argued by Max Weber and contemporary economic historians.[89]

The RoL has been accepted in many countries for developmental or legitimacy reasons, without being embedded in the legal and social traditions of those countries. In many developing countries, and in others in transition to democracy, the RoL is formally recognized because foreign investors and the international community insist on it. It became a matter of formal international evaluation and contest with possibly fundamental consequences for a whole state, as is the case with the European Union. According to Article 7 of the Lisbon Treaty, the voting rights of a Member State can be suspended where there is a clear risk of a serious breach by a Member State of the values of the EU, which include, among others, the rule of law and respect for human rights. But the RoL remains a cultural phenomenon, and a matter of social habits. It presupposes a culture of legality (and even fairness) among lawyers and in society. In the absence of a proper legal culture it remains superficial and does not actually animate social regulation. The imposition of the RoL has generated new conflicts. In Asia many countries pursue a form of 'economic rule of law' where the legal system operates (for the most part) independently of political influence with respect to commercial issues but where other areas of law are subject to greater, if varying, degrees of politicization.[90] Moreover, transitional justice or the creation of new RoL institutions (a decent judiciary and public administration) may require measures that challenge textbook concepts of the RoL.

The RoL and socio-economic development. After the fiasco of the 'law and development' reforms of the sixties and, at least since the collapse of communism, an investment-friendly RoL has been advocated. The RoL was a condition of becoming a member of the European Union

---

[88] M. Krygier, 'Re-imagining the Rule of Law', Denis Leslie Mahoney Prize Public Lecture (7 September 2017).

[89] D.C. North and R.P. Thomas, *The Rise of the Western World: A New Economic History* (Cambridge University Press, 1973).

[90] R. Peerenboom (ed.), *Varieties of Rule of Law: An Introduction and Provisional Conclusion Asian Discourses of Rule of Law* (Routledge, 2004), xviii–xix.

(Copenhagen criteria) and in the case of two Member States where the conditions were deemed not to be fully met the monitoring is now in its second decade. Economists and investors insist on the need of a reliably working legal system which will make foreign investment safe and competitive and the political system reliable for purposes of international cooperation. This was reflected in the Washington Consensus that shaped RoL missions of governments and organizations such as the World Bank. According to one of the definitions provided by the World Bank: the RoL is 'the extent to which agents have confidence in and abide by the rules of society, and in particular the quality of contract enforcement, the police and the courts, as well as the likelihood of crime and violence'.[91] Here public trust in the institutions is central, instead of respect to citizens. The actual programmes were concerned with laws and administration (e.g. land registry) necessary for market transactions and formal dispute settlement. These may have served the security of investment but often remained alien or irrelevant to citizens.

RoL in transitional countries. It is often argued, especially by external observers, that in post-conflict and post-totalitarian situations countries are in need of the RoL. This expectation is included regularly in the mandate of peacekeeping international operations. Post-totalitarian countries, especially if they seek international recognition, are keen to have a RoL-based legal system. Sometimes the RoL became a central socio-political concern as in Poland after 1989. (See also the Portuguese Constitution above.) Here the not-fully-revised 1952 communist constitution continued to be in force until 1997. The text did not provide clear guidance on institutional arrangements and it was restrictive of, or silent on, fundamental rights. The Polish Constitutional Tribunal relying on the RoL principle has created the right to judicial review where the inherited communist statutes made the decision of the administration final. Substantive RoL protection was also central in the Tribunal's finding that the liberalization of abortion is unconstitutional: a RoL state is bound to protect dignity and abortion is contrary to human dignity, therefore it has to be criminalized (decision of 28 May 1997).

The transition to a RoL state may necessitate a certain departure from its own tenets; in this context the RoL turned out to be rather ambiguous,

---

[91] World Governance Indicators, http://info.worldbank.org/governance/wgi/pdf/rl.pdf (accessed 12 December 2017).

especially in property restitution cases and when it came to calling to account perpetrators of past injustices.[92] When dealing with past injustices, issues of retroactive legislation emerged and arguably the *nullum crimen* principle was violated. Vetting laws (restrictions applied to former communist leaders and secret service collaborators) were held unconstitutional in Hungary because of RoL considerations but employment bans on former communist functionaries were upheld by the Czechoslovak and Czech constitutional courts.[93] International law respects the principle that there is no punishment without law. However, a person can be tried in violation of this requirement for an 'act which, at the time when it was committed, was criminal according to the general principles of law recognised by civilised nations'.[94]

The use and meaning of the RoL can became controversial in institution building too. In the creation of an independent judiciary, corruption or political bias of the judiciary may be of such gravity that revolutionary solutions (i.e. mass dismissal) are held necessary. However, to dismiss judges without individualized due process and good cause clearly contradicts the principles that apply in an established constitutional system. It is telling that three different positions were held applicable regarding three comparable post-communist countries. The *en masse* changes in the judiciary in Georgia were objected to by the Venice commission and in Ukraine it was argued that the dismissal of all judges with reapplication was too harsh but the measure was held acceptable for Albania.[95]

---

[92] See *Rekvényi v. Hungary,* Application No. 25390/94 (20 May 1999).

[93] See No. Pl. ÚS 03/92 (judgement Lustration I); No. Pl. ÚS 09/01 (judgement Lustration II); BVerfGE 30, 367 (383 and ff); BVerfGE 72, 200 (258).

[94] ECHR Art. 7(2).

[95] Joint opinion of the Venice Commission and the Directorate of Human Rights (DHR) of the Directorate General of Human Rights and Rule of Law (DGI) of the Council of Europe on the Draft Law Making Changes to the Law on Disciplinary Liability and Disciplinary Proceedings of Judges of General Courts of Georgia: www.venice.coe.int/webforms/documents/?pdf=CDL-AD(2014)032-e; Joint opinion of the Venice Commission and the Directorate of Human Rights (DHR) of the Directorate General of Human Rights and Rule of Law (DGI) of the Council of Europe on the Law on the Judicial System and the Status of Judges and amendments to the Law on the High Council of Justice of Ukraine: www.venice.coe.int/webforms/documents/default.aspx?pdffile=CDL-AD(2015)007-e; Final Opinion in the Revised Draft Constitutional Amendments on the Judiciary of Albania: www.venice.coe.int/webforms/documents/default.aspx?pdffile=CDL-AD(2016)009-e (accessed 12 December 2017).

Conclusion

Notwithstanding important ideological differences, there are certain similarities in the practice of important constitutional courts. The most striking is a methodological one, namely a certain reluctance to apply the RoL as a principle directly. Instead there is a tendency to rely on specific constituent components of the RoL such as certainty or foreseeability. Beyond formal criteria regarding the structure of law, procedural considerations appear in many legal systems. This can be explained by the minimalist attitude of courts. Constitutional courts seem to prefer formal criteria of the RoL and extend their control over laws and state practices under review by taking a procedural position. This fits into the effort of juridification: while judges are uncomfortable with substantive issues (including substantive justice) they feel at ease when it comes to the review of procedural fairness (equality of arms, hearing, notice). The comparative analysis indicates that, depending on the nature of judicial review, the RoL may have different meanings in different branches of law (e.g. references to legal certainty are preferred to naked RoL arguments) and procedural fairness is often used to achieve substantive goals. When it comes to institutional solutions serving the RoL (e.g. safeguards of judicial independence, impartiality) the agreement that exists in principle at the level of constitutions almost disappears because the actual institutional solutions are varied due to historical differences. Finally, when it comes to the general evaluation of the RoL within a legal system, which is rather common in political discourse and international politics, the disagreements are rather marked and the debate about the social and political functions and consequences of the RoL will continue in the future.

Further Reading

T. Carothers, 'Rule of Law Temptations', *Fletcher Forum of World Affairs*, (2009). 33, 49–61.

T. Ginsburg and T. Moustafa (eds.), *Rule by Law: The Politics of Courts in Authoritarian Regimes* (Cambridge University Press, 2008).

M. Krygier, 'The Rule of Law: Pasts, Presents, and Two Possible Futures' (2016) 12(1) *Annual Review of Law and Social Science* 199–229.

G. Palombella and N. Walker (eds.) *Relocating the Rule of Law* (Hart Publishing, 2009).

B. Tamanaha, *On the Rule of Law: History, Politics, Theory* (Cambridge University Press, 2004).

J. Waldron, 'Is the Rule of Law an Essentially Contested Concept (in Florida)?' (2002) 21(2) *Law and Philosophy* 137–164.

M. Weber [1922], *Economy and Society*, G. Roth and C. Wittich (eds.), Volume II, (University of California Press, 1968).

Human Rights Law 11

Conor Gearty

Introduction

Any analysis of the role of human rights in domestic constitutional law must grapple with a central tension lying at the core of the relationship between the two. Whereas constitutional law is inevitably grounded in a particular place covering defined sets of people, human rights aspire, as the term makes clear, to transcend the political in the name of entitlements that inhere in people wherever they are from and regardless of the governmental arrangements under which they live. National constitutional law can almost always point to a specific moment when the foundational document from which all else follows is agreed and brought into effect, and even in those very few places where this is not the case (the United Kingdom, for example) the 'constitution' is made up of a bundle of documents (statutes; judicial decisions; shared practices) which are similarly rooted in time as well as in place and people. In this way too human rights appear different: the vast ambition of the phrase involves a claim to stand outside a history made up not only of people and places but of foundational turning points as well.

The bridge between these antithetical perspectives in the national constitutional environment is human rights law. Here the universalist instincts of human rights are given a voice but in a way that harnesses their impulsive ethical force. The term is tamed by being forced to take a legal shape recognizable to (local) constitutional law while the latter is compelled through its reception of human rights to make some concessions to the universal. As we shall see, the tension between the two is played out in different ways around the world but in our contemporary democratic polities there can be little doubting that the two need each other. Human rights without law are (merely) a bunch of activists' claims or philosophers' dreams. But constitutional law without human rights (or whatever the relevant document chooses to call them: more on this shortly) looks altogether too morally neutral to be entirely trustworthy. There was a time when in at least some places it was thought that democratic society could get along just fine with no moral basis to government other than agreement on how laws were made, enforced and interpreted (with even these structures themselves being up for grabs). That is rarely now believed to be the case even in those places where it had once held sway, and 'human rights law' is what has rushed to fill what has increasingly come to be believed was an ethical gap at the core of democratic government.

In this chapter our task is to unravel the practical implications of the tension just identified and assess how effective human rights law has proved to be at managing the constitutional conflicts that it produces, across various jurisdictions. There are three large-scale paradoxes generated by this sterling effort of human rights law at bridge-building, and before we turn to the substance we shall elaborate on these now: understanding them will help guide us through the constitutional thickets to follow.

First – in a subset of the central tension with which we started – there is this dependence of human rights law for its very existence on the sort of grounded constitutional moments that human rights appear by their very nature to demand to transcend. How does human rights law escape the claim to ahistorical universalism that is so much the rationale of the field of which it is the legal offshoot? Does the bridge to the grounded from the ethereal not inevitably drag the latter down with it? Now it is true that there are rare moments when even in democratic societies adjudicators of disputes find in 'natural law' a source of right and wrong that trumps not only ordinary law but (even) the constitution to which that ordinary law is itself uncontroversially subject. A famous dissenting judgment from Ireland in the 1930s did exactly this, with no less a figure than the Irish Free State's inaugural chief justice Hugh Kennedy reaching into a quasi-religious space to find constraints on a government that were rooted not in the apparently authorizing words of the constitution he was interpreting but rather in a timeless sense of right and wrong.[1] Such attempts are rarely made and when they come along they invariably fail. For all his stature Kennedy's reflections were unpersuasive; no democracy can allow judicial interventions like these to gain the upper hand if it wishes to avoid a drift to theocracy at worst, juristocracy[2] at best. But this being the case, how then does the universal stay afloat in the sea of localism in which it finds itself? As we shall see, the answer to this varies from place to place and across time. The extent to which human rights law is able to reach beyond its moment of national birth depends (ironically, it might be thought) on the sort of birth it has, how many rights it produces, how robust and ambitious it is.

Our second paradox leaps out at us the moment we acknowledge how indelibly our subject is rooted in democratic governance: human rights appear to thrive best of all in the political cultures whose commitment to the popular will appear to leave no room for them. This is another way of saying that the protection of human rights via an independent rule of law is now regarded as a key component in a properly functioning, modern democratic state.[3] We must distinguish here between such places and the sort of polities in which in this chapter we have no interest: states with declarations of commitments to human rights which are either creatures of the executive will[4] or those in which sentiments such as these are designed merely to function as camouflage for the exercise of despotic power.[5] Totalitarian states can have 'human rights' – Stalin's constitution of 1936 is full of them.[6] Fascist regimes likewise – Hitler deployed his human rights conscience in the pre-war 1930s when he expanded his territorial reach under cover of interventions to protect maligned German

---

[1] *The State (Ryan)* v. *Kennedy* [1935] 1 IR 170, at 204: 'every act, whether legislative, executive or judicial, in order to be lawful under the Constitution, must be capable of being justified under the authority thereby declared to be derived from God'. (Note the 'thereby' – even here the invoker of natural law is hedging his bets about their source).

[2] K.D. Ewing, 'The Bill of Rights Debate: Democracy or Juristocracy in Britain', in K.D. Ewing, C.A. Gearty and B.A. Hepple (eds.), *Human Rights and Labour Law. Essays for Paul O'Higgins* (Mansell Publishing, 1994), ch. 7.

[3] H. Brunkhorst, 'Constitutionalism and Democracy in the World Society', in P. Dobner and M. Loughlin (eds.), *The Twilight of Constitutionalism?* (Oxford University Press, 2010), ch. 9.

[4] P. Brooker, *Non-Democratic Regimes,* 3rd ed. (Palgrave Macmillan, 2014).

[5] C. Gearty, *Liberty and Security* (Polity Press, 2013).

[6] See in particular Chapter 10 of that constitution: www.departments.bucknell.edu/russian/const/36cons04.html#chap10 (accessed 26 September 2017).

minorities in neighbouring states.[7] In this chapter we are not concerned with the 'bad-faith' use of human rights in this way. Our assumption is that the phrase is being deployed in tandem with those other benchmarks of civilized democratic living, popular elections and an uncompromised judiciary.

But if this is the case, then how can we be describing democratic government? The whole point of the democratic revolution was surely to sweep away constraints on the 'people's will' whatever shape they happened to take in their subtle or not-so-subtle defence of vested interests? How can a 'proper' democratic regime submit to human rights law when this inevitably entails genuflection before the judicial branch, a cohort of personnel who may well (depending on where we are looking) have been in the van of anti-democratic reaction in the years of struggle? The only way out of this paradox – and the point is hinted at in our reference a moment ago to human rights backed by the rule of law as a 'key component' in any such system – is to dissolve it by redefining democracy, as Ronald Dworkin and other key rights-thinkers have done: the will of the people ruling as they will becomes just a type (and the wrong type) of democracy, 'majoritarianism', whereas true, authentic democracy involves expression of the will of the people of course, but now hemmed in by a set of moral boundaries that guard against populist transgression.[8] Representative democracy does not get to play free-style on the whole playing surface but only on a pitch with boundaries set by the referee to prevent any straying out-of-bounds. Constitutional human rights are the lines on the pitch that ensure the democratic game is played within those proper limits. And inevitably, given the way we construct representative government with its high emphasis on separation of powers, it is the judges who play the role of referees.

Our final paradox concerns claim and delivery. There is an immense mismatch between the loud ethical claims of human rights law on the one hand and their singular impotence when viewed in isolation from other branches of the state on the other. Here are claims that talk big but carry no stick at all. The bark is not only 'worse' than their bite; without

---

[7] As with Danzig and Poland: see Hitler's speech to the Reichstag on 1 September 1939: http://avalon.law.yale.edu/wwii/gp2.asp (accessed 26 September 2017).

[8] R. Dworkin, *Taking Rights Seriously* (Gerald Duckworth and Co, 1977); R. Dworkin, *Law's Empire* (Harvard University Press, 1986).

the help of others there is no bite at all. The dependence of human rights on the various organs of the state to give them any kind of effect is total. Human rights are, after all, not an organ of the state, jostling to achieve a position where they can get things done, an executive branch at odds with the legislature or vice versa. At bottom they are merely claims on (constitutional) bits of paper whose potential wholly depends on a group of interpreters, the judges, who are themselves (as 'the least dangerous branch')[9] dependent on the goodwill of their colleagues across the polity if their constitutional commands are to have any effect. In this regard the probably apocryphal remark attributed to US President Andrew Jackson about a particularly controversial ruling by the then US chief justice and his colleagues on the Supreme Court, 'John Marshall has made his decision; now let him enforce it!',[10] stands as a warning against excess of which all judges tempted by the first phrase rather than the last word in the term 'human rights law' need to be mindful. (And the case about which the remarks were supposedly made, *Worcester* v. *Georgia*,[11] was what we would today regard as an important ruling on the rights of indigenous people.) Practice (in terms of what actually happens) does not necessarily follow from what the constitutional text declares to be the case by way of enforcement mechanisms and duties. How do constitutions avoid human rights merely adding to the beauty of the instrument, ethical adornments on the outside of the civic building but offering precious little shelter for anyone within?

In this chapter the aim is to grow a deeper understanding of our subject by seeking to resolve as much as we can each of these paradoxes in turn, thereby doing the best we can to understand the central tension between the universal and the particular that lies at the heart of our subject (and with which we began). First, though, there are unavoidable issues of definition, not about what democracy means this time but rather concerning the sorts of rights with which we are about to concern ourselves.

---

[9] A. Bickel, *The Least Dangerous Branch. The Supreme Court at the Bar of American Politics*, 2nd edn (Yale University Press, 1986).

[10] 'The decision of the Supreme Court has fell still born, and they find that it cannot coerce Georgia to yield to its mandate' is less glamorous but more accurate: New Georgia Encyclopaedia www.georgiaencyclopedia.org/articles/government-politics/worcester-v-georgia-1832 (accessed 26 September 2017).

[11] 31 US (6 Pet) 515 (1832).

1 What Are (Constitutional) Human Rights?

The parenthetic qualifier in this question does a lot of work. 'Constitutional' dramatically narrows the range of potential answers, driving (as we have seen) the response mainly into the field of national frameworks of government: 'mainly' because while we are still in the (Westphalian) mindset of assuming that all sovereign power is inevitably exercised by independent states, new arrangements for the pooling of sovereignty have recently been creating supra-national constitutional law (more on this shortly). For now though, restricting ourselves to the national raises a predictable problem of nomenclature: does a state have to refer to certain items in its constitutional in-tray as 'human rights' for them to be treated as such here? The answer can hardly be yes as this would drive us down a nominalist route that would put the scholastic ancients to shame; ignoring this place or that not because they have not raised questions of great importance of the sort we have just been discussing but because their basic constitutional document happens not to describe them as 'human rights' is, surely, an obvious wrong turning. But if the subject is not to be limited to 'human rights' what control can we place upon it?

The discussion of the second paradox in the last section contains the key clue. We are not concerned only to find the 'human rights' term; it is what the term signifies in a constitution that matters. We are after the constitutional arrangement that it connotes, howsoever this is described. So we can deploy other phrases and words just as well where we find on close examination that they are doing exactly the same kind of constitutional labour as 'human rights'. Put shortly, as we described a moment ago, that work involves the demarcation of the democratic pitch, the name we give to the boundary lines. In more 'constitutional' terms what we are looking for are those arrangements under which individual entitlements are to be found sitting above the democratic bustle to which the legal outputs of the political sphere need (or are expected or are asked) to conform. What exactly these are called – human rights; civil rights; constitutional rights; or whatever – ought to be neither here nor there: it is its essence as an intrusive supra-legislative engagement that captures our interest. And this invasive vigilance can itself take many shapes, across a spectrum from confident command to diffident dialogue: it is not the consequences of such interventions that define our subject so much as it is the existence of this court-policed layer of morality above the political.

Approached in this way it becomes clear that 'human rights law' is an altogether more nuanced and contextually driven subject than the term might seem to suggest. We can confidently assert that human rights law predates (even if it anticipates) the rise of democracy and has long co-existed successfully with it. Less confidently we can also say that there are, broadly speaking, five historical situations out of which, if we have to generalize, we can say that human rights law has emerged.[12] First up are those situations where such laws flow out of internal revolution. The most famous epitome of this is of course the France whose revolution in 1789 produced that dramatic claim to universal freedom in the shape of the Declaration of the Rights of Man and of the Citizen.[13] Following from this was the Constitution of 1793, setting out a range of rights that were proclaimed to sit above the polity as guarantors of the promises made during the years of struggle.[14] At the same time as these French initiatives, the civil rights set out in a series of amendments to the constitution of the newly formed United States of America reveal a second kind of 'human rights' construction, one driven this time not by internal revolution but by a vibrant anti-colonial impetus.[15] A couple of years after these American guarantees had been given credible legal force, in *Marbury* v. *Madison*,[16] came the Haitian constitution of 1805, another consequence of fundamental change wrought by resistance to a foreign status quo.[17]

In these earliest of human rights instruments, the authority of the judicial branch was available even in such pre-democratic times to protect citizens from abuse by the government across the board. And both kinds of situation have arisen regularly ever since, well into the democratic era, generating bills of rights which stand out as celebratory features of a new system of government achieved by a people liberated from

---

[12] See for an acute study of constitutionalism in one region, with a strong emphasis on social rights, R. Gargarella, *Latin-American Constitutionalism, 1810–2010: The Engine Room of the Constitution* (Oxford University Press, 2013).

[13] See http://avalon.law.yale.edu/18th_century/rightsof.asp (accessed 26 September 2017).

[14] Para. 122: http://oll.libertyfund.org/pages/1793-french-republic-constitution-of-1793 (accessed 26 September 2017).

[15] Amendments 1–10 of the US Constitution: www.archives.gov/founding-docs/bill-of-rights-transcript (accessed 26 September 2017).

[16] 5 US (1 Cranch) 137 (1803).

[17] See http://faculty.webster.edu/corbetre/haiti/history/earlyhaiti/1805-const.htm (accessed 26 September 2017).

within (post-Soviet states, for example) or from without, as with so many post-colonial states in the years after World War II.[18] Sometimes the two merge, combining features of both, as with post-Soviet satellite states for example and arguably also South Africa and Zimbabwe, whose pre-constitutional domestic overlords were leftovers from previous periods of colonial domination that had turned themselves into domestic minority overlords. What is common to both of these constitutional situations is the existence of a dramatic moment of change, a point on which history turns. The deployment of supra-legislative guarantees of better govern-mental behaviour is in each case driven from within by the domestic agents of change – 'we will not repeat the oppression of those whom we supplant' is the rallying cry.

The third situation has a different kind of turning point. In this category, the emergence of human rights (broadly defined) has arisen where a state has needed to be rebuilt after violent armed conflict, against an external enemy (as in the case of Germany, Japan and Italy, for example) or within its own borders (the United States after its Civil War of 1860–1865). In each case there is a victor-party for whom the imposition/agreement of a human rights oversight mechanism in the defeated jurisdictions is seen not only as a moral intervention similar to the first two of our categories ('never again') but also as a shrewd move in post-conflict regeneration. Reconstruction in the post-Civil War United States was an exercise in assimilation heavily dependent on law and on the renewal of 'civil rights' in particular. For their part, the embracing of written guarantees to which the new democratic systems of Germany and Italy were required to be subject may have most obviously guarded against the revival of fascism but they also served as a deterrent against the emergence of a majority-sanctioned move towards socialist government, as embodied in the then powerful Soviet Union, its armies located intimidatingly close by.[19]

The fourth instance of human rights resurgence, that of Neo-Enlightenment as it may perhaps be tentatively called, is different in every way. It arises at a moment of relative political stability, one that is experiencing none of the productive trauma common to our first three categories. In this kind of case, the domestic system largely works, but

---

[18] D. Grimm, *Constitutionalism: Past Present and Future* (Oxford Constitutional Theory, Oxford University Press, 2016).
[19] S. Gill and C.A. Cutler (eds.), *New Constitutionalism and World Order* (Cambridge University Press, 2014).

gets human rights law nonetheless. If nothing is broken, why the need to embark on a large-scale programme of repair? The answer lies in how these states imagine themselves, as places where things can be even better, and also where such improvement is needed to tackle problems which though not so severe as colonial or domestic oppression or defeat in war are, to the minds of those exposed to them, bad enough to warrant tackling in this radical way. The Canadians enacted a bill of rights in 1958 before a grand scheme of national improvement produced its well-known Charter of 1982, designed to bring all the Provinces and peoples more closely into the Canadian family while also establishing a new framework of basic individual rights. Often, as with Canadian Premier Pierre Trudeau and the desire to tame the rebellious province of Quebec, there will be political calculation behind the embracing of rights-talk. In the first term of Tony Blair's New Labour administration of 1997–2001 in the United Kingdom, a human rights law was enacted as part of a package of constitutional measures designed to display radical intent on the part of a government that was in fact adopting highly conservative fiscal measures at the time. Similar rights-interventions have occurred in New Zealand and a number of Australian states, a 'new Commonwealth model of constitutionalism' as one scholar has perceptively called it.[20]

The final way in which constitutional human rights are likely to emerge is as part of a coherent framework of state-building. This might be in a situation where a fresh constitutional settlement has been devised as a means of transitioning out of a long-term state of disorder into one of greater stability and with more widely accepted governing institutions.[21] Unlike our third category just referred to, here there is no victor-party imposing human rights as part of its triumph; rather the guarantees set out in a new human rights law of this sort become themselves an important element in an emerging pathway to peace.[22] Northern Ireland is an outstanding example of this sort of situation, with both of the relevantly engaged states (the United Kingdom and the Republic of Ireland) enacting

[20] S. Gardbaum, *The New Commonwealth Model of Constitutionalism: Theory and Practice* (Cambridge University Press, 2013).

[21] And in such situations the breadth of the rights embraced can be very wide: S. Liebenberg, *Socio-Economic Rights: Adjudication under a Transformative Constitution* (Juta, 2010).

[22] Reflecting on how South Africa might well fit this category as well as into the second just discussed reminds us of the inevitability of some degree of fluidity as between these various models of constitutional origins.

a regional human rights instrument (the European Convention on Human Rights) into their domestic law as one of a number of a menu of options deliberately chosen to signal to all the communities in the Province that there was to be no turning away from the agreements reached in the Good Friday Agreement of 1998. The field of transitional justice contains many similar examples.[23]

In this category, there is also the case of the aspirant state realizing its potential through the embracing of rights. We occasionally see human right law as an element in state-building playing out on a larger scale, as a key ingredient in the creation of a new framework of government covering multiple, previously sovereign entities. Something like this happened in the United States in the early to middle twentieth century when the widening application of constitutional rights to state as well as federal authorities played an important part in the holding of all the states in that Union to account for the conduct of their agents towards the individuals under their control. The federal Supreme Court had already done early judicial work in hewing a central federal authority out of a constitutional framework that had been at best uncertain about this demarcation, at worst positively better disposed towards state power.[24] Much the same process has repeated itself in what we now think of and call the European Union but which began as a loose affiliation of sovereign states combining to improve their overall trading effectiveness. The European Court of Justice has done pioneering federalizing work in a way that echoes that of the nineteenth-century US court, but (unlike in that jurisdiction) from the start it has deployed the language of fundamental rights as a means of securing its desired outcome, a more unified Europe of shared values and agreed basic laws to which all domestic constitutions must adhere.[25] As the Common Market has taken on this more state-like demeanour, first as a set of Communities and then as a Union, its emphasis on rights has become clearer and more pronounced. The embracing of a social aspect to Union activities in the 1980s led to a sharp increase in human rights oriented initiatives on such topics as

---

[23] R. Buchanan and P. Zumbansen (eds.), *Law in Transition: Human Rights, Development and Transitional Justice* (Hart Publishing, 2014).

[24] A. Cox, *The Courts and the Constitution* (Houghton Mifflin, 1987) is a compelling, highly readable account.

[25] R. Schütze, 'Constitutionalism and the European Union', in C. Barnard and S. Peers (eds.), *European Union Law* (Oxford University Press, 2014).

workers' rights, equality and non-discrimination. As the Union's ambition has grown and its remit deepened, so the articulation of its rights agenda has become clearer, culminating in the Charter of Fundamental Rights agreed in 2000 and of binding legal character since the coming into force of the Treaty of Lisbon in 2009.[26] It is not surprising to see the rights of EU citizens and the status of the EU Charter at the forefront of discussions about the United Kingdom's planned exit from the European Union: those who see the EU as merely a tool of the markets have not been paying attention to developments over the last two decades. And human rights and the rule of law are key – perhaps the key – principles underpinning this new emerging, state-like power.[27]

If these then are the various ways in which constitutional 'human rights' (however they happen to be described) can come about – and our five cannot be definitive because by definition our enquiry has been empirical and can change with the emergence of new forms of constitution-making – what then is to be found in these various rights' instruments? It is time now to return to the three paradoxes with which we began and through which we hope to make deeper sense of our subject, beginning with our first and the one that most demands our attention, the conceit that with human rights we have a set of transcendent truths that the necessities of history mean can only be realized in highly particular sets of circumstances.

2 The Range of Human Rights

The German constitution of 1949 took effect as a basic law and contained in its opening set of articles what are called 'basic rights'.[28] Pride of place is given to the bald statement with which the document opens: 'Human dignity shall be inviolable'[29] and then, almost immediately, '[t]he German

---

[26] See http://ec.europa.eu/justice/fundamental-rights/charter/index_en.htm (accessed 26 September 2017).
[27] See S. Weatherill, *Law and Values in the European Union* (Clarendon Law Series, Oxford University Press, 2016). I have argued that these values are at the core of an emerging European culture: 'Unpicking Europe's Cult of Culture', *The New European*, 21–27 September 2017, 30–31: www.theneweuropean.co.uk/culture/conor-gearty-europe-culture-1-5211899 (accessed 18 October 2017).
[28] The constitution can be read at www.btg-bestellservice.de/pdf/80201000.pdf (accessed 26 September 2017).
[29] Art. 1(1).

people therefore acknowledge inviolable and inalienable human rights as the basis of every community, of peace and of justice in the world'.[30] The rights that follow (personal freedoms; equality before the law; freedom of faith and conscience; freedom of expression, arts and sciences are the first five, with assembly, association, religious, privacy property and asylum rights following) are specifically stated to 'bind the legislature, the executive and the judiciary as directly applicable law'[31] and while restrictions are permitted, the 'essence of a basic right' may never be affected.[32] Now consider in contrast the rights to be found in the South African constitution: extensive, wide-ranging and ambitious, running to some twenty-seven substantive articles.[33] The reach is much wider: the German equivalents for sure, but also such matters as access to information, environmental protection, cultural rights, health and social security. The difference between the two can hardly be explained away by some claimed distinction between 'basic' and other rights. Nor does some supposed historical movement (the unfolding of the three 'generations of rights' say) make any immediate sense. As has already been intimated in our more general discussion, each is a creature of its specific moment, the German a victors' anti-Communist constitution for sure but also a reaction to the Nazi hegemony which had first twisted the country's moral compass out of recognition and then destroyed it physically in war; and in South Africa a concerted effort to contrive a rights document so comprehensive as to be a vital act of nation-building and of national reconciliation in itself. The exercise could be multiplied writ-large across the canvass of global constitutional law. Constitutions, and constitutional rights within them, are like siblings in a large family – sharing broad resemblances, each nevertheless remains individually distinct.

While this makes comparative work difficult it does not make it impossible.[34] We have already seen that credible generalizations are possible so far as the origins of constitutional rights' instruments are concerned, and the same can be said for their content. Broadly speaking three family resemblances are detectible, at least within the democratic culture which as we have already explained must be our starting assumption so far as

---

[30] Art. 1(2).

[31] Art. 1(3).

[32] Art. 19(2).

[33] See www.gov.za/documents/constitution/chapter-2-bill-rights (accessed 19 October 2017).

[34] See generally M. Rosenfeld and A. Sajó (eds.), *The Oxford Handbook of Comparative Constitutional Law* (Oxford University Press, 2012).

the constitutional rights of interest to us here are concerned. For reasons that will become obvious shortly these can usefully be called 'thin', 'thick' and 'innovative' democratic rights. Let us deal now with each in turn.

First, there are 'thin' democratic rights, those that grow out of the 'majoritarian' approach to our subject that we earlier discussed. If there is any role for rights in a system which allows the democratic legislature to produce whatever laws it wishes,[35] then it can only be as a means of keeping that democracy in shape, stopping it from straying into other, more authoritarian forms of government. On this analysis, if the building blocks for a properly functioning democratic system are in place then what the representative assembly speaking through law chooses to do with that power is neither here nor there – but constitutional rights are the guardians of the strength of those blocks. To change the metaphor from construction to locomotion, they are the oil that enables the democratic machine to be driven by its electoral victors. This points us in the direction of what were in British law known as civil liberties[36] and what in more contemporary constitutional human rights terms we think of as civil and political rights. The freedoms of thought and of conscience are pre-eminent here, as are the freedoms of expression, association and assembly. This is because you cannot have a properly functioning democracy where thoughts cannot be conceived or even if they can be articulated cannot then be made the focus of active debate. The right to non-discrimination ensures that these freedoms are not protected unevenly, favouring one 'acceptable' political community over others. What we now call 'due process' ensures that dissent is given its day in court, judged by independent persons (judge and, in the common law tradition, jury) rather than partisans. On its outer margins, rights such as those to life, liberty and not to be tortured ensure that the political environment is not polluted by fear. At the apex of any such system is the right to vote.

Here we have a major preoccupation of very many constitutional rights instruments.[37] Civil and political rights have become the most predictable content to be found in such documents; they may contain more (as we shall see shortly) but it is a rare framework that does not contain such

---

[35] Such systems are often conceived of as Republican in nature: see R. Bellamy, *Political Constitutionalism: A Republican's Defence of the Constitutionality of Democracy* (Cambridge University Press, 2007).

[36] C.A. Gearty, *Civil Liberties* (Clarendon Law Series, Oxford University Press, 2007).

[37] See the data-base constructed by the University of Texas *Constitute* project: www.constituteproject.org/ (accessed 17 October 2017).

rights. Building on the US, French and Haitian early models at the turn of the eighteenth/nineteenth centuries, as enlightenment culture grew into the modern, the idea took hold that the civil and political freedoms that had been denied the drafters in their revolutionary struggles should from their moment of victory onwards take pride of place in the new regime that they were creating, pious guarantees of good behaviour on the part of future rulers, capable of binding even impeccably elected leaders. This supra-political setting of the boundaries of the polity is to be found in constitutions in all five categories we have discussed. It is strongly reinforced by international and regional human rights law: an example of the first being the International Covenant on Civil and Political Rights of 1966 and of the second the European Convention on Human Rights and Fundamental Freedoms (1950).

Two further points about the nature of these rights when they take this constitutional (rather than philosophical) shape can be usefully noted. First, while such rights may begin life as political, their generalized character as constitutional rights inevitably gives them reach beyond the democratic necessities that they have been designed to protect. Here the conjunction between the civil and political is a useful reminder that what works for politics plays for civil society as well: the freedom to express oneself reaches literature and art as well as its more direct targets; the right to a fair trial covers the petty criminal as well as the political trouble-maker; and so on. Second, it is always immediately obvious once rights are being translated into real-life situations that there have to be exceptions to many of them or the democratic society that is their beneficiary will soon descend into anarchy. If the original document does not acknowledge this fact (as the US constitutional amendments, on the whole, did not) then the judges will have to fill these drafting gaps. Even if the caveats are there, it is in the determination of the range of the exceptional that the judges as arbiters of constitutional meaning find most of their work. How could this not be, to pick one salient example, when a rights framework like that of the Canadian begins with a declaration that 'the rights and freedoms set out in it [are] subject only to such reasonable limits prescribed by law as can be demonstrably justified in a free and democratic society'.[38] The word

---

[38] Canadian Charter of Rights and Freedoms 1982, section 1: see http://laws-lois.justice.gc.ca/eng/Const/page-15.html (accessed 17 October 2017).

'only' here cannot hide the extent of qualification contained in the move from the philosophical to the politico-legal.

The need for qualifications to rights, expressed perhaps as an acceptance of their progressive realization, is generally thought to be especially marked with regard to our second set of rights in the human rights family, those that are concerned with the protection of 'thick' democratic rights. Here the version of democracy that rights are required to protect is richer and more wide-ranging than that which we have just been discussing, driven by the strategic redefinition of what democracy entails that we have earlier observed.[39] The machine of government is not only given the oil with which to function but it is required also to drive in a particular direction, one that heads towards a society which cherishes the equal dignity of all, and in which life opportunities are guaranteed while protections against calamitous misfortune are also built into the design of the vehicle. The constitutional route towards realization of this ambitious democratic plus model is via the entrenchment of social and economic rights. A well-known example of these is to be found in the South African Constitution, whose rights provisions (as we have already briefly noted) extend well beyond the civil and political to embrace rights of access to, for example, adequate housing, health care, food and social security.[40] To the same effect are the constitutions of scores of constitutions worldwide.[41] Constitutions without explicit protection along these lines have on occasion been tempted to develop them by a process of interpretation, as in India where the 'right to life' has been given a very much broader texture than its drafters may have anticipated,[42] and even the United States toyed with innovation along these lines at the height of its Warren/Burger court activism.[43] Of course, how far these rights are allowed to dictate democratic decision-making with regard to policy and

---

[39] See text at n. 8 above.

[40] The Bill of Rights is set out at www.justice.gov.za/legislation/constitution/SAConstitution-web-eng-02.pdf (accessed 26 September 2017). The housing guarantees are in Art. 26, those to health care, food and social security in Art. 27. See generally Liebenberg, n. 21 above.

[41] See www.constituteproject.org/search?lang=en (accessed 17 October 2017).

[42] Art. 21 of the Indian Constitution; *Unni Krishnan JP* v. *State of Andhra Pradesh* 1993 AIR 217, 1993 SCR (1) 594. See generally M. Langford (ed.), *Social Rights Jurisprudence: Emerging Trends in International and Comparative Law* (Cambridge University Press, 2009).

[43] *Shapiro* v. *Thompson* 394 US 618 (1969); *Goldberg* v. *Kelly* 397 US 254 (1970).

budget-making has been a difficult issue in most jurisdictions from time to time, and not only because of the perceived need for qualifications just referred to but also because, and we have seen this recently with the rise of neoliberalism, the mood of politics might well turn hostile to the very assumptions about equality and socially just allocation of resources upon which social and economic rights depend.[44]

And finally, less commonly but always interestingly there are those constitutions which develop a range of innovative rights as a way of meeting the particular concerns of their political communities. Canada provides another good example: its Charter of Rights and Freedoms contains many provisions aimed at supporting the cultural rights of French-speaking communities within this largely Anglophone polity.[45] New Zealand's bill of rights has a general clause guaranteeing the rights of minorities[46] and chapter 2 of South Africa's constitution, devoted to rights, includes guarantees related to the environment, language and culture, and cultural, religious and linguistic communities.[47] The innovative website developed at the University of Texas, *Constitute*, ambitiously seeks to provide a user-friendly database of the world's constitutions.[48] It finds no fewer than 146 constitutions with a right to culture, forty with provisions on disability and ten guaranteeing indigenous rights of representation. And at the outer reaches of the possible there is Bolivia's (non-constitutional) Law of Mother Earth,[49] showing how far this language of rights can be pushed, even beyond the human (and therefore the remit of this chapter).

As we have moved through the family of rights from thin to thick to innovative, we cannot help but observe how the range of rights has been expanding. More and more issues that might have been thought to belong to the cut and thrust of the democratic process are being recategorized as rights, thereby (to recall our earlier analogy) shrinking the playing field

---

[44] P. O'Connell, 'The Death of Socio-Economic Rights' (2011) 74(4) *Modern Law Review* 532–554; C.A. Gearty, 'Neo-Democracy: "Useful Idiot" of Neo-Liberalism' (2016) 56(6) *British Journal of Criminology* 1087–1106.

[45] See in particular general language rights (ss. 16–19) and minority language educational rights (s. 23).

[46] s. 20.

[47] See ss. 24, 30 and 31 respectively.

[48] www.constituteproject.org/ (accessed 17 October 2017).

[49] www.worldfuturefund.org/Projects/Indicators/motherearthbolivia.html (accessed 17 October 2017).

of politics in favour of ever-narrowing and more intrusive boundaries. Where does this leave the referee, the adjudicator of when such politics ends and these (human) rights begin? We have already observed his or her importance in the policing of the exception. Our second paradox, about such an elevation of the judicial being possible only in a democratic polity that would seem to leave no room for it, combines now with our third, about the contrast between what courts are empowered to do and what actually happens, to put the judges at the centre of this final part of our comparative human rights journey. How do democratic constitutions manage the great power that appears to flow from entrusting human rights to the courts? How do the judges approach the exercise of the powers with which they have been entrusted in the name of human rights?

3 The Least Dangerous Branch?

A dramatic recent development in constitutional law has been the willingness of courts to deliberate on, and sometimes reject, the validity of elections that have been held in democratic states. *Bush* v. *Gore*[50] will live on in the memories of not just constitutional specialists, and more recently we have seen declarations of invalidity affecting elections in Thailand,[51] Austria[52] and Kenya.[53] Arguably these remarkable interventions, which go well beyond the application to a specific issue of this or that right to assert control over the very way in which the political field arranges its players, both vindicate the status of the affected states as democratic and in doing so display the courts in their role as guardians of the fundamental right of citizens to live in a truly (rather than bogus or corrupt) democratic system. That is as may be but the feeling is unavoidable that something bigger is going on here than the enforcement of human rights of the sort we have been discussing, even those civil and political rights with which we began the last section.

---

[50] 531 US 98 (2000).

[51] 'Court Annuls Thai Election Adding to Political Crisis' *Financial Times* 21 March 2014: www.ft.com/content/b73523cc-b0c9-11e3-bbd4-00144feab7de (accessed 17 October 2017: pay wall).

[52] 'Austria Presidential Poll Result Overturned', BBC News, 1 July 2016: www.bbc.co.uk/news/world-europe-36681475 (accessed 17 October 2017).

[53] 'Kenyan Presidential Election Cancelled by Supreme Court', BBC News, 1 September 2017: www.bbc.co.uk/news/world-africa-41123329 (accessed 17 October 2017).

The same issues arise at the more prosaic level of conventional constitutional analysis. There are it is true (and against the generality of an
assumption we earlier made) sometimes occasions when rights are stated in
absolute terms and furthermore presented in ways that allow no scope for
democratic retaliation. The most famous examples are the US Constitution's
first amendment stipulation that 'Congress shall make no law respecting
an establishment of religion, or prohibiting the free exercise thereof; or
abridging the freedom of speech, or of the press; or the right of the people
peaceably to assemble, and to petition the government for a redress of
grievances', and the German basic law's succinct declaration at its outset,
already noted earlier, that 'human dignity shall be inviolable'[54] and that the
'essence' of any right can never be overridden.[55] Where context demands it,
however, the courts find themselves compelled to manage the risk of absurd
absolutism by reading caveats into words regardless of how bald they
appear in the text.[56] The moral force of human rights cannot help but be
diluted by contact with practical necessity. It is the same for those few pure
human rights prohibitions that are to be found scattered across the globe's
constitutions, those which, unusually, permit of no exception (on torture for
example or slavery/forced servitude), though here the leeway is to be found
in tightening definitions rather than in the contriving of exceptions.[57]

    More frequent than unequivocal language of the sort we have just been
discussing are the purpose-built limitations on rights that one finds in most
rights instruments, across all the family members that we have earlier been
discussing. The examples here could be multiplied to numbing effect but
one or two may be permitted to make general points on behalf of all the
rest. Thus we can recall our earlier observation about that generally impec-
cable rights' instrument the Canadian charter, which starts with a general get-out clause, permitting 'such reasonable limits prescribed by law
as can be demonstrably justified in a free and democratic society'. The
South African equivalent allows limitations 'only in terms of law of general
application to the extent that the limitation is reasonable and justifiable

---

[54] Art. 1 German Constitution.
[55] Art. 19(2) German Constitution.
[56] As with the first amendment to the US Constitution: A. Lewis, *Freedom for the Thought
We Hate: A Biography of the First Amendment* (Basic Books, 2007).
[57] D. Luban, *Torture, Power and Law* (Cambridge University Press, 2014) deals well with
direct acts of torture and covers the Bush presidency's definitional efforts to debilitate the
reach of the term: see especially Part IV.

in an open and democratic society based on human dignity, equality and freedom' and even then only after taking into account all relevant factors (only some of which are enumerated). Both are typical in interpreting (and perhaps striking down) democratic laws by reference to the needs of democratic society: the irony of this being done by unelected referees[58] is neither noticed nor appreciated given how such vigilant oversight is assumed in both places (and in others of which these are typical) to be of the essence of rather than in violation of democracy. A separate exculpatory avenue for rights-violation is the emergency route. No liberal democratic state wants to be so open-minded that its brains fall out;[59] as a result prohibitions on assaults on the 'free democratic basic order'[60] can often be found, as can permissions to act in controlled violation of constitutional norms in situations of crisis.[61] Once again we see resolution of the paradox of judicial power being resolved in favour of a reworking of what democracy requires, and in particular of the obligation required of all such polities, and supported by the courts, not to facilitate their own destruction.

A different tack is taken in those rights' frameworks where the courts are intentionally disabled from conclusive legislative override. The new commonwealth model already alluded to when we were discussing the origins of constitutional rights instruments is of particular interest in this regard.[62] The New Zealand bill of rights does not allow any kind of ruling against primary legislation,[63] while the Canadian equivalent does but then permits democratic retaliation in the shape of rights-proofed re-enactment of the offending measure (with pre-emptive parliamentary strikes also possible).[64] Somewhere in the middle is the United Kingdom's approach, followed in Ireland[65] and the Australian Capital Territory,[66] under which

---

[58] On which see R. Hirschl, *Towards Juristocracy: The Origins and Consequences of the New Constitutionalism* (Harvard University Press, 2004).

[59] A variation on a well-known observation: see https://quoteinvestigator.com/2014/04/13/open-mind/ (accessed 17 October 2017).

[60] German Constitution, art. 18.

[61] J. Ferejohn and P. Pasquino, 'The Law of the Exception: A Typology of Emergency Powers' (2004) 2(2) *International Journal of Constitutional Law* 210–239. See generally A. Nolan (ed.), *Economic and Social Rights After the Global Financial Crisis* (Cambridge University Press, 2014).

[62] Gardbaum, n. 20 above.

[63] New Zealand Bill of Rights Act 1990, s. 4.

[64] Canadian Charter of Rights and Freedoms, s. 33.

[65] European Convention on Human Rights Act 2003, s. 5.

[66] Human Rights Act 2004, s. 32.

primary legislation may be declared to be in breach of human rights but without this involving any loss in the impugned law's validity.[67] Lawyers may condemn this as useless but there remain in the sorts of places that enact such laws strong commitments to human rights and the rule of law which have led to these declarations being implemented, albeit by executive and legislative choice rather than duress,[68] and the same is true of the override allowed the Canadian parliament which has never been deployed in (now) over thirty-five years.

This last observation is a reminder to us that the law is not always what it seems, that the theoretically weak (in terms of enforcement) can be stronger (in reality) than it appears. The reverse also holds true: courts often hang back from deploying to full effect the powers with which they have been entrusted, deploying the language of justiciability, remedy-deferral, deference and respect for separation of powers in order to do so.[69] If they do go so far as to rule in a way that provokes a legislative reaction then even higher levels of reticence kick in when it comes to assessing the validity of that response.[70] Judicial pugilism often seems to exhaust itself after one battle.[71] Courts exploit the paradox of their strength lying in their weakness so as to ensure that sometimes, in the wider public interest as they see it, the latter must be allowed to triumph over the former.

Conclusion

Human rights law is so often about proportionality. The courts use this tool of rational engagement to assess whether any given incursion into a 'human right' is warranted by a legitimate aim identified by the state, and also whether the state action affecting the right is causally linked to that aim. If it passes muster on both of these, the next step is to ask whether other less human-rights-intrusive means could have

---

[67] Human Rights Act 1998, s. 4.

[68] Joint Committee on Human Rights, *Human Rights Judgments*. Seventh Report of Session 2014–15. HL 130. HC 1088, 11 March 2015.

[69] M. Tushnet, *Weak Courts, Strong Rights: Judicial Review and Social Welfare Rights in Comparative Perspective* (Princeton University Press, 2008).

[70] R. Dixon, 'The Core Case for Weak-Form Judicial Review' (2017) 38 *Cardozo Law Review* 2193–2232.

[71] Ibid.

been deployed instead, and then finally if this is not the case whether the balance between the public need and the private interest has been properly drawn.[72] Looking at this technical legal term with a consciously broader set of eyes than usual, what is proportionality if not a means of managing the paradoxes with which we have been concerned here, between individual entitlement and public necessity, between the democratic will and the need for its occasional defiance in the name of democracy, and between the availability of intrusive judicial power and the necessity not to exercise it? Human rights law is surely the same exercise in proportionality albeit written on a larger canvass: the courts must engage with the ethical while not losing sight of the real-world situation they are adjudicating; they must be brave when they can be but reticent when the wider public interest demands; litigants with just claims must occasionally be disappointed in the interests of keeping the whole show on the road. Democracy thrives on grey areas, on uncertainty, on nuance and nudge. Human rights law is no exception.

Further Reading

R. Buchanan and P. Zumbansen (eds.), *Law in Transition: Human Rights, Development and Transitional Justice* (Hart Publishing, 2014).

J. Christoffersen and M.R. Madsen, *The European Court of Human Rights: Between Law and Politics* (Oxford University Press, 2011).

C. Gearty and C. Douzinas (eds.), *Cambridge Companion to Human Rights Law* (Cambridge University Press, 2012).

S. Gill and C.A. Cutler (eds.), *New Constitutionalism and World Order* (Cambridge University Press, 2014).

D. Grimm, *Constitutionalism: Past Present and Future* (Oxford Constitutional Theory, Oxford University Press, 2016).

K. Möller, *The Global Model of Constitutional Rights* (Oxford University Press, 2012).

M.J. Perry *Toward a Theory of Human Rights: Religion, Law, Courts* (Cambridge University Press, 2008).

A. Young, *Democratic Dialogue and the Constitution* (Oxford University Press, 2017).

---

[72] K. Möller, *The Global Model of Constitutional Rights* (Oxford University Press, 2012); P. Daly, *A Theory of Deference in Administrative Law: Basis, Application and Scope* (Cambridge University Press, 2012), ch. 5; A.D.P. Brady, *Proportionality and Deference under the UK Human Rights Act: An Institutionally Sensitive Approach* (Cambridge University Press, 2012).

12 Federalism

Raffaele Bifulco

Introduction: Federalism and Connected Areas

The term 'federalism' refers to a plurality of historical experiences and features both a static-structural and a dynamic-procedural dimension. The first dimension refers to the concrete organizational forms assumed by federalism (such as in the United States or India); the second dimension, on the other hand, concerns federal processes, that is to say the historical evolution and the progressive development of a union between several communities (for example, the European Union or the United Provinces of the Netherlands in the modern era).

The first structural dimension studies federalism mostly as a juridical-constitutional organization and traditionally belongs to legal studies, while the second dimension is a form of reaction to the predominance of the juridical approach. Friedrich, who was the main theorist

supporting this political science approach, believes that the word federalism concerns:

> the process of federalizing a political community, that is to say, the process by
> which a number of separate political communities enter into arrangements for
> working out solutions, adopting joint policies, and making joint decisions on joint
> problems, and, conversely, also the process by which a unitary political commu-
> nity becomes differentiated into a federally organized whole. Federal relations are
> fluctuating relations in the very nature of things.[1]

In these pages, I will try to merge the two approaches following
Elazar's suggestion, according to which 'federalism must combine both
structure and process', because '[t]hat combination, indeed, is what
creates a federal system'.[2]

A semantic clarification is also important at the outset. The concepts of
federalism and federal state are often used in an undifferentiated manner.
Here, the concept of *federal state* (Bundesstaat, Federation) will be used
to indicate a certain type of legal system, characterized by a particular
territorial organization. The concept of *federalism* (Föderalismus, federalism), on the other hand, will be used to indicate a concept often coin-
ciding with the federal state, not in its legal-organizational dimension,
but rather in the dynamics of different processes such as the creation,
change and dissolution of federal experiences.[3]

Finally, a brief warning. A few 'classic' examples will inevitably need to
be highlighted. These are the federal states that arose between the eighteenth and nineteenth centuries, namely the United States, Switzerland,
Australia, Canada, Germany and Austria (the latter formed in 1919–
1920), since they became reference models for every subsequent historical experience. These concrete historical forms of federalism tend to have
common features because they were formed through association into a
single and comprehensive state entity composed of pre-existing smaller
entities (*coming-together federalism*). They are opposed to more recent

---

[1] C.J. Friedrich, *Trends of Federalism in Theory and Practice* (Pall Mall Press, 1968), 7.
[2] D.J. Elazar, *Exploring Federalism* (University of Alabama Press, 1987), 68.
[3] M. Burgess, 'Federalism and Federation in Western Europe', in M. Burgess (ed.), *Federalism and Federation in Western Europe* (Croom, 1986).

federal formations, which were created through processes of disintegration of pre-existing state units (*holding together federalism*).[4]

After examining the specificities relating to the study of the federal phenomenon in the first part of this chapter, the analysis will focus on the current reasons for federalism and the federal state. In the central part of this analysis, the features characterizing the federal state will be identified in order to reaffirm the long-lasting usefulness of some legal categories for the understanding of the concept of federal state. The final part will try to clarify the reasons for a renewal of a common category, which is composed of the experiences of 'classic' federal states, more recently formed unions and the so-called 'Regional states'.

1 The Plurality of Models

The identification of a single model of federal state is not possible. This impossibility is due not only to the specificities that each federal experience presents but also to the interaction that a federal organization develops with other central institutions (form of government), with intermediate State-society institutions (parties), and with local communities.

Our starting point is therefore characterized by the *plurality of federal state models and by the specificity of federal processes*.[5]

a Plurality of Approaches and Methods of Study

Analytical difficulties may also be found in the plurality and diversity of methodologies applied to the study of federal experiences. If the

---

[4] The terminological distinction between 'coming together' federalism, i.e. by association, and 'holding together' federalisms, i.e. by dissociation, belongs to A. Stepan, 'Toward a New Comparative Politics of Federalism, (Multi) Nationalism, and Democracy: Beyond Riker Federalism', in A. Stepan (ed.), *Arguing Comparative Politics* (Oxford University Press, 2001), 315, who used it to mark a clear difference between the two types of federalism and, above all, to emphasize the asymmetries characterizing 'holding together' federalisms.

[5] W.H. Riker, *Federalism: Origin, Operation, Significance* (Little, 1964), 5–6; M. Bothe, 'Föderalismus – ein Konzept im geschichtlichen Wandel', in T. Evers (ed.), *Chancen des Föderalismus in Deutschland und Europa* (Nomos, 1994), 22.

contribution of the legal dimension (in particular constitutionalism and internationalism) has undoubtedly been fundamental because of the close relationship created between the federal state and the development of constitutionalism, this is not enough to affirm the self-sufficiency of the legal approach.

The contribution of political science has indeed also been rich and fundamental. Suffice to say that without it the political conditions that allowed the formation of the most long-lived federal states would not yet be clear;[6] and the practical functioning of federal institutions in their daily contact with political actors,[7] in particular with the parties,[8] would not be clear either. However, above all, an analysis of federalism both as an associative process that federalises separate political organizations, and as a dissociative process through which a previously unified political community is split into separate and distinct political communities, would not be available.[9]

It should also be added that limiting the spectrum of relevant disciplinary contributions to a legal and political approach is of course not possible. Indeed, a concept such as the asymmetric federal state or the asymmetric regional state, frequently used by constitutionalists for the analysis of some federal experiences, is a contribution brought by sociology to the study of the federal state.[10] It is also useful to remember that the principle, according to which 'the essence of federalism lies not in the institutional or constitutional structure but in the society itself',[11] has been developed by a sociological approach that has become common

[6] *Ex multis* Riker, *Federalism* (n.5).

[7] For a practical case, F.W. Scharpf, B. Reissert and F. Schnabel, *Politikverflechtung: Theorie und Empirie des kooperativen Föderalismus in der Bundesrepublik* (Scriptor, 1977).

[8] As far as the German party system is concerned, G. Lehmbruch, *Parteienwettbewerb im Bundesstaat* (Kohlhammer, 1976).

[9] Friedrich, *Trends of Federalism in Theory and Practice* (n.1); Elazar, *Exploring Federalism* (n.2), 55–56.

[10] C.D. Tarlton, 'Symmetry and Asymmetry as Elements of Federalism: A Theoretical Speculation', (1965) 27 *The Journal of Politics* 861.

[11] W.S. Livingston, 'A Note on the Nature of Federalism' (1952) 67 *Political Science Quarterly* 84. For a different approach, centred on the role of the State (State-centred model), cf. H. Bakvis and W.M. Chandler, 'Federalism and Comparative Analysis', in H. Bakvis and W.M. Chandler (eds.), *Federalism and the Role of the State* (University of Toronto, 1987), 5.

to other disciplines. And, finally, we must not forget the fundamental contribution of economic science to the study of the financial aspects of federalism.

In sum, an interdisciplinary approach is essential in studying the federal phenomenon. However, the special characteristics of each discipline must not be neglected. These specificities, which imply different methods of analysis, also affect the way of understanding the object of study as a whole.

b Diachronic and Synchronic Perspectives in the Study of Federalism: From the Dual to the Cooperative Federal State

The organization and functioning mode of federal states – especially federal states that have a considerable historical continuity – changes over time; and their evaluation can thus vary according to the historical phase taken into consideration. To illustrate this point: the assessment of the US federal system in its first seventy years of life is decidedly different to an assessment of its current form. A juridical analysis of the US, Swiss and German federal systems that is limited to the first years of their existence will thus clearly underline the influence of confederal 'residuals' on the functioning of the system, because the Member States' resistance towards the new federal entity is generally particularly strong in the early years. (For a theoretical elaboration here, consider the works of Calhoun as to the US and von Seydel on the European side,[12] which equally mirror this 'natural' resistance to the excessive strengthening of a central power). The outcome of a synchronic analysis is often, by contrast, very different: it would here be difficult to deny the strong centralization process that federations often exercise over the Member States.[13]

---

[12] J.C. Calhoun, *A Discourse on the Constitution and Government of the United States* (Johnston, 1851); M. von Seydel, *Commentar zur Verfassungs-Urkunde für das Deutsche Reich* (Mohr, 1897).

[13] K.C. Wheare, *Federal Government* (Oxford University Press, 1951), 252, notes in this regard that the tendency towards centralization 'is not surprising. For after all when these governments were initiated they began from almost nothing at all'.

The two perspectives – diachronic and synchronic – are indispensable to understand not only the reality of the single federal experience but also the evolution it has undergone. Indeed, without a diachronic perspective it would not have been possible to grasp the importance of the historical-social changes that transformed the relations between a federation and its member states from a dual federal approach,[14] inspired by the separation of the respective attributions and competences, to a cooperative one that was based on the powers of intervention and coordination in areas falling even within the competence of the member states.

This rise of cooperative federalism, represented by the *marble cake* image,[15] is of fundamental importance if one wishes to understand the organization and functioning of the modern federal state. It represents, in theoretical and practical terms, the response offered by the federal state to the challenges arising from the decline of the liberal era. The arrival of the welfare state forced public authorities to engage in a larger degree of intervention in various social spheres. In the federal legal system, this led to greater intervention, not only by the member states, but also especially by the federation. The first signs of this great transformation occurred in the United States with President Roosevelt's New Deal: the federal grants to the Member States (grants-in-aid) became its principal application.[16] Following the New Deal, the phenomenon subsequently spread to

---

[14] The expression *dual federalism* belongs to E. Corwin, 'The Passing of Dual Federalism', (1950) 36 *Virginia Law Review* 1.

[15] M. Grodzins, *The American System: A New View of Government in the United States*, (Rand McNally, 1966), 265: 'The American form of government is often, but erroneously, symbolized by a three-layer cake-federale-state-local government. A far more accurate image is the rainbow or marble cake, characterised by an inseparable mingling of differently colored ingredients, the colors appearing in vertical and diagonal strands and unexpected whirls. As colours are mixed in marble cake, so functions are mixed in the American federal system.'

[16] Corwin, *The Passing of Dual Federalism* (n.14) 20, wrote that as for grants-in-aid 'the greater financial strength of the National Government is joined to the wider coercive powers of the State... The culmination of this type of National-State cooperation to date, however, is reached in *The Social Security Act* of August 14, 1935'. The phenomenon is already well absorbed by the *Foreword* to the *Symposium on cooperative federalism*, published in (1935) 23 *Iowa Law Review* 455.

all federal states (also in new federal experiences such as the European Union[17]), taking different forms and proportions.[18]

From this moment onwards, a fundamental change occurred in the very understanding of the federal state. For a definition of the federal state as 'a system of division of powers that allows central and regional governments to be coordinated and independent, each in a given sphere, was no longer possible'.[19] The federation and the Member States began to establish relationships of 'mutual interdependence'.[20] And this cooperation has paved the way for a greater power centralization on behalf of the Federation.[21]

This transformation, in many ways irreversible, has changed the features of the federal state in at least two ways. First, cooperative federalism (this is the name given to the political interdependence of different levels of government) has itself transformed into a competition over competence.[22] This undermined the benefits of the dual organization within the nineteenth-century federal state, in which each level of government had a clearly delimited sphere of competences, in that citizens lose the

---

[17] R. Schütze, *From Dual to Cooperative Federalism: The Changing Structure of European Law* (Oxford University Press, 2009).

[18] On these aspects, see M. Venkatrangaiya, *Competitive and Cooperative Trends in Federalism* (R.R. Kale Memorial Lecture, Modak, Poona, 1951), 20; G. Kisker, *Kooperation im Bundesstaat* (Mohr, 1971); G. Bognetti, 'L'evoluzione del federalismo moderno e i diversi modelli dello Stato federale', in A.M. Petroni (ed.), *Modelli giuridici ed economici per la costituzione europea* (Il mulino, 2001), 46; G. de Vergottini, *Stato federale*, in *Enc. dir.*, XLIII, 1990, 854; and generally R. Bifulco, *La cooperazione nello Stato unitario composto. Le relazioni intergovernative di Belgio, Italia, Repubblica federale di Germania e Spagna nell'Unione Europea* (Cedam, 1995).

[19] Wheare, *Federal Government* (n.13) 11, who adds that 'What is necessary for the federal principle is not merely that the general government, like the regional governments, should operate directly upon the people, but, further, that each government should be limited to its own sphere and, within that sphere, should be independent of the other' (ibid., 15).

[20] M.J.C. Vile, *The Structure of American Federalism* (Oxford University Press, 1961), 197, who wrote that federalism is a system of government in which neither level of government is wholly dependent upon the other, nor wholly independent of the other. There is, in fact, a mutual interdependence which allows each of them to act independently in some circumstances, but which means that where the vital interest of one level are involved in actions of the other, the former will be able to affect the decision taken, even though they concern matters formally outside its competence'.

[21] Wheare, *Federal Government* (n.13) 382; Corwin, *The Passing of Dual Federalism* (n.14), 20.

[22] On this point Wheare was already critical towards the federal government (n.13), 147.

ability to distinguish the individual responsibilities of each governmental level with respect to one determined policy.[23] The second change, also analysed in depth below, concerns the effect of 'deparliamentarization' caused by cooperative federalism. Political interdependence, specifically the need for coordination, here calls to the fore executive powers with the federal and state governments taking decisions that are subsequently 'imposed' on their respective legislative assemblies.

The concrete intergovernmental relations, the federal organization and the ideological orientations of the main political actors, especially the parties, all play a decisive role in the practical structuring of cooperative forms. This explains why in some federal systems, like the German one, cooperative federalism has become a pervasive model that characterizes the generality of all political relations between the Federation and the *Länder* (Politikverflechtung).[24] In contrast to the nineteenth-century federal state, in modern federal states there is an everlasting tension between a dual aspiration and the cooperative needs of the system.[25]

2 The 'Reasons' for Federalism and the Federal State

Let us briefly examine the causes and reasons behind the origin of federal phenomena, some of which are considered to be obsolete in today's world.[26]

The protection against 'external' threats, particularly of a military nature, or the need to preventively eliminate the possibility of an internal conflict, are often identified as the main reasons behind classic federal processes. The federal solution here offers the main alternative to an empire or a consolidation under a single government.[27] This applies in

---

[23] Among many, W.M. Chandler, 'Federalism and Political Parties', in Bakvis, Chandler (eds.), *Federalism and the Role of the State* (n.11), 157–158.

[24] See especially Scharpf, Reissert, Schnabel, *Politikverflechtung* (n.7).

[25] J.F. Zimmerman, 'National-State Relations: Cooperative Federalism in the Twentieth Century' (2001) *Publius: The Journal of Federalism* 29.

[26] H. Laski, 'The Obsolescence of Federalism (1939) 98 *New Republic* 367. The radical position of Laski does not find contemporary followers, as M. Bothe observes, 'Die Entwicklung des Föderalismus in den angelsächsischen Staaten (1982) 31 *Jahrbuch des öffentlichen Rechts* 163.

[27] See only Riker, *Federalism* (n.5), 12–13; I. Duchacek, *Comparative Federalism: The Territorial Dimension of Politics* (Holt, 1970), 199.

particular to 'classic' federal states. However, external pressure on its own cannot explain the federal *foedus* because, in other contexts, the path followed to resist external pressure was something different to federalism,[28] namely a unitary and centralized solution. And indeed external pressure was not the origin of all 'classic' federal states, as in the case of Australia, Germany and Austria.

A second cause can be sought in the 'democratic' factor. In fact, a federal organization entails a closer relationship between institutions and citizens, contributing at the same time to the increase of democracy (as well as pluralism and a limitation of power),[29] as well as a control of the rigidity of majority rule.[30] However, it is difficult to establish a secure one-way relationship between federalism and democracy.[31]

A third factor can be identified in the need for greater institutional and economic efficiency. This element is controversial, with some scholars highlighting the instability and inefficiency related to federal solutions;[32] and, which will in any case be more expensive.[33] At the same time, one must recall that many of the most economically advanced states have a federal organization; and a federal solution is often able to guarantee greater economic advantages because wider domains of action are open to economic actors, especially in large markets.[34]

Conflict management and resolution can be considered a fourth driving force behind federal processes. This force is especially (but not exclusively)

---

[28] In addition to the experience of the United Provinces of the Netherlands, born in 1579 with the Union of Utrecht, consider the early phases of some well-known federal processes: the United States from 1777 to 1787; Switzerland from 1815 to 1848; Germany from 1815 to 1867.

[29] Elazar, *Exploring Federalism* (n.2), 5, according to which 'federal principles are concerned with the combination of self-rule and shared rule'; Friedrich, *Trends of Federalism in Theory and Practice* (n.1), 260; Wheare, *Federal Government* (n.13), 382–383.

[30] H. Bakvis, 'Alternative Models of Governance: Federalism, Consociationalism, and Corporation', in H. Bakvis and W.M. Chandler (eds.), *Federalism and the Role of the State*, (University of Toronto Press, 1987), 279–280, which pulls together with federalism, in such anti-majoritarian function, also consociativism and corporatism.

[31] F. Neumann, *The Democratic and The Authoritarian State. Essays in Political and Legal Theory* (The Free Press, 1955), 227.

[32] It is the well-known (provocative) conclusion of the research carried out by Riker, *Federalism* (n.5), 145–155; similarly Burgess, 'Federalism as Political Ideology', cit., 112.

[33] Wheare, *Federal Government*, cit., 110–111.

[34] Duchacek, *Comparative Federalism* (n.27), 199.

strong in federalism-by-dissociation and in the creation of regional states, in which spatial, historical, economic, socio-cultural, political-cultural, and ethnic conflicts are particularly accentuated (think, for instance, of Belgium, India and Canada).[35] And in the most recent experiences, multiculturalism and/or multinationalism are at the origin of dissociative federal processes, as in the case of Spain or the United Kingdom.

From what has been observed, some quick conclusions can be drawn. First, a discontinuity in the causal factors behind federal processes can be observed: while the first factor (Riker's *military condition*) is at the origin of many classical federal states, the management of conflict resolution characterizes most recent historical experiences. (Of course, this last factor may well have also played a role in 'classic' federal states, but the resolution of internal conflicts, especially of a multicultural nature, has today become a driving force behind many federal processes). The asymmetry that characterizes more recent federal processes is yet another strong differentiating feature between older federalisms and contemporary federal states.

This leads to another interim conclusion: the most recent illustrations of federal processes prove how difficult it has become for a contemporary State to preserve its original unitary and centralized form. In all federal experiences, however, the relationship between the federal-constitution-State process remains paramount, even if its organizational forms are changing.

The formation of 'classic' federal states thereby coincided with the parallel rise of general institutions fundamental for constitutionalism, such as a constitutional division of competences, the right of the Member States to participate in the exercise of the main state functions through a representative assembly, and the presence of an arbiter impartial and independent of the federal government and the state governments.[36] Only the European federal process, perhaps, could explain whether this

---

[35] For the typologization of conflicts cf. R.-O. Schultze and T. Zinterer, 'Föderalismus und regionale Interessenkonflikte im Wandel: Fünf Fallbeispiele (2001) 32 *Politische Vierteljahresschrift* 254–255.

[36] Once again Wheare, *Federal Government* (n.13), 72.

relationship has been interrupted or in any case is no longer strictly necessary.[37]

These profound historical-cultural differences, which characterize 'classic' federal states when compared to more recent federal states, help to understand the diversity of institutional solutions. This diversity may explain (at least in part) the importance that associative federalisms have given to the participation of the Member States in the exercise of the federal will through second 'territorial' chambers and the current relevance of mechanisms of intergovernmental negotiation through the executive and/or administrative branch. In this perspective, the form of government plays a decisive role, since in federal states with a parliamentary form of government (Canada, Australia, Germany, India) the importance of intergovernmental conferences in managing inter-state relations is much greater than in federal states with a presidential system.[38]

Finally, it is necessary to underline the different role played by political parties in these different scenarios. Parties that are formed within a pre-existing federal context act and organize themselves very differently compared to parties that, having developed in unitary states, must then adapt themselves to the new federal context. In this regard, it should be noted that the most recent federal processes by dissociation are characterized by the presence of strong regional parties, probably originating from the disruptive effect that, on the one hand, produces proper mechanisms of cooperative federalism and, on the other, results from the absence of a second territorial chamber.[39]

3 The Characterizing Features of Federal States

Before examining the characterizing aspects of federal states, it is useful to reflect on the distinction between a federal state and a confederation.

---

[37] As many scholars state: I. Pernice and F.C. Mayer, 'De la constitution composée de l'Europe' (2000) *Revue Trimestrielle de droit Européen* 634; I. Pernice, 'Does Europe Need a Constitution? Achievements and Challenges After Lisbon', in A. Arnull, C. Barnard, M. Dougan and E. Spaventa (eds.), *A Constitutional Order of States? Essays in EU Law in Honour of Alan Dashwood* (Hart Publishing, 2011), 82.

[38] R.L. Watts, *Executive Federalism: A Comparative Analysis* (Institute of Intergovernmental Relations, Queen's University 1989), 4.

[39] R. Bifulco, *Partiti politici e autonomie territoriali*, in *Associazione italiana dei costituzionalisti*, Annuario 2008.

The distinction is not just a *locus classicus* in the study of federal systems; it has in fact been the subject of several more recent theoretical proposals. Yet even if theoretically sound, these new theories, as we will see below, do not help one understand federal experiences properly.

a The Distinction between Confederation and Federal State

Undoubtedly, a distinct process of formation is the most common feature in all 'classical' federal states. This common formation is represented by the pre-existence of sovereign legal entities (states, cantons, principalities, etc.) that conclude a pact of a constitutional nature and status, which gives rise to a new entity (Union, *Bund*, Federation, etc.).

Confederations present different structural traits, while sharing the same dynamic and procedural dimension as federal states. Normally, a confederation has few and limited powers with respect to the Member States; indeed, the powers of a confederation are typically under the control of the Member States. The confederation thus only holds powers expressly delegated by the unit members; and often, these members exercise a veto power over the decisions of the confederation with such decisions generally not directly addressing the citizens but rather the unit members themselves. Finally, since the unit members do not surrender their sovereign powers to the confederation, they are allowed to leave the confederation legally.[40]

As previously mentioned, in recent years this dichotomy between federal state and confederation has faced elegant criticism aimed at diluting the differential features of these two forms of State. However, this critical perspective does not fully convince. Is is indeed a victim of a methodology problem that concerns the different perspectives from which a federal experience can be analysed. The synchronic approach, which looks at the concrete structure of the organization and the federal process at a given historical moment, here tends to overemphasize the role of the federation with respect to the Member States; whereas, on the other hand, the diachronic approach looks at the historical and progressive development

---

[40] In this sense, Wheare, *Federal Government* (n.13), 35–36, 80; Duchacek, *Comparative Federalism* (n.27), 231.

of the federal experience, and thus favours the confederal 'residuals'.[41] Both perspectives are however indispensable for an understanding of individual federal experiences. The diachronic approach is fundamental in understanding the transition from dual to cooperative federalism; but the synchronic approach is just as important in order to understand how a federal organization works today or how it worked yesterday.

The unilateral use of either of these approaches leads to inevitable conceptual distortions. This will happen when the characteristics of the initial phase are extracted from a federal experience in which the Member States are still in a very 'strong' position *vis-à-vis* the federal state, and these characteristics are then represented as the characteristic features of each federal state.

Conflating the confederal phenomenon with the federal phenomenon is therefore a mistake. For the absorption of the confederal phenomenon within the federal model neglects the historical reasons that led to the creation of a confederal system and the shift towards the federal system. This is certainly true for those countries that had a confederal experience, like the United States, where the adoption of the 1787 Constitution was not an obvious and automatic choice; and the same is true for Switzerland, where the passage from the 1815 Confederation to the 1848 Constitution was marked by the 1847 war; and this is also the case for Germany, in which the 1871 Constitution was only adopted after a long and troubled confederal period that had started in 1815.

Classifying the confederation as a weak federal model also means neglecting the different nature of the constitutive acts at the basis of the two phenomena: an international act in the first case, a constitution in the second.[42] And there are profound differences in terms of effects on the constituent bodies and on the individuals that make up the constituent bodies of the two entities.

The conflation of federal state and confederation moreover obscures the role of the Member States within the federal states. Within confederations,

---

[41] O. Beaud, *Théorie de la Fédération* (PUF, 2007), who deals exclusively with federalisms in their constitutive, emerging phase (in part ibid., 96, 108, 275). However, in this direction, see also the earlier research by S. Ortino, *Introduzione al diritto costituzionale federativo* (Giappichelli, 1993), 36 and A. La Pergola, *Residui «contrattualistici» e struttura federale nell'ordinamento degli Stati Uniti* (Giuffrè, 1969).

[42] On this point, see: C. Durand, *Confédération d'états et état fédéral* (Rivière, 1955), 22.

the protagonists are still the Member States, whereas in federal states the main role is held by the central entity.[43] The federal state thus corresponds better to the current reality in which the Union (the central State) holds a decisive and preponderant role in the organization and functioning of the federal system.

b Structural Aspects

An examination of the structural elements does not allow us to identify a principle, an institution or a characteristic element capable of indicating the *principium individuationis* of the federal state with respect to similar state phenomena, such as the regional state. It is however equally true that, taken as a whole, the structural aspects that shape the constitutional organization of federal states nonetheless express different and often more intense levels of autonomy that in turn, represent actual differences between these separate federal experiences. For practical purposes, this justifies the distinction between federal and regional states.

aa Constitutional Review and Second Chambers

In light of the above, two elements of constitutional organization characterize a federal state: the Member States' participation in constitutional review and the existence of a second chamber representing the interests of the Member States.

The first institution is structured in such a way as to ensure the effective participation of the Member States in the constitutional review process. This special involvement in the review power here confirms the very close relationship between the classical federal state and constitutionalism: the constitutional pact represents a guarantee that the will of the member states will not be overlooked when a change in the original agreement is brought about.[44] This guarantee has worked so well that constitutional revisions in federal states may even occur in an extra-constitutional way.[45]

---

[43] Beaud, *Théorie de la fédération* (n.41), 108.

[44] Wheare, *Federal Government* (n.13), 57, 222; Duchacek, *Comparative Federalism* (n.27), 230–231.

[45] R.L. Watts, *Comparing Federal Systems*, 3rd ed. (McGill-Queen's University Press, 2008), 165.

The other institution characterizing classical federal states is the second chamber filled with representatives of the Member States.[46] Undoubtedly, the more a federal state distances itself from its initial phase, when confederal residuals are still strong, the more its second chamber (and its members) lose the ability to represent the States' interests. This applies regardless of the second chamber model within the individual federal state, as highlighted by the cases of the United States and the Federal Republic of Germany.[47]

This observation should however not lead one to believe that second chambers are not important in a broader federal logic since it is true that their presence is able to co-determine the concrete development of federal systems.

Firstly, the nature of a second chamber for the Member States affects the ways in which the interests of the states are represented at the federal level. In this regard, the well-known distinction between *intrastate* and *interstate federalism* should always be remembered.[48] In the case of *intrastate federalism*, state interests are *directly* represented in federal institutions (government and/or parliament); as for *interstate federalism*, state interests are only *indirectly* represented at the federal level, for example through intergovernmental negotiations carried out between executive powers (as in Canada, Spain and Italy). The 'classic' federal states tend to fall into the first category. (The theoretical proposal by Smiley and Watts is useful as it allows the observation that the presence of second chambers prevents institutional relations between the federation and the Member States from taking place exclusively via intergovernmental solutions).

The second chambers of federal states are usually heterogeneous in their composition and relatively symmetrical in terms of their powers when compared to first chambers (this is the well-known case of the United

---

[46] From different perspectives Wheare, *Federal Government* (n.13), 93, for whom the institution is not logically essential, even though essential for the proper functioning of a federal government and Elazar, *Exploring Federalism* (n.2), 183–184.

[47] On this point please refer to R. Dehousse, 'Il paradosso di Madison: riflessioni sul ruolo delle camere alte nei sistemi federali' (1989) *Le Regioni* 1365, who underlines a paradox linked to second federal chambers: the more powers they are attributed, the higher the likelihood of their escape from the influence of regional authorities.

[48] D.V. Smiley and E.L. Watts, *Intrastate Federalism in Canada* (University of Toronto Press, 1985).

States, Switzerland, Germany and Australia); and territorial interests tend to be represented through the chambers themselves.

The role of second chambers however changes according to the form of government chosen for the federal level. With regard to the legislative function, federal states characterized by a separation between government and parliament, as in the case of the United States and Switzerland, here feature second chambers that are substantially of equal strength when compared to first chambers. In these systems, the representation of state interests often struggles to be implemented through intergovernmental negotiations entrusted to executive powers.[49]

Yet in federal states originating from dissociation or in regional states, entities with the same characteristics are not easily identified.

bb Other Structural Aspects Characterizing Federal States

There are other elements that typically structure federal orders. However, unlike those previously examined, they are also found in federal systems created by dissociation or in regional states.

One such element is the vertical division of powers and, in particular, the division of legislative powers that is present in all federal constitutions.[50] In many 'classical' federal states, it takes the form of a mandatory list of Union competences, accompanied by the allocation of all the remaining powers to the Member States (residual clause). In others, such as Canada or India after 1935, the criterion consists in the double enumeration of competences; one in favour of the Union and one in favour of the States; and in yet other cases, the material enumeration only covers the competences of the Member States, with a residual clause in favour of the Union (as, above all, in the so-called Regional States).

The study of the allocation of competences confirms, once again, the usefulness of a syncretic method in the study of federal systems. The mere analysis of constitutional data, unrelated to the reality of political relations, would here not allow one to understand the innovations

---

[49] R. Bifulco, 'The Italian Model of State-Local Autonomies-Conferences (also) in the Light of Federal Experience', in J. Luther, P. Passaglia and R. Tarchi (eds.), *A World of Second Chambers: Handbook for Constitutional Studies on Bicameralism* (Giuffrè, 2006) 1045–1083.

[50] Wheare, *Federal Government* (n.13), 33, already excludes this as the essence of a federal state.

introduced by executive federalisms, such as those in Germany and
Austria (and partly, Switzerland) in which the effectiveness of intergovernmental relations has led to the following set-up: the Federation tends
to legislate, the Member States tend to enforce laws.[51]

The adoption of the residual clause in favour of the Member States here
did not prevent the progressive expansion of the Union's jurisdiction,[52]
partly because of the elastic and indeterminate nature of the allocation
criteria.[53] And a final role in the configuration of the allocation criteria is
of course assumed by the *supremacy clause*, which establishes the prevalence of the federal constitution and of federal laws in case of conflict
with the state laws. In the interpretation of the supremacy clause, a key
role is held by constitutional jurisdictions, which need to adapt the federal constitution to ever-changing demands.[54]

As for the other functions, the organization of the executive function
can have a significant impact on the concrete functioning of the federal
state. Consider, in particular, Germany, Austria and, partially, Switzerland,
India and Malaysia, where the executive function is mostly attributed to
the Member States. This particular division of the executive function –
defined, as was previously mentioned, as executive federalism – has
greatly encouraged the development of cooperative solutions.

In federal states, with Austria as an important exception, the judicial
function is also vertically distributed between the Union and the Member
States. This characteristic is however not a feature of regional states, such
as Italy and Spain.

In many 'classical' federal states, the Member States have the power
to form a constitution. This power finds its explanation in the formation

---

[51] On this point, please refer to the analysis made by Watts, *Executive Federalism: A Comparative Analysis* (n.38).

[52] C.J. Friedrich, *Constitutional Government and Democracy: Theory and Practice in Europe and America*, 4th ed. (Blaisdell Publishing Company, 1968).

[53] The phenomenon is explained through different factors according to Duchacek, *Comparative Federalism* (n.27), 273, who indicates, among these, changes in time, the difficulty of 'quantifying' portions of political power and the explicit will of constitutional legislators to maintain general terms.

[54] Wheare, *Federal Government* (n.13), 352–353; Venkatrangaiya, *Competitive and Cooperative Trends in Federalism* (n.18), 14; Bothe, 'Die Entwicklung des Föderalismus in den angelsächsischen Staaten' (n.26), 167, which emphasizes the naturally conservative tendency of constitutional jurisdictions (with the exception of the Warren Presidency at the US Supreme Court).

of classical federal states, generally of an associative nature. Since the constitutive entities existed before the federal state, they retained their constitutions even after voluntarily concluding a federal pact.

This constitutional autonomy has nevertheless limitations. Generally speaking, a federal constitution will often require the constitutions of the Member States to comply with certain principles adopted by the federal constitution. This is the reason why there is substantial homogeneity between federal constitutions and the constitutions of the Member States. This constitutional homogeneity may be expressly required by the federal constitution; or, it can instead be established in the course of the federal process initiated by a federal pact.[55] In any case, homogeneity is essential for the preservation of the federal pact, which could not sustain the presence of entities governed by extremely different or even conflicting constitutional principles.[56]

Having said that, constitutional autonomy does not appear to be a distinguishing feature of classic federal states, because either this characteristic is not present (with equal intensity) in all federal states, or because the constitutive bodies of the regional states also enjoy a statutory autonomy that may even be higher than the constitutional autonomy of the Member States within a federal state. Consider for example the five Italian regions granted special autonomy and the statutory powers of the autonomous Spanish Communities.

Federal States are also often characterized by the so-called *existence guarantee* that is aimed at protecting the federal structure of the State. Normally this guarantee is considered as an implicit limitation on constitutional review, even though, in the German constitutional order, it is expressly foreseen by Article 79(3) GC. According to some scholars, the guarantee of the states' existence should thereby be understood with reference not only to the federal principle, but also to each individual constituent entity (State, *Land*, Canton, Province).[57]

---

[55] It is interesting to note that Beaud, *Théorie de la fédération* (n.41), 330 ss, takes into account the German Confederation born in 1815 as an example of a federation in which Member States coexisted, some characterized by monarchical orders, others (the free cities) by a republican form of government. The chosen example only confirms the usefulness of keeping a distinction between federal state and confederation.

[56] In a partially different sense, see Friedrich, *Constitutional Government and Democracy* (n.52), 194, according to whom constitutional uniformity or homogeneity is not a necessary component of a federation.

[57] In this light Beaud, *Théorie de la fédération* (n.41), cit., 325–328.

The right of secession of the Member States is much discussed and a controversial question within federal states. While according to some scholars it is not an antithesis to the federal state; according to others, a right to secession is incompatible with the very nature of the federal phenomenon.[58] An evaluation aimed at bringing together a structural approach (which underlines the presence of clauses formally allowing the right of secession) and a procedural approach (which highlights that the looser the federal community is, the easier the withdrawal)[59] makes it possible to state that consolidated federal states do not allow, as a matter of fact, the withdrawal of the Member States.[60]

The concrete autonomy of the Member States is ultimately determined by the so-called *financial constitution*, which is that part of the federal constitution that regulates the financial relations between governmental levels. If it is true that financial discipline is useful to give an actual content to the autonomy of the Member States, it is equally true that it cannot be considered among the characteristic features of classical federal states. It is indeed easy to see that in some of these states, financial discipline is deficient or generic or contradicted by reality and that, at the same time, even in regional states, constitutions are aimed at guaranteeing regional financial autonomy. Usually, the financial dominance enjoyed by central governments promotes the unitary drive that characterizes all federal states, especially in the period following the initial phase of the federal process.[61]

A final aspect that characterizes classic federal states is the so-called *federalization of the constitutional bodies*, which indicates that the Member States should contribute to their formation. However, it should be noted that, apart from the existence of monocratic bodies legitimized by the population of the entire nation (as in the case of the US President), the federalization of constitutional bodies is not only variably modulated, but often only formal (think about the different role of the Member States in the formation of constitutional bodies in the United States and in Germany). It should, however, be added that compensation for the loss

---

[58] As for this first interpretation, please see Wheare, *Federal Government* (n.13), 91, as for the second Duchacek, *Comparative Federalism* (n.27), 217.

[59] Same goes for Friedrich, *Man and his Government* (McGraw-Hill, 1963), 605.

[60] Watts, *Comparing Federal Systems* (n.45), cit., 170.

[61] Wheare, *Federal Government* (n.13), 381; Bothe, 'Die Entwicklung des Föderalismus in den angelsächsischen Staaten' (n.26), 165–166.

of importance of second chambers can be sought precisely in the federalization of the executive branch, as in Switzerland, Canada, Australia (and the European Union), where the composition of the federal executive often reflects the federal character of the State.[62]

Conclusion: The Usefulness of a Syncretic Approach

The analysis of the various elements of federal states has shown the differences between 'classic' federal states, the more recently formed federal states (generally created by dissociation from previous unitary state entities) and regional states. Can these three different types be placed under the same federal umbrella?

The differences between 'classic' federal states and federal states by dissociation and regional states are many and concern aspects that are either purely historical-social or relate to constitutional organization. The main differences lie in the formation process; however, this genetic difference does not necessarily affect the federal process as such. The case of Belgium exemplifies the process of dissociation from a unitary, centralized state to a federal one. It clearly shows how a federal solution, while responding to very different causal factors, compared to federalism by association, is still oriented towards a common goal. Similar processes, though less accentuated, can be found in the so-called regional states (Spain, but also Italy).

In both cases, the federal process is able to produce or maintain unity. This indeed seems to be the essence of federalism and the federal state: the creation or conservation of a degree of unity among individuals, groups or political communities.[63] This perspective also seems to justify the joint analysis of the experiences of 'classic' federal states, federal states formed through dissociative processes and of regional states.

But while the aforementioned processual perspective greatly contributes to the study and understanding of federal phenomena, it must nevertheless

---

[62] On this point, Dehousse, 'Il paradosso di Madison: riflessioni sul ruolo delle camere alte nei sistemi federali' (n.47), 1374.

[63] Elazar, *Exploring Federalism* (n.2), 109: 'The essence of federalism should not be sought in a particular set of institutions, rather in the institutionalization of particular relationships between political life actors. Consequently, federalism is a phenomenon that provides many options for the organization of authority and political power'.

be combined with a structural perspective, that is to say a perspective focused on the juridical and organizational structure of the federal phenomenon. Only this view, albeit more static, makes it possible to better understand the differences within federal processes that may be linked to the historical phase that the process itself undergoes or to the different constitutional configurations that the process itself takes on.

Further Reading

O. Beaud, *Théorie de la fédération* (Presses Universitaires de France, 2007).

I.D. Duchacek, *Comparative Federalism: The Territorial Dimension of Politics* (Holt, 1970).

C. Durand, *Confédération d'états et état fédéral* (Rivière, 1955).

D.J. Elazar, *Exploring Federalism* (The University of Alabama Press, 1987).

C.J. Friedrich, *Trends of Federalism in Theory and Practice* (Pall Mall Press, 1968).

T.O. Hueglin and A. Fenna, *Comparative Federalism: A Systematic Inquiry* (University of Toronto Press, 2015).

L. Le Fur, *État fédéral et confédération d'états* (Marchal et Billard, 1896).

S. Ortino, *Introduzione al diritto costituzionale federativo* (Giappichelli, 1993).

W.H. Riker, *Federalism: Origin, Operation, Significance* (Little, 1964).

C. Schmitt, *Verfassungslehre* (1928) (Duncker & Humblot, 1993).

R.L. Watts, *Comparing Federal Systems*, 3rd ed. (McGill-Queen's University Press, 2008).

K.C. Wheare, *Federal Government* (Oxford University Press, 1951).

Part IV

State Institutions

Parliaments 13

Nicola Lupo

Introduction

In a modern sense, parliaments and constitutions are born together as two essential elements of the liberal state. Both of course had their own ancestors – in royal advisory assemblies and in legal documents binding the monarch in some way, respectively – but both reached maturity together, mutually presupposing and reinforcing each other. No (modern) constitution could be recognized as such had it not provided for a representative assembly, elected by all the citizens at that time entitled to political rights. Reciprocally, no (modern) parliament could define itself as a political representative assembly without one or more fundamental charters designing its main structural and functional features, attributing to it some prerogatives, and protecting the main political rights of the

citizens, such as freedom of speech, of the press and of meeting and association, in addition, of course, to the right to vote.

The times and the evolutionary paths through which this maturity was
reached by parliaments and constitutions vary according to the geographical area taken into consideration. In England, as is well known,
the evolution started earlier and has progressed (relatively) smoothly
since the Middle Ages, without the adoption of a codified constitution, but ensuring the clear recognition of the role of the representative assembly even during the eighteenth century. In North America,
instead, both the US Constitution and a representative Congress were
conceived and implemented as instruments for achieving simultaneously
both liberal-democratic government and independence. In continental
Europe, this process was even more traumatic: liberal constitutions and
representative parliaments were obtained as necessary outcomes of
revolutionary events, which took place at the end of eighteenth century
within the nation-states and in polemics against the formerly predominant absolute State.

The first two sections of this chapter seek to depict the main structural and functional features of parliaments, as deriving from this evolutionary path and as normally defined by each constitution. First, the main
structural features (unicameralism or bicameralism; standing committees;
parliamentary groups) will be analysed, then the functional ones (the
different classifications of the essential functions of parliaments that have
been proposed) will be looked at. Specific attention will be devoted to parliamentary rules of procedure, as they represent a very peculiar and atyp-
ical source of law to which some constitutions refer, and which are aimed
at ensuring the good functioning of any parliament. They are a bunch
of procedural and rational rules, sometimes 'codified' – among others
by Jeremy Bentham and Thomas Jefferson – during or just after the two
revolutions that took place in France and in North America at the end of
the eighteenth century, and then integrated and adapted, according to the
features of each parliament and institutional system. They are a way of
rationalizing and putting legal limitations and constraints on the political
process, when it takes place in parliament, and may be seen as part of the
joint origins of constitutions and parliaments.

In Section 3, the chapter analyses, instead, the moments when
parliamentarism and constitutionalism diverge. The first crisis of
parliaments and parliamentary democracy, particularly in continental

Europe, came about when parliaments were called to be elected by universal suffrage and to thus face the new demands of the working class. In other words, when liberal constitutions were asked to transform themselves into democratic constitutions, the transformation was not always smooth and successful and, especially in the cases of Italy, Germany, Greece, Spain and Portugal, it passed through the tragic experiences of totalitarian or authoritarian regimes (by definition devoid of any representative and freely elected parliament and a constitution in the modern sense). In the middle of this crisis, and in the wake of the rise of the Nazi regime in Germany, an intense debate on the role of parliamentarism took place between two famous legal scholars: Hans Kelsen and Carl Schmitt. During the twentieth century, it thus became clear that constitutional rights needed to be protected not only by the legislator, which in many cases had infringed and violated them on purpose, but also by constitutional courts. These courts tended to be seen – especially by legal constitutionalism theories – as enemies or rivals of parliaments, as they were the only institutions entitled by the legal order to strike down legislative acts; with courts enforcing the principles stated in the (rigid) constitution against the will of the parliamentary majority.

In the conclusion, the opposite reading of political constitutionalism will finally be recalled so as to ponder whether these theories are more consistent with the main trends emerging in the twenty-first century. In fact, it is argued that constitutional adjudication nowadays tends to become, at least on some occasions, a 'protector' of parliaments and parliamentary democracy, which has come to be seen as menaced by globalization, populism and direct democracy (empowered by the technological evolution). And because constitutional courts, in doing so, are also protecting themselves, this indeed might be a further demonstration of the persistence (or revival) of the genetic alliance between parliaments and constitutions.

1 The Structure of Parliaments

At least from an historical perspective, the existential connection between parliamentarism and constitutionalism helps to explain why, among the mandatory content of any constitution – often even of non-democratic constitutions, there are some constitutional provisions regarding the structural features and main functions of parliaments, while other and more specific elements are left to parliamentary procedures. The following paragraphs are devoted to addressing these provisions, without going into too much detail, but by trying to draw some guidelines from their historical evolution and to discuss the main categories used by scholars and constitutional documents.

a Unicameralism or Bicameralism?

A first constitutional choice regarding parliaments relates to their unicameral or bicameral configuration. A global overview of parliaments offers a clear predominance of unicameral parliaments, with almost 60 per cent of the total.[1]

It is true and rather obvious that the configuration of each parliament is the result of the specific history, context and parliamentary tradition of each country, but it seems incorrect to state that the choice between unicameralism or bicameralism is completely unrelated to the size of the population. The mere fact that China (population 1.3 billion) has a unicameral parliament, while the parliament of Saint Lucia (in the Commonwealth Caribbean: population 170,000) is bicameral does not prove much (also because the two countries are not exactly examples of solid democracies). But data within the European Union confirms the existence of a correlation between bicameralism and the size of a country: all the Member States of the European Union with over 11 million inhabitants have a bicameral parliament (and among those that are under this threshold, only Austria, Ireland and Slovenia are characterized by bicameralism). Similar results were registered, two decades ago, in respect of all Western democracies, and in which only Portugal stood out as the sole Western democracy with a unicameral system to exceed the threshold of ten million inhabitants (by less than one million).[2]

---

[1] Out of 193 parliaments, included in the Inter-parliamentary Union PARLIN database, only 78 are bicameral (http://archive.ipu.org/parline-e/ParliamentsStructure.asp?REGION=All&LANG=ENG, consulted on 10 December 2017).

[2] Cf. D. Shell, 'The History of Bicameralism', in N.D.J. Baldwin and D. Shell (eds.), *Second Chambers* (Frank Cass, 2001), 5–18.

Therefore, it can be affirmed that the bicameral parliament is 'the standard model in use by large democratic states'.[3] More precisely, the choice for bicameral over unicameral systems has been deemed to be correlated with four variables: federalism or devolutionary arrangements; a large population; size; and the presence of a stable democracy.[4]

Historically, the main reason for the establishment of upper chambers derived from the need to represent the upper classes, formed by the nobility and the clergy so as to preserve their power.[5] Yet once this reason was deemed no longer consistent with the democratic principle, the existence of two houses was subsequently reconnected to other founding values of constitutionalism, such as the separation of powers or the protection of minorities.[6] Both values are however often linked to territorial articulations (of powers and minorities) in order to be fully acceptable;[7] because in all the other cases, the argument – attributed to Sieyès[8] – has been made that if a second chamber disagrees from the first, it is mischievous, if it agrees it is superfluous; and attempts have therefore been made to either reform or suppress upper houses in the past.[9]

---

[3] M. Russell, *Reforming the House of Lords: Lessons from Overseas* (Oxford University Press, 2000), 22.

[4] L. Massicotte, 'Legislative Unicameralism: A Global Survey and a Few Case Studies' (2001) 7 *The Journal of Legislative Studies*, 151–170, 152.

[5] On the bases of bicameralism see, among many, J. Uhr, 'Bicameralism', in R.A.W. Rhodes, S.A. Binder and B.A. Rothman (eds.), *The Oxford Handbook of Political Institutions* (Oxford University Press, 2008), 474 ff. See also G. Tsebelis and J. Money, *Bicameralism* (Cambridge University Press, 1997), esp. 35 ff; S.C. Patterson and A. Mughan, 'Senates and the Theory of Bicameralism', in S.C. Patterson and A. Mughan (eds.), *Senates: Bicameralism in the Contemporary World* (Ohio State University Press, 1999), 1 ff; and M. Russell, *Reforming the House of Lords: Lessons from Overseas* (note 3), 19 ff.

[6] See P. Popelier, 'Conclusion: Bicameralism in Multi-tiered Systems', in R. Albert, A. Baraggia and C. Fasone (eds.), *Constitutional Reform of National Legislatures* (Edward Elgar, 2019).

[7] On the connection between federalism, quasi-federalism and bicameralism see A. Gamper, 'Representing Regions, Challenging Bicameralism: An Introduction' (2018) 10 *Perspectives on Federalism* I.

[8] Indeed, the attribution to Sieyès is not confirmed: see N. Aroney, 'Four Reasons for an Upper House Representative Democracy, Public Deliberation, Legislative Outputs and Executive Accountability' (2008) 29 *Adelaide Law Review* 205–246, 213, and J. Waldron, 'Bicameralism and the Separation of Powers' (2012) 65 *Current Legal Problems* 31–57, 37.

[9] In the twentieth century a trend in favour of unicameralism is generally detected, although with some exceptions, especially around the end of the century: see J. Coakley, 'The Strange Revival of Bicameralism' (2014) 20 *The Journal of Legislative Studies* 542–572. On the difficulties of reforming upper houses see M. Russell and M. Sandford,

b Plenary and Committees

The public image of any parliament is represented by its plenary (also often called the 'floor'). It is there that parliaments seem to express all their potentiality, in terms of pluralism, rhetoric, transparency and democratic legitimacy. The existence of a plenary is therefore essential for a body to be called a parliament.

For example: due to a lack of a plenary in the Council of the European Union (formerly called, before the Treaty of Lisbon, the Council of Ministers), the latter cannot qualify as a parliament in the full sense. And although many scholars, pointing to the functional features, as defined by Articles 14 and 16 TEU, tend to argue in favour of its being an upper house, with the European Parliament as the lower one, its structure does not seem compatible with that of a parliament. Council members, as representatives of each Member State 'at ministerial level', meet only in one of its (currently, ten) different configurations and never convene in plenary. Moreover, according to the Treaty on European Union there is no freedom of mandate, as the Member States' representatives 'commit the government of the Member State in question and cast its vote' (Article 16 TEU). Furthermore, its concrete way of functioning, based on a series of specialized committees, coordinated by the Committee of Permanent Representatives (COREPER), looks rather distant from the high levels of political engagement, formality and transparency that generally characterize parliamentary procedures. If included in the group, and notwithstanding some recent progress, the Council would inevitably be considered 'the most secretive legislature west of Beijing'.[10]

However, moving again to more general terms, it has been remarked that 'both the strength and weakness of Parliament lie in the heterogeneity of its membership'.[11] This explains why there is a rather general agreement

'Why are Second Chambers so Difficult to Reform?' (2002) 8(3) *Journal of Legislative Studies* 79–89.

[10] In these terms, see the evidence of Simon Hix at the European Scrutiny Committee of the House of Commons, on 18 June 2008, question 41 (https://publications.parliament.uk/pa/cm200708/cmselect/cmeuleg/563/8061803.htm) (accessed on 6 April 2019).

[11] See J.A.G. Griffith, 'The Place of Parliament in the Legislative Process: Part I' (1951) 14 *Modern Law Review* 279–296, esp. 295.

on recognizing that the real influence or strength of a parliament is not dependant on its plenary, but rather on its committees. Therefore: when the level of heterogeneity is too high, and the members of a collegial body are too numerous, it is almost impossible for this body to exercise any decisional function and it is inevitably confined to symbolic and theatrical roles. Especially in the first half of the twentieth century, when parliaments were called upon to represent more pluralist societies and when party cleavages became more relevant, the powers given to parliamentary committees – themselves existing since 'the earliest time of which record[s] exist'[12] – have increased and there has been a wider awareness of their strategic function in determining the role of the parliament in the institutional system.

It is remarkable that in those years, and in very different parliamentary contexts, important figures such as Woodrow Wilson in the United States, Joseph Barthélemy in France, and Leopoldo Elia in Italy, all underlined the crucial role of committees in a parliament. The first stated that 'Congress in session is Congress on public exhibition, whilst Congress in its committee rooms is Congress at work' and showed that US Congressional Government required effectively working standing committees.[13] The second demonstrated that the existence of a system of standing parliamentary committees makes possible a 'methodical, organic, organized and effective oversight' over the executive,[14] and his lesson has been learned by the designers of France's Fifth Republican Constitution, which successfully managed to avoid the establishment of too powerful committees that would hurdle the daily initiative and activity of the government.[15] The third, finally, remarked that nineteenth century's parliaments were 'Parliaments in Plenary', while twentieth century's parliaments were 'Parliaments in Committees'.[16]

---

[12] In these terms, with reference to the House of Commons, I. Jennings, *Parliaments*, 2nd ed. (Cambridge University Press, 1957), 268 ff.

[13] W. Wilson, *Congressional Government: A Study in American Politics* (Riverside Press, 1885, reprinted 1956), 69.

[14] J. Barthélemy, *Essai sur le Travail Parlementaire et le Système des Commissions* (Librairie Delagrave, 1934), 58–59. On Barthélemy's role see F. Saulnier, *Joseph Barthélemy: 1874–1945. La crise du constitutionnalisme libéral sous la IIIe République* (LGDG, 2004), esp. 450 ff.

[15] See P. Türk, *Les commissions parlementaires permanentes et le renouveau du Parlement sous la Ve République* (Dalloz, 2005), esp. 35 ff.

[16] L. Elia, 'Le Commissioni parlamentari italiane nel procedimento legislativo', in (1961) *Archivio giuridico 'Filippo Serafini'*, 42.

The reasons for success of parliamentary committees are thereby many: among them, there is the ability of finding a kind of balance between political representation and technical and sectorial expertise and, most of all, the fact that within each committee negotiations can more easily take place. The latter reason has been specifically analysed by political scientists, who have demonstrated how committees make possible the deferral of 'reciprocal compensations', based on the intensity of preferences and a continuous decisional context permitting a flow of decisions.[17]

c Parliamentary Groups and Political Parties

Furthermore, as has been shown,[18] parliamentary committees are able to better exercise their functions when the simplification that they bring in terms of a reduction of heterogeneity is not too relevant. This means that their composition should rely on real, effective and stable divisions among MPs which happens when the plenary members can themselves be divided according to strong and clear cleavages that can themselves be mirrored, although on a smaller scale, within the committees.

This element helps to explain why parliamentary committees rose especially during the twentieth century, when parliamentary groups tended to appear on the scene, reflecting or in some cases even stimulating the existence of political parties.[19] For once the cleavages within a society tend to be clearly recognizable as ideological or teleological issues, it becomes easier to reproduce them within each parliamentary committee. If cleavages are strong and political groups properly organized, the decisions taken by each committee are more likely to correspond to those

---

[17] G. Sartori, 'Will Democracy Kill Democracy? Decision-Making by Majorities and by Committees' (1975) 10(2) *Government and Opposition* 131–158. For a comparative picture see J.D. Lees and M. Shaw (eds.), *Committees in Legislatures: A Comparative Analysis* (Duke University Press, 1979); D.M. Olson, *The Legislative Process: A Comparative Approach* (Harper, 1980), 269 ff.; L.D. Longley and R.H. Davidson (eds.), *The New Roles of Parliamentary Committees* (Frank Cass, 1998).

[18] See C. Fasone, *Sistemi di commissioni parlamentari e forme di governo* (Cedam, 2012), 94 ff.

[19] Especially in the UK, the setting-up of parliamentary groups normally anticipates that of (mass) political parties, see: *inter alia*, P. Norton, *Parliament in British Politics*, 2nd ed. (Palgrave, 2013), 20 ff. On the evolution of parliamentary committees in the UK see L. Thompson, *Making British Law: Committees in Action* (Palgrave, 2015), esp. 31 ff.

that the plenary would have come to, yet obviously with a significant reduction of time and transaction costs.

Indeed, the existence of parliamentary groups, often composed according to party affiliation, is a general organizational feature of every democratic parliament. Throughout the twentieth century, parliamentary groups have gradually increased their own functions, and have become the most recurrent way of simplifying the actual functioning of a rather numerous and differentiated body. So, for instance, in many plenary debates just one representative from each group is often allowed to speak; or time allotments are assigned according to groups and in proportion with their size (and sometimes also according to the level of interest on that topic). Even the possibility to submit or to vote on amendments tends to be restricted on the basis of groups. However, some (limited) time must of course also be left for those members of parliament who want to dissent from their group.

In some cases, this feature of contemporary parliaments has even led to identify the host institution with its main guests: that is, the political parties. Yet this reduction of parliaments to parties tends to underestimate the institutional resources of parliaments and the autonomy still recognized to each of its members.

2 The Functions of Parliaments in the Institutional System

The functions of each parliament are defined, more or less explicitly or specifically, in the respective constitution. Before examining these functions, a preliminary question should however be asked. One may indeed wonder whether it is possible to abstractly define the functions of parliaments; that is, whether it is possible to determine which functions a parliament should exercise in a democratic state.

a The Classifications of Parliamentary Functions

Those who have tried to answer this question in a positive way[20] have been obliged to rely on very vague features of a parliament. For example,

---

[20] Underlining the difficulties of giving a positive answer see M.L. Mezey, 'The Functions of Legislatures in the Third World', in G. Loewenberg, S.C. Patterson and M.E. Jewell (eds.), *Handbook of Legislative Research* (Harvard University Press, 1985), 733–772.

political scientists often speak of essentially two main functions of every parliament: representation and decision-making (with the latter being very differently understood).[21] Yet this very basic classification looks both incomplete and misleading. First, it is incomplete, because it is clear that parliaments are not only decision-making bodies and, wherever assessed exclusively on the basis of their decision-making function, they inevitably end up being losers, as less efficient and less performative, when compared to any other institution.[22] Second, the classification is also misleading, because representation, far from being a mere function of parliaments, is one of their essential features: representativeness is indeed one of those quintessential elements that define a parliament as such (at least in a democratic state). In other words, a parliament that is not representative cannot be defined as a parliament in a full sense.

This last insight leads to another point that needs to be clarified. Parliaments should pass a sort of 'representativeness test' in order to be qualified as such. In some cases, the result of this test can be controversial, like in the case of the German *Bundesrat*, the Council (of Ministers) of the European Union, or in the UK House of Lords. It is not by chance, however, that in all these cases the controversy relates to only one of the two (alleged) chambers of a bicameral system, while the other chamber's representativeness, as directly elected by the citizens, is deemed out of question. This means that the parliament as a whole is seen as representative, and that some different kinds of legitimation can be allowed but only for a part of it.

This dissatisfaction with the current classification of parliamentary functions probably explains why the pages of *The English Constitution* devoted to the 'functions of the House of Commons' by Walter Bagehot in 1867 are still very successful today. In this book he famously identified five functions that the House of Commons was called upon to

---

[21] For instance, see M. Cotta, D. Della Porta and L. Morlino, *Scienza Politica* (Il mulino, 2001), 331 ff; G. Pasquino and R. Pelizzo, *Parlamenti democratici* (Il mulino, 2006), 74 ff; S. Fabbrini, *Politica comparata* (Laterza, 2008), 108 ff.

[22] On the 'organizational puzzle' of legislatures see G. Loewenberg, *On Legislatures* (Paradigm, 2011), esp. 49 ff. On the disadvantages relating to size, and on the contradiction in assuming that they have 'independent minds' or act according to party directives, see B. Crick, *The Reform of Parliament*, 2nd ed. (Weidenfeld and Nicolson, 1970), 12 ff.

exercise: the elective function; the legislative function; the teaching function; the expressive function; and the informing function:

> That a House of Commons may work well it must perform, as we saw, five functions well: it must elect a ministry well, legislate well, teach the nation well, express the nation's will well, bring matters to the nation's attention well.[23]

Although specifically referring to the British Parliament of that time, and thus without any intention of designing a general theory, this classification nonetheless presents many advantages even to contemporary scholars. At least three advantages can be highlighted here. First, Bagehot did not start with the legislative function, which he considered less important than the elective function as well as the informative and teaching functions.[24] Second, he powerfully underlined the relationship with public opinion: parliament is seen not only as a part of the institutional setting of the State, but it has an essential relationship with the voters and the public opinion in general (considering its representativeness). Finally, he stressed the relations with the executive by proposing a very effective depiction of the parliamentary form of government, in which the parliament chooses but is at the same time directed by the government:

> Because the House of Commons has the power of dismissal in addition to the power of election, its relations to the Premier are incessant. They guide him and he leads them [...] A good horse likes to feel that it is under worthy guidance; and a great deliberative assembly likes to feel that it is under worthy guidance.[25]

b The Denomination Issue: A Distinction between Parliaments and Congresses?

Bagehot's classification of the functions of the House of Commons contains a very important methodological clue: the functions exercised by a parliament are necessarily linked to the form of government in which that parliament operates and to the way in which the power of political direction is distributed among constitutional bodies.[26]

---

[23] W. Bagehot, *The English Constitution* (Chapman and Hall, 1867), 195.
[24] See also W. Wilson, *Congressional Government: A Study in American Politics* (n.13), 333.
[25] W. Bagehot, *The English Constitution* (n.23), 164 ff.
[26] For this definition see C. Mortati, *Le forma di governo* (Cedam, 1973), 91 ff.

According to some scholars, this feature should even lead to the distinction between parliamentarism and presidentialism – or, more precisely, between parliamentary and presidential forms of government. This distinction differentiates between parliaments (in the strict sense: those operating in a system in which the executive is selected by the legislature and responsible to it throughout its tenure) and Congresses (those operating in a system in which the legislative and the executive are selected independently, and neither has the ability to dissolve or remove the other from office).[27] According to this scholarship, the word 'Legislature', as a body of persons having the power to legislate,[28] here offers the more comprehensive term that includes both parliaments and congresses.[29]

Two main criticisms may be raised against this classification. First, it is not always the case that the institutional reality and the denominations actually adopted by the different bodies are consistent with this reading, as that same scholarship itself concedes.[30] Second, by using 'legislature' as the most general term, there is an implicit but clear recognition of the legislative function as the most essential function of elective assemblies; yet this neglects Bagehot's lesson and, paradoxically, at a moment when even in the United States the attention tends to be focused on the non-legislative functions of Congress.[31] As has therefore been correctly

[27] See G. Pasquino and R. Pelizzo, *Parlamenti Democratici* (note 21), 73 ff. and A. Kreppel, 'Legislatures', in D. Caramani (ed.), *Comparative Politics*, 4th ed. (Oxford University Press, 2017), 118 ff.

[28] See the classical definition by M.L. Mezey, *Comparative Legislatures* (Duke University Press, 1979), 6 ff., as a 'predominantly elected body of people that acts collegially and that has at least the formal but necessarily the exclusive power to enact laws binding on all members of a specific geopolitical entity'. On the origins of this terminology see G. Loewenberg, *On Legislatures* (note 22), 19 ff.

[29] J.A.G. Griffith, 'The Place of Parliaments in the Legislative Process: Part I' (1951) 14 *Modern Law Review* 279–296, 290 ff. demonstrates the ambiguity of the terminology: 'when Parliament is called the Legislature [...] what is meant is that no body or person can issue an order, rule, regulation, scheme or enactment having the force of law without Parliamentary authority', but 'it does not follow that Parliament is responsible for the whole of the legislative process or that an enactment which Parliament has not specifically examined is invalid'. In other words, if to legislate means 'to carry through the whole legislative process', then 'legislation today is more a Governmental than a Parliamentary function'.

[30] See A. Kreppel, 'Understanding the European Parliament from a Federalist Perspective: The Legislatures of the United States and European Union Compared', in A. Menon and M. Schain (eds.), *Comparative Federalism: The European Union and the United States in Comparative Perspective* (Oxford University Press, 2006), 245–274.

[31] See J. Chafetz, *Congress's Constitution: Legislative Authority and the Separation of Powers* (Yale University Press, 2017).

remarked, the use of the name 'legislature' can be misleading as 'for a large part of the time of these bodies is not devoted to law-making at all'.[32]

For these reasons, it looks preferable to stick to the more common and traditional terminology of parliaments. At the same time, the official denomination matters of course when determined by each constitution or when adopted by each elective assembly. For an example of the first kind, one can cite the case-law of the Italian Constitutional Court, which denied to the Regional Assemblies the possibility to call themselves parliaments, as the word 'parliament' is uniquely reserved by the Italian Constitution to bodies that express a national political representation. For an example of the second kind, it is easy to recall the European Parliament, which decided to give itself this name in 1962, notwithstanding the fact that the EU Treaties originally qualified it as an 'Assembly', as is the case with many international organizations.[33]

This nominalist issue becomes even trickier when it relates to international treaties, which often present a higher degree of ambiguity. This is shown, for instance, by the European Convention on Human Rights, whose Article 3 of its Protocol No. 1 protects the right to freely elect a 'legislature' ('corps législatif', according to the French version);[34] or else, in the EU legal order, in which Protocol No. 2 on the Early Warning System refers to 'Regional Parliaments with legislative Powers' – ignoring the above-mentioned *dictum* of the Italian Constitutional Court.[35]

---

[32] See K.C. Wheare, *Legislatures* (Oxford University Press, 1968), 1. See also G. Loewenberg and S.C. Patterson, *Comparing Legislatures* (University Press of America, 1979), 49 (noting that 'law-making is not unique to legislatures' and that 'law-making is not the only activity in which legislatures engage'). However, often parliaments tend to self-represent themselves mainly as lawmakers: see C. Leston-Bandeira, 'Parliamentary Functions Portrayed on European Parliaments' Websites' (2009) *Revista de Sociologia e Política* 13–27.

[33] For the first example, see judgment no. 106/2002 of the Italian Constitutional Court. For the second example, see R. Corbett, F. Jacobs and D. Neville, *The European Parliament* (Harper, 2016), 8. The denomination of 'European Parliament' officially appeared in the Treaties since the Single European Act (1986).

[34] 'The High Contracting Parties undertake to hold free elections at reasonable intervals by secret ballot, under conditions which will ensure the free expression of the opinion of the people in the choice of the legislature.'

[35] See C. Fasone, 'Italian Regional Councils and the Positive Externalities of the Early Warning Mechanism for National Constitutional Law', in A. Jonsson Cornell and

When adopting a legal perspective, the functions of each parliament are compulsorily determined by the respective constitution, and each parliament is constitutionally obliged to exercise them. The constitution includes, of course, the constitutional text which always devotes specific attention to parliamentary functions.[36] However, other legal provisions are also relevant. These provisions can sometimes be derived from a different legal order (for EU Member States the clearest example is Article 12 TEU, which entitles each national parliament to a series of 'European powers');[37] or, they are embedded in parliamentary rules of procedure, especially when the latter are allowed to bring about tacit modifications to the constitution.[38] In some cases, parliamentary functions are even laid down in non-written norms, which often fill the many gaps within parliaments' written norms.

For all these reasons, a comparative analysis of parliaments is never an easy job and requires multiple scholarly approaches: legal, political and historical, at least, as well as a constant contact with those who work in parliaments and who have direct experience with the political culture that every parliament, every chamber and often every committee creates.

c Parliamentary Rules of Procedure: Rational Principles in Politics

Constitutions contain the main legal provisions regarding parliaments. However, these provisions are far from self-sufficient. The daily activity

---

M. Goldoni (eds.), *National and Regional Parliaments in the EU-Legislative Procedure post-Lisbon: The Impact of the Early Warning Mechanism* (Hart Publishing, 2017), 155–179, 157.

[36] For a wide comparative analysis of the powers of legislatures, mainly based on a survey sent to country experts complemented with an analysis of national constitutions, see M.S. Fish and M. Kroenig, *The Handbook of National Legislatures: A Global Survey* (Cambridge University Press, 2009).

[37] N. Lupo, 'National Parliaments in the European Integration Process: Re-aligning Politics and Policies', in M. Cartabia, N. Lupo and A. Simoncini (eds.), *Democracy and Subsidiarity in the EU* (Il mulino, 2013), 107–132. Others prefer to speak of 'European functions': see M. Olivetti, 'Parlamenti nazionali nell'Unione europea', in *Digesto discipline pubblicistiche: Aggiornamento V* (Utet, 2012), 485.

[38] On silent constitutional change deriving from parliamentary rules of procedure see S. Tosi, *Modificazioni tacite della Costituzione attraverso il diritto parlamentare* (Giuffrè, 1959), 94 ff.

of every parliament is made up of many procedures that need to be regulated in detail; and the rules and principles of the so-called parliamentary law and practice are normally not placed within constitutions; and, when some of them are, it is mainly with the aim of limiting parliamentary autonomy.[39] Normally, it is thus for the plenary to adopt parliamentary rules of procedure, with the constitution only determining how these rules have to be approved and which matters are reserved to it.

It is not by chance that the first codifications of parliamentary law and practice appear soon after the French and the US revolutions and refer precisely to the experiences of the French Parliament and the US Congress. Indeed, the initial impetus for Jeremy Bentham's *Essay on Political Tactics* was the summoning of the French Estates Generals (États-Généraux) in 1789.[40] Given that this body – composed of over 1,100 delegates, half of whom represented the third estate – had not met for 175 years, it urgently needed rules for its activity; and it was precisely this deficiency that Bentham attempted to address.[41] Twelve years later, on the other shore of the Atlantic, and within a similar cultural environment,[42] Thomas Jefferson's *Manual of Parliamentary Practice for the Use of the Senate of the United States* derived from his experience as US Vice President (and therefore as a Speaker of the Senate), aimed at different finalities. Explicitly, his aim was to avoid giving an excessive discretionary power to the Speaker, so that 'he may neither leave himself

---

[39] A good example could be the parliaments of the German States in the nineteenth century (F. Wittreck, 'Parliamentary Law: The German Experience', in K.S. Ziegler, D. Baranger and A.W. Bradley (eds.), *Constitutionalism and the Role of Parliaments* (Hart Publishing, 2007), 55 ff., 60 ff.) and, even more clearly, the French Constitution of the Fifth Republic (1958, on which see E. Thiers, 'Ontologie du droit parlementaire', in O. Rozenberg and E. Thiers (eds.), *Traité d'études parlementaires* (Bruylant, 2018), 165–192, esp. 173).

[40] J. Bentham, *Essay on Political Tactics* (1791). The book was first printed in French and then translated into English only much later. On its story see C. Blamires, *The French Revolution and The Creation of Benthamism* (Palgrave, 2008), 194 ff. and P. Seaward, 'Parliamentary Law in the Eighteenth Century: From Commonplace to Treatise', in P. Evans (ed.), *Essays on the History of Parliamentary Procedure: In Honour of Thomas Erskine May* (Hart Publishing, 2017), 97–114, esp. 110.

[41] As it is well known, the first struggles within the États-Généraux, on the second day of its summoning, arose precisely on a procedural issue: whether to vote according to the estate or *per capita*.

[42] Indeed, Thomas Jefferson spent five crucial years in France (1784–1789): see A. Burstein and N. Isenberg, *Madison and Jefferson* (Random House, 2010), 108 ff.

free to indulge caprice or passion, nor open to the imputation of them'.[43] Implicitly, it was to move away from the prevailing practice put in place by his rival Adams (who preceded him as Speaker of the Senate and against whom he conducted two presidential campaigns).[44]

Both codifications shared a common point of reference: the parliamentary law and practice of the British Parliament, which was the first to be written down, although only in part (after the Glorious Revolution of 1688).[45] This commonality of the main source of inspiration explains also the fact that, although without quoting each other, in some parts Bentham's and Jefferson's rules of procedure tend to coincide, even literally.

British rules of procedure thus represented the main point of reference for Bentham's assistance to the new French States-Generals so as to work as a proper parliament by avoiding 'the inefficiency and inutility so justly imputed to all former assemblies of the Estates-General of France'.[46] He showed how the British rules of procedures were much better suited than those derived from the French tradition, which he inferred, with some difficulty, from some French provincial assemblies.

Jefferson, on the other hand, also reported and discussed the main precedents of the British Parliament, together with the rules applied by some States' legislatures. In this, he used as his main source John Hatsell's collection of precedents of the House of Commons and referred to them as points of reference to be employed by the US Senate.[47] Jefferson was trained in parliamentary law and, even when in charge as US Vice President, was still in close contact with his mentor, George Wythe, who

---

[43] See T. Jefferson, *A Manual of Parliamentary Practice Composed for the Use of the Senate of the United States* (1801) (Clark, Austin & Smith, 1856), v.

[44] On the lifelong relations between Jefferson and Adams see G.S. Wood, *Friends Divided: John Adams and Thomas Jefferson* (Penguin, 2017), esp. 279 ff. The rules for electing the US President and Vice president were changed after the controversial 1800–1801 election.

[45] See G. Philips, *Lex parlamentaria* (or, *A treatise of the law and custom of the Parliaments of England*), December (1689).

[46] J. Bentham, *Essay on Political Tactics* (n.40), 332 ff.

[47] J. Hatsell, 'Precedents of Proceedings in the House of Commons' which was published, in four volumes, between 1776 and 1796.

had been a clerk and a member of the Virginia House of Burgesses and later of the Constitutional Convention.[48]

Whereas Bentham's attention was focused mainly on the content of the procedural rules to be applied and on their philosophical foundations,[49] Jefferson gave less importance to these elements. In his view, the content of a rule did not matter much. Quoting Hatsell's book, he affirmed that '[w]hether these forms be in all cases the most rational or not, is really not of so great importance. It is much more material that there should be a rule to go by, than what the rule is; that there may be a uniformity of proceeding in business, not subject to the caprice of the Speaker, or captiousness of the members'.[50] Jefferson's Manual won the day and has been for a long time and, indeed, still is, for the US House of Representatives (more than for the US Senate itself), a 'book of authority', even if it constitutes today a subsidiary source.

A couple of conclusions can be derived from this experience and at a first glance they look contradictory. On the one hand, the founding milestones of parliamentary law were both constructed using a comparative approach, thus assuming, at least up to a certain degree, the transferability of parliamentary procedures from one parliament to another.[51] On the other hand, both Bentham and Jefferson highlighted the peculiarities of their institutional system and their parliamentary procedure. For instance, Bentham argued that the House of Commons was not corrupt or, as we would say, anarchical; because in its ordinary course, it was led

---

[48] See D. Patnode, *A History of Parliamentary Procedure*, 4th ed. (Infinity, 2006), 43 ff. Wythe is also known for being appointed (by Jefferson, in 1779) as the first law professor in the United States.

[49] See K. Palonen, 'Parliamentary Procedure as an Inventory of Disputes: A Comparison between Jeremy Bentham and Thomas Erskine May' (2012) 27 *Res Publica: Revista de Filosofía Política* 13 ff., esp. 15.

[50] *Jefferson's Manual* (n.43), 14.

[51] On transferability of parliamentary procedures and its limits see G. Loewenberg, *On Legislatures* (n.22), 56 ff., R. Ibrido, *L'interpretazione del diritto parlamentare. Politica e diritto nel 'processo' di risoluzione dei casi regolamentari* (FrancoAngeli, 2015), 383 ff., and O. Rozenberg, 'Comparer les parlements', in Y. Déloye and J.M. de Waele (eds.), *Politique Comparée* (Bruylant, 2018), 303–363. On the rather peculiar features of these rules see S. Bach, 'The Nature of Congressional Rules' (1989) 5 *Journal of Law and Politics* 725–757.

by ministers (something that, of course, could not be the situation with regard to the US Congress).

This cannot be the place for an in-depth analysis of parliamentary rules and principles. What can however be observed is that their aim is always to insert some elements of rationality into parliamentary activity. They contain a series of prescriptions directed at easing the creation of a democratic result in which the majority can prevail, but in which the minority can also feel that it had its chances for taking part in a (fair) process. Some of the basic rules codified in those documents still represent the essential core of any parliamentary procedure: the exclusion of written discourses; the need for every speaker to stand, in plenary, and to always address the President; the rule according to which amendments should be voted on; or, the role and functions of the Presiding Officer.[52]

Finally, it is almost superfluous to remark that both the French and American codifications of parliamentary rules were the result of the personal work of extraordinary figures, who achieved great results in their political and intellectual life (interestingly, in their lives, both founded important universities): in the first case, a renowned philosopher and founder of modern utilitarianism; in the second case, one of the American Founding Fathers and the principal author of the Declaration of Independence, who, after being the second Vice President, served for two mandates as the third US President (from 1801 to 1809).

3 The Crisis of Parliamentarism in the Twentieth Century

The crisis of parliaments and parliamentary democracy, particularly striking in continental Europe, came when these institutions were called to coexist with universal suffrage and the new demands of the working classes (to whom the Russian revolution offered a fascinating answer). Indeed, when liberal constitutions were asked to transform themselves into fully democratic constitutions, the process was not always smooth and successful and, especially in the cases of Italy, Germany, Greece, Spain and Portugal, it passed through

---

[52] On the latter, see the comparative analysis conducted by P. Laundy, *The Office of Speaker in the Parliaments of the Commonwealth* (Quiller Press, 1984), esp. 62 ff.; and, highlighting Bentham's legacy, A. Torre, *Il magistrato dell'assemblea: Saggio sui presidenti parlamentari* (Giappichelli, 2000), esp. 177 ff.

the tragic experiences of totalitarian or authoritarian regimes, by definition devoid of any representative and freely elected parliament.

a The Debate between Kelsen and Schmitt

In the middle of this crisis, and against the background of the rise of the Nazi regime, an intense debate on the role of parliamentarism took place in Germany between two major legal scholars and political thinkers of the twentieth century: Hans Kelsen and Carl Schmitt. Their different ideas on the role of parliaments derived from very different conceptions of the constitution, which most famously clashed over the question as to who should be the 'guardian of the constitution'.

Carl Schmitt did not recognize pluralism and argued that the parliamentary state needed 'complete homogeneity' of its people to exist.[53] In the nineteenth century the main function of parliamentarism had been to integrate 'the bourgeoisie – that is, a segment of the population characterised by the two traits of property and education – into the then existing monarchic state'. In the twentieth century this task of parliamentarism had been replaced by a much more challenging one: 'today the issue is to integrate the proletariat, a propertyless and uneducated mass, into a political unity'. Yet for Schmitt, neither the constitution nor the parliament could successfully assume this new task and both consequently appeared inadequate and 'artificial'.[54]

Hans Kelsen, by contrast, started from a full recognition of pluralism and a positive concept of parliamentary legislation. His 'pure theory of law' may indeed be seen as an attempt at keeping the law 'pure', that is: outside ideological struggles and social contrasts. Consistent with these premises, Kelsen thus attributed a central role to parliaments and parliamentary procedures: 'The aim of the entire parliamentary process is to achieve a compromise between opposing interests, to produce a resultant of the various conflicting social forces'. It is the parliamentary procedure that 'guarantees that the various interest of the groups represented in

---

[53] C. Schmitt, *Die geistesgeschichtliche Lage des heutigen Parlamentarismus* (1923), translated by E. Kennedy, *The Crisis of Parliamentary Democracy* (MIT Press, 1988), 1–50.

[54] C. Schmitt, *Der bürgerliche Rechtsstaat* (1928), translated by B. Cooper, in J. Jacobson and B. Schlink (eds.), *Weimar: A Jurisprudence of Crisis* (California University Press, 2002), 297–300.

parliament are given a voice'.[55] This led him to express his preference in favour of parliamentarism (defined as 'government by an organ democratically elected by the people based on universal, equal suffrage and the principle of majority'), and seen as 'the only realistic form of government capable of putting the democratic ideal into practice', and of proportional electoral systems generally, which would help the formation of strong parties and party coalitions.[56]

Of course, Kelsen was fully aware of the anti-parliamentary and anti-democratic tendencies dominating the twentieth century at that moment: the Russian revolution and Italian fascism had shown that party dictatorship was undermining democracy from both the Left and the Right. At the same time, he was conscious of the fictitious nature of political representation: parliament is a proxy for the people (although legally independent from it), yet the people can only express its will in and through parliament. That is why he advanced several proposals to reform and modernize parliamentarism, which indeed were adopted by some constitutions throughout the twentieth century. For instance: the introduction of referenda (both constitutional and 'on laws') as a way to soften parliamentarism; the reduction of parliamentary privileges; the promotion of specialized parliamentary committees as a response to the lack of technical qualifications of democratically elected parliaments; as well as the promotion of a stronger link between the representatives and their party, even to the extent that representatives must lose their mandate, if they no longer belong to the party that sent them to parliament.

b The Rise of Constitutional Adjudication

It is to this famous debate between Schmitt and Kelsen that some of the elements of the divergent paths between parliamentarism and constitutionalism can be traced. Because the constitution, and especially the fundamental rights and liberal values it aims to preserve, could no longer be sufficiently protected by parliaments alone. Parliaments were

---

[55] H. Kelsen, 'Vom Wesen und Wert der Demokratie (1920)', translated by B. Graf in N. Urbinati and C. Invernizzi Accetti (eds.), *The Essence and Value of Democracy* (Roman & Littlefield, 2013).

[56] H. Kelsen, *The Essence and Value of Democracy* (ibid.), 47–62.

'vulnerable' institutions, all without exceptions.[57] As history was beginning to show, parliamentary majorities could infringe and compress the rights and freedoms that liberal constitutions had called upon them to protect.

Once the Italian, the German and the Spanish Constitutions – just to quote the most significant cases in Europe – were deprived of their original function of guaranteeing civil and political liberties, due to the actions of parliamentary majorities, the protection of these liberties had to be found elsewhere. And following Kelsen's ideas, this new guarantee could only be found in rigid constitutions and in special constitutional courts, which would be called upon to enforce fundamental rights even against parliamentary legislation.

The concept of constitutional rigidity plays a crucial role in this regard. Between the alternatives of the French revolution, in which the constitution fully trusted the legislative power and assigned to it the task of protecting fundamental rights (through the *reserve de loi*), and the US Constitution, which instead aimed at constraining and limiting legislation approved by Congress ('Congress shall make no law' to quote the initial words of the First Amendment),[58] the latter alternative has prevailed. Following what the US Supreme Court affirmed in its famous judgment *Marbury* v. *Madison* of 1803, it nevertheless took more than a century for constitutional adjudication to affirm itself outside the United States: i.e., to entrust the courts with the task of ensuring the superiority of the Constitution over ordinary legislation. In Europe, important steps in this process took place in 1919–1920, in Czechoslovakia and Austria respectively, under Kelsen's influence, and then shortly after World War II, especially in Italy and in Germany.[59] It subsequently spread elsewhere in Western Europe and from there all over the world in the last decades,

[57] C. Malaparte, *Tecnica del colpo di Stato* (1931) (Adelphi, 2011), esp. 116.

[58] For a re-reading here, see J.H. Ely, *Democracy and Distrust* (Harvard University Press, 1980), 105 ff.

[59] See M. Cappelletti, *Judicial Review in the Contemporary World* (Bobbs-Merrill, 1971), 45 ff., M. De Visser, *Constitutional Review in Europe: A Comparative Analysis* (Hart Publishing, 2014), 53 ff. and M. Olivetti, 'La giustizia costituzionale in Austria (e in Cecoslovacchia)', in T. Groppi and M. Olivetti (eds.), *La giustizia costituzionale in Europa* (Giuffrè, 2003), 25 ff.

especially after the end of authoritarian regimes,[60] in which it became an essential element in their democratic transitions.[61]

As a result of this process, constitutionalism tends to rest today more on the shoulders of courts, and especially of constitutional courts, and less on those of parliaments. Judicial decisions are able to grant a fuller protection of fundamental rights. They are also able to provide a more accurate balancing of fundamental rights that is itself shaped by the features of the concrete case at stake.

Up to a certain extent, there is a kind of natural rivalry between parliaments and courts in protecting fundamental rights and values declared by the constitution. This rivalry is extremely intense in the United States, where the Supreme Court has played, and is continuing to play, a crucial role in shaping and adapting the constitutional norms and the principles that regulate many essential aspects of society; but it can also be seen wherever constitutional courts strike down parliamentary legislation deemed in violation of the constitution.

Constitutional courts tend to be seen as negative – and sometimes even positive[62] – legislators, and are therefore usually qualified as counter-majoritarian institutions.[63] In any case, they are seen as a way of constraining, and thus denying, parliamentary sovereignty,[64] and as a means for enforcing and protecting the fundamental rights granted by the constitution. As has been noted throughout the twentieth century,[65] fundamental rights and the principle of justice have increasingly

---

[60] See T. Ginsburg, *Judicial Review in New Democracies* (Cambridge University Press, 2003), 90 ff. and A. Barbera, *I parlamenti* (Laterza, 1999), 98 ff.

[61] See S. Issacharoff, *Fragile Democracies: Contested Power in the Era of Constitutional Courts* (Cambridge University Press, 2015), esp. 189 ff. On the different waves of the global spread of judicial review see D. Lustig and J.H.H. Weiler, 'Judicial Review in the Contemporary World: Retrospective and Prospective' (2018) 16 *International Journal of Constitutional Law* 315 ff.

[62] A.R. Brewer-Carías (ed.), *Constitutional Courts as Positive Legislators: A Comparative Law Study* (Cambridge University Press, 2011), esp. 31 ff.

[63] The definition is due to A.M. Bickel, *The Least Dangerous Branch: The Supreme Court at the Bar of Politics*, 2nd ed. (Yale University Press, 1962), 16 ff. On the subsequent debate see, among many, C. Pinelli, *Il dibattito sulla legittimazione della Corte Suprema*, in *Associazione italiana dei costituzionalisti, Annuario 2006. La circolazione dei modelli e delle tecniche di costituzionalità in Europa* (Jovene, 2010), 21 ff.

[64] See T. Ginsburg, *Judicial Review in New Democracies* (n.60), 2 ff.

[65] G. Zagrebelsky, *Il diritto mite* (Einaudi, 1992), esp. 57, 123 ff.

been detached from the legislator and found new homes in the rigid constitutions and in the courts entitled to ensure their respect.

These divergent paths between constitutionalism and parliamentarism have been theorized under the label of 'legal constitutionalism', according to which parliamentarism and parliamentary democracy are something completely different from, if not enemies of, constitutionalism.[66] The dominant reading by legal constitutionalist theories has depicted parliaments as the realms of majorities: majoritarian decision-making aggregates interests, while arranging trade-offs between them and 'encouraging compromises that may subordinate important issues of principle'.[67] This reading has thereby adopted 'a "mechanical" or "statistical" form of majoritarian democracy, where legislation needs only to be endorsed by a majority or plurality of voters to pass'.[68] And following that view, judicial review of legislation would be more effective, in the United States and elsewhere, in protecting fundamental rights and the values on which constitutionalism is based.

Conclusion

In stark contrast to the reading proposed by legal constitutionalism, so-called political constitutionalism argues that depoliticizing constitutional values in the manner of legal constitutionalism undermines the individual autonomy and self-rule protected by liberal constitutions. Instead, politics is called to perform the 'crucial function of reconciling differences through negotiation and debate';[69] and far from merely being the realm of majorities, parliamentary processes, more than court judgments, here allow all citizens to count equally.[70]

---

[66] Among others K.S. Ziegler, D. Baranger and A.W. Bradley, 'Constitutionalism and the Role of Parliaments', in K.S. Ziegler, D. Baranger and A.W. Bradley (eds.), *Constitutionalism and the Role of Parliaments* (note 39), 1, observing that 'constitutionalism and parliamentary government are often seen as potential adversaries or rivals, rather than as natural allies'.

[67] The reference is to the theories of R. Dworkin, *Freedom's Law: The Moral Reading of the American Constitution* (Oxford University Press, 1996), esp. 30 ff.

[68] Critically on Dworkin's theories, see R. Bellamy, *Political Constitutionalism: A Republican Defence of the Constitutionality of Democracy* (Cambridge University Press, 2007), 93 (from which the expressions are taken).

[69] Ibid., 102.

[70] Ibid., 175.

According to this view, the task of protecting fundamental rights is assigned first of all to the parliament, and then also to the other branches of government. Even with regard to US history, normally considered the classic example of legal constitutionalism, it has thus been noted that Congress has played a major role in the protection of individual rights and that 'the constitutional system is strengthened when members of Congress, Presidents, courts, academics, reporters, the media, and the public at large treat all three branches of government as legitimate parts of a political system that debates and decides the meaning of the Constitution'.[71]

Indeed, the evolution that took place in the first two decades of the twenty-first century seems to show that the idea of a rivalry between courts and parliaments is no longer so dominant. In some recent judgments, courts pertaining to three larger European countries have thus been acting as 'guardians of Parliaments' by exercising their function of constitutional adjudication in the name of ensuring the good functioning of representative democracy. The famous references here are first of all the case-law of the German *Bundesverfassungsgericht* on the European integration process, especially the judgment of June 2016 on the Outright Monetary Transactions (OMT) program;[72] then, to the judgments of the High Court of England and Wales in *Miller* v. *The Secretary of State on Exiting the European Union* (November 2016) and, on the subsequent appeal, of the UK Supreme Court (January 2017);[73]

---

[71] Cf. L. Fisher, *Congress: Protecting Individual Rights* (University Press of Kansas, 2016), chapter 1.

[72] See, BVerfG, Jan. 14, 2014, 2 BvR 2728/13, arguing *inter alia* that 'Public deliberation on arguments and counterarguments, public debate, and public discussions are essential elements of democratic parliamentarianism'. Among many, see M. Payandeh, 'The OMT Judgment of the German Federal Constitutional Court: Repositioning the Court within the European Constitutional Architecture' (2017) 13 *European Constitutional Law Review* 400–416.

[73] See, respectively, *R (Miller)* v. *Secretary of State for Exiting the European Union* [2016] EWHC 2768, [2017] 1 and *R (Miller)* v. *Secretary of State for Exiting the European Union* [2017] UKSC 5. The former judgment maintained that the 2015 Referendum Act needs 'to be interpreted in light of the basic constitutional principles of parliamentary sovereignty and representative parliamentary democracy which apply in the United Kingdom'. Among many, see M. Elliott, J. Williams and A.L. Young, 'The *Miller* Tale: An Introduction', in M. Elliott, J. Williams and A.L. Young (eds.), *The UK Constitution after Miller: Brexit and Beyond* (Hart Publishing, 2018), 1–38.

and, finally, one should mention the order of the Tribunale di Milano on the Italian constitutional referendum.[74]

These are judgments that came from very different courts and originated in specific issues and facts. They do not deal with the protection of the parliaments in themselves; nor do they safeguard their traditional prerogatives (such as immunities, regulatory, administrative or budgetary autonomy); they aim at protecting the reasons of parliamentary democracy generally, and especially the negotiation process and the dynamics between political parties, including opposition and parliamentary minorities.

It is too early to say whether this 'democratic' role of courts is just an occasional phenomenon or something more profound and stable. Several elements, however, suggest the latter. Representative democracy currently faces existential challenges in the form of globalization, populism and direct democracy – phenomena that could even endanger constitutionalism and courts too. Courts, in protecting parliaments, are thus also protecting themselves and their function of constitutional adjudication from the same risks. If all this is true, it might mean that the divergent paths of constitutionalism and parliamentarism may move, again, towards a possible convergence.

Further Reading

P. Avril and J. Gicquel, *Droit Parlementaire* (LGDJ, 2014).

N. Besly and T. Goldsmith (eds.), *How Parliament Works*, 8th ed. (Routledge, 2018).

R. Corbett, F. Jacobs and D. Neville, *The European Parliament* (Harper, 2016).

B. Crick, *The Reform of Parliament* (Weidenfeld and Nicolson, 1968).

---

[74] See, Tribunale di Milano, order 6 November 2016, no. 54353, highlighting that according to the logic of the Italian Constitution (Article 138) the political decision to revise the Constitution is attributed first to parliamentary representatives, as the fundamental choices of national community are reserved to the political representation, on which the people cannot intervene, except in the typical forms provided'. On it see G. Rivosecchi, 'La tutela del voto referendario. Note a margine del ricorso "Onida-Randazzo" al Tribunale civile di Milano', in *Osservatorio costituzionale*, 2017, no. 1 (available at: www.osservatorioaic.it/it/osservatorio/ultimi-contributi-pubblicati/guido-rivosecchi/la-tutela-del-voto-referendario-note-a-margine-del-ricorso-onida-randazzo-al-tribunale-civile-di-milano) (accessed on 6 April 2019) and G. Menegus, 'L'accesso al giudizio di costituzionalità in via incidentale alla luce della decisione sul ricorso "Onida-Randazzo"', in *Forumcostituzionale*, 2017, no. 1 (available at: www.forumcostituzionale.it/wordpress/wp-content/uploads/2016/12/menegus.pdf) (accessed on 6 April 2019).

W. Ismayr, *Der Deutsche Bundestag* (Springer, 2012).

P. Jan, *Les assemblées parlementaires françaises* (La Documentation Française, 2010).

I. Jennings, *Parliament* (Cambridge University Press, 1969).

G. Loewenberg, *On Legislatures: The Puzzle of Representation* (Paradigm, 2011).

A. Manzella, *Il parlamento* (Il mulino, 2003).

W. McKay and C.W. Johnson, *Parliament and Congress: Representation and Scrutiny in the Twenty-First Century* (Oxford University Press, 2010).

P. Norton, *Parliament in British Politics* (Palgrave Macmillan, 2013).

W.J. Oleszek, M.J. Oleszek, E.E. Rybicki and W.A. Heniff, *Congressional Procedures and the Policy Process* (CQ Press, 2016).

D. Olson, *The Legislative Process: A Comparative Approach* (Harper, 1980).

M. Russell, *The Contemporary House of Lords: Westminster Bicameralism Revived* (Oxford University Press, 2013).

K.C. Wheare, *Legislatures* (Oxford University Press, 1963).

Governments 14

Philipp Dann

Introduction

Governments can pose a threat to constitutional authority. As institutions, they pre-date constitutional regimes and are structurally least sympathetic to its limitations. Their sceptical predisposition towards constitutionalism has only grown in the twentieth and twenty-first century, when the rise of the bureaucratic state and internationalization coupled with government-led international law-making have only heightened the potential dominance of executive power. Functions and competences of governments are hence a central battlefield of constitutional calibration.

This chapter studies the principles of gubernative organization by focusing on the political leadership of the executive branch and on its institutional structures.[1] Using the lens of presidential and parliamentary systems, it contrasts two models of gubernative organization and their evolution by proceeding in four sections.

In Section 1, it observes that in theory presidential and parliamentary systems differ most starkly at the top. While the presidential system is based upon the idea of a government of one person, the President, in whom all executive power is vested, the parliamentary system is characterized by a plural government, composed of a prime minister or chancellor and ministers. Furthermore, while in the presidential system the executive is strictly separated from the legislature by rules of incompatibility, the government in the parliamentary system is regularly composed of the leading members of the majority party in parliament. Hence, where singularity and separation characterize the presidential concept of organizing the gubernative, plurality and fusion shape it in the parliamentary system.[2]

But where theory is clear, reality often is not. Current governments more often than not depart from the theoretical model and from their original design. In Section 2, the chapter examines the US–American system as a prototype of a presidential system, observing that it has witnessed a certain pluralization of the gubernative and today features several institutions surrounding the President. Likewise, the German gubernative, analysed as an example of a parliamentary system of cabinet government in Section 3, has seen a centralization, so that it is often called a 'Kanzlerdemokratie' (chancellor's democracy), implying a system in which the Chancellor has a marginalized Cabinet. Both models thus share a strong trend towards the institutionalization of governmental structures, often beyond the constitutional frame.

In Section 4, this chapter finally compares these distinct systems of gubernative organization with regard to two common functions, namely to

---

[1] The notion of the 'gubernative' is not very common, but captures more precisely than the notions of 'executive', 'government' or 'administration' what is meant here. The notion is based on the distinction between the politically responsible leadership of the executive branch (the gubernative) and the hierarchically subordinated administration or bureaucracy. Both together form the executive branch. Cf. C.O. Jones, The Presidency in a Separated System, 2nd ed. (Brookings, 2005), 73–74; generally A. von Bogdandy, Gubernative Rechtsetzung (Mohr Siebeck, 2000), 108–115.

[2] On these models of governmental systems, see G. Sartori, Comparative Constitutional Engineering, 2nd ed. (New York University Press, 1997); A. Lijphart, Patterns of Democracy, 2nd ed. (Yale University Press 2012).

provide leadership and to ensure the coherence and coordination of governmental policy. It contrasts the different starting points but also argues that a gradual convergence of both systems with regard to the increased institutionalization of the chief executive's office can be observed. This convergence is largely due to similar functions and similar context factors.[3] A similar context can be seen in the general developments in the political and constitutional systems worldwide that every government has to react to. Chief among those developments, so it is argued, are the growing complexity of societal structures and of governing more specifically, along with internationalization in the exercise of public authority and hence the need to cooperate much more widely with other states and actors. Finally, the last couple of years have also seen a polarization in the political spectrum of most states, which makes cooperation between the branches of government and especially the role of the gubernative trickier.

By studying gubernative organizations in a comparative perspective, this chapter hopes to shed light on a topic that is seldom considered by comparative constitutional lawyers (with the field being dominated by political scientists or comparative government scholars).[4] Constitutional lawyers often rather discuss the powers and not the institutional structures of gubernatives – mostly in domestic settings, and only sometimes in comparative ways.[5] Despite this neglect, the area is a particularly fruitful field for constitutional lawyers too, as it examines the conditions under which the implementation of governmental policies, and democratic

[3] On the convergence of parliamentary and presidential systems see also R. Albert, 'The Fusion of Presidentialism and Parliamentarism' (2009) 57 *The American Journal of Comparative Law* 531; J.A. Cheibub, Z. Elkins and T. Ginsburg, 'Beyond Presidentialism and Parliamentarism' (2014) 44 *British Journal of Political Science* 515.

[4] L. Helms, *Presidents, Prime Ministers and Chancellors: Executive Leadership in Western Democracies* (Palgrave Macmillan, 2005); T. Poguntke and P. Webb (eds.), *The Presidentialization of Politics: A Comparative Study of Modern Democracies* (Oxford University Press, 2005); R.A.W. Rhodes, J. Wanna and P. Weller, *Comparing Westminster* (Oxford University Press, 2011); W.G. Howell, 'Executives – The American Presidency', in S.A. Binder, R.A.W. Rhodes and B.A. Rockman (eds.), *The Oxford Handbook of Political Institutions* (Oxford University Press, 2008); J.A. Cheibub, *Presidentialism, Parliamentarism, and Democracy* (Cambridge University Press, 2006).

[5] For a comparative perspective, J. Martinez, 'Inherent Executive Power: A Comparative Perspective' (2006) 115 *Yale Law Journal* 2480; P. Craig and A. Tomkins (eds.), *The Executive and Public Law: Power and Accountability in Comparative Perspective* (Oxford University Press, 2005); T. Ginsburg, Z. Elkins and J. Cheibub, 'Still the Land of Presidentialism? Executives and the Latin American Constitution' in D. Nolte and A. Schilling-Vacaflor (eds.), *New Constitutionalism in Latin America: Promises and Practices*

choices can take place. Gubernative organization is thus also a mirror of general global developments.[6]

1 Two Models of Gubernative Organization

In the late eighteenth century, roughly at the same time, two models of organizing the gubernative emerged. But while the model of a presidential gubernative was intentionally drafted at the constitutional drawing table by the framers of the American Constitution,[7] the parliamentary model of cabinet government evolved only slowly, starting in the 1780s and continuing through the nineteenth century, most prominently in England.[8] Both models are concerned with the efficiency and accountability of government, and both advance different strategies to enhance these values.

a Unitary Government in the Presidential System – Alexander Hamilton

The basic idea and components of a presidential gubernative are best described in Alexander Hamilton's contributions to the *Federalist Papers*.[9]

(Routledge, 2016), 73–99. For domestic studies, see S. Dam, *Presidential Legislation in India: The Law and Practice of Ordinances* (Cambridge University Press, 2014); E.A. Posner and A. Vermeule, *The Executive Unbound: After the Madisonian Republic* (Oxford University Press, 2011); S.G. Calabresi and C.S. Yoo, *The Unitary Executive: Presidential Power from Washington to Bush* (Yale University Press, 2008).

[6] See for instance C. Möllers, *The Three Branches: A Comparative Model of Separation of Powers* (Oxford University Press, 2013); E. Carolan, *The New Separation of Powers: A Theory for the Modern State* (Oxford University Press, 2009); K.S. Ziegler, D. Baranger and A.W. Bradley, *Constitutionalism and the Role of Parliaments* (Hart Publishing, 2007). See also references in n. 3.

[7] On *Hamilton* and his concept of a single executive see R. Loss, 'Alexander Hamilton and the Modern Presidency' (1984) 14 *Presidential Studies Quarterly* 6–22; on the influence of the British example for the North American drafters see E. Fraenkel, *Das amerikanische Regierungssystem: Eine politologische Analyse*, 4th ed. (Westdt. Verlag, 1981), 244–251.

[8] The idea of an executive council is certainly older. But its specific combination with a parliamentary claim on the composition of this council emerged only in that time, see K. Löwenstein, British Cabinet Government (Oxford University Press, 1967) 77–99; K. von Beyme, *Parliamentary Democracy: Democratization, Destabilization, Reconsolidation* (Palgrave Macmillan, 2000), 415–516.

[9] J. Madison, A. Hamilton and J. Jay, *The Federalist Papers* (ed. I. Kramnick, Penguin Classics, 1987), No. 67–77 'Concerning the constitution of the president'.

To drum up support for the new constitution in 1787, Hamilton argued for a strong and powerful gubernative. The new constitution was intended to heal the major disadvantages of the former Articles of Confederation, especially their failure to establish an effective central government. The key notion to describe what he expected from such government was therefore energy. 'Energy in the executive is a leading character in the definition of good government ... A feeble executive implies a feeble execution of the government. A feeble execution is but another phrase for a bad execution.'[10] The salient prerequisite for an energetic government, according to Hamilton, is its unity. Other aspects, such as an adequate duration of its term, provisions for its support and even powers, range only second to this requirement of unity. Unity, and hence dispatch and leadership, will best be ensured by vesting the gubernative in one person. Energy and unity of the executive are achieved, however, not only through a single gubernative, but through a set of institutional and constitutional arrangements. One such arrangement, Hamilton argued, is the incompatibility between a seat in the legislature and a position in the executive branch. Incompatibility between offices in both branches is not only a 'guard against the danger of executive influence upon the legislative body',[11] it also separates two styles of decision-making. While the decision-making procedures in the legislature are based on differences in opinion and on deliberation, in the executive, by contrast, swift and unambiguous decision-making is preferable.[12]

Hamilton's presidential gubernative is counterbalanced in a system of separated powers.[13] The President as single executive is checked by a plural, deliberating and slow legislature[14] and by the judicial branch, headed by one Supreme Court, controlling the rules.[15] The executive post,

---

[10] *Federalist Papers* (n. 9), No. 70, 402. The need for a strong government is expressed in several of the *Federalist Papers*, cf. No. 1, 23 and 37.

[11] *Federalist Papers* (n. 9), No. 76, 431.

[12] *Federalist Papers* (n. 9), No. 70, 405.

[13] *Federalist Papers* (n. 9), No. 47–51.

[14] *Federalist Papers* (n. 9), No. 52–66.

[15] *Federalist Papers* (n. 9) No. 78–83.

however, is filled only by the chief executive, strictly separated from the other two branches, and without any need for consultation, deliberation or compromise. His task and duty is to act alone.[16]

b Cabinet Government in the Parliamentary System – Walter Bagehot

Although concerned with the same problems as Hamilton – efficiency and accountability – an entirely different concept of organizing the gubernative is presented by Walter Bagehot's concept of the parliamentary system. Analysing the English constitution of the mid-nineteenth century, Bagehot considered the 'efficient secret' of the parliamentary system to be the 'nearly complete fusion of executive and legislative powers'.[17] This fusion is institutionalized in the Cabinet, which serves as a link connecting both branches, or as Bagehot put it, as 'a hyphen which joins, a buckle which fastens the legislative part of the state to the executive part of the state'.[18] The Cabinet, as plural government, is thus the heart of the entire system. Bagehot describes it as 'a committee of the legislative body selected to be the executive body'. The legislature, he goes on, 'has many committees, but this is its greatest. It chooses for this, its main committee, the men in whom it has most confidence'.[19] The head of the Cabinet is the Prime Minister. With regard to the selection of cabinet members, the Prime Minister is only free to organize, not to choose them since he has to select his cabinet associates from the distinct circle of most honoured members of the legislature (the 'charmed circle'[20]).

Bagehot outlines the advantages of the parliamentary system in direct comparison with the American presidential system. Central to him are the enhanced opportunities in the parliamentary system to communicate and cooperate between the executive and legislative branches. In a

[16] Hamilton explains the need for a cabinet in the British system (as opposed to the American) with the fact that the British system would otherwise lack a legally responsible government, since 'the Crown can do no wrong'. The American chief executive would be legally responsible though by way of impeachment, thus a Cabinet was not needed.
[17] W. Bagehot and P. Smith (ed.), *The English Constitution* (Cambridge University Press, 2001), 9.
[18] Ibid., 14.
[19] Ibid., 11.
[20] Ibid., 12.

presidential, separated system, he argues, not only legislative power but also executive power is weakened.

Bagehot takes issue with the incompatibility rule and hence the relation between the executive and legislative branches. The arguments for a plural gubernative are less pronounced in his text, while other writers mainly present three arguments for the Cabinet as a plural gubernative.[21]

First of all, the existence of the Cabinet facilitates coordination and cooperation between the different ministries and executive agencies. Cabinet is the place where information between ministers can be directly exchanged and inter-ministerial coordination is organized. Secondly, the Cabinet contributes to the coherence of governmental policies. It is the place for exchange and debate among the ministers and locus of final decision-making in all major governmental affairs, where divergent interests can be balanced and departmental egoism can be checked. A single executive, by contrast, would have difficulties in controlling what is going on in the different executive institutions. Finally, and in contrast to Hamilton's assumption, the plurality in the gubernative is often seen as the best bulwark against the abuse of power. Different members in the gubernative, it is argued, would rather check each other's power than conspire to collectively abuse it.[22]

In sum, two different sets of arguments for two characteristically different systems have crystallized: one argument prizes the independence of a single chief executive to ensure his energy and dispatch and his sole and clear responsibility; the other cherishes the fusion of executive and legislature in the name of effective cooperation and the opportunity to communicate and coordinate within a plural gubernative, in which all relevant executive actors are represented.

How do these models translate into constitutional systems and their gubernative institutions? The following two sections describe the organization of the gubernative in two constitutional systems: the US American system based on the Constitution which Hamilton commented on, and the German system, based on the Constitution of 1949 (the *Grundgesetz*).[23]

---

[21] See I. Jennings, *Cabinet Government*, 3rd ed. (Cambridge University Press, 1969), 1, 232 with further references.

[22] K. Löwenstein, *Political Power and the Governmental Process*, 2nd ed. (University of Chicago Press, 1965), 167.

[23] An interesting point of comparison could also be the German *Kaiserreich*. There, problems with the coordination of executive departments under a one-man-executive

2 The Organization of the Gubernative in the American Presidential System

a The President in a System of Separated Powers

The American Constitution places the President at the centre of the executive branch of government.[24] Article II, § 1, cl. 1 determines that 'the executive power shall be vested in a President of the United States of America'. It is the President who carries the ultimate responsibility for the faithful execution of the laws; s/he is the Commander in Chief of Army and Navy and who has – with the advice and consent of the Senate – the power to make treaties and to appoint ambassadors and other public officials. This concentration of power is based on the President's exceptional political legitimacy. He is elected by the people, not by Congress. He is politically responsible only and directly to the electorate.[25] Yet, it is also a core value of the American governmental system that power is balanced and there therefore exists a division of political power between the branches of government so that each branch checks and balances the other.[26] For the President this means that he is not alone in charge of the executive.[27] In fact, the President's control of the administration is surprisingly weak and has been famously described as being the power of persuasion only.[28] Instead, Congress has extensive powers to shape and

---

played an important role. See E. Rosenthal, *Die Reichsregierung* (Fischer, 1911), 62–74; H. Goldschmidt, Das Reich und Preußen im Kampf um die Führung (Heymann, 1931); cf. S. Schöne, Von der Reichskanzlei zum Bundeskanzleramt (Duncker & Humblot, 1968), 18–28.

[24] On the original concept of presidency, see L. Lessig and C.R. Sunstein, 'The President and the Administration' (1994) 94 *Columbia Law Review* 14; for foreign perspective see H. Laski, *The American Presidency*, 1940 (Transaction, 1980). On alternative concepts in the Constitutional Convention, see G. Hoxie, 'The Cabinet in the American Presidency' (1984) 14 *Presidential Studies Quarterly* 209.

[25] The President is also legally responsible and can be impeached for 'Treason, Bribery and other high Crimes and Misdemeanors', Art. II, § 4. On the meaning of this instrument for the American system of government, see Fraenkel (n. 7) 244–251.

[26] For the classic explanation of this concept, see *Federalist Papers* (n. 9), No. 51, 318–322 (Madison).

[27] See extensively Jones (n. 1).

[28] R.E. Neustadt, *Presidential Power and the Modern Presidents: The Politics of Leadership from Roosevelt to Reagan* (Free Press, 1990), 33. The question of whether the Constitution establishes the President as the only head of the executive (concept of a unitary executive) or whether he has to share this position with Congress, has been a hotly debated question in recent years. See Bradley and Morrison, 'Presidential Power, Historical Practice, and Legal Constraint' (2013) 113 *Columbia Law Review* 1097.

control the administration through organizational, financial and substantial means.[29] Next to the executive departments, established by Congress but directly subordinate to the President, Congress also established a large number of independent executive agencies over which the President has hardly any direct influence.[30]

To cope with this disaggregated administration and to compete with Congress's influence, the President has to rely on institutional help for oversight and advice – this is where first the Cabinet and, since the 1920s, increasingly the White House administration come into play.[31]

b The President's Cabinet

The American Cabinet holds no formal powers. It is neither a forum for collective deliberations of governmental policies; nor is it a place where central decisions are taken. It is a merely an advisory body, while the power to take a decision rests solely with the President. An anecdote about President Lincoln is telling. He once asked his Cabinet for advice on a crucial political matter and met with opposition from the entire Cabinet. Lincoln got up and concluded: 'Seven nays, one aye – the ayes have it.'[32] The story strikingly underlines the difference in status between the President and the members of his Cabinet.

What is called the 'Cabinet' in the American context is not mentioned in the Constitution. Instead, it evolved as an advisory body to the President and never became a central decision-making or coordinating body. The President's Cabinet is a gathering of the heads of the executive departments and other senior advisors of the President, convened at his leisure and without any formal powers. Legally obscure, the Cabinet evolved from practical demand and was shaped by practice and each President's personal style.

---

[29] It is central for the reader from a parliamentary system to keep in mind that the basic argument for congressional control of the executive is not democracy (as it would be in the parliamentary German context), but separation of powers. The US is a system of dual legitimacy, with democratic legitimacy equally vested in President and Congress.

[30] See G. Lawson, *Federal Administrative Law*, 7th ed. (West Academic, 2015), 7–10; see also R. Steinberg, Politik und Verwaltungsorganisation (Nomos, 1979), 107.

[31] The Vice Presidency is another example for the need in the American system to support the chief executive. On the vice presidency generally, see T.E. Cronin and M.A. Genovese, *The Paradoxes of the American Presidency*, 5th ed. (Oxford University Press, 2017), 288.

[32] Hoxie (n. 24), 219; J.W. Davis, *The American Presidency*, 2nd ed. (Longman, 1987), 196.

The American Cabinet is not to be confused with its namesake in a parliamentary system. The differences are profound, both with respect to composition and function. Since the presidency of George Washington, Presidents have traditionally assembled the heads of the executive departments as well as the Vice President in the Cabinet.[33] The composition, however, is flexible. Different Presidents chose to extend the circle according to the weight they wanted to give certain personalities, offices or the Cabinet itself.[34] The President's power to include somebody into the Cabinet is not restricted.

At the same time, the president's power to appoint the heads of the executive departments or agencies is constrained by two provisions. Art. II, § 2, cl. 2 prescribes that the President has to 'seek advice and consent of the Senate' on his nominees, thus giving the Senate a veto power on presidential nominees. Practically, this is more a formality than a serious burden;[35] and legally it has seldom raised any problems with regard to cabinet officers.[36] Equally constrained are the removal powers of the President. In 1935, the Supreme Court qualified an earlier ruling and stated that the President could not at his pleasure remove from office a Federal Trade Commissioner before the end of his statutory term, when Congress had sought to deny such discretion to the President. Instead, the President's unqualified removal power was limited to 'purely executive officers'.[37] In other words, the removal power of the President does not depend on the formal status of the secretary, but more so on his function. As long as his office can be regarded as being 'purely executive', the President's removal power is unlimited. With officers who do have rather independent, or even quasi-legislative or quasi-judicial functions, his power of removal is curtailed.

---

[33] On the composition, see A.J. Bennett, *The American President's Cabinet* (Macmillan, 1996), 139–141.

[34] Davis (n. 32) 195, table 8.1; J.P. Pfiffner, *The Modern Presidency*, 6th ed. (Cengage Learning, 2010), 40.

[35] R.F. Fenno, *The President's Cabinet: An Analysis in the Period from Wilson to Eisenhower* (Harvard University Press, 2013), 54. During the thirty-two years from the Kennedy to the first Bush administration there were 148 appointments for cabinet officers and only one of them were not confirmed (cf. Bennett (n. 33), 121).

[36] See L.H. Tribe, *Constitutional Law*, 3rd ed. (Foundation Press, 2000), § 4–8.

[37] *Humphrey's Executor v. United States*, 295 US 602 (1935).

Another legal constraint is also characteristically different from the Cabinet in a parliamentary system: The constitution's incompatibility rule determines that members of Congress cannot hold an executive office and this changes the recruitment pool and recruitment process for cabinet members profoundly – as well as the character of the Cabinet. Cabinet members in the United States are not chosen from the group of leading parliamentarians or party politicians. They are individual and rather spontaneous choices of the President-elect.[38] Accordingly, they are not shaped by common political goals or battles, normally do not know each other before entering the Cabinet and hardly make up a coherent group of politicians.[39] Reflecting the openness of the American political system the knowledge of private professionals is often tapped into.[40]

The main functions of the Cabinet are twofold. The primary function is to advise the President and provide for direct communication between the President and the departmental heads. As the President has only limited powers to direct and control the departments, it is one of the main challenges for each incoming President to establish a hold on the standing bureaucracy. His appointment power for the department heads and his direct link to them is thus of central importance. The other function of the Cabinet as a college is rather symbolic but no less important. The President, surrounded by his Cabinet's members, is a familiar picture on TV and conveys the impression of a unified and proactive government with the President as its leader. This message is directed not only at the general public, but also at the cabinet members themselves. It reminds them of their common commitment to the President, and not only to their respective departments.

c White House Staff: The Presidential Branch

In the twentieth century, the Cabinet became overshadowed by a new institution: the White House administration. In fact, the growth of the

---

[38] Fenno (n. 35), 51–87.

[39] Often enough, Presidents do not know their appointees before they meet them for their 'job interview', J.W. Riddlesberger and J.D. King, 'Presidential Appointments to the Cabinet, Executive Office, and White House Staff' (1986) 16 *Presidential Studies Quarterly*, 695–6.

[40] With respect to the secretaries of the defence department, see S. Hess, *Organizing the Presidency*, 3rd ed. (Brookings, 2012), 193; as to the composition of the cabinets from Kennedy to Clinton see also Bennett (n. 33), 125.

White House administration has been a dramatic development, perceived by many as resulting in the establishment of a fourth branch of government. What has been baptised the 'presidential branch' is 'separate and apart from the executive branch',[41] which is no longer just the personal bureau of the chief executive, but has developed into a virtual parallel bureaucracy and a super-ministry overseeing all departments. The need for coordination and oversight of the executive branch has immensely contributed to the growth of the White House administration. Today, some two thousand people work for the President (five hundred thereof in the White House Office), administering a budget of more than $500 million dollars.[42]

The White House is marked today not only by its remarkable size, but also by its astonishing organizational complexity. All in all, the White House administration comprises some 125 offices of varying shape and importance.[43] They are assembled under the umbrella of the Executive Office of the President (EOP), but beyond that their organizational structure is hardly formalized. Instead, it can best be described as a solar system. Its 'sun' is the President to whom all units exclusively report. They encircle and influence the President with different degrees of proximity. Legally, there is no formal hierarchy between the units and hardly a clear delineation of substantial and exclusive responsibilities. All in all, the White House administration under the umbrella of the EOP has evolved into a super-ministry, which basically covers and oversees all areas of policy and politics. It is a parallel bureaucracy, next to the actual departments and agencies. It is easy to imagine that managing the complexity of the modern White House has become a major problem for any presidency.[44]

[41] N. Polsby, 'Some Landmarks in Modern Presidential-Congressional Relations', in A. King (ed.), *Both Ends of the Avenue* (AEI Press, 1983), 20. While the White House was only a small bureau throughout the nineteenth and early twentieth century, the 'modern' White House began emerging in the 1920s (see also J. Hart, *The Presidential Branch* (Pergamon, 1987)).

[42] P. Burke, 'The Institutional Presidency', in M. Nelson (ed.), *The Presidency and the Political System*, 11th ed. (CQ Press, 2018), 419.

[43] On the structures within the EOP, see J. Pfiffner, *The Modern Presidency*, 6th ed. (Cengage Learning, 2011), 109–114.

[44] One reason for this complexity lies in the power to establish the presidential branch, which can be exercised by act of Congress, by executive order of the President, or by a presidential submission of a reorganization plan to Congress. From a legal perspective the lack of any constitutional limit to Congress' authority to organize the White House and

Two models of dealing with this complexity have emerged and both revolve around a central figure in the White House administration below the President: the Chief of Staff.[45] One model, which has been described as a pyramid, is based on a strong Chief of Staff.[46] It is an attempt to run the White House, despite all complexity, in a structured and (rather) hierarchical way. The Chief of Staff is here entrusted by the President to manage the internal White House administration and to shield himself from managerial tasks.[47] The other model, metaphorically labelled as a circle, tries to avoid a dominant Chief of Staff and is built on the idea of direct access of (senior advisors) to the president.

Another factor adds to the complexity of the White House administration and contributes to its specific character: the staff. The White House has almost no permanent staff. Every new President brings along his own and completely new personnel. But there is more that distinguishes the White House staff from normal bureaucratic personnel. White House staff are rarely composed of former government officials or civil servants, they are mostly recruited from those people who campaign for and with the candidate and thus prove their strong commitment and loyalty even before the candidate is elected. As John Ehrlichman put it, there is only one qualification for working in the White House and that is the confidence of the President.[48]

The White House administration covers a wide range of tasks, but four main functions can be distinguished. The core units in the EOP perform, first of all, coordination and enforcement functions. They basically oversee the executive departments and agencies, coordinate the governmental policy and are supposed to make sure that narrower departmental perspectives do not prevail over the President's priorities. The Office of Management and Budget (OMB), the National Security Council and the Office of Policy Development mainly serve this function. Other units have

---

thus the heart of the executive branch is noteworthy. The idea of a core area of executive authority with regard to organizational aspects, which is well grounded in German constitutional law, does not exist in American law.

[45] C.E. Walcott, S.A. Warshaw and S.J. Wayne, 'The Chief of Staff' (2001) 31 *Presidential Studies Quarterly* 464 with further references.

[46] J.P. Pfiffner, *Strategic Presidency*, 2nd ed. (University Press of Kansas, 1996), 19–21.

[47] On famous and infamous chiefs of staff, see Pfiffner (n. 46), 21–22, 32.

[48] J. Ehrlichman, quoted in Pfiffner (n. 46) 18; also compare Hess (n. 40), 180–1.

primarily advisory functions: they provide information to the President and are, from their structure and staff number, not built to oversee departments and agencies. Thirdly, there are units which have primarily outreach and communication functions, such as the Office of Global Communications, Public Liaison or Press Secretary. These are mainly located in the White House Office itself. And finally, there are those units that serve mainly administrative functions.[49]

These functions, most importantly in the first two categories, demonstrate to what extent the growth of the White House staff has also affected the role of the Cabinet. Although originally planned as anonymous assistants to the President, the White House staff is today his primary advisor, partly even policy-maker on its own terms, and coordinator of policy affairs. On both accounts it is more important than the Cabinet.[50] The White House staff has indeed eclipsed the Cabinet.

This development had practical as well as structural reasons. Practically, it is the White House staff that organizes the presidential timetable, the information flow to him and thus functions as gatekeeper. White House staff also has the advantages of proximity and confidence based on loyalty. It is mostly composed of long-term acquaintances or devoted campaigners for the President. Cabinet members, by contrast, are often hardly acquainted with the President and torn between their loyalty to the presidential agenda and that of their departments.[51] As department heads they depend not only on the President, but also on money from Congress and are in the spotlight of relevant interest groups.

The increased importance of the presidential branch has also structural reasons, which have been mentioned before. Presidents have only very limited influence over departments and agencies. Their attempts to establish agency control are doomed if they only rely on direct communication between President and Cabinet members. Instead, it is now the task of several White House offices to coordinate and control departmental and agency policies. The relationship between White House staff and cabinet members is therefore often filled with distrust and frustration. The White

---

[49] E.g. the Executive Residence at the White House, or the Office of Administration.
[50] On relations between the Cabinet and White House, see A.S. Warshaw (n. 45), 228–233; J. Pfiffner, 'White House Staff versus Cabinet' (1986) 16 *Presidential Studies Quarterly* 666–690.
[51] Bennett (n. 33), 165–167.

House staff considers the cabinet members as 'natural enemies'.[52] Cabinet members, on the other hand, might question the expertise and legitimacy of the White House staff. Perceiving themselves as authorized by law and politically legitimized by Senate approval, they see the younger, short-term-oriented staff in the White House as only a half-serious partner of policy making.[53]

In sum, the White House is characterized by a curious volatility as an institution. There is a surprising disconnect between the organizational structures and a striking discontinuity of personnel. One could say that while the offices remain, the officers change. In effect, the White House turns out to be an institution without institutional memory, run on the principle of discontinuity. For the presidency, however, it has become the central institutional pillar.

3 The Organization of the Gubernative in the German Parliamentary System

The organization of the gubernative within the parliamentary system of Germany stands in clear contrast to the American system: the Chancellor is elected by parliament, the Federal government consists of both Chancellor and ministers, and there are no incompatibility rules that would prevent cabinet members from sitting in parliament. It is a system of cabinet government, the basic rationale of which Bagehot described. At the same time, however, the German governmental system has been characterized as a *Kanzlerdemokratie*, meaning a parliamentary system which is dominated by the Chancellor as a constitutionally resourceful and dominant leader of the Cabinet.[54] By constitutional design, the German system therefore strikes a balance between the need for gubernative coordination (through the Cabinet) and the need for gubernative leadership (in a strong Chancellor). The German system too, however has seen modifications.

---

[52] C.G. Dawes, quoted in H. Seidman, *Politics, Position, and Power: The Dynamics of Federal Organization*, 5th ed. (Oxford University Press, 1998), 72.

[53] Bennett (n. 33), 179–180.

[54] The notion was coined with respect to the first Chancellor of the Federal Republic, Konrad Adenauer, but is used today to describe a general characteristic of the system. Cf. G. Smith, 'The Resources of a German Chancellor, (1991) 14 *Western European Politics* 57.

The Chancellor's office, called the Federal Chancellery, plays a more dominant role today than was originally planned and the Cabinet has been undermined by the rise of informal procedures and institutions.

a The Chancellor and the Cabinet

In the German context, the Cabinet is the institution in which coordination takes place and coherence is established.[55] The Cabinet is the regular and central meeting place of all ministers and the Chancellor. All major topics have to be tabled and formally decided in its weekly sessions. Constitutionally (although not always in reality) the German Cabinet has the powers and the organizational and procedural structures to ensure that governmental actions and substantial matters are coordinated.

The characterization of the German system as *Kanzlerdemokratie* is based on assumptions both about the political skills of the Chancellor and on his or her constitutional powers. As Wilhelm Hennis put it: 'The powers of his office leave nothing to be desired. At the moment of his election his stallion is bridled and saddled; he only needs to be able to ride.'[56] Our question then is: what is the saddle made off?

The Chancellor's role is constitutionally designed along three central competences.[57] First, the Chancellor has the power to determine the general policy guidelines of the government (*Richtlinienkompetenz*). This is grounded in her superior democratic legitimacy, since she is the only member of the Cabinet who is directly elected by parliament, but it is ultimately based on her skills of political leadership. There are no formal procedures to issue political guidelines and no legal instruments to ensure compliance,[58] but there are also no legal limits on how to use this competence. The right to set the course thus places the Chancellor politically at the top of the Cabinet and gives her the constitutional basis to press

---

[55] See especially section 4(b) below.

[56] W. Hennis, 'Richtlinienkompetenz und Regierungstechnik', in *Regieren im modernen Staat* (Mohr Siebeck, 2000), 129 (my translation).

[57] For a basic description of the position of the German Chancellor in English, see K. Niclauß, 'The Federal Government: Variations of Chancellor Dominance', in L. Helms (ed.), *Institutions and Institutional Change in the Federal Republic of Germany* (Palgrave, 2000), 65–83; Smith (n. 54), 48–61. For a historical and comparative perspective on Prime Ministers in parliamentary systems (in German) see Beyme (n. 8), 438–456.

[58] G. Hermes, Art. 65, para. 27, in H. Dreier, *Grundgesetzkommentar*, Vol. 2, 3rd ed. (Mohr Siebeck, 2015).

in certain directions.[59] Although it is formally the Federal President who appoints the Cabinet, it is the Chancellor, who has the constitutional right to select and nominate them. The Chancellor's power of appointment is complemented by her right to dismiss her ministers. Here again, the Federal President only performs the formal part of the procedure as a kind of notary, whereas the material decision rests solely with the Chancellor.[60] In contrast to the American President, she faces no formal challenges to this power from the legislature.[61]

There are considerable *political* constraints, however, on whom the Chancellor can nominate.[62] In contrast to the American President, who is fairly free to appoint his cabinet secretaries, the German Chancellor has to select from the 'charmed circle', as Bagehot put it: the group of leading politicians from her party and party group. The Cabinet in the German parliamentary system is dependent for its existence and success on the support of parliament. The Chancellor therefore has to ensure this support by assembling the most respected and influential members of her party. The Chancellor's choice is restrained for yet another reason: Germany normally has coalition governments. It is an (unwritten) rule for the formation of these governments that every party within the government decides autonomously about its ministers and the Chancellor has no influence on the decisions of other parties.[63] Both constraints demonstrate that parliament and the parties forming the government are not out of the picture once the Chancellor is elected, but remain the basis of support and power.[64] The third element of the Chancellor's power is the competence to organize the scope and structure of the ministries. The Chancellor determines the overall structure of the Cabinet, the number of ministers

---

[59] W. Hennis (n. 56), 106–141; K. Stern, Staatsrecht der Bundesrepublik, Vol. 2 (Beck, 1980), 303.

[60] M. Oldiges, in M. Sachs, *Grundgesetz* (C.H. Beck, 2018), Art. 64, para. 19.

[61] See section 2 above.

[62] On German Cabinets from a sociological perspective, see U. Kempf, 'Die Regierungsmitglieder als soziale Gruppe', in U. Kempf and H.G. Merz (eds.), *Kanzler und Minister 1949–1998: Biblliografisches Lexikon der deutschen Bundesregierung* (Springer-Verlag, 2001), 7–35.

[63] K. Sontheimer, W. Bleek and A. Gawrich, *Grundzüge des politischen Systems Deutschlands*, 13th ed. (Piper, 2007), 312.

[64] H. Meyer, 'Das parlamentarische Regierungssystem des Grundgesetzes' (1975) 33 *Veröffentlichungen der Vereinigung der Staatsrechtslehrer* 86; Hermes (n. 58), Art. 64, para. 6.

and their respective fields of responsibility through special ordinances or executive orders.[65] Certain limits to this prerogative hardly abridge its width; the *Grundgesetz*, for example, prescribes the existence of some ministries (such as the Ministry of Defense, or the Ministry of Finance), but these are hardly disposable anyway. Parliament's power of the purse offers another means to control organizational arrangements, but even this is no real threat since under German constitutional law the executive prerogative and its organizational powers are considered to be shielded against parliamentary 'blackmail'.[66] Equally important is the fact that the Chancellor's organizational acts are not dependent on an approval by the legislature, but are based directly on the Constitution. Parliament cannot, even by statute, legally interfere.[67]

The competences at the Chancellor's disposal are consequently strong but the *Grundgesetz* equally determines that the Federal Government is a collective body. Article 62 states that only Chancellor and all ministers together form the government. Most importantly, the Cabinet has to discuss all matters that are of general political concern, be it in the realm of domestic or foreign policies. In particular: every draft of a statute (*Gesetz*), an executive order (*Rechtsverordnung*), a memorandum to the Upper House (*Bundesrat*) and every matter on which individual ministers could not agree has to be tabled in the Cabinet. Further, high-ranking appointments have to be discussed in Cabinet before a final decision is possible.[68]

The Cabinet not only discusses but also makes decisions about issues of major political importance; it has the power to issue executive orders, i.e. general rules binding private individuals or rules that primarily bind the administration; and finally, it can introduce bills in parliament (Art. 76(2)), which is of special importance since most bills are prepared in the

---

[65] G. Lehnguth and K. Vogelsang, 'Die Organisationserlasse des Bundeskanzlers seit Bestehen der Bundesrepublik im Lichte der politischen Entwicklung' (1998) 113 *Archiv des öffentlichen Rechts* 531.

[66] Hermes (n. 58), Art. 64, para. 20; G. Lehnguth, Die Organisationsgewalt des Bundeskanzlers und das parlamentarische Budgetrecht, (1985) Deutsche Verwaltungsblätter (DVBl.) 1359, 1362.

[67] V. Busse, Regierungsbildung aus organisatorischer Sicht: Tatsächliche und rechtliche Betrachtungen am Beispiel des Regierungswechsels 1998, (1999) 52 DÖV 313, 317, with further references.

[68] Hermes (n. 58), Art. 65, para. 33–34.

ministries. Considering these powers, the Cabinet is not just an advisory board for the Chancellor but a formidible decision-making body.

The actual decision-taking procedures in the Cabinet are thereby based on the cabinet principle, according to which important decisions are to be taken by vote of the Cabinet as a college.[69] One of the rare decisions of the Federal Constitutional Court concerning the organizational provisions deals with the decision-taking procedure in the Cabinet.[70] In that decision, the Court held that every such decision has to be made in a procedure which ensures that: (a) every member of the Cabinet was informed about the upcoming decision; (b) a certain quorum of ministers actually take part in the decision; and (c) it is a majority which adopts the decision.[71]

In sum, the powerful position of the Chancellor is constitutionally balanced by a strict framework on the role and competences of the Cabinet. Its members are not only independent within their respective ministry, but also formal equals to the Chancellor in the process of decision-making within the Cabinet; and the Cabinet has to decide about all major political initiatives of the government. However, as is often the case, a look at the Constitution alone does not provide for the whole picture. The German system, like the US, has seen a certain departure from its original structure and the evolution of new structures that today play a significant role in the gubernative.

b The Federal Chancellery (*Bundeskanzleramt*)

The Federal Chancellery is not mentioned in the German Constitution but is today the 'institutional center of the executive'.[72] It plays an irreplaceable part in the governmental process and is more than just the secretariat of the Cabinet that it is mentioned as in the Rules of Procedure of the Federal Government.[73] It is also the personal bureau of the Chancellor, a central coordinator of gubernative processes and enjoys a pivotal place for policy planning. For the Chancellor, who has no individual portfolio,

---

[69] Hermes (n. 58), Art. 65, para. 37.

[70] BVerfGE 91, 148, 166; V. Epping, Die Willensbildung von Kollegialorganen, (1995) 48 DÖV 719–724.

[71] These requirements were established with regard to the circulation procedure (*Umlaufverfahren*, § 20(2) RoP), in which a decision is not taken during a meeting but by written consent of the members of the Cabinet.

[72] Sontheimer, Bleek and Gawrich (n. 63), 298.

[73] § 21 RoP.

it is the central institutional basis of power.[74] The Chancellery, in its organizational structure, is a classical bureaucracy and is organized hierarchically from top to bottom.[75] Head of the Chancellery is a senior civil servant who is also given cabinet rank as a Minister for Special Affairs.[76] Its central principle of organization derives from its intended relation to the ministries. Every ministry is mirrored in the Chancellery, which means that every subdivision in a ministry finds a counterpart or mirror department (*Spiegelreferat*) in the Chancellery. Thereby, the Chancellery is able to overview and accompany every development in the ministry. It is a structure parallel to the ministries, not just observing some, but all ongoing projects in the gubernative. The civil servants of the Chancellery often create close links to the civil servants in the ministries and build up their own expertise.[77]

The Chancellery has mainly three functions.[78] As mentioned above, it serves as the secretariat of the Cabinet, scheduling Cabinet meetings, coordinating their agenda and preparing the necessary papers. The Chancellery also serves as a coordination point for what the ministries work on. It has the duty to check every proposal for a bill that comes from the ministries in a legal as well as political sense, and that particularly means to ensure that they are in sync with the general political direction of the government. This finally provides the link to the third, more vague but most important function: to plan and to conceptualize policy, to spell out and transform the political guidelines that the Chancellor sets, into concrete action, projects and law.[79] The Chancellery is more than just a coordinating bureau, it is a political bureaucracy, which is developing projects, planning programs, and steering the process of governance. In

---

[74] On the Chancellery F. Möller-Rommel, 'The Chancellor and his Staff', in S. Padgett (ed.), *Adenauer to Kohl* (Hurst and Co, 1994), 106–126; in comparative perspective, see Beyme (n. 8), 456–459. On the history of the institution that dates back to the German *Kaiserreich,* when it was set up as *Reichskanzlei* and personal bureau for Chancellor *Bismarck* (Schöne (n. 23), 59–70).

[75] Busse (n. 67), 106–116; K. König, 'Vom Umgang mit Komplexität in Organisationen: Das Bundeskanzleramt' (1989) *Der Staat* 55–58.

[76] This has led to much political and legal criticism, since the Chancellery is supposed to have only a servicing function and is not to compete with the ministries. See E.-W. Böckenförde, *Die Organisationsgewalt im Bereich der Regierung* (Duncker and Humblot, 1964), 241–242; Brauneck (n. 76), 30–59.

[77] Busse (n. 67), 119–121.

[78] Brauneck (n. 76), 12–30.

[79] König (n. 75), 60–63.

that respect, the Chancellery secures the Chancellor's influence on all policy.[80]

The relationship between the Chancellery and the Cabinet or individual ministries is peculiar and, to that extent, comparable to the American example.[81] The limits of the Chancellery's competences are vague but strict. The legal yardstick is Article 65 and its three principles which outline the Chancellor's power to set general policy directions, departmental independence and the Cabinet's collective decision-making. The Chancellery has to find its place between these principles.[82] It shall coordinate the Cabinet, prepare the Chancellor's agenda and make sure that the ministries comply with them; yet at the same time it must not instruct the ministries. There is no line of command since this would violate the principle of departmental independence. It also cannot place itself between the Chancellor and the ministries, receiving guidelines from her and issuing them on to the ministries, since this would violate the principle of collective decision-making. Further, it shall not grow into a kind of proxy government, with the civil servants in the Chancellery substituting the ministers.

The Chancellery's staff is another important feature. It is generally composed of (often highly qualified ministerial) civil servants who are mostly lawyers. Only in the press department, the Chancellor's personal bureau or the speech-writing unit would one find non-civil servants.[83] This has important consequences: their primary qualification is their professional quality, not their party affiliation. The career of a civil servant in Germany is still, and despite all party-grip on the state, more dependent on job performance than on the colour of the party. Especially in the ministerial bureaucracy, party affiliation plays a less significant role than, for example, on a local level. In the federal bureaucracy, the competition is too fierce to rely on party patronage systems; and the German law of civil service contains hurdles against mere political appointments. Although § 31 *Beamtenrechtsrahmengesetz*[84] has a provision for so-called 'political civil servants' (*politische Beamte*), this is applicable only to a

[80] Smith (n. 54), 50 (calling the Chancellery 'the indispensable voice and ears of the chancellor').
[81] See especially section 4 below.
[82] Brauneck (n. 76), 22–28.
[83] König (n. 75), 65–70.
[84] 'Civil Servant Framework Law'.

very small number of enumerated positions. In the case of the Federal Chancellery, this category covers only six (!) employees.[85] The chances of the incoming incumbent to change its staff and to politicize it are therefore extremely limited.[86] In sum, the development, described here, has been one of centralization rather than politicization. The Chancellery is far from comparable to the one in the White House, but its extension and development certainly have had an impact on the importance of the Cabinet. Major decisions have become much more likely to be pre-determined by decisions in the Chancellery than by deliberation in the Cabinet.[87] Another central reason for this has to be seen in informal institutions.

c The Rise of Informal Institutions: Coalition Rounds and Expert Groups

The cabinet system in Germany appears strong as long as one limits one's view to constitutional law. In political reality, and also in infra-constitutional rules, the role and importance of the Cabinet has nevertheless been severely restricted over the past thirty years. Two dynamics have contributed to this development: first, the superimposition of cabinet rules by party logic, and secondly, a self-deprivation of the Cabinet through the deliberate transfer of decision-making powers to smaller, external bodies.

The superimposition of cabinet rules by party logic has to be seen in the broader context of the German party system and its effect on the formation and functioning of governments. The German party system is a multi-party system; and governments therefore are almost always coalition governments of two or more parties. Understandably therefore, the coordination between the governing parties in a coalition has always played a crucial role.[88]

[85] König (n. 75), 69.

[86] On consequences of this provision, see H.-U. Derlien, *Repercussions of Government Change on the Career Civil Service in West Germany*, IPSA SOG Conference Paper, 1986.

[87] Smith (n. 54), 50. For a comparative perspective see F. Müller-Rommel, 'Ministers and the Role of Prime Ministerial Staff', in J. Blondel and Ferdinand Müller-Rommel (eds.), *Governing Together* (Palgrave, 1993), 131–152.

[88] Smith (n. 54), 53–54; W. Rudzio, 'Informelle Entscheidungsmuster in Bonner Koalitionsregierungen', in Hartwich and Wewer (eds.) (n. 63), 123–133; Wewer (n. 63), 145–150.

The relation between cabinet rule and party demands thereby took on a new quality under the chancellorship of Helmut Kohl who installed a so-called coalition round (*Koalitionsrunde*) next to his Cabinet.[89] This group brought together the chairmen of the governing parties, their general secretaries, the leaders of their party groups in parliament and certain, but not all, ministers.[90] It was formed in accordance to party logic, not governmental rank; and it served to accommodate the demands of coordination between the coalition forming parties, not to coordinate between ministries. Over the years, the group developed into an increasingly institutionalized body with invitations, fixed agendas, written memoranda and the logistical support of the Chancellery and certain ministries.[91] The group may negotiate bills and major reforms, discuss general approaches to new issues, clear treatment of the media and, consequently, developed into the salient body of policy-planning and decision-making in the federal government.[92] Ultimately, the constitutional rules of the Cabinet system here compete with the dynamics of party politics. The formal rules are increasingly circumvented by more flexible, informal arrangements, which better accommodate the demands of political realities.

The second dynamic that has contributed to an undermining of the Cabinet's role is the deliberate shift of decision-making prerogatives from the Cabinet to informal bodies, such as expert commissions, civil society councils and, most importantly, negotiations between the parties holding the majority in the *Bundestag* (and hence forming the Federal Government) and those holding the majority in the Upper House, the *Bundesrat*.[93] This development is often discussed under the heading of de-parliamentarization because it is primarily seen as a threat to the

---

[89] The idea of the coalition rounds as informally coordinating groups dates back to 1961, when the liberal party (FDP) initiated such a round on the occasion of returning to the government with the CDU.

[90] W. Schreckenberger, 'Informelle Verfahren der Entscheidungsvorbereitung zwischen der Bundesregierung und den Mehrheitsfraktionen: Koalitionsgespräche und Koalitionsrunden', (1994) ZParl 330, 334.

[91] Ibid., 331–333.

[92] Schreckenberger (n. 90), 335.

[93] For a description of different types of these bodies, see J. von Blumenthal, 'Auswanderung aus den Verfassungsinstitutionen' (2003) 43 Aus Politik und Zeitgeschichte, 9/10.

autonomy of the parliament;[94] yet at the same time, these bodies also undermine the autonomy of the decisions of the Cabinet. Certainly, this development was driven by the government itself and by the institutional structure of executive federalism in the *Grundgesetz*, but that does not preclude it from threatening the role of the Cabinet and the idea of collective decision-making. It indicates a shift of power within the gubernative to the Chancellor and a few central or concretely involved ministers, who prepare and influence these bodies. It is also a shift to informal procedures of decision-making, which seem more effective.

4 Comparative Summary

The gubernatives in the United States and Germany are organized according to different construction plans: the US plan of a presidential system stipulates a unitary top, supported today by a number of auxiliary but subordinate bodies. The German system, following a parliamentary plan, rests on the idea of a collective gubernative composed of Chancellor and ministers. However, the description of the two systems in the previous sections has also underlined that they serve mainly two similar functional expectations. Firstly, both systems aim to facilitate political leadership, i.e. to provide for an institution which can set political goals, formulate policy agenda and has the means to pursue them. And second: both systems have to ensure the coordination and coherence of governmental policies, i.e. to make sure that the different departments adhere to the general policy direction, that departmental special interests do not prevail and that all relevant aspects are heard and integrated.

At the same time, serving these functions takes place in a context that is similar for most governments, in particular an increased importance of the executive branch more generally. This rests on several factors: the growing complexity of societal structures and expectations; globalization, in both the transnational nature of many problems, and the ensuing internationalization in the exercise of public authority; and, finally, a polarization in the political spectrum of most states, which makes cooperation between the branches of government and hence the role of the

---

[94] On this discussion, see M. Morlok, 'Informalisierung und Entparlamentarisierung politischer Entscheidungen als Gefährdung der Verfassung' (2003) 62 *Veröffentlichung der Vereinigung deutscher Staatsrechtslehrer* 72 with abundant further references.

gubernative harder. All of these trends strengthen the role of the executive branch and, in turn, the role of the chief executive.

a Facilitating Leadership: Chief Executives and their Offices

The two systems present two different concepts of leadership, each rooted in their respective composition. The American system enables swift policy-formulation and decision-taking through a radical concentration of power in one person. The President may seek advice, but he is ultimately independent and solely responsible.[95] 'Energy in the executive', as Hamilton called it, is the basic rationale of the American scheme of the gubernative, and this is ensured through its unity.

The German system, in contrast, prescribes a plural gubernative and combines collective and monocratic elements of leadership. In the Cabinet, Chancellor and ministers are equals and take decisions collectively.[96] Agenda setting is to some extent a deliberating process, in which the Chancellor is not the only overriding authority; the Ministers of Finance and Justice have veto positions and a majority of ministers could even overrule the Chancellor (though this is politically improbable). At the same time, the German Constitution also vests considerable powers in its chief executive to enable its 'energetic' lead.[97]

It became apparent, though, that neither President nor Chancellor could play their leading role without massive institutional support. In both systems separate offices of the chief executives evolved with considerable staff attached: the White House administration in the United States and the Federal Chancellery in Germany. They form today the organizational backbone of the gubernative lead of President and Chancellor and signal a significant centralization of governmental power in the office of the chief executive.

Both institutions have (at least to some extent) similar functions. They provide the chief executive with information and advice, they organize the Cabinet and they are instrumental in overseeing or directing the policies of the different ministries. However, they could hardly be more different with respect to their size, organization and staff: the White House employs by far more people than the Chancellery. Where the latter has all

[95] See section 2(a).
[96] See section 3(a).
[97] See section 3(b).

in all some five hundred employees, the inner bureau of the President, the White House Office, is alone as big as that. The Chancellery is organized in strict hierarchy and as a pyramid with a respective line of command from top to bottom. The White House, in contrast, has almost no hierarchy. All its officers are directly responsible to the President alone, which encircle him like planets encircle the sun in the solar system. The White House is also characterized by a confusing complexity with regard to the responsibilities and influence of its units. Most dramatic and far reaching, however, is the difference of their staff. The staff in the White House is mostly composed of campaign loyalists of the President, often young and without prior governmental experience. Moreover, staff is almost entirely exchanged with each new incumbent so that there is no personal continuity in the White House, nor is there any institutional memory. The Chancellery, in contrast, is filled with long-time civil servants, contractually independent of the Chancellor and normally longer in the Chancellery than any incumbent.

The reasons for these differences are certainly various. The organizational complexity of the White House, for example, results to a good degree from the American system of separated powers. This gives Congress great influence over the White House' organization, which uses it incrementally, unsystematically and not seldom against the will of the President. The difference of staff continuity might be explained by the radical concentration on one incumbent in the American system and its instrumental and somewhat pragmatic understanding of government in general. In Germany, the bureaucracy has traditionally a more grounded standing than the short-time inhabitants of political offices.

b Ensuring Coherence: Cabinet and Non-Cabinet Coordination

The gubernative also has to ensure the coherence of gubernative policies and the coordination of executive branch activities. The gubernative, as the politically responsible top of the executive branch, has to ensure that democratically endorsed policies are enforced by the executive, and that this happens in an organized, coordinated and hence efficient way. This function highlights a central organizational difference between the German parliamentary and the American presidential systems: the status and role of the Cabinet.

In the German context, the Cabinet is the institution in which coordination takes place and coherence is established.[98] The Cabinet is the regular and central meeting place of all ministers and the Chancellor where all major topics have to be tabled and formally decided in its weekly sessions. Constitutionally (although not always in reality) the German Cabinet has the powers; and, infra-constitutionally, it also posseses the organizational and procedural structures to ensure that governmental actions and substantial matters are coordinated.

The United States lacks a direct functional equivalent. What is called the 'Cabinet' in the American context is an informal institution, not mentioned in the Constitution.[99] It evolved as an advisory body to the President, and never became a central decision-making or coordinating body. The difference is reflected in their respective recruitment pools. The German Cabinet, typically for a parliamentary system, is recruited from the strongest politicians of the governing party, normally the leading figures of the party group in parliament, or the 'charmed circle', as Bagehot put it. The fusion of executive and legislative power is the fundament on which the parliamentary system is built and institutionalized in the Cabinet. The American Constitution, by contrast, separates the gubernative from the parliament by a strict incompatibility rule. Presidential power is not (and is not supposed to be) based on the integration of strong party figures; they are meant to manage their department on behalf of the President, not to ensure the compliance of the President's party group in the legislature.

Coordination in the American presidential system takes place in the White House and its numerous offices, which have taken on more and more the task of monitoring the executive departments and agencies. The White House administration is now the institution which tries to make sure that presidential directives and policy goals are complied with, that departmental activities do not collide with the President's agenda and that governmental policies are somehow coordinated.[100] In effect, the White House and what has been baptised the 'presidential branch' (as opposed to the executive branch) is not just a personal bureau for the chief executive anymore. It has developed into a virtual parallel bureaucracy

---

[98] See section 3(a).
[99] See section 2(b).
[100] See section 2(c).

that constitutes a super-ministry overseeing all departments. The need for coordination and oversight of the executive branch has immensely contributed to the growth of the White House administration.

In a comparative perspective, the American system of coordination still seems deficient since it lacks a central meeting point where the President is not only surrounded by loyalists (i.e. White House staff), but confronted with senior experts. It also lacks a place where voices from all areas of the executive branch are heard. Finally, the system of White House oversight creates a continued tension between the executive departments and the presidential branch.

At the same time, the German Cabinet does not fulfil the coordination role in the German system by itself. The Federal Chancellery is important as a secretariat to the Cabinet and as manager of inter-ministerial conflicts. The Chancellery also faces similar conflicts to the White House since, in Germany too, it is a fine line between admissibly disciplining the ministries and unconstitutionally commandeering them. However, the conflict between the Chancellor's office and ministries is not as grave as in the United States and a central reason for this is to be found in the collective leadership of the Cabinet as a political team. In the German parliamentary system, the Cabinet is composed of politically close actors and meets regularly, which fosters coherence. Such a committed team can have a strong grip on the executive branch departments whereas the US President is often alone in confronting the executive when his Cabinet secretaries are much less committed to him or to a party agenda. They are much more easily captured by the special interests of their respective department and in effect, the President is much more dependent on his own institutional support to rule the executive branch than the German Chancellor is.

Problems of coordination in Germany result less from recalcitrant bureaucracies but rather from political parties as external centres of power. The dynamics of coalition governments and the importance of the political parties in the parliament have resulted in the need to involve the party chairmen or women in the political decision-making, even if they are not formally part of the Cabinet. This takes place in informal meetings, most notably in the so-called coalition rounds.[101]

---

[101] See section 3(c).

Conclusion

Ultimately, systems of gubernative organization serve their functions in very distinct ways. The presidential and the parliamentary system thereby converge in the increasing institutionalization of the chief executive's office: the White House and the Chancellery. This convergence, in turn, is an echo to the increased importance of the executive branch more generally, which can be explained by several factors. There is the growing complexity of societal structures and expectations in general, which is connected also to globalization and the transnational nature of many problems and the ensuing internationalization in the exercise of public authority. Finally, a polarization has taken place in the political spectrum of most states, which makes the formation of governments more difficult and makes cooperation between the branches of government and hence the role of the gubernative trickier. All of these trends strengthen the role of the executive branch and in turn the role of the chief executive and his or her need to rely on institutionalized help.

These trends, while demonstrated here in two case studies in Sections 2 and 3 above, can be observed in many governmental systems around the world. What happened in the presidential system of the United States is mirrored in other presidential systems, in particular in Latin America and Francophone Africa. Many of these systems have witnessed an institutional pluralization as well as the increased importance and institutionalization of the presidency.[102] Similarly, what characterizes the development in the German parliamentary system finds echoes in other parliamentary systems, in particular in the Commonwealth states. The prime minister, together with the executive generally, gains importance and is institutionally strengthened not only by political clout but also through institutional

---

[102] For the African context see C. Fombad (ed.), *Separation of Powers in African Constitutionalism* (Oxford University Press, 2016); H.K. Prempeh, 'Presidential Power in Comparative Perspective: The Puzzling Persistence of Imperial Presidency in Post-Authoritarian Africa' (2009) 35 *Hastings Constitutional Law Review* 761; M. Ndulo, 'Presidentialism in the Southern African States and Constitutional Restraint on Presidential Power' (2002) 26 *Vermont Law Review* 769. For Latin America see R. Gargarella, *Latin American Constitutionalism, 1810–2010: The Engine Room of the Constitution* (Oxford University Press, 2013), 148 ff.

means.[103] This goes hand in hand with a certain 'presidentialization' of the prime minister, as was observed in Germany.[104]

Further Reading

K. von Beyme, *Parliamentary Democracy: Democratization, Destabilization, Reconsolidation* (Palgrave Macmillan, 2000).

J. Blondel and F. Müller-Rommel (eds.), *Governing Together* (Palgrave, 1993).

E.-W. Böckenförde, *Die Organisationsgewalt im Bereich der Regierung* (Duncker & Humblot, 1964).

P. Craig and A. Tomkins (eds.), *The Executive and Public Law: Power and Accountability in Comparative Perspective* (Oxford University Press, 2005).

C. Fombad (ed.), *Separation of Powers in African Constitutionalism* (Oxford University Press, 2016).

R. Gargarella, *Latin American Constitutionalism, 1810–2010: The Engine Room of the Constitution* (Oxford University Press, 2013).

L. Helms, *Presidents, Prime Ministers and Chancellors: Executive Leadership in Western Democracies* (Palgrave Macmillan, 2005).

S. Hess, *Organizing the Presidency*, 3rd ed. (Brookings, 2002).

T. Poguntke and P. Webb (eds.), *The Presidentialization of Politics: A Comparative Study of Modern Democracies* (Oxford University Press, 2005).

H. Laski, *The American Presidency*, 1940 (Transaction, 1980).

R.E. Neustadt, *Presidential Power*, 3rd ed. (Free Press, 1990).

G. Sartori, *Comparative Constitutional Engineering*, 2nd ed. (New York University Press, 1997).

---

[103] C.f. Rhodes, Wanna and Weller (n. 4).

[104] T. Poguntke, 'A Presidentializing Party State? The Federal Republic of Germany', in T. Poguntke and P. Webb (eds.), *The Presidentialization of Politics: A Comparative Study of Modern Democracies* (Oxford University Press, 2005).

Administration 15

Susan Rose-Ackerman

Introduction

Honest and competent administration is essential to legitimate consti-tutional government. Administrators make rules with the force of law and apply the law to particular cases. The case-by-case implementation of established policies requires citizens to trust in the impartial applica-tion of the law. However, impartiality is not sufficient for administrative legitimacy. In addition, policymaking by the executive and the agencies needs to be consistent both with the competent use of expertise and with accountability to citizens and interest groups. Policymaking delegation is the inevitable result of the weakness of the legislative process as a site for detailed policy prescriptions. Gaps and ambiguities are inevitable.

I wish to thank Thomas Perroud, Athanasios Psygkas and Matthias Rossbach for assistance on France, the UK, and Germany, respectively. All errors are my own.

Furthermore, the electoral process is too aggregated and episodic to be the only legitimate route for citizen influence on policymaking. Referenda and surveys are not a responsible option for most policy choices; they risk measuring the views of uninformed individuals, often reacting to emotional appeals. Hence, other routes to public involvement beyond voting and surveys are a crucial aspect of legitimate, representative democracy. Administrative law scholarship needs to articulate practical ways to combine public input with the competent application of technical information to policy.

The chapter begins by arguing that public input into executive policymaking is consistent with the democratic principles that undergird constitutional democracies. The next section unpacks the concept of public participation and outlines alternative ways for an administration to elicit outside input. It draws especially on the cases of the United States, Germany, France and the United Kingdom.

1 Democracy and the 'Public' in Public Administration

Two contrasting models of democracy frame the debate over the role of public administration in supporting democratic values. The first focuses on the 'chain of legitimacy' from voters to public officials; the second emphasizes direct input from groups and individuals outside of government.

a The Chain of Legitimacy

Germans invoke the *legitimationskette* or 'chain of legitimacy'. Democratic accountability in a parliamentary system is seen as a chain from the voters at election time to a party coalition charged with forming a government and proposing legislation, and then from top officials to those below them in a chain on down to the citizens.[1] Reversing direction, citizens who are subject to official actions can make their views known to lower-level bureaucrats who pass their concerns back up the chain to politically responsible officials. Under this view, it would be undemocratic and risk special interest influence to introduce public involvement into executive rulemaking or even into

---

[1] E.-W. Böckenförde, *Staat, Verfassung, Demokratie* (Suhrkamp, 1992), 291–326.

statutory drafting. Those engaged in statutory drafting or rulemaking should not rely on non-expert outsiders who might provide biased and emotional responses. Even if public consultations occur, the final decision must be made by a person embedded in the chain. 'Lobbying', borrowed from English in both German and French, is a pejorative term that signals illicit influence. However, this model needs to confront the limitations of the legislative process in translating public views into legislative language. There may be a weak link between a person's vote for a party or an individual candidate and support for particular statutory language. The democratic chain that extends back to the voters is not strong or well articulated. Furthermore, because statutes are often compromises between different points of view, they may be vague or inconsistent on purpose, especially when there are diffuse benefits and concentrated costs.[2]

In parliamentary systems the executive generally drafts statutes that are debated and passed by the parliament – many times with few changes in the submitted text. The chain of legitimacy continues into the bureaucracy where statutes may delegate certain policy choices to the executive. Under the German constitution, statutes that delegate must include the 'content, purpose and scope of the authority'.[3] Ideally statutes resolve all vexed policy issues, leaving it to the executive to carry out these policies as technical exercises that rely on competence, not political legitimacy.

In the United Kingdom, 'in its traditional form, ministerial responsibility [to Parliament] has been highly non-deliberative through shrouding discussions between civil servants and ministers in secrecy.'[4] Transparency has increased in recent years through review mechanisms both within the Government and in Parliament, but, outside some specialized regulatory agencies, the reforms mainly facilitate Parliamentary oversight.[5] The 2000 Freedom of Information Act (FOIA) requires greater openness to outsiders'

[2] J.Q. Wilson (ed.), *The Politics of Regulation* (Basic Books, 1980).
[3] German Grundgesetz, article 80(1). Article 80(2) requires consent of the Bundesrat (the upper house) for a subset of such rules.
[4] T. Prosser, *The Economic Constitution* (Oxford University Press, 2014), 248.
[5] T. Prosser, *The Regulatory Enterprise: Government Regulation, and Legitimacy* (Oxford University Press, 2010); Most secondary norms must be placed before Parliament, but the requirement is usually pro-forma (P. Craig, *Administrative Law*, 7th ed. (Sweet & Maxwell, 2012), 440–442).

demands for information, but it is a relatively weak law described by one critic as a 'sheep in wolf's clothing'.[6]

The French semi-presidential system permits delegations but also gives the Government some independent decree authority.[7] The French Constitution lists the topics that must be determined by statute; executive decrees can regulate topics not on the list if no statute is in force.[8]

The executives in all three countries have great freedom to issue and enforce decrees with legal force, and they face little legislative pressure to allow public participation or to provide public justifications except from backbenchers and minority parties outside of government. The Government consults technical experts,[9] but, under this model, involving either the general public or 'stakeholders' in post-enactment policy-making would be undemocratic because participation is likely to be concentrated among those with intense personal or economic interests in the outcome.[10] Direct public input ought to enter through the ballot box, not citizen engagement, under this view.

In Germany, if rulemaking occurs inside the executive, the process escapes judicial oversight for two contrasting reasons. On the one hand, the production of rules is political and, as such, is immune from judicial oversight if the statute is silent.[11] On the other hand, if the underlying statute sets policy and resolves political controversies, competent legal and technical experts draft secondary norms that implement the statute's policy commitments. Then, the judiciary might check the rules for consistency with the statute and with expert opinion, but the rulemaking

---

[6] R. Austin, 'The Freedom of Information Act 2000 – A Sheep in Wolf's Clothing?' in *The Changing Constitution* 387, J. Jowell and D. Oliver eds., 6th ed. (Oxford University Press, 2007), 387–406

[7] S. Rose-Ackerman and T. Perroud, 'Policymaking and Public Law in France: Public Participation, Agency Independence, and Impact Assessment', *Columbia Journal of European Law* 2013 19(2) 225–312.

[8] French 1958 Constitution arts. 34, 37, 38.

[9] Böckenförde, n. 1; M. Weber, 'Politics as a Vocation', in *Max Weber: Essays in Sociology*, translated and edited by H.H. Girth and C. Wright Mills (Oxford University Press, 1946) 77–128; Rose-Ackerman and Perroud, n. 7; S. Rose-Ackerman, *Controlling Environmental Policy: The Limits of Public Law in Germany and the United States* (Yale University Press, 1995).

[10] O. Renn, T. Webler and P. Wiedemann (eds.), *Fairness and Competence in Citizen Participation: Evaluating Models for Environmental Discourse* (Kluwer Academic Publishers, 1995), 25–26.

[11] If a statute includes procedural requirements, the courts will enforce them, see BVerfGE 127, 293 – Legenhennenhaltung (2010).

process would be off-limits. This institutional framework is explicable as a matter of positive political theory not only in Germany but also in the United Kingdom. Given the unitary nature of parliamentary governments, governments have little reason to support statutes that would limit their freedom to issue degrees with legal force.[12] Opposition parties might support procedural constraints on executive policymaking, but they do not have the power to enact such laws, and they would not favour them if they took power. In Germany, the Grundgesetz does not interfere with that logic; so long as the delegation itself is constitutional, it imposes no other procedural constraints on the executive. In the United Kingdom, EU law has pushed some regulatory agencies towards more public involvement, perhaps in tension with government wishes.

The situation could well be different in France with its independently elected president. However, in practice, France is close to the German and UK cases. The French legislature does little to check the administration because in recent years the majority has been politically allied with the Government. The main examples of independence are periods of co-habitation when President and Prime Minister are of different parties – an increasingly unlikely situation under current electoral timing. Furthermore, the National Assembly is very large with 577 members, and neither individual members, nor committees, nor the political parties have adequate staff fully to vet legislative texts from the executive or routinely to propose statutes that challenge executive prerogatives.[13] France has a constitutionally mandated third chamber, the Economic, Social, and Environmental Council (CESE) organized on neo-corporatist lines. It might be a route for greater public input into policy, but, in practice, it is a low-profile advisory body with little power or visibility.[14]

However, even without legislation requiring public input into executive rulemaking, no system avoids outside input. Consultation is often

[12] Rose-Ackerman, n. 9, S. Rose-Ackerman, S. Egidy, and J. Fowkes, *Due Process of Lawmaking: The United States, South Africa, Germany and the European Union* (Cambridge University Press, 2015). Of course, coalition governments are not 'unitary' in one sense, but the coalition controls both the legislature and the executive so requiring broader outside involvement in government policymaking seems an unlikely legislative response.

[13] K. Strøm, 'Parliamentary Committees in European Democracies' (1998) 4 *Journal of Legislative Studies* 21–59.

[14] French Constitution articles 69–71. Articles 32 to 36 of the Constitutional law no. 2008-724, 23 July 2008 added the environment.

politically expedient, but it may occur selectively and behind closed doors, avoiding not only broad public input but, in some cases, legislative involvement as well.[15] However, especially in the environmental area, civil society groups are challenging the traditional aversion to transparent, participatory procedures, and they have won some victories in Europe based on judicial interpretations of constitutional and treaty language.

b Public Input into Policymaking

The second model, reflected in US practice, argues that public input should occur at all stages of the policymaking process. Elections provide a democratic check on government policymaking, but that check is more attenuated for administrative actions than for legislation, even with a separately elected president. The weakness of voters' influence implies that both legislative and executive procedures must guard against undue special interest influence while accepting public input. In this view, the lack of a clear electoral chain supports the introduction of executive rulemaking procedures that further democratic accountability. In the United States these procedures involve public notice, broad consultation, transparency and reason-giving. Similar legal requirements do not apply to the legislative process, even if, as a practical matter, consultation generally occurs.[16]

The US model recognizes that policymaking in the executive is necessary but that such choices need a legal framework to enhance their democratic legitimacy. The attenuated 'chain' that stretches back to the voters is an unrealistic source of popular control. The citizenry as well as organized stakeholders and interest groups need to help promulgate rules that set policy. However, the best way to that goal is unclear. The archetypal US process of notice and comment rulemaking satisfies some of the conditions for democratic accountability, but it has many weaknesses and does not always live up to the ideals that justify its use.

[15] J.R. Heilbrunn, 'Oil and Water? Elite Politicians and Corruption in France' (2005) 37 *Comparative Politics* 277–296, D. Dulong, *Moderniser la politique: aux origines de la Ve République* (l'Harmattan, 2006). In the summer of 2017 the French legislature accepted President Emmanuel Macron's plan to reform the French labour code by decree after closed-door consultations with business and labour unions.

[16] Rose-Ackerman, Egidy and Fowkes, n. 12.

Positive political theory can account both for the notice and comment provisions of the Administrative Procedures Act [APA][17] and for Republican Party initiatives designed to constrain rulemaking. Given the separation of powers, Congress may want to constrain executive policy-making, even as Members recognize the necessity of delegation. The APA permits Congress to find out what agencies are doing and allows private parties to contest executive actions without Congressional involvement. Even with a president of the same party as the Congressional majority, constraints on executive policymaking may be a good long-term invest-ment. A President may sign such a statute into law to bind the hands of future administrations.

I proceed under two premises – one factual and the other normative. First, delegation of policymaking to the executive or to independent agencies is inevitable in representative democracies. Legislatures are not capable of writing statutes that resolve all policy issues. Second, such delegated political/policy decisions need to be democratically legitimate. Invoking the chain of legitimacy is insufficient and leaves loopholes for self-interested public officials to ignore the interests of the citizenry and to further their own aims or those of particular groups.

2 Public Involvement in Executive Rulemaking: Alternative Routes

By 'public involvement' I mean: 'forums of exchange that are organized for the purpose of facilitating communication between government, citizens, stakeholders and interest groups, and businesses regarding a specific decision or problem.'[18] The definition excludes protests, expert workshops, and government service, and includes public hearings, public meetings, focus groups, surveys, citizen advisory councils, negotiations. An important subset focuses on resolving conflicts through consensus.[19] However, that model has limited application to large-scale polities, espe-cially for decisions based on technocratic expertise and probabilistic

---

[17] US Federal Administrative Procedure Act 5 U.S.C. §§ 551–559, 701–706.
[18] Renn, Webler and Wiedemann, n. 10 at 2.
[19] Ibid. at 3; J. Habermas, *The Theory of Communicative Action. Vol. 1: Reason and Rationalization of Society*, translated by Thomas McCarthy (Beacon Press, 1984).

assessments. I am especially interested in such cases where consensus is unlikely.

However, even accepting the democratic legitimacy of public participation, the best techniques are not obvious. Not everyone can be consulted, and those willing to provide input may not be knowledgeable or may represent narrow, minority viewpoints. In a constitutional democracy, the ultimate policy decisions ought to remain ones for politically accountable officials. Nevertheless, important questions remain about how to integrate the concerns of citizens, businesses and other interest groups with the political and technical demands of public programs. I consider three alternatives with different purposes: finding facts, reaching consensus and improving democratic accountability.

a Participation to Find Facts: 'The 18th Specialist'

Some emphasize the 'wisdom of crowds' where the information needed to make good policy is widely distributed in the population and can be tapped through participatory methods.[20] Citizens are the '18th specialist'.[21]

In an often-used example, the task is to guess the number of jelly beans in a jar. Everyone independently guesses the true value through random draws from a distribution that is symmetric about the true value. Each individual has a very small chance of guessing correctly, but if the 'crowd' is large enough, pooling the random draws reflects the underlying distribution, and the mean of the guesses will be close to the true value.[22] The draws must be independent; thus the participants must not communicate. The aim is to find a fact not to debate policy options or value premises. In other cases, information is additive or, at least, complementary. In one example, mass transit riders reported their bus routes.[23] The city then produced a city-wide bus route map. The goal was not contested;

---

[20] J. Surowiecki, *The Wisdom of Crowds: Why the Many are Smarter than the Few and How Collective Wisdom Shapes Business, Economics, Societies, and Nations* (Doubleday 2004).

[21] M. Martini and S. Fritzsche, 'E-Participation in Germany: New Forms of Citizen Involvement between Vision and Reality', in C. Fraenkel-Haeberle, S. Kropp, F. Palmero and K.-P. Sommermann (eds.), *Citizen Participation in Multi-Level Democracies* (Brill/Nijhoff, 2015), 121–160 at 128.

[22] The Condorcet Jury Theorem, dating from 1785, is summarized in D.C. Mueller, *Public Choice III* (Cambridge University Press, 2003), 128–133.

[23] Surowiecki, n. 20.

citizen input generated knowledge at low cost. Similarly, surveys can elicit opinions to feed into policy decisions. The information includes expressions of values and policy preferences. There is no discussion, and answers are usually multiple choice. These procedures help answer pre-set questions – the number of jelly beans, where and when buses travel, which option has the most support from what groups. They tap into distributed knowledge to solve problems.[24]

Important as these innovations are for public policymaking, they are little concerned with democratic accountability. Rather, to enhance government legitimacy, processes designed to reach consensus might seem ideal. However, as outlined below, I reject that ideal as a norm for democracies. The final section then turns to options that accept the inevitability of disagreement and invite both citizens and groups to engage in discussion with other citizens and with public decision-makers.

b Consensual Processes

Taking consensus as an ideal is utopian and of limited value outside homogeneous communities. Some imagine that if citizens take a disinterested, public-regarding perspective when they debate public choices, a 'general will' will emerge.[25] In France the 1789 Declaration states, '*La Loi est l'expression de la volonté générale*' ('The Law is the expression of the general will'). This ideal permeates French discussions of public policy and public law, but it is invoked by politicians and policymakers with very different agendas. It is problematically associated with the choices of representative legislatures and with the decisions of professional bureaucrats.[26]

Consensus reached through bargaining is quite different; here, the gainers compensate the losers so that everyone is at least as well off with the new policy as they were in the status quo. Convincing others is not a goal.[27] This standard limits policy options to those that can earn

---

[24] B.S. Noveck, *Smart Citizens, Smarter State: The Technologies of Expertise and the Future of Government* (Harvard University Press, 2015).

[25] J.-J. Rousseau, *An Inquiry into the Nature of the Social Contract, or Principles of Political Right*, English translation (A. Heywood, 1840).

[26] Rose-Ackerman and Perroud, n. 7.

[27] J. Black, 'Proceduralizing Regulation, Part I' (2002) 20 *Oxford Journal of Legal Studies* 597–614.

unanimous consent based on private benefits and costs. If taken as the primary guide to policy, it rules out redistributive policies.

Consensual processes might aim to produce satisfied participants, analogous to satisfied market participants. New Public Management (NPM) views citizens as customers whom public officials should accommodate, but this goal ignores the mismatch between satisfied customers and good policy.[28] Of course, a service orientation is valuable at the implementation stage, and bureaucrats ought to consult beneficiaries to discover ways to improve performance. However, when public agencies make policy, the aim is good policy not only the satisfaction of beneficiaries.[29] Thus, consensus reached through negotiation between 'stakeholders' may lack democratic legitimacy.[30]

In short, consensus based on persuasion is too idealized a standard, consensus based on payoffs is normatively impoverished, and satisfying 'consumers' of public services is too narrow. Representative democracy is premised on managing disagreements, often over quite fundamental issues.

c Enhancing Democratic Legitimacy

Participatory processes that enhance democratic legitimacy can be organized in many ways. Consider three familiar options: civic forums, stakeholder advisory groups and open-ended public input. The first encourages dialogue and learning. The second is similar to a bargaining session. The third, an open-ended procedure, produces a rule accompanied by a statement of reasons.[31] Each responds to the infeasibility of having the mass public make public policy choices.

---

[28] A. Psygkas, *From the 'Democratic Deficit' to a 'Democratic Surplus': Constructing Administrative Democracy in Europe* (Oxford University Press 2017), 19, 193–199; P. Laegreid, 'New Public Management', in *Oxford Research Encyclopedia of Politics* (Oxford University Press, 2017).

[29] C. Coglianese, 'Is Satisfaction Success? Evaluating Public Participation in Regulatory Policymaking,' in R. O'Leary and L.B. Bingham (eds.), *The Promise and Performance of Environmental Conflict Resolution* (Resources for the Future 2003), 69–86.

[30] S. Rose-Ackerman. 'Consensus versus Incentives: A Skeptical Look at Regulatory Negotiation' (1994) 43 *Duke Law Journal* 1206–1220.

[31] US APA§553.

aa Civic Forums

In organizing 'civic forums', citizens may be chosen through strati-
fied random sampling, or anyone may volunteer with a lottery or other
method selecting participants.[32] Some processes are advisory and produce
reports to government agencies. The category also includes participatory
budgeting exercises and New England town meetings that are open to
all citizens in a neighbourhood or small polity and that produce binding
choices. The ideal is citizens who 'come together as political equals to
engage in public reasoning in a search for agreement about how to rule
themselves'.[33]

Karpowitz and Raphael highlight two normative values. The first is
the equality of participants' involvement in the forum, and the second
is publicity of the results to help legitimize policy choices. They stress
the tension between hearing from a broad range of views and locating
new and innovative options. If a forum does not engage in dialogue, it
is equivalent to a citizen survey. The risks are of two kinds: the general
public might reject the conclusions as biased, elitist or uninformed, and
experts and elites may complain that the conclusions do not incorporate
the expertise needed to make good policy.

Most advanced democracies have experimented with this model.
Germany has carried out many forums, especially in the environmental
and energy areas.[34] In France the Poitou-Charentes region has been a
centre of participatory activities, and Paris has carried out participatory
processes that allocate 5 per cent of its investment fund through civic
forums and residents' votes.[35]

Some observers are sceptical. One French critic calls the activities 'mini-
publics'[36] and argues that they do not reflect the general will because
most people do not participate. He worries that the organizers will set the
agenda and influence the process. But often the proposals from citizen

---

[32] C.F. Karpowitz and C. Raphael, *Deliberation and Democracy, and Civic Forums: Improving
Equality and Publicity*, (Cambridge University Press, 2014); J.S. Fishkin, *When the People
Speak: Deliberative Democracy and Public Consultation* (Oxford University Press, 2009).

[33] Karpowiz and Raphael, n. 32 at 16.

[34] Rose-Ackerman, n. 9.

[35] Rose-Ackerman and Perroud, n. 7. The Parisian activities are described in https://
budgetparticipatif.paris.fr/bp/.

[36] L. Blondiaux, 'Démocratie Délibérative vs. Démocratie Agonistique?' (2008) 30 *Raisons
politiques* 131–147.

forums are just that – proposals. The government will not enact them into law if they fly in the face of popular opinion. Furthermore, even when the processes determine some government spending choices, the fears of the critics seem exaggerated because of the programs' small scale. With only 5 per cent of one part of the budget at issue in Paris, the projects on offer suggest that most will have a positive but marginal effect on city life.

bb Stakeholder Groups

Under the second variant, the public agency limits participation to 'stakeholders'. Those involved may represent groups with policy agendas, such as environmental organizations, and include representatives of business, labour, academia, etc. as well as public officials. Notice the different goal of participation compared with civic forums. Here, the goal is a reasonable compromise in light of the positions and interests of the organizations behind the stakeholders. Participants may face tensions between their roles as members of the negotiating group and as representatives of organized groups. Stakeholder groups merge into citizen forums if unorganized citizens have a voice along with organized associations.

Mark Reed reviews some of the experiences with stakeholder participation in environmental management.[37] The processes were mostly site-specific management issues and had widely varying results. The outcomes depended upon differing definitions of 'success' as well as on the way the participatory process operated. To him, the selection of participants is a key issue. In some cases he recommends that the selection itself be done through a participatory process. One sees an infinite regress looming. Other recommendations involve clarity about goals, education in technical matters, and trained facilitators – all attempts to manage and contain the activity. He recommends early and ongoing stakeholder involvement, a proposal that might clash with the need to educate participants.

Germany: In Germany stakeholder groups seek to incorporate input from organized groups. These processes arose from a model of labour/management relations that goes back to the nineteenth century – a model

---

[37] M.S. Reed, 'Stakeholder Participation for Environmental Management: A Literature Review' (2008) 141 *Biological Conservation* 2417–2431.

that has been copied in Eastern Europe.[38] Outside of the labour/management area the success of stakeholder negotiations has been mixed and their experiences echo Reed's caveats and recommendations. The problem of merging citizen forums and stakeholder input has been especially acute as illustrated by German efforts to use public input to develop a climate policy.

The 'participation and dialogue' process fed into the German government's Climate Action Plan 2050 that the coalition government adopted on 11 November 2016, before the UN Global Climate Conference in Marrakesh, Morocco.[39] The ministry did not produce a draft for comment. Rather, 'stakeholders and citizen workshops were to suggest climate protection measures that would then be consolidated into the Plan by the ministry'.[40] The stakeholders were local communities, federal states, associations from industry and civil society, and citizens. Their four hundred proposals were consolidated in 'measures set 1.0'. Each stakeholder group had a representative on a 'delegates' committee' that produced 'measures set 2.0'. In November 2015, '472 randomly chosen citizens in five German cities participated in workshops' that made nineteen further proposals, with twelve citizens added to the delegates' committee. They voted on the measures, leading to 'measures set 3.0' that was subject to a final review by the delegates' committee.

The Environmental Ministry's resulting draft plan included very general proposals with no specifics or sense of priorities and no explicit trade-offs. One has to sympathize with the German industry associations that criticized the process as 'highly complex, in-transparent, and prone to be instrumentalized'. Of course, those groups had their own interests in limiting the stringency of the plan, but the basic point is that public consultation in an open-ended forum that mixes organized stakeholders and unorganized citizens can do little more than highlight the major issues.

---

[38] Rose-Ackerman, n. 9 at 103–106; S. Rose-Ackerman, *From Elections to Democracy: Building Accountable Government in Hungary and Poland* (Cambridge University Press, 2005).

[39] P. Oltermann, 'German Coalition Agrees to Cut Carbon Emissions Up to 95% by 2050', *The Guardian*, 11 November 2016.

[40] K. Appunn, 'Climate Action Plan 2050: Negotiating a Path to Decarbonisation', *Clean Energy Wire*, 6 May 2016. The quotes are from that document.

The group was unable to negotiate concrete policies and make practical trade-offs.

France: France has carried out several organized large-scale concertations with stakeholders other than political parties. Called 'Grenelles', they produce legislative drafts, not secondary norms, but the process could cover either.[41] The 2007 Environmental Grenelle involved almost 2,000 people with business, labour and environmental groups sitting together around the negotiating table.[42] The working group proposals were discussed in public meetings followed by round tables with representatives of the same groups. Some potential participants agonized over whether to join the process or to stand outside and maintain a critical stance. A counter-Grenelle argued that the environmental participants had sold out, labelling the Grenelle a 'Munich of ecology'.[43] Although the number of participants was large, they were mainly professionals from the sector concerned and users of its services. The traditional hierarchy of actors often reappeared in the debate because some actors were more experienced than others.[44] Furthermore, these debates are organized at the discretion of the government; they create no legal rights and are not subject to any judicial review.[45]

Citizens and Stakeholders: In short, neither citizen forums nor stakeholder negotiations are an adequate response to demands for public participation in executive branch policymaking. Each one taken alone or in combination can inform executive policy deliberations, but they ought not to be the only route to public input. The third type of participation, represented by US notice-and-comment rulemaking, is also not a complete response, but it does counteract some of the weaknesses of the above options.

---

[41] Rose-Ackerman and Perroud, n. 7; P. Lascoumes, 'Des acteurs aux prises avec le 'Grenelle Environnement': Ni innovation politique, ni simulation démocratique, une approche pragmatique des travaux du Groupe V' (2011) 1 *Revue Participations* 277.

[42] *Le Grenelle Environment*, legrenelle-environnement.fr (accessed May 4, 2019).

[43] Lascoumes, n. 41, at 285; K. Whiteside et al., 'France's 'Grenelle de l'environnement': Openings and Closures in Ecological Democracy (2010) 19 *Environmental Politics* 449.

[44] J. Chevallier, 'Le débat public en question', in *Pour un droit commun de l'environnement: Mélanges en l'honneur de Michel Prieur* 489 (2007).

[45] At the regional level, the Poitou-Charentes region organized a stakeholder process involving school budgets; those invited were students, teachers, other staff and parents. People participated as individuals, not necessarily as designated spokespeople for their group. After engaging in debate, the process concluded with a vote on a range of options to be implemented by the school board. Rose-Ackerman and Perroud, n. 7.

cc Open-Ended Notice and Comment[46]

Notice and comment rulemaking is the bedrock of the American regulatory process. This process does not involve public deliberation but rather requires the government to inform the public about its plans, to hold hearings where anyone can submit a statement and consult the docket, and to provide public reasons for its final policy choice that take account of the comments. The agency cannot limit participation, thus minimizing the chance of an echo chamber. Rather the agency must weigh the probity of the comments before it issues a final rule.[47] Comments are not treated as votes; rather, the agency must bring its own judgement and expertise to evaluate the comments against the statute's policy goals.

Organized groups view participation as an important part of their strategy to influence public policymaking. Participation involves written comments and participation in oral hearings, but informal contacts also occur before the notice and comment process begins with the publication of a proposed rule in the Federal Register and again after the rule has been issued.[48]

The notice and comment process can be costly and time consuming for both agencies and interest groups. A major rulemaking at the US Environmental Protection Agency (EPA) takes several years and requires many hours of input from both bureaucrats and outside interests.[49] Judicial challenges introduce further delays. If a rulemaking generates public concern, the number of comments can be very large. For example, when the Forest Service was considering a rule on roadless areas in national forests, it received over one million comments.[50] However, most were form letters that could be easily processed. The average rulemaking is much less contested and time consuming. A review of eleven dockets covered rules

---

[46] Rose-Ackerman, n. 38 at 219–233.

[47] *US* v. *Nova Scotia Food Prods. Corp.*, 568 F. 2d 240 (2d Cir. 1977).

[48] S.R. Furlong and C.M. Kerwin, 'Interest Group Participation in Rulemaking: What Has Changed in Ten Years? (2005) 15 *Journal of Public Administration Research and Theory* 353–370; W. Wagner, 'Participation in the US Administrative Process', in F. Bignami and D. Zaring (eds.), *Elgar Research Handbook on Comparative Law and Regulation* (Edward Elgar, 2016), 109–128.

[49] C. Coglianese, 'Assessing Consensus: The Promise and Performance of Negotiated Rulemaking' (1997) 46 *Duke Law Journal* 1255–1349, at 1283–1284.

[50] N.A. Mendelson, 'Agency Burrowing: Entrenching Policies and Personnel Before a New President Arrives' (2003) 78 *New York University Law Review* 557–666, at 623.

that attracted from one to 268 comments.[51] A random sample of forty-two rulemakings found that the median number of comments was about thirty.[52] A study of thirty-six US Department of Transportation (DOT) 'completed actions' between 2002 and 2005 found that DOT received 2,857 public comments, ranging from 3 to 387 per rule.[53] In general, agencies do not seem to be overwhelmed with comments.

Delays, when they exist, may not relate to the number of comments. One study of 150 EPA rules asked if the time between the start of the process and the issuance of the final rule was associated with the number of internal participants and the number of comments. Surprisingly, neither factor had a positive impact; the number of internal participants even had a small negative impact – the greater the number of such participants, the shorter the elapsed time. The authors suggest that rulemaking is facilitated by inclusive procedures.[54] Delay can be strategic and depend upon whether the agency, the White House, or Congress wants to hold up resolution of an issue. However, delay times at the Department of the Interior between 1950 and 1999 increased in the second half of the period. The study, however, covered only one agency and was unable to distinguish between unjustified delays and those resulting from complexity and public interest.[55]

More fundamental is the claim that notice and comment processes are biased towards business interests that public officials must counteract in writing the rule. One study of the Resource Conservation and Recovery Act documents the dominance of business comments.[56] Business both participates more actively than other interests in rulemaking and has an

---

[51] M.M. Golden, 'Interest Groups in the Rule-making Processes: Who Participates? Whose Voices Get Heard?' (1998) 8 *Journal of Public Administration and Theory* 245–270.

[52] W.F. West, 'Formal Procedures, Informal Processes, Accountability, and Responsiveness in Bureaucratic Policy Making: An Institutional Analysis' (2004) 64 *Public Administration Review* 66–80.

[53] S. Webb Yackee, 'Participant Voice in the Bureaucratic Policymaking Process' (2014) 25 *Journal of Public Administration Research and Theory* 427–449).

[54] C.M. Kerwin and S.R. Furlong, 'Time and Rulemaking: An Empirical Test of Theory' (1992) 2 *Journal of Public Administration Research and Theory* 113–138, at 125–131.

[55] J. Webb Yackee and S. Webb Yackee, 'Testing the Ossification Thesis: An Empirical Examination of Federal Regulatory Volume and Speed, 1950-1990' (2011–2012) 80 *George Washington Law Review* 1414–1492.

[56] C. Coglianese, *Challenging the Rules: Litigation and Bargaining in the Administrative Process* (UMI Dissertation Services, 1994), 228–232.

impact on the content of rules when it does. Nevertheless, public interest groups can influence outcomes.[57]

Submitted comments affect the content of rules,[58] but apparently business regards its influence as insufficient. If the regulatory process had been entirely captured by business, it would be difficult to explain business efforts to roll back regulatory constraints through legislation. Furthermore, industries often disagree on the best outcome. For example, efforts to deregulate the automobile industry were challenged by the auto insurance industry.[59]

Officials make independent judgements and do not react mechanically to the volume of comments. Thus, one study evaluated US EPA rulemakings that determined the 'best practical technology currently available' for controlling water pollution. The results were optimistic about the ability of officials to resist pressure from regulated industry. Comments that supported weaker standards did not tend to produce weaker standards, and industries with more firms out of compliance with proposed rules did not get weaker standards. However, well-organized industry groups with a consistent message influenced outcomes.[60] On the other side of the ledger, a study of the Forest Service Roadless Areas Rulemaking found that the notice and comment period produced modifications that responded to comments from those favouring a strong rule.[61] Two researchers also evaluated public participation in over 200 environmental decisions covering federal, state, local and regional processes over a thirty-year period. Involving the public 'not only frequently produces decisions that are responsive to public values and substantially robust, but it also helps to resolve conflict, build trust, and educate and inform the public about the environment'.[62]

[57] J. Webb Yackee and S. Webb Yackee, 'A Bias toward Business? Assessing Interest Group Influence on the Bureaucracy' (2006) 68 *Journal of Politics* 128–139.

[58] Yackee and Yackee, n. 55; S. Webb Yackee, 'Reconsidering Agency Capture During Regulatory Policymaking', in D. Carpenter and D.A. Moss (eds.), *Preventing Regulatory Capture: Special Interest Influence and How to Limit It* (Cambridge University Press, 2014), 292–325.

[59] *Motor Vehicle Manufacturers' Association* v. *State Farm Mutual Automobile Insurance Co.*, 463 US 29 (1983).

[60] W.A. Magat, A.J. Krupnick and W. Harrington, *Rules in the Making: A Statistical Analysis of Regulatory Agency Behavior* (Resources for the Future, 1986).

[61] Mendelson, n. 50 at 628.

[62] T.C. Beierle and J. Cayford, *Democracy in Practice: Public Participation in Environmental Decisions*, (Resources for the Future, 2002), 74.

Cases ranked highly by the participants in terms of process, also scored highly on measures of success.[63]

Many proposed rules change little after the end of the comment period.[64] However, if a rule is overtly biased, the publicity attendant on the notice and comment process would provide unfavourable public relations for the agency. It will also spur the losers to go to court to have the rule remanded to the agency for a more balanced result. These possibilities affect the agency's willingness to buckle under pressure in the first place. A rule that survives notice and comment unchanged may indicate that the government successfully anticipated objections.

The American experience suggests that the most important problems with notice and comment rulemaking are delay, bias, irrelevance, displacement to other methods, and curbs on agency implementation.[65] The existing studies provide examples of these problems, but they appear mostly to be the result of poorly designed and biased procedures, not participation per se. Some delay is the inevitable counterpart of expanded participation.

If Congress imposes procedural hurdles on agencies to undermine a statute's stated purposes, that is a special case of narrow interests overcoming broader public goals. Regulatory 'reform' efforts proposed by some in the US Congress seek to make rulemaking an unattractive option for regulatory bodies.[66] They are supported by those who want to make environmental and health and safety regulations more difficult to promulgate.

dd Public Participation in Germany, the United Kingdom and France

Neither Germany, France, nor the United Kingdom legally requires procedures equivalent to US notice and comment rulemaking for the

---

[63] Ibid. at 29, 60–61.

[64] Golden, n. 51; Kerwin and Furlong, n. 54.

[65] For a critical view of US practice see R.A. Kagan, *Adversarial Legalism and American Government: The American Way of Law* (Harvard University Press, 2001).

[66] The Regulatory Accountability Act, H.R. 5, passed the House in 2017, but it died with the House's return to Democratic control in 2019. For a critique, see S. Rose-Ackerman, 'A Regulatory Revolution Is Underway,' *The Hill*, 2 March 2017, http://thehill.com/blogs/pundits-blog/the-administration/322127-a-regulatory-revolution-is-underway (accessed May 4, 2019).

promulgation of most secondary norms (*Rechtsverordnungen, réglements juridiques*, delegated legislation), although political expediency will often encourage consultations with outsiders. In contrast, public hearings or consultations are legally required for many individual licensing and public investment decisions.

In Germany, the debate over public participation mainly concerns legislative drafts, not government rules, although there have been successful efforts to increase public involvement in environmental policymaking based on the Aarhus Treaty.[67] Public input is widespread at the local level where the law requires public participation in the drafting of development plans.[68] Furthermore, as Germany phases out nuclear power and promotes renewable energy, electric power must be transported from the windy north to the industrial south. Disputes concern the details of exactly where new grid lines will be built, and the law requires public input, but only on local issues dealing with route choices.[69] Participants seek to avoid costs by shifting them to other localities or to the federal government; they are not debating the trade-offs behind the broad policy. The decisions are divide-the-pie choices. When the law was enacted, both the phase-out of nuclear power and the shift to renewables were broadly popular with voters, but there was no focused debate on the implications of the law. The costs for consumers and citizens were not central to the debate but are now becoming more salient as a result of lawsuits by the power companies for compensation,[70] of subsidies paid to renewable providers, and of exemptions for some industries.

---

[67] UN Economic Commission for Europe, Convention on Access to Information, Public Participation in Decisionmaking and Access to Justice in Environmental Matters (Aarhus Convention), 25 June 1998: www.unece.org/env/pp/treatytext.html (accessed 9 September 2016).

[68] Baugesetzbuch, section 3, www.gesetze-im-internet.de/bbaug/__3.html (accessed May 4, 2019).

[69] S. Kropp, *'Federalism, People's Legislation and Associative Democracy'*, in C. Fraenkel-Haeberle, S. Kropp, F. Palermo and K.-P. Sommermann (eds.), *Citizen Participation in Multi-Level Democracies* (Brill/Nijhoff, 2015), 48–66.

[70] Decisions by the German Constitutional Tribunal will further increase costs for taxpayers. A 6 December 2016 decision, BVerfG, 1BvR 282/11, 1BvR 321/12, 1BvR 1456/12, finds that even though the underlying law on the nuclear power phase-out is constitutional, the utility firms must obtain compensation for losses based on their legitimate expectations. Furthermore, in BVerfG, Order of April 13, 2017, 2BvL 6/13 the Tribunal struck down a tax on nuclear energy companies, requiring refunds.

The United Kingdom incorporated public input under the 'Citizens' Charter' that encouraged a service orientation in the civil service and the regulatory agencies. It followed the New Public Management principles of running government like a business that tries to satisfy its 'customers' or 'clients'. This orientation is not equivalent to inviting 'citizens' to provide input into public policymaking. Under NPM, the underlying policy framework is given, and public involvement helps the government to provide services, regulates private firms, and imposes costs using techniques that are efficient and fair. Those are worthy aims, but they differ from mandating public participation in executive and agency policymaking.

However, at least in the regulation of communications, the UK has moved closer to the notice and comment model, albeit under a legal mandate from the EU. The Office of Telecommunications (Oftel) was charged with regulating the industry after privatization in the 1980s. Directors General of Oftel supported transparency, reason-giving, and public consultations, but their actions were personal, discretionary decisions, not required by law. They were 'matters of personal choice in keeping with the British tradition of personalized, informal, and discretionary decisionmaking'.[71] However, Oftel's practices did put pressures on other agencies to follow suit. In 2003, in response to an EU directive, the UK passed a statute mandating public participation in the electronic communications sector. As a result, the Office of Communications (Ofcom) has a robust consultation process. A 'consultation champion' inside the agency, along with agency management and judicial review, has moved public involvement beyond viewing citizens as 'customers' towards consulting them as 'citizens'.

France is moving cautiously towards more public participation in rulemaking.[72] In 2015 it promulgated its first Code of Administrative Procedure that largely codifies the jurisprudence of the *Conseil d'État* and the state of the law; it permits but does not require public consultations. The Code does not go as far as a *Conseil Constitutionnel* (CC) decision that applies to environmental matters. The Constitution's Charter for the Environment states: 'Each person has the right, in the conditions and to the extent provided by law ... to participate in the public decision-making process likely to affect the environment.' The CC held that the procedural

[71] Psygkas, n. 28 at 229.
[72] See the 2011 *Conseil d'État* report: *Consulter Autrement Participer Effectivement*: www. conseil-etat.fr/Decisions-Avis-Publications/Etudes-Publications/Rapports-Etudes/Rapport-public-2011-Consulter-autrement-participer-effectivement (accessed May 4, 2019).

requirements in article 7 were reviewable after an association of environmental groups argued that there had been insufficient consultation. The CC confirmed that article 7 created a constitutional right to consultation and that this right had been violated by the air pollution statute. It held that the Charter requires a balance between legal and environmental expertise, on the one hand, and public consultation, on the other. Whenever Parliament takes measures that affect the environment, it must incorporate public participation into executive regulatory procedures. However, the *Conseil* provided no guidance on how to satisfy the constitutional provisions.[73]

Subsequently, the legislature passed a statute to comply with the ruling, but to US eyes it seems a grudging accommodation. A proposed environmental rule must be made available to the public along with its context and objectives. The public can submit observations within a minimum of twenty-one days. During that period, the comments are not publicly available. After the close of the comment period, the government must wait at least four days before issuing the final rule and must provide a statement of reasons, a response to the comments, and a synopsis of the comments. The comments must be on the ministry website for three months but can then be removed.[74]

The 2015 Administrative Code is even weaker and leaves more discretion to government policymakers. Public consultations are either 'purely' optional or can substitute for existing 'stakeholder' consultations.[75] Even when the government does carry out a consultation, the provisions are much less robust than US notice and comment procedures; in particular, the government need not give public reasons and the extent of judicial review is unclear. Dominique Custos argues, however, that in one respect the code is more expansive than US law because she interprets it to apply to non-legislative rules.[76]

---

[73] *Association France Nature Environnement (AFNE)* CC Decision No. 2011–183/184QPC, Oct. 14, 2011, J.O. 78.

[74] *Ministère de L'écologie, du Développement Durable et de L'énergie, Consultations publiques*, www.consultations-publiques.developpement-durable.gouv.fr/projet-de-loi-relatif-a-la-mise-en-oeuvre-du-principe-de-participation-du-public (accessed May 4, 2019).

[75] D. Custos, 'The 2015 French Code of Administrative Procedure: An Assessment', in S. Rose-Ackerman, P. Lindseth and B. Emerson (eds.), *Comparative Administrative Law*, 2nd ed. (Edward Elgar, 2017) 284–301.

[76] Ibid. at 294–295. Unlike US independent agencies, comparable French agencies cannot issue rules with the force of law and hence rely on non-legislative rules that often have de facto binding effects.

Conclusion

Some claim that public participation in executive rulemaking is undemo-cratic because the resulting policies may flout the will of the legislative majority. Only a small subset of the population will participate, and it is likely to be a biased sample. Furthermore, if the process welcomes input from organized groups – industry associations, large firms, labour unions, professional associations and civil society advocacy groups – their input may be similarly unbalanced. This has led some to argue against outside participation in government rulemaking. Such distrust of outside input seems overblown. One can accept the importance of using competent and up-to-date technical information without concluding that public input will distort the ultimate policy choices.

A commitment to majority rule is a central challenge to public involve-ment beyond the ballot box. Do participatory processes perfect majority rule or dilute and supersede it? Can governments defend acting on the basis of participatory processes that draw on both specialized expertise and citizen input, even if the policy would be unable to obtain majority support in a referendum? Is public participation an effective route to good policy, and is it democratically legitimate in the eyes of voters?

To answer these questions, agencies, first, ought to organize partici-pation processes so that the public exercises genuine judgement on the merits of policies, rather than engaging in quarrels over the distribu-tion of a fixed basket of benefits and costs. Second, techniques that are too close to a corporatist or stakeholder model may not reflect broad public concerns if the agency consults with a fixed number of organized interests. The risk, as shown in Hungary and Poland after the transition from socialism, is a membership frozen at one point in time that does not respond to changing interest group patterns.[77] Open-ended opportuni-ties, as under the US notice and comment process, avoid that problem. However, they may produce an overwhelming number of comments from a biased sample. The process is not designed for debate and dia-logue. The bureaucracy reviews the written comments, holds hearings, and must have the capacity to make technically competent decisions. To be consistent with democratic values, however, officials must give public reasons for their choices and submit to limited court review. Thus,

[77] Rose-Ackerman, n. 38.

in a choice between deliberation between stakeholders or among a few select members of the public (civic forums), on the one hand, and deliberation by public officials who must take public input into account, on the other, the latter comes closer to democratic values, in my view. In spite of critiques of the notice and comment process in the United States, the process complies with two basic principles. First, the process is consistent with democratic values because agency has an obligation to accept comments from anyone, not just from experts or selected 'stakeholders'. Second, executive policy decisions further public accountability because they must be justified through public reasons provided to the citizenry, not just to experts and focus groups.

Further Reading

F. Bignami and D. Zaring (eds.), *Elgar Research Handbook on Comparative Law and Regulation* (Edward Elgar, 2016).

T. Prosser, *The Regulatory Enterprise* (Oxford University Press, 2010).

O. Renn, T. Webler and P. Wiedemann (eds.), *Fairness and Competence in Citizen Participation: Evaluating Models for Environmental Discourse* (Kluwer Academic Publishers, 1995).

S. Rose-Ackerman, P. Lindseth, and B. Emerson (eds.), *Comparative Administrative Law*, 2nd ed. (Edward Elgar, 2017).

S. Rose-Ackerman, S. Egidy and J. Fowkes, *Due Process of Lawmaking: The United States, South Africa, Germany and the European Union* (Cambridge University Press, 2015).

C. Fraenkel-Haeberle, S. Kropp, F. Palmero and K.-P. Sommermann (eds.), *Citizen Participation in Multi-Level Democracies* (Brill/Nijhoff, 2015).

16 Courts with Constitutional Jurisdiction

Cheryl Saunders

Introduction: Comparing Courts

All courts perform functions of a broadly constitutional kind. They provide a key mechanism for ensuring compliance with law and the peaceful resolution of disputes between people, according to law. Viewed from this perspective, they are integral to the capacity of a state to carry out its responsibility to establish and maintain internal peace and security.[1] In one form or another, courts also are likely to be the forum for the resolution of that most challenging category of legal disputes: enforcing compliance with law by the institutions of the state itself. In each of these respects, courts are central to the rule of law. They may be analysed in terms of separation of powers or representative democracy, as well, where these are features of the constitution of the state.

---

[1] The point applies whether the state is 'reactive' or 'activist': M.R. Damaska, *The Faces of Justice and State Authority: A Comparative Approach to the Legal Process* (Yale University Press, 1986) 73, 80.

This chapter is primarily concerned with one category of courts: those with jurisdiction to interpret and apply the Constitution. Because, in some states, multiple courts may have a jurisdiction of this kind, the ambit of the chapter is further confined to apex courts, where final decisions are made. In the world of the twenty-first century, most states have adopted codified constitutions with superior legal status, which are likely to empower one or more courts, expressly or by implication, to evaluate the validity or applicability of legislation by reference to the constitution. Even where a constitution is uncodified, however, as in the United Kingdom and New Zealand, an apex court is likely to apply norms of a constitutional kind and so falls within the scope of the chapter as well.

Most of the 200 or so states or comparable polities of the world have courts with a constitutional jurisdiction.[2] The subject thus offers a rich field for comparison, offering all the familiar opportunities for greater self-understanding, improved knowledge and understanding of others and insights into options for change. The size and diversity of the field, however, also offers equally familiar challenges.[3] To manage these, four cross-cutting schemes of classification, or taxonomies, may be useful. These should not be treated as water-tight compartments, but as aids to the formulation of some initial hypotheses, to be informed or even rebutted by more targeted research for the purposes of more jurisdiction-specific projects.

One category distinguishes between states by reference to the degree of adherence to the rule of law, including constitutional law. The distinction maps, very roughly, onto categorizations of states by reference to regime type and to constitutionalism.[4] Hybrid practices on the part of states that occupy an extensive middle ground make bright lines based on any of these criteria notoriously difficult to draw. As a generalization, nevertheless, it is likely to be relevant to consider, in many comparative projects, the extent to which an apex court engages seriously with the task of

---

[2] See the listing compiled by the Venice Commission: Venice Commission, 'Constitutional Courts' (*Council of Europe*, 2014), www.venice.coe.int/webforms/courts/ (accessed 29 March 2018).

[3] C. Saunders, 'Towards a Global Constitutional Gene Pool' (2009) 4(3) *National Taiwan University Law Review* 1.

[4] A.H.Y. Chen, 'The Achievement of Constitutionalism in Asia', in A.H.Y. Chen (ed.), *Constitutionalism in Asia in the Early Twenty-First Century* (Cambridge University Press, 2014) 1. This and other work by Chen examines earlier schemes of classification by regime type or constitution to determine their relevance to current conditions, generally and in particular in Asia.

constitutional review within the limits of its jurisdiction. Unless otherwise specified, courts considered in this chapter broadly comply with this prescription.

A second scheme of classification on which the chapter draws distinguishes between diffuse (or decentralized) and centralized constitutional review.[5] In systems of diffuse review apex courts and, generally, some other courts as well, resolve legal disputes by reference to all sources of law, of which the constitution is one. By contrast, centralized review confers on a Constitutional Court or Tribunal what typically is a monopoly over the interpretation and application of the Constitution, at least in relation to legislation. In various ways, in contemporary conditions of globalization, these two distinct approaches to review are converging. The differences still are sufficiently marked, however, to make the distinction a useful framework for analysis.

Third, in analysing courts with a constitutional jurisdiction it may be relevant to consider the legal system in which review occurs. Granted, this consideration is complicated by the existence of mixed legal systems and the phenomenon of convergence: this time of world legal systems. The prevalent legal system nevertheless may affect both the design of an apex court with constitutional jurisdiction and its operation in practice. Most relevantly, for present purposes, there is a degree of correlation between the legal system and the choice of diffuse or centralized review, insofar as diffuse review tends to be associated with common law legal systems and centralized review with the civil law. While the correlation is by no means invariable, as instances on both sides of the divide show, in each of these cases, the legal system has an impact of a different kind on their operation in practice.[6]

Finally, insights into the design and behaviour of apex courts with a constitutional jurisdiction may be derived from the region or subregion in which they are located. Courts of states that are grouped together in a region may exhibit distinctive tendencies stemming from cultures, including histories, that their states share as neighbours. Ideas and practices concerning courts as well as other aspects of government

---

[5] Other terms may be used to describe this distinction: A.H.Y. Chen and M.P. Maduro, 'The Judiciary and Constitutional Review', in M. Tushnet, T. Fleiner and C. Saunders (eds.), *Routledge Handbook of Constitutional Law* (Routledge, 2013), 97.

[6] The Venice Commission listing shows that the apex courts of around eighteen states depart from this rule of thumb: Venice Commission (n. 2).

may spread more readily within regions than to other parts of the world. Regional integration affects the apex courts of Member States in ways that are not replicated elsewhere and are necessary for an understanding of the role and functions of courts of this kind.

These categories are used as guides to analysis in the rest of the chapter, which is organized as follows. The next two substantive parts describe and explain the two principal prototypes of courts with constitutional jurisdiction by reference to, respectively, diffuse and centralized review.[7] Each of these parts considers the principal characteristics of the form of review with which it is concerned; its spread; and some of the variations to which it is subject. Each also examines two other key aspects of constitutional review: its legitimacy, in terms of the authority for it and the approach to reasoning that is characteristic of this form of review. A brief conclusion draws attention to indicators of future trends.

1 Prototypes: Diffuse Review

a Design and Function

The prototype for diffuse review is a judicial system in which multiple courts apply all sources of law, including constitutional law, to resolve disputes properly brought before them. The courts typically are organized in a hierarchy, in which the apex court has the final word on the meaning and application of the constitution. In common law courts, which are the norm in a system of review of this kind, decisions of higher courts including, quintessentially, the apex court bind all lower courts through a doctrine of precedent, reinforced by stare decisis.[8] Examples include the Supreme Courts of the United Kingdom, the United States, Canada and India and the High Court of Australia.

It follows that the courts engaged in diffuse review are ordinary or general courts, subject to all the laws and practices that apply to such courts, many of which predate constitutional review. Where diffuse review is embedded in a common law legal system, judges tend to be appointed

---

[7] These two parts draw on earlier work on this subject: C. Saunders, 'Constitutional Review in Asia: A Comparative Perspective', in A.H.Y. Chen and A. Harding (eds.), *Constitutional Courts in Asia* (Cambridge University Press, 2018).

[8] H. Patrick Glenn, *Legal Traditions of the World* 3rd ed. (Oxford University Press, 2007), 246 notes that the doctrine in its current form emerged over the course of the nineteenth century.

at a relatively late stage in a successful legal career, typically as legal practitioners and, especially, in a divided profession, as barristers, but occasionally also as government lawyers or legal scholars. In civil law systems, by contrast, judging is more likely to be treated as a career, on which lawyers embark at a much earlier stage. In either case, nevertheless, the independence that is at least as necessary for constitutional review as for other forms of adjudication is protected by the same means that apply to the courts as a whole. The framework of relevant rules usually includes appointment of judges for life or until retirement, guaranteed maintenance of the level of remuneration during a judge's time in office and strict limits on removal for cause.[9] Other forces for protection of judicial independence, which also are important, draw on constitutional convention, legal culture and the political influence of the legal profession.[10]

Courts in most, although not all, states that provide for diffuse constitutional review apply the constitution even against legislation. Where constitutional review is not available to invalidate legislation, as in the United Kingdom and New Zealand, courts nevertheless review executive action and may interpret legislation to bring it closer to accepted constitutional norms. In either case, courts exercising a function of constitutional review typically do so when a concrete legal dispute is brought before them, by a competent applicant, for which a judicial remedy is available. Generally, no distinction is drawn between the parts of a constitution that can be applied and enforced in this way, as long as the relevant provisions are deemed to be justiciable. It follows that courts engaged in constitutional review may eschew determination of questions in the abstract, in the form of advisory opinions.[11] There are notable examples to the contrary, however, of which Canada and India are examples, in which constitutional questions can be raised before courts in an abstract form, typically at the instance of specified state institutions.[12]

---

[9] H. Patrick Glenn traces the historical reasons for the evolution of judicial independence as generally understood in common law legal systems: ibid. 244.

[10] The Honourable Sir A. Mason, 'The Independence of the Bench; the Independence of the Bar and the Bar's Role in the Judicial System' (1993) 10(1) *Australian Bar Review* 1.

[11] While a refusal to deal with cases in the abstract may sometimes be attributable to the text of the Constitution, as in the United States and Australia, in both those jurisdictions the relevant case law also relies on assumptions about the nature of adjudication: *Muskrat v. United States* 219 US 346 (1911); *In Re Judiciary and Navigation Acts* (1921) 29 CLR 257.

[12] *Supreme Court Act*, RSC 1985, c S-26, s 53 (Canada); Constitution of India 1950 art. 143.

Courts in this category may also play a role in resolving disputes over election returns. When they do so, they may be identified distinctively as courts of 'Disputed Returns'. While on one view, this is merely another dimension of the legal function of settling disputes according to law, it has been complicated in the British constitutional tradition by an historical understanding, derived from conflict between the Crown and Parliament, that such matters are for the Parliament itself to decide, should it choose to do so.[13]

b Diffusion and Variation

Diffuse review is more prevalent in the common law world, where it also is broadly consistent with common law theory and practice. Common law legal systems have never drawn a sharp distinction between public and private law. Legal disputes to which entities with a public character are a party have always been resolved in ordinary courts, together with disputes of an indisputably private nature. From this vantage point, once norms of a constitutional kind were recognized as having superior legal status, it was a logical, if significant, step to conclude that they could be applied, even against the legislature, by general courts as well. Credit for taking this step first is widely, although not necessarily accurately,[14] attributed to the Supreme Court of the United States in *Marbury* v. *Madison*,[15] not least because of the clarity with which the rationale for applying the Constitution, as a source of superior law, was articulated by Chief Justice Marshall in that case. Even before the advent of the Constitution of the United States, however, general courts in British colonies had applied Imperial law as superior law that would override inconsistent local legislation, offering an alternative source, rooted in practice, for diffuse review. As decolonization progressed, moreover, at least some Constitutions, including that of Australia, initially relied on their status as Imperial legislation for their overriding legal effect. From these twin foundations, diffuse review spread with relatively little controversy across

---

[13] K. Walker, 'Authority of the High Court of Australia', in C. Saunders and A. Stone (eds.), *The Oxford Handbook of the Australian Constitution* (Oxford University Press, 2018) 449, 466–467.
[14] M. Schor, 'Mapping Comparative Judicial Review' (2008) 7 *Washington University Global Studies Law Review* 257, 262.
[15] 5 US (1 Cranch) 137 (1803).

the otherwise diverse countries that inherited the common law as a consequence of colonization. In the twenty-first century, almost all countries in which the common law is the sole or dominant formal type of law use diffuse review in some form. The small number that do not, including South Africa and Zimbabwe, are considered in the next part.

Diffuse review is by no means confined to states with a common law legal system, however. It is provided also by courts in, for example, parts of continental Europe, including Switzerland and the Nordic states; in a range of countries in Latin America; and in Japan. The explanation for the reliance on diffuse review in these states variously reflects the earlier influence of the Constitution of the United States particularly, but not only, in federated states[16] or, as in the case of the Nordic states, the distinctiveness of a positivist legal system in which Parliament plays a central role and there has been relatively little pressure for judicial review of legislation.[17]

Given the diversity of the states in which diffuse review is used, significant variations are inevitable in its operation and effects, resulting both from initial design and from evolution over time.

These are observable even between states in the British constitutional tradition, in which the role of apex courts superficially is most similar. Here, variations are attributable to the different contexts in which judicial review operates and to the divergence of constitutional arrangements over time.

Some have been mentioned already. In most, but not all such states, judicial review of the constitutionality of legislation is accepted. The United Kingdom and New Zealand are outliers in this regard, in the absence of codified constitutions with superior legal status, enabling parliamentary sovereignty to persist, giving rise to some distinctive theoretical and doctrinal issues.[18] At the other end of the spectrum, the courts of some states have significantly expanded the function of judicial review to assume authority to invalidate constitutional amendments that are

[16] A. Tschentscher and C. Lehner, 'The Latin American Model of Constitutional Jurisdiction: Amparo and Judicial Review' (2013) SSRN: https://papers.ssrn.com/abstract=2296004 (accessed 16 April 2018); S. Matsui, 'Why is the Japanese Supreme Court so Conservative?' (2011) 88 *Wash U L Rev* 1375, 1376–1377.

[17] J. Husa, 'Guarding the Constitutionality of Laws in the Nordic Countries: A Comparative Perspective' (2000) 48 *American Journal of Comparative Law* 345.

[18] These include, for example, the implications of the disapplication of UK law in the face of conflict with valid EU law and the scope of judicial authority to interpret legislation to comply with constitutional norms.

found to be inconsistent with the 'basic structure' of the Constitution[19] or to accept the standing of anyone to initiate litigation on public interest grounds.[20] The Supreme Court of India has been at the forefront of each of these developments, which have been accepted also by the courts of some other states in South Asia.

Similarly, while concrete review is the norm some, but by no means all, such states accept abstract review in limited circumstances, raising yet another set of issues about the types of abstract questions that might be put to a court and the legal status of the answers.[21] In an example of another kind, there also now is significant variation in the manner of appointment of judges in states that provide for diffuse review, and in particular in relation to appointments to apex courts. There always was a difference between the British and United States traditions in this regard, with appointments by the Head of State on the advice of executive government in the former and an additional requirement for Senate consent in the latter.[22] The obvious potential for effective appointment by the executive government alone to impinge over time on judicial independence has been countered in India by interpretation of the relevant constitutional provisions to require, in effect, approval of appointments by a judicial collegium, creating further difficulties of its own.[23] In other Commonwealth countries, including the United Kingdom itself, there has been a trend towards the introduction of Judicial Commissions or other comparable bodies to broaden the range of voices involved in judicial selection and to provide a greater measure of transparency for it.[24] In some

[19] Famously in India, in *Kesavananda Bharati* v. *State of Kerala* (1973) 4 SCC 225, but with influence elsewhere, including Bangladesh and Pakistan, as shown by Y. Roznai, *Unconstitutional Constitutional Amendments: The Limits of Amendment Powers* (Oxford University Press, 2017), 47–52.

[20] S. Divan, 'Public Interest Litigation', in S. Choudhry, M. Khosla and P.B. Mehta (eds.), *The Oxford Handbook of the Indian Constitution* (Oxford University Press, 2016), 662.

[21] In relation to Canada, see C. Mathen, 'Access to Charter Justice', in P. Oliver, P. Macklem and N. Des Rosiers (eds.), *The Oxford Handbook of the Canadian Constitution* (Oxford University Press, 2017), 639, 651–655.

[22] US Const art. 2, § 2.

[23] N. Robinson, 'Judicial Architecture and Capacity', in S. Choudhry, M. Khosla and P.B. Mehta (eds.), *The Oxford Handbook of the Indian Constitution* (Oxford University Press, 2016), 330, 345–346.

[24] Bingham Centre for the Rule of Law, 'The Appointment, Tenure and Removal of Judges Under Commonwealth Principles: A Compendium and Analysis of Best Practice' (British Institute of International and Comparative Law 2015), 16.

states, however, of which Australia is an example, judicial appointments continue to be made by the executive branch alone.

Yet another variation brings diffuse review somewhat closer to the contrasting system of centralized review, at least in outward form. Some states including, again, several in South Asia, restrict judicial review by lower courts and may, in addition, enable or require the apex court to be specially constituted for some or all constitutional cases. Thus, in Bangladesh, review jurisdiction is conferred only on the High Court Division, as the lower division of the Supreme Court;[25] in India, review is confined to the High Courts and the Supreme Court, with a constitution bench of at least five Supreme Court judges required for important constitutional cases;[26] and the 2015 Constitution of Nepal requires a Constitutional Bench of five judges for specified categories of constitutional cases.[27] Developments of this kind not only emphasize the role of the apex court as a constitutional court but may also accentuate the tendency of constitutional law to dominate the sources of law applied in the resolution of disputes, at the expense of other branches of public and private law.

A final set of variations between systems of diffuse review derives from characteristics of the legal system in which review occurs. These potentially affect all aspects of review, from procedure to judicial reasoning to outcomes.[28] One such characteristic, which deserves particular mention on account of its significance, is the treatment of precedent in common law and civil law legal systems. In common law legal systems, stare decisis assists to make diffuse review practicable, while its absence from civil law legal systems helps to explain the turn to centralized review. Where diffuse review is provided in a civil law system, an alternative to stare decisis must be found. The manner in which some Latin American states have adjusted their otherwise civil law legal systems to the conditions of diffuse constitutional review offers a striking example. The writ of amparo, developed initially in Mexico in the nineteenth century before

---

[25] Constitution of Bangladesh, art. 102.

[26] Constitution of India 1950, art. 145(3); this clause has become increasingly important, in principle if not in practice, as the case load of the Supreme Court of India has expanded and two-judge benches have become the norm.

[27] Constitution of Nepal, art. 137.

[28] V. Ferreres Comella, 'The European Model of Constitutional Review of Legislation: Toward Decentralisation?' (2004) 2 *International Journal of Constitutional Law* 461, 462.

spreading to other jurisdictions, was designed broadly to emulate judicial review in the United States, in the absence of a comparable procedure.[29] Amparo decisions derive binding force in Mexico once delivered in five consecutive judgments by a Supreme Court majority of at least eight votes.[30]

c Authority

The source of authority for constitutional review underpins the legitimacy of a process that otherwise could be regarded as inconsistent with both democracy and separation of powers. In systems of diffuse review, the authority for constitutional review draws in large part on the authority of the courts themselves. This offers an important foundation, where courts are protected by a tradition of independence, entrenched through convention and law. In such states, compliance with judicial decisions about the meaning and effect of the Constitution is likely to be regarded as an attribute of the rule of law.[31]

The basis for the authority for diffuse constitutional review typically is reinforced by the provisions of the Constitution itself, together with any supporting legislation. In most states the constitutional jurisdiction of courts and in particular of the apex court, is likely to be drawn directly from the Constitution, expressly or by implication. In either case, constitutional jurisdiction may be able to be regulated by legislation, but otherwise will be entrenched. Authority may be strengthened somewhat when explicitly conferred, which may occur in diverse ways. Where authority is regarded as implicit, courts may be more vulnerable to critique on the grounds of self-aggrandisement in exercising their review function, as the example of the Supreme Court of the United States shows.[32]

At least in common law legal systems with an entrenched codified constitution, judicial review by the ordinary courts is unlikely to raise

[29] R.D. Baker, *Judicial Review in Mexico: A Study of the Amparo Suit* (University of Texas Press, 1971), 33.
[30] Tschentscher and Lehner (n. 16).
[31] K. Hayne, 'Rule of Law', in C. Saunders and A. Stone (eds.), *The Oxford Handbook of the Australian Constitution* (Oxford University Press, 2018), 167.
[32] For an early classic account, see E.S. Corwin, '*Marbury* v. *Madison* and the Doctrine of Judicial Review' (1914) 12 *Michigan Law Review* 538. The issue has also been raised, but in muted form, in Australia: J.A. Thomson, 'Constitutional Authority for Judicial Review: A Contribution from the Framers of the Australian Constitution', in G. Craven (ed.), *The Convention Debates 1891–1898: Commentaries, Indices and Guide* (Law Books, 1987), 173.

separation of powers concerns on that ground alone.[33] Judicial review
may be contested, however, where a court is deemed to have overstepped
the bounds of what is considered the appropriate judicial function. Exactly
what this involves varies, sometimes considerably. The common core of
judicial review is shaped by the general judicial function of resolving
disputes according to law. Constitutional review presents particular
challenges, however, stemming both from its interface with legislative
and executive power and from the distinctive character of constitutions
themselves, in terms of status, rigidity, longevity and generality. How
courts respond to these challenges varies between states. The acceptable
limits of constitutional review are shaped at the considerable margins
by constitutional and political context. The point could be illustrated by
plotting the understanding of the scope of the function of courts exercising diffuse review that is assumed and accepted in, say, India, Australia
and Singapore along a spectrum. The Supreme Court of India would be
placed at one end, the Supreme Court of Singapore at the other and the
High Court of Australia would lie somewhere in between.

d Reasoning

Judicial reasoning is an emerging field of comparative constitutional law.
All constitutions present similar challenges for interpretation, in terms of
relative generality, potential longevity, political significance and status
vis-à-vis ordinary law. Recent work in the field demonstrates, however,
both quantitatively and qualitatively, that there are significant differences
in constitutional reasoning between apex courts, notwithstanding global
forces for convergence.[34] These stem from a range of factors, including
the history, character and substance of the Constitution and the political,
legal and social context in which it applies.

Some similarities between approaches to reasoning between courts in
this category nevertheless follow from the character of diffuse review
itself. Concrete review with a competent plaintiff is likely to be the default
position, even when abstract review also is allowed, shaping the context in which cases are decided. Courts that are in a position to draw on

---

[33] C. Saunders, 'Theoretical Underpinnings of Separation of Powers' in G. Jacobsohn and
M. Schor (eds.), *Comparative Constitutional Theory* (Edward Elgar, 2018), 66.
[34] A. Jakab, A. Dyevre and G. Itzcovich, *Comparative Constitutional Reasoning* (Cambridge
University Press, 2017).

sources of law apart from the Constitution, as is the case with diffuse review, may choose to do so where the issues at stake allow, so as to avoid invoking fundamental law, with all the consequences that follow. Where multiple concurrences and dissenting opinions are acceptable in non-constitutional cases, they are likely to be a feature of constitutional cases as well, providing alternative ways of articulating and resolving constitutional questions and freeing the majority view from the need to find more broad-based consensus.[35]

The legal system in which diffuse review is embedded is a cause of both similarity and difference in judicial reasoning. Courts operating within the same legal system are likely to share some assumptions and practices that feed into the reasoning process. Thus, for example, in common law legal systems, the habits associated with stare decisis reinforce the reluctance of apex courts to depart from their own earlier decisions about the meaning of the Constitution, although they may well refine them or distinguish them, using familiar common law techniques. Similarly, judicial process in common law courts is typically adversarial, with arguments from either side playing a significant role in shaping the course of a court's reasoning. Common law judicial reasoning tends to be inductive rather than deductive and to draw on analogy to shape the development of the law. Perhaps not surprisingly, in these circumstances, the citation of foreign decisions is an accepted practice in apex courts in most common law legal systems, although as a source of guidance, rather than binding authority.[36] Courts exercising diffuse review in civil law legal systems tend to differ from their common law counterparts in all these ways, reflecting civil law methodology. Here as elsewhere, however, generalization requires caution. Neither system is monolithic; exceptions can be found to most such propositions; and both systems are evolving in any event influenced, in part, by each other.[37]

One final factor that deserves brief mention for its effect on the reasoning of courts engaged in judicial review is the status of international or supranational law. While this factor affects courts exercising either diffuse or centralized review, practice may be more variable amongst the former category of courts. For these purposes, the status of such norms depends

---

[35] Ibid. 771.
[36] C. Saunders, 'Judicial Engagement with Comparative Law', in T. Ginsburg and R. Dixon (eds.), *Comparative Constitutional Law* (Edward Elgar, 2011), 571.
[37] Jakab et al. (n. 34), 782.

on whether at least some international law norms take direct effect in domestic law; whether courts are authorized or directed to take international law into account; or whether the state concerned is a member of a regional arrangement directed to economic integration or human rights protection. Courts operating in a state where none of these conditions apply may nevertheless consider international law, as in India;[38] equally, however, they may not, as in Australia.[39] Where one or more of these conditions applies a court has, at least in principle, additional sources of law on which it can or must draw, forged by bodies beyond the state. Such a court also may need to engage with other categories of legal question, going to the scope of the authority of regional or international judicial bodies and the issue of which court, ultimately, decides where the boundary lies.[40]

2 Prototypes: Centralized Review

a Design and Function

In apparently stark contrast, the prototype for centralized review is a single, specialist court, usually termed Constitutional Court, Constitutional Tribunal or, occasionally, Constitutional Council, organized separately from the rest of the court system and with exclusive jurisdiction over the constitutional matters assigned to it.[41] Examples include the Federal Constitutional Court of Germany, the Constitutional Court of the Republic of Korea, the Constitutional Court of South Africa and the Constitutional Court of Chile.

The concept of such a body is associated with Hans Kelsen, although it has deep historical roots and has been significantly developed and adapted over the century that followed its implementation in Austria in

---

[38] L. Rajamani, 'International Law and the Constitutional Schema' in S. Choudhry, M. Khosla and P.B. Mehta (eds.), *The Oxford Handbook of the Indian Constitution* (Oxford University Press, 2016), 143.

[39] S. Donaghue, 'International Law', in C. Saunders and A. Stone (eds.), *The Oxford Handbook of the Australian Constitution* (Oxford University Press, 2018), 237.

[40] On the relationship between the Supreme Court of the United Kingdom and the European Court of Human Rights in this regard, for example, see Roger Masterman, 'Supreme, Submissive or Symbiotic? United Kingdom Courts and the European Court of Human Rights' (The Constitution Unit, 2015) www.ucl.ac.uk/constitution-unit/sites/constitution-unit/files/166.pdf (accessed 9 April 2019).

[41] Ferreres Comella (n. 28), 65.

1920. A Constitutional Court always has jurisdiction over the interpretation and application of the constitution to test the validity of legislation and may have jurisdiction over other constitutional questions as well. Typically, decisions of a Constitutional Court about the constitutionality of legislation are expressed to be binding, with erga omnes effect, producing an outcome broadly equivalent to diffuse review in conditions of stare decisis, although the two are conceptualized quite differently.[42] Constitutional Courts may be given authority over other, related functions as well, of which the unconstitutionality of acts of political parties, proceedings against officers of the state and disputes over elections or referendum outcomes are examples.[43]

The separation of constitutional from other legal questions necessarily represents a boundary between Constitutional Courts and the general judicial system, which may cause friction and which needs to be anticipated and managed. Details vary, with the scope of the jurisdiction of the Constitutional Court and the provisions of the empowering constitution and supporting legislation. Familiar points of tension, however, are the authority of a Constitutional Court to interpret statutes so as to comply with the Constitution, the authority of general courts to determine the meaning of the Constitution in the course of interpreting statutes and the authority that attaches to the reasoning of a Constitutional Court on which a decision is based.[44]

Almost by definition, the composition of a Constitutional Court differs from that of other courts, in at least some respects. It is customary, although not invariable, for the power of appointment to a Constitutional Court to be shared between key political institutions on a basis that allocates a certain number of places to each, often requiring special majorities, in ways that assist to underpin the political legitimacy of the Court in the context of the state in question.[45] While legal expertise generally is a criterion

---

[42] G.F. de Andrade, 'Comparative Constitutional Law: Judicial Review' (2001) 3 *University of Pennsylvania Journal of Constitutional Law* 977, 979.

[43] A. Mavcic, 'Historical Steps in the Development of Systems of Constitutional Review and Particularities of Their Basic Models' (Concourts.Net): www.concourts.net/introen. php (accessed 7 May 2018).

[44] For helpful insight into these difficulties, see L. Garlicki, 'Constitutional Courts Versus Supreme Courts' (2007) 5 *International Journal of Constitutional Law* 44.

[45] For description of this approach as the 'representation model' see W.-C. Chang, L. Thio, K.Y.L. Tan and J. Yeh, *Constitutionalism in Asia: Cases and Materials* (Hart Publishing, 2014), 369–370. The rationale for the combination of appointment by different institutions

for appointment, a Constitutional Court is likely to comprise members from a range of legal backgrounds, which may include the general judiciary, legal practice, politics or academia, enabling diverse perspectives to be brought to bear on constitutional decisions. Consistently with this concept of the constitution of such a court, non-judicial members are appointed for a term of years, which is likely to be lengthy and may be managed so that retirements are staggered, ensuring both continuity and renewal. Immediate reappointment usually is not permitted, in the interests of the independence of the court.

b Diffusion and Variation

The contemporary concept of a distinct Constitutional Court is generally attributed to Hans Kelsen, who drafted the provisions for it in the Austrian Federal Constitution of 1920 and theorized its fit within the Austrian federal constitutional system as it evolved in the wake of World War I.[46] In this initial form, the Court offered abstract review, at the instance of the two chambers of the legislature, primarily in relation to questions of federal competence although it had other responsibilities as well. Its rationale stemmed, at least in part, from the absence of a formal doctrine of stare decisis, threatening considerable 'non-uniformity' of constitutional interpretation were the task to be entrusted to ordinary courts instead.[47] Decisions effectively annulled the statute, from the time they were made, consistently with conception of the Court as a 'negative legislator'.[48]

with special majorities is explained with reference to various examples and in critique of the arrangements in France by D. Rousseau, 'The *Conseil Constitutionnel* Confronted with Comparative Law and the Theory of Constitutional Justice (or Louis Favoreu's Untenable Paradoxes)' (2007) 5 *International Journal of Constitutional Law* 28, 32.

[46] On the complexity of both evolution and credit for authorship see G. Schmitz, 'The Constitutional Court of the Republic of Austria 1918–1920' (2003) 16 *Ratio Juris* 240. A Constitutional Court also was established in Czechoslovakia in 1920: T. Langasek, 'Constitutional Court of the Czech Republic and its Fortunes in Years 1920–1948' (Ustavni Soud),   www.usoud.cz/en/constitutional-court-of-the-czechoslovak-republic-and-its-fortunes-in-years-1920-1948/ (accessed 11 May 2018).

[47] H. Kelsen, 'Judicial Review of Legislation: A Comparative Study of the Austrian and the American Constitution' (1942) 4 *The Journal of Politics* 183.

[48] Ibid.

In the period of constitutional reconstruction that followed World War II, centralized review was adapted by other European states as an approach that would assist to protect the new, entrenched Constitutions but that also was consistent both with the modalities of the civil law and with a conception of the separation of powers that could be traced to the French Revolution.[49] The Constitutional Courts of Germany and Italy were the first such courts to be established at this time; the Austrian Court was re-established during this period as well. Over the course of the rest of the twentieth century and into the twenty-first, most European states adopted centralized constitutional review in some form.[50] France was a partial and important exception, in the sense that the Constitutional Council established in 1958 was originally designed as a body to control the actions of the legislature vis-à-vis the executive, providing only a priori review. Over time, however, as it evolved, it has taken on more of the characteristics of constitutional courts elsewhere. The introduction of the priority preliminary rulings procedure in 2010, as a means by which statutes might be challenged after promulgation, is the most recent of a long line of developments to this end.[51]

The institution of centralized review spread widely to other parts of the world as well. There are now Constitutional Courts or their broad equivalents throughout Africa, the Middle East, Asia and Latin America. Examples, to give an idea of the range, include Algeria, Bahrain, Benin, Bolivia, Colombia, Guatemala, Indonesia, Korea, Mali, Mongolia, Morocco, Peru and Taiwan.[52] In at least some cases, establishment of a Constitutional Court accompanied democratization for functional or expressive reasons or both.[53] The experiences of Latin America are particularly noteworthy for this purpose; in the latter part of the twentieth century, a range of states including, for example, Chile, Colombia and Peru, created specialist

---

[49] G. Dietze, 'Constitutional Courts in Europe' (1955) 60 *Dickinson Law Review* 313, 315–317. Dietze notes that the idea of a special court to protect the constitution could be traced to the French revolution as well: at 315.

[50] G. Delledonne, 'Relation of Constitutional Courts to Supreme Courts', *Max Planck Encyclopaedia of Comparative Constitutional Law* (2017): http://oxcon.ouplaw.com/view/10.1093/law-mpeccol/law-mpeccol-e571 (accessed 11 May 2018).

[51] X. Philippe, 'Constitutional Review in France: The Extended Role of the *Conseil Constitutionnel* through the New Priority Preliminary Rulings Procedure (QPC)' (2012) 53 *Annales* 65.

[52] Venice Commission (n. 2).

[53] Delledonne (n. 50).

Constitutional Courts or Tribunals that were superimposed in different ways on the earlier arrangements for diffuse review.[54]

Centralized review is well adapted to the principles and practices of civil law systems, but occasionally is found in common law or mixed legal systems as well. South Africa is a well-known example; Zimbabwe is another; and centralized review was considered for Sri Lanka in the constitutional reform process that followed the elections in 2015.[55] In these cases, centralized review is not needed for the purposes of legal certainty or to overcome difficulties associated with a conception of the separation of powers that draws a sharp distinction between public and private law. Rather, in these as in other states undertaking the challenging task of transition to a more democratic form of government, centralized review offers the opportunity to create a new court, constituted by members who had no necessary association with the previous regime and are more likely to have the vision and commitment to interpret the new Constitution.[56] The same opportunity could also be abused, of course, if a new court were established to circumvent existing courts, adapting features of centralized review in a way that weakened its independence.[57]

The diversity of the states by which centralized review has been adopted and adapted is a catalyst for significant diversification. Points of difference include the appointment procedures used;[58] the qualifications of members of Constitutional Courts, including the extent to which membership draws on judges of other courts; the length of terms of appointment; whether or not the Court can review the constitutionality of administrative as well as executive action;[59] the other functions that Constitutional

---

[54] P. Navia and J. Rios-Figueroa, 'The Constitutional Adjudication Mosaic of Latin America' (2005) 38 *Comparative Political Studies* 189.

[55] T. Daly, 'A Constitutional Court for Sri Lanka? Perceptions, Potential and Pitfalls' (April 2017) CPA Working Papers on Constitutional Reform No 15, http://constitutionalreforms. org/wp-content/uploads/2016/06/CPA_WP_CR_No_15_Final-TDrevno-tracks.pdf> (accessed 14 May 2018).

[56] H. Corder, 'Judicial Authority in a Changing South Africa' (2004) 24 *Legal Studies* 253. The opportunity was not taken in Zimbabwe, where the new Constitution of 2013, which established a Constitutional Court, provided that it should be constituted for seven years by existing judges: 6th schedule, para. 18(2).

[57] The final paragraph of the Venice Commission opinion on the High Constitutional Court of Palestine makes the point, albeit subtly: Venice Commission, 'Opinion on the Law on the High Constitutional Court of the Palestinian National Authority' (2009) CDL-AD(2009)014.

[58] In relation to Asia, see Chang et al. (n. 45), 369–370.

[59] ibid. 357–358.

Courts are empowered to perform;[60] the possibility or acceptability of differing opinions, whether in concurrence or dissent;[61] the need for an ordinary or special majority vote in holding legislation invalid.[62] Typically, the detail of these and other features constitute a package that responds to the context of the state concerned. Three other points of variation also mix the spread of the influence of centralized review with local context, but merit more specific consideration.

First, in some states a Constitutional Court does not have a monopoly over constitutional review, which also is available from other courts, to some extent and on some conditions. Typically, this 'mixed' arrangement results when a Constitutional Court is superimposed onto a pre-existing system of constitutional review. In Latin America, Colombia, Ecuador, Guatemala and Peru are examples.[63] South Africa offers an example of a different kind, where a Constitutional Court is embedded in a legal system with marked common law characteristics, unaccustomed to drawing a sharp distinction between constitutional and other sources of law. In each of these systems, the details of the responsibilities of the various courts and of the relationship between them varies.[64] To illustrate, however: the Constitutional Court of South Africa can also deal with non-constitutional matters on appeal; and while other courts can make an order of constitutional invalidity, the order must be confirmed by the Constitutional Court before it 'has any force'.[65] As a generalization, which is explicit in the case of South Africa, specialist constitutional courts that share constitutional jurisdiction with other courts in the system are likely to be considered as part of the judiciary, rather than separate from it.[66]

---

[60] For an illustrative taxonomy of those in use in Europe, see M. De Visser, *Constitutional Review in Europe: A Comparative Analysis* (Hart Publishing, 2014), 123.

[61] K. Kelemen, 'Dissenting Opinions in Constitutional Courts' (2013) 14 *German Law Journal* 1345.

[62] By way of example, the Constitutional Courts of both the Republic of Korea and Taiwan require supermajorities for this purpose: Chang et al. (n. 45), 444.

[63] Venice Commission (n. 2). On the variety of 'mixed' arrangements in Latin America see, for example, Navia and Rios-Figueroa (n. 54).

[64] Delledonne (n. 50).

[65] Constitution, Republic of South Africa, section 167. The drafting history of the provisions establishing the Constitutional Court show the framers of the South African Constitution grappling with these issues: A. Chaskalson, 'Constitutional Courts and Supreme Courts – A Comparative Analysis with Particular Reference to the South African Experience', in I. Pernice, J. Kokott and C. Saunders (eds.), *The Future of the European Judicial System in a Comparative Perspective* (Nomos, 2006), 97.

[66] Delledonne (n. 50).

Secondly, the conceptual and design differences between Kelsenian style Constitutional Courts in Europe and the *Conseil Constitutionnel* of the Fifth French Republic can also be found elsewhere in the world. The distinctive features of the latter, in terms of its more overtly political character and limitation to a priori review sometimes are adopted by former French colonies and other states in the French orbit of influence: Algeria, Morocco, Mozambique and Cambodia are examples.[67] The influence of the *Conseil Constitutionnel* can readily be seen in many other French colonies as well, although the path has not necessarily been linear and there are numerous variations on the original theme. Thus, in the context of francophone West Africa, Babacar Kante has noted that Constitutional Courts were introduced in connection with democratization in the 1990s, rather than at the point of decolonization, in a variety of forms and with a variety of functions, which typically included at least some capacity for ex ante review.[68] It may be expected that over time the French variation on centralized review will continue to take on more of the characteristics of the Kelsenian approach, globally and in France itself.

Thirdly, there is now considerable variation between systems of centralized review in relation to the related issues of access to the court and the type of questions a court can entertain.[69] As originally conceived, a Constitutional Court determined a question about the constitutionality of a statute in the abstract, at the instance of an organ of state or a level of government. More usually now, however, there are also other ways to approach a Constitutional Court. One, which is relatively common, involves reference to the Constitutional Court of a constitutional question that has arisen before an ordinary court in the course of concrete proceedings, in a form of 'incidental' review.[70] The referring court suspends the proceedings until the specialist court has reached a decision on the constitutional question, enabling the case to be determined. In addition, in some systems of centralized review, an individual may bring a 'constitutional complaint' to claim that his or her fundamental rights have been violated

[67] Venice Commission (n. 2).
[68] B. Kante, 'Models of Constitutional Jurisdiction in Francophone West Africa' (2008) 3(2) *Journal of Comparative Law* 158. Kante attributes the developments in the 1990s to regional fallout from the National Conference in Benin in 1990: 'having the same significance in Africa as the fall of the Berlin Wall in Europe', at 159.
[69] This and the next paragraph closely follow my chapter in Chen and Harding (n. 7).
[70] Garlicki (n. 44), 46.

or not vindicated by earlier judicial proceedings.[71] Both these avenues of access to a Constitutional Court establish a closer and more complex relationship with ordinary, or general courts, offering additional points at which the tensions of divided authority can play out.[72]

The convergence between forms of review noted in the earlier part can also be seen from the perspective of centralized review. The diversification of avenues to access Constitutional Courts, the expansion of the jurisdiction of some Constitutional Courts to include executive as well as legislative action; recognition that other courts might entertain constitutional issues, subject to the authority of the Constitutional Court; and the increasing prevalence of separate opinions are amongst a range of developments in design and practice that contribute to blurring a distinction already being eroded by parallel changes in arrangements for diffuse review. Superficial differences nevertheless remain, in the composition, constitution, modes of proceeding and jurisdiction of courts in systems of diffuse and centralized review. More importantly still, the underlying assumptions on which the respective systems are based continue to explain differences in discourse, doctrine and practice, which cannot be understood on other bases.

c Authority

Centralized review was originally conceived as a mechanism for constitutional control of legislation that overcame legitimacy concerns as far as possible in that most sensitive of all contexts to which a constitution now applied. In composition, functions, procedure and status, the new institution was quite distinct from the familiar notion of a court. The function of pronouncing a statute contrary to the constitution was 'constitutive', not 'declaratory', facilitating characterization of the body as a 'negative legislator'.[73] Appointments were 'political' rather than 'bureaucratic' in the manner of ordinary judges, appropriately for the functions Constitutional Courts were to perform, although engineered so as to shore up their independence.[74] Determination of constitutional questions in the abstract, on

---

[71] Delledonne (n. 50).

[72] Ibid.; De Visser (n. 60), 377–392.

[73] T. Bustamante and E. de Godoi Bustamante, 'Constitutional Courts as "Negative Legislators": The Brazilian Case', in A.R. Brewer-Carias (ed.) *Constitutional Courts as Positive Legislators* (Cambridge University Press, 2013), 283.

[74] Ferreres Comella (n. 28), 468.

the application of emanations of the state and in the absence of private parties was consistent with the idea of a Constitutional Court as a new addition to the legislative process, acting in the public interest.[75]

In most states with centralized review the institution has long since evolved. Constitutional Courts are acknowledged and generally respected as courts, whether formally tied to the general court hierarchy or not. Their jurisdiction has expanded, enabling engagement with concrete cases, sometimes at the instance of the parties, typically in claims for the protection of rights. Their methodologies have changed too, to encompass the interpretation of statutes so as to avoid annulment or even the pre-scription of temporary rules to fill a legislative gap.[76] These changes have fuelled characterization of such courts as 'positive' rather than 'negative' legislators, although by reference to a range of different phenomena.[77] Even so, many characteristic features remain, including the generally dis-tinctive and somewhat more political basis on which appointments to Constitutional Courts are made. In any event, despite the changes that have occurred, the original conception of concentrated review has proved remarkably robust in providing legitimacy for it.

The conferral of specific authority on Constitutional Courts, by posi-tive law, generally in the form of a Constitution, to control the consti-tutional consistency of legislation, further underpins their political and social, as well as legal legitimacy. By definition, Constitutional Courts are new institutions, which must deliberately be created for the purpose they are specifically designed to serve, namely, constitutional control. Other key issues, including the effect of Constitutional Court decisions, necessarily are specified too. It follows that Constitutional Courts are free from one challenge to legitimacy that is occasionally levelled at older apex courts in systems of diffuse review, where the authority to review legislation on con-stitutional grounds is assumed or implied, rather than explicitly conferred.

Nevertheless, whenever a court annuls or invalidates legislation for inconsistency with a constitution there is potential for conflict with representatives of a past or current political majority, creating what has

---

[75] Kelsen (n. 47), 193, 195.

[76] A.R. Brewer-Carias, *Constitutional Courts as Positive Legislators* (Cambridge University Press, 2011).

[77] Compare, for example, Brewer-Carias (n. 76) and Alec Stone Sweet, 'The Politics of Constitutional Review in France and Europe' (2007) 5 *International Journal of Constitutional Law* 69.

been described in the United States as the 'counter-majoritarian' difficulty or dilemma.[78] It is ironic in some respects that this argument does not have greater purchase in systems of centralized review, where Constitutional Courts do not have the same range of options to avoid difficult constitutional questions to determine challenges on other bases. Presumably, the explanation lies again, at least in part, in the underlying rationales for centralized review. On the other hand, recent backlash against what were claimed as over-active Constitutional Courts in Hungary, Poland and elsewhere in central and eastern Europe show that, in this context too, the potential for tension between constitutional control and political forces is real and must be taken seriously.[79]

d Reasoning

Enough has been said in this part to make it clear that, notwithstanding a broadly shared core conception of centralized review, there are significant differences in the design and functions of Constitutional Courts around the world. Coupled with other contextual differences, some of which stem from the nature and purposes of individual Constitutions, these complicate generalization about approaches to constitutional reasoning. A degree of commonality nevertheless follows from features typically or often associated with centralized review, including the authority of Constitutional Courts to entertain constitutional questions in the abstract without a factual setting, the typical inability of such courts to draw on other sources of law to resolve the issue before them and the reliance on a single opinion of the court, rather than multiple opinions.

Constitutional Courts embedded in a civil law context also may share approaches to reasoning associated with that legal tradition. Characteristics of civil law reasoning are claimed to include working deductively from principle, rather than inductively from other analogous cases; less reliance on precedent; and a relatively formalistic style.[80] To

---

[78] For an account of some of the strands of this rich and complex debate, after the term was first coined by Alexander Bickel, see L. Solum, 'Legal Theory Lexicon: The Counter-Majoritarian Difficulty' (*Legal Theory Blog*, 9 September 2009): http://lsolum.typepad.com/legaltheory/2012/09/legal-theory-lexicon-the-counter-majoritarian-difficulty.html (accessed 16 May 2018).

[79] For an account in relation to Hungary: I. Stumpf, 'The Hungarian Court's Place in the Constitutional System of Hungary' (2017) 13 *Civic Review* 239.

[80] Jakab et al. (n. 34), 768–769.

the extent that this is so, the approach is not confined to courts offering centralized review in civil law legal systems but is likely to apply to any form of constitutional review in a civil law setting. The broad association between centralized review and civil law legal systems makes it a relevant consideration here, however. Systematic research on comparative legal reasoning shows that these claims about Constitutional Courts in civil law legal systems have some substance, as long as the contrast with common law and mixed legal systems is not pushed too far.[81] It also shows variations between groupings within Constitutional Courts of this kind, with the French *Conseil Constitutionnel* an outlier in its formulaic reasoning style, with close adherence to text.[82] Finally, it draws attention to the 'richer and more discursive style' of reasoning found in some Constitutional Court, including the German Federal Constitutional Court, hypothesizing that this may be due to common law influence, further blurring the distinction between the two.[83]

One final aspect of reasoning in Constitutional Courts concerns the ability or willingness of courts to look outside the national constitutional system to explicitly consider international or foreign law. In some cases, of which South Africa is one, the Constitution requires the Constitutional Court to consider the former in interpreting the constitutional rights provisions and permits it to consider the latter.[84] In other states, the answer may depend on whether international law has direct effect or on whether the state is a member of regional arrangements for human rights protection or economic integration. These possibilities aside, practice varies considerably, within and between courts in systems of diffuse and centralized review. As a generalization, which does not always hold true, courts in systems of diffuse review are more likely to draw on foreign constitutional experience in the course of judicial reasoning and Constitutional Courts are less likely to do so.[85] In this context as well, however, the prevalent legal system is a factor. Famously, moreover, there are apex courts within common law systems for diffuse review that are reluctant to take foreign experience into account: the Supreme Court of the United States is one court in which this has been an issue and the

[81] Ibid. 769, 774.
[82] Ibid. 763–764, 770, 779.
[83] Ibid. 782.
[84] Constitution of the Republic of South Africa 1996, s. 39.
[85] Saunders (n. 36).

Supreme Courts of Malaysia and Singapore are others.[86] New courts also may be more willing than those with an established jurisprudence to draw on foreign case law, whether operating within the context of diffuse or centralized review. The Constitutional Courts of Hungary and Indonesia are, or have been, examples.[87]

Conclusions

In the second decade of the twenty-first century, judicial review of the constitutionality of legislation, other state action and, sometimes, forms of private action is prevalent throughout the world. While judicial review first emerged, in both diffuse and centralized systems, in connection with the enforcement of federal Constitutions, it has since expanded to encompass most provisions, in most constitutions including, quintessentially, protection of rights. By this means, judicial review became a building block for liberal democracy and, in divided societies, a guarantee of minority rights. Expansion continued, well into the twenty-first century as, in many states, courts assumed the authority to review the constitutionality of constitutional amendments, even in the absence of express constitutional authority to do so and sometimes in the teeth of apparent constitutional prohibition.[88]

There are various generic theories about the causes of the expansion and acceptance of a role for courts in supervising compliance with the constitution, ranging from perception of the need for judicial review as a safeguard to protect both institutions and rights to claims about strategic behaviour on the part of political actors.[89] No one theory is likely to be universally valid, to explain a phenomenon that in any event clearly draws impetus as well from the forces of globalization, including the degree of external involvement in constitution making. Whatever the cause, however, once in place any arrangements for constitutional review will have similarities to others elsewhere in the world, as well as

---

[86] Ibid. 574.

[87] Ibid.

[88] Y. Roznai, *Unconstitutional Constitutional Amendments: The Limits of Amendment Powers* (Oxford University Press, 2017).

[89] D. Landau, 'Substitute and Complement Theories of Judicial Review' (2017) 92 *Indiana Law Journal* 1283; R. Hirschl, *Towards Juristocracy: The Origins and Consequences of New Constitutionalism* (Harvard University Press, 2007); T. Ginsburg, *Judicial Review in New Democracies: Constitutional Courts in Asian Cases* (Cambridge University Press, 2003).

distinctive features of its own, not all of which are self-evident. One purpose of this chapter has been to provide a map by which some of these similarities and differences can be identified and understood.

At least three issues bear watching for the future.

First, there is considerable cross-fertilization between courts and court systems, due to various forces of globalization, including the ease of communication and travel. This process is not necessarily eradicating difference, which remains responsive to context, broadly conceived. Cross-fertilization is eroding some of the more predictable indicators of difference, however, including the distinction between diffuse and centralized review and between legal systems, rendering comparison all the more difficult. This trend can be expected to continue. Its significance should not be overstated, however, to the point at which these still relevant distinctions are ignored.

Secondly, many courts provide constitutional review in states that are parties to one or more arrangements for regional human rights protection or economic integration. Not all regions have such arrangements in a form that is relevant for present purposes: notably, there are no regional arrangements with a significant institutional framework in Asia and the Pacific. Regional arrangements also vary considerably across the world in purpose, depth, design and operation, adding more comparative considerations to the mix. Where regional arrangements exist, and have institutions, including courts of their own, a new set of issues is presented for national courts, including those with a constitutional jurisdiction, in conditions of legal and, arguably, constitutional pluralism. Some of the questions that arise include the implications of regional norms and decisions of regional institutions for national constitutions; the national constitutional validity of regional arrangements or decisions taken pursuant to them; and the respective authority of regional and national courts in the interpretation and application of regional norms and instruments.[90] This chapter has not considered this aspect of the operation of courts with a constitutional jurisdiction, but its relevance to the framework within which some courts operate and the challenges that

---

[90] In relation to Europe, where these questions have emerged in the most sophisticated form, see G. Davies, 'Interpretative Pluralism within EU Law', in G. Davies and M. Avbelj (eds.), *Research Handbook on Legal Pluralism and EU Law* (Edward Elgar, 2018), 323.

they face should be noted at this stage. Regional arrangements are likely to continue and their range may well expand, including in regions of the world where they presently are undeveloped. There are no present signs, however, that they will further overtake the authority of national constitutional courts.

The third issue is, or may be, connected. It is possible that judicial review has, at least for the moment, reached its zenith. National courts have, by and large, preserved the final word for themselves vis-à-vis relevant regional counterparts; but some of the more ambitious national courts themselves are subject to new constraints in various ways. In some cases, of which Hungary and Poland are examples and Israel may be another, this is due to political action to change the authority or composition of the court. In others, of which the United States and India are quite different instances, it is due to vigorous debate about the proper limits of judicial action, inside and outside the court. At their best, courts with a constitutional jurisdiction are sensitive to the context in which they operate; aware of the limits to which they should go and beyond which they should not. This development, if it continues, will not neuter courts with a constitutional jurisdiction as important players in constitutional systems, but may constrain the continued expansion of judicial review.

Further Reading

A.R. Brewer-Carias, *Constitutional Courts as Positive Legislators* (Cambridge University Press, 2011).

A.H.Y. Chen and M.P. Maduro, 'The Judiciary and Constitutional Review' in M. Tushnet, T. Fleiner and C. Saunders (eds), *Routledge Handbook of Constitutional Law* (Routledge, 2013).

T. Daly, *The Alchemists: Questioning our Faith in Courts as Democracy Builders* (Cambridge University Press, 2017).

G. Delledonne, 'Relation of Constitutional Courts to Supreme Courts', *Max Planck Encyclopaedia of Comparative Constitutional Law* (2017) http://oxcon.ouplaw.com/view/10.1093/law-mpeccol/law-mpeccol-e571 (accessed 11 May 2018).

B. Kante, 'Models of Constitutional Jurisdiction in Francophone West Africa' (2008) 3(2) *Journal of Comparative Law* 158.

M. De Visser, *Constitutional Review in Europe: A Comparative Analysis* (Hart Publishing, 2014).

L. Garlicki, 'Constitutional Courts Versus Supreme Courts' (2007) 5 *International Journal of Constitutional Law* 44.

C. Saunders, 'Constitutional Review in Asia: A Comparative Perspective', in Albert HY Chen and Andrew Harding (eds.), *Constitutional Courts in Asia* (Cambridge University Press, 2018).

Cal Viney and Thomas Poole

Introduction

This chapter examines the rise of the Independent Fiscal Institution (IFI) within the institutional structures of modern states. A new feature of the regulatory landscape in most of the jurisdictions where they are to be found, these institutions are designed to encourage fiscal responsibility on the government's exercise of its budgetary responsibilities. The IFI often forms part of post-Global Financial Crisis (GFC) regulatory architecture[1] and is familiar to students of political economy and financial

The authors would like to thank David Kershaw, Martin Loughlin, Niamh Moloney and Joachim Wehner for their detailed and helpful comments and criticisms on an earlier version of the chapter.

[1] See E. Ferran, N. Moloney, J.G. Hill and J.C. Coffee, Jr, *The Regulatory Aftermath of the Global Financial Crisis* (Cambridge University Press, 2012); J. Black, 'Paradoxes and

regulation. But even though their activities relate directly to government in a way that is less true of other post-GFC innovations, IFIs have been largely ignored in the specialist public law literature, a by-product of the tendency among public lawyers to overlook the political economy dimensions of their field.[2]

This chapter seeks to bring the IFI into the public law fold. The project in general seeks to map the terrain for the benefit of public lawyers and to consider the institution from the perspective of public law. This chapter provides a fine-grained comparative analysis of two examples of the genre that were introduced at roughly the same time: the UK Office for Budget Responsibility (OBR) and the Australian Parliamentary Budget Office (PBO). It examines the origins, duties and functions of the two institutions – but not at this point their effectiveness[3] – and the way they have developed since their introduction. Our focus is to situate these bodies within their constitutional and institutional environment. This aim has influenced the process of selection.

The chapter provides a detailed comparative analysis of the selected bodies, framed by a general discussion of the rise of the IFI as a distinctive fiscal and political institution. Our analysis of the OBR and the PBO shows how these bodies were set up for somewhat different, if overlapping, reasons, and that their responsibilities and functions are correspondingly distinctive, again overlapping. But it also suggests some underlying commonalities, the most important of which is that they offer a technocratic attempt at counterbalancing the short-term bandwidth of modern fiscal politics. On the basis of this observation, we argue that the IFI ought to be understood as an institutional expression of what we call *intergenerational constitutional justice*. It provides, that is, a technology

Failures: "New Governance" Techniques and the Financial Crisis' (2012) 75 *Modern Law Review* 1037.

[2] See G.E. Metzger, 'Through the Looking Glass to a Shared Reflection: The Evolving Relationship between Administrative Law and Financial Regulation' (2015) 78 *Law & Contemporary Problems* 129, 145: 'in the 1960s and 1970s ... as financial regulation dropped off the political and administrative [law] radar, it became more identified with the business and private-law side of law schools ... This academic division has meant that scholars from each field often have limited familiarity with the analytic paradigms and core concerns that dominate the other, further reinforcing their divergence.'

[3] As such, we do not discount the possibility that IFIs in practice turn out to be window dressing – examples of virtue signalling on the part of governments facing pressure from bewildered citizenries post-GFC and looking to shore up (or restore) confidence in their fiscal decision-making competence.

by means of which the interests and concerns of future generations are given voice and forced upon the consciences of today's decision makers.

1 The Rise of the Independent Fiscal Institution

Independent Fiscal Institutions (IFI) – or independent parliamentary budget offices, fiscal policy councils or independent fiscal watchdogs as they are all but interchangeably termed – exist to provide independent and authoritative analysis of the public finances.[4] The International Monetary Fund (IMF) has employed the following broad definition:

a permanent agency with a statutory or executive mandate to assess publicly and independently from partisan influence government's fiscal policies, plans and performance against macroeconomic objectives relating to the long-term sustainability of public finances, short-medium-term macroeconomic stability, and other official objectives. In addition, a fiscal council can also (i) contribute to the use of unbiased macroeconomic and budgetary forecasts in budget preparation, (ii) facilitate the implementation of fiscal policy rules, (iii) cost new policy initiatives, and (iv) identify sensible fiscal policy options, and possibly, formulate recommendations.[5]

Applying this definition identifies thirty-nine IFIs globally[6] (including eighteen within the OECD).[7] IFIs of one sort or another have existed for decades in countries such as Belgium (1936), the Netherlands (1945), Denmark (1962), Austria (1970) and the United States (1974). But most owe their origins to the surge in government deficits and debts during the 2008–2009 GFC, which gave impetus to the suggestion that states should apply some of the experience of independent central banking to the fiscal sphere. Governments resorted to the IFI in part to lend legitimacy to their fiscal decision-making, and bound up in the reaction to the socialization

---

[4] IFIs are 'independent public institutions with a mandate to critically assess, and in some cases provide non-partisan advice on, fiscal policy and performance': L. von Trapp, I. Lienert and J. Wehner, 'Principles for Independent Fiscal Institutions and Case Studies' (2015) 2 *OECD Journal on Budgeting* 11.

[5] X. Debrun and T. Kinda, 'Strengthening Post-Crisis Fiscal Credibility: Fiscal Councils on the Rise – A New Dataset' (IMF Working Paper WP 14/58, International Monetary Fund, April 2014), 9.

[6] International Monetary Fund, 'Fiscal Councils Data Set', IMF Website: www.imf.org/external/np/fad/council/ (statistics as of end of December 2016).

[7] von Trapp et al., 10.

of fiscal risk that was such a feature of post-crisis politics, draws support from the evidence: the number of IFIs has more than tripled since the GFC. The largest growth can be seen in the European Union (EU) following reforms in the fiscal framework,[8] part of 'the massive reform agenda' undertaken by the EU in respect of its financial markets supervision and regulatory structures.[9] Outside the EU, new IFIs have been set up – as in Canada (2008) and Australia (2011) – to increase fiscal transparency and enhance the role of the legislature in the budget process.

a Rationale 1: Deficit Bias

Specific reasons for introducing an IFI vary according to national context, a point our case studies will illustrate. But two general (related but not subsumable) rationales tend to be advanced to explain the potential contribution of the IFI from a political economy standpoint. One prominent rationale offers the IFI as a technology for certain 'credible commitment' problems that pertain in this area, specifically the tendency of governments to depart from the long-term interests of the populace in fiscal sustainability for short-term gain, electoral popularity or sectional interest. The argument connects the IFI to the persistence in advanced economies of deficits across the economic cycle. Robert Hagemann notes that this is a long-term trend: 'the overall fiscal balance of OECD economies, as well as in the large majority of its member countries, was in

---

[8] According to the Treaty on Stability, Coordination and Governance 2012 (TSCG), euro area member states must have an independent body to monitor compliance with national fiscal rules. For analysis of the TSCG see P.P. Craig, 'The Stability, Coordination and Governance Treaty: Principle, Politics and Pragmatism' (2012) 37 *European Law Review* 231. The requirement to have IFIs was subsequently enhanced by the so-called 'two-pack' set of EU Regulations: EU Regulation 472/2013 on the strengthening of economic and budgetary surveillance of euro area members states experiencing or threatened with serious difficulties with respect to financial stability (EU Budget Surveillance Regulation); and EU Regulation 473/2013, which set out a common budgetary timeline applying to all euro area states for the publication and adoption of national medium-term fiscal plans and draft budgets. As part of this process, all euro area states were required to establish IFIs by October 2013 (EU Budget Monitoring and Assessing Regulation). For analysis see S. De la Parra, 'The Two Pack on Economic Governance: An Initial Analysis' (*Background Analysis*, European Trade Institute, Brussels 2013).

[9] N. Moloney, 'Reform or Revolution? The Financial Crisis, EU Financial Markets Law, and the European Securities and Markets Authority' (2011) 60 *International & Comparative Law Quarterly* 521, 523.

deficit throughout virtually the entire three decades to 2007.'[10] This is a problem in as much as one subscribes to the macroeconomic theory that government should run a counter-cyclical fiscal policy (i.e. deficits in a recession and surpluses in boom times so that public debt is kept stable across the economic cycle).[11] Yet the persistence of deficits indicates a different practice – 'a tendency to adopt and implement pro-cyclical positions during cyclical upswings, resulting in high levels of public debt'.[12]

On this rationale, the problem the IFI responds to is a predisposition to favour tax and spend policies that produce deficits at all times within the economic cycle arising from the tendency among elected politicians 'not to consolidate the budget during good times in order not to hurt their electorates'.[13] The intuition is that politicians, perceiving the importance of economic conditions for electoral success, will generate a 'political business cycle' so as to foster favourable conditions at election time.[14] It represents as such an example of the principal–agent problem that looms large in the public finance literature.[15] The term 'deficit bias' often deployed in such analyses trades on the idea of 'inflation bias' used in the monetary policy context which postulates that governments are unlikely to stick to long-term inflation targets due to *time inconsistency* pressures (the notion that policy makers' short-term objectives, such as adjusting interest rates in response to rising unemployment, conflict with the long-term objective of price stability,[16] a problem said to

[10] R. Hagemann, 'How Can Fiscal Councils Strengthen Fiscal Performance?' (2011) 1 *OECD Journal: Economic Studies* 75, 77.

[11] As one might expect, this model is contested. For an entry into the debate see J.M. Buchanan and R.A. Musgrave, *Public Finance and Public Choice: Two Contrasting Visions of the State* (MIT Press, 1999).

[12] Hagemann, 77.

[13] J. von Hagen, 'Scope and Limits of Independent Fiscal Institutions', in George Kopits (ed.), *Restoring Public Debt Sustainability: The Role of Independent Fiscal Institutions* (Oxford University Press, 2013), 38. This relates to the practice of 'deficit finance': expenditure is raised in a context where additional outlays are deficit-financed (rather than through raising taxes). On this scenario, the principal of today in effect colludes with its agent to put the cost burden on the principal of tomorrow.

[14] R.A. Musgrave and P.B. Musgrave, *Public Finance in Theory and Practice* (McGraw-Hill, 5th ed., 1989), 105.

[15] For an application of the insights of public finance theory into the domain of constitutions and constitutional arrangements see J.-J. Laffont, *Incentives and Political Economy* (Oxford University Press, 2000).

[16] C. Wyplosz, 'Fiscal Policy: Institutions versus Rules' (2005) 191 *National Institute Economic Review* 64, 67: 'the long-term discipline objective is systematically overlooked

be amplified in democracies).[17] Some economists argued that monetary policy functions – including the decision and execution of that policy, not just advice – should be outsourced to independent central banks,[18] a proposal that had significant take-up in practice.[19] By analogy,[20] some argue that IFIs can address some of the presumed causes of deficit bias, including information asymmetry (both between voters and politicians and between the legislature and the executive), economic forecasting bias (the tendency among governments to over-optimism in their economic forecasts)[21] and time inconsistency (as defined above).[22]

b Rationale 2: Information Asymmetry

If the first rationale sees the IFI as a technocratic tool that can mitigate deficit bias through a strategy of *de-politicization*, the second rationale understands the office in terms of an institutional response to the decline of legislative influence in the budget process, and is as such arguably a strategy of *re-politicization*. Its starting point is the observation that the executive now typically controls the budget process. This new executive financial hegemony has implications for the democratic ideal of elected

---

when short term discretion is being used.' But see Wren-Lewis, 'Comparing the Delegation of Monetary and Fiscal Policy', 58–62 and X. Debrun, 'Democratic Accountability, Deficit Bias and Independent Fiscal Agencies' (IMF Working Paper WP/11/173, International Monetary Fund, 2011) 10, both rejecting the claim that the specific type of time inconsistency that applies to inflation bias also applies to deficit bias.

[17] P. Tucker, *Unelected Power: The Quest for Legitimacy in Central Banking and the Regulatory State* (Princeton University Press, 2018), 130: 'elected politicians face a bit of a problem in committing to a stable and prudent debt management strategy because their expected life in office is so much shorter than the life of the debt'.

[18] See e.g. C. Goodhart, *The Evolution of Central Banks* (MIT Press, 1988); Tucker, *Unelected Power*.

[19] See e.g. C. Crowe and E.E. Meade, 'The Evolution of Central Bank Governance around the World' (2007) 21 *Journal of Economic Perspectives* 69.

[20] See e.g. S. Wren-Lewis, 'Comparing the Delegation of Monetary and Fiscal Policy', in Koptis, *Restoring Public Debt Sustainability*.

[21] L. Calmfors and S. Wren-Lewis, 'What Should Fiscal Councils Do?' (2011) 26 *Economic Policy* 651.

[22] Other problems associated with deficit bias include government impatience – governments know their time in power is limited and are therefore unlikely properly to internalize the long-term implications of fiscal decisions – and the 'common pool' problem – that those who press governments for increased spending, or greater tax cuts, fail to internalize the overall costs of higher spending and debt. See P. Posner and M. Sommerfield, 'The Politics of Fiscal Austerity: Democracies and Hard Choices' (2013) 13 *OECD Journal on Budgeting* 141.

legislators checking and controlling government tax and spending policies. From this perspective, the primary goal of the IFI is to enhance the fiscal capabilities of the legislature.

Articulating this rationale, Allen Schick offers a long-term narrative according to which legislatures initially wrested control over executive (usually the monarch's) spending through appropriations legislation until the expansion of government altered the balance of financial power. The result was that budgeting came to be viewed as a core function of the executive (aided by its growing bureaucratic apparatus).[23] Joachim Wehner subjects the constitutional notion that legislatures control the power of the purse to rigorous comparative quantitative and qualitative examination and concludes that, with the exception of the United States, legislatures within the OECD often have a low ability to scrutinize, influence and shape budgets.[24]

Observations of this sort have led to calls for a redefined role for legislatures in tackling debt and deficit, ideally in a manner that is not hostile to the service delivery demands of citizens. Schick calls for a strengthened legislature capable of 'promoting fiscal discipline, improving allocation of public money, and stimulating administrative entities to manage their operations more efficiently.'[25] These insights often cash out in terms of the need to provide non-partisan analysis to legislators in order to 'break the executive's monopoly on budget information'.[26] The IFI can be modelled as an institution that can help legislators by simplifying complex executive proposals, thereby enhancing the credibility of forecasts (through greater contestability) and promoting fiscal transparency and accountability.[27]

---

[23] A. Schick, 'Can National Legislatures Regain an Effective Voice in Budgetary Policy?' (2002) *1 OECD Journal on Budgeting* 15. For the 'long history' of this topic see C. Webber and A. Wildavsky, *A History of Taxation and Expenditure in the Western World* (Simon and Schuster, 1986) and, specifically from the perspective of British constitutional history, P. Einzig, *The Control of the Purse: Progress and Decline of Parliament's Financial Control* (Secker & Warburg, 1959).

[24] J. Wehner, *Legislatures and the Budget Process – The Myth of Fiscal Control* (Palgrave Macmillan, 2010). The UK Parliament performs particularly poorly in this comparative examination.

[25] Schick, 'Can National Legislatures Regain an Effective Voice in Budgetary Policy?', 28.

[26] J.K. Johnson and R. Stapenhurst, 'Legislative Budget Offices: International Experience' in R. Stapenhurst, R. Pelizzo, D.M. Olsen, L. von Trapp (eds.), *Legislative Oversight and Budgeting: A World Perspective* (World Bank, 2008), 152.

[27] B. Anderson, 'The Value of a Nonpartisan, Independent, Objective Analytical Unit to the Legislative Role in Budget Preparation', in Stapenhurst et al., *Legislative Oversight and Budgeting.*

More specifically, some argue that the IFI can reduce two types of information asymmetry. First, principal–agent information asymmetry can be improved.[28] By opening up the budgeting process, the IFI can create a more capable principal (the citizens) who, better informed by the expert and independent bystander, is able to use their voting power to reward good policy or sanction bad policy on the part of its agent (the government). Second, legislature-executive information asymmetry: the problem being that the executive has enormous resources (including expert resources) at its disposal, while the legislature typically does not. One way of responding to this problem is to provide a greater range of independent fiscal information either by providing a legislative-aligned IFI or by means of an official forecaster independent of the executive.[29]

c Design Variation

While it is legitimate to talk about the IFI in the singular, it is important to acknowledge considerable flexibility in design. IFIs form a 'hetero-geneous group', as one might expect, that 'vary considerably in terms of their governance provisions, breadth of their mandate and functions, leadership and staff arrangements, and budget'.[30] Path-dependency is a strong factor, as it almost always is in the context of agency design where local needs and the local institutional environment remain paramount. For Member States within the Euro area, initiatives take place within the relatively specific terms of EU regulatory structure developed under the TSCG.[31] Elsewhere, design choices – as well as being influenced by more mundane political factors – often come down to which of the rationale(s) for the IFI attracted more institutional support at the time of conception.

---

[28] See e.g. Debrun, 'Democratic Accountability, Deficit Bias and Independent Fiscal Agencies'.

[29] For a good discussion and summary of the literature see Hagemann, 'How Can Fiscal Councils Strengthen Fiscal Performance?'. See also G. Kopits, 'Independent Fiscal Institutions: Developing Good Practices' (2011) 11 *OECD Journal on Budgeting* 3.

[30] See von Trapp et al., 'Principles for Independent Fiscal Institutions and Case Studies', 13.

[31] Although even here, considerable variation is to be found. Compare e.g. the French High Council for Public Finances (HCFP), closely networked with the existing Court of Auditors, and which has a direct (if non-binding) role in the budget process but no role in assessing the status and outlook – or sustainability of public finances, with the Spanish Independent Authority for Fiscal Responsibility (AIReF), which enjoys a broad mandate to ensure effective compliance by all public administrations with the budgetary stability principle established by Article 135 of the Spanish Constitution. This includes

Von Trapp et al. identify three basic models of IFI: the *fiscal council*, which tend either to be small councils comprised mainly of academics (e.g. Sweden, Ireland) or follow a corporatist tradition in that members of a larger council are proposed by different stakeholders (e.g. Austria, Denmark); the *parliamentary budget office*, where the focus is on assisting parliamentary oversight of the budget and supporting the work of the main budget committee (e.g. Canada, United States); and the *audit model*, in which the IFI is an autonomous part of the national audit institution (Finland, France).[32]

What is common to these models is that the institutions they model are not simply a functionary of the existing fiscal policy arm of the state (the Treasury or Finance Ministry). In design terms, they represent various (path-dependent) attempts to establish an entity with fiscal responsibilities that inputs into government at the highest level but remains free from direct political control or interference. IFIs are structured so as to incline voters and decision makers of today to give more weight than they otherwise might to the impact their vote or decision will have on the fiscal situation future generations are likely to encounter.

2 United Kingdom: The Office for Budget Responsibility

The genesis of the OBR in many ways reflects the overall story of the rise of the IFI. Established after the GFC in response to local political concerns, the OBR was designed to address structural problems with the existing framework for maintaining fiscal discipline and to prevent unsustainable public debt. The OBR also has some unique design features, notably its responsibility for supplying official fiscal and economic forecasts.

a Origins

The OBR grew out of a critical account of the fiscal performance of the previous (Labour) government pre- and post-GFC. The Conservative Party argued in the lead-up to the 2010 general election that previous Treasury

---

the continuous role of the budgetary cycle and public indebtedness, as well as analysis of economic forecasts. See von Trapp et al., 'Principles for Independent Fiscal Institutions and Case Studies', 118–123 and 214–219.

[32] von Trapp et al., 'Principles for Independent Fiscal Institutions and Case Studies', 13.

economic and fiscal forecasting had been too optimistic,[33] an argument supported by the Institute for Fiscal Studies (IFS).[34] The central claim was that the Labour government, assisted by this supposed forecasting bias, had overspent in the boom years, leaving state finances less well prepared when the crisis arrived and causing higher public debt as a result.[35] Existing fiscal rules established by the Treasury as self-binding mechanisms against such a scenario, which were in any case suspended in late 2008 as the GFC started to bite, were now seen as insufficient.[36] Given this narrative, the creation of an arm's-length body embedded within the interstices of fiscal administration but distinguished by its sole interest in fiscal responsibility must have seemed a natural progression.

b Legal Status and Functions

The OBR was established (initially on an interim basis)[37] on the formation of the Conservative-led Coalition Government in 2010,[38] with the primary 'objective of removing any possibility of political interference from official forecasts'.[39] Taking up its forecasting functions, the OBR became the

[33] Conservative Party, *Reconstruction: Plan for a Strong Economy* (Conservative Party, 2008).

[34] See e.g. Institute for Fiscal Studies, *The IFS Green Budget, January 2008* (Institute for Fiscal Studies, 2008). The IFS is a politically non-aligned economic research institute that specialises in UK taxation and public policy.

[35] See e.g. R. Chote and S. Wren-Lewis, 'United Kingdom: Fiscal Watchdog and Official Forecaster', in Kopits, *Restoring Public Debt Sustainability*, 235.

[36] The Labour-led governments of 1997–2010 committed itself to two main fiscal rules: the *golden rule* that 'over the economic cycle, the Government will borrow only to invest and not to fund current spending' and the *sustainable investment rule* that 'over the economic cycle, the ratio of net public sector debt to GDP will be set at a stable and prudent level' (defined by the Treasury as no more than 40 per cent of GDP): Finance Act 1998, Part VI; UK Government, 'Code of Fiscal Stability: Budget 1998' (March 1998). The framework was largely retrospective and the Government could also gain fiscal leeway through its determination on the dates on which the economic cycle started and finished. Pre-2010 arrangements did not, then, address the potential 'time inconsistency' problem noted in our conceptual introduction. For analysis see C. Emmerson, C. Fayne and S. Love, 'The Government's Fiscal Rules' (Institute of Fiscal Studies Briefing Note No. 16, November 2006).

[37] HM Treasury Press Notice, 'Chancellor announces policy on fiscal credibility', 17 May 2010.

[38] For its place within the Coalition agreement see P. Johnson and D. Chandler, 'The Coalition and the Economy', in A. Seldon and M. Finn (eds.), *The Coalition Effect, 2010–2015* (Cambridge University Press, 2015).

[39] Sir A. Budd, 'Letter to the Chancellor: Advice on the Establishment of OBR as a Permanent Body', 12 July 2010, para. 7.

first IFI anywhere to be charged with making official fiscal and economic forecasts. The Budget Responsibility and National Audit Act 2011 (Budget Responsibility Act) put the OBR on a permanent footing, with former IFS Director and economic journalist Robert Chote as chair.[40]

The OBR is an executive non-departmental public body or executive agency. It is primarily responsible to government not Parliament, but is an independent, arms-length entity. As its sponsor department is the Treasury, it is the Chancellor of the Exchequer who accounts for the OBR's business in Parliament. The Chancellor also appoints the chair and the two other members of the Budget Responsibility Committee, the unit that heads the OBR.[41] An Oversight Board, comprising the three members of the BRC plus two non-executive members,[42] and an Advisory Panel of economic and fiscal experts (mostly academics and financial practitioners) complete the corporate structure.

The House of Commons Treasury Select Committee (Treasury Committee) must approve those appointments[43] and more generally has oversight over the OBR. For a select committee to have a veto power over appointments and dismissals is extremely rare in the UK context,[44] and gives the Treasury Committee more leverage in its dealings with government in relation to the OBR.[45] The OBR is supported by a staff of twenty-seven permanent civil servants, which makes the body relatively small both within the IFI context and compared to other domestic institutions – the Office for National Statistics, for instance, has a staff of over 3,000.

---

[40] Chote remains chair at the time of writing, having been reappointed for another five-year term in September 2015.

[41] At the time of writing, the other two members of the BRC are former Deputy Governor for Monetary Policy at the Bank of England Professor Sir Charlie Bean and Graham Parker CBE, who had worked previously at the Treasury, the Inland Revenue and the IMF. The latter stepped down in August 2018, replaced by Andy King, civil servant and currently Chief of Staff at the OBR.

[42] Currently Christopher Kelly (career civil servant) and Bronwyn Curtis (global financial economist and consultant).

[43] Budget Responsibility Act, Schedule 1, s. 1.

[44] Indeed, it was the Treasury Committee itself, in a 2010 Report, that suggested this innovative veto mechanism over BRC appointments and dismissals, thereby exerting a critical influence over the OBR's design: House of Commons Treasury Committee, 'Fourth Report of Session 2010–11 Volume I – Office for Budget Responsibility' (21 September 2010), p. 3.

[45] The Treasury Committee has not been shy in exerting its influence to ensure non-interference with the OBR's functions. See e.g. 'Treasury Select Committee raises red flags after emails reveal Treasury meddling with Office for Budget Responsibility (OBR)', *City AM*, 22 February 2016.

While there are efficiency arguments for making the body no bigger than necessary, it may impact on perceptions of independence, as we shall see.

The fact that the OBR is accountable to both Government and Parliament has perplexed some commentators (we think without good reason). The first external review,[46] conducted in 2014 by former Canadian Parliamentary Budget Officer Kevin Page, found that 'the OBR's legally defined sources of accountability (the Chancellor and Parliament) are in tension, challenging its independence'.[47] But this double-headed accountability is not at all unusual within the UK agency context, where agencies tend to work for government but within a set of accountability conventions structured around the principle of Parliamentary democracy. It nonetheless serves to highlight the dual nature of the OBR as an institution of government that aspires to be both a service provider and an accountability mechanism.

The 2011 Act mandates the OBR 'to examine and report on the sustainability of the public finances'.[48] In fulfilling this duty the OBR must (1) produce the official five-year economic and fiscal forecasts twice a year;[49] (2) assess the government's progress in achieving its fiscal targets alongside its forecasts; (3) assess the accuracy of its previous forecasts;[50] and (4) analyse the long-term sustainability of the public finances, based

---

[46] An external review of the OBR must be undertaken at least once every five-year period: Budget Responsibility Act, Schedule 1, s. 16.

[47] Kevin Page, 'External Review of the Office for Budget Responsibility' (September 2014), 34. Recommendation 4 of that Review noted that 'the particularly narrow legal framework of the OBR and its interdependencies with the executive branch may risk creating perceptions of conflicts-of-interest'.

[48] Budget Responsibility Act, s. 4(1). The Act also requires the Government to produce a Charter of Budget Responsibility (s. 1), a Treasury document laid before the House of Commons and brought into force by a resolution of the Commons, which sets out the Government's approach to fiscal policy, management of the National Debt, and guidance to the OBR about how it should perform its legislative duties. This and other documents are supplemented with a number of other primary governance documents, including a Memorandum of Understanding between the OBR and the Treasury (and HM Revenue and Customs, the Department for Work and Pensions) on the joint governance, management and development of the macroeconomic model used by both the OBR and Treasury in forecasting.

[49] These forecasts are published in the OBR's Economic and Fiscal Outlook (EFO) publication. Its spring EFO is published at the same time as the budget and incorporates the impact of any tax and spending policy measures announced in the budget.

[50] The Treasury Review of the OBR recommended that the OBR should work systematically with forecasting departments on model development, building on existing practice to ensure key models are fit for practice.

on fifty-year projections.[51] The OBR can also undertake analysis at its own initiative. While its focus is on the public finances at a UK-wide level, the UK government also asks the OBR to forecast the receipts from taxes it has devolved, or intends to devolve, to the Scottish and Welsh governments.

This set of functions indicates that the OBR tacks towards the first rationale outlined in the previous section. It aims to tackle 'deficit bias', specifically by targeting economic forecasting bias (the tendency among governments to over-optimism in their economic forecasting) by the simple expediency of taking that responsibility from the hands of Government altogether.[52]

The other critical task at Budget time for the OBR, beyond forecasting, is certifying the Government's costings. The principal legal restriction on the OBR is the prohibition on alternative policy analysis. (At his Treasury Committee pre-appointment hearing, Chote argued that OBR independence would be better served by allowing it to respond to costings requests from other political parties.)[53] While the Budget Responsibility Act prescribes that where 'any Government policies are relevant to the performance' of its duties, the OBR must have regard to those Government policies only, it notes specifically that the OBR 'may *not* consider what the effect of any alternative policies would be'.[54] This is a subtle provision, but marks an important difference between the OBR and some other IFIs, including the PBO as we shall see. This restriction on the OBR can be explained in part by the political controversy surrounding the Government's austerity programme, instigated at the same time as the OBR was formed. Had the OBR been able to analyse not just that programme 'but also the more gradual tightening proposed by the opposition, it would have been at the centre of political debate' and may well as a result 'have lost the appearance of impartiality'.[55]

The prohibition on alternative policy costing precludes the OBR from producing election policy costings, which is a major function of the PBO.

<hr>

[51] Budget Responsibility Act, s. 4.
[52] There is a point of possible convergence between the UK and Australia, since it is now Labor Party policy for the PBO to be granted an official forecasting role in addition to its existing functions.
[53] 'Robert Chote tells MPs: open OBR to all parties', *The Telegraph*, 17 September 2010.
[54] Budget Responsibility Act, s. 5(3), emphasis added.
[55] Chote and Wren-Lewis, 'United Kingdom: Fiscal Watchdog and Official Forecaster', 243.

There is an ongoing debate about whether the OBR's remit should be expanded to include the certification of costings of political parties' tax and spending policies in the run-up to general elections. The OBR itself (perhaps unsurprisingly) seems keen to expand its remit in this direction, believing that independent scrutiny of pre-election policy proposals could contribute to better policy making, to a more informed public debate, and facilitate coalition-formation when party programmes need to be reconciled.[56] A 2015 Treasury review of the OBR concluded that 'the costs of relaxing the restricting on alternative policies are likely to outweigh the benefits at this stage, and by potentially undermining the OBR, it may serve to reduce rather than increase fiscal credibility in the UK.'[57] Responding to this review, the Treasury Committee accentuated the positive aspects of the proposal, while ultimately leaving the matter an open question for further consideration. 'The benefits to fiscal credibility of the OBR carrying out party policy costings before general elections are now becoming clear', it said, and cited with approval the Institute for Government's balanced argument in favour of the move.[58]

The legal structure of the OBR contains a number of mechanisms aimed at shoring up the OBR's independence and impartiality. The primary legislation stipulates that the OBR 'has complete discretion' in performing its main forecasting duty but 'must perform that duty objectively, transparently and impartially.'[59] The Charter of Budget Responsibility, which sets out the OBR's remit, contains a number of independence-related provisions. These relate to forecasting methods, content of publications, work programme and own-initiative research. The Budget Responsibility Act provides a right of access 'to all Government information which it may reasonably require for the purposes of the performance of its [main] duty.'[60] The Framework Document, a more detailed governance and management specification, states that the OBR's duty to work 'objectively, transparently and on the basis of government policy' fundamentally 'protects the independence of the OBR and ensures a clear separation

---

[56] See Letter from Robert Chote (Chair of the OBR) to Andrew Tyrie (Chair of the Treasury Committee), 'The costing of pre-election policy proposals', 15 January 2014.

[57] HM Treasury, 'HM Treasury review of the Office for Budget Responsibility', 3 September 2015, para. 3.92.

[58] House of Commons Treasury Committee, 'Reviewing the Office for Budget Responsibility' (Seventh Report of Session 2015–16, 9 February 2016), paras. 45, 50 & 54.

[59] Budget Responsibility Act, s. 5.

[60] Budget Responsibility Act s. 9(1).

between analysis (which is the role of the OBR) and policy-making (which is the responsibility of ministers)'.[61]

The absence of a guarantee in respect of the OBR's budget in the framing legislation (or the Charter) is sub-optimal from the perspective of securing an IFI's autonomy, as the Page Review noted.[62] A five-year funding allocation from the Treasury was agreed in 2016–2017.[63] This reduces the possibility of politically motivated budget fiddling. BRC members are restricted from engaging in 'controversial political activity' as part of their terms of employment.

But the OBR's reasonably robust legal and corporate structure (input legitimacy)[64] is complicated by aspects of its working life (output legitimacy). The objective of holding government to account may be tempered by the reality that in providing economic forecasting the OBR performs what has hitherto been seen as a basic function of modern government. The tension that ensues is captured in the last line of the Government response to the Treasury Committee 2010 Report: 'The Government agrees that the OBR should not run education campaigns.'[65] While it was never intended that the OBR run campaigns, the line is indicative of a view that while the OBR should publish 'user-friendly' reports, it ought not to go out of its way to educate the public. The stronger this sentiment, the more the OBR begins to resemble a mechanism internal to government rather than a tool to enhance democratic decision-making.

The prevailing practice among existing IFIs was for an independent body which comments on government forecasts or produces its own forecasts. The OBR broke that mould in that it was set up to provide forecasts *for*

---

[61] HM Treasury, 'Office of Budget Responsibility and HM Treasury Framework Document' (May 2014), at 1.7.

[62] 'External Review', 32.

[63] Letter from the Treasury Permanent Secretary to OBR Chair (31 March 2016).

[64] As Gillian Metzger notes, calibrating agency independence can be a complicated affair in which many variables are in play 'including budgetary autonomy, bipartisan and multimember composition, and the extent of substantive oversight in addition to removal protection': 'Through the Looking Glass to a Shared Reflection', 134. We might also note that independence is only one variable when assessing an agency's overall social value (e.g. its fit within a pre-existing administrative network; structures of accountability; constitutional principles). On the importance of 'background conditions' in agency design in the financial regulation context see C. Ford, 'New Governance in the Teeth of Human Frailty: Lessons from Financial Regulation' (2010) *Wisconsin Law Review* 441.

[65] 'Government Response to the House of Commons Treasury Committee 4th Report of Session 2010–11: Office for Budget Responsibility' (November 2010), at 5.20.

the government. But that role means that the OBR inevitably operates close working relationships with various government departments, above all the Treasury. The OBR, with its small permanent staff, relies on extra staffing largely seconded from the Treasury during forecasting periods in particular.[66] The sense of a revolving door between OBR and the Treasury has the potential to undermine perceptions of independence. The Treasury Committee in its 2016 Report homed in on the opportunity enjoyed by Ministers to offer views to the OBR during the pre-release access period of the Economic and Fiscal Outlook. If the OBR 'is to remain demonstrably institutionally independent', the Committee concluded, 'the terms of engagement with Government departments must be clarified. At a minimum, a revised Memorandum of Understanding should explain the purpose of exceptional pre-release access, which Ministers and officials are granted access and why, and the sort of changes to OBR documents that are envisaged during this period.'[67]

c Lines of Development

In its early years, the emphasis of the OBR appears to have been more on independent and impartial service delivery rather than on developing an expert and external 'check' on government. This is a familiar pattern for an early-career IFI. Chohan and Jacobs identify two basic functions such a body might perform. IFIs 'can be relegated to a perfunctory and mechanical role of costing policies that are brought to them' by government or political parties (the *mechanistic-costing* role). Alternatively, IFIs can also provide 'a more active engagement, a presentation of budget options, and sense of 'right' policies in a variety of fields' including government borrowing and expenditure (the *normative-advisory* role). The authors see the latter role as 'more advanced, and more valuable, but also more politically contentious'.[68] The OBR, as currently modelled, sits squarely within the former category.

---

[66] For details see 'HM Treasury review of the Office for Budget Responsibility', paras. 5.30–5.31.

[67] Treasury Committee, 'Reviewing the Office for Budget Responsibility', para. 37.

[68] U.W. Chohan and K. Jacobs, 'Public Value in Politics: A Legislative Budget Office Approach' (2017) 40 *International Journal of Public Administration* 1063, 1064.

Despite its relatively limited remit, the OBR has not been free from controversy. We have already noted the Treasury Committee's concern for the independence of the OBR from Government (especially the Treasury). That investigation was triggered by the revelation that the Government had used the pre-release access period as an opportunity to induce not entirely insignificant changes of language from the Economic and Fiscal Outlook in late 2014. As well as the robust Treasury Committee Report, the incident also brought critical headlines.[69] The OBR has also received criticism for the quality of its economic forecasting. Generally this has concerned its predictive capacities: in its early years (2010–2012) its growth forecasts were over-optimistic; later on (2012–2014) they proved to be more negative than the actual figures.[70] More sophisticated criticism has targeted modelling blindspots. Future spending on welfare and other benefits is calculated independently by the OBR by projecting forward the costs of current policies. For other Departmental spending, the OBR effectively uses the Chancellor's numbers, regardless of whether they are compatible with the Government's current detailed spending policies, undermining to some extent the robustness of the relevant OBR forecasts.[71]

These sorts of criticisms go largely with the grain of the institution, in that they accept that the OBR can in principle produce 'public value' through exerting government numbers on present and future public expenditure to rigorous examination.[72] It is not necessarily implausible to count them as symptoms of success. They show that the OBR has not been ignored – though perhaps given its official forecasting role it is not really ignorable, especially given challenging economic conditions since 2010. If the OBR is to realize any of its aims, whether improving efficiency or raising the level of transparency and accountability in the budget process, then it really has to be in the public eye. The friction generated by at least some of these critical moments may facilitate productive reform of the institution.

---

[69] See e.g. 'Treasury has sought to meddle with OBR forecasts', *The Times*, 14 September 2015.
[70] See e.g. 'Four times the OBR has been wrong', *The Telegraph*, 24 November 2016.
[71] Julian McCrae, 'Securing the long-term credibility of the OBR: four key changes are needed', *Institute for Government*, 30 November 2015.
[72] Chohan and Jacobs, 'Public Value in Politics: A Legislative Budget Office Approach'. The underlying source of this approach is M. Moore, *Creating Public Value: Strategic Management in Government* (Harvard University Press, 1995).

3 Australia: Parliamentary Budget Office

As noted in the introduction, there has been a notable increase in the number of IFIs since the GFC (especially within the Eurozone). But we also observed that the impetus underlying the creation of such institutions is both longer term and more general, aided in no small measure by international and transnational governmental institutions such as the G20[73] and the IMF.[74] Australia provides an interesting example in this context. Its Parliamentary Budget Office, while it dates from the relevant period – it commenced operations on 23 July 2012 – has almost nothing directly to do with the GFC, which left Australia largely unscathed. The immediate context for the genesis of the PBO was political deal making involving a Labor Prime Minister without a majority courting a supply agreement from independent parliamentarians. One of the things those MPs wanted, and which the Prime Minister was prepared to grant, was an interesting example of the parliamentary budget office model of IFI.

The catalyst for the PBO may have arisen out of the need to form a working majority, but the primary impetus behind its creation was the perceived need (at least among some independent MPs) for greater fiscal transparency and accountability regarding the cost of election promises and more broadly costings outside of an election period requested by independents. One of the key issues was that while the government, opposition, and any minority party with at least five elected members enjoyed access to the Ministry of Finance and Treasury to cost their election commitments under the Charter of Budget Honesty Act, similar access was not available to smaller political parties or independents, an important feature of the modern Australian political landscape.[75] A secondary impetus came from the view among some that Parliament would

---

[73] See e.g. M. Dolls, A. Peichl and K.F. Zimmermann, 'A Challenge for the G20: Global Debt Brakes and Transnational Fiscal Supervisory Councils' (2012) 47 *Intereconomics* 31, discussing inter alia the steps taken on this front at G20 conferences in Seoul and Toronto in 2010 and Cannes in 2011.

[74] See e.g. IMF, *Fiscal Councils: Rationale and Effectiveness* (IMF Working Paper 16/86, International Monetary Fund, April 2016).

[75] Charter of Budget Honesty Act 1998 (Cth), Parts 2 & 8. For a recent explanation of how this process operates, including interaction with the PBO, see Joint Secretaries of the Treasury and Department of Finance, *Charter of Budget Honesty Policy Costing Guidelines*, Treasury, 2016 (https://static.treasury.gov.au/uploads/sites/1/2017/06/charter-of-budget-honesty-guidelines.pdf).

benefit from specialized and independent research and analysis on fiscal and economic policy.

a Origins

The 2010 general election resulted in a hung parliament. As part of the negotiation process between the Australian Labor Party (ALP) and the cross-bench independents, a deal was struck between the then leader of the ALP, Julia Gillard, and two independent MPs, Rob Oakeshott and Tony Windsor, which agreed a set of reforms to the parliamentary process. Some of these reforms were for additional resources for Parliament. This agenda included reform 16.1: that a Parliamentary Budget Office 'be established, based in the Parliament Library, to provide independent costings, fiscal analysis and research to all members of parliament, especially non-government members. The structure, resourcing and protocols for such an Office be the subject of a decision by a special committee of the Parliament which is truly representative of the Parliament.'[76] A Joint Select Committee on the Parliamentary Budget Office was appointed, reporting in March 2011. The Government agreed or agreed-in-principle to all of its twenty-eight recommendations in July. The agreement included allocating $24.9 million over four years in the 2011–2012 Budget to establish the PBO,[77] a provision which makes it one of the most effectively endowed budget institutions in the world.[78]

Its functions and organizational arrangement indicate that, in contrast to the OBR, the PBO tacks towards the second rationale for IFIs outlined earlier. Its immediate goal is to address 'information asymmetry' associated with the politics of modern public financing, specifically by empowering both minority parties and independents within Parliament and Parliament more generally through the provision of specialized, independent fiscal information. This is not to say, of course, that countering the problem of

---

[76] See The Australian Labor Party and the Independent members (Mr Tony Windsor and Mr Rob Oakeshott) – Agreement, 7 September 2010, and 'Appendix B: Agreement for a Better Parliament – Parliamentary Reform'.

[77] Government Response to the Joint Select Committee on the Parliamentary Budget Office Inquiry into the Proposed Parliamentary Budget Office, July 2011.

[78] U.W. Chohan, 'How does Australia's policy costings body, the Parliamentary Budget Office, compare?', *The Conversation*, June 2016.

'deficit bias' (Rationale 1) is not present in these arrangements as a deeper lying goal.

b Legal Status and Functions

The PBO was established by the Parliamentary Service Amendment (Parliamentary Budget Officer) Act 2011 (which amended a number of pieces of legislation, most notably the Parliamentary Service Act 1999) as one of four parliamentary departments supporting the Australian Parliament.[79] Its primary clients are parliamentarians. Accountability to Parliament is secured in the first instance through the appointments process. The PB Officer is appointed for a four-year term (and can only be removed) by the Presiding Officers, i.e. the Speaker of the House of Representatives and the President of the Senate, following approval by the Joint Committee of Public Accounts and Audit ('the Committee').[80] The legislation also grants significant over-sight powers to the Committee, which has a duty to consider the PBO's annual work plans and budget.[81]

Unlike the OBR whose primary functions concern forecasts and budget estimates, the PBO is specifically prohibited from preparing economic forecasts or preparing budget estimates, whether at the government, agency or programme level.[82] Rather, its mandate is 'to inform the Parliament by providing ... independent and non-partisan analysis of the budget cycle, fiscal policy and the financial implications of proposals.'[83] This translates into two more specific functions: (1) election policy costings; and (2) policy costings on request by senators and members.

(1) The *election policy costings* function is a distinctive feature of the Australian version of the IFI. A survey of OECD countries found only one other jurisdiction – the Netherlands – where the IFI has a role in costing elections.[84] This part of its mandate equates to two powers,

---

[79] Parliamentary Service Act 1999 – as amended by the Parliamentary Service Amendment (Parliamentary Budget Officer) Act 2013 – s. 64A.

[80] s. 64X.

[81] s. 64S.

[82] s. 64E(2).

[83] s. 64B.

[84] von Trapp et al., 'Principles for Independent Fiscal Institutions and Case Studies', 19 and 181. Although established in 1945, the tradition has grown since the mid-1980s of requesting costing and economic impact forecasts of election manifestos from the CFB

the first being a power for parliamentarians to request that a policy be costed on a public basis during the 'caretaker period' leading up to polling day. The second is a mandatory reporting requirement, a responsibility introduced in 2013[85] which requires the PBO 'to report on election commitments of designated Parliamentary parties' within thirty days of the end of the caretaker period of a general election. The report must set out for each designated parliamentary party costings of (a) all election commitments that would have 'a material impact on the Commonwealth budget sector and Commonwealth general government sector fiscal estimates'; and (b) 'the total combined impact those election commitments would have on the Commonwealth budget sector and Commonwealth general government sector fiscal estimates' over the next four financial years.

In practice this entails that each party must, before 5pm on the day before polling day, give the PBO a list of the policies that the party has publicly announced it intends to seek to have implemented after the election. The ensuing report must be publicly released. This means that when parties announce a policy, with their own costing, they know that it will be subject to serious post-election scrutiny by an independent body. As then Treasurer Wayne Swan observed during the second reading of the 2013 legislation: 'The Bill will impose discipline on the promises of political parties and incentivize all political parties to be up front and honest about the cost of their promises.'[86]

The fact that the scrutiny of costings proposals occurs *after* polling day may look curious, causing a sceptic to wonder how the PBO can influence a vote if its work on election policies only comes out after the election. It is true that the arrangement represents a trade-off between, on one hand, the goal of encouraging fiscal responsibility in election promises and, on the other, the over-politicization and the over-exposure that would ensue if the PBO could put out a statement shortly before election day confirming or dismissing the purported costs of a party's election policies (cf. Former FBI Director James Comey's intervention in

---

Netherlands Bureau for Economic Policy Analysis. Although voluntary, all major parties now ask for such costings.

[85] By the Parliamentary Service Amendment (Parliamentary Budget Officer) Act 2013.

[86] Hansard, Thursday 14 March 2013, 2093.

the 2016 US Presidential election is a cautionary tale).[87] The PBO may still exert influence, casting a shadow over campaigning. That presence, more particularly the sanction of having the PBO issue a statement thirty days after a party is elected (or even after defeat) to the effect that its costings were seriously in error, provides a non-negligible incentive to politicians not to make extravagant promises. Financial credibility is a hard won reputation in the political arena, and easily lost, and a party's reputation for fiscal competence – or incompetence – does not track a single electoral cycle but operates over the medium-to-long term. (Consider how the British Labour Party still suffers from a reputation for fiscal irresponsibility picked up a decade ago.)

(2) The *policy costings* function involves a requirement on the PBO to prepare responses to requests from individual Senators and Members (and also parliamentary committees) outside the caretaker period, a power that notably includes the preparation of costings in relation to proposed policies and bills. This function might seem on the face of it to enable a party to 'officially' cost another party's policy proposal or initiative. However, in practice this is unlikely. PBO Guidance Note 01/2013 provides that since the PBO must operate at all times in an independent and non-partisan manner, it 'will not prepare costings of policies attributed to an individual parliamentarian or a political party without the knowledge and active participation of the individual parliamentarian or political party in the costings process'.[88]

The PBO's fundamental role in relation to this part of its remit, then, is to empower members of opposition parties, and more specifically minor parties, to cost *their own* policies. Both the guidance notes and the practice of the PBO as evidenced by its website, which publishes all costings unless requested to be kept confidential, indicates that the key to the PBO's work is power asymmetry between Government (which has the Treasury to hand) and minor parties and independents, especially in the Senate. Much of the costing work concerns proposals that independents or small party Senators put to the PBO often in the context of negotiations with Government on amendments to legislation that they would like to see. The

---

[87] See for example, A. Chozick 'Hillary Clinton Blames F.B.I. Director for Election Loss' *New York Times*, 12 November 2016, www.nytimes.com/2016/11/13/us/politics/hillary-clinton-james-comey.html.

[88] PBO Guidance Note 01/2013, 'Costing of policy proposals at the request of a parliamentarian or political party that are attributed to another parliamentarian or political party'.

fact that such a request (outside the caretaker period) may be confidential enables parliamentarians and parliamentary parties to develop and cost their policies in a measured fashion in the lead-up to an election. They are then able to publicly release policies that have been professionally costed by the PBO.

Again, details of these arrangements may appear counter-intuitive. In particular, if the rationale behind the PBO is to counteract information asymmetry, the option to keep costings confidential seems odd. That criticism would be more compelling if the PBO were designed to address information between the public and the executive (principal–agent asymmetry). While this is one of the roles of the PBO – possibly an increasing one – it remains a subsidiary function. Its primary objective is to overcome information asymmetry (and resource asymmetry) between MPs who are not members of a major party, and the elected government (legislature–executive information asymmetry). The possibility of confidential costings does nothing to address public/government information asymmetries but may be part of an effective response to legislature/executive asymmetries. The central innovation is that MPs can now get their hands on genuine costings, when previously this would not have been a realistic prospect.

The PBO's mandate does not extend to oversight of the budget process, although it does include the duty to prepare responses to requests by Senators or Members to the budget. It also has a fairly broad capacity to conduct on its own-initiative research on and analysis of the budget and fiscal policy settings.[89] Exercise of this own-motion power has produced fourteen Reports to date, for instance on the budgetary impact of the National Broadband Network[90] and the Higher Education Loan Programme.[91] The impression is of an IFI that is busy doing independent policy thinking and forecasting.

Two own-initiative reports on economic forecasting within the budget process are particularly salient.[92] Although based on the economic forecasts and other parameters underpinning the Budget, analysis in these reports goes beyond the forward estimates contained in the official

---

[89] s. 64E(1)(c).

[90] Report 4/2016: National Broadband Network: Impact on the Budget (14 December 2016).

[91] Report 2/2016: Higher Education Loan Programme: Impact on the Budget (6 April 2016).

[92] Report 02/2015: 2015/16 Budget: Medium-term projections and Report 02/2017: 2017/18 Budget: medium-term projections (5 July 2017).

budget papers prepared by the Treasury (in the more recent report, to the years 2027–2028). These 'medium-term' reports are not dissimilar to the 'financial sustainability' reports produced on an annual basis by the OBR.

In the course of its ordinary business, the PBO is under an obligation to use the budget parameters set out by the Treasury, which are considerably shorter than the fifty-year horizon deployed by the OBR. Even so, the PBO can be said to have made a concerted effort to insert a degree of comparative rigour into the forecasting exercise. It is here that we can see perhaps most clearly the ambition of the PBO to become more than an election policy costing machine, reactive to the wishes of often marginal MPs and Senators. The PBO appears to be engaged, in the exercise of its own private-motion power, in a much broader analysis. It has chosen to examine some of the largest and most contentious areas of policy,[93] and has done so while projecting their impacts over the forward estimates and undertaking forecasting work over a longer horizon than the Treasury.

c Lines of Development

While a relatively new entity on the Australian landscape, the PBO has become a creature of some interest. Two examples demonstrate its increasingly embedded nature. First, in the lead-up to the 2016 national election, the Labor Party (by that time in opposition) announced an intention to expand the PBO's remit, specifically by transferring the official forecasting role for the budget from the Treasury to the PBO. As Shadow Treasurer Chris Bowen noted, this innovation would 'ensure that economic forecasts are undertaken at arm's length from government, giving the public more confidence in the budget process'.[94] Party political considerations naturally played a part in this proposal. Even so, it indicates a deepening commitment to the OBR within the political elite and more

[93] The national broadband network has been one of the most expensive and controversial projects in recent Australian policy making history. See e.g. T. Alizadeh, 'The NBN: how a national infrastructure dream fell short' *The Conversation*, 5 June 2017; P. Manning, 'Network Error', *The Monthly*, April 2017; K. Middleton, 'The Politics of the NBN', *The Saturday Paper*, 28 October 2017. Likewise the Higher Education Loan Programme remains a fundamental battleground between major parties. For a brief history, and the role of the PBO within it, see J. Hare and K. Loussikian, 'Higher education, higher costs in student loan scheme nightmare' *The Australian*, 8 April 2016.
[94] C. Bowen, National Press Club Address, May 2016, quoted in Michelle Grattan, 'Aspiring treasurer Chris Bowen looks fit for purpose' *The Conversation*, 10 May 2016, https:// theconversation.com/aspiring-treasurer-chris-bowen-looks-fit-for-purpose-59187.

particularly an intention to give the institution more responsibility for mainstream fiscal management functions. The effect of such reform would be to bring the PBO closer to the OBR, by adding to its existing rationale of combatting 'information asymmetry' the additional rationale of tackling 'deficit bias'.

In politics as in life, imitation is often the sincerest form of flattery. As a federation, Australia offers plenty of scope for copycat innovation, and there has been a significant uptake of IFIs within state legislatures since the PBO was formed. In late 2010 – after the federal election that led to the establishment of the PBO – New South Wales introduced a Parliamentary Budget Officer. Like its federal counterpart, its focus is on election policy costings, with a statutory duration of less than a year before state elections.[95] In South Australia, the Parliamentary Budget Advisory Service – led by the Parliamentary Budget Officer – operated for the first time at the 2018 state election, although at the time of writing it has no firm statutory underpinning.[96] The focus of that model is once again non-compulsory election policy costings. Another institution similar in design to the federal PBO has recently been instituted in Victoria.[97]

Entities with a special focus on costings used during the election process are proliferating in Australia. It is reasonable to wonder if the present (and rather narrow) focus on election policy costings will persist, or whether their role might expand, influenced by the possible direction of travel of the federal PBO, to include more general fiscal policy advisory functions. Recalling Chohan and Jacob's framework, one possible direction of travel would be from the current staunchly mechanistic-costing

---

[95] See Parliamentary Budget Officer Act 2010; see also: www.parliament.nsw.gov.au/pbo/Pages/Parliamentary-Budget-Office.aspx.

[96] See http://pbas.sa.gov.au/about.

[97] Parliamentary Budget Officer Act 2017. The Victorian scheme allows for election related policy costings and will operate at three levels: in the election policy costing period, a parliamentary leader may request the PBO officer prepare a policy costing (which can then be made public by the leader); if the leader asks for more than one policy to be costed in this period, they may instead request a 'pre-election report' enabling a party to list, and then have costed, those policies they would like costed, with the pre-election report going public only at the request of the leader; there is a separate post-election report, under which the PBO Officer must prepare a post-election report on the policies of each parliamentary leader that were publicly announced before the date of the general election. The second plane of this body enables any MP to request a costing of a policy or proposed policy at any time during the parliamentary term.

role towards a more ambitious normative-advisory role. (Although we might note that such a transition can be met with strong resistance.)[98]

Conclusion: Comparative Analysis

The OBR and the PBO owe their existence to particular confluences of political events. The former represents a key policy initiative connected to a critique of the previous Government's supposedly profligate handling of the public finances, an issue that became especially pressing after the GFC. The latter happened to be one of the demands made by a handful of independent MPs in return for an agreement to supply a minority administration.

For all the serendipity of their origins, the two institutions mirror quite closely the two central rationales underlying the global proliferation of IFIs. The OBR, under the aegis of the executive (albeit with substantial parliamentary oversight and protection) and with a focus on budget forecasting and the long-term sustainability of the public finances, reflects the 'deficit bias' rationale – the idea that governments ought not to be trusted to run the numbers alone (if at all). The PBO, a parliamentary body with a focus on supplying MPs with fiscal information (including important election costings functions), reflects the 'information asymmetry' rationale – more especially the idea that legislatures should be empowered by making inroads into the executive's fiscal hegemony ('legislature–executive information asymmetry').

Once instituted, IFIs are drawn into the game of party political point-scoring. We have just seen how the current ALP is seeking to use the PBO to its advantage. The politics of economic sustainability are equally a source of contestation in the UK. In late 2017, Shadow Chancellor John McDonnell introduced a policy that the government should include the fiscal risks posed by global warming in future economic forecasts. The reform would put climate change on an equal footing with other complex challenges affecting the public finances such as demography. McDonnell also announced that a future Labour Government would give the OBR total independence, allow it to audit party manifestos, and said that the forecaster would report directly to Parliament rather than the Treasury.[99] This last initiative is particularly interesting. Not only does it provide

---

[98] Chohan and Jacobs, 'Public Value in Politics', citing the experience of the Canadian PBO.
[99] 'Labour vows to factor climate change risk into economic forecasts', *The Guardian*, 14 November 2017.

more evidence for a 'convergence thesis' between the two IFIs – since if it were to occur the OBR would become, like the PBO, in effect a *parliamentary* budget office. It also indicates the current standing the OBR has among politicians. Given its origins, one could well imagine the Labour Party to take a much less supportive line towards the institution.

Both the OBR and the PBO are young entities, with presumably much growing still to be done. But it looks as though they might be on a path of convergence. The OBR (with the support of the Treasury Committee and some MPs) looks to move into election policy costing, something that is central to the PBO's existing mandate. The PBO looks as though it might gain an official forecasting role should the Labor Party win the next general election, an addition that would align it more closely with the OBR. It is unwise to generate descriptive generalizations or predictions on so limited a case study. But we introduce, very tentatively at this point, a set of hypotheses that we hope to test in future research: (i) whatever its starting point, an IFI will seek to add functions to its portfolio; (ii) these will include both more inward-facing functions (e.g. official forecasting) and more outward-facing functions (e.g. election policy costings); and (iii) this expansion is likely to be facilitated by the logic of inter-party competition. The extent to which this process of expansion and alignment is a transnational phenomenon – whether the product of comparative or copycat behaviour and/or as a result of pressure from transnational bodies such as the G20 – is something we intend to explore in future work.

We have made observations about the immediate take-up in political culture, but a fuller evaluation of an IFI's 'public value' contribution is only plausible over the long term. If we assume that the two IFIs studied in this chapter embed themselves in the fiscal pathways of the state, it is possible to detect at least one serious possible downside about their current operations. The existence of an IFI may make it easier for governments to perform a type of virtue signalling in fiscal affairs.[100] This is particularly likely where an IFI has a limited remit and performs its functions tamely, allowing politicians to talk the talk of fiscal responsibility without really facing up to hard choices. Drawing on recent Australian practice, Chohan and Jacobs observe that the incantation of terms such as fiscal

[100] Critics suggest that this is what has happened in respect of the Irish Fiscal Advisory Council. For evaluation, see L. Jonung, I. Begg and M.G. Tutty, *How is the Irish Fiscal Advisory Council Performing? An Independent Evaluation of the First Years of IFAC* (Working Paper 2016:3, Department of Economics, Lund University).

'sustainability' and 'responsibility' combine with the release of budget documents at regular intervals to give contemporary fiscal politics a ritual flavour. Given the contradictory stance that citizens often have on issues of expenditure and restraint, politicians can be tempted to 'prioritize between those values that will be addressed through resources and those that will be addressed through rhetoric'.[101]

The intersection between the genesis of IFIs and the rhetoric of fiscal trust politics is revealing. IFIs operate without the hard sanction powers of other gatekeepers – e.g. ratings agencies can increase or decrease the cost of borrowing through a revision of the institution's credit rating – and may be said as such to be incapable of imposing any real costs (beyond rhetorical damage) on the governments they monitor.[102] This more sceptical line of enquiry prompts the Aristotelian[103] question: are IFIs merely institutions of deliberative rhetoric, to be deployed (as a sword) in order to dissuade the demos from following a fiscally heterodox politician whose position independent analysis has 'proved' will bring only bad things or (as a shield) against speculative challengers, enabling the politician in power to refute assertions of fiscal incompetence with recourse to 'independent' fiscal truth?

Should the rhetoric (as opposed to the reality) of public value take hold in the arena of budget politics, one could speculate about where that leaves the goal of rebuilding public confidence, the ultimate political goal of the endeavour. Dawn Oliver uses the term 'stewardship' to capture the constitutional role of various arm's-length public bodies (including the OBR) that provide information or other resources to government.[104] But for which constituencies do they act as steward? The

---

[101] U.W. Chohan and K. Jacobs, 'Public Value as Rhetoric: A Budgeting Approach' (2017) *International Journal of Public Administration* 1, 4 and 10.

[102] But, as Philip Pettit reminds us, 'attitude-dependent goods' – such as trust or good standing – are desirable to agents and so important to society at large. They are also (instrumentally) essential to politicians in order to achieve their goals and ultimately to the state if it is to function effectively: 'The Cunning of Trust' (1995) 24 *Philosophy & Public Affairs* 202, 212–217. To inflict a sanction on a politician's (or political institution's) good reputation is thus a material cost.

[103] Aristotle, *Rhetoric*, Book I, Ch 3, ss. 3–4: 'The deliberative kind [of rhetoric] is either hortatory or dissuasive; for both those who give advice in private and those who speak in the assembly invariably either exhort or dissuade.' With deliberative forms of rhetoric, there is always a focus on the future: 'to the deliberative the future, for the speaker, whether he exhorts or dissuades, always advises about things to come.'

[104] D. Oliver, 'Constitutional Stewardship: A Role for Public or State Sector Bodies?' (2017) 15 *New Zealand Journal of Public and International Law* 21.

obvious (but not quite complete) answer is the public. IFIs may be able to serve an important role in the democratization of financial governance. As Annelise Riles argues, the technicalities of fiscal decision-making are its core element. To democratize the practice requires political debate to be at 'once *more technical* and *more political*'. Institutions like the OBR and PBO, not least by providing independent and transparent fiscal information, can help bring together 'finance's many publics' into the political debate at the requisite level of sophistication.[105] But that debate not only concerns today's citizens, who constitute only a small – and perhaps relatively insignificant – part of the political equation. Alessandro Spano observes that 'if a government decides to finance today's expenses with long term debt, a clear intergenerational clash emerges: today's generation is going to enjoy a higher value whose cost will be paid by tomorrow's citizens'.[106] We argue that IFIs work really in the interests of the citizens of the future, as the exceptionally long timelines through which IFIs tend to think indicate.

From the public law perspective, fiscal sustainability is ultimately a question of intergenerational constitutional justice. The general idea, though sometimes overlooked, is familiar. Burke's idea that the essential constitutional relationship takes the form of 'a partnership not only between those who are living, but between those who are living, those who are dead, and those who are to be born'[107] still exerts considerable influence. The French mathematician Condorcet, critical of the presentism of much of the incipient democratic theory, provided the prose to Burke's poetry in the form of detailed constitutional specifications for the political value of time.[108] The IFI represents a similarly detailed and material specification of the classic constitutional task of self-binding. It is a technique aimed ultimately at retying the now unbound fiscal decision maker to the mast by means of fiscal restraints in the interests of future *demoi* incapable of asserting that capacity but who are the inheritors of current

---

[105] A. Riles, *Collateral Knowledge: Legal Reasoning in the Global Financial Markets* (University of Chicago Press, 2011), 223.

[106] A. Spano, 'Public Value Creation and Management Control Systems' (2009) 32 *International Journal of Public Administration* 328, 333.

[107] Edmund Burke, *Reflections on the Revolution in France* [1790].

[108] See e.g. E.F. Cohen, *The Political Value of Time: Citizenship, Duration, and Democratic Justice* (Cambridge University Press, 2018), 68–76.

fiscal choices.[109] The immediate goal is a modest resetting of expectations on present decision makers and, by highlighting the impact current policies will have on the demos of the future, a subtle reminder that in making decisions they ought to bring into view a longer term horizon.

Further Reading

P. Einzig, *The Control of the Purse: Progress and Decline of Parliament's Financial Control* (Secker & Warburg, 1959).

J. Elster, *Ulysees and the Sirens: Studies in Rationality and Irrationality* (Cambridge University Press, 1979).

P.G. Joyce, *The Congressional Budget Office – Honest Numbers, Power, and Policy Making* (Georgetown University Press, 2011).

G. Kopits (ed.), *Restoring Public Debt Sustainability: The Role of Independent Fiscal Institutions* (Oxford University Press, 2013).

P. Tucker, *Unelected Power: The Quest for Legitimacy in Central Banking and the Regulatory State* (Princeton University Press, 2018).

C. Webber and A. Wildavsky, *A History of Taxation and Expenditure in the Western World* (Simon and Schuster, 1986).

J. Wehner, *Legislatures and the Budget Process – The Myth of Fiscal Control* (Palgrave Macmillan, 2010).

A. Wildavsky, *The Politics of the Budgetary Process* (Little, Brown, 1964).

[109] J. Elster, *Ulysees and the Sirens: Studies in Rationality and Irrationality* (Cambridge University Press, 1979).

Part V
Transnational Constitutionalism

Multi-Layered Constitutions 18

Roger Masterman

Introduction

Examination of the state-centric dynamics of constitutions can only partially illuminate the multi-faceted characteristics of constitutional law. A statist focus often obscures both internal and external dimensions of constitutions themselves, and of the broader structures and patterns of governance that exist within and beyond nations. Either explicitly or implicitly, constitutions speak to the sub- as well as to the inter- and

Underpinning work on this chapter was carried out while I held a MacCormick Fellowship at the University of Edinburgh. My thanks are due to Stephen Tierney and Elisenda Casanas Adam in Edinburgh, to Nick Kilford and Aoife O'Donoghue in Durham and to Ruth Houghton in Newcastle for discussions and suggestions.

supra-national, and provide a lens through which obligations and pressures arising in each differing context might be reflected. Constitutions are, as such, inherently multi-layered.

The focus of this chapter is not primarily on the forms taken by multi-level governance structures,[1] but rather on the accommodation and integration of multiple layers of government via national constitutions and the tensions to which multiple layers of constitutional authority give rise. The chapter takes as a point of departure the suggestion that though national constitutions can be accepted and interpreted as monolithic, or standalone, entities, understanding their place as a conduit between sub-national, national and international norms and institutions is vital to a full appreciation of their character and qualities. Constitutions are often explicitly contingent upon sub-national and international sources of authority, others may be centralized to the virtual exclusion of other sources of normative power. But – as Vandenbruwaene has observed – the place of national structures of government is, regardless, increasingly seen as but one source of normative authority among many of varying, potentially intersecting, geographical ranges:

The 21st century is marked by an increased recognition, both empirical and normative, of a complex world, which is simultaneously fragmented and inter-dependent. These co-existent trends, one of globalization and one of localization, yield a bifurcated pressure on the unitary nation-state: on the one hand, the circumspection of the relevant polity is subjected to change because of particular claims – the rise of regional authority based on identity politics springs to mind. On the other hand, the necessity of effective governance suffers from interdependencies and mobility, frequently exceeding national borders.[2]

In the United Kingdom the diffusion of power away from Westminster and Whitehall – once seen as bywords for centralized national government – during the last fifty years provides a case in point. Acceptance of the right of individual petition to the European Court of Human Rights in 1966 and accession to the European Community (as was) in 1973 combined to permit extra-jurisdictional institutions a significant role in shaping domestically applicable norms and policy. The internal devolution of

---

[1] On which see the chapters by Raffaele Bifulco, Jan Klabbers and Kaarlo Tuori in this volume.

[2] W. Vandenbruwaene, 'Multi-Level Governance through a Constitutional Prism' (2014) 21 *Maastricht Journal of European and Comparative Law* 229, 230.

legislative powers to institutions in Northern Ireland, Scotland and Wales saw – from 1999 onwards – the wholesale geographical transfer of powers previously exercisable at Westminster to three sub-national legislatures (and executives).[3] The cumulative effect of these developments was a significant reconfiguration of governmental power posing a series of challenges to the established unitary understanding of the UK constitution.[4] These decentralizing and internationalizing initiatives have seen the United Kingdom constitution take on 'the appearance of a structure with multiple, but inter-connected and sometimes overlapping layers'.[5]

For many jurisdictions, of course, a geographical distribution of powers (and the division of sovereignty between local and national-level units) is an inherent feature of constitutional government. Notwithstanding this, trends towards 'sub-state nationalism'[6] and a 'new regionalism'[7] have led to the establishment of governmental structures that have been pragmatically retrofitted onto an established constitutional architecture or have otherwise prompted refinement of accepted understandings of constitutional structures of national government.[8] Federal and non-federal solutions to the accommodation of sub-national government alike recognize intra-state diversity and the imperative of subsidiarity, but do so through either constitutionalized arrangements (e.g. Australia, Canada, Germany) or other sub-constitutional mechanisms of governmental decentralization (e.g. France, Spain, the United Kingdom). Both present alternative loci of power which might be seen to

---

[3] The United Kingdom's experience of devolution pre-dates the initiatives of the late twentieth century. Between 1921 and 1972, devolved government had operated in Northern Ireland as a result of the Government of Ireland Act 1920. Political conflict in Northern Ireland saw the reestablishment of direct rule in 1972, and the Parliament of Northern Ireland was abolished by the Northern Ireland Constitution Act 1973. The late 1970s also saw failed efforts to establish devolved institutions in Scotland and Wales (see V. Bogdanor, *Devolution in the United Kingdom* (Oxford University Press, 2001), esp. chs. 3 and 6).

[4] N. Walker, 'Beyond the Unitary Conception of the United Kingdom Constitution?' [2000] *PL* 384.

[5] N. Bamforth and P. Leyland, 'Public Law in a Multi-Layered Constitution', in N. Bamforth and P. Leyland (eds.), *Public Law in a Multi-Layered Constitution* (Hart Publishing, 2003), 3.

[6] S. Tierney, 'Sub-State Nations and Strong States: The Accommodation Impasse?' in S. Tierney (ed.), *Nationalism and Globalisation* (Hart Publishing, 2015).

[7] M. Keating, *The New Regionalism in Western Europe: Territorial Restructuring and Political Change* (Edward Elgar, 1998).

[8] See e.g. R. Schütze and S. Tierney, *The United Kingdom and the Federal Idea* (Hart Publishing, 2018).

challenge – or at the very least prompt refinement of – state-centric visions of constitutional authority.

The jurisdictional integrity of the state and ability of the constitution to map the allocation of governmental powers may also be challenged by developments on the international plane. As states have sought to operate collectively (e.g. via treaty-based organizations such as the Council of Europe, the African Union, the Association of Southeast Asian Nations) and to pool sovereignties in semi-autonomous supra-national legal structures (e.g. the European Union) the exercise of competences 'above' state-level institutions has become commonplace. Though the extent to which such upward dispersals of constitutional authority impact on domestic affairs may vary – both as a result of the substantive powers exercised beyond the state and the means by which such powers will be domestically effective or enforced – the transfer of powers away from the state may challenge jurisdictional autonomy, raise questions relating to resolving issues of contested competence and see the political and economic authority of state institutions apparently diminished.

In this age of 'post-sovereignty'[9] or 'constitutional pluralism,'[10] state-level institutions – the typical receptacles of supreme legal power – are but one component of an increasingly complex series of governance networks across which constitutional authority is dispersed (and contested). For national legal systems, often characteristically wedded to the idea of law's emanation from a single authority or institution, the diffusion of authority towards supra- and sub-national loci of power may pose particular difficulties for the continuing integrity of the notional 'sovereign' and therefore for one of the defining characteristics of the national constitution.

1 Internal Layering

a Structure and Sovereignty

Federal, regional and devolutionary approaches each share the common purpose of recognizing and accommodating diversity within a larger 'national' framework.[11] As such, the allocation of governmental powers

---

[9] N. MacCormick, *Questioning Sovereignty: Law, State and Nation in the European Commonwealth* (Oxford University Press, 1999), ch. 8.
[10] See e.g.: N. Walker, 'The Idea of Constitutional Pluralism' (2002) 65 *MLR* 317.
[11] *Reference re Secession of Quebec* [1998] 2 SCR 217, 244–245, 250–252.

between state-level and sub-national institutions through both federal and regional/devolved arrangements can be seen to give broad effect to the principle of subsidiarity.[12] Beyond this however, a range of motivations for the maintenance of distinct institutions of sub-national government are discernible. These include a desire to limit the range of powers exercisable by central government (e.g. the United States), an intention to recognize through self-government a particular regional or national identity (e.g. Basque, Catalonia, Scotland, Quebec), the need to provide stability and continuity during a period of transition (e.g. Hong Kong), and may seek to provide a conciliatory mechanism by which politically divided communities might be brought together in shared government (Northern Ireland).

Within federal constitutions the division of power to provincial/regional institutions is frequently uniform, established by the constitution and immune from unilateral amendment by either national or state legislature. Devolutionary arrangements, by contrast, may be underpinned by legislation (as distinct from the constitution), may be more *ad hoc* and may tend more towards an asymmetric division of competence between territories.[13] In theory at least, the latter may be more sensitive to the specific, potentially differing, needs of the territory or territories in question. Spain's autonomous communities (*comunidad autónoma*), for instance, enjoy varying degrees of autonomy, within a state framework otherwise considered to be unitary.[14] Equally, devolved structures may – as in the United Kingdom – also include the *absence* of sub-national structures of government (as in England) as well as the devolution of power to city-level administrations (as in the Greater London Authority). As such, the legislative basis of the United Kingdom's devolutionary arrangements has allowed structural change to be partially led by demand, or, indeed, by an

---

[12] Here taken as encapsulating the principle that 'decisions affecting the life and activities of the citizen should generally ... be made at the lowest level of government consistent with economy, convenience and the rational conduct of public affairs' (Lord Bingham, 'The Evolving Constitution' [2002] *EHRLR* 1, 2. See generally: D. Halberstam, 'Federalism: Theory, Policy, Law', in M. Rosenfeld and A. Sajó (eds.), *The Oxford Handbook of Comparative Constitutional Law* (Oxford University Press, 2012).

[13] Federations may also display asymmetry. In Australia, for instance, there is a distinction drawn between State and territory governments.

[14] Constitution of Spain 1978, Article 2: 'The Constitution is based on the indissoluble unity of the Spanish Nation, the common and indivisible homeland of all Spaniards; it recognises and guarantees the right to self-government of the nationalities and regions of which it is composed and the solidarity among them all.'

absence of such demand.[15] Consistently with this relative flexibility – and indeed with the statutory framework upon which devolution in the United Kingdom rests – devolutionary arrangements may be established and/or amended without the need for fundamental (state-level) constitutional renewal and see the sovereign legal power of the central/unitary legislature at least formally preserved.

By contrast with such pragmatic allocations of power, separations of power between national/federal level institutions of government and a federation's component states, provinces or regions provide an *essential* division of powers and foundational architecture for numerous constitutional systems. While the constitutional, geographical, division of power is therefore fundamental to the internal constitutional order, so too is the idea of an essentially divisible sovereignty. As Wheare famously claimed, the core of the federal principle is the division of power 'so that the general and regional governments are each, within a sphere, co-ordinate and independent' with 'neither general nor regional government ... subordinate to the other'.[16] The ability of federal systems to 'split the atom of sovereignty'[17] sees divisible sovereignty treated as a quality of constitutionalism, rather than a threat to it.

Though it is commonplace for federated divisions of power to be referred to as 'vertical' the description is not entirely apt. While the existence of a supremacy clause may ensure the primacy of federal laws over those of the state components,[18] the implication of a hierarchy as between federal and states governments does not accurately capture the vital formative, or centripetal, role played by the state or regional components of federal systems such as the United States. In those states in which the influence of unitary government remains, the notion of hierarchical constitutional ordering may appear to be more appropriate, given that devolved/

---

[15] A proposed scheme to establish elected regional assemblies throughout England (*Your Region, Your Choice: Revitalising the English Regions*, Cm.5511 (2002)) was – following the rejection of such a body in a pilot referendum held in the North East of England 2004 – abandoned. Since 2014 enhanced powers have been devolved to local government in England in a range of areas under the Cities and Local Government Devolution Act 2016.

[16] K.C. Wheare, *Federal Government* (4th ed.) (Oxford University Press, 1963), 10 and 12.

[17] *US Term Limits, Inc* v. *Thornton* 514 US 779 (1995) (Kennedy J), 838: 'The Framers split the atom of sovereignty. It was the genius of their idea that our citizens would have two political capacities, one state and one federal, each protected from incursion by the other.'

[18] For instance, Article VI, cl.2, Constitution of the United States.

regional competences may be the product of a centrifugal redistribution of central authority. If federal systems are predicated on the divisibility of sovereignty within the federation, then the maintenance of a 'sovereign' central authority is perhaps the characteristic that most clearly delineates unitary/devolutionary systems. Though unitary government persists in a range of jurisdictions (for instance, Denmark, Ireland, Sweden) the adoption of regional or devolutionary approaches in previously highly centralized states indicates something of a trend towards sub-state constitutionalism. In France, considered to be 'the cradle of the unitary state', the 'hierarchical subordination of [local authority] to central authorities was intended to guarantee unity in the direction of public power'.[19] The recognition of the French Republic as being 'indivisible' has not however prevented the redistribution of central authority; 'recent decades have witnessed decentralization, and even some forms of regional autonomy, within a unitary state, resulting in a new division of competences between the central state and the *collectivités territoriales* (sub-state administrative units) and a constitutional principle of subsidiarity in territorial organization.[20] As Roobol has observed, '[m]ost European states are by now either decentralized unitary states with increasing autonomy for the regions or federations with historically or linguistically defined Member States.'[21] Beyond Europe, the tendency towards sub-state constitutions is equally pronounced: 'documents that can fairly be described as constitutions govern the affairs of some two hundred sub-national divisions of nations around the world.'[22]

b Competences

Though maintenance of the form of the unitary state may be the consequence of sub-constitutional decentralization that is not to say that the advent of regionalization or devolution will be accompanied by the

---

[19] S. Bartole, 'Internal Ordering in the Unitary State', in M. Rosenfeld and A. Sajó (eds.), *The Oxford Companion to Comparative Constitutional Law* (Oxford University Press, 2012), 610, 614.

[20] E. Daly, 'The indivisibility of the French republic as political theory and constitutional doctrine' (2015) *European Constitutional Law Review* 458, 462.

[21] W.H. Roobol, 'Federalism, Sovereignty, etc' (2005) *European Constitutional Law Review* 87, 88.

[22] J.A. Gardner, 'Perspectives on Federalism: In Search of Sub-National Constitutionalism' (2008) 4 *European Constitutional Law Review* 325, 325.

continued *exercise* of centralized powers; in practice the involvement of the central power in the exercise of devolved competences may be limited. The United Kingdom's devolutionary arrangements reflect a system that maintains the form of a legal hierarchy but in which *political* control over areas of devolved competence is substantial. While the legislative bases of the United Kingdom's territorial governance structures contemplate the continuing *legal* power of the Westminster Parliament to legislate on any matter[23] the exercise of such power is limited by (*ordinarily* binding) constitutional convention[24] with the structural allocation of power to sub-national units accompanied by a shared political commitment to self-government.

In substance therefore the establishment of sub-national governmental structures in otherwise unitary states may result in significant practical decentralization. In practice it has been argued that devolution amounts to a formal redistribution of power not dissimilar to that resulting from federal arrangements.[25] Statutory recognition of the 'permanence' of devolved institutions in Wales and Scotland serves to underscore the potential for devolved government to morph into something with a more overtly constitutional character. Spain, similarly (and in spite of the formal indivisibility of the State), has been referred to as a 'federation in all but name'.[26]

Extraordinary circumstances may however permit the reassertion of central power. The collapse of the power-sharing arrangements in Northern Ireland (under which members of the nationalist and unionist communities are required to govern in effective perpetual coalition) has seen 'direct rule' from Westminster re-established on a number of occasions since the devolution of power to institutions in Northern Ireland pursuant to the Belfast/Good Friday Agreement 1998. Similarly, the unilateral issue of the Catalan declaration of independence in October 2017 – issued following a disputed referendum and annulled shortly after by the *Tribunal Constitucional de*

---

[23] Scotland Act 1998, s. 28(7). See also *Tribunal Constitucional de España* Decision STC 4/1981: 'autonomy makes reference to a limited power ... autonomy is not sovereignty ... in no case can the principle of autonomy be opposed to that of unity.'

[24] Scotland Act 1998, s. 28(8) as amended by the Scotland Act 2016, s. 2: 'it is recognised that the Parliament of the United Kingdom will not normally legislate with regard to devolved matters without the consent of the Scottish Parliament' (the Sewel convention).

[25] V. Bogdanor, *Devolution in the United Kingdom* (Oxford University Press, 2001), ch. 8.

[26] R.L. Watts, *Comparing Federal Systems* (McGill-Queens University Press, 2008), 42.

España – resulted in the suspension of the Catalan statute of autonomy (*Estatutos de Autonomía*) and the imposition of centralized government. By contrast then with the formal division of sovereignty by federal structures, extraordinary political circumstances *may* render the devolution or decentralization of power susceptible to reassertions of central authority. Elsewhere, however, political circumstance may well dictate that central involvement in otherwise local power be entirely routine. Though the position of Hong Kong as a Special Administrative Region (SAR) under the 'one country, two systems' model operational in the Peoples' Republic of China the 'genuine autonomy' provided for under Hong Kong's 'mini-constitution' is in practice also 'subject to potentially far-reaching political control by the PRC central government.'[27]

c Integration and Cooperation

Even if the result of federal structuring is that similar assertions of central authority may not necessarily enjoy overriding status, this is not to say that there is no potential for competence disputes between state and federal authorities. Nor does the constitutional delineation of functions mean that the potential for competence creep is eradicated. The 'judicial nationalization of individual rights'[28] by the United States Supreme Court in the post-New Deal era provides a salient example, with the Court seeking to ensure uniformity – a common standard of rights protection – at the apparent expense of State autonomy.[29] While the accommodation of diversity within a national framework is an objective of both federal and non-federal systems of decentralized government, means of ensuring unity between states/regions may also be apparent.[30] It is therefore commonplace for the role of the Supreme Court in a federal system to be to determine 'between what is truly national and what is truly local'.[31]

---

[27] Q. Zhang, *The Constitution of China: A Contextual Analysis* (Hart Publishing, 2012), 112–113.

[28] C. Warbrick, 'Federal Aspects of the European Convention on Human Rights' (1989) 10 *Michigan Journal of International Law* 698, 703.

[29] Cf. M. Tushnet, *A Court Divided: The Rehnquist Court and the Future of Constitutional Law* (W. W. Norton and Co., 2006), ch. 10.

[30] On the necessity of, for instance, a unified Australian common law see: *Lange* v. *ABC* (1997) 189 CLR 520, 563.

[31] *United States* v. *Morrison* (2000) 529 US 598, 617–618.

Political and bureaucratic means through which national and sub-national government might be managed may be less obviously adversarial than litigation. As Russell observes, many second chambers – in federal and non-federal systems alike – are tasked with 'binding different levels of government together'.[32] The extent to which second chambers may provide for regional participation in government may vary; some may be elected on a territorial basis but otherwise provide only a relatively weak connection to sub-national government (for instance, the Australian and Canadian Senates), others might properly be described as a representational and operational 'fulcrum' of the system of government (for instance the German *Bundesrat*).[33] The appointment by the autonomous communities of a proportion of members of the Spanish *Senado* illustrates that the representation of regional affairs in national institutions is not the sole preserve of federal systems.[34]

Alongside formal accommodation of sub-state representation within legislatures, many systems exhibit executive-driven machinery of intergovernmental relations. The well-established machinery of intergovernmental relations in Canada, for instance, revolves around First Minsters' Conferences and Ministerial Meetings and is supported by both national- and province-level Ministers of Intergovernmental Affairs and a dedicated central secretariat. The advent of devolution in the United Kingdom was accompanied by the establishment of a Joint Ministerial Committee, comprising Ministers from national and devolved administrations, as well as a range of soft-law instruments designed to regulate interactions between Westminster and Whitehall and the devolved administrations.[35] As the experience of devolution to Northern Ireland also demonstrates, the establishment of mechanisms of intergovernmental relations may also serve political and/or diplomatic ends that resound beyond the boundaries of the territory to which power has been devolved.[36]

---

[32] M. Russell, *Reforming the House of Lords: Lessons from Overseas* (Oxford University Press, 2000), ch. 10.

[33] Ibid.

[34] Article 69, Constitution of Spain.

[35] On which see: R. Rawlings, 'Concordats of the Constitution' (2000) 116 *LQR* 257; J. Poirier, 'The Functions of Intergovernmental Agreements: Post-Devolution Concordats in a Comparative Perspective' [2001] *PL* 134.

[36] See Strands 2 and 3 of the Belfast Agreement 1998 (available at: www.gov.uk/government/publications/the-belfast-agreement) (accessed 10 May, 2019) and Part V of the Northern Ireland Act 1998 in relation to the activities of the North-South Ministerial Council and the British Irish Council.

2 Internalizing the External

a Monism/Dualism

The necessary implication of subsidiarity is that just as particular governmental functions might be most appropriately administered at the local
level, certain governmental functions are better addressed on a national,
or indeed international, plane.[37] The logic of this dimension of subsidiarity
is that particular (external) issues or problems which transcend national
borders are better confronted via state collaborations (addressing the
causes and implications of climate change provides an obvious example).
Participation in structures at the international level is, in turn, generally
motivated by concerns relating to the greater influence or effectiveness of
inter-state arrangements in relation to particular governmental activities.
The extent to which inter-state agreements might impact upon domestic
legal affairs is however contingent on a range of factors.

In the first instance, the translation of external norms into the domestic
polity will also be a matter either explicitly addressed by, or a necessary
implication of, national constitutional law. In relation to the nature of
national constitutional orders, it remains a relevant start point to distinguish monist and dualist constitutions.[38] Monist constitutions essentially
treat international norms as being as one with those of domestic origin.
The impact of translating international legal norms in a monist system
may not be immediately pronounced, as they are effective without the
need for domestic legislative implementation. Dualist systems, by contrast,
will require that treaty obligations should be implemented (translated) by
domestic legislative means in order that the formal supremacy of the
domestic legislature or constitution – and the jurisdictional integrity of
the domestic constitutional order – be better maintained. Dualist systems
may be able to preserve the impression that international obligations
resound only as against the state, and may not permit those obligations

---

[37] D. Halberstam, 'Federal Powers and the Principle of Subsidiarity', in V.D. Amar and
M. Tushnet (eds.), *Global Perspectives on Constitutional Law* (Oxford University Press,
2009), 34.

[38] Though it should be noted that doubts exist as to the continuing utility of the
labels: G. Gaja, 'Dualism – A Review', in J.E. Nijman and A. Nollkaemper (eds.),
New Perspectives on the Divide Between National and International Law (Oxford
University Press, 2007).

to be employed in domestic adjudication in the absence of domestic implementing legislation.[39]

b Incorporation and Receptivity

Even in the event that 'incorporating' legislation gives some degree of domestic effect to the relevant international norm, the precise terms of that legislation will be conditioned both by the nature of pre-existing constitutional arrangements and the extent to which the international norm might compel, or provoke, change in the domestic sphere. As to the first of these, the long-standing and robust commitment to the protection of constitutional rights evident in the German Basic Law (*Grundgesetz*) has seen the direct influence of the jurisprudence of the European Court of Human Rights limited by comparison with experience in those states historically lacking a domestic Bill of Rights or comparable tradition of enforceable individual rights. As a point of contrast, the United Kingdom's Human Rights Act 1998, for instance, serves the specific purpose of 'giving further effect to rights and freedoms guaranteed under the European Convention on Human Rights'. To that end, the human rights standards against which public authority activities and legislation are measured are those contained in the ECHR and partially defined by the European Court of Human Rights. As a result – and perhaps also as a product of the previous *absence* of legally enforceable individual rights in the United Kingdom's legal orders – the Convention rights enjoy a prominence and immediacy in the UK context that is not necessarily evident in other states within the Convention system.

Though specific domestic legislation may allow local actors to claim ownership of the standards to be upheld/enforced[40] – and will adhere to the form required by the doctrine of dualism – perceptions of excessive external influence may still permit accusations of over-reach by extrajurisdictional actors into the national political domain.[41] In response to the tensions prompted by such external drivers there have been notable moves

[39] See *R* v. *Secretary of State for the Home Department, ex parte Brind* [1991] 1 AC 696.
[40] *Re McKerr* [2004] UKHL 12, [65] (Lord Hoffmann).
[41] In the context of the reach of the European Court of Human Rights into national affairs in the United Kingdom see: R. Masterman, 'Federal Dynamics of the UK/Strasbourg Relationship', in R. Schütze and S. Tierney (eds.), *The United Kingdom and the Federal Idea* (Hart Publishing, 2018).

to reassert the authority of national institutions in the face of perceived or potential encroachment from outside. The Russian Constitutional Court has, for instance, declared the ability to find decisions of international bodies 'impossible to implement'[42] while the German Federal Constitutional Court reserved to itself the right to review European legislation for compliance with the rights protected in the Basic Law.[43]

The 'alien' heritage of the translated norms may also hamper their effective deployment at the domestic level.[44] This tendency is all the more prominent in those spheres in which the subject matter of the constitutional arrangement is 'perceived as going to the core of national sovereignty'.[45] The so-called 'sovereignty clause' in the UK's European Union Act 2011 provides evidence of an unsuccessful attempt to reiterate that the influence of external norms was solely the product of a domestically taken legislative decision. The United Kingdom's decision to leave the European Union, and the unresolved question of whether the Human Rights Act should be replaced by a *British* Bill of Rights, are both symptomatic of a concern to insulate the national from external influence.

While legislative and constitutional instruments may condition the extent to which the importation of external norms is possible, the degree to which external norms will permeate the domestic constitutional order is also a question of (inter alia) constitutional culture and judicial technique. As to the first of these, monism may encourage receptivity to external influence; in the words of the President of the *Bundesverfassungsgericht*, '[t]he Basic Law is open, or as we say friendly, to European Law (*Europa rechtsfreundlichkeit*)'.[46] Constitutional reasoning from an originalist perspective may drive a species of jurisdictional exceptionalism limiting the influence of international norms, as well as the decisions of other national courts. By contrast, the shared traditions of common law jurisdictions may permit the importation (or influence) of constitutional standards that

---

[42] M. Smirnova, 'Russian Constitutional Court affirms Russian Constitution's Supremacy over ECtHR decisions', *UK Const. L. Blog*, 17 July 2015.

[43] See: 37 BVerfGE 271 (*Solange I*); 73 BVerfGE 339 (*Solange II*).

[44] See: *Hirst* v. *United Kingdom (No. 2)* (2006) 42 EHRR 41; Joint Committee on the Draft Voting Eligibility (Prisoners) Bill, *Draft Voting Eligibility (Prisoners) Bill*, HL103/HC924 (December 2013), [67]–[113].

[45] D. Nicol, 'Lessons from Luxembourg: Federalisation and the Court of Human Rights' (2001) 26 *EL Rev* HR3, HR3.

[46] A. Voβkuhle, 'European Integration and the *Bundesverfassungsgericht*' Sir Thomas More Lecture, Lincoln's Inn, 31 October 2013.

the doctrine of dualism would otherwise appear to preclude. In practice, care should be taken to guard against over-generalization. Systems which may be in one sense appear open to the influences of international norms[47] may prove in another to be resistant to external stimuli;[48] systems that otherwise maintain the form of dualism, might occasionally display monist traits;[49] systems displaying exceptionalist tendencies may simultaneously belong to a broader grouping of systems sharing, and exchanging, characteristics.[50] In other words, monist and dualist constitutions should not be thought of as neatly defined categories, but rather should be considered as predominating tendencies which may permit degrees of fluidity.

3 External Layering (I): Regional/Continental Regimes

a Hierarchy or Heterarchy?

Regional human rights regimes – in their efforts to place limitations on the ability of governments to interfere with certain norms – share common ground with the constitutionalist motivations behind the internal power divisions visible in certain federal systems. While domestic constitutional arrangements provide a start point for the importation (and therefore influence) of such external norms, the specific nature of the international agreement will determine the extent to which its norms infiltrate the domestic sphere. While both the European Convention on Human Rights and Inter-American Convention require state compliance with their terms, the extent to which each permeates the national sphere falls short of requiring direct effect. In both regimes, however, the extent to which states have taken steps to internalize the norms originating in the treaties has led Gardbaum to conclude that the formal

---

[47] See e.g.: US Constitution, Article VI.

[48] See e.g.: *Sosa* v. *Alvarez-Machain* (2004) 124 S. Ct. 2739, 2776 (Scalia J): 'The notion that a law of nations, redefined to mean that consensus of states on *any* subject, can be used by a private citizen to control a sovereign's treatment of *its own citizens* within *its own territory*, is a twentieth-century invention of internationalist law professors and human-rights advocates.'

[49] English courts, for instance, have traditionally regarded customary international law as being a part of the common law (See: *Triquet* v. *Bath* (1764) 3 Burr 1478; W. Blackstone, *Commentaries on the Laws of England* (1st edn, Clarendon Press, 1765–1769) Vol. IV, 67).

[50] On which see generally: M. Elliott, J.N.E. Varuhas, and S. Wilson Stark, *The Unity of Public Law? Doctrinal, Theoretical and Comparative Perspectives* (Hart Publishing, 2018).

absence of direct effect is a matter of form as opposed to substance.[51] As to the Strasbourg regime, though the ECHR might only be characterized as a partial – or 'abstract'[52] – constitution, the Convention is regarded as being a 'European Bill of Rights'[53] or – as the Court has recognized – an analogous 'instrument of European public order ('*ordre public*')'.[54] While decisions of the European Court of Human Rights may lack the supremacy or finality typically enjoyed by those of domestic constitutional courts, they otherwise enjoy significant gravitational pull.[55] The ability of the Court to adjudicate on inter-state applications also provides a parallel to the constitutional functions of a centralized supreme court within a 'federal' structure.[56] The ECHR's devolution of remedial action to the Member States, by contrast, is reflective of a system in which state responsibility for compliance with the Convention's requirements remains pronounced.

It is the development of the European Union that provides the most salient example of a fully formed supra-national constitutional system. Since the creation of the EEC in 1958, the EU has grown from an economic collaboration into a quasi-federal structure concerned with diverse social and political initiatives, now displaying many structural and constitutionalist features commonly internal to national constitutions (including quasi-federal characteristics,[57] a separation of powers broadly adhering to the tripartite model,[58] a hierarchy of norms,[59] and a bill of rights[60]). The sui generis nature of the EU clearly sets it apart from other international

---

[51] S. Gardbaum, 'Human Rights as International Constitutional Rights' (2008) 19(4) *European Journal of International Law* 749, 760–762.

[52] S. Greer, *The European Convention on Human Rights: Achievements, Problems and Prospects* (Cambridge University Press, 2006), 172.

[53] On which see: E. Bates, *The Evolution of the European Convention on Human Rights: From its Inception to the Creation of a Permanent Court of Human Rights* (Oxford University Press, 2010).

[54] *Loizidou* v. *Turkey* (1995) 20 EHRR 99, [75].

[55] Gardbaum characterizes the Convention case-law as having '*de facto* rather than *de jure* direct effect' within the Member States as a result (S. Gardbaum, 'Human Rights as International Constitutional Rights' (2008) 19 *EJIL* 749, 760).

[56] For instance: *Ireland* v. *United Kingdom* (1979–1980) 2 EHRR 25 (and now (2018) 67 EHRR SE1).

[57] On which see: R. Schütze, *From Dual to Cooperative Federalism: The Changing Structure of European Law* (Oxford University Press, 2009); R. Schütze, 'From Rome to Lisbon: "Executive Federalism" in the (New) European Union' (2010) 47 *Common Market Law Review* 1385.

[58] G. Conway, 'Recovering a Separation of Powers in the European Union' (2011) 17 *ELJ* 304.

[59] *Costa* v. *ENEL* [1964] CMLR 425.

[60] The EU Charter of Fundamental Rights became operative on the coming into effect of the Lisbon Treaty, in 2009.

agreements and structures. It is clear, for instance, in the jurisprudence
of the Court of Justice of the European Communities that the establishment of the EEC, as it then was, was to be understood generating a new
'legal order' that would have a profound transformative effect on the
competences of national-level governmental structures:

> the Treaty giving effect to the European Economic Community, as well as the
> other two so-called European Treaties, creates its own legal order which is sep-
> arate from that of each of the Member States but *which substitutes itself partially
> for those* in accordance with rules precisely laid down in the Treaty itself and
> which consist in a transfer of jurisdiction to Community institutions.[61]

The self-conscious establishment of a supra-national legal order, the
norms of which enjoy supremacy over the ordinary and constitutional
laws of the Member States,[62] underpins the ability of EU law to permeate,
and – potentially[63] – disrupt the constitutional laws of the EU's Member
States and speaks to its transformative influence.

Yet while the EU legal order outwardly claims supremacy over the laws
of the Member States, it also 'envisages the co-existence of national constitutional orders within [its] supra-national constitutional order'[64] much
as federal or regional states envisage the coexistence of sub-national governmental units. Reflecting an external dimension of the federal principle,
the German Basic Law recognizes that sovereign power may be divided
externally, with Article 23(1) of the *Grundgesetz* acknowledging that 'the
Federation may transfer sovereign powers by a law with the consent of
the Bundesrat'. While such provision formally recognizes that constitutional powers can be allocated to supra- or international institutions, it is
accompanied by a more informal acceptance that national authorities may
not hold a monopoly over constitutional authority. This openness comes
with limits however, and the influence of external norms cannot come
at the expense of the constitutional 'identity' of the Basic Law. As such,
the Federal Constitutional Court's *Lisbon* decision confirms that the Basic
Law does not permit accession to a European Federal State, and that –
while sovereignty may be transferrable – it cannot be relinquished.[65] The

---

[61] *Costa* v. *ENEL* [1964] CMLR 425, 439 (emphasis added).
[62] *Costa* v. *ENEL* [1964] CMLR 425.
[63] *R* v. *Secretary of State for Transport, ex parte Factortame Ltd* (No. 2) [1991] 1 AC 603.
[64] E. de Wet, 'The International Constitutional Order' (2006) 55 *ICLQ* 51, 52.
[65] See: 123 BVerfGE 267.

powers allocated to the Federal Constitutional Court by the Basic Law do not give rise to the suggestion that the national court is hierarchically inferior to the CJEU:

[t]he relationship between the two courts is not one of supremacy and subordination. Instead it should be seen as a sharing of responsibility within a complex multilevel cooperation of courts. We call this cooperation the *Gerichtsverbund*.[66]

The perceived *absence* of a similar constitutional resilience in the face of external incursions can be seen in the counter-integration pressures that culminated in the United Kingdom's decision to exit the European Union.[67]

b Self-Government and Subsidiarity

While sub-national constitutionalism is supported in order to address democratic deficits, inter- or supra-national constitutionalism is often argued to exacerbate such shortfalls.[68] The transfer by national institutions of decision-making competence to external bodies, often perceived as being 'remote' from national concerns and therefore lacking accountability to a national electorate, contributes to an absence of democratic legitimacy that is potentially damaging to the perceived legitimacy and implementation of associated norms in the domestic constitutional framework.[69] The Treaty-based origins of enterprises such as the European Union and European Convention on Human Rights are undoubtedly grounded in the principle of State-consent. But the increased constitutionalization of those regimes – and concurrent ability of each system to autonomously

---

[66] A. Voβkuhle, 'European Integration and the *Bundesverfassungsgericht*' Sir Thomas More Lecture, Lincoln's Inn, 31 October 2013.

[67] Cf. *R (on the application of Buckinghamshire County Council)* v. *Secretary of State for Transport* [2014] UKSC 3; [2014] 1 WLR 324.

[68] The widespread antipathy towards 'European' human rights law in the United Kingdom is one such symptom of such a perception. It should be noted that this antagonism to decisions of the European Court of Human Rights is not confined to the United Kingdom (see generally: P. Popelier, S. Lambrecht and K. Lemmens (eds.), *Criticism of the European Court of Human Rights: Shifting the Convention System – Counter-Dynamics at the National and EU Levels* (Intersentia, 2016).

[69] The establishment of a Caribbean Constitutional Court, however, serves to illustrate that the establishment of a supra-national judicial organ can be presented as an exercise in subsidiarity, given that part of its jurisdiction was previously exercised by the (generally London-based) Judicial Committee of the Privy Council.

generate norms – challenges what was once seen as the foundation of the international legal order.

By way of a partial response, the language of constitutional law has developed in order to explain (or attempt to resolve) some of the tensions between national and international structures of government. As a result, despite speaking directly to the issue of *local* governance, subsidiarity has come to be seen as a distinct principle of 'European' law,[70] and the European Court of Human Rights has employed the terminology of the margin of appreciation in order to accommodate difference and policy variance within and among the Convention signatories.[71] Through articulating the parameters of such concepts, international courts – in common with many of their domestic counterparts – play a role in delineating between local (national) and central (international) spheres of competence. And in so far as notions such as subsidiarity and the margin of appreciation allow for a degree of deference to be permitted to national-level decision-makers, they enable supra-national constitutionalism to be presented as being both partially parasitic upon domestic, or state-level, authority and also grounded in the terminology of deference which is so familiar to national constitutional adjudication. However, de Wet argues that expectations that international legal structures display characteristics common to national institutions are rooted in a flawed 'mythologizing of national democratic governance as a model for international governance', suggesting that the legitimacy of post-national constitutionalism is not solely the product of democratic inputs.[72] Though it is undoubtedly the case that international constitutionalism rests on a footing that is materially different to that supporting a national constitution, international actors have nonetheless sought to respond: the Council of Europe has recently re-emphasized the fundamentality of national democratic institutions as holding primary responsibility for upholding the

---

[70] Lord Bingham, 'The Evolving Constitution' [2002] *EHRLR* 2, 2. On which see Article 5(3) Treaty of European Union: 'Under the principle of subsidiarity ... the Union shall act only if an in so far as the objectives of the proposed action cannot be sufficiently achieved by the Member States, either at central level or at regional and local level, but can rather, by reason of the scale or effects of the proposed action, be better achieved at the Union level.'

[71] The margin of appreciation has also shown itself able to accommodate sub-national variation (see e.g. *Otto-Preminger Institute* v. *Austria* (1995) 19 EHRR 34).

[72] E. de Wet, 'The International Constitutional Order' (2006) 55 *ICLQ* 51, 71–74.

ECHR standards,[73] while the implementation of the Lisbon Treaty saw a conscious effort to democratize the European Union. Similar pressures are evident (but perhaps not so keenly felt) outside of Europe,[74] for it remains the case that the development of regional international institutions with such reach and influence remains 'a partial development, felt more in Europe than elsewhere'.[75]

4 External Layering (II): The Influence of 'Global' Norms

a Symbiosis and Circularity

International law undoubtedly displays constitutional characteristics – '[t]he Charter of the United Nations is ... described as a constitution for the international community, and the World Trade Organization as an economic charter'[76] – and is subject to the processes of constitutionalization.[77] Each is the topic of independent inquiry. But the increasing range and influence of instruments, institutions and laws with a potentially global reach has also impacted upon understandings of the concept of constitutional law,[78] and on the extent to which the external is able to permeate the domestic constitution. The relationship between the internal and the external in this particular sphere is somewhat circular, and is driven by developments within and without state institutions. Discourse on 'global' constitutional law has therefore been given succour as a result of the

---

[73] Protocol 15 amending the Convention on the Protection of Human Rights and Fundamental Freedoms.

[74] For a South American comparison see: T.G. Daly, 'Baby steps away from the State: Regional Judicial Interaction as a Gauge of Postnational Order in South America and Europe' (2014) 3 *Cambridge Journal of International and Comparative Law* 1011.

[75] S. Tierney, 'Sub-State Nations and Strong States: The Accommodation Impasse?' in S. Tierney (ed.), *Nationalism and Globalisation* (Hart Publishing, 2018), 58.

[76] See for instance J.-R. Yeh and W.-C. Chang, 'The Emergence of Transnational Constitutionalism: Its Features, Challenges and Solutions' (2008–2009) 27 *Penn State Int. L. Rev.* 89, 90.

[77] A. O'Donoghue, *Constitutionalism in Global Constitutionalisation* (Cambridge University Press, 2014).

[78] Peters has argued that globalization 'means that state constitutions can no longer regulate the totality of governance in a comprehensive way, and the state constitutions' original claim to form a complete basic order is thereby defeated' (A. Peters, 'Compensatory Constitutionalism: The Potential and Function of Fundamental International Norms and Structures' (2006) 19 *Leiden Journal of International Law* 579, 580).

cross-jurisdictional conversations on 'universal' values[79] and gradual convergence of constitutional idea(l)s[80] evident in the decisions of national courts *as well as* through the proliferation of international governance regimes and constitutional instruments with a potentially global reach.[81]

Though many global instruments have not been internalized in the same manner as – for instance – the European Convention on Human Rights in many European states, they may nonetheless exercise an indirect effect in influencing the contours of domestic laws as templates for national legislation and bills of rights,[82] or as influences upon judicial decision-making. International law writ large also plays a role in the shaping of domestic constitutional standards. Beyond the basic incorporationist stance of formally monist systems, international law may be allocated a specific role in the interpretation and application of domestic constitutional laws. The Constitution of the Republic of South Africa, for instance, is receptive to the broad influence of international law, making it mandatory for the courts to consider relevant international law in the interpretation of the Bill of Rights:

When interpreting the Bill of Rights, a court, tribunal or forum

(a) must promote the values that underlie an open and democratic society based on human dignity, equality and freedom;

(b) must consider international law; and

(c) may consider foreign law.[83]

By contrast however with the comparatively direct influences of the bodies of European Union and European Convention norms (both reinforced by the extensive jurisprudence of their specialized judicial bodies), the domestic influence of law with a *global* reach is often rather

---

[79] See e.g.: C. McCrudden, 'A Common Law of Human Rights? Transnational Judicial Conversations on Constitutional Rights' (2000) 20 *OJLS* 499.

[80] See e.g.: M. Tushnet, 'The Possibilities of Comparative Constitutional Law' (1999) 108 *Yale Law Journal* 1225.

[81] The paradigm example being the so-called International Bill of Rights (comprising the Universal Declaration of Human Rights 1948, the International Covenant on Civil and Political Rights 1966 (and its two optional protocols) and the International Covenant on Economic, Social and Cultural Rights 1966). For a more focused account of constitutional 'transplants', see Gábor Halmai, Chapter 22 in this volume.

[82] The substantive rights protected by the New Zealand Bill of Rights Act 1990 and the Hong Kong Bill of Rights Ordinance 1991, for instance, are taken from the ICCPR.

[83] Constitution of the Republic of South Africa 1996, s. 39(1). See also Constitution of India 1949, s. 51(c).

less pronounced. In part, this is due to the relatively small body of constitutional rules that are binding upon *all* states (including the prohibitions
on genocide, torture, enslavement, refoulement, and so on), the absence
(barring perhaps in the sphere of UN Security Council Resolutions) of an
effective equivalent to 'direct effect' and may also be due to the non-
judicial means of enforcement that underpin instruments such as the
ICCPR and ICESCR.

b Minimalist Universalism

The aspirations of human rights law to universal application provide
perhaps the paradigmatic case of a global set of norms. Lord Bingham
has described, for instance, the 1948 Universal Declaration of Human
Rights as setting 'a common standard of rights to be *universally* observed
and secured'.[84] The vindication of this objective necessitates that rights
must resound within the national sphere; as Thomas Poole has observed,
'[r]ights drive an international discourse the objective of which is to infiltrate and influence the national.'[85] In the face of the claimed ubiquity of
human rights protections, the doctrine of dualism may still present an
obstacle to importation of such norms.[86] In the Australian context, for
instance, the absence of a national bill of rights and a long-standing and
influential tradition of judicial formalism have combined to render the
influence of external human rights standards heavily contested.[87]

Even where the influence of international human rights instruments is
in evidence in domestic measures, this may fall well short of an equivalent to direct effect. By contrast with the previously-considered United
Kingdom Human Rights Act, the Victorian Charter of Human Rights and
Responsibilities 2006 – though similarly taking its substantive inspiration
from the rights enshrined in an international charter (the ICCPR) – is

---

[84] T. Bingham, *Widening Horizons: The Influence of Comparative Law and International Law on Domestic Law* (Cambridge University Press, 2010), 56 (emphasis added).
[85] T. Poole, 'Between the Devil and the Deep Blue Sea: Administrative Law in an Age of Rights', in L. Pearson, C. Harlow and M. Taggart (eds.), *Administrative Law in a Changing State: Essays in Honour of Mark Aronson* (Hart Publishing, 2008), 16.
[86] *R* v. *Secretary of State for the Home Department, ex parte Brind* [1991] 1 AC 696; *Al-Kateb* v. *Godwin* [2004] HCA 37, [62]-[73] (McHugh J).
[87] See generally: F. Wheeler and J. Williams, '"Restrained Activism" in the High Court of Australia', in B. Dickson (ed.), *Judicial Activism in Common Law Supreme Courts* (Oxford University Press, 2007).

not tailored towards ensuring domestic consistency with the requirements of that specific international agreement. Indeed, the meaning of the Victorian Charter's protected rights may be determined by reference to a rather more diffuse body of laws, including 'international law, and the judgments of domestic, foreign and international tribunals' so far as they are 'relevant' to the human right under consideration.'[88] The operation of the Victorian Charter – by contrast to the Human Rights Act – is not therefore intimately intertwined with the decisions of an extra-jurisdictional judicial body, either as a matter of international law, or on the terms of the Charter itself. As such, the influence of international law in the Victorian Charter context is more a partial template for constitutional design than a normative guide to implementation.[89]

The 'universal' character of certain other constitutional principles – such as the rule of law, and perhaps proportionality – has both spurred the process of constitutional borrowing and transplantation, and been deployed in national courts as a tool of judicial argumentation. While reference to such principles may provide evidence of the symbiosis of domestic and international constitutional norms, it is not uncommon to find reference to the 'global' values attaching to principles such as the rule of law[90] and the employment of common analytical tools, such as proportionality,[91] in the decisions of national apex courts.

If 'global' standards of constitutional law are to some extent derivative of the standards visible in national constitutions, then global constitutional law assumes a homogeneity amongst constitutional orders[92] that is in tension with the diversity of constitutional models and practice. Though it is common to contrast systems of parliamentary sovereignty with those of constitutional sovereignty even this binary distinction obscures the diversity of constitutions in terms of their form and substance. At the very least, if a system of global constitutional law is apparent, it is rather more fragmentary than its regional (European) and domestic counterparts. As de Wet has observed, the 'contrast between a well-developed European

---

[88] Victorian Charter of Human Rights and Responsibilities 2006, s. 32(2).

[89] In practice – due to largely internal constitutional factors – the impact of the Victorian Charter has been limited (see: *Momcilovic* v. *The Queen* [2011] HCA 34).

[90] For instance: *R (on the application of Evans)* v. *Attorney-General* [2015] UKSC 21; [2015] AC 1787.

[91] For instance: *McCloy* v. *New South Wales* [2015] HCA 34.

[92] See for instance J.-R. Yeh and W.-C. Chang, 'The Emergence of Transnational Constitutionalism: Its Features, Challenges and Solutions' (2008–2009) 27 *Penn State Int. L. Rev.* 89.

public order that benefits from the enforcement of a centralized court, and a much more fragile international value system that has to be enforced in a decentralized fashion'[93] is marked. It is perhaps the absence of robust centralized enforcement mechanisms and any equivalent to direct effect however that sustains the emergence of a looser, less prescriptive, framework of global constitutional norms. Though global constitutional law is just – if not more – susceptible to the charges of democratic deficit that beset European constitutionalist institutions, its incomplete and remote nature mean that its ability to penetrate the national is less acutely felt.

Conclusion

The division of governmental power along territorial lines is an accepted characteristic of constitutional systems. While State boundaries may once have provided the primary parameters within which such divisions were historically evident, the advent and expansion of international governance structures has seen a similar philosophy deployed beyond the state, as governments have sought to establish structures and institutions to operate for the collective benefit or the achievement of a particular set of political/legal objectives. The accommodation of diversity within a common unifying framework – one of the animating principles of federal structures – has become a principle of international legal governance. Though the importation of external norms is conditioned in part by the design of national constitutions, international institutions have increasingly sought to demonstrate that subsidiarity operates effectively alongside the homogeneity that inter-state collaboration requires. This is especially the case where some degree of direct effect is operative. As the former US Supreme Court Justice Sandra Day O'Connor has written, '[a]s salutary as national and supra-national bodies can be, we must not let their potential obscure the simple truth that government often governs best when it governs close to the people.'[94]

Just as decentralization might prompt the dilution of the sovereign power within an otherwise unitary state, the upward transfer of power to inter- or supra-national institutions sees sovereignty

---

[93] E. de Wet, 'The Emergence of International and Regional Value Systems as a Manifestation of the Emerging International Constitutional Order' (2006) 19 *Leiden Journal of International Law* 611, 631.

[94] S. Day O'Connor, 'Altered States: Federalism and Devolution at the "Real" Turn of the Millennium' (2001) 60 *CLJ* 493, 508.

further challenged through its subjection to the rulings and directions of extra-jurisdictional structures. While for many such developments should have proven fatal to traditional notions of sovereign national institutions, sovereignty has arguably shown itself to possess a fluidity – in its sometimes uncomfortable acceptance of intra- and extra-jurisdictional sources of authority – that has seen it take on pluralistic characteristics. Such are the constitutional pressures now exerted by forces within and beyond states that MacCormick has argued that the stifling effect of 'monocular' conceptions of sovereignty *must* give way to conceptions that accommodate a more systems-based approach to constitutional/legal power.[95] It does not necessarily follow, however, that the general direction of travel is towards the diminution of centralized national institutions. In the United Kingdom, Brexit has provoked tensions between the Westminster Parliament and devolved Governments in Wales and – in particular – Scotland relating to the London-centric pressures evident in the proposed division of EU competences once returned to domestic stewardship. The governance of Spain, similarly, continues to display considerable centrist tendencies, while the experience of regional government in Italy demonstrates an ebb and flow between centralizing and decentralizing initiatives.[96] But the concept of *national* sovereignty – as the prospect of Brexit and insular trends in politics in the United States, Italy, the Netherlands and elsewhere illustrates – is showing itself to be resilient:

The squeeze on statehood both from above and below has its limits. Either because the state remains strong in unexpected ways, or because it feels threatened and ... will not allow its shrinking power to be diminished further.[97]

---

[95] N. MacCormick, 'Beyond the Sovereign State' (1993) 56 *MLR* 1, 8: 'To escape from the idea that all law must originate in a single power source, like a sovereign, is this to discover the possibility of taking a broader, more diffuse, view of law. The alternative approach is system-oriented in the sense that it stresses the kind of normative system law is, rather than some particular or exclusive set of power relations as fundamental to the nature of law. It is a view of law that allows of the possibility that different systems can overlap and interact, without necessarily requiring that one be subordinate or hierarchically inferior to the other to some third system.'

[96] B. Guastaferro and L. Payero, 'Devolution and Secession in Comparative Perspective: The case of Spain and Italy', in R. Schütze and S. Tierney, *The United Kingdom and the Federal Idea* (Hart Publishing, 2018), esp. 141–145.

[97] S. Tierney, 'Sub-State Nations and Strong States: The Accommodation Impasse?' in S. Tierney (ed.), *Nationalism and Globalisation* (Hart Publishing, 2015), 69.

The statist narrative of constitutional law clearly no longer holds a monopoly on constitutional thought, but its influence – in, among other things, prescribing or conditioning much of the interplay between (subnational, national and international layers) of government, in animating the democratic critique of international constitutional norms, in providing a language through which constitutional change can be expressed or interrogated – remains pervasive.

Further Reading

N. Bamforth and P. Leyland, *Public Law in a Multi-Layered Constitution* (Hart Publishing, 2003).

T. Bingham, *Widening Horizons: The Influence of Comparative Law and International Law on Domestic Law* (Cambridge University Press, 2010).

E. de Wet, 'The International Constitutional Order' (2006) 55 *International and Comparative Law Quarterly* 51.

P. Dobner and M. Loughlin, *The Twilight of Constitutionalism?* (Oxford University Press, 2010).

B. Fassbender, 'The United Nations Charter as Constitution of the International Community' (1998) 36 *Columbia Journal of Transnational Law* 529.

S. Gardbaum, 'Human Rights as International Constitutional Rights' (2008) 19(4) *European Journal of International Law* 749.

D. Held, *Democracy and the Global Order: From the Modern State to Cosmopolitan Governance* (Polity Press, 1995).

N. MacCormick, *Questioning Sovereignty: Law, State and Nation in the European Commonwealth* (Oxford University Press, 1999).

A. Peters, 'Compensatory Constitutionalism: The Function and Potential of Fundamental International Norms and Structures' (2006) 19 *Leiden Journal of International Law* 579.

S. Tierney (ed.), *Nationalism and Globalisation* (Hart Publishing, 2015).

19 International Constitutionalism

Jan Klabbers

Introduction

International law has always been conceived as a project involving sovereign and equal states, who would be forever locked in battle with each other – if not literally, then at least metaphorically. The international legal order, such as it is, was always conceptualized as a horizontal order, mostly geared towards facilitating the co-existence of states, and with scant attention for planetary unity, or even for the interests of individual human beings. International law was made by states, to regulate relations between states, and for the benefit of states. What happened within those states was long considered anathema, and nothing was supposed to exist above those states.

If this has always and invariably been the dominant strand in conceptualizations of the global legal order, eventually to be confirmed by the Permanent Court of International Justice in some of its classic decisions, individual thinkers through the ages have nonetheless occasionally dared to dream of something bigger. Grotius, for one, dreamt of collective security, of a legal order that would distinguish between just and unjust wars and collectively punish the wrongdoer. Christian Wolff posited the existence of a *civitas maxima*, a world government with authority over states. Immanuel Kant, worried about the possible tyrannical side of world government, posited a confederation of republics as the recipe for eternal peace, a stand which at least presupposes peace as a legitimate *telos* for the society of states, as opposed to the proto-Darwinian (or Hobbesian) struggle of all against all.[1]

But such dreams notwithstanding, for all practical purposes international law long remained a system of rules created by, between and for equals enjoying the status of sovereignty, serving no higher goals than the peaceful (if at all possible) co-existence between those same states. Some may have identified a connection to the domestic law of those states, and Wolfgang Friedmann may have famously posited that the law of co-existence was in the process of being joined by a law of co-operation,[2] but until the late 1960s, early 1970s, these changes were little more than window-dressing.

During the 1960s, however, some states started to think that there might be some norms which were simply intransgressible, and formalized this into the idea of *jus cogens* norms: some norms exist from which no derogation is permitted.[3] The International Court of Justice added, in 1970, the idea that there exist norms which affect the legal interests of all states: these give rise to so-called *erga omnes* obligations.[4] And less than a decade later, people had started to think it might be possible to distinguish between state torts and state crimes.[5] It never became very clear what either of these developments meant, and the tort–crime distinction rather rapidly proved difficult to operationalize, but somehow the seeds had been planted. *Jus cogens* norms, *erga omnes* obligations, and state crimes, they all presuppose something of a hierarchical, vertical element

---

[1] For a fine overview, see M. Mazower, *Governing the World* (Allen Lane, 2012).

[2] See W. Friedmann, *The Changing Structure of International Law* (Columbia University Press, 1964).

[3] The concept came to be solidified in Article 53 Vienna Convention on the Law of Treaties.

[4] See *Case Concerning the Barcelona Traction, Light and Power Company* (Belgium v. Spain), second phase (1970) ICJ Reports 3.

[5] Most notably the International Law Commission. For discussion, see N. Jorgensen, *The Responsibility of States for International Crimes* (Oxford University Press, 2000).

in the order that had traditionally been made up of sovereign equals, and had been based on the consent of those sovereign equals.

These seeds would come to fruition for a brief period, roughly the first decade of the new millennium, with many proclaiming the constitutionalization of international law, either as an ontological reality or at least as a desideratum. For about a decade, the putative constitutionalization of international law captured the interests of international lawyers – for reasons to be discussed in Section 1. Sections 2 to 5 discuss different manifestations of thinking about constitutionalization; section 6 provides a view of the field after the smoke has cleared, while the final section concludes.

1 The Setting

Perhaps inspired by millennial angst, during the first decade of the twenty-first century many international lawyers explored the possibilities of and for international constitutionalism. The reasons for doing so were varied and manifold. For some, constitutionalism was merely the obvious next step, following the fall of the Wall and the proclaimed 'end of history': a liberal world order required, or mandated, a liberal international constitutional order, and with human rights and democracy firmly in place – or so it seemed from a Western European vantage point, a good few years before Trump and Erdogan – it made sense to complete the Enlightenment project: global peace through a global constitutional order. There may have been faint echoes of 1950s rallying cries here ('world peace through world law'), but nonetheless, if ever, this was the moment.

Others, more pragmatic perhaps, saw in constitutionalism a response to the much-feared image of the fragmentation of international law: if the domains of international law were becoming increasingly independent and international environmental lawyers could no longer communicate with international trade lawyers, then something was required to bind them together, and what could be more obvious and beneficial than international constitutionalism? In an international constitutional order, trade law and environmental law would both be part of the same overarching system and, so the argument implicitly continued, both be subject to the higher goals of the international community – although what exactly those higher goals were was usually, wisely perhaps, left unspecified.

And yet for others, worried about the risks and dangers posed by unfettered globalization, constitutionalism provided something of a political response: if globalization was ideology, used to sell political projects of exploitation to influential Western elites, then something of a counter-ideology was required, and constitutionalism could fit the bill.

The story of international constitutionalism can be told in a variety of ways, but it is important to realize that there is no constitutionalization going on without a story, a larger narrative that places disjointed occurrences into a single coherent whole. One way to tell the story is to focus on concrete legal developments: the emergence of notions such as *jus cogens* norms or *erga omnes* obligations in international case law; or the rise of human rights after World War II; or the post-war mushrooming of international organizations and multilateral agreements; or the increase in the number of international courts and tribunals since the 1990s. All of these can be seen as markers of constitutionalism for those wishing to see them as such; indeed, *jus cogens* becomes a feature of constitutionalism only for those who look at the world through constitutionalist lenses; those who refuse to don such spectacles may think of *jus cogens* as an aberration, or as a harbinger of future developments, or even simply as political correctness.[6]

This suggests that much depends on how international constitutionalization is conceptualized by proponents and discontents alike. There is no single, generally agreed and accepted notion of international constitutionalization available: instead, it seems that every author has used his or her (surprisingly often her, given the still overwhelmingly male composition of international law academia) own vocabulary, based on his or her own insights and intuitions and background understandings – not to mention his or her own value systems. Hence, the current chapter discusses those authorial interpretations, not so much to search for common denominators, but rather in order to highlight what international constitutionalization was, and is, and could be, all about. This also entails that I am hard-pressed to adopt standard definitions: much depends, after all, on how various authors have employed various terms. Nonetheless, I will generally distinguish

---

[6] This owes something to F.V. Kratochwil, *Rules, Norms, and Decisions* (Cambridge University Press, 1989).

between the material process of constitutionalization and the idea of constitutionalism.

International constitutionalization and constitutionalism manifested themselves predominantly in four broad strands in the literature. First, there were those who observed or endorsed constitutionalization as a process, taking place in international law broadly conceived, and in various ways – I will refer to them as the cosmopolitans. A second group thought of constitutionalization primarily in connection with specific international organizations: the institutionalists. A third group shifted attention away from full constitutionalization to a more modest and less demanding strand, concentrating on administrative control and, in the process, filling a gap curiously left wide open by most constitutionalist proposals: few of these proposals occupied themselves meaningfully with control of public authority. For this group I coin the neologism administrativists. Finally, some proved more sceptical, and suggested that full-fledged constitutionalization might not work or would be undesirable (or both), but nonetheless borrowed elements deemed normatively commendable – the sceptics. In what follows, I will discuss these four strands, mindful of the circumstance that boundaries between the various groups of authors were porous and fluid, so much so that some authors – including myself – can be placed in more than one group. I will finish by taking stock of what is left of the debate, for a curious characteristic is that it seems to have disappeared just as rapidly as it burst on to the scene – the intellectual equivalent of a one-hit wonder. On the other hand, it is not impossible that while it has changed its colours and its tone, something of a constitutionalization debate still persists.

2 The Cosmopolitans

It is no exaggeration to state most of the international lawyers writing about constitutionalism displayed strong liberal sensitivities. For the likes of Mattias Kumm, Erika de Wet and Anne Peters, for all their differences, constitutionalization has something to do with human rights, with democracy, with rule of law and, for de Wet, also with the market economy. International constitutionalization is also, it seems, a peculiarly German affliction, and has been especially noted in precisely its German manifestations. While others, from other traditions, have written approvingly about international constitutionalization, their work has been less influential, and markedly different in tone.[7]

There are, one would think, at least three reasons for this Germanic orientation. One is the legacy of the Nazi era, which inspired post-war German international lawyers to adopt a strong liberal orientation. Second, in the absence of a central authority in international law, much of the systematizing in that discipline needs to be done by law professors – and this dovetails nicely with the German tradition of systematization by dogmatic scholarship. Third, Germany's legal academia has traditionally had a strong public law orientation, and constitutionalization thus fell into a fertile tradition; recent antecedents can be detected in the works of Verdross going back to the 1930s,[8] but also in Mosler's conception of the international community as a *legal* community rather than, as many non-German contemporaries would have it, an anarchical society.[9] Even Kelsen can be seen as a forerunner: his monism, characterized by the supremacy of international law, hinged on a conception of a global community able to delegate tasks to states and others, and was inspired, as Jochen von Bernstorff has so compellingly shown, by his social-democratic liberalism.[10]

Following this strong tradition, perhaps the *pater familias* of millenarian constitutionalism was Christian Tomuschat, whose 1999 lectures to the Hague Academy set the tone.[11] These lectures were devoted to the survival of mankind, and imbued with an anxiety that could only be relieved by global liberal thought. In addition, Tomuschat wrote and edited tomes about human rights protection by international authorities – which in itself can be seen as a manifestation of constitutionalism – as well as about supreme norms – another manifestation. Tomuschat therewith constructed a careful edifice of a constitutional legal order, with certain norms for the protection of the individual at

---

[7] Examples include the work of French author Pierre-Marie Dupuy, or the very personal constitutionalism of Philip Allott.

[8] See, e.g., A. O'Donoghue, 'Alfred Verdross and the Contemporary Constitutionalization Debate' (2012) 32 *Oxford Journal of Legal Studies* 799–822.

[9] See H. Mosler, *The International Society as a Legal Community* (Sijthoff, 1980).

[10] See J. von Bernstorff, *Der Glaube an das universale Recht: zur Völkerrechtstheorie Hans Kelsens und seiner Schüler* (Nomos, 2001).

[11] See C. Tomuschat, 'International Law: Ensuring the Survival of Mankind on the Eve of a New Century' (1999) 297 *Recueil des Cours* 9–438.

the apex, as norms from which no derogation was permitted. All of this, of course, had been floating around for a few decades already, but Tomuschat was arguably the first to systematize and place it in a constitutionalist framework.

Still, other German international lawyers (Bruno Simma, Jochen Frowein, Rüdiger Wolfrum, Jost Delbrück) followed suit, or worked on the basis of similar premises, even if they did not always use the constitutionalist vocabulary. Even those outside the discipline of international law would come to discuss international constitutionalism in one way or another. This applied, for instance, to individuals working in the private law tradition: Christian Joerges posited that private law could exercise constitutional values and functions, while Gunther Teubner used constitutionalism as a prism for discussions of functionally differentiated regimes. Constitutional lawyers too, such as the above-mentioned Kumm, rather naturally extended the reach of their domestic domain to international affairs, and as we will see, even the renowned philosopher Jürgen Habermas came to embrace international constitutionalism.

But possibly the most discussed versions of constitutionalism stemmed from two female authors,[12] Erika de Wet and Anne Peters, in two articles published almost simultaneously and, while related, with some crucial differences. De Wet possibly qualifies as the most outspoken proponent of constitutionalism or, as she would say at the time, the constitutionalization of international law.[13] For her, constitutionalization was not a mental structure or a normative project (not just a political dogma) but empirically observable reality – a process that could be, and ought to be, identified: her seminal article confidently discusses the international constitutional order as ontological reality, without question mark.[14]

Still, for all the confidence of the article, both the premises and the theory could be scrutinized. In particular her catalogue of human rights was question-begging in its embrace of the market economy: while she no doubt had a point in insisting on the prohibition of torture being

---

[12] This has the risk of confirming gender prejudices of course: the women write about soft topics (constitutionalism) while at roughly the same moment in time the men flock to the hard law of investment arbitration.

[13] For the record, de Wet is not a German national, but has spent time in the German-speaking world, and defended her *Habilitation* thesis at the University of Zürich.

[14] See E. de Wet, 'The International Constitutional Order' (2006) 55 *International and Comparative Law Quarterly* 51–76.

widely recognized as a human right, the same could not be said about the right to contract, or the right to engage in trade and commerce. Rights these may be, but they are not necessarily recognized as part of any human rights catalogue, and neither do they carry the same normative expectations as the prohibition of torture – or, put differently: if human rights flow from human dignity, the connection to the torture prohibition is a lot easier to make than to freedom of contract or the right to trade. These rights flowed straight from the ordo-liberal hymn-sheet, tapping into a kind of liberalism briefly popular in the interbellum and the years immediately following World War II, but rarely endorsed in this particular form. In the end, then, de Wet's constitutionalization thesis found itself at the more extreme end of the political spectrum: read and referred to by many, but not generally considered persuasive.[15]

The work of Anne Peters, by contrast, possesses more traction. The main thrust of Peters' brand of constitutionalism emphasized democracy. In a classic piece, published the same year as de Wet's,[16] she suggested strongly that constitutionalism is leaking away at the domestic level – meaning in particular, if not exclusively, that democratic control in the nation-state was no longer viable if decision-making was transferred to international levels. Hence, this leak needed to meet with a response: compensatory constitutionalism. But, as she elaborated a few years later,[17] this was not a matter of either/or: in fact, there ought to be, as she called it, a system of 'dual democracy': democracy both domestic and on the international level. And what is more, this is not mere 'ideal theory' but, instead, is slowly but surely materializing. Non-democratic decision-making suffers from a legitimacy deficit that its output, no matter how useful or welcome, cannot compensate for.

Peters has a point, both on normative and empirical grounds – it is difficult to argue against democracy, on any level of decision-making. Indeed, some might think that her fondness of democracy is too limiting: carving

---

[15] Her own later writings are more sober in tone: see, e.g., E. de Wet, 'The Constitutionalization of Public International Law', in M. Rosenfeld and A. Sajó (eds.), *The Oxford Handbook of Comparative Constitutional Law* (Oxford University Press, 2012), 1209–1229.

[16] See A. Peters, 'Compensatory Constitutionalism: The Function and Potential of Fundamental International Norms and Structures' (2006) 19 *Leiden Journal of International Law* 579–610.

[17] See A. Peters, 'Dual Democracy', in J. Klabbers, A. Peters and G. Ulfstein (eds.), *The Constitutionalization of International Law* (Oxford University Press, 2009), 263–341.

a particular, thin concept in stone, makes it more difficult for thicker concepts of democracy to rise to prominence.[18]

If de Wet made a strong empirical claim, a more overtly normative version of international constitutionalization was posited by Kumm.[19] For him, the domestic legitimation of international law was no longer fully available, and thus needed to be replaced by an international constitutional framework. To this end, he posited that the legitimacy of international law would be enhanced through four principles: formal legitimacy (legality), jurisdictional legitimacy (subsidiarity), procedural legitimacy (participation and accountability) and output legitimacy (achieving reasonable outcomes). In doing so he anticipated the work of what I refer to below as the administrativists, although not by much and possibly not by happenstance: being, like some of them, based at New York University may have sensitized him to the need to address in particular participation and accountability in a constitutionalist framework, something that in particular de Wet had never emphasized.

Kumm's approach was also different in another way: he was not interested in sketching an international constitutional order, but rather in sketching and justifying constitutionalism beyond the state – and this was how he explicitly presented his project, thinking of the legal setting not as one with strictly separated 'international' and 'domestic' spheres, but rather as overlapping and cross-cutting 'legal practices'. In this sense, as I will argue below, he also foreshadowed more current manifestations of international constitutionalization, which take the existence of overlapping legal spaces as their starting point.

3 The Institutionalists

a The EU

If one might think that constitutionalization of the international order is, well, a tall order, there might be solace in looking forward to the constitutionalization of bits and pieces thereof, and typically, such

---

[18] The seminal representation of such an argument, pre-dating Peters' work, is S. Marks, *The Riddle of All Constitutions: International Law, Democracy, and the Critique of Ideology* (Oxford University Press, 2000).

[19] See M. Kumm, 'The Legitimacy of International Law: A Constitutionalist Framework for Analysis' (2004) 15 *European Journal of International Law* 907–931.

is operationalized by looking at specific international organizations. This is not a particularly German affectation, although Germans have played a prominent role here as well, and quite possibly the first to approach the matter had fled from German occupation of his native Czechoslovakia: Eric Stein. Stein wrote what must have been the first piece on the constitutionalization of the EU (then still the EEC), noting that the Court of Justice of that organization played a strong constitutional role: it had posited that EU law was directly effective in the Member States; that EU law was superior to Member State national law; and that the EU could boast implied powers in the external sphere. All this added up to far more than a regular international organization.[20]

Stein was right, of course, although one may question whether the process he observed was well-served by referring to it as 'constitutionalization'. In a sense, this unmasked the poverty of the legal-political vocabulary, itself reflective of the limited nature of political imagination. The EU was constitutionalizing in that it could no longer plausibly be regarded as a mere contractual undertaking between fully independent Member States (even if the Member States are generally thought to remain, in ironic German, *Herren der Verträge*), but its constitutional structure showed fairly little resemblance to that of the constitutional state – Stein's interest was in describing the solidification of the EU rather than discussing controls on executive authority or other staples of constitutional thought – and that suggests a radically different notion of 'constitutionalization'.

What is more, in this limited sense a great many international organizations can be considered 'constitutional': in many international organizations, the executive organ plays a role of its own, and in many, the accepted sphere of action includes implied powers. Still, it would be decidedly unorthodox to pin the label 'constitutional' on, say, the Universal Postal Union, or the International Olive Council, or the European University Institute.

Nonetheless, a lively and long-lasting debate ensued on how constitutional the EU was, and whether it should have a formal constitution, and whether such a constitution could take the form of a treaty between Member States to begin with.[21] More to the point though, some started to

---

[20] See E. Stein, 'Lawyers, Judges and the Making of a Transnational Constitution' (1981) 75 *American Journal of International Law* 1–27.

[21] See J.H.H. Weiler, *The Constitution of Europe* (Cambridge University Press, 1999); Gráinne de Búrca and J.H.H. Weiler (eds.), *The Worlds of European Constitutionalism* (Cambridge University Press, 2012).

investigate whether other organizations could somehow be seen as constitutional, and attention focused on two such organizations: the newly created World Trade Organization, and the well-established United Nations.

b The WTO

The constitutionalization of the WTO had been posited, in various ways and, it seems, varying degrees, by seasoned trade lawyers, including Ernst-Ulrich Petersmann.[22] Ordo-liberal in outlook, he based himself on the integrative workings of the CJEU, which had observed that the right to trade and the right to contract were fundamental rights. These now were exemplified most of all in the WTO. Hence, an argument could be made that the WTO was protecting and stimulating fundamental rights and, *ergo*, could thus be seen as a constitutional order, however embryonic perhaps. It would, moreover, also deliver the goods associated with (ordo-)liberal constitutionalism: the WTO, by insisting on the freedom to trade and contract, would increase global welfare, and that would be good for everyone. As the slogan goes: a rising tide lifts all boats.

It was here, naturally, that critics started to object: a rising tide may lift all boats, but the analogy is deceptive, in that some boats are likely to be lifted higher than others. All legal rules and institutions have distributive effects, and Petersmann's, so it was feared, would rapidly make the rich richer and the poor poorer. His outlook was unmasked as blatantly free-market oriented, with little regard for other values that some may deem constitutional: solidarity, equality, or the entire catalogue of social and economic rights. Plus, there remained the unanswered question as to who would be responsible for the constitutionalization process. The most obvious candidate would be the WTO's Member States (these were *Herren des Vertrags*, after all), but this seemed unlikely: if so, they could have created a constitutional order from the start, rather than set in motion a process. Moreover, a large number of those Member States cannot claim internally to be liberal, or democratic, or even much more than nominally market-oriented, and the accession of China and Russia would do little to change this.

---

[22] See e.g. E.-U. Petersmann, 'Time for a United Nations "Global Compact" for Integrating Human Rights into the Law of the World Trade Organization' (2002) 13 *European Journal of International Law* 621–650.

Hence, one would have to look elsewhere for the engine of the constitutionalization process, and in a pioneering article Deborah Cass suggested that this engine consisted of the dispute settlement mechanism of the WTO: its panels and especially its highest judicial organ, the Appellate Body.[23] Yet, upon closer scrutiny, Cass retreated considerably: in her monograph published a few years[24] later she took distance from her earlier views, and suggested that there was not all that much constitutionalization going on in the WTO. Much of this change of heart stemmed from having adopted a different, more comprehensive and demanding, notion of constitutionalization. If the earlier article assumed constitutionalization as a means for addressing some particular concerns (including the WTO's own position), the later monograph viewed constitutionalization more on a par with domestic constitutional thought, highlighting such issues as inclusiveness of participation, political community, and deliberation. And on such a conception, there is all of a sudden a lot less constitutionalization visible in the WTO.

c The United Nations

The most well-known version of organizational constitutionalism is, in fact, a combination of the institutional and cosmopolitan versions. The German scholar Bardo Fassbender, currently a law professor at St. Gallen in Switzerland, published a famous piece in 1998 in which he suggested, invoking the German tradition, that the UN Charter was best seen as constitution for the international community.[25] The claim therewith contains two distinct sub-claims, although these remained largely implicit: first, that the international order has a constitution, known as the UN Charter; and second, the claim includes the sub-claim that the UN, as an organization, must be viewed as constitutional.

Fassbender's argument was picked up and endorsed by none other than Habermas,[26] and indeed it contains a few plausible elements. Thus, if

---

[23] See D. Cass, 'The Constitutionalization of International Trade Law: Judicial Norm-generation as the Engine of Constitutionalization' (2001) 12 *European Journal of International Law* 39–77.

[24] See D. Cass, *The Constitutionalization of the World Trade Organization: Legitimacy, Democracy and Community in the International Trading System* (Oxford University Press, 2005).

[25] See B. Fassbender, 'The United Nations Charter as the Constitution of the International Community' (1998) 36 *Columbia Journal of Transnational Law* 529–619.

[26] See J. Habermas, *The Divided West* (Polity, 2006).

the hallmark of constitutions is that they are hierarchically superior to ordinary law, the same applies to the Charter, by virtue of the supremacy clause of article 103. And if constitutions usually apply to all within the same political community, article 2(6) of the Charter displays a similar ambition, although in terms more guarded than Fassbender suggests perhaps: the provision calls upon the cooperation of third parties, but does not (and cannot) order such cooperation.

On other points, Fassbender's claim was less plausible, even within its own four corners. For instance, the suggestion that the drafters of the Charter chose the term Charter precisely because it referred to a constitution and no similar term was available, is historically untenable. If nothing else, they could have just referred to their instrument as a 'constitution', without needing to resort to the term 'charter' – indeed, the constitutive instruments of some other organizations are called 'constitution'; the World Health Organization, a contemporary of the UN, is an example.

More important though than these cosmetics is how Fassbender conceptualized his constitution. It turned out that Fassbender's constitution does little by way of separation of powers and says nothing at all about the accountability of the UN and any of its organs. If one of the functions of a constitution is to place limits on the exercise of public power, as many would agree, then the UN Charter à la Fassbender is a very, very relaxed example of constitution: it does not limit the UN's activities in any way and, on at least one reading of the Charter, does not even limit the scope of activities of the supreme international public organ, the Security Council. In the end, then, Fassbender's constitutionalism is in effect a hyper-functional concept,[27] allowing the UN to do as it pleases, without placing any limits on the scope and reach of public power. And if the UN were deemed constitutional in theory, one cannot escape the practical observation that much of what it does would be difficult to reconcile with any version of constitutionalist thought: if the UN is considered to be 'constitutional', one can only reach the conclusion that much of what does is actually 'unconstitutional' – and how helpful is that?

---

[27] See J. Klabbers, 'Functionalism, Constitutionalism and the United Nations', in A. Lang, Jr. and A. Wiener (eds.), *Handbook on Global Constitutionalism* (Edward Elgar, 2017).

4 The Administrativists

As transpired from the above, most versions of international constitutionalism suffered from two major blind spots. First, much constitutional thought was modelled, explicitly or implicitly, on Western values. That is not surprising, of course; it would be much more surprising if Western scholars would not reflect Western values. It would be problematic if the Western-born plans would result in global domination, yet that is something that is less easily demonstrated. The critique that such projects are neo-colonial or Western-dominated is a bit facile, but it does have bite – politically, such allegations are often enough to kill off any ambitions a project may have.

Second though, and much more surprising given the usual associations that come with the term 'constitution', few of the constitutionalist proposals pay much attention to the control of public authority. Yet, if there is one single normative element to constitutionalism, it is the idea that public power should be kept in check: this is the hallmark of one of the foundational texts of constitutionalism, the Federalist Papers.[28] A constitution, in other words, is expected to include provisions on the organization of public power, and therewith also on limits on the exercise of public power – even if only in terms of a separation of powers. Yet, as noted, much of the constitutional discourse related to specific international organizations was geared towards solidifying the position of the institution in question, while the more general constitutional discourse of the cosmopolitans posited the existence of universal values (with greater or lesser cogency) but, in most versions, was never explicit about controlling public power. Peters' work, with its emphasis on democracy, comes closest, but at best represents an important exception rather than the rule. Thus, one might say that international constitutionalism collapsed under its own weight: it posited a universalizing project, while closing its eyes for the one thing that would have fit such a universalizing project.

Perhaps in response, several projects aimed to play down constitutionalism's 'conceits'[29] and relied on an administrative law

---

[28] See A. Hamilton, J. Madison and J. Jay, *The Federalist Papers* (Bantam, 1982).

[29] See J.L. Dunoff, 'Constitutional Conceits: The WTO's "Constitution" and the Discipline of International Law' (2006) 17 *European Journal of International Law* 647–675.

approach instead. This had two distinct advantages (at least) over inter-national constitutionalism, or so it seemed. First, being administrative in nature, it never needed to demonstrate the universality of big polit-ical values. All it needed to do was to suggest the universality of cer-tain procedural ideas: the idea that decisions should be reasoned; or the idea that all relevant stakeholders should participate in decision-making affecting them; or the idea that decisions should be proportional. And this, so proponents thought, was much easier to achieve than agreement on whether or not torture would be acceptable in extreme circumstances, or where the limits of free speech should lie. And second, being adminis-trative in nature, it would automatically be concerned (so it was thought) with the control of public power, and perhaps even the control of some manifestations of private power as well.[30]

For ease of reference, two versions will be distinguished. The first became known as global administrative law, and was developed by international lawyers such as Benedict Kingsbury and Nico Krisch, in conjunction with administrative lawyers, including Richard Stewart and Sabino Cassese.[31] It worked on the basis of the posited existence of a global legal space (empir-ically verifiable), in which decisions are taken which thus (or so it seemed to follow) ought to be subject to some kind of review. These decisions could emanate from public authorities, local as well as international: refugee applications, e.g., can be handled both by domestic authorities and by UNHCR. Sometimes, pertinent decisions can even emanate from private authorities, at least in those cases where private authorities assume public or semi-public functions, or their standards have been adopted by public authority. Thus, GAL scholars have paid attention to private certification schemes as well as to the work of, e.g. international sports bodies.

A second approach was pioneered in Heidelberg, at the Max Planck Institute for Foreign Public and International Law, under the heading of International Public Authority (IPA).[32] Here, the scope was more

---

[30] It is for this reason that Anne-Marie Slaughter's work does not fit the bill: while she acknowledges the rise of multi-stakeholder decision-making, she is rather cavalier about issues of accountability. See A.-M. Slaughter, *A New World Order* (Princeton University Press, 2004).

[31] See B. Kingsbury, N. Krisch and R. Stewart, 'The Emergence of Global Administrative Law' (2005) 68 *Law and Contemporary Problems* 15–62; S. Cassese (ed.), *Research Handbook on Global Administrative Law* (Edward Elgar, 2016).

[32] See A. von Bogdandy *et al.* (eds.), *The Exercise of Public Authority by International Institutions: Advancing International Institutional Law* (Springer, 2010).

restrictive: IPA concentrated on public institutions, and aimed to develop a framework for understanding the standard-setting activities of these international institutions, on the basis of the observation that much of this work is done through governance that may not utilize specifically legal instruments, and therewith may escape legal scrutiny. Hence, IPA tried to reconstruct international public governance in public law terms (often borrowed from administrative law), with the ambition to highlight control.[33]

While GAL in particular proved a hugely popular and successful academic project, not all of its ambitions could be met. For one thing, the posited distinction between procedure and substance, used to justify a procedural perspective, proved difficult to sustain. Proportionality testing, e.g., always involves a substantive choice: something must be tested against something else, and the choice for the 'something else' can have huge political effects. Likewise, it is one thing to claim that decision-making should include the relevant stakeholders, but the choice for the relevant stakeholders in any given procedure is never politically innocent either. Here too, the neo-colonial critique reared its head: the administrative notions relied on were often borrowed from the United States or the EU, so how universal were they really? Plus, even the premise proved problematic: for Anglo-Saxons, administrative law may function so as to limit public authority; but for some civil law traditions, it functions rather to empower public authority. In response, GAL scholars have done much to clarify what they mean by 'public' and even what they mean by 'law', and have further investigated different techniques of governance, including in particular governance that does not rely on standard instruments (regulations, directives) but instead takes place through indicators.[34]

And then there is the circumstance that if one of the inspirations for re-introducing public law thinking into international law resided in the perceived fragmentation of international law, the administrative approaches do little to overcome fragmentation. GAL works best when it comes to applying norms from a single regime – in such circumstances, proportionality (for instance) may make some sense. But it makes less

---

[33] See also E. Benvenisti, *The Law of Global Governance* (Hague Academy of International Law, 2014).

[34] Seminal is K. Davis et al. (eds.), *Governance by Indicators* (Oxford University Press, 2012).

sense when norms from different regimes are cast against each other, and that is precisely where guidance is mostly needed. How can one decide proportionally between trade and the environment? Or between security and human rights?[35]

5 The Sceptics

Some of the pitfalls of international constitutionalism were discovered early enough: thus, it was observed that the constitutionalization of different regimes or organizations would only serve so as to deepen political cleavages: instead of pitting rule against rule, it would pit constitution against constitution, therewith making any compromise that much harder to achieve.

The sceptics can, by and large, be divided into two groups, with some overlapping membership, on the basis of whether they look for alternatives within the law or outside of it. Both groups accept that the world is highly pluralist, not merely normatively, in that people may endorse different agendas, but epistemological as well. We do not mean the same things even if we use the same terms, let alone that we can agree on anything substantive. For some, such as Nico Krisch, this meant that lawyers would have to reach 'beyond constitutionalism', and would need to try and devise methods of settling conflicts within and between functional regimes. In a pluralist world, conflicts between norms or regimes would demand a political solution, and the law ought to do as much as possible to facilitate such a solution.[36] Klabbers, in turn, aimed to posit a sources-doctrine for a constitutional global order: under what circumstances can a constitutional global order accept normative utterances as law?[37] In order to achieve this, he suggested a 'presumptive positivism': normative

[35] See F.V. Kratochwil, *The Status of Law in World Society: Meditations on the Role and Rule of Law* (Cambridge University Press, 2014).
[36] N. Krisch, *Beyond Constitutionalism: The Pluralist Structure of Postnational Law* (Oxford University Press, 2010).
[37] See J. Klabbers, 'Law-making and Constitutionalism', in Klabbers et al., n. 17, 81–124; see also J. Klabbers, 'International Legal Positivism and Constitutionalism', in J. Kammerhofer and J. d'Aspremont (eds.), *International Legal Positivism in a Post-Modern World* (Cambridge University Press, 2014), 264–290.

utterances should be regarded as (international) law unless the reverse could be demonstrated.

Others, however, doubted whether the law could do much work here, although they accepted that much of the work to be done was to be done by lawyers, utilizing their expertise when acting in a decision-making capacity. It followed, that much would come to depend on how those individuals would come to utilize their expertise. Koskenniemi suggested that the one thing worth saving from a duty-based constitutionalism was the mindset: lawyers ought to realize that when making decisions, they ought to be mindful of the effects of their actions, and give effect to a 'culture of formalism'.[38]

Klabbers had likewise suggested, early on, that the most proper constitutionalism would be a 'constitutionalism lite',[39] and later fleshed this out more explicitly in terms borrowed from Aristotelian virtue ethics. This approach accepts the premise that the application of legal rules always involves a human element: rules do not decide on their own application, or how they shall be interpreted, or whether the exception is applicable – all this involves human intervention, and thus there is merit in thinking about what sort of individual gets to apply the law. It may make a difference, for instance, beyond differences in technical competence, whether legal officers are courageous or not, humble or not, or honest or not, even if notions of honesty or humility or courage may differ across time and space. And emphatically, it may matter whether they are compassionate, or display empathy.[40]

6 The Current State of Affairs

After the broad and intense debates in the first decade of the twenty-first century, the discussion on international constitutionalism seems to have calmed down considerably. Looking back, it seemed that the debate received several final contributions in the forms of a volume edited by Tsagourias,

---

[38] See M. Koskenniemi, 'Constitutionalism as Mindset: Reflections on Kantian Themes about International Law and Globalization' (2007) 8 *Theoretical Inquiries in Law* 9–36.

[39] See J. Klabbers, 'Constitutionalism Lite' (2004) 1 *International Organizations Law Review* 31–58.

[40] See J. Klabbers, 'Doing Justice: Bureaucracy, the Rule of Law and Virtue Ethics', (2017) 6 *Rivista di Filosofia del Diritto* 27–50.

a study by Klabbers, Peters and Ulfstein and a volume edited by Dunoff and Trachtman,[41] after which the caravan of international lawyers moved on to different matters, symbolized in the title of Krisch's work: *Beyond Constitutionalism*. And once the caravan had moved on, it became time to reflect not on constitutionalization itself, but on the debate that had taken place: several of the post-2009 contributions aimed to make sense first and foremost of that debate.[42] To the extent that the debate itself is still engaged in, it seems to have been taken over by political theorists.[43]

Perhaps the parochial, Western foundations espoused by many international constitutionalists has come to place constitutionalism in a bad light; perhaps the belated discovery by international lawyers of a principle of systemic integration, laid down in the Vienna Convention on the Law of Treaties, has eased many worries about the fragmentation of international law; perhaps the rejection by Dutch and Frech electorates of the EU constitution has slowed down the discussion even in EU circles (note though that much of the rejected constitutional treaty has found its way, uncontroversially, in the Lisbon Treaty: a constitution in all but name); and if it is true, as it seems, that globalization is less popular these days, it stands to reason that there is less need for an antidote in the form of international constitutionalism.

That said, international constitutionalism has not disappeared altogether, but it does appear to have changed some of its colours. Perhaps the most remarkable development has been the creation of two relevant journals.[44] The first of these is the *International Journal of Constitutional Law*, first published in 2003 and especially inspired by the dual circumstance that constitutional norms were globalizing and comparative constitutional law was considered to be on the rise. Its editorial policy does not sharply

---

[41] See N. Tsagourias, *Transnational Constitutionalism: International and European Perspectives* (Cambridge University Press, 2007); Klabbers et al., n. 17, and J.L. Dunoff and J. Trachtman (eds.), *Ruling the World? Constitutionalism, International Law, and Global Governance* (Cambridge University Press, 2009).

[42] See C. Schwöbel, 'Situating the Debate on Global Constitutionalism' (2010) 8 *International Journal of Constitutional Law* 611–635; O'Donoghue, n. 8.

[43] See J. Cohen, *Globalization and Sovereignty: Rethinking Legality, Legitimacy, and Constitutionalism* (Cambridge University Press, 2012); T. Isiksel, *Europe's Functional Constitution: A Theory of Constitutionalism Beyond the State* (Oxford University Press, 2016). It is possibly no coincidence that a recent overview is edited by two political theorists: see Lang and Wiener, n. 27.

[44] Or perhaps even three, counting the less well-known *Vienna Journal of International Constitutional Law*.

distinguish, as it could have done, between the internationalization of constitutional law on the one hand and the constitutionalization of international law on the other hand, and neither does the more recently created, and intimately related, International Society of Public Law.

The second and more specifically dedicated journal is titled *Global Constitutionalism*, edited by an interdisciplinary mix of lawyers and political scientists. Remarkably, the latter journal saw the light not at the crest of the constitutionalist wave, but when the wave had already receded, in 2012, and this circumstance alone suggests that there is something fundamental about international constitutionalization that renders it more than just another academic fad or fashion.

That 'something', however, does not appear to be anything grandiose such as the putative constitutionalization of the international legal order. Instead, perusing the table of contents of the journal suggests it focuses on the philosophical niceties of global constitutionalism, and on comparative constitutional law and politics. There is fairly little talk in its pages about *jus cogens*, hierarchy or, indeed, globalization; but quite a bit of attention for developments in Turkey or Colombia, and for what theorists mean when they speak of 'the people', or of 'judicial review'. And this suggests the making of a second wave, smaller perhaps and less ambitious than its predecessor, but possibly longer-lasting.

This makes sense, if only because, appearances notwithstanding, some of the problems that inspired the earlier wave of scholarship have continued to persist. Public power is still exercised on a transnational level, beyond the reach of most national parliamentarians, and often escaping the reach of judicial organs as well. Private power, moreover, often uses public authorities for its own purposes, again often unimpeded, and public authorities outsource tasks to private actors, therewith redistributing social and economic capital.

And to the extent that international constitutionalism owed much to the emergence of the individual – or humanity – as independent carrier of rights and obligations under international law,[45] legal issues can be expected to multiply. Put differently, when the legal position of a specific individual is affected by rules coming from different sources and saying

---

[45] It is probably no coincidence that Peters has moved on to demonstrate precisely the relevance of the individual (and humanity) for today's international law: A. Peters, *Beyond Human Rights* (Cambridge University Press, 2016).

different things, some device is needed to decide the situation – and that device can no longer be simply the claim that one jurisdiction applies and the other does not, or the claim that one is superior to the other. Even if technically that may be the case, deciding cases by technical competence without taking the individual concerned into account is no longer fully acceptable. This is, ultimately, the main lesson (one of many, to be sure) of the *Kadi* case before the CJEU: it suggests that doing justice in individual cases is becoming an inherent element of legal decision-making across boundaries – and this, if anything, may well be characterized as a form of 'constitutionalization from below' and driven by incidental litigation rather than grand design.[46]

Additionally, even if the vocabulary of constitutionalization is no longer fully applied, there remains the strongly felt need to provide global public goods and common goods, ranging from putting a stop to climate change to such things as peace and security, and in these matters the traditional international law vocabulary revolving around state consent is clearly not up to the task. Hence, something else is needed, and that something else may well be a different manifestation of constitutionalism, however 'light' perhaps.[47]

Conclusion

International law lacks central authorities, and thus the task of systematizing what otherwise seem like random events and creations falls upon academics. Yet, the absence of central authority also suggests the absence of any specific authorial intent: it is left to international lawyers, or more specifically international law academics, to make sense of what goes on around them. This helps explain the circular structure of much academic international legal debate: it aims to work through whatever it is that people think they observe. Those people then adopt a vocabulary that may, *prima facie*, seem to suit their observations, only to discover that actually, it is not all that suitable, or that it comes with loads of normative baggage that no one anticipated at the time, or even that the initial observations were not all that accurate really.

---

[46] See J. Klabbers and G. Palombella (eds.), *The Challenge of Inter-legality* (Cambridge University Press, forthcoming).

[47] See N. Krisch, 'The Decay of Consent: International Law in an Age of Public Goods' (2014) 108 *American Journal of International Law* 1–40.

So too with international constitutionalism. It kicked off in earnest, arguably, once Tully had compellingly suggested that constitutions could co-exist.[48] Thereafter, people started to think that international and domestic constitutionalism were not mutually exclusive, and that, lo and behold, some international phenomena could perhaps be explained with the help of a constitutional vocabulary – how else to make sense of *jus cogens*? Or *erga omnes* obligations? It is no coincidence that traditional international lawyers, raised on a diet of sovereignty and state consent, were abhorred by these notions, but the new Latin terms seemed amenable to a constitutional discourse, and once such a discourse was adopted, they seemed to pop up everywhere; which in turn created doubts about the accuracy or usefulness of the observation: if all norms are *jus cogens*, then the concept does little specific work. Moreover, once it was realized that constitutionalism comes with normative connotations, the question quickly arose whether it was needed in the wake of the seeming retreat of globalization and the pragmatic way to solve fragmentation, or whether it was even desirable: classic fears about world government could come to the fore, for it seemed that global constitutionalism was only one step removed from such a spectre.

As a result, the debate died down about as quickly as it had arisen. It dominated the discipline for about a decade, and then fizzed out. Still, some of the underlying issues are persistent. There is a movement towards global law,[49] including through overlapping legal spaces. There is the need to provide for public and common goods, made crystal clear by climate change, and for this, the traditional existence on sovereignty and state consent seems insufficient, outdated, probably even dangerous. In one form or another then, some of the thoughts underlying constitutionalization are bound to persist or, perhaps, return.

Further Reading

E. Benvenisti, *The Law of Global Governance* (Hague Academy of International Law, 2014).

J. Klabbers, A. Peters and G. Ulfstein, *The Constitutionalization of International Law* (Oxford University Press, 2009).

---

[48] See J. Tully, *Strange Multiplicity: Constitutionalism in an Age of Diversity* (Cambridge University Press, 1995).

[49] See N. Walker, *Intimations of Global Law* (Cambridge University Press, 2015).

M. Koskenniemi, 'Constitutionalism as Mindset: Reflections on Kantian Themes about International Law and Globalization' (2007) 8 *Theoretical Inquiries in Law* 9–36.

N. Krisch, *Beyond Constitutionalism: The Pluralist Structure of Postnational Law* (Oxford University Press, 2010).

E. Stein, 'Lawyers, Judges and the Making of a Transnational Constitution', (1981) 75 *American Journal of International Law* 1–27.

N. Walker, *Intimations of Global Law* (Cambridge University Press, 2015).

European Constitutionalism 20

Kaarlo Tuori

Introduction

In this chapter, 'European constitutionalism' refers to European Union constitutionalism. European constitutionalism will be examined as an epitome of transnational constitutionalism; i.e. as a species of constitutionalism distinct from state or national constitutionalism.

Adopting the conceptual framework of transnational constitutionalism implies approaching the EU and its legal system from a particular disciplinary perspective and relating them to a particular legal order. The debate on the basic legal characteristics of the EU manifests the impact of legal perspectivism, prevalent in all law but especially conspicuous in EU law, lying on the interface of diverse legal orders and defying an unambiguous compartmentalization in the conventional divisions of legal disciplines. Yet, acknowledging the possibility of differing conceptual frameworks and perspectival commitments does not amount to buffering them against criticism coming from other perspectives. Thus, I shall claim that questioning the constitutional characterization of the EU by prominent scholars, such as Dieter Grimm and Peter Lindseth, reflects the persistent impact of state constitutionalism, which forms a major obstacle to probing into the specificity of European transnational constitutionalism. So the distinct features which have led these observers to doubt the existence of European constitutionalism can – and in my mind should – be understood as peculiarities of this variant of constitutionalism. These include the evolutionary, process-like nature of European constitutionalism; its multidimensionality, due to the constitutionalization of particular policy fields; and its dependence on Member State, national constitutionalism. Analysis of the peculiarities will be the main focus of this chapter.

Catching the European specificities requires adopting a thin notion of constitutionalism, summarizing the shared features of different variants of constitutionalism; i.e. the common denominator of constitutionalism. In this chapter the common denominator will be sought in constitution's position as higher law and in the functions this higher law is expected to accomplish.

1 Does the European Union Possess a Constitution?

a Perspectivism of Legal Disciplines and Legal Orders

Much ink – too much, one could say – has been spilled in debating whether the EU possesses a constitution or not. This is not an issue where an objectively valid answer could be found. What is at stake is the basic legal vocabulary with which the EU is characterized. Alternative conceptual frameworks exist. More or less convincing arguments can be presented in favour of opting for each of these, but no second-order criteria exist for declaring any of them the winner of the argumentative game.

Alternative conceptual frameworks reflect, not only scholarly disagreements and individual efforts to stand out in scholarly debates, but also a more profound and interesting backdrop; namely, the perspectivism which labels law in general but which is especially accentuated in the context of the EU. We always approach the law from a particular perspective, and our perspective inevitably affects the legal cultural *Vorverständnis* (pre-understanding) through which our legal knowledge is filtered. Legal concepts form a central part of this *Vorverständnis*. Legal cultural perspectivism comes in three main guises: perspectivism of legal disciplines, legal orders and legal roles. Here we can focus on the perspectivism of legal disciplines and legal orders and skip that of legal roles, manifesting the different relations to law of, say, judges, scholars and legislators.

Different legal disciplines employ different legal concepts and offer different conceptualizations of 'surface-level' legal phenomena; say, the Founding Treaties of the EU. A constitutional lawyer may see in the Treaties a (formal) constitution – or, at least, a quasi-constitution; an administrative lawyer a delegation of administrative powers from the Member States to the EU; and an international lawyer an international treaty establishing an international organization. Such disciplinary perspectives are not wholly exclusive. In her account, a constitutional lawyer may find space even for administrative and international law aspects; an administrative lawyer for constitutional and international law viewpoints; and an international lawyer for constitutional and administrative law considerations. However, the main disciplinary perspective dictates the emphasis in the account and the legal vocabulary employed.

Yet, not only do disciplinary commitments affect our conceptual choices. Legal phenomena are always analysed in relation to a distinct legal order; a referential legal order, as we can call it. Especially when analysing legal phenomena which lie in the intersection of several legal orders – as does the EU – the conscious or unconscious choice of the referential legal order is of crucial importance. Obviously, the basic choice here is between the EU legal order and a Member State legal order. Evidently, conceptual frameworks which lead to negating or at least downplaying European-level constitutionalism, such as an administrative or international law approach, imply commitment to the latter, Member State perspective. Within the constitutional approach both the EU law and a Member State law perspective are possible. This has been made conspicuous by fundamental conflicts of authority between the ECJ and, say, the German Constitutional Court. Both courts employ a constitutional approach, but the ECJ examines the issue at stake from the perspective of EU constitutional law, while the German Court adopts the perspective of German constitutional law. Still, the perspectivism of legal orders is not exhausted merely by the choice of the surface-level constitutional norms which are deemed applicable to the issue at hand. Legal orders do not consist merely of surface-level norms but include legal cultural layers, informing the *Vorverständnis* of legal actors. This also holds for constitutional law: constitutional culture, consisting of constitutional concepts, principles, theories and methods, possesses features specific to the legal order at issue.

In sum, when examining the debates on European constitutionalism we should be attentive to the perspectivism of both legal disciplines and legal orders. Commitment to a constitutional law approach does not necessarily imply acknowledgement of European constitutionalism. When the constitutional law approach is combined with the perspective of Member State law, rejection of the constitutional claims of European law is wholly conceivable, perhaps even probable. To speak of European constitutionalism requires a combination of constitutional law and European law perspectives. Such a combination defines the legal cultural starting-point of this chapter.

Emphasizing the significance of legal cultural perspectivism does not imply immunizing scholarly arguments from criticism anchored in another perspective or negating the possibility of a wide divergence of views within each perspective. Thus, adopting the combination of constitutional law and European law perspectives does not exclude disagreements with other accounts sharing the same perspectival commitments. Indeed, because of the still emergent and contested nature of EU law culture, including EU constitutional culture, theoretical controversies are rather to be expected.

b The Persistence of the State Template

Modern constitutionalism in both senses of the term, i.e. as specific constitutional practices and as the specific ideational basis of these practices, emerged in the context of modern states; to constitute, organize and delimit public power as state power. Constitutional concepts, starting from the very concept of constitution, bear traces of their origin. When transferred to the transnational level, to examine, say, the EU, we face the dilemma of translatability. On the one hand, concepts elaborated in the state setting offer the only available starting-point for transnational constitutional analysis. Furthermore, if national and transnational constitutionalism had nothing in common, it would be difficult to justify in the first place employing constitutional vocabulary at the transnational level. On the other hand, our conceptual framework should allow for the possibility that some typical features of national constitutionalism[1] are wanting at the transnational level and that at this level constitutionalism displays aspects which do not find correspondence in the state setting. We should avoid thick concepts which may be warranted at the level of national constitutionalism but which tend to negate transnational constitutionalism or at least obscure the view to its particularities.

Scholars who reject transnational European constitutionalism or denigrate it to the status of quasi-constitutionalism employ a thick notion of constitutionalism, manifesting the state template. In the administrative law account of the EU, represented most prominently by Peter Lindseth,[2] constitutionalism is located exclusively at the pole of Member States, while the relationship between Member States and the EU is explored through the (US) administrative law conceptual relationship of delegation and control between a principal and an agent. In this analysis, constitutionalism does play an important role but at issue is the polyarchic constitutionalism of the Member states; at the level of the EU, nothing worth the term of constitutionalism exists.

The administrative law account implies a thick normative notion of constitutionalism corresponding to the American understanding of a constitutional democracy and the European understanding of a democratic *Rechtsstaat* defined through the requirements of democracy and fundamental rights. In this conceptual setting, 'constitutionalism' is intimately linked to legitimacy: 'constitutionalism' implies that the legitimacy of a polity and its law should be achieved through democratic procedures and fundamental rights. While Lindseth refuses to examine putative European constitutionalism in its interaction with national constitutionalism, he ends up by denying the justification for a constitutional depiction of the Union and its law.[3]

---

[1] In this chapter, 'national constitutionalism' and 'state constitutionalism' are used as synonyms. On the state-centricity of classic constitutionalism, see Chapter 2.

[2] P. Lindseth, *Power and Legitimacy: Reconciling Europe and the Nation-State* (Oxford University Press, 2010).

[3] D. Halberstam, 'Constitutional Heterarchy: The Centrality of Conflict in the European Union and the United States', in J. Dunoff and J. Trachtman (eds.), *Ruling the World? Constitutionalism, International Law, and Global Governance* (Cambridge University Press, 2009), 326–355.

Dieter Grimm's writings[4] offer another example of adoption of a state perspective – in Grimm's case, the perspective of German constitutional law; reliance on a thick definition of basic constitutional concepts; and a consequent scepticism of the constitutional credentials of the EU. Grimm defines modern constitution through five characteristics:

1.   A constitution consists of legal norms and not of philosophic principles or a description of the actual power relationships in a polity.
2.   Constitutional norms address the establishment and exercise of political rule (public power). It not only regulates and modifies public power but constitutes it.
3.   The constitution regulates political rule in a systematic, comprehensive manner, tolerating neither extraconstitutional powers nor extraconstitutional ways and means of rule. Historically, the emergence of a modern constitution was preceded by the emergence of the modern state; i.e. the concentration of the rights to rule into a state power as a uniform public power.
4.   Political rule is only legitimate when constituted and limited by the constitution, and consequently constitutional law takes precedence over all other legal acts, which are valid only when they comply with the constitutional framework.
5.   Constitutional norms must originate with the people, since every other principle for the legitimation of political rule would undermine the other elements of a modern constitution and prevail over the constitution in the event of a conflict.

Grimm emphasizes the significance for modern constitutionalism of the distinction between constituent and constituted power (*pouvoir constituant* and *pouvoir constitué*), made famous by abbé Siéyes: the constituent, constitution-making power lies with the people, while the bodies established by the constitution exercise constituted power. Closely related to the distinction between constituent and constituted power is another distinction; namely, that between procedures and principles of political decision-making and political decision-making itself. The procedures and principles of political decision-making fall

---

[4] Two volumes of Grimm's writings in constitutional law have recently appeared in English. D. Grimm, *Constitutionalism: Past, Present, and Future* (Oxford University Press, 2016); D. Grimm, *The Constitution of European Democracy* (Oxford University Press, 2017).

under constituent power and belong to the domain of the constitution, while political decision-making itself should be left to the constituted power, i.e. to the bodies established by the constitution. Grimm does not explicitly mention democracy and fundamental rights – the main elements of a constitutional democracy or a democratic *Rechtsstaat* – as conceptual elements of a constitution but labels them achievements or standards of modern constitutionalism.

In Grimm's assessment, the Founding Treaties of the EU fall short of the criteria of a modern constitution mainly because of the lack a democratic *pouvoir constituant* as their source. The Treaties are treaties under international law which have been ratified in accordance with national constitutional requirements and which cannot be amended without the consent of the Member States. The Member States remain Masters of the Treaties. The Treaties may enjoy democratic legitimacy in individual Member States but they are not emanations of the sovereignty, i.e. the constituent power, of a European people. If the term 'constituent power' can in general be used in the European context, the constituent power falls to the Member States and not to the European people. Grimm concedes that a process of constitutionalization has occurred in the sense that in particular in the jurisprudence of the ECJ, the Treaties have been assigned constitutional functions and treated as 'higher law'. Grimm invokes the introduction of the direct effect of European law in *van Gend en Loos* and the principle of the supremacy of European law in *Costa* v. *Enel*, as well as the extension of supremacy to cover even national constitutional law in *Internationale Handelsgesellschaft*.[5] However, these developments have not transformed the Treaties into a constitution in the full sense of the term; at most, the Treaties deserve the denomination of a quasi-constitution. The minimum requirement for reaching the rank of a constitution would be the detachment of future Treaty amendments from the acceptance of the Member States, i.e. the abolishment of the Member States' position as Masters of the Treaties.

In Grimm's view, the EU's quasi-constitution also falls short of the achievements of modern constitutionalism, especially democracy. In line with many other observers, Grimm points to the legal, sociological and cultural obstacles to the development of the European parliament

---

[5] Case C-26/62 *Van Gend en Loos* [1963] ECR 3; Case C-6/64 *Flaminio Costa* v. *ENEL* [1964] ECR 585; Case C-11/70 *Internationale Handelsgesellschaft* [1970] ECR 1125.

to a body representative of the European *demos*. However, he sees the main impediment to European level democracy in the violation of the crucial distinction between the conditions and the substance of political decision-making. The Treaties as a quasi-constitution do not regulate merely the procedure and principles of political decision-making but include substantive policy provisions in, for instance, competition law. The Treaties spill over to policy issues which at the state level belong to the domain of ordinary laws and ordinary democratic decision-making. In this sense, constitutionalization of the Treaties has led to over-constitutionalization: to the narrowing of the field of political decision-making by the Council and the European Parliament, and the enhancement of the role of judicial decision-making by the Court and executive decision-making by the Commission. Constitutionalization has not been accompanied by a restriction of the substantive scope of the Treaties to issues of constitutional character.

Thick concepts of constitution and constitutionalism, such as those employed by Lindseth and Grimm, reflect the persistent dominance of the state template of constitutions and hence risk blocking the view to the specificity of European constitutionalism. This specificity comprises extension of constitutionalism to sectoral policy fields, its process-like, evolutionary nature and its constant interaction with national, Member State constitutionalism. The state template focuses on the juridical and political constitutions, and tends to neglect sectoral constitutionalization; a distinct feature of European constitutionalism which corresponds to the basic teleological, policy orientation of European law. Rather than seeing in sectoral constitutionalization an anomaly it should be treated as a particularity of European constitutionalism, distinguishing it from its state counterpart. In addition to the framing juridical and political constitutions, in the EU constitutionalization has covered policy fields, such as economy, social welfare and security.

Obsession with the concept of *pouvoir constituant*, labelling Grimm's contributions, leads easily to downplaying the process-like character of the European constitution and ignoring the centrality of evolutionary concepts for its examination. Finally, rejecting the existence of constitutionalism at the European level because of the putative failure to meet the legitimacy exigencies of a constitutional democracy intimates bypassing the constant interaction with Member State constitutionalism, i.e. the third distinctive feature of European constitutionalism.

In order to probe into the specificity of European constitutionalism, we should not burden our basic constitutional concepts with too demanding normative assumptions. 'Constitution' and 'constitutionalism' can and should also be used in a thinner, normatively more neutral sense, which detaches them from the state template and allow for examining the particularities which mark out European constitutionalism. Yet, of course, we must also keep in mind that in order to justify the use of constitutional vocabulary in the first place, European constitutionalism must be shown to display, not only divergences from, but also similarities to state constitutionalism. Similarities include the position of constitution as higher law and the basic functions this higher law is expected to perform.

c Constitution as Higher Law

The idea of constitution as higher law can be given both a formal and a substantive reading. Ever since the *Les Verts* ruling in 1986,[6] the ECJ has characterized the Founding Treaties as the constitutional charter of the EC (the EU), implying that these amount to a formal constitution. The ECJ's claim of the Treaties as a constitutional charter obviously involves the idea of higher or superior law. But superior to what law? One of the constitutional particularities of the EU is that superiority works in two directions: with regard to other EU law and with regard to the national law of the Member States. In the internal relations of EU law, the Treaties both enjoy primacy in norm conflicts and provide the competence basis for lower-level normative acts, such as regulations and directives. This corresponds to how Hans Kelsen, for instance, defined the superiority of the constitution in his hierarchical view of the legal order.[7]

With regard to Member State law, superiority is a more complicated issue and breaks with the clarity and unambiguity of Kelsen's conception. The superiority of EU law is reflected by the principle of supremacy of which the primacy of EU law over national Member State law in norm conflicts before national courts is a sub-principle. However, only directly effective Treaty norms enjoy primacy over conflicting national norms, but, to further complicate matters, so do other directly effective European norms, too, regardless of their position in the internal

---

[6] Case C-294/83 *Parti Ecologiste 'Les Verts' v. Parliament* [1986] ECR 1365.
[7] H. Kelsen, *Pure Theory of Law* (Peter Smith, 1989).

hierarchy of EU law. Moreover, the other characteristic of superiority which Kelsen attached to the hierarchical structure of law is wholly missing in relations between European and national law: EU law is not the basis of national law's validity. In sum, EU law and national law do not constitute a unitary hierarchical structure or *Stufenbau* as the application of Kelsen's ideas of constitutional superiority would require.

As regards a qualified amendment procedure as a formal criterion of the superiority of constitutional law, the Treaties clearly stand out from other EU law. The Treaty on the European Union sets out a particular drafting and decision-making procedure for Treaty revisions. Moreover, as amendments to international treaties revisions have to be ratified by every Member State in accordance with the national constitution. Those sceptical of the constitutional claims of the EU are prone to emphasize that the Treaties remain part of international law and the Member States Masters of the Treaties. According to the tenets of an either-or logic, the Treaties cannot possess both an international law and a constitutional character. Yet dichotomous thinking may be misleading. Why could the Treaties not both obey international law in their amendment procedures and function as constitutional law with respect to other EU law and Member State national law? Kelsen, for one, did not see any difficulty in an international treaty functioning as the constitution of a legal order.[8]

What further complicates labelling the Treaties as a formal constitution is the role of general principles in EU constitutional law. Some of the most pertinent constitutional principles are not enshrined in the Treaties but have been articulated in the case law of the ECJ; these include supremacy and direct effect, as well as efficacy (*effet utile*) and uniformity as meta-level justificatory principles. Initially, fundamental rights, too, were introduced into EU law as general principles through ECJ jurisprudence. The ECJ has expressly granted general principles constitutional status.[9] Thus, even if the Treaties as a constitutional charter were characterized as

---

[8] H. Kelsen, *Allgemeine Staatslehre* (Springer, 1920), 194. See also the discussion in R. Schütze, *From Dual to Cooperative Federalism: The Changing Structure of European Law* (Oxford University Press, 2009), 37–39.

[9] Case C-101/08 *Audiolux and Others* v. *Groupe Bruxelles Lambert and Others* [2009] ECR I-9823, Para. 63.

a formal constitution, it is crucial to remember that not all constitutional norms are enshrined in explicit Treaty provisions.

The ECJ is a hybrid court with many functions, reflecting the hybrid character of the EU legal system and polity.[10] It is not a mere constitutional court, but among its many tasks it does exercise functions which equal those of state constitutional courts: through judicial review, it guards the EU constitution as a higher law with regard to both lower-level EU law and national Member State law; it engages in protection of fundamental rights; it resolves conflicts of competence between the EU and the Member States in a way reminiscent of the role of a constitutional court in a federal state; and it settles disputes among the main EU institutions, such as the European Parliament, the Council and the Commission. Indeed, these functions of the ECJ are a major argument for applying constitutional concepts to the European level.

A typical vagueness can be observed in the formal contours of the EU constitution, brought about by the central role of the ECJ. A similar ambiguity affects the substance of this constitution in all its diverse dimensions, i.e. the substantive reading of the European constitution as higher law. The premise, however, should be clear enough: time and again, we are dealing with a *loi fondamentale*, a law of the basics, whether the juridical, political, economic, social or security constitution is at issue. These basics can be identified only through reconstructing the cultural or theoretical layers underlying 'surface-level' Treaty law and doctrine. Yet, in its 'subsurface' movement, too, European constitutionalism differs from typical state constitutionalism.

In the state setting, legal cultural principles, which also produce the substantive coherence of the legal order, are typically closer to Ronald Dworkin's morally laden principles – principles in *sensu stricto* – than policies related to goals and programmes concerning the desired state of society.[11] What has detached European law from an ideal typical state legal order is its fundamental policy orientation which has left its impact on constitutional law, too. The policy orientation is most conspicuous in sectoral constitutions, but it has affected juridical constitutionalization as

---

[10] R. Dehousse, *The European Court of Justice: The Politics of Judicial Integration* (Macmillan, 1998) analyses the ECJ as an international, constitutional and administrative court.

[11] R. Dworkin, *Taking Rights Seriously* (Duckworth, 1978).

well. Such key principles of the juridical constitution as direct effect and
supremacy were also motivated by policy considerations; by the effective
and uniform application of European law which aimed at the establishment and functioning of the common market.

Accordingly, the substantive coherence which European law has
achieved has been a result of policies rather than principles. However,
building up sub-surface, legal-cultural foundations for policy-oriented
law, including constitutional law, has been an arduous process. Within
sectoral constitutions, Member State constitutional traditions can offer
but meagre support for the development of EU constitutional culture. In
central fields, EU law, comprising constitutional law too, has started cultural sedimentation from scratch: no national free movement law exists,
and even national competition law is a relative newcomer.

In their sub-surface foundations, the juridical and political dimensions
partly differ from the general picture. General policy orientation affects
the European framing constitutions, too, as is shown by the backdrop to
direct effect and supremacy, and the justificatory principles of efficacy
and uniformity. Yet an important sub-field of the juridical and political
constitutions exists which EU constitutional law shares with its national
counterparts, where national constitutional traditions have been an
important source and where morally laden principles temper the policy
emphasis; namely, fundamental rights law. Maastricht enshrined in Treaty
law the contribution of national constitutional traditions to fundamental
rights as general principles of European law.[12] In respect of fundamental
rights law, it is also evident that EU and national legal systems share the
same 'deep culture' where the universalist values now listed in Article 2
TEU find their place.[13]

---

[12] Present Article 6(3) TEU provides that 'fundamental rights, as guaranteed by the European
Convention for the Protection of Human Rights and Fundamental Freedoms and as they
result from the constitutional traditions common to the Member States, shall constitute
general principles of the Union's law'. In the Preamble to the TEU, the Member States
confirm 'their attachment to the principles of liberty, democracy and respect for human
rights and fundamental freedoms and of the rule of law'.

[13] 'The Union is founded on the values of respect for human dignity, freedom, democracy,
equality, the rule of law and respect for human rights, including the rights of persons
belonging to minorities. These values are common to the Member States in a society in
which pluralism, non-discrimination, tolerance, justice, solidarity and equality between
women and men prevail.'

d Constitutional Functions

The functions the European constitution is expected to accomplish should be examined in a differentiated manner, attending to the specific features of distinct constitutional dimensions. The functions of the sectoral constitutions are not necessarily identical to those of the framing political and juridical constitutions. Constitutional functions must primarily be examined in the relationship of constitutional law and its object of regulation, i.e. the juridical and political subsystems for the framing constitutions and specific policy fields for the sectoral ones. However, as even the term 'framing constitution' intimates, the juridical and political constitutions accomplish important functions with regard to, not only their specific constitutional objects, but also the other, i.e. sectoral, constitutional dimensions. Thus, they provide the necessary legal and institutional means without which sectoral constitutionalization would not be possible. In particular through their fundamental rights part, they also play a restrictive role with regard to the sectoral ones.

The functions constitutions are expected to fulfil at both the national and transnational level can be discussed in the following framework:

- a constitutive function: bringing about the constitutional object;
- a positioning function: defining the position of the constitutional object in relation to other entities of the same kind;
- an organizing function: bringing order and stability into the constitutional object;
- a restrictive function: preventing the constitutional object from exceeding its limits;
- a legitimizing function: promoting the acceptance of the constitutional object among relevant addressees.

In the EU, the above functions can be discerned in both framing and sectoral constitutions. In the following, examples will be taken from the European political constitution. Analogously to typical state constitutions, it has fulfilled a constitutive function in respect of European polity. The institutional part of the political constitution defines the main institutions of the EU, as well as their competences and mutual relationships. The constitution is also supposed to render the institutional organization the order and stability necessary for its effective and frictionless operating. In a polity aspiring to meet the criteria of a democratic *Rechtsstaat*, the constitutive and organizing functions are accompanied by a restrictive one. Through fundamental rights, the constitution restricts the power that the institutions of the polity are allowed to wield with regard to individuals. Fundamental rights are not the only constitutional limitation on the powers of EU institutions. As a transnational, policy-oriented polity and differing from states, the EU does not possess a universal scope of activity, but its competences are limited to the substantive fields defined in the Treaties. The principle of conferral is an essential restrictive principle of the EU political constitution, distinguishing it from its Member States where the principle of comprehensive powers reflects the universality of a sovereign state's claim to political authority.

A political constitution defines the individual pole of the polity as citizens, endowed with citizenship rights, among which fundamental rights possess a privileged position. From the perspective of individuals, fundamental rights protect them against abuse of power by the institutional pole of the polity and guarantee them spheres of private and public autonomy. The exercise by citizens of their public autonomy renders a polity its democratic character.

In a nascent polity, such as the European one, the constitutive function should be examined in even broader, foundational terms. The political constitution is expected to contribute to the emergence of the polity itself, i.e. to accomplish a polity-building function. For polity building, establishing and stabilizing the institutional organization and relating it to the individual pole of citizens does not suffice. Individual citizens should be interlinked as a citizenry; a *demos* capable of engendering the communicative power without which democracy would remain an empty promise of the formal constitution. Here the constitutional practices where European citizens jointly, across national borders, exercise their political autonomy are of crucial importance; it is only through these practices that European belongingness and solidarity or a European civil society and public sphere can develop. In polity building, the emergence of a constitutional culture shared by European legal or political elites does not suffice. What is needed is a civic constitutional culture forging individual citizens into a European citizenry; a source of communicative power controlling European political institutions and infusing them with democratic input legitimacy. As is well known from the intensive debate of the EU's democratic deficit, the European polity-building process is only taking its first steps.

The constitutive function, so important for the political constitution of an emergent European polity, is accompanied by an equally important positioning function: defining the relations of the polity to other polities. This is a function of state constitutions, too, but it is particularly pertinent in a transnational polity, such as the EU. The basic positioning relates to the claim to autonomy that a constitution typically involves. Discussing the relevance of the claim to autonomy takes us back to the overall characterization of the EU and its law. Opting for the language of transnational constitutionalism entails attaching to the European constitution a claim to autonomy as well. Through this claim, the European political constitution distinguishes the EU polity from Member States and international organizations under public international law.

The organizational and restrictive functions are inseparable from the legitimizing one. For individuals, the political constitution of a democratic *Rechtsstaat* promises autonomy, citizenship and democracy. These promises are linked to the claim to legitimacy, so intimately associated with constitutionalism in its thick normative sense. The legitimizing function takes us to the constant interaction which EU constitutionalism maintains with national Member State constitutionalism; i.e. one of the distinctive features of EU constitutionalism. This interaction will be discussed in the last section of this chapter.

2 Multidimensionality of the European Constitution

As the 'constitutional charter' of the EU, the Founding Treaties are bewildering reading for someone approaching them through the state template. Indeed, the general embarrassment among the citizenry confronted with the substance of the abortive Constitutional Treaty in the mid-2000s has been identified as one of the reasons for its rejection in the French and Dutch referenda. The Treaties contain an abundance of provisions which do not pertain to typical *materia constitutionis* of state constitutions; most conspicuously provisions on diverse policy fields. The European constitution is not only about European law and polity; it is also about European economy, European social welfare and European security. For scholars adopting the perspective and standards of state constitutionalism, such as Dieter Grimm, policy-related provisions blur the boundary which distinguishes principles and procedures of politics from its substance and which also should delimit constitutional from ordinary law. Such provisions are seen as an anomaly which attests to the quasi-nature of the European constitution and which should be removed.

State constitutions usually limit themselves to regulating the political and legal subsystems of society. The political and juridical dimensions exist in the European constitution as well. In the political dimension, constitutional law regulates the EU as a polity and in the juridical dimension the EU legal system. But EU constitutional law also constitutionalizes sectoral fields which at state level are usually the province of ordinary policy- and law-making. In state constitutions, the basic premise is the universality of the political and legal claim to authority within state territory; the principle of comprehensive powers, as we can also put it. State constitutions follow a territorial principle of authority, and, consequently, no sector-specific constitutional authorizations are needed. By contrast, the European Union does not adhere to a territorial but to a functional or substantive principle of authority. In accordance with the basic policy orientation of the EU, its juridical and political claim to authority is substantially (functionally) limited. Neither is the assumption of comprehensive powers valid for the European transnational polity and legal system; the principle of conferral substitutes for that of comprehensive powers. Not only must the European constitution provide the general juridical and political framework for sectoral policies, it must also set sectoral objectives and create sectoral competences. Consequently, the framing political and juridical constitutions are complemented by sectoral constitutions, such as economic, social and security constitutions. Furthermore, economic constitutionalization has produced a differentiation of two subfields: a microeconomic constitution, based on the Treaty of Rome but in important respects elaborated by the ECJ, and a macroeconomic one, based on the Maastricht provisions on Economic and Monetary Union (EMU). The microeconomic constitution is centred around free movement and competition law, and focuses on the economic activity of individual economic actors. In turn, the macroeconomic constitution addresses macroeconomic objectives and policies.

The sectoral constitutions possess distinct constitutional objects: European economy, social welfare and security. A corresponding differentiation is noticeable in Treaty law, as well as constitutional doctrine and theory. The exact contours of the sectoral constitutions can, though, be debatable. Should education be included in the constitutional object of the social constitution? Does the constitutional object of the security constitution cover both internal and external security? It might also be asked whether the sectoral constitutions should include, say, an environmental dimension. The decisive criterion consists of differentiation: arguably, neither primary environmental law nor the accompanying constitutional doctrine and theory have reached the required level of differentiation.

The term 'juridical constitution' may cause some confusion. All the constitutional dimensions possess a legal character in the sense that constitutional law always occupies one of the two poles of the constitutional relation; all the constitutional dimensions are about the constitutional relation between constitutional law and its constitutional object. What distinguishes the juridical constitution is the fact that here both poles of the constitutional relation are legal in nature. In the juridical constitution, the law establishes a reflexive relation to itself.

Thus, distinct dimensions can be discerned in the European constitution. Yet, their distinctness is not absolute but they enter into specific relations with each other. The very term 'framing constitutions' implies such interrelationality. How, exactly, do the political and juridical constitutions frame the sectoral ones? Put briefly, the political constitution provides the institutional framework for sectoral constitutionalization, while the juridical constitution offers the legal instruments. The political constitution regulates the EU institutions to which sectoral competences are granted: such as the European Council, the European Parliament, the Council of Ministers, the Commission and the ECJ. At the individual pole of the polity relationship, the political constitution establishes and defines European citizenship, with potential implications in all sectoral dimensions. Correspondingly, sectoral constitutional dimensions rely on the legislative and judicial instruments, institutions and procedures provided by the juridical constitution. Moreover, the general principles developed in the course of juridical constitutionalization, such as direct effect, supremacy, the rule of law and fundamental rights, are pertinent in all sectoral dimensions. The framing constitutions exercise both a constitutive and a restrictive function with regard to the sectoral constitutions.

All the sectoral constitutions possess distinct political and juridical features as well: they have their characteristic institutional structures and legal particularities. The economic constitution cannot be examined without including the role of the Commission as the European

Competition Authority or – after Maastricht – the ECB as the executor of European monetary policy. Correspondingly, in addition to general EU legal instruments sectoral constitutions have resorted to particular means, too, such as the Maastricht Social policy Protocol and Agreement in the social dimension or framework decisions in the security constitution. Institutional or juridical particularities should be discussed in the context of sectoral constitutionalization. But they should also be conceived of as elements in the overall European political and juridical constitutions. The political and juridical constitutions do not merely facilitate sectoral constitutionalization. They also react to and summarize its implications and consequences. In this sense the political and juridical constitutions are not only framing but also summarizing constitutions.

In a way, the EU reverses the relationship between the political and juridical constitutions and the sectoral policy fields to which we are accustomed at the state level. A state constitution is usually equated with the political and juridical dimensions which, according to the traditional understanding, establish the political and legislative sovereignty of the state. In turn, sectoral policies result from the exercise of this sovereignty. The political and juridical constitutions are primary in relation to sectoral policy fields which, as a rule, do not enjoy constitutional dignity. In a policy-oriented transnational polity and legal system, such as the EU, the claim to authority is substantively (functionally) limited. Juridical and political constitutionalization are not ends in themselves but largely respond to the needs and implications of sectoral constitutionalization. Economic constitutionalization would not have been possible without simultaneous juridical constitutionalization, which for instance produced the crucial principles of direct effect and primacy. Sectoral constitutionalization displays both formal and substantive aspects; by and large, the formal aspect of sectoral constitutionalization coincides with juridical constitutionalization. In turn, the Maastricht Treaty, which for instance reinforced the position of the European Parliament and introduced European citizenship, signified a leap in political constitutionalization. An important backdrop to this leap consisted of the legitimacy deficit which was perceived to have ensued from the preceding economic constitutionalization driven by the ECJ. In the European constitution, too, the framing political and juridical dimensions enjoy constitutive primacy. But they are subjected to the functional primacy of sectoral constitutions. The relationship between framing and sectoral constitutions is recursive: through their functional primacy sectoral constitutions trigger juridical and political constitutionalization, the results of which will then be available for subsequent framing purposes.

European integration has primarily been an economic project, and in spite of the expansion of EU activities into new policy domains, economic integration still retains a dominant position. This has left its imprint on inter-dimensional relations within the European constitution. The economic constitution has benefited from a functional primacy with regard not only to the framing constitutions but to other sectoral constitutions as well. The functional primacy of the economic constitution can be observed not only in juridical constitutionalization but in the emergence and further development of non-economic sectoral constitutions, too. The social policy provisions of the Treaty of Rome had an economic rationale: they served free movement of workers and securing a level playing field for the industries of different Member States. In turn, the origins of the security dimension lie in the consequences of opening internal Community borders in order to implement free movement of workers, which is an essential element of the economic constitution. The functional primacy of the economic constitution has also limited the developmental options of the non-economic constitutions, as can be seen in the subjection of healthcare and social security to free movement and competition law.

Still, the functional primacy of the European economic constitution should not be understood in absolute terms. Although owing their initial momentum to the economic constitution, in their further development non-economic constitutional dimensions may have obtained at least partial independence from economic considerations. The original institutional organization of the Community – the nascent institutional pole of the European polity – was largely tailored to the needs of the economic constitution, but subsequently, say in and since Maastricht, specific political values, such as democracy and transparency, have gained in importance in political constitutionalization. In the security dimension, the scope of the risks to which the security constitution responds has expanded and transcends those deriving from the opening of internal borders. Similar signs of independence – or at least striving for independence – are detectable in the social constitution, too. A model example of growing autonomy is offered by the way the Treaty provision on equal pay was progressively detached from its economic rationale and turned into a nucleus of EU antidiscrimination law. The gradual development of constitutional social rights also reflects an aspiration for independence, although cross-border social rights in particular owe much of their initial dynamics to the implications of the economic constitution. Free movement of workers has provided the impetus to the right to cross-border social security and free movement of services to the right to cross-border healthcare.

The at least partial independence of the social constitution points to yet another type of relations between constitutional dimensions: relations of conflict. Increasing autonomy may lead to normative results which contradict the requirements of the economic constitution. The normative implications of the economic constitution may clash with those of, say, the political or social one. Before the ECJ, such constitutional conflicts often assume the guise of a contestation between different types of rights. Economic rights derived from free movement law may clash with social rights, or civil or political fundamental rights. In a standard constellation before the ECJ, the issue is whether protection of other types of rights justifies derogating from economic rights; reference can be made to such celebrated rulings of the ECJ as *Omega, Schmidberger, Viking* and *Laval*.[14] The functional primacy of the economic constitution is obvious in the very posing of the issue: in conflicts of rights, what needs justification is restricting not a fundamental right but an economic right. Yet, as *Omega* and *Schmidberger* demonstrate, functional primacy does not necessarily dictate the result of the balancing exercise.

Economic rights possess an instrumental character; they serve the basic policy objective of establishing and securing the functioning of the common (internal) market. The conflictual relations between the economic and the political or social constitutions can often be conceptualized as a tension between policy-oriented economic rights and principle-based fundamental rights. The above-mentioned landmark cases also point to an aspect of conflict resolution in the framing function of the juridical constitution. The juridical constitution may be called upon to resolve inter-dimensional constitutional conflicts.

Constitutionalism is not only about surface-level constitutional law, enshrined in constitutional provisions and precedents. It is also about

14 Case C-36/02 *Omega Spielhallen* [2004] ECR I-9609; Case C-112/00 *Schmidberger* [2003] ECR I-5659; Case C-438/05 *International Transport Workers' Federation and Finnish Seamen's Union* [2007] ECR I-10779; Case C-341/05 *Laval un Partneri* [2007] ECR I-11767.

the constitutional culture animating constitutional practices, informing the *Vorverständnis* of constitutional actors and acting as a filter through which surface-level constitutional material is approached. As the Treaties constitutionalize sectoral policy areas and objectives, they also constitutionalize disagreements on the background assumptions of sectoral policies. In sectoral constitutionalization, European constitutionalism has not been able to draw on Member State constitutional traditions, and the contestedness of the theoretical underpinnings has delayed development of a distinct constitutional culture, impregnating the *Vorverständnis* of European constitutional actors.

In accordance with the basic teleological nature of the EU, the constitutional theories which in the diverse sectoral dimensions have created coherence in EU constitution have been policy-oriented. However, policy issues are controversial issues, and the constitutional theories underlying constitutional law have been subject to contestation, too. Examination of sectoral constitutionalization shows how controversial constitutional theories in the various dimensions are. Within the microeconomic constitution, the main frontline separates advocates of market liberalization from those who accept the possibility and need of national or European public regulation; within the macroeconomic constitution Monetarists have been confident of EMU becoming an optimal currency area while Economists have stressed the necessity of common economic policies as a precondition for common monetary policy; within the social constitution the primacy of national welfare regimes collides with the prevalence of the economic constitution, and national solidaristic justice confronts European access justice; and, finally, within the security constitution, security and fundamental rights considerations clash with each other, as does transnationalism with state-sovereigntism and intergovernmentalism.

3 The Evolutionary Nature of the European Constitution

State constitutions are usually examined as unitary normative entities, the tacit assumption being that juridical and political constitutions emerge and develop parallel to each other. By contrast, the multidimensional European constitution has resulted from a differentiated process, displaying diverse temporalities. The European constitutional dimensions have not appeared simultaneously but, rather, successively. Nor have they followed exactly the same developmental path. Typical of European constitutionalism is – to borrow Ernst Bloch's expression – *Gleichzeitigkeit des Ungleichzeitigen.*

The upsurge of theoretical interest in European constitutionalism has involved efforts to apply to the European context the tripartite conceptual cluster of constituent power (*pouvoir constituant*), *demos* as the subject of this power and constitutional moment as the instance when this power is wielded. These efforts have not been particularly successful. The elevation of 'constituent power' to a central constitutional concept has led Dieter Grimm to denigrate the Treaties to a quasi-constitution. Conceptual dilution is an alternative consequence of clinging to concepts coined in a specific branch of constitutional culture: revolutionary American and French constitutionalism. We have drifted far from the original conceptual connotations if we define the Member States as Masters of the Treaties (*Herren der Verträge*) as a European *demos* or their treaty-making power as a *pouvoir constituant* the exercise of which has produced the European constitution. The concepts of revolutionary constitutionalism are not applicable to the European constitution, which has not resulted from the exercise of constituent power by a European *demos* at an identifiable constitutional moment.

Instead of a revolutionary break, the many constitutions of Europe are a continuously evolving outcome of an ongoing process. This process does include such high-profile occasions as agreements on new Treaties and Treaty amendments, but to label these as constitutional moments is rather far-fetched. Furthermore, they do not exhaust the process of constitutionalization. Even more fanciful would be to employ concepts of the revolutionary constitutional tradition in the context of landmark decisions by the ECJ, such as *van Gen den Loos* and *Costa* v. *Enel*; decisions which were crucial for juridical constitutionalization but whose constitutional significance was, outside of a narrow circle of initiates, realized only long afterwards. Instead of the cluster of revolutionary-tuned concepts of constituent power, *demos* and constitutional moment, the European constitution(s) should be examined through the evolutionary concept of constitutionalization, as a multidimensional and multitemporal process of constitutionalization. In the European context, 'constitutionalization' simply refers to the gradual, incremental development of the European constitution in its various dimensions and by various constitutional actors; not only by the Member States as a constitutional legislator but also the ECJ as a constitutional court, assisted by European law scholars.

Distinct periods can be discerned in European constitutionalization. These receive their particular colouring from a particular constitution; a pacemaker constitution, as it were. Reflecting the temporal and functional primacy of economic integration, the first wave, initiated by the Treaty of Rome, or even earlier by the Treaty of Paris (1951) establishing the European Coal and Steel Community (ECSC), proceeded under the auspices of the economic constitution. The rulings of the ECJ defining the basic principles characterizing Community law as an independent legal system manifested the significance of the juridical constitution: juridical and economic constitutionalization proceeded in tandem. The Maastricht Treaty epitomized the at least temporary dominance of the political constitution. In turn, the Amsterdam Treaty (1998), with its new provisions on the Area of Freedom, Security and Justice, inaugurated the prominence of the security constitution, which was further reinforced by European reactions to 9/11. Subsequently, the Eurozone crisis catapulted the economic constitution back to the pacemaker role. However, if the emphasis in the Rome Treaty and the succeeding case law of the ECJ lay on the microeconomic constitution, the crisis highlighted the role of the macroeconomic layer. The pacemaker role of the macroeconomic constitution entailed that the constitutional mutation launched by the Eurozone crisis was not restricted to the economic aspect. It extended to the political and social dimensions as well; it also affected democracy and transparency, as well as social values and rights. Finally, the immigration crisis which broke out in 2015 and the vote for Brexit in June 2016 shifted the emphasis to, respectively, the security and the political dimension.

Related to 'constitutionalization', other process-oriented concepts are of particular relevance for European constitutional analysis. These include 'transnationalization' and 'individualization'. In important respects, constitutionalization has signified transnationalization: superseding intergovernmental institutional and decision-making structures, typical of international organizations, as well as detaching European law from the international law background. However, when examining European constitutionalization 'transnational' and 'intergovernmental' should not be straightforwardly opposed. In the institutional organization of the EU, the Commission, the ECJ and the European Parliament make up the transnational core. But even the European Council and the Council of Ministers are institutions of a transnational polity, and the transnational setting leaves its imprint on institutions with an intergovernmental composition, too. In turn, the Treaties still possess the dual character of 'a constitutional charter' and an agreement under international law. Moreover, in both the social and security dimensions, international law agreements have played an important role as precursors to constitutionalization through Treaty provisions. In combating the Eurozone crisis, Member States resorted to agreements under international law as an alternative to primary or secondary Union law. The third-Pillar Treaty provisions in force from 1993 to 2009 even explicitly constitutionalized international law conventions as an EU legal instrument.

Constitutionalization has implied individualization: establishment of direct links between European institutions and European citizens in their diverse attires. From the perspective of European individuals, the multidimensional process of constitutionalization has involved a gradual enrichment of European citizenship, adding successive layers to the initial market citizenship of the economic constitution: the judicial citizenship of the juridical constitution; the social citizenship of the social constitution; and finally the political citizenship which grants individuals not only the specific citizenship rights of the Treaty but European fundamental rights as well. Still, European citizens also remain citizens of Member States, and the relations between European institutions and individual citizens hint at the relevance of the Member State level, too.

In sum, 'constitutionalization' is an evolutionary alternative to the revolutionary concepts of *pouvoir constituant*, *demos* and constitutional moment. Particular relations exist among the constitutional dimensions, such as the functional – and temporal – primacy of the economic constitution and the general functional primacy of sectoral constitutionalization in respect of the framing juridical and political constitutionalization. Such relations hint at a particular internal logic guiding European constitutionalization. Still, it is important to stress that European constitutionalization should not be reconstructed as a closed, linear and pre-determined evolutionary process. Different constitutions may well clash with each other, and constitutional backlashes form part of the picture as well. And even more crucially, we should always bear in mind that the ultimate factors accelerating or impeding constitutionalization are of an extra-legal and extra-constitutional, economic, political and ideological, nature. These factors may include high-profile, even crisis-like events, such as the fall of the Berlin wall and the reunification of Germany (the Maastricht Treaty as a high-point of political constitutionalization); 9/11 (acceleration of the development of the security constitution); the global financial crisis which in the autumn of 2008 broke out following the collapse of Lehman Brothers (the teetering of the Maastricht principles of the European economic constitution); the eruption of the migration crisis in the winter 2015–2016 or the Brexit referendum in 2016. Still, equally well constitutionalization may be influenced by contingent events which on their occurrence have aroused no public attention but which have, for instance, produced constitutionally relevant case law of the ECJ.

4 Transnational and National Constitutionalism

a Constitutional Pluralism and Federal Constitutionalism

During the last twenty years, constitutional pluralism has largely dominated scholarly discussion on the relations between the European constitution and its national counterparts. The debate does address an important aspect in the relations that the European transnational constitution entertains with Member State national constitutions: the overlapping and rival claims of authority that these constitutions raise. Indeed, the very concept of legal or constitutional pluralism can be defined as a constellation where two legal regimes raise such overlapping and conflicting claims of authority. Pluralist constellations are typical of our age of postnational law. Conflicts of authority seem to be inevitable between transnational law, such as EU law, and national law, such as Member State law. Transnational and national law follow different principles of authority; the scope of their authority is circumscribed through different criteria. National law adheres to the territorial principle of authority and claims universal jurisdiction in in its territory. By contrast, transnational law's claim of authority is substantially or functionally defined and limited. Territorial and functional principles of authority are bound to clash, producing at regular intervals fundamental conflicts of authority; that is, conflicts turning on the autonomy and identity of the colliding legal regimes. The celebrated cases involving the German Constitutional

Court and the Luxembourg Court – the OMT case[15] is the latest but will not remain the last example – intimate how high the stakes are: the German Constitutional Court sees itself as the guardian of German constitutional identity and the autonomy of German law, while the ECJ defends the autonomy and constitutional identity of EU law. Such fundamental conflicts of authority are widely different from the border skirmishes that are addressed by private international law or, as the Anglo-American term goes, conflict of laws. However, the exchange of arguments between the German Constitutional Court and the Luxembourg Court in, for instance, the OMT case not only shows the inevitability of fundamental conflicts of authority under the pluralism of postnational law. It also testifies to the possibility of a dialogical resolution or, at least, pacification of these conflicts. The relationship between the function-specific EU constitution and universalist Member State constitutions is not labelled only by actual or latent conflicts. It is also marked by dialogue and co-operation, facilitated by a shared constitutional deep culture; in brief, by normative and institutional *interlegality*.

In addition to its conflictual focus, the debate on constitutional pluralism has been one-sided in another respect, too. It has addressed the consequences of the overlap of national and transnational claims of authority merely in the juridical and political dimensions. However, Member States' defence of their political and legislative sovereignty – the universality of their political and legal claims to authority – has had implications for European sectoral constitutions, too. Member States have raised sovereignty concerns vis-à-vis EU action with regard to fiscal and other economic policy; welfare policy and the choice of welfare regimes; and use of the coercive power of the state, the state's 'monopoly of legitimate use of violence'.

In fundamental conflicts of authority, typical of the pluralist constellation, each party – say, the ECJ and a national constitutional court – approaches the issue from the perspective of its referential legal order – say, EU law and the national legal order, respectively. Perspectivism of legal orders is inevitable. As constitutional pluralists have emphasized, no second-order legal principle or neutral arbiter exists to resolve the conflict. In this sense, the conflicts are undecidable. This observation has

---

[15] The contributions of the German Constitutional Court are Beschluss vom 06. Juli 2014 – 2 BvR 2728/13 and Urteil vom 21. Juni 2016 – 2 BvR 2728/13, and the ECJ interventions Opinion of Advocate General Cruz Villalón delivered on 14 January 2015, C-62/14 – *Gauweiler and Others* and C-62/14 – *Gauweiler and Others*.

been picked up by theorists of federal constitutionalism, such as Robert Schütze, and related to notion of *Staatenverbund* or – in Schütze's translation – federal union. What is considered characteristic of a federal union is the very undecidability of fundamental conflicts of authority (sovereignty). If such conflicts were to be resolved in favour of the union, it would develop into a federal state; if, in turn, in favour of the states, the union would be degraded to the status of an international organization.[16] In line with the debate on constitutional pluralism, federal constitutionalism points to an important aspect in the relationship of European and Member state constitutionalism. However, it also shares the one-sided conflictual focus and the reduction of the European constitution to its juridical and political dimensions.

b Relations of Complementarity

The conflict-oriented view of constitutional pluralism tends to obscure another, equally important aspect in the relationship between the transnational European constitution and the national Member State constitutions: complementarity. Treaty provisions on the respective competences of the Union and the Member States may be read to imply a division of labour, based on a relationship of complementarity. Yet this can be an erroneous reading. Complementarity in the sense of division of labour presupposes common objectives; only with regard to common objectives can an expedient division of labour and corresponding allocation of competences be adopted. But division of competences, such as it is enshrined in the Treaty on the European Union, does not necessarily imply a division of labour: division of competences may free the Union and Member States to pursue their distinct objectives and policies within their fields of competence. It is misleading to assume that the Union and its Member States constitute in every relevant respect a multilevel *Verfassungsbund* where relations between the transnational and the national are primarily characterized by intertwinement and complementarity.[17] In the field of shared competences, the principle of

---

[16] R. Schütze, 'Constitutionalism and the European Union', in C. Barnard and S. Peers (eds.), *European Union Law* (Oxford University Press, 2014), 71–96.

[17] The idea of a multilevel *Verfassungsverbund* was propounded, first of all, by Ingolf Pernice. See, e.g., I. Pernice, 'The Treaty of Lisbon: Multilevel Constitutionalism in Action' (2009) 15 *Columbia Journal of European Law* 349–407.

subsidiarity, as formulated in Article 5(3) TEU, does presuppose the existence of common objectives; the Union will step in only if the objective at issue cannot be better achieved by lower-level action. A presumption of common objectives, grounded in a common value basis whose existence Article 2 TEU postulates, also facilitates an understanding of the demarcation between national and Union fundamental rights review in terms of complementarity.

All the sectoral European constitutions imply relations of complementarity. Take the economic constitution. EU constitutional law does not comprise all the constitutional guarantees which must be in place to enable a European internal market, based on undistorted competition. The fundamental rights that a market economy requires are mainly ensured by national constitutions; by national constitutional provisions on the right to property, freedom of contract and freedom of trade. Hence, the European microeconomic constitution, covering primarily the fundamental market freedoms and competition law, is premised on the complementary contribution of Member State constitutions. In turn, the European macroeconomic constitution has presupposed, say, Member State financial and economic policy autonomy, although its use has been subjected to European constraints. In the social dimension, the European constitution has relied on the existence of national redistributive welfare regimes. Finally, in the security dimension, too, core security functions and their judicial supervision have been retained under Member State sovereignty and taken by the European security constitutions as a given premise.

The relation of complementarity is also conspicuous in the field of citizenship, which brings us to the dimension of the political constitution. European citizenship builds on national citizenship, and not only in the sense of the identification of individual citizens – by definition, Member State citizens are also EU citizens. Complementarity labels the participatory rights of European citizens as well. In their EU constitutional practices, in debating EU issues and in participating in the European public sphere, EU citizens rely on the public autonomy guaranteed to them as Member State citizens; the freedoms of assembly, association and the press enshrined in national constitutions. And if we in general can speak of European citizenship in collective terms, as European citizenry, this collective political subject can only exist as a result of the networking of national citizenries and national public spheres.

c Two-Stage Legitimation

Opting for thin notions of constitution and constitutionalism does not imply denying the relevance for European constitutionalism of the normative ideas of a constitutional democracy (a democratic *Rechtsstaat*) or the conception of legitimacy they imply. However, efforts to secure democratic constitutional legitimacy should be examined through the interaction between transnational and national constitutionalism. As an epitome of transnational constitutionalism European constitutionalism has been, and still is, in some vital respects, parasitic on Member State national constitutionalism. This also holds for constitutional and democratic legitimacy, where the complementary relationship between national and transnational constitutionalism – alongside its process-like and multidimensional character the third distinctive feature of European constitutionalism – is particularly important.

Paradoxically, perhaps, the Treaties owe their original constitutional legitimacy to their international law aspect, to the fact that they have been ratified by national parliaments or in referendums, in accordance with the provisions of the national constitution. However, the initial legitimacy which the EU may derive from Member States' acting as Masters of the Treaties does not suffice. The claim to legitimacy must be constantly re-redeemed. This concerns both system legitimacy – the overall legitimacy of the EU – and the policy legitimacy of individual policies and institutions responsible for these. Let us rely on Fritz Scharpf's distinction between democratic input legitimacy and result-based output legitimacy.[18] In state constitutions, provisions on legislative and budgetary procedures, as well as participatory citizenship rights, aim to produce democratic input legitimacy at both system and policy level. In turn, provisions on independent expert bodies, such as courts or central banks, seek to facilitate output legitimacy in terms of, say, impartial and reasoned adjudication or monetary policy objectives, such as monetary stability.

At the European level, the distinction between system and policy legitimacy has not been very sharp. Especially in the early, pre-Maastricht decades, European integration as a whole could be understood as a

[18] F. Scharpf, *Governing in Europe: Effective and Democratic?* (Oxford University Press, 1999), 6–8.

cluster of specific policies[19] and assessed in terms of output legitimacy. Bracketing the second-order objective of maintaining peace in Europe, what was decisive was whether the promise of increased economic prosperity (re)distributed through national mechanisms was kept or not. However, enlargement of European competences through ECJ case law and the prominent role of the ECJ in European law- and constitution-making in general raised concerns about the need for democratic input legitimacy. The boost to political constitutionalization in Maastricht responded to these concerns.

Reflecting the initial technocratic policy orientation of European integration, prominent in, for instance, Jean Monnet's functionalism, the Treaty of Rome largely ignored the issue of democratic legitimacy. The Member States ratified the Treaties according to their constitutional requirements, and the democratic legitimacy this produced was considered sufficient. However, embryos of democratic legitimation of European policy-making, too, were inserted even in the Treaty of Rome through the Council and the Assembly (European Parliament). These embryos manifested the two-stage mechanism of democratic legitimacy which is such a distinct feature of European constitutionalism and the significance of which has grown in line with the widening of European competences. The contribution of national democratic procedures to the legitimacy of European policies is a vital epitome of the complementary relation between national and European constitutionalism. Peter Lindseth's administrative law portrayal of the EU not only ignores sectoral constitutionalization. From its exclusive Member State perspective, it also refuses to examine European constitutionalism through interaction between the transnational and national levels, and declines to place national democratic procedures of control, oversight and implementation in the context of European constitutionalism.

In the course of political constitutionalization, efforts have been made to create direct legitimating relations between European citizenry and European institutions, most notably through direct election of the European Parliament and the introduction of European citizenship. However, as the low turnout in European elections has most dramatically

---

[19] Such an understanding was implicit in Hans Peter Ipsen's often-cited characterization of the European Communities as *Zweckverbände funktioneller Integration*. H.P. Ipsen, Europäisches Gemeinschaftsrecht (J.C.B. Mohr, 1972).

proved, the cultural and social prerequisites for the formation of a European civil society and public sphere, capable of sustaining a Europe-wide democracy, are still largely lacking. On their own, European constitutional practices, culminating institutionally in the election of the European Parliament and its legislative and supervisory powers, can hardly live up to the high expectations of the thick normative concept of constitutionalism. This has only accentuated the importance of the contribution of national constitutionalism to the democratic legitimacy of the EU.

Intergovernmental EU institutions work under the guidance of national democratically legitimated bodies, and national parliaments even participate directly in Union law-making. Furthermore, the major part of Union legislative and other measures are implemented and enforced by national authorities. EU directives are transposed into the municipal legal order by the national legislator, thereby receiving an injection of democratic input legitimacy. Furthermore, nationally applicable EU law is integrated into the whole of the national legal order and, as it were, scrounges off the general legitimacy of the latter. In Jürgen Habermas's distinction between regulatory law (law as a medium) and law as an institution,[20] EU law has mainly fallen into the former category. Law as an institution is intimately related to the moral and value texture of society; hence, this department of law is vital to the overall substantive legitimacy of the legal order. Insofar as EU law enjoys substantive legitimacy, it is at least partly parasitic on the substantive legitimacy of national legal orders. In sum, the fact that the general public has primarily confronted EU measures, not directly, but indirectly, through the political and administrative institutions and the legal system of the respective Member State, has been crucial for the legitimacy that the Union and its individual policies have enjoyed among European citizenry.[21]

As Lindseth has shown, Member State parliamentary oversight of European policies has intensified during recent decades. Yet, contrary to what Lindseth contends, this is not an argument for rejecting the existence of European constitutionalism. The interaction between the transnational and national levels belongs to the distinct of European constitutionalism. This interaction is vital for providing European institutions

---

[20] J. Habermas, *The Theory of Communicative Action*, Vol. 2 (Polity Press, 1989), 365.

[21] F. Scharpf, *Legitimacy Intermediation in the Multilevel European Polity and its Collapse in the Euro Crisis* (Max Planck Institute for the Study of Societies, 2012), 19.

and policies with democratic legitimacy. Although this can hardly be seen as a decisive argument, it might still be worth mentioning that the Treaty of Lisbon explicitly recognizes the role of Member State constitutionalism in realizing the democratic principle. Article 10 TEU proclaims that the functioning of the Union is founded on representative democracy. Not only are citizens directly represented at Union level in the European Parliament; in addition, Member States are represented in the European Council by their heads of state or government and in the Council by their governments. In turn, these representatives are themselves democratically accountable either to national parliaments or citizens. Article 10 TEU expressly confirms the complementarity of direct European democracy and the two-level mechanism which harnesses national procedures to the service of European-level democratic legitimacy.

Conclusion

So in some crucial respects, European constitutionalism calls for complementing by Member State national constitutionalism. In particular, this concerns the legitimacy function of the constitution. The critics of constitutional conceptualization of the EU seem to have a point. European constitutionalism seems to be deficient or dependent constitutionalism; quasi-constitutionalism as one could also put it. However, employing the thin notion of constitutionalism, I would consider the intimate relationship with Member State constitutionalism a specific feature of European constitutionalism, rather than a deficiency. Transnational constitutionalism only exists in interaction with national constitutionalism.

The complementarity relationship between European and national constitutionalism manifests the plurality of postnational law; a plurality which can no longer be depicted in accordance with the black-box model, as a mere coexistence of self-contained and self-sufficient legal regimes, shut in their respective boxes. Another important manifestation of postnational plurality consists in the overlapping and rival claims of authority, discussed in the European context under the heading of constitutional pluralism. This discussion, initiated by the late Neil MacCormick,[22] has thematized vital issues but appears now to have come to a standstill.

---

[22] N.D. MacCormick, *Questioning Sovereignty: Law, State and Nation in the European Commonwealth* (Oxford University Press, 1999).

New insights into the interrelationship between European and Member state constitutionalism require overcoming the limitations of the constitutional pluralism debate. These include one-sided conflictual emphasis and exclusive focus on the juridical and political constitutions and ignorance of the sectoral constitutions, so characteristic of the multidimensional and multitemporal European constitution.

It is no wonder that historical expositions occupy a prominent place in accounts of European constitutionalism. European constitutionalism is primarily about constitutionalization; it is an evolutionary and not a revolutionary phenomenon. That is why the central concepts of revolutionary constitutionalism – such as *pouvoir constituant*, demos and constitutional moment – seem so unconvincing at the European level. However, this testifies to the specificity rather than the non-existence of European constitutionalism.[23]

Further Reading

R. Dehousse, *The European Court of Justice: The Politics of Judicial Integration* (Macmillan, 1998).

D. Grimm, *The Constitution of European Democracy* (Oxford University Press, 2017).

D. Halberstam, 'Constitutional Heterarchy: The Centrality of Conflict in the European Union and the United States', in J. Dunoff and J. Trachtman (eds.), *Ruling the World? Constitutionalism, International Law, and Global Governance* (Cambridge University Press, 2009), 326–355.

H.P. Ipsen, *Europäisches Gemeinschaftsrecht* (J. C. B. Mohr, 1972).

H. Kelsen, *Pure Theory of Law* (Peter Smith, 1989).

P. Lindseth, *Power and Legitimacy: Reconciling Europe and the Nation-State* (Oxford University Press, 2010).

N.D. MacCormick, *Questioning Sovereignty: Law, State and Nation in the European Commonwealth* (Oxford University Press, 1999).

I. Pernice, 'The Treaty of Lisbon: Multilevel Constitutionalism in Action' (2009) 15 *Columbia Journal of European Law* 349–407.

F.W. Scharpf, *Governing in Europe: Effective and Democratic?* (Oxford University Press, 1999).

R. Schütze, 'Constitutionalism and the European Union', in C. Barnard and S. Peers (eds.), *European Union Law* (Oxford University Press, 2014), 71–96.

K. Tuori, *European Constitutionalism* (Cambridge University Press, 2015).

---

[23] On the specificity of European constitutionalism see also K. Tuori, *European Constitutionalism* (Cambridge University Press, 2015).

21 A New Commonwealth Constitutionalism?

Claudia Geiringer

Introduction

Until recently, standard accounts of the global constitutional landscape assigned the world's constitutions to one of two dichotomous models for the constitutional protection of human rights: legislative supremacy or judicial supremacy. According to this binary taxonomy, the first model is characterized by the absence of any codified bill of rights and by the allocation of final authority on human rights questions to the legislative branch of the state. The second is characterized, to the contrary, by the presence of an entrenched and supreme law bill of rights, interpreted and enforced (including as against the legislature) by courts of some kind.[1]

During the late twentieth century (with the spread of constitutionalism after World War II and, again, following the break-up of the Soviet Union), it was the latter model that moved into triumphant ascendency with only a small handful of constitutional democracies holding out against constitutionalized and judicially enforced human

---

[1] A further recognized division is into systems that allocate judicial authority over the constitution to ordinary versus special (constitutional) courts.

rights protections.[2] Even so, doubts persisted (and continue to persist) in some quarters about the legitimacy of this form of court-enforced constitutionalism. Ironically, but perhaps understandably, it is from within the jurisdiction paradigmatically associated with judicial supremacy – the United States – that doubts of this kind have been most insistently expressed. The counter-majoritarian objection to judicial review (that is, the concern about the democratic legitimacy of allocating final authority on constitutional issues to judges) is a leitmotif of US constitutional scholarship.[3] On the other hand, the proponents of judicial review worry, for example, about the vulnerability of minorities and the systematic under-enforcement of human rights that they say can result from unrestrained majoritarianism.[4] Resolution of this so-called constitutionalism/democracy dilemma has resisted generations of scholarly creativity, and has been described by some as an enduring fixation of the US academy.[5]

It is against this backdrop that comparative scholarship on the new generation of Anglo-Commonwealth bills of rights (in Canada, New Zealand, the United Kingdom and Australia) has emerged. As is well known, these four jurisdictions each have strong historic links to the Westminster-derived doctrine of parliamentary sovereignty, with its traditional hostility to codified human rights protection. New Zealand and the United Kingdom remain to this day the clearest proponents of unwritten (or small-c) constitutionalism, with judges in both jurisdictions continuing to ascribe to the view that – except, perhaps, in extreme and as-yet hypothetical circumstances – judges will always obey a sufficiently clear expression of legislative will. Prior to the late twentieth-century developments with which we are now concerned, Canada and Australia – which are federal states – had written constitutions, enacted at the point of federation by the Westminster Parliament. (This is still the position in Australia.) But beyond establishing the organs of federal government and specifying the horizontal and vertical division of powers, neither

---

[2] See, e.g., L.E. Weinrib, 'The Postwar Paradigm and American Exceptionalism', in S. Choudhry (ed.), *The Migration of Constitutional Ideas* (Cambridge University Press, 2006), 89–92.

[3] See, e.g., B. Friedman, 'The Birth of an Academic Obsession: The History of the Countermajoritarian Difficulty, Part Five' (2002) 112 *Yale Law Journal* 153.

[4] E.g., E. Chemerinsky, 'In Defense of Judicial Review: A Reply to Professor Kramer' (2004) 92 *California Law Review* 1013.

[5] Friedman (n. 3).

constitution placed significant substantive limits on legislative power. In these jurisdictions, too, the doctrine of parliamentary sovereignty remained an important feature of constitutional discourse.

Against that background, one might expect this block of Anglo-Commonwealth states to be particularly resistant to the spread of US-style constitutionalism. And so they have proved to be. On the other hand, these jurisdictions have not been entirely immune to the mounting international pressure to conform to the post-war constitutional (and juridical) paradigm of court-enforced human rights protection.[6] Out of these countervailing forces have emerged novel forms of human rights protection that adopt some of the characteristics of traditional codified bills of rights but that accommodate, in various ways, the ongoing claims of majoritarianism. Thus, between 1960 and 2006, Canada, New Zealand, the United Kingdom, and two Australian sub-national jurisdictions each moved to adopt codified human rights protections in statutory (rather than capital-C constitutional) form. And in 1982, as part of the patriation of its federal constitution, Canada adopted a supreme law charter of rights but made it formally subject to majoritarian override in certain circumstances.

If nothing else, these developments break new ground by accommodating codified human rights protections (of some kind) to the Westminster parliamentary tradition. Some scholars have, however, attributed to these developments a broader significance for the study of comparative constitutional law. They have suggested that this 'new Commonwealth model' of human rights protection might constitute a distinct third form of constitutionalism that disrupts the traditional dichotomy between legislative and judicial supremacy and that, in doing so, has the potential to solve the impasse between constitutionalism and democracy.

This chapter discusses these developments. It documents the emergence of this new generation of Anglo-Commonwealth bills of rights, and of a body of comparative scholarship that explores its potential as a distinct and normatively advantageous model of human rights protection. The chapter pays tribute to the important contribution this 'new Commonwealth model scholarship' (as we might call it) has made both to constitutional theory and to constitutional design. But it also documents the emergence of a counter-literature that questions the empirical assumptions on which this scholarship rests. This counter-literature argues that claims about the

---

[6] On that paradigm, see Weinrib (n. 2).

distinctiveness of the new Commonwealth model rest on an oversimplified picture of inter-branch interactions under the 'traditional' systems of legislative and judicial supremacy, on an oversimplified picture of inter-branch interactions in the systems that supposedly constitute the new Commonwealth model, and on a failure to engage with the extent to which hybridism is a feature of the comparative constitutional landscape more generally.

If scholarship on the distinctiveness of the new Commonwealth model has not provided us with all the right answers, nor even asked all the right questions, it has succeeded nonetheless in opening up new vistas of comparative constitutional engagement. Whether intentionally or not, it has also exposed important questions about comparative method – for example, about the taxonomic function of comparative law, and the trade-off between broad-brush typologies and fine-grained contextualism. These questions are addressed briefly at the conclusion of the chapter.

1 The Anglo-Commonwealth Bills of Rights – History and Main Features

a Two Canadian Innovations

As others have done, we begin this story of constitutional experimentation in the Anglo-Commonwealth with two Canadian innovations. The first is the *Canadian Bill of Rights*, SC 1960, c 44 (the Canadian Bill of Rights) – an ordinary Act of the federal Parliament constraining federal, but not provincial, government.[7] It catalogues a short list of classic political and legal rights, and declares that those rights 'have existed and shall continue to exist'.[8]

The novelty of the Canadian Bill of Rights at the time of its enactment lay in its drafters' intuition that some of the advantages of codified bill of rights protection might be able to be achieved through a statutory, rather than a formal constitutional, instrument. That potentiality is exemplified most strikingly in section 2 of the Act, which stipulates that, unless expressly declared by an Act of Parliament to operate 'notwithstanding'

---

[7] There was an earlier provincial experiment with codifying rights in statutory form, enacted in Saskatchewan in 1947, but this has had less impact and is not discussed further.

[8] Section 1.

the Canadian Bill of Rights, Canadian federal laws are to be 'construed and applied' so as not to 'abrogate, abridge or infringe' the rights or freedoms contained in it. In *R* v. *Drybones*, a majority of the Supreme Court of Canada treated section 2 as an enforceable primacy clause, requiring irreconcilable federal enactments (at least in the absence of an express legislative override) to be treated as inoperative to the extent of the inconsistency.[9] This was strong stuff. The Westminster tradition of parliamentary sovereignty did not, at least in its orthodox iterations, recognize any hierarchy of statutes other than the pre-eminence of the most recent expression of legislative will.[10]

The Canadian Bill of Rights also pioneered another important idea. It conferred on the Minister of Justice (who also serves as Attorney-General) a duty to examine Bills and regulations for consistency with the Act's 'purposes and provisions' and to report any perceived inconsistency to the House of Commons. As we shall see, this experiment in pre-legislative executive scrutiny was to be reproduced and refined elsewhere.

Despite these interesting (and, with hindsight, influential) ideas, the Canadian Bill of Rights soon became a by-word for the impotence of statutory protection. A timid judicial approach to the scope of protected rights ensured that the reach of the instrument remained narrow, and that the section 2 primacy clause was rarely invoked.[11] Although it is still in force, in 1982, the Act was largely superseded by the second Canadian innovation: the Canadian Charter of Rights and Freedoms (the Canadian Charter).[12]

The Canadian Charter was enacted as Part I to the Constitution Act 1982 (which patriated Canada's Westminster-derived constitution). The Charter regulates federal and provincial governments, and guarantees a broad array of civil and political rights drawn from both the United States and the emerging international law traditions, as well as responding to local circumstance.

The Charter (and the Constitution Act in toto) is part of the supreme law of Canada.[13] Further, a broadly worded remedies clause has forestalled any

---

[9] *R* v. *Drybones* [1970] SCR 282.

[10] E.g. *Ellen Street Estates* v. *Minister of Health* [1934] 1 KB 590.

[11] See P.W. Hogg, *Constitutional Law of Canada* (5th ed., Carswell, 2007), [35].

[12] But for a discussion of its continued relevance to administrative law, see L. Sossin, 'The Quasi-Revival of the Canadian Bill of Rights and its Implications for Administrative Law' (2004) 25 *Supreme Court Law Review (2d)* 191.

[13] Section 52.

real doubt that the Canadian courts are entitled to enforce the Charter, as against the legislative branch, through the disapplication of conflicting legislation.

But the Charter's supremacy is tempered by an unusual provision. Section 33 of the Charter protects the validity of (federal and provincial) legislation expressly declared to operate 'notwithstanding' certain provisions of the Charter. This language owes an obvious debt to section 2 of the Canadian Bill of Rights. But in the Charter, it serves a starkly different function: no longer an assertion of relative priority for a statute (vis-à-vis other statutes) but, instead, as an avenue for majoritarian override of a supreme law constitution. Section 33 specifies that a statutory 'notwithstanding clause' (as they have become known) is only valid for five years, and that some rights cannot be overridden. Nevertheless, at least on its face, it signals a significant departure from the classic model of a judicially enforced supreme law bill of rights exemplified by Canada's immediate neighbour.

Two other institutional features ground (or are said to ground) the Charter's claim to carve out distinct constitutional territory. The first is the idea of pre-legislative executive scrutiny, which was lifted from the Canadian Bill of Rights. Although not mandated by the Charter itself but, rather, set out in an Act of Parliament, it has become an established element of the Charter's enforcement regime.

The second is the Charter's approach to accommodating limits on rights. Its drafters considered, but ultimately rejected, two approaches utilized elsewhere: of leaving the existence and scope of any limits to judicial discretion (as in the United States); or of attaching individualized limitation clauses to particular rights on a case-by-case basis (as in the International Covenant of Civil and Political Rights and the European Convention on Human Rights (ECHR).[14] Instead, they adapted an approach trialled in the Universal Declaration of Human Rights: of including a generally applicable limitation clause, guaranteeing all the rights in the Charter 'subject only to such reasonable limits prescribed by law as can be demonstrably justified in a free and democratic society'.[15]

---

[14] See J. Hiebert, 'The Evolution of the Limitation Clause' (1990) 28 *Osgoode Hall Law Journal* 103.
[15] Section 1.

b The New Zealand, United Kingdom and Australian Statutes

Although these latter two institutional features of the Canadian Charter have been widely exported, the model of a supreme law charter of rights subject to majoritarian override has not.[16] To the contrary, it is the statutory model exemplified by the Canadian Bill of Rights that has since been taken up throughout the Anglo-Commonwealth world. This can perhaps be put down to two factors: on the one hand, the strong attachment in these jurisdictions to a tradition of legislative supremacy (and the obstacle this creates to adopting a supreme law constitution); on the other hand, the comparative success of the statutory model in New Zealand – the first jurisdiction to follow in Canada's footsteps.

The New Zealand Bill of Rights Act 1990 (the NZ Bill of Rights) was enacted in 1990 after a proposal for a supreme law instrument failed to attract widespread support. On paper, the Act looks even weaker than its Canadian predecessor (in any event, it contains no equivalent of the Canadian Bill of Rights' primacy clause). It was enacted without much enthusiasm even from its proponents. But it defied expectations that it would prove as ineffective as the Canadian precedent. From the start, New Zealand's judiciary interpreted the rights contained in the NZ Bill of Rights generously and purposively, and developed a range of judicial remedies (such as exclusion of evidence and damages) for breach. Unambiguously rights-incompatible legislative language remained inviolable. But much else, it seemed, was up for grabs.

By thus rehabilitating the credibility of the statutory bill of rights model, the NZ Bill of Rights opened the way for its subsequent utilization throughout the Anglo-Commonwealth world. Statutory bills of rights have since been enacted in the United Kingdom, in the Australian Capital Territory (the ACT) and in the (Australian) state of Victoria. In late February 2019, a similar statute was enacted by the Queensland Parliament.[17] The Republic of Ireland has also enacted a similar instrument to discharge its responsibilities under the ECHR but that Act operates in the shadow of human rights protections found in the Irish Constitution. Perhaps for

---

[16] I put to one side the case of Israel, where a Canadian-influenced 'notwithstanding clause' has been added to one of Israel's Basic Laws – laws enacted through the ordinary legislative process, but elevated to the status of a formal constitution by the Israeli Supreme Court.

[17] Human Rights Act 2019 (Qld) (Austl). This development came too late to be further discussed in this chapter.

that reason, it has been interpreted restrictively by the Irish courts and is regarded as of limited significance even within the jurisdiction.[18] For want of space, I do not discuss it further.

The statutory instruments with which we are concerned are variously self-identified as bills of rights, charters of rights, and human rights Acts. With one exception, these terminological differences do not reflect differences in form or function. The exception relates to the Human Rights Act 1998 (the UK Human Rights Act) which, one might argue, is not strictly a 'bill' or 'charter' of rights at all. Rather, it is an Act to implement the United Kingdom's obligations under the ECHR. It is to that instrument and its successive protocols (albeit as scheduled to the Act) that one must look to discover which rights are protected. Similarly, the approach to accommodating limits on rights is settled by the law and practice of the ECHR (which, as we have seen, adopts a clause-by-clause approach).

In contrast, the NZ Bill of Rights, the Human Rights Act 2004 (ACT) (Austl) (the ACT Act), and the Charter of Human Rights and Responsibilities Act 2006 (Vic) (Austl) (the Victorian Charter) are freestanding bills of rights that enumerate, on their own terms, the rights that are to be protected – albeit with an eye to international and comparative precedents. These three Acts also follow the lead of the Canadian Charter in the inclusion of a generally applicable limitation clause.

Despite this important structural difference, all four instruments share a number of regulatory impulses.[19] First, these regimes all borrow from Canada the idea of pre-legislative vetting – requiring, at a minimum, that the executive arm of government engage with the human rights compatibility of prospective legislation. There are, however, some important differences in how this is achieved including on whom the relevant duty is conferred (the government's law officer or the government minister responsible for the relevant Bill) and whether a compatibility report must be tabled on all Bills or only on those deemed to be incompatible with the respective human rights instrument. Perhaps the most important difference is that, in the United Kingdom and the two Australian jurisdictions,

---

[18] See C. Kelly, 'A Tale of Two Rights-Based Reviews or how the European Convention on Human Rights Act 2003 has Impacted on the Irish Model of Review', in J. Bell and M. Paris (eds.), *Rights-Based Constitutional Review: Constitutional Courts in a Changing Landscape* (Edward Elgar, 2016).

[19] The ACT Act has been amended on a number of occasions. The summary here relates to the Act's operation at the time of writing.

dedicated parliamentary committees play an independent role in scrutinizing the compatibility of legislation and the adequacy of the executive's compatibility statements.[20] In New Zealand, no such dedicated committee has been established. Since 2014, however, any report from the Attorney-General indicating inconsistency with the NZ Bill of Rights stands referred to the relevant subject matter committee that would otherwise scrutinize the legislation.[21]

Secondly, none of these instruments follow the Canadian Bill of Rights in according primacy to the respective human rights statute vis-à-vis other primary legislation.[22] To the contrary, all four instruments expressly preserve the validity and continuing operation of conflicting enactments. On the other hand, all four instruments stipulate that, where possible, legislation is to be interpreted and applied in a manner that is consistent or compatible with the protected rights. There are variations both in the way these interpretive directions are expressed and, perhaps even more so, in how they have been applied in practice.[23] But, in general terms, each of the four instruments preserves a distinction between rights-consistent 'interpretation' (which is mandated) and disregard or disapplication of a statute (which remains off-limits).

Thirdly, where (following application of the relevant interpretive direction) primary legislation is in irredeemable conflict with the protected rights, the United Kingdom, ACT and Victorian statutes each confer on the superior courts a power to issue a formal declaration to that effect. Such a declaration is non-binding and does not affect the validity or continuing operation of the impugned provision. On its face, the NZ Bill of Rights Act contains no equivalent power. Since 2001, however, a specialized tribunal has been statutorily empowered to make non-binding declarations of legislative 'inconsistency' specifically in relation to the right to freedom from discrimination. In early 2018, the New Zealand

---

[20] This is achieved by legislative direction in the ACT and Victoria, and by parliamentary and executive practice in the United Kingdom.

[21] Standing Orders of the House of Representatives (2017), SO265(5).

[22] In the United Kingdom, however, enactments produced by the devolved legislatures in Scotland, Wales and Northern Ireland are considered 'subordinate' for the purposes of the UK Human Rights Act, and must accordingly give way in the face of inconsistency.

[23] See, e.g., C. Geiringer, 'The Principle of Legality and the Bill of Rights Act: A Critical Analysis of *R* v. *Hansen*' (2008) 6 *New Zealand Journal of Public and International Law* 59.

Government announced an in-principle intention to introduce a similar power to the NZ Bill of Rights but has not (at the time this chapter was finalized) provided further details. In any event, the New Zealand courts have now supplied the omission. After years of prevarication, New Zealand's Supreme Court confirmed in November 2018 that, notwithstanding the Act's silence on the subject, the High Court has a power to make declarations of inconsistency with the NZ Bill of Rights.[24]

Fourthly, in general terms, all the instruments provide that, *unless* shielded by primary legislation, rights-incompatible exercises of public power are unlawful. There are significant variations both in how this is accomplished, and in the remedies that are available for breach. But, in general terms, specific legislative authorization is required to protect exercises of governmental or public power (variously defined) that are incompatible with the protected rights. (The two Australian Acts place an additional and novel obligation on public authorities to give 'proper consideration' to protected rights when making a decision.)

Fifthly and finally, in all four instances, the legislature retains the formal power to override judicial interpretations (or applications) of the protected rights.[25] So, for example, the judicial power to issue a non-binding declaration of legislative incompatibility does not tie the hand of the legislative branch. The only statutory consequences of such a declaration are either procedural or at the option of the executive.[26] The political branches are not legally required to remedy the incompatibility. Similarly, if the political branches are unhappy with a judicial interpretation of a statute, or with a judicial finding of public authority unlawfulness, they retain the power to promote and enact legislation that reverses it.

---

[24] *Attorney-General* v. *Taylor* [2018] NZSC 104; [2019] 1 NZLR 213 (upholding the decisions of the High Court and Court of Appeal).

[25] Again, in the United Kingdom, this does not include the devolved legislatures.

[26] Most commonly, to table in the legislature the declaration itself, and a statement of the executive's intended response. But the UK Human Rights Act provides, instead, an optional fast-track process for remedying the identified incompatibility by executive order where there are compelling reasons to do so. The in-principle announcement of the New Zealand Government suggests that this legislation, if it is enacted, may go further and require Parliament to 'reconsider' the issue, although not to reach any particular result. It is not clear, at this stage, how that would be achieved.

2 A New Constitutionalism?

In short, the period since the end of World War II has witnessed a significant evolution in the forms of human rights protection deployed within
the Westminster-style parliamentary democracies that comprise the
Anglo-Commonwealth world. From a situation in which the very idea of
a bill of rights was regarded as incompatible with the Westminster tradition, we have seen the emergence of codified human rights protections in
all four Anglo-Commonwealth jurisdictions (although, in Australia, only
at the sub-national level). This new generation of Anglo-Commonwealth
bills of rights does not, however, conform to the classic ideal of a formal,
supreme law and judicially enforced bill of rights. Instead, the Anglo-
Commonwealth bills of rights subvert that idea – either (in the case of the
Canadian Charter) by providing for majoritarian override of a supreme
law instrument or (in other instances) through the utilization of statutory
(rather than capital-C constitutional) protection.

This latter model, in particular, has proved of undoubted significance
to those jurisdictions wedded to the Westminster parliamentary tradition
because it has provided a vehicle to secure at least some of the benefits
of codified human rights protection while respecting constitutional
orthodoxies relating to the supremacy of legislative power. But on that
basis alone, we might be forgiven for questioning the relevance of these
developments to those located outside the Anglo-Commonwealth world.
Is this model of human rights protection perhaps nothing more than,
as Eoin Carolan suggests, a 'limited upgrade on a parliamentary model
which has now been withdrawn from sale'?[27]

A number of scholars of comparative constitutional law suggest otherwise and have freighted the emergence of this new generation of Anglo-
Commonwealth bills of rights with broader significance.[28] In general

[27] E. Carolan, 'Leaving Behind the Commonwealth Model of Rights Review: Ireland as
an Example of Collaborative Constitutionalism', in J. Bell and M. Paris (eds.), *Rights-
Based Constitutional Review: Constitutional Courts in a Changing Landscape* (Edward
Elgar, 2016) invoking Mark Tushnet's suggestion that: 'For all practical purposes, the
Westminster model has been withdrawn from sale.' M. Tushnet, 'New Forms of Judicial
Review and the Persistence of Rights- and Democracy-Based Worries' (2003) 38 *Wake
Forest Law Review* 635 at 814.
[28] E.g., Tushnet (n. 27); S. Gardbaum, *The New Commonwealth Model of Constitutionalism:
Theory and Practice* (Cambridge University Press, 2013); S. Stephenson *From Dialogue to
Disagreement in Comparative Rights Constitutionalism* (Federation Press, 2016).

terms, scholars of this ilk begin (as we did at the start of this chapter) with the traditional either/or dichotomy between two competing paradigms of constitutionalism: judicial supremacy and legislative supremacy. Jurisdictions falling within the former paradigm, they say, allocate the 'final word' on human rights questions to the courts under a formal constitutional document. On the other hand, jurisdictions falling within the latter paradigm lack anything that might resemble a codified bill of rights, and confer on the legislature the 'final word' on human rights questions.

For these comparative scholars, the point of interest in the new generation of Anglo-Commonwealth bills of rights is its potential to disrupt and problematize this traditional dichotomy. Viewed from this perspective, the key distinguishing feature of these instruments is that they seek to apportion constitutional responsibility for the protection of human rights between all three branches of government without formally allocating the 'final word' on human rights issues to the courts. In this way, these scholars suggest, this new model seeks to carve out a distinct third form of constitutionalism and, in doing so, to break the longstanding impasse between constitutionalism and democracy. It is to assessing whether (and how) that potential is realized in practice that these writers address themselves.[29]

We can further illustrate the claims of this group of scholars by expanding on some specific examples. Mark Tushnet, an early contributor to this school, coined the term 'weak-form judicial review' to describe the forms of non-conclusive review of legislation exercised by the courts within such systems of human rights protection (non-conclusive in the sense that the final word on the content of legislation remains with legislatures).[30] In a series of articles and essays and a 2008 monograph,

---

[29] A number of terms have been deployed in the literature to describe this so-called model. These include the new Commonwealth model (Gardbaum (n. 28)); weak-form judicial review (Tushnet (n. 27)); parliamentary bills of rights (J.L. Hiebert and J.B. Kelly, *Parliamentary Bills of Rights: The Experiences of New Zealand and the United Kingdom* (Cambridge University Press, 2015)) and multi-stage rights review (Stephenson (n. 28)). The term 'Anglo-Commonwealth bills of rights' is mine and is deployed to preserve the neutrality of Gardbaum's description while addressing the problem of over-inclusiveness associated with his terminology: see C. Geiringer, 'Moving Beyond the Constitutionalism/ Democracy Dilemma: 'Commonwealth Model' Scholarship and the Fixation on Legislative Compliance', in M. Elliott, J.N.E. Varuhas and S.W. Stark (eds.), *The Unity of Public Law? Doctrinal, Theoretical and Comparative Perspectives* (Hart Publishing, 2018) 301 at 303, n. 14.

[30] E.g., Tushnet (n. 27).

he poses a range of questions directed at assessing whether weak-form review can fulfil the promise it holds out of reconciling constitutionalism and self-governance.[31] Tushnet is simultaneously fascinated by, and sceptical about, this promise – worrying that weak-form review might be inherently 'unstable' (that is, prone in practice either to 'degenerate' into parliamentary supremacy or, more likely in his view, 'escalate' into strong-form review).

Stephen Gardbaum's systematic and ground-breaking study of the 'new Commonwealth model' of human rights protection (as he calls it) reflects similar preoccupations.[32] For Gardbaum, like Tushnet, the key point of interest is the ability of this new model to 'transcend the either/ or nature of the existing choice' and to offer a 'third institutional form of constitutionalism' that sits in between 'the two traditional and dichotomous ones' (of parliamentary sovereignty and judicial supremacy).[33] The new Commonwealth model does this, he says, by combining two novel techniques for protecting rights: pre-enactment political rights review (requiring both executive and legislative review of prospective legislation) and weak-form judicial review. The key to understanding the latter is that it decouples judicial review from judicial supremacy, conferring on the courts *some* powers of review but formally allocating to the legislature the final authority to determine the law. In this way, Gardbaum says, the new Commonwealth model blends elements of legal and political constitutionalism, exploiting the key strengths but avoiding the key weaknesses of each. This more balanced apportionment of constitutional power results in an intermediate form of constitutionalism that, in its various iterations, occupies a series of points on a continuum between the two traditional poles.

Following detailed examination of practice in the specific jurisdictions in which the model operates, Gardbaum also presents some conclusions

[31] E.g., M. Tushnet, 'Policy Distortion and Democratic Debilitation: Comparative Illumination of the Countermajoritarian Difficulty' (1995) 94 *Michigan Law Review* 245; M. Tushnet, 'Weak-Form Judicial Review: Its Implications for Legislatures' (2004) 2 *New Zealand Journal of Public and International Law* 7; M. Tushnet, *Weak Courts, Strong Rights: Judicial Review and Social Welfare Rights in Comparative Constitutional Law* (Princeton University Press, 2008) (Tushnet, '*Weak Courts, Strong Rights*').

[32] S. Gardbaum, 'The New Commonwealth Model of Constitutionalism' (2001) 49 *American Journal of Comparative Law* 707 (Gardbaum 2001); S. Gardbaum, 'Reassessing the New Commonwealth Model of Constitutionalism' (2010) 8 *International Journal of Constitutional Law* 167; Gardbaum (n. 28).

[33] See Gardbaum (n. 28) at 25.

on whether this intermediate form of constitutionalism has been, and can be, sustained in practice. He concludes that the model is working in 'at least a minimally distinct way'[34] in all its iterations but that, in practice, the Canadian Charter operates too close to the pole of judicial supremacy, and the two sub-national Australian statutes operate too close to the pole of parliamentary supremacy. On the other hand, while by no means perfect, both New Zealand and, to a lesser extent, the United Kingdom have generated distinctively intermediate versions of constitutionalism that succeed in retaining the strengths, while avoiding the major weaknesses, of the traditional alternatives.

Tushnet and Gardbaum have both toyed with the language of 'dialogue' to describe the institutional interactions promoted by this new generation of Anglo-Commonwealth bills of rights.[35] In this, they are not alone. There is a voluminous body of scholarship (some of it self-consciously comparative, and some of it generated from within each of the respective Anglo-Commonwealth jurisdictions) suggesting that what is interesting or distinct about these instruments is the way they promote such dialogue.[36]

The prominence in contemporary Anglo-Commonwealth discourse of this idea of inter-branch dialogue began with Peter Hogg and Allison Bushell's seminal 1997 article, suggesting that the terms of the Canadian Charter leave room for legislative-judicial dialogue over the protection of human rights, and that this manifests in frequent 'legislative sequels' to Charter-invalidating judicial decisions.[37] Hogg and Bushell identified a number of features of the Charter that they thought promoted such

---

[34] See Gardbaum (n. 28) at 237.

[35] M. Tushnet, 'Dialogic Judicial Review' (2008) 61 *Arkansas Law Review* 205; Gardbaum 2001 (n. 32) at 745–747. Gardbaum, though, has since disowned the metaphor: see Gardbaum (n. 28) at 15–16.

[36] A small selection might include: R. Clayton, 'Judicial Deference and "Democratic Dialogue": The Legitimacy of Human Rights Intervention under the Human Rights Act 1998' [2004] *Public Law* 33; J. Debeljak, 'Parliamentary Sovereignty and Dialogue under the Victorian *Charter of Human Rights and Responsibilities*: Drawing the Line between Judicial Interpretation and Judicial Law-Making' (2007) 33 *Monash University Law Review* 9; R. Dixon, 'The Supreme Court of Canada, Charter Dialogue, and Deference' (2009) 47 *Osgoode Hall Law Journal* 235; K. Roach, *The Supreme Court on Trial: Judicial Activism or Democratic Dialogue* (Irwin Law, revised ed., 2016).

[37] P.W. Hogg and A.A. Bushell, 'The *Charter* Dialogue between Courts and Legislatures (Or Perhaps the *Charter of Rights* Isn't Such a Bad Thing After All)' (1997) 35 *Osgoode Hall Law Journal* 75.

dialogue – most prominently, the section 33 'notwithstanding clause' and the section 1 limitations clause. As the former has fallen, in practice, into desuetude, recent accounts of dialogue under the Canadian Charter tend to focus more particularly on the latter.[38] At the risk of oversimplification, the claim is that the terms of section 1, and the proportionality test that it has generated, leave room for a significant exercise of political judgement in whether to, and how to, respond to the judicial invalidation of a statute.

In Canada itself, Hogg and Bushell's metaphor gripped the imagination, generating a deluge of defences, elaborations and refutations.[39] Scholars elsewhere in the Anglo-Commonwealth world (as well as those observing from the outside) have found the metaphor hardly less absorbing. At least at first glance, Hogg and Bushell's metaphor seems even *more* apposite to the statutory bills of rights, which rather obviously leave room for a political response to judicial decisions generated in reliance on the respective human rights instruments. Thus, by the time the statutory bill of rights model migrated to Australia in 2004, the metaphor of dialogue had taken such hold that it was to be found at the centre of official conceptions of the two Australian sub-national instruments. The final reports of the two consultation committees that gave rise to the ACT and Victorian statutes each explicitly proposed a 'dialogical' model of human rights protection – one that would create multiple sites of inter-institutional engagement, rather than allowing the legislature or the judiciary a monologue on human rights protection.[40]

The idea of 'dialogue' can be accused of signifying all things to all people.[41] As Aileen Kavanagh points out, the term is used sometimes as a metaphor, sometimes as a descriptor and sometimes as a normative theory.[42] Its meaning is not stable as between the different jurisdictions

---

[38] E.g., Roach (n. 36) at 297–298 (although acknowledging an ongoing role for s. 33 in providing an outlet for 'extraordinary dialogue').

[39] E.g., Dixon (n. 36); C.P. Manfredi and J.B. Kelly, 'Six Degrees of Dialogue: A Response to Hogg and Bushell' (1999) 37 *Osgoode Hall Law Journal* 513; Roach (n. 36).

[40] ACT Bill of Rights Consultative Committee, *Towards an ACT Human Rights Act* (2003); Victorian Human Rights Consultation Committee, *Rights, Responsibilities and Respect: The Report of the Human Rights Consultation Committee* (2005).

[41] A. Kavanagh, 'The Lure and Limits of Dialogue' (2016) 66 *University of Toronto Law Journal* 83.

[42] Kavanagh (n. 41).

that comprise the so-called new Commonwealth model,[43] nor even within those jurisdictions.[44] There are almost as many dialogue theories as there are dialogue theorists. At its heart, however, the metaphor of dialogue embodies a claim that what counts about these Anglo-Commonwealth bills of rights is not which institution has the 'final word' on human rights questions, but the opportunities they create for multiple institutional perspectives to be brought to bear on those questions along the way.

Dialogue theory has many critics.[45] One of those is Scott Stephenson, whose 2016 monograph *From Dialogue to Disagreement in Comparative Rights Constitutionalism* is one of the most recent systematic contributions to the comparative literature on the Anglo-Commonwealth bills of rights.[46] Like Tushnet and Gardbaum, Stephenson's preoccupation is the extent to which this system of 'multi-stage rights review' (as he calls it) has succeeded in generating distinct patterns of institutional practice that distinguish it from the traditional poles of judicial and parliamentary supremacy.[47] The concept of 'dialogue' does not, he says, assist. It is too vague, it does not constitute a true point of distinctiveness (because inter-branch dialogue is present in all constitutional systems), and it obscures the difficulties and trade-offs associated with the new model.

As the title to his monograph suggests, Stephenson seeks instead to shift the focus to 'disagreement'. Specifically, he suggests that what is distinctive about this model of human rights protection is that it seeks to expand and facilitate *direct* forms of inter-institutional disagreement about rights. Within the traditional paradigms of judicial and parliamentary supremacy, opportunities for inter-institutional disagreement exist but are mainly indirect.[48] In Stephenson's view, direct forms of

---

[43] See S. Stephenson, 'Constitutional Reengineering: Dialogue's Migration from Canada to Australia' (2013) 11 *International Journal of Constitutional Law* 870.

[44] See, e.g., T. Hickman 'Constitutional Dialogue, Constitutional Theories and the Human Rights Act 1998' [2005] *Public Law* 306.

[45] Three recent examples are: E. Carolan, 'Dialogue isn't working: the case for collaboration as a model of legislative-judicial relations' (2016) 36 *Legal Studies* 209; Kavanagh (n. 41); L. Sirota, 'Constitutional Dialogue: The New Zealand Bill of Rights Act and the Noble Dream' (2017) 27 *New Zealand Universities Law Review* 897.

[46] Stephenson (n. 28). See C. Geiringer, 'Review: Scott Stephenson, From Dialogue to Disagreement in Comparative Rights Constitutionalism' (2017) 15 *International Journal of Constitutional Law* 1247.

[47] Stephenson (n. 28) at 2–3. Stephenson, though, objects to the characterisation of this distinct form of constitutionalism as 'weak' or 'intermediate': Stephenson (n. 28) at 112–113.

[48] Stephenson (n. 28) at Chapters 4 and 5.

inter-institutional disagreement are normatively desirable – they are, for example, more transparent, more consistent and predictable, and more calculated to facilitate the bringing to bear of multiple institutional perspectives on the determination of rights issues. On the other hand, Stephenson also acknowledges and explores a set of 'normative trade-offs' associated with the model – competing constitutional principles or values which he sees as being in tension with it.[49] Stephenson suggests that the particular emphasis placed on these competing normative commitments within each of the jurisdictions to have adopted the Commonwealth model helps to explain the different patterns of institutional practice that have emerged.

3 The 'Commonwealth Model' Interrogated

Perhaps the surest mark of scholarship of enduring significance is the deluge of reactive scholarship that follows in its wake. If this is so, we must acknowledge this body of work about the constitutional distinctiveness of the new Anglo-Commonwealth bills of rights as truly groundbreaking. For it has been met with a veritable avalanche of refutations, elaborations and refinements.[50]

Before turning to consider some of the main critiques, we should pause to consider why the contribution of this body of comparative scholarship has been so important. First, this body of work has rightly been lauded for the innovative contribution that it has made to constitutional theory. It engages with what is undoubtedly a central dilemma of Western constitutionalism – the counter-majoritarian nature of judicial review – and recasts the debate in new terms. It moves the focus from the normative justifiability of giving the 'final word' on human rights questions to one particular branch of government to the question of what kinds of constitutional arrangements succeed at bringing multiple institutional perspectives to the table (and on whether that produces, in the

[49] Stephenson (n. 28) at Chapter 7. The other competing principles or values he explores are bureaucratic independence, the rule of law, the hierarchy of laws and comity.
[50] In addition to the literature on inter-branch dialogue listed at nn. 39 and 45 see, e.g., Carolan (n. 27); R. Dixon, 'Weak Form Judicial Review and American Exceptionalism' (2012) 32 *Oxford Journal of Legal Studies* 487; Geiringer (n. 29); A. Kavanagh, 'What's So Weak About 'Weak-Form Review'? The Case of the UK Human Rights Act 1998' (2015) 13 *International Journal of Constitutional Law* 1008; J. King, 'Rights and the Rule of Law in Third Way Constitutionalism' (2015) 30 *Constitutional Commentary* 101.

round, more robust and enduring solutions on human rights questions). Whatever its vagueness as a fully formed theory or model, the metaphor of 'dialogue' has succeeded in capturing the imaginative essence of that idea, and has thereby acted as an important catalyst for reflection and debate – both inside and outside the common law world.

Secondly, this body of scholarship on the constitutional distinctiveness of the Anglo-Commonwealth bills of rights has also made a significant contribution to the taxonomic enterprise which dominates the discipline of comparative constitutional law. It is in the nature of comparison that it involves the elaboration of similarity and of difference. For this reason, comparative study is often preoccupied with taxonomy; with the search for models, systems, families, traditions and phenomena that can help us to transcend the parochial and to speak in a common language across legal and constitutional divides.[51] The scholarship on the constitutional distinctiveness of the Anglo-Commonwealth bills of rights is deeply embedded in, but fundamentally reconfigures, this exercise of map-drawing. Once upon a time, two polar continents were separated by a sea of nothingness. Now, instead, our eyes are drawn to an equator, populated by an archipelago of constitutional hybridism. For navigators of the constitutional high seas, life has become altogether more interesting.

In the very brilliance of these ideas, however, we find the source of their frailty. For once we refocus our gaze (as these scholars suggest we should) on an ocean of endless possibility, we are forced to question whether perhaps it was there all along. Could it be that the polar continents of judicial and parliamentary supremacy were never as bleak and unvarying as scholars such as Stephen Gardbaum have suggested? And might the 'new Commonwealth model' not, in fact, be the only archipelago to populate the constitutional equator?

So, for example, some critics argue that the problem with claims about the distinctiveness of the 'new Commonwealth model' is that they depend on a set of stereotypical assumptions about the characteristics associated with the two polar extremes of judicial and legislative supremacy.[52] Critics point out, for example, that even in strong-form systems such

---

[51] See K. Young, 'A Typology of Economic and Social Rights Adjudication: Exploring the Catalytic Function of Judicial Review' (2010) 8 *International Journal of Constitutional Law* 385 at 388.

[52] Carolan (n. 27); Dixon (n. 36); A. Kavanagh, 'A Hard Look at the Last Word' (2015) *Oxford Journal of Legal Studies* 825 at 828–830, 843–845.

as the United States, courts have a range of devices at their disposal (Bickel's 'passive virtues') to avoid wrestling the 'final word' from the elected branches in all but exceptional circumstances. Even when the courts do exert the power of legislative invalidity, their decisions often leave room for 'legislative sequels' not dissimilar from those celebrated by Hogg and Bushell as evidence of the dialogic nature of the Canadian Charter. Proportionality analysis (one of the supposed engines of such dialogue) is an embedded element of US constitutional discourse. Indeed, the very idea of inter-branch dialogue was stolen by Hogg and Bushell from US constitutional theorists.[53]

Critics point to a similar element of stereotyping of legislative supremacy. Not only does scholarship such as Gardbaum's tend to over-simplify the nature of inter-branch interactions under this model,[54] it also errs in treating the model as static. So, for example, common law techniques of interpretation (such as the principle of legality) are evolving in parallel with (and arguably in dynamic relationship with) the new statutory forms of protection.[55] Thus, on one reading (and perhaps in some jurisdictions more than others), the Anglo-Commonwealth bills of rights are inextricably entwined with, rather than a point of contrast from, the evolving Westminster tradition of legislative supremacy.[56]

A striking example of parallel common law evolution can be found in the common law's embrace of the idea inherent in section 2 of the Canadian Bill of Rights that the Westminster tradition can accommo-date the attribution of hierarchical superiority to certain constitutionally significant statutes. As we have seen, the drafters of the New Zealand, United Kingdom and Australian statutory bills of rights all declined to follow the lead of the Canadian Bill of Rights in requiring irreconcil-able enactments to be treated as inoperative in the absence of express

---

[53] E.g., B. Friedman, 'Dialogue and Judicial Review' (1993) 91 *Michigan Law Review* 577.

[54] Kavanagh (n. 52) at 830.

[55] An even more striking example can be found in the decision in *Attorney-General* v. *Taylor* [2017] NZCA 215, [2017] 3 NZLR 24, [109], in which New Zealand's Court of Appeal located the power to make declarations of legislative incompatibility with the NZ Bill of Rights not in the text of the NZ Bill of Rights but in the common law authority of the courts to expound on questions of law. On appeal, however, the Supreme Court neither adopted nor clearly overruled this line of reasoning: see *Attorney-General* v. *Taylor* [2018] NZSC 104, [2019] 1 NZLR 213.

[56] C. Geiringer, 'The Constitutional Role of the Courts under the NZ Bill of Rights: Three Narratives from *Attorney-General* v. *Taylor*' (2017) 48 *Victoria University of Wellington Law Review* 547 at 566–569.

legislative override. Outside of the statutory bill of rights context, however, that idea has since been embraced by common law courts in Canada,
the United Kingdom and, more equivocally, New Zealand. Not only have
these courts affirmed the enforceability of statutory primacy clauses in
other legislative contexts; they have gone further and suggested that, by
dint of the common law, legislation protecting important constitutional
values might be treated as hierarchically superior (and thus overcome
the doctrine of implied repeal) even in the *absence* of a primacy clause.[57]
In this respect at least, the common law has outstripped the reach of the
statutory bills of rights.

The point made so far is that claims about the distinctiveness of the
new Commonwealth model often rest on an oversimplified picture of
the nature of inter-branch interactions under the 'traditional' systems of
legislative and judicial supremacy. Critics also suggest that these claims
about distinctiveness overlook the extent to which hybridism is a feature of the comparative constitutional landscape more generally. Thus,
a number of critics point to other constitutional systems that, they say,
cannot be located at the so-called polar extremes. Rivka Weill suggests
that Israel's constitutional arrangements constitute a 'hybrid Constitution
of the Commonwealth model type' and is the 'missing case' in discussions
of the Commonwealth model.[58] She also speculates that similar examples
of weak-form constitutionalism might be found in Eastern Europe.[59]
Lavapuro, Ojanen and Scheinin suggest that a form of 'intermediate'
third-way constitutionalism distinct, but not dissimilar, from the so-
called new Commonwealth model has emerged in Finland.[60] Similar
developments in other Nordic countries led Ran Hirschl to posit that: 'In
many respects ... the Nordic model of judicial review, not the so-called

---

[57] For example, *Winnipeg School Division No 1* v. *Craton* [1985] 2 SCR 150, [8]; *Quebec*
v. *Montreal* 2000 SCC 27, [2000] 1 SCR 665, [27]; *Thoburn* v. *Sunderland City Council*
[2003] QB 151, [60]-[64]; *H.* v. *Lord Advocate* [2012] UKSC 24, [2013] 1 AC 413, [30];
R v. *Pora* [2001] 2 NZLR 37 (Elias C.J. concurring).

[58] R. Weill, 'Hybrid Constitutionalism: The Israeli Case for Judicial Review and Why We
Should Care' (2012) 30 *Berkley Journal of International Law* 349 at 355.

[59] R. Weill, 'The New Commonwealth Model of Constitutionalism Notwithstanding: On
Judicial Review and Constitution-Making' (2014) 62 *American Journal of Comparative
Law* 127 at 130, 144, 168.

[60] J. Lavapuro, T. Ojanen and M. Scheinin, 'Rights-Based Constitutionalism in Finland and
the Development of Pluralist Constitutional Review' (2011) 9 *International Journal of
Constitutional Law* 505.

"commonwealth model," is the true, genuine weak-form judicial review.'[61] Eoin Carolan suggests that the Republic of Ireland 'does not confirm to the prescriptions of either political or legal constitutionalists' but neither to the 'third way' provided by the so-called new Commonwealth model.[62] And Joel Colón-Ríos documents a number of variants on weak-form review to be found in some nineteenth- and twentieth-century Latin American constitutions[63] – a claim that suggests (contra Gardbaum) that there is, after all, nothing new under the sun.[64]

Mark Tushnet, the scholar who coined the term 'weak-form review', draws explicit linkages in his own scholarship between the Anglo-Commonwealth bills of rights, and other forms of constitutional hybridism. Thus, he regards the weak enforcement regimes associated in the South African Constitution and elsewhere with the constitutional protection of social and economic rights as other examples of 'weak-form review'.[65] And, writing with Rosalind Dixon, he suggests that, although weak-form review is largely absent in Asia at the level of formal constitutional design, a study of Asian constitutionalism discloses some functional equivalents. These are to be found, on the one hand, in judicial reluctance (in some jurisdictions) to exercise formal powers of constitutional review and, on the other, in the presence in some Asian constitutions of relatively flexible powers of formal constitutional amendment.[66]

Intentionally or not, these analogies suggest that 'weak-form review' may be a very large church indeed. But that, as others have suggested, casts into doubt the tripartite typology as a whole.[67] And it also underscores two further (and closely related) critiques made of

---

[61] R. Hirschl, 'The Nordic Counternarrative: Democracy, Human Development and Judicial Review' (2011) 9 *International Journal of Constitutional Law* 449 at 451.

[62] Carolan (n. 27) at 95.

[63] J. Colón-Ríos, 'A New Typology of Judicial Review of Legislation' (2014) 3 *Global Constitutionalism* 143–169. Colón-Ríos also proposes a more extended typology that supplements the weak-form/strong-form distinction with two variants on 'basic structure' review.

[64] See Gardbaum (n. 28) at 1: 'the new Commonwealth model of constitutionalism may be something new under the sun.'

[65] Tushnet, *'Weak Courts, Strong Rights'* (n. 31).

[66] M. Tushnet and R. Dixon, 'Weak-form Review and its Constitutional Relatives: An Asian Perspective', in R. Dixon and T. Ginsburg (eds.), *Comparative Constitutional Law in Asia* (Edward Elgar, 2014).

[67] Carolan (n. 27) at 97.

scholarship on the distinctiveness of the 'new Commonwealth model'. The first is that this scholarship focuses too exclusively on text and formal institutional design at the expense of culture and context.[68] As we know, 'function does not necessarily follow form in constitutional law'.[69] The Anglo-Commonwealth bills of rights may, on paper, exhibit some coherent and distinctive features. But arguably, the political and operational reality is much less tidy. Thus, the claims of 'third way' constitutionalism made on behalf of a number of other (non-Commonwealth) constitutional systems – Israel, Ireland, Finland, and so on – are based as much in political and judicial practice as in formal institutional design. Conversely, many scholars argue that a focus on actual experience casts into doubt the true distinctiveness of at least some, if not all, of the Anglo-Commonwealth regimes.[70] They point out, for example, that the design feature in the Canadian Charter on which claims to constitutional distinctiveness most obviously rest – the notwithstanding clause – has been rendered almost obsolete by the reluctance of political actors to rely on it. And they suggest that the close to perfect rate of compliance by political actors in the United Kingdom with judicial declarations of legislative incompatibility casts into doubt the plausibility of portraying the UK Human Rights Act as functionally distinct from a system of strong-form review.

Scholars of the 'new Commonwealth model' variety acknowledge, up to a point, these discrepancies between prescription and description. They treat them either as evidence of potential instability in the weak-form model (Tushnet), or as examples of imperfection in the way the model is being realized in practice (Gardbaum), or as the outcome of the normative trade-offs that need to be reconciled in each jurisdiction (Stephenson). But perhaps, as Aileen Kavanagh suggests, this divergence between theory and practice reflects 'deeper problems and instabilities inherent in the distinction itself'.[71] If the normative model of weak-form review

---

[68] E.g., Carolan (n. 27) at 96–97, 111–112, 118–119; Dixon (n. 50) at 503–506; R. Hirschl, 'How Consequential is the Commonwealth Constitutional Model?' (2013) 11 *International Journal of Constitutional Law* 1086 at 1089–1091; Kavanagh (n. 52) at 836–837; R. Leckey, *Bills of Rights in the Common Law* (Cambridge University Press, 2015); Weill (n. 59) at 129–130.

[69] Kavanagh (n. 50) at 1031. See, also, Lavapuro, Ojanen and Scheinin (n. 60) at 506.

[70] E.g., Dixon (n. 50) at 493–495; Kavanagh (n. 50) at 1026–1029; Weill (n. 59) at 129.

[71] Kavanagh (n. 50) at 1030.

(and its various scholarly counterparts) does not mirror reality in the very jurisdictions from which it purports to have been derived, surely we must question whether it is a helpful lens to deploy.[72]

The second and related critique is that claims about the distinctiveness of the new Commonwealth model chart the strength of human rights protection almost entirely along one plane: that relating to the circumstances in which political versus judicial actors are empowered to pronounce on the human rights compatibility of primary legislation.[73] Even if we focus solely on text, this uni-dimensionality fails to capture the complexity of constitutional design. As a number of scholars have suggested, the strength or weakness of a system of human rights protection depends on a multifarious and interlocking range of structural features, including the substantive rights to which protection is extended, the full range of remedies that are available, the presence or absence of structural barriers to judicial intervention, the ease or difficulty of constitutional amendment, the provision that is made in the instrument for the constraint of non-legislative forms of public power, and the interface with any relevant regime of international or regional human rights protection.[74] It is only once we overlay these formal design features with a similarly nuanced list relating, for example, to the institutional and political norms that govern the actual behaviour of political (including judicial) actors within the respective jurisdiction, that we can begin to make an accurate assessment of the comparative strength of constitutional protection. Indeed, the very metric of 'strength' may serve to obscure, rather than to reveal, the 'matrix of interbranch and extrabranch relations' on which constitutional protection depends.[75]

Conclusion

Like the European explorers who sought a new trade route to Asia and stumbled across the New World, Tushnet, Gardbaum and their ilk have

---

[72] Geiringer (n. 46) at 1251–1253.

[73] Carolan (n. 27) at 98.

[74] Carolan (n. 27) at 98, 109–110; C. Geiringer, 'Inside and Outside Criminal Process: the Comparative Salience of the New Zealand and Victorian Human Rights Charters' (2017) 28 *Public Law Review* 219; Geiringer (n. 29); Lavapuro, Ojanen and Scheinin (n. 60) at 530–531; Tushnet and Dixon (n. 66). See also Weill (n. 59), arguing that the main determinant of whether a system gravitates towards weak-form or strong-form review is in fact the process by which the document was first adopted.

[75] Young (n. 51) at 391.

set us off on an ocean voyage that has not taken us quite where they anticipated. We were told to expect an equatorial archipelago of constitutional hybridism, stretched sparsely between two polar land masses. Instead, we find ourselves in a vast ocean, in which multiple islands of constitutional distinctiveness stretch out on the horizon in all directions. '[W]hat began as quite a polarized picture of different *systems* of review,' Kavanagh suggests, 'ends up being a more complex picture of multiple "blended systems," all of which combine some "strong-form" and "weak-form" features in various ways and to varying degrees'.[76]

But if scholarship on the distinctiveness of the new Commonwealth model has not provided us with all the right answers, nor even asked all the rights question, it has succeeded nonetheless in opening up new vistas of comparative constitutional engagement. It has lifted us out of the stale and polarized debate between constitutionalism and democracy, into a more nuanced conversation about the nature of inter-institutional engagement under a liberal democratic constitution. It has pushed us to think more creatively about the possibilities, as well as the limits, of constitutional design. And it has provoked a rich counter-literature on the role of context and culture in mediating the effect of formal constitutional design features.

Along the way, scholarship on the distinctiveness of the new Commonwealth model has opened up important questions about the very nature of the comparative enterprise. Thus, critics of this body of scholarship argue that it reflects a superficial kind of 'macro-constitutional' inquiry that relies on constitutional archetypes or caricatures and that is divorced from the messy and contingent reality of how constitutional power is actually exercised.[77] Stephen Gardbaum, though, has a rejoinder to this call for 'fine-grained contextual comparison'.[78] In comparative inquiry, he says, typologies or classifications serve a useful function. Yet such typologies 'necessarily involve generalization; they inevitably and deliberately abstract from the thick level of "the lived life of the law" and do not purport to be accurate in all empirical details'.[79]

---

[76] Kavanagh (n. 50) at 1034, citing Young (n. 51) at 387.

[77] Carolan (n. 27) at 96–97; Kavanagh (n. 50) at 1036–1037.

[78] Kavanagh (n. 50) at 1037.

[79] S. Gardbaum, 'What's so Weak about 'Weak-form Review'? A reply to Aileen Kavanagh' (2015) 13 *International Journal of Constitutional Law* 1040 at 1048.

Gardbaum has a point. Typologies may create 'blind spots and contradictions'.[80] But they also serve an important function in comparative law. They enable us, for example, to 'classify previously disjointed features and present clusters of analysis that were previously kept apart'.[81] In order to do this, some degree of simplification or generalization is inevitably required.[82]

The counter-literature on the 'new Commonwealth model' nevertheless contains two important warnings for those engaged in this taxonomic enterprise. The first is that the use of such typologies ought not to be allowed to obscure more than it reveals. Their broad outlines, as Aileen Kavanagh suggests, 'should map onto constitutional reality to some meaningful degree.'[83]

The second is that if constitutional design typologies (of the 'new Commonwealth model' variety) do not, as Gardbaum says, purport to be accurate in all empirical details, that must surely have implications for the purposes to which such scholarship ought to be put. As has been suggested elsewhere, this body of scholarship on the distinctiveness of the new Commonwealth model is perhaps best thought of as 'reflective' or 'dialogical': an idealized reconstruction of the Anglo-Commonwealth bills of rights, produced from within the American academy in order to critique dominant traditions of American constitutionalism, and to challenge assumptions about the limits and possibilities of constitutional design.[84] To the extent that it holds itself out as a fully realized assessment of the systems of human rights protection in the four Anglo-Commonwealth jurisdictions it must, however, be treated with rather more caution.

Further Reading

S. Gardbaum, *The New Commonwealth Model of Constitutionalism: Theory and Practice* (Cambridge University Press, 2013).

C. Geiringer, 'Moving Beyond the Constitutionalism/Democracy Dilemma: 'Commonwealth Model' Scholarship and the Fixation on Legislative Compliance', in M. Elliott, J.N.E. Varuhas and S.W. Stark (eds.), *The Unity*

---

[80] Young (n. 51) at 388.

[81] Young (n. 51) at 388.

[82] Dixon (n. 50) at 503.

[83] A. Kavanagh, 'What's so Weak about 'Weak-form Review'? A Rejoinder to Stephen Gardbaum' (2015) 13 *International Journal of Constitutional Law* 1049 at 1052.

[84] Geiringer (n. 29) at 323–324; Dixon (n. 50) at 503.

of Public Law? Doctrinal, Theoretical and Comparative Perspectives (Hart Publishing, 2018) 30.

J.L. Hiebert and J.B. Kelly, *Parliamentary Bills of Rights: The Experiences of New Zealand and the United Kingdom* (Cambridge University Press, 2015).

P.W. Hogg and A.A. Bushell, 'The *Charter* Dialogue between Courts and Legislatures (Or Perhaps the *Charter of Rights* Isn't Such a Bad Thing After All)' (1997) 35 *Osgoode Hall Law Journal* 75.

A. Kavanagh, 'What's so Weak About 'Weak-Form Review'? The Case of the UK Human Rights Act 1998' (2015) 13 *International Journal of Constitutional Law* 1008.

A. Kavanagh, 'The Lure and Limits of Dialogue' (2016) 66 *University of Toronto Law Journal* 83.

K. Roach, *The Supreme Court on Trial: Judicial Activism or Democratic Dialogue* (Irwin Law, revised ed, 2016).

S. Stephenson, *From Dialogue to Disagreement in Comparative Rights Constitutionalism* (Federation Press, 2016).

M. Tushnet, *Weak Courts, Strong Rights: Judicial Review and Social Welfare Rights in Comparative Constitutional Law* (Princeton University Press, 2008).

22 Constitutional Transplants

Gábor Halmai

Introduction

This chapter investigates the problem of how the transplant and borrowing of foreign constitutional law and international law can influence constitution-making processes and constitutional interpretation – state actions which are still considered sovereign. International law, especially international human rights laws, are of pre-eminent importance in this context since they are virtually by definition based on limitations on national constitutional law to assert internationally shared constitutional principles. In other words, the chapter seeks to answer the question of how far the process of the internationalization of (national) constitutional law has progressed; to what extent are the framers of constitutions and the courts that interpret constitutions willing to accept alien, foreign, or international principles and rules? What underlies the decision by the con- stitutional organs of certain states to accede to such constitutional migra- tion, and the rejection of such migration by their respective counterparts in other countries?

A growing constitutional cross-fertilization is taking place between national constitutional systems. This process may contribute not only to the emergence of better constitutions and improved (constitutional) court decisions, but also to the rise of a 'global legal system'.[1] Ultimately, the globalization of constitutional law implies that constitutionalism is no longer the sole prerogative of nation-states, but emerges instead as a set of standards for an international community that is now in the process of taking shape.[2] This internationalization is bolstered especially by the expansion of commercial ties and communication, and the increasing depth of political, economic, cultural and legal relations. In certain analyses they emphasize the potential effects of globalization via market processes on constitutional rights.[3] As economic globalization also implies rivalry – for investments and labour – between states, however, internationalization is primarily limited to countries that partake in the international competition for capital and labour;[4] and at least those among the latter segment that use international models for designing, amending or interpreting their constitutions. Also, modern computer technology, personal connection between justices, and developments in legal education have made the circulation of case law easier and more frequent.[5]

To illustrate the various ways in which comparative law materials are used, academic literature frequently turns to the use of metaphors. One of these is the so-called legal transplant, which designates the translation of rules between legal systems. In his early work Alan Watson argued that he needed to address the transplantation of the science of comparative law.[6] Watson himself has been careful to note that his conclusions were properly applicable to the development of private law. Christopher Osakwe is even more certain that public law, much more than private law, is infused with indigenous political, social and economic realities,

---

[1] This possibility is proposed by A.-M. Slaughter, *A New World Order* (Princeton University Press, 2004), 65–103.

[2] Bruce Ackerman has already envisioned this future towards the end of the 1990s. See B. Ackerman, 'The Rise of World Constitutionalism' (1997) 87 *Virginia Law Review* 771.

[3] Cf. D.S. Law, 'Globalization and the Future of Constitutional Rights' (2008) 102 *Northwestern University Law Review* 1277, and especially 1280.

[4] See M. Tushnet, 'The Inevitable Globalization of Constitutional Law' (2009) 49 *Virginia Journal of International Law* 985–1006.

[5] See T. Groppi and M.-C. Ponthoreau, 'Introduction. The Methodology of Research: How to Assess the Reality of Transjudicial Communication?', in T. Groppi and M.-C. Ponthoreau (eds.), *The Use of Foreign Precedents by Constitutional Judges* (Hart Publishing, 2013), 7.

[6] See A. Watson, *Legal Transplants: An Approach to Comparative Law* (Scottish Academic Press, 1974).

and therefore is closely linked to national traditions.[7] In his critique of Watson, Pierre Legrand claims that transplantation is not a viable enterprise; in rejecting convergence he emphasizes differences.[8] Csaba Varga reports on the role that transplantation played during the Hungarian regime transition,[9] while Angelika Nussberger on the transfer of constitutional law from West to East.[10]

Another metaphor employed is the opposite of the aforementioned, namely constitutional borrowing.[11] Those who employ the metaphor of the 'migration' of constitutional ideals argue that that is the only concept capable of capturing the versatile impact of constitutional ideals on the judicial practices that incorporate them, as well as to express both constitutional differences and the commitment to a comparative approach, though the latter does not necessarily imply the assertion that constitutions and judicial practices converge.[12] In another study Sujit Choudhry uses the term 'dialogical interpretation' in the context of constitutional interpretation, which falls outside the scope of 'constitutional borrowing', but is within the scope of the 'migration' of constitutional principles.[13] This model of comparative constitutional law interpretation bears similarities to Vicki C. Jackson's 'engagement' model,[14] as well as to Sarah K. Harding's model, which is also based on 'dialogue'.[15] The political scientist, Ran Hirschl argues that the question, why is the migration of constitutional migration happening cannot be answered by a juristic methodology or by legal

---

[7] See C. Osakwe, 'Introduction: The Problems of Compatibility of Notions in Constitutional Law' (1984) 59 *Tulane Law Review* 875, 876.

[8] Cf. P. Legrand, 'What "Legal Transplants"', in D. Nelken and J. Feest (eds.), *Adapting Legal Cultures* (Hart Publishing, 2001).

[9] See C. Varga, 'Transfer of Law. A Conceptual Analysis', in *Hungary's Legal Assistance. Experience in the Age of Globalization* (Nagoya, 2006).

[10] See A. Nussberger, 'Verfassungstransfer von West nach Ost: Illusion, Desillusion, Neubeginn' (*Osteuropa*, 2010), 81–96.

[11] See the published materials of the scientific symposium on 'constitutional borrowing': (2003) 1 *International Journal of Constitutional Law* 177–324.

[12] On the metaphors see S. Choudhry, 'Migration As a New Metaphor in Comparative Constitutional Law', in S. Choudhry (ed.), *Migration of Constitutional Ideas* (Cambridge University Press, 2006).

[13] See S. Choudhry, 'Globalization in Search of Justification: Toward a Theory of Comparative Constitutional Interpretation' (1999) 74 *Indiana Law Journal* 819, 835.

[14] See V. Jackson, *Constitutional Engagement in a Transnational Era* (Oxford University Press, 2010).

[15] See S.K. Harding, 'Comparative Reasoning and Judicial Review' (2003) 28 *The Yale Journal of International Law* 409–467.

argumentation alone. Therefore, he suggests to turn from comparative constitutional law to comparative constitutional studies.[16]

The migration of constitutional ideals may manifest itself in the use of foreign constitutional solutions, in the process of drafting constitutions, as well as in the application of comparative law in construing constitutions. This is the context in which Frederick Schauer distinguishes between imposed, transplanted, indigenous and transnational constitutions.[17] Addressing these important manifestations of constitutional migration must begin by addressing the preliminary theoretical question of how far the sovereignty of the branches of powers that make and interpret constitutions, respectively, extend in terms of applying external constitutional solutions or completely disregarding them.

Rosalind Dixon and Eric A. Posner describe four paths to constitutional convergence.[18] The first one is represented by superstructure theories, which argue that constitutions reflect deeper forces – technological, demographic, economic – and therefore constitutions converge across countries just when those factors converge.[19] This means that constitutional borrowing is not within the direct control of constitution-makers, while the other three mechanisms assume that decision-makers do control constitutional change. One means of borrowing is via learning theories, which argue that judges, political actors who produce constitutional norms copy what they see in other legal orders, mostly using of course the more successful or older counties' solutions, as it happened with the postcommunist countries, like Hungary after the transitions in 1989–1990, using many German constitutional approaches. The next theory is of coercion, which argues that countries try to compel other countries to use their constitutional norms. From a different point view one can state that

---

[16] Cf. R. Hirsch, *Comparative Matters* (Oxford University Press, 2014), 281. In contrast to Hirschl's social scientific approach, Armin von Bogdandy in his critique of the book favours a more lawyerly approach. See A. v. Bogdandy, 'Comparative Constitutional Law as a Social Science? A Hegelian Reaction to Ran Hirschl's Comparative Matters' (2016) 49 *VRÜ Verfassung und Recht in Übersee* 278–290.

[17] See F. Schauer, 'On the Migration of Constitutional Ideas' (2005) 37 *Connecticut Law Review* 907.

[18] See R. Dixon and E. Posner, 'The Limits of Constitutional Convergence' (2011) 11(2) *Chicago Journal of International Law* 400.

[19] The scholars representing this theory are writing in economic and political science literature, treating constitutions as endogenous, like the work of D. Acemoglu and J.A. Robinson, *Economic Origins of Dictatorship and Democracy* (Cambridge University Press, 2006). Cited by Dixon and Posner, id., on p. 408.

the countries of East-Central Europe after becoming democratic, believed that they have no choice but to adopt liberal democratic constitutions, if they were have a chance at attracting global trade and investment. Finally, competition theories argue that countries change their norms to attract migration, or trade, and this should also lead to constitutional convergence. Assessing these theories, Dixon and Posner conclude that probably the best case for constitutional convergence comes from the superstructural approach.[20]

1 The Use of International Law in Constitutional Drafting

National constitution-makers are influenced or constrained by standards of international law. This influence may be direct in states that rely on international help to reframe their constitutional system following a crisis situation, or indirect, as a result of global international agreements that bind nation-states in designing their constitutional systems.

International law, traditionally understood, does not have an impact on the constitutional arrangements of nation-states. Article 2(7) of the Charter of the United Nations also prohibits the UN from intervening in matters within the domestic jurisdiction of states – except in cases when it applies enforcement measures, which will be discussed separately – and it does not oblige Member States to submit issues to a settlement procedure compatible with the Charter. Global and regional international human rights conventions, whose main function is precisely to compel states to respect universal human rights norms, constitute the main exceptions to this ban on interventions.

As of today, the international community lacks a global constitutional document. At most we can speak of the growing influence of transnational standards of national constitution-making and constitutional interpretation in some regions of the world. At the same time, in a global context, international *ius cogens* constitutes a higher order of norms in international norms and prevails over international agreements or common law when they conflict. In other words, in a formal sense it qualifies as constitutional law. Furthermore, many argue that under *ius cogens* the UN Charter, too, may be considered a constitutional document

---

[20] Cf. Dixon and Posner, id., at 421.

of international law.[21] This means, in other words, that in addition to the external hierarchical relations between international law and national law, there is also an internal hierarchy in international law.

The adoption in 1948 of the United Nations Universal Declaration of Human Rights was the first step in the direction of making human rights legally binding requirements. Richard Falk traces the emergence of international human rights back to the Declaration, which questioned the notion of unfettered state sovereignty within national boundaries. Through the Declaration, signatory governments made a pledge of sorts to undertake everything in their power to avert genocides similar to the Holocaust.[22] Jürgen Habermas also argues that human rights were endowed with posterior moral content derived from the notion of human dignity, which emerged in response to the Holocaust. This was first manifested in the UN documents and then in the constitutions of the successor states of those regimes that bore responsibility for the grand moral catastrophe of the twentieth century, to wit Germany, Italy and Japan.[23] Nevertheless, once the Declaration was adopted it was seen more as a non-binding principle for states – as a guiding standard rather than a document that served as a basis for decisions rendered by national judicial or administrative bodies. This situation changed with the Spanish and Portuguese democratic transformations, and then, in the 1990s, with the regime transitions in Central and Eastern Europe. The constitutional framers in these countries drew from the Declaration and its bill of rights, which offered a wider spectrum of rights – including economic, social and cultural rights – than the European Convention on Human Rights. Correspondingly, it is no coincidence that the countries in which judicial decisions explicitly refer to the Declaration and the rights therein most frequently in international comparison are Spain, Portugal and Poland. Interestingly, in Hungary, which was not a UN member in 1948, the Declaration was subjected to severe criticisms by prevailing political and legal attitudes at the time of its adoption, especially with respect to Article 19, on account of the latter's all too libertarian approach towards freedom of speech and its failure to interdict fascist propaganda. Following regime transition, the

---

[21] See for example B. Fassbender, 'The United Nations Charter as Constitution of the International Community' (1998) 36 *Columbia Journal of Transnational Law* 529.

[22] See R. Falk, *Achieving Human Rights* (Routledge, 2009), 84.

[23] See J. Habermas, 'Das Konzept der Menschenwürde und die realistische Utopie der Menschenrechte', in *Zur Verfassung Europas: Ein Essay* (Suhrkamp, 2011), 15.

Constitutional Court expressly based its understanding of the freedom of expression as a pre-eminent right on the very same Article 19, among other things. Despite these changes, it is still fair to assert that even today the Declaration cannot be considered a universally accepted principle of international law, nor is it part of the documents that fall in the domain of *ius cogens*. Nevertheless, certain articles therein, such as, for instance, its Article 5 on the prohibition of torture, are obviously part of international common law.

The second step was the creation of the two comprehensive UN human rights covenants, the International Covenant on Civil and Political Rights (ICCPR) and the International Covenant on Economic, Social and Cultural Rights (ICESCR). Precisely because they enjoyed such widespread acceptance in the community of nations, these two agreements can serve as frameworks of sorts for international human rights, and they undoubtedly exert some effect even on states that are not parties to the Covenants. Hence some experts also treat these as an International Bill of Human Rights, which provides a basis for examining the legitimacy of any government.[24]

The two Covenants had discernible impacts on both constitution-making and the constitutional jurisprudence of national courts. As far as constitutions are concerned, in certain countries the adopted wording of constitutional texts, or their amendment occurring after the adoption of the Covenants, reflected a direct influence of the Covenants in their entirety. This was the case for the 1993 interim and the 1996 final constitutions of the Republic of South Africa, the 1982 Canadian Charter of Rights, and the 1995 amendment to the Finnish constitution.[25] At the same time, in other countries – Columbia, the Czech Republic, Estonia, the Philippines, Spain and Russia – individual provisions of the Covenants are reflected in constitutional provisions.[26] In certain countries references to

---

[24] See C. Tomuschat, *Human Rights. Between Idealism and Realism*, 2nd ed. (Oxford University Press, 2008), 4.

[25] See the results of the research (conducted in 20 countries: Australia, Brazil, Canada, Columbia, Czech Republic, Egypt, Estonia, Finland, India, Iran, Jamaica, Japan, Mexico, Philippines, Romania, Russia, Senegal, South Africa, Spain, Zambia) about the impact of the United Nations' Human Rights treaties on the legislation and jurisprudence of the member states, in Ch. Heyns and F. Viljoen, *The Impact of the United Nations Human Rights Treaties on the Domestic Level* (Kluwer International, 2012), 16.

[26] Id. Note that Hungary (which was not part of the research), in its 1989 constitution-making process used the philosophy, and often the wording, of the covenants in many of

UN human rights documents, including the two Covenants, are regularly recurring features of constitutional jurisprudence: 844 such references were found in Australia, 169 in Canada, 36 in Finland, and 28 each in South Africa and Spain.[27]

2 Foreign and International Law in Constitutional Interpretation

Judicial use of foreign law is a product of globalization of the practice of modern constitutionalism: it has been made possible by a dialog among high court judges with constitutional jurisdiction around the world, conducted through mutual citation and increasingly direct interactions. This growing 'transjudicial communication'[28] can afford not only a tool for better judgments, but also for the construction of a global legal system. The globalization of constitutional law means that constitutionalism is no longer the privilege of the nation-state, but has instead become a world-wide concept and standard. Globalization is especially encouraged by advances in transportation and communication, and by the deepening of political, economic, cultural and legal ties. Since economic globalization includes competition among nations for investment and human capital, globalizing processes are limited to countries that compete internationally for investment and human capital, or at least to those among them which use foreign law. Constitutional jurisdictions tend to fall into one of three different categories: those that do not use foreign law (as we will see, the US Supreme Court seldom cites foreign court decisions); those that do use foreign law, but do not do so explicitly (e.g. Hungary) and, those that do so explicitly (e.g. South Africa).[29]

A recent research project focusing on sixteen different countries' constitutional and supreme court explicit citations uses only two categories of

---

its laws. From the countries included in the research, only Egypt and Iran did not observe the impact of the covenants on their national constitutions.

[27] Id. 18. Even though references in the remaining countries researched were not systematic, there were only three, Iran, Mexico and Senegal, out of the twenty investigated where courts did not refer at all to the Human Rights documents of the UN.

[28] For this expression, see A.-M. Slaughter, 'A Typology of Transjudicial Communication' (1994) 29 *University of Richmond Law Review* 99.

[29] See this categorization concerning the use of human rights law in C. McCrudden, 'A Common Law of Human Rights? Transnational Judicial Conversations on Constitutional Rights' (2000) 20 *Oxford Journal of Legal Studies* 511.

courts: the ones that often resort to foreign precedents (Australia, Canada, India, Ireland, Israel, Namibia, South Africa), and the others that only rarely cite such precedents (Austria, Germany, Hungary, Japan, Mexico, Romania, Russia, Taiwan, United States) according to a common methodology.[30] This means that there is almost perfect correlation between the two groups of courts as presented in the research and the legal traditions to which the courts belong: to the first group belongs the common law countries, or those with a mixed tradition, while to the second belongs the civil law countries, with the exception of the US Supreme Court.[31] In the common law countries, the more frequent use of foreign precedents is a direct product of 'openness' of the legal systems, as demonstrated in the case of Australia, and of the legal culture of jurists, like in India, South Africa, Israel and Namibia. The refusal of use can have different reasons, but in the case of both the United States and Russia, one of them can be a psychological resistance: great countries must be seen to act independently, preserving their national uniqueness.

Even though the research clearly shows that citations of foreign case law prevail in both groups of countries in human rights decisions, whereas they appear less frequently in institutional decisions, the differences between the two groups are significant. For instance, in the first group, 93 per cent of the decisions of the Namibian Supreme Court refer to foreign cases.[32] 52 per cent of the decisions of the South African Constitutional Court cite foreign case law. Just to provide an example, the famous case of *S* v. *Makwanyane* on the abolishment of the death penalty contains 220 citations to foreign cases.[33] Ireland provides another relevant example: since 1937, 396 decisions of the Supreme

---

[30] See T. Groppi and M.-C. Ponthoreau (eds.), *The Use of Foreign Precedents by Constitutional Judges* (Hart Publishing, 2013).

[31] See T. Groppi and M.-C. Ponthoreau, 'Conclusion. The Use of Foreign Precedents by Constitutional Judges: A Limited Practice, An Uncertain Future', in T. Groppi and M.-C. Ponthoreau (eds.), *The Use of Foreign Precedents by Constitutional Judges* (Hart Publishing, 2013), 412–413.

[32] I. Spigno, 'Namibia: The Supreme Court as a Foreign Law Importer', in T. Groppi and M.-C. Ponthoreau (eds.), *The Use of Foreign Precedents by Constitutional Judges* (Hart Publishing, 2013), 171.

[33] Ch. Rautenbach, 'South Africa: Teaching an "Old Dog" New Tricks? An Empirical Study of the Use of Foreign Precedents by the South African Constitutional Court (1995–2010)', in T. Groppi and M.-C. Ponthoreau (eds.), *The Use of Foreign Precedents by Constitutional Judges* (Hart Publishing, 2013), 185–209, 194.

Court on constitutional cases out of 902 (43.9 per cent) cite foreign precedents.[34] The High Court of Australia during the period from 2000 to 2008 cited foreign case law in 99 out of 193 constitutional cases (51.3 per cent).[35] The Supreme Court of Canada from 1982 to 2010 cited foreign precedents in a total of 377 constitutional cases out of the 949 it decided (39.7 per cent).[36] From 1994 to 2010 the Supreme Court of Israel quoted foreign case law in 121 cases out of 431 constitutional cases, representing 28 per cent of the total, with a peak of 54 per cent in 1995, the year when the landmark decision *United Mizrahi Bank ltd.* v. *Migdal Cooperative Village*, which introduced judicial review of legislation in Israel, was issued. This decision alone refers to thirty-five foreign precedents.[37]

In the second group of courts, the Taiwanese case represents sixty-six decisions out of 680 (9.7 per cent), which is almost equal to the figure of 179 out of 1908 (9.3 per cent) of the Indian court in the first group, but all but four of the Taiwanese citations are located in dissenting opinions.[38] In Mexico only eleven majority decisions and eighteen separate opinion citing foreign cases have been detected.[39] In Romania only fourteen out

---

[34] C. Fasone, 'The Supreme Court of Ireland and the Use of Foreign Precedents: The Value of Constitutional History', in T. Groppi and M.-C. Ponthoreau (eds.), *The Use of Foreign Precedents by Constitutional Judges* (Hart Publishing, 2013), 117.

[35] C. Saunders and A. Stone, 'Reference to Foreign Precedents by the Australian High Court: A Matter of Method', in T. Groppi and M.-C. Ponthoreau (eds.), *The Use of Foreign Precedents by Constitutional Judges* (Hart Publishing, 2013), 29.

[36] G. Gentili, 'Canada: Protecting Rights in a "Worldwide Rights Culture" – An Empirical Study of the Use of Foreign Precedents by the Supreme Court of Canada (1982–2010)', in T. Groppi and M.-C. Ponthoreau (eds.), *The Use of Foreign Precedents by Constitutional Judges* (Hart Publishing, 2013), 53.

[37] S. Navot, 'Israel: Creating a Constitution – The Use of Foreign Precedents by the Supreme Court (1994–2010)', in T. Groppi and M.-C. Ponthoreau (eds.), *The Use of Foreign Precedents by Constitutional Judges* (Hart Publishing, 2013), 141.

[38] See W-C. Chang and J-R. Yeh, 'Judges as Discursive Agent: The Use of Foreign Precedents by the Constitutional Court of Taiwan', in T. Groppi and M.-C. Ponthoreau (eds.), *The Use of Foreign Precedents by Constitutional Judges* (Hart Publishing, 2013), 381 about Taiwan. On the Indian case, see V.R. Scott, 'India: A "Critical" Use of Foreign Precedents in Constitutional Adjudication', in T. Groppi and M.-C. Ponthoreau (eds.), *The Use of Foreign Precedents by Constitutional Judges* (Hart Publishing, 2013), 85.

[39] E.F. MacGregor and R.S. Gil, 'Mexico: Struggling For an Open View in Constitutional Adjudication', in T. Groppi and M.-C. Ponthoreau (eds.), *The Use of Foreign Precedents by Constitutional Judges* (Hart Publishing, 2013), 308.

of the total of 13,250 decisions of the Constitutional Court display a clear reference to foreign precedents (0.1 per cent).[40] Even less, 6 out of 11,000 decisions contain foreign citations in the Russian Constitutional Court jurisprudence, all in separate opinions.[41] Austria, the oldest Constitutional Court, did not produce significantly more citations between 1980 and 2010: only 60 out of 13,251 cases (0.45 per cent), and even less, only sixteen out of the sixty were parts of the Court's reasoning. In all the other instances, the quotation was only made by one of the parties.[42] In Germany, out of a sample of 1,351 decisions selected by analysing the decades of the 1950s, 1970s and 2000s, only thirty-two of them cite foreign cases (2.4 per cent).[43] In Hungary, between 1999 and 2010, out of 1,016 decisions, nineteen cited foreign cases (1.8 per cent).[44] In Japan, in the period analysed (1990–2008), there has been one single explicit citation out of 234 constitutional cases in a dissenting opinion.[45] The research shows that in the United States during the years of the Rehnquist Court (1986–2004) only 0.3 per cent of the cases cite foreign case law, while citations are almost absent in the years of the Roberts Court (2005–2010).[46]

[40] E.S. Tanasescu and S. Deaconu, 'Romania: Analogical Reasoning as a Dialectic Instrument', in T. Groppi and M.-C. Ponthoreau (eds.), *The Use of Foreign Precedents by Constitutional Judges* (Hart Publishing, 2013), 329.

[41] S. Belov, 'Russia: Foreign Transplants in the Russian Constitution and Invisible Foreign Precedents in Decisions of the Russian Constitutional Court', in T. Groppi and M.-C. Ponthoreau (eds.), *The Use of Foreign Precedents by Constitutional Judges* (Hart Publishing, 2013), 367.

[42] A. Gamper, 'Austria: Non-cosmopolitan, but Europe-friendly – The Constitutional Court's Comparative Approach', in T. Groppi and M.-C. Ponthoreau (eds.), *The Use of Foreign Precedents by Constitutional Judges* (Hart Publishing, 2013), 221.

[43] S. Martini, 'Lifting the Constitutional Curtain? The Use of Foreign Precedents by the German Federal Constitutional Court', in T. Groppi and M.-C. Ponthoreau (eds.), *The Use of Foreign Precedents by Constitutional Judges* (Hart Publishing, 2013), 241.

[44] Z. Szente, 'Hungary: Unsystematic and Incoherent Borrowing of Law. The Use of Foreign Judicial Precedents in the Jurisprudence of the Constitutional Court, 1999–2010', in T. Groppi and M.-C. Ponthoreau (eds.), *The Use of Foreign Precedents by Constitutional Judges* (Hart Publishing, 2013), 259.

[45] A. Ejima, 'A Gap between the Apparent and Hidden Attitudes of the Supreme Court of Japan towards Foreign Precedents', in T. Groppi and M.-C. Ponthoreau (eds.), *The Use of Foreign Precedents by Constitutional Judges* (Hart Publishing, 2013), 284.

[46] A. Sperti, 'United States of America: Attempts of Judicial Use of Foreign Precedents in the Supreme Court's Jurisprudence', in T. Groppi and M.-C. Ponthoreau (eds.), *The Use of Foreign Precedents by Constitutional Judges*, Hart Publishing, 2013), 406.

According to the findings of the research, despite the declining influence of US constitutionalism[47] and the corresponding decline in the US Supreme Court's influence,[48] the nine justices still remain the main references for almost all courts examined. This is also a consequence of the influence of US legal culture on legal higher education, and the 'Americanization' of law schools, for instance in Israel. Decisions of the South African Constitutional Court, the Canadian Supreme Court and the European Court of Human Rights are experiencing an increase in influence, and UK courts are also still frequently quoted in Commonwealth countries. On the other hand, the influence of non-English language courts, like the very active German Federal Constitutional Court, is made difficult by the linguistic barrier. Almost exclusively the bilingual Canadian Supreme Court quotes the French *Conseil Constitutionnel*.

According to some scholars the explicit and non-explicit reference to judicial decisions in other jurisdictions can lead to a convergence among the importer's and exporter's constitutional systems, even if this globalization does not entail uniformity. But the findings of the comparative research show that among the sixteen countries examined, the practice of citation is rather circumscribed and belongs to a limited 'family' of courts.

Before going further we should clarify that 'using' foreign law in this work will typically mean the application of national law to another national jurisdiction. (In some cases we will also deal with the use of international law to national, and national law to international jurisdiction.) The use to which this foreign law is put is in the context of the interpretation of a domestic legal provision, and not of a direct application of the foreign law in the domestic court's jurisprudence. Thus the focus is here on foreign law used transnationally.[49] As we will see, the cited foreign

---

[47] See D.S. Law and M. Versteeg, 'The Declining Influence of the United States Constitution' (2012) 87 *New York University Law Review* 762.

[48] About this tendency see first C. L'Heureux-Dubé, 'Importance of Dialogue: Globalization and the International Impact of the Rehnquist Court' (1998) 34 *Tulsa Law Journal* 15. Later also A. Barak, 'A Judge on Judging: The Role of a Supreme Court in a Democracy' (2002) 116 *Harvard Law Review* 16, 114.

[49] This is also the approach of McCrudden's study. See McCrudden, 2000, 510. Rex D. Glensy argues for the distinction of the use of foreign domestic law and international law, by claiming that comparing a domestic law to another domestic law means comparing apples to apples, but the use of international law, which by definition is not domestic, in this context is more akin to comparing apples to oranges. See R.D. Glensy, 'Constitutional Interpretation Through a Global Lens' (2010) 75 *Missouri Law Review* 1174. The other difficulty concerning the use of external sources with international law is that the issue

cases can have different degrees of influence. Least influential is when judges just mention the foreign law. The next step is when they actually 'follow' such cases as some sort of authority. They can also 'distinguish' them. With the exception of some rarely discussed binding international law, the authority of the cited foreign law is only persuasive in the process of judicial interpretation.[50] The rise of persuasive authority is the most important factor of 'constitutional cross-fertilization'.[51] Even in the case of the South African Constitution, in which the interpretative rule is codified in Section 39, Justice Chaskalson, the then-President of the Constitutional Court, one of the most strenuous supporters of citations of foreign cases, has not treated foreign precedents as having more than persuasive authority. In the famous *Makwanyane* case on the constitutionality of the death penalty he wrote: 'We derive assistance from public international law and foreign case law, but we are in no way bound to follow it.'[52]

After looking at the normative basis of the use of citations I will investigate the questions why and where these uses takes place.

a Normative Underpinning

It is generally agreed that the notion that foreign materials should be used to interpret constitutions is gaining currency, and that the migration of constitutional ideas has been identified at a descriptive level. But many

---

of precedent is controversial in international law. Most international tribunals are asked to limit themselves to the dispute at hand. For example, Article 59 of the Statute of the International Court of Justice (ICJ) proclaims that 'the decision of the Court has no binding force except between parties and in respect of that particular case.' Exceptions from the rare use of precedents are the European Court of Justice (ECJ) and the European Court of Human Rights (ECtHR), which rely heavily on their past decisions, but even these courts refer very rarely to other courts' decisions. For instance, only 29 majority judgments of all 7,319 decisions that the ECtHR made before 30 October 2006 cited one or more decisions of foreign constitutional courts or international courts. (This proportion is higher in the separate opinions of the judges.) See E. Voeten, 'Borrowing and Nonborrowing among International Courts' (2010) 39 *The Journal of Legal Studies* 557.

[50] This is the situation in countries like Canada where practice of the courts often results in the rethinking of the domestic interpretation of international law. See K. Knop, 'Here and There: International Law in Domestic Courts' (2000) 32 *New York University Journal of International Law and Politics* 501 about the decision of the Supreme Court of Canada on the Baker-case.

[51] See A.-M. Slaughter, *A New World Order* (Princeton University Press, 2004), 75–78.

[52] *S* v. *Makwanyane* (1995) 3 SA 391 (CC) 39.

scholars complain that the basic conceptual issues, the methodology of migration, as well as the normative underpinning are lacking, and yet proponents of this practice cannot offer a theoretical justification for it. While some scholars argue that constitutional theory is just a vehicle to make sense of a constitutional practice, others raise the even more general question about the legitimacy of constitutional comparativism, and whether comparativism is only a methodology that is employed on a judge's particular theory, or alternatively whether a special comparative constitutional theory is possible. This theory is profoundly procedural in seeking a particular comparativist methodology, but also substantive in that it maintains the existence of universal norms. One, less convincing methodological reason for a comparative theory is that a parochial methodology places the countries following it (e.g. the United States) at odds with international norms and creates diplomatic tensions with foreign allies. Another explanation is to enhance transnational dialogue and the global rule of law through a global jurisprudence. The substantive reasons include the maintenance of the existence of universal norms and the advocacy of the internalization of international norms into the constitutional jurisprudence, together with the ability to promote political democracy and substantive justice by respecting a morally defensible set of individual rights.

In the scholarly controversy over the uses of comparative constitutionalism, especially the judicial recourse to foreign law, there are three broadly defined positions.[53]

a) Those scholars supporting the idea of the use of foreign law legitimate this practice with the sameness of both the problems and solutions of constitutional law for all constitutional democracies. One of the most well-known scholarly representatives of this position is David Beatty,

---

[53] See this categorization in M. Rosenfeld, 'Principle or Ideology? A Comparativist Perspective on the US Controversy Over Supreme Court Citations to Foreign Authorities', in Z. Gaspár and A. Hanák (eds.), *Sajó 2009* (Prime Rate, 2009), Vicki C. Jackson very similarly talks about three postures toward the transnational. See V.C. Jackson, 'Constitutional Comparisons: Convergence, Resistance, Engagement' (2005) 119 *Harvard Law Review* 109. But there are also authors who are talking only about two positions in this debate: the first is that the constitutional law of one country is, or should be, largely independent of the constitutional law of other countries; the second is that the constitutional law of one state inevitably influences, and should influence, constitutional law in other states. See R. Dixon and E.A. Posner, 'The Limits of Constitutional Convergence' (2011) 11 *Chicago Journal of International Law* 400.

who claims that the ultimate goal of all constitutional adjudication is to subject constitutional controversies to resolutions according to the dictates of the principle of proportionality, which Beatty describes as the 'ultimate rule of law'.[54] This test for justification of rights' limitations articulated by many constitutional systems is a component of 'generic constitutional law', which offers a formula for limiting rights.[55] This position tends to national identification with transnational and international legal norms, and towards constitutional universalism. This means that the representatives of this model claim a process of transnational norm convergence.

b) The second position's starting point is that although the problems of constitutional law are the same for all democratic countries, the solutions to these problems should differ from one constitutional system to another. This position, which is advocated by Mary Ann Glendon in her writings,[56] highlights differences and tries to explain how different one constitutional system is from the other, and why they differ from each other. This is also the very idea behind Vicki C. Jackson's engagement approach, considering foreign or international law without a presumption that it necessarily be followed.[57] In other words the engagement model does not treat foreign and international law as binding sources. Jackson argues that the appropriate posture for the US Supreme Court is one of engagement.

c) The followers of the third position claim that neither the constitutional problems nor their solutions are likely to be the same for different constitutional democracies. Vicki Jackson calls this a resistance posture. This position goes back to Montesquieu's observation that 'the political and civil laws of each nation [...] should be so appropriate to the people for whom they are made that it is very unlikely that the laws of one nation can suit another'.[58] This other extreme position concludes that comparisons are likely to be arbitrary, and that

[54] See D.M. Beatty, *The Ultimate Rule of Law* (Oxford University Press, 2004), 159–188.
[55] See M. Tushnet, 'Comparative Constitutional Law', in M. Reimann and R. Zimmermann (eds.), *The Oxford Handbook of Comparative Law* (Oxford University Press, 2008), 1226–1257.
[56] See M.A. Glendon, 'Rights in Twentieth-Century Constitutions' (1992) 59 *U.Chi.L.Rev.* 532, and M.A. Glendon, *Comparative Legal Traditions*, 2nd ed. (West, 1994), 10.
[57] See V. Jackson, *Constitutional Engagement in a Transnational Era* (Oxford University Press, 2010).
[58] C. de Secondat, Baron de Montesquieu, *The Spirit of Laws*, 1989 (A. M. Cohler et al. eds. and trans.), 8.

comparativists' choices are driven mostly by ideology. For instance, Günther Frankenberg criticized comparativists who impose Western hegemonic approaches for acting as a colonialist, and characterized constitutional comparativism as 'a post-modern form of conquest executed through legal transplants and harmonization strategies'.[59] Another objection, raised by O. Kahn-Freund, is that constitutional law is much less amenable to legal transplantation from one country to another than is private law.[60]

Richard A. Posner claims that the citations of foreign decisions by US Supreme Court Justices such as Antony Kennedy is related to moral vanguardism. Posner labels Justice Kennedy as a kind of 'judicial Ronald Dworkin', and marks him (like Professor Dworkin) as a natural lawyer, arguing that the basic idea of natural law is that there are universal principles of law that inform and constrain positive law.[61] Indeed, some scholars argue that the citation to foreign law is best understood as an application of natural law or post-modern natural law, while according to others it is only a theory articulated in terms of *ius gentium*, i.e. 'the accumulated wisdom of the world on rights and justice from the decisions of judges and lawmakers'. In other words, a consensus among 'civilized' or 'freedom-loving' countries' justifies the citations.[62] At the same time, some believe that even if there is no consensus, adaption by judges is justified based on the cosmopolitan view

---

[59] G. Frankenberg, 'Stranger than Paradise: Identity and Politics in Comparative Law' (1997) 259 *Utah Law Review* 262–263.

[60] O. Kahn-Freund, 'On Uses and Misuses of Comparative Law' (1974) 37 *Modern Law Review* 1, 17–18.

[61] See R.A. Posner, 'Forward: A Political Court' (2005) 110 *Harvard Law Review* 32, 84–89. Besides this scholarly attack, there were also some political attempts leading members of Congress to call for the potential impeachment of Supreme Court Justices. For instance, Congressman Tom Feeney stated: 'To the extent [judges] deliberately ignore Congress's admonishment [about the use of foreign law in court decisions], they are no longer engaging in "good behaviour" from the meaning in the Constitution and they may subject themselves to the ultimate remedy, which would be impeachment.' See T. Curry, *A Flap Over Foreign Matters at the Supreme Court*, MSNBC.com (11 March 2004), http://masnbc.com/id/4506232. Quoted by D. Fontana, 'The Rise and Fall of Comparative Constitutional Law in the Postwar Era' (2011) 36 *The Yale Journal of International Law* 1, 44. The most radical consequence for Justices Ruth Bader Gingsburg and Sandra Day O'Connor, who showed their favour towards citation of foreign law in several extrajudicial speeches, was not only criticism, but death threats: See A.L. Parrish, 'Storm in a Teacup: The US Supreme Court's Use of Foreign Law' (2007) *University of Illinois Law Review* 637, 645.

[62] See J. Waldron, 'Foreign Law and the Modern Ius Gentium' (2005) 119 *Harvard Law Review* 129–147.

of constitutional law.[63] Arguments for the use of comparative law in human rights are based on the universality of rights concepts, or at least on their regionally divided existence, like the existence of the European *ius commune,* as the cultural relativism approach would make the comparison meaningless.[64]

The different normative arguments concerning the relevance of foreign materials in constitutional cases, especially in the US Supreme Court's practice, can be followed in a conversation between the late Justice Antonin Scalia and Justice Stephen Breyer.[65] They both agreed that the use of comparative law is not 'authoritative', i.e., that it is not binding as a precedent. But for Justice Scalia, such citations were neither legitimate nor useful, while for Justice Breyer, they were useful and legitimate so long as they were considered for their insights and not regarded as authoritative. Breyer offered a pragmatic rationale, suggesting that foreign court 'have problems that often, more and more, are similar to our own... If here I have a human being called a judge in a different country dealing with a similar problem, why don't I read what he says if it's similar enough? Maybe I'll learn something...' From Scalia's originalist viewpoint, foreign law 'is irrelevant with one exception: old English law, which served as the backdrop for the framing of the constitutional text'. Scalia also stated that judges using foreign materials cite comparative law selectively, such that 'when it agrees with what the justices would like the case to say, we use the foreign law, and when it doesn't agree we don't use it'.[66] This means that the citation of comparative case law 'lends itself to

---

[63] See V. Perju, 'Cosmopolitanism and Constitutional Self-Government' (2010) 8 *International Journal of Constitutional Law* 326.

[64] See this recognition at C. McCrudden, 'Judicial Comparativism and Human Rights', in E. Örücü and D. Nelken (eds.), *Comparative Law: A Handbook* (Hart Publishing, 2007), 373.

[65] The transcript was published in (2005) 3 *International Journal of Constitutional Law* 519–541.

[66] Id., at 521. As one possible explanation McCrudden mentions that the use of foreign judgments is simply result driven: that advocates and judges use the foreign decision that will support the result they want in the particular case before the court. He even raises the suspicion that the selective use of foreign judgments is inevitably associated with a rights-expanding agenda. But then he rejected this premise by referring to Justice Frankfurter, who was the US Supreme Court justice most consistently disposed to citing foreign cases favourably, and who was certainly not pursuing a rights-expanding agenda. See McCrudden, 2000, 527. The role of ideology as a motivating force for the use of foreign and international sources is also suggested by Bork's words: 'Perhaps it is significant that the justices who [borrow] are from the liberal wing of the [US Supreme] Court. This trend is not surprising, given liberalism's tendency to search for the universal and to denigrate

manipulation'. For Breyer, one of the justifications for citing the case law of other national courts is to consolidate judicial review in transitional democracies. As Justice Breyer emphasized in the discussion, even where there are no apparent firm convergences, human beings across cultures and national borders confront many of the same problems. What is at stake in these situations is a 'dialogue' (à la Choudhry) or 'engagement' (à la Jackson) with foreign decisions, which does not mean necessarily any disposition to endorse or adopt particular foreign approaches.

The positions of Scalia and Breyer can also be seen as the dichotomy of American exceptionalism, i.e., the refusal of many US courts and justices, including those of the Supreme Court, to engage in comparative interpretation, and the 'postwar juridical paradigm' of rights protection, a common constitutional model found in a variety of liberal democracies. As Scalia's arguments demonstrate, the starting points of American exceptionalism are that constitutional judicial review is undemocratic and illegitimate, and consequently the use of foreign law is a form of judicial activism, which further undermines the legitimacy of judicial review. American exceptionalism forbids not only the use of foreign law, but also international law.[67] Jed Rubenfeld argues for instance that American constitutionalism is based on the idea of containment by domestic law only, and not by international law. On this basis he argues that two diverging conceptions of constitutionalism, namely a genuinely 'European' one and a different 'American' one, exist. In that view, 'international constitutionalism' is a genuinely European conception.[68] According to this argument,

---

the particular.' See R. Bork, *Coercing Virtue: The Worldwide Rule of Judges* (AEI Press, 2003), 22. Eric Voeten surveying the borrowing among international courts, especially in the jurisprudence of the European Court of Human Rights says that judges who refer to external decisions in their separate opinions are more activist than are the judges who refrain from doing so on the same cases. See E. Voeten, 'Borrowing and Nonborrowing among International Courts' (2010) 39 *The Journal of Legal Studies* 547–576.

[67] The past decade has seen international lawyers and political scientists discuss 'American exceptionalism'. This debate was characterized by the concern about perceived hegemonic and unilateral conduct of the 'last remaining superpower'. See e.g. M. Ignatieff (ed.), *American Exceptionalism and Human Rights* (Princeton University Press, 2005); H.H. Koh, 'On American Exceptionalism' (2003) 55 *Stanford Law Review* 1479.; N.T. Saito, *Meeting the Enemy – American Exceptionalism and International Law* (New York University Press, 2010), 54–55; S. Walt, 'The Myth of American Exceptionalism', *Foreign Policy*, November, 2011; J. Karabel, '"American Exceptionalism" and the Battle for the Presidency', *Huffington Post*, 22 December 2011.

[68] Cf.: J. Rubenfeld, 'The Two World Order' (2003) 27 *Wilson Quarterly* 28. Obviously the different concepts of 'international constitutionalism' contributed to the very fact that while there were almost no international public law concerns expressed in the US after

nations are bound by international law only if it is legitimate, but international law is not democratically legitimate and therefore not really law, which means that the United States is not legally bound by it.

In contrast, the postwar juridical paradigm model views judicially enforced constitutional rights as subjects of comparative constitutional interpretation. This 'constitutionalist' concept is of course in favour of the legitimacy and thus of the bindingness of international law as a source of constitutional interpretation.[69]

b   Jurisprudential Aspects

In this part I try to identify some criteria that can explain why particular judges and courts decide to use or not use foreign materials. Christopher McCrudden lists the following factors that seem to lead judges to engage with foreign materials: a) type of political regime in which the foreign court is situated; b) pedagogical impulse to look at more established democracies, or wanting not to use certain laws; c) audience; d) existence of common alliances; e) filling vacuum of temporary absence of (preferred) indigenous jurisprudence; f) perceived nature of the constitution as transformative or conservative; g) theories of law and legal interpretation; h) foreign law empirical fact; i) perceived judicial competence in the area of foreign law in issue; j) differences in constitutional structure.[70] But the most important criterion common in all of these factors is the search for good persuasive ideas in other national jurisprudences, which would help to solve similar constitutional problems through interpretation. The very few empirical surveys show that for many judges, foreign judicial colleagues form a reference group on the resolution of constitutional questions. But the data indicate that this globalist conception of judges citing foreign law as a source of persuasive authority may apply to only a minority of judicial comparativists.[71] A survey study of forty-three

the killing of Osama bin Laden, several such concerns were published in Germany. See S. Ulrich, *Darf man Terrorsiten einfach töten? Juristen befürchten, dass Aktionen wie die Erschießung Osama bin Ladens das Völkerrecht verwässern* (2011), Süddeutsche Zeitung, 4 Mai 2011.

[69] Cf.: M. Kumm, 'The Legitimacy of International Law. A Constitutionalist Framework of Analysis' (2004) 15 *EJIL* 907–931.

[70] See McCrudden, 2000, 516–527.

[71] See B. Flanagan and S. Ahern, 'Judicial Decision-Making and Transnational Law: A Survey of Common Law Supreme Court Judges' (2011) 60 *International and Comparative Law Quarterly* 28.

judges from the British House of Lords, the Caribbean Court of Justice, the High Court of Australia, the Constitutional Court of South Africa, and the Supreme Court of Ireland, India, Israel, Canada, New Zealand and the United States on the use of foreign law in constitutional rights cases has shown that twenty out of forty-three judges felt that they used foreign law occasionally or rarely while twenty-three felt they used it regularly. To the question, whether they use comparative materials to justify their legal conclusions, 42 per cent considered themselves frequent users, so the frequency with which judges used comparative materials to justify their conclusions was significantly related to the frequency with which they cited foreign law.

As the number of liberal democratic countries is constantly increasing, the migration of constitutional ideas within this community cannot be a one-way process: some courts being always 'givers' of law while others always 'receivers'. Of course, the courts in the countries of the 'postwar juridical paradigm' (Weinrib) of rights protection use more case law from the courts of older and more established democracies, like that of the US Supreme Court. As Justice Albie Sachs of the South African Constitutional Court writes:

If I draw on statements by certain United States Supreme Court Justices, I do so not because I treat their decisions as precedents to be applied in our Courts, but because their dicta articulate in an elegant and helpful manner problems which face any modern court dealing with what was loosely been called state/church relations. Thus, though drawn from another legal culture, they express values and dilemmas in a way which I find most helpful in elucidating the meaning of our own constitutional text.[72]

Another example of juridical transplant is the case of the Hungarian Constitutional Court. As Catherine Dupré's book[73] on the import of the concept of human dignity shows, the judges first carefully chose the German as a suitable model, and than instrumentalized it through a very activist interpretation of the Hungarian constitution. As Andrea Zimmermann observes, the influence of the German Federal Constitutional Court was decisive on the jurisprudence of political and civil rights in East-Central

[72] *S.* v. *Lawrence, S.* v. *Negal, S.* v. *Solberg,* (4) SA 1176, 1223 (South Africa 1997). Quoted by Slaughter 2004, 77.
[73] C. Dupré, *Importing the Law in Post-Communist Transitions: The Hungarian Constitutional Court and the Right to Human Dignity* (Hart Publishing 2003).

Europe.[74] On that basis, the Hungarian Constitutional Court developed its own, autonomous concept of human dignity. Describing the genesis of a new legal system in Hungary, Dupré states that relying on law importation to develop its case law in the transitional period the Hungarian Constitutional Court discovered new rights in the wake of human dignity and the general personality rights. The main characteristic of this imported law is that it is between natural law and globalization, or more precisely 'not global but German' as the author highlights the particular nature of Hungarian law importation. The discourse on law importation can be likened to a modern form of natural law.

Conclusion

We can conclude that despite the different postures towards the transplant and borrowing of foreign law, constitutionalism and judicial review have 'gone global', that there is definitely a growing horizontal communication between constitutional systems, and given this dramatic development, the traditional neglect of the study of comparative law is becoming harder to justify.[75] This means that there are more and more countries engaging with foreign, international and transnational norms. The expanding universe of law through the internet also makes much harder nowadays to avoid taking a position on the role of international or foreign law.[76] Whether the consequence of this development will be the emergence of a 'transnational or cosmopolitan constitutionalism'[77] or

---

[74] See A. Zimmermann, 'Bürgerliche und politische Rechte in der Verfassungsrechtsprechung mittel- und osteuropäischer Staaten unter besonderer Berücksichtigung der Einflüsse der deutschen Verfassungsgerichtsbarkeit', in Jochen Abr. Frowein (eds.), *Grundfragen der Verfassungsgerichtsbarkeit in Mittel- und Osteuropa* (Springer, 1998), 89–124. In the same volume the then-President of the Hungarian Constitutional Court and his advisor acknowledge this use of German law in the constitutional interpretation. See L. Sólyom, Anmerkungen zur Rezeption auf dem Gebiet der wirtschaftlichen und sozialen Rechte aus ungarischer Sicht, at 213–227, G. Halmai, Bürgerliche und politische Rechte in der Verfassungsrechtsprechung Ungarns, at 125–129.

[75] Cf. R. Hirschl, *Towards Juristocracy* (Harvard University Press, 2004), 222.

[76] See this argument in V.C. Jackson, *Constitutional Engagement in a Transnational Era* (Oxford University Press, 2010), 5–6.

[77] As Goldsworthy formulates: 'We live in an era of "cosmopolitan constitutionalism" in which lawyers and judges increasingly look beyond their own borders and borrow ideas from other jurisdictions.' J. Goldsworthy, 'Introduction', in J. Goldsworthy (ed.), *Interpreting Constitutions: A Comparative Study* (Oxford University Press, 2006), 3.

the international community becoming a constitutional community,[78] is
to be seen.

One of the signs of this global trend is that more and more polities accept
supra-national core principles of the rule of law in their constitutions,
and these principles cannot be changed and can be regarded as intrinsic
to its specific identity. As we have seen, the international trend is moving
towards accepting the Indian basic structure doctrine, explicitly through
constitutional provisions that are deemed unamendable, or implicitly
through judge-made laws.[79] There are two kinds of protected supra-
constitutional principles: universal and particular. The universal ones
are common to all modern democratic societies, such as the democratic
nature of the state, human dignity of the individual, and the rule of law.
Others, such as federalism, official language, and a state religion might
be regarded as particular, as they reflect the specific ideals and values of
a distinct constitutional culture.

Constitutional transplantation and borrowing contributes to the state of
constitutional law in a given country. But, there is a dialectic relationship
between constitutional law and constitutional culture: the former is based
on the latter, and it also influences it.[80] This means that it is very hard
to make legitimate constitutional law accepted by the people without a
pre-existing constitutional culture. For instance, it was difficult to import
constitutions after the political transition into the region of the former
Communist countries of East-Central Europe in the early 1990s, because
constitutionalism was a minor element of the political culture at best.[81]

---

[78] The Italian philosopher, Massimo Cacciari uses the metaphor archipelago to describe the
type of mutual interdependence between cultural, linguistic, national or ethnic groups
as islands, communicating with each other as part of an archipelago. See M. Cacciari,
L'arcipelago (1997), referred to by A. Lollini, 'Legal Argumentation Based on Foreign Law.
An example from Case Law of the South African Constitutional Court' (2007) 3(1) *Utrecht
Law Review* 60, 74.

[79] See C. Fusaro and D. Oliver (eds.), 'Towards a Theory of Constitutional Change', in D.
Oliver and C. Fusaro (eds.), *How Constitutions Change: A Comparative Study* (Hart
Publishing, 2011), 428.

[80] See R. C. Post, 'The Supreme Court 2002 Term. Foreword: Fashioning the Legal
Constitution: Culture, Courts, and Law' (2003) 117 *Harvard Law Review* 4–112, at 7. Here
Post uses the term 'constitutional culture' referring to the beliefs and values of non-
judicial actors, most of all the people, while the term 'constitutional law' according to
Post refers to constitutional law as it is made from the perspective of the judiciary.

[81] See U.K. Preuss, 'Perspectives on Post-Conflict Constitutionalism: Reflections on Regime
Change Through External Constitutionalization' (2006) 51 *New York Law School Law
Review* 7, 28.

In such situations constitutional law, including the transplantation of it, must necessarily be an elitist project with the hope that it contributes to the development of constitutional law.

This is the reason that some scholars are more cautious, emphasizing the difficulties in changing constitutional culture,[82] or saying that the direction in which constitutional identity might evolve trough engagement with foreign law might be at stake.[83] Others argue against the existence of convergence,[84] or at least talk about a dual tendency of globalization and 'balkanization'. Michel Rosenfeld observes that paradoxically, while the world becomes bound together, ideas migrate; at the same time it also becomes violently split and divided due to ethnic-based nationalistic identity politics and religious fundamentalism.[85] Some scientists even raise doubts whether a convergence through transplant and borrowing would be a good thing at all, since significant variations necessarily continue to distinguish different liberal constitutions.[86]

Further Reading

S. Choudhry, *Migration As a New Metaphor in Comparative Constitutional Law*, in Sujit Choudhry (ed.), *Migration of Constitutional Ideas* (Cambridge University Press, 2006).

D.M. Davis, 'Constitutional Borrowing: The Influence of Legal Culture and Local History in the Reconstruction of Comparative Influence: The South African Experience' (2003) 1 *International Journal of Constitutional Law* 181.

C. Dupré, *Importing the Law in Post-Communist Transitions: The Hungarian Constitutional Court and the Right to Human Dignity* (Hart Publishing, 2003).

J. Goldsworthy, 'Questioning the Migration of Constitutional Ideas. Rights, Constitutionalism and the Limits of Convergence', in S. Choudhry (ed.), *Migration of Constitutional Ideas* (Cambridge University Press, 2006).

---

[82] See V. Perju, 'Constitutional Transplants, Borrowing, and Migrations', in M. Rosenfeld and A. Sajó (eds.), *The Oxford Handbook of Comparative Constitutional Law* (Oxford University Press, 2012), 1323–1326.

[83] See G.J. Jacobsohn, 'The Formation of Constitutional Identity', in T. Ginsburg and R. Dixon (eds.), *Comparative Constitutional Law* (Edward Elgar, 2011), 138.

[84] Cf. Michel Rosenfeld and András Sajó, 'Spreading Liberal Constitutionalism: An Inquiry into the Fate of Free Speech Rights in New Democracies', in S. Choudhry (ed.), *Migration of Constitutional Ideas* (Cambridge University Press, 2006).

[85] See M. Rosenfeld, *Law, Justice, Democracy, and the Clash of Cultures. A Pluralist Account*, (Cambridge University Press, 2011), 2–3.

[86] See J. Goldsworthy, 'Questioning the Migration of Constitutional Ideas: Rights, Constitutionalism and the Limits of Convergence', in S. Choudhry (ed.), *Migration of Constitutional Ideas* (Cambridge University Press, 2006).

T. Groppi and M.-C. Ponthoreau (eds.), *The Use of Foreign Precedents by Constitutional Judges* (Hart Publishing, 2013).

G. Halmai, *Perspectives of Global Constitutionalism* (Eleven International Publishing, 2014).

C. McCrudden, 'A Common Law of Human Rights?: Transnational Judicial Conversations on Constitutional Rights' (2000) 20 *Oxford Journal of Legal Studies* 499–532.

M. Rosenfeld, 'Constitutional Migration and the Bounds of Comparative Analysis' (2001) 58 *NYU Annual Survey of American Law* 67.

M. Siems, 'Malicious Legal Transplants' (2018) 38 *Legal Studies* 103–119.

E. Voeten, 'Borrowing and Nonborrowing among International Courts' (2010) 39 *The Journal of Legal Studies* 547–576.

A. Watson, *Legal Transplants: An Approach to Comparative Law* (Scottish Academic Press, 1974).

Index

Page numbers in **bold** refer to figures; those in *italic* to tables.